EX-ITALIAN SOMALILAND

THE COLOUR BAR IN THE ITALIAN COLONIES
as represented by an officially published Italian monthly magazine, dated August, 1938, under the direction of Telesio Interlandi, and edited by Dr. Guido Landra, Dr. Lidio Ciprini, Dr. Leone Franzi, Dr. Marcello Ricci and Dr. Lino Businco.

The sword is supposed to divide the Italian of Indo-European race (left) from the Jew (centre) and the African (right).

The head of the Jew is taken from a sculpture of the third century A.D. in the Rheinisches Landesmuseum, at Treves in the Rhineland.

EX-ITALIAN SOMALILAND

By
E. SYLVIA PANKHURST
Editor " New Times and Ethiopia News "

With a Foreword by
PETER FREEMAN, M.P.

PHILOSOPHICAL LIBRARY
NEW YORK

PUBLISHED, 1951, BY THE PHILOSOPHICAL LIBRARY, INC.,
15 EAST 40TH STREET, NEW YORK 16, N.Y.

All rights reserved.

COPYRIGHT 1951 BY E. SYLVIA PANKHURST

PRINTED IN GREAT BRITAIN BY
PERCY BROTHERS LTD., MANCHESTER AND LONDON
ISBN 978-0-8065-3054-3

Contents

		Page
Foreword by Peter Freeman, M.P.		7
Introduction		9
I	How the Coast was Acquired	11
II	The Advance Inland: Negotiations with the Emperor Menelik II	20
III	The Rise of the Mullah: "Italy has no Money to Waste"	29
IV	Government of the Colony: Parliamentary Disclosures of Chartered Company Misrule	38
V	From Inside the Colony: Chiesi-Travelli Revelations	46
VI	Italian Government Legalises Slavery	77
VII	How the Colony was Conquered	84
VIII	Land Seizures and Concessions	90
IX	The Fascist Era	96
X	The Wal Wal Incident	99
XI	The Colony as a Base for War	114
XII	The Italian Collapse: the Slaves Desert	118
XIII	How the British Found It	132
XIV	British Military Administration and Somali Aspirations	147
XV	Somali Youth League	175
XVI	Contemporary Somaliland	185
XVII	The Colony in Suspense	215
XVIII	Four Power Commission of Investigation	222
XIX	At the Bar of the United Nations	260
XX	Background.—(i) Economic Stranglehold	270
	(ii) Italian Political Retrospect	275
XXI	Count Sforza's New Compromise	288
XXII	Drafting the Italian Trusteeship Agreement	355
	Appendix 1 Italo-Ethiopian Treaty, 1908	397
	,, 2 Draft Trusteeship Agreement	398
	,, 3 U.N.O. Charter concerning Trusteeship	408
	,, 4 Italian Draft Trusteeship Agreement	410
XXIII	Italian Return to Somaliland	417
	Report from Somaliland	439
XXIV	Somaliland and the Future	448

List of Illustrations

	Page
The Colour Bar in the Italian Colonies	Frontispiece
The Emperor Menelik II of Ethiopia..	Facing 20
Somali Fishermen—circa, 1920	,, 28
The Mullah's Stronghold at Tale	,, 29
Marshal Graziani	,, 114
The Juba River in 1935	,, 115
The Collapse of Italian Morale	,, 118
One of the Colossal Effigies of Mussolini	,, 119
A Notorious Italian Punishment	,, 145
Italian Armed Labour Battalion	,, 146
Italian Armed Labour Battalion Parade before the Viceroy in Mogadishu	,, 146
Somali Agriculturists	,, 194
Receipt for Animals Requisitioned without Payment ..	,, 195
Cartoon on the Mogadishu Riot	.. 227
Old Colonials at work	Facing 262
Homeless Unemployed Camp out in Rome	,, 263
Italian Colonisation Propaganda	,, 263
Tents for Somaliland	,, 416
Stuart tanks and Staghound armoured cars were assembled at Caserta for use in Somaliland ..	,, 417
Volunteers enrolling for Somaliland	,, 421
Awaiting for Execution .. .. (Photograph by the Italians found at their Headquarters after their defeat in 1941)	,, 422

MAPS

Map of Ethiopia showing boundary Treaties with Italy and other Powers	Facing 22
Ethiopia and Surrounding Territories (the Wal Wal incident)..	,, 99
Ex-Italian Somaliland: Land Utilisation..	.. 112
Ex-Italian Somaliland: Administrative Region ..	.. 113
Map of Present-day Ethiopia	.. 187

Foreword

By PETER FREEMAN, M.P.

The Ethiopians have a noble champion in Miss Sylvia Pankhurst. She acquired her capacity to fight for a just cause in the struggle for the rights of women in Great Britain in 1905 and onward. Largely as a result of the efforts of the Pankhurst family, who brought the matter to the fore by their intrepid courage, women throughout the British Commonwealth now enjoy equal constitutional rights with men. The participation of women in public work is now recognised as of paramount importance to the civilised world.

Having won this great fight and having devoted herself to alleviating the misery of the poorest of our own people in the East End of London during the first World War, she saw the misery through which the Ethiopians and their near neighbours in Eritrea and Somaliland were passing. Italian oppression was rampant, abject poverty, starvation and cruelty were being forced on a peace-loving people by the Italians. Miss Pankhurst traces with careful accuracy, citing exact dates, quotations and references, the unworthy part Italy took in this sorry affair.

From the beginning of their occupation of Somaliland territory in 1889, the Italian Government connived at the breaking of treaty obligations, encouraged the traffic in slaves, evicted the people of the territory from their cultivated land, and eventually used the colony as a base of aggression against Ethiopia.

In struggling to resist further Italian penetration, the Ethiopians came into inevitable conflict with the Italian invaders at Wal Wal, and—to its shame—Great Britain left them to their fate.

Although Ethiopia was a loyal member of the League of Nations, no effective action was taken by any member of the League to protect the Ethiopian people from the Italian invasion; they were left as the helpless victims of the modern armed might of Mussolini and his Fascist State.

The Ethiopians bravely stood their ground, but were powerless against poison gas, bombs and aeroplanes. Italy obtained complete sovereignty, though the Ethiopian struggle for liberty was never relinquished.

This was the first step that led to the European War of 1939-45. Had we supported the Ethiopians in the first place, the war might have been avoided.

The war against the Fascists and Nazis being won, to hand back any of the former colonies to Italy would be an act of supreme injustice.

The world should be grateful to Miss Pankhurst for her timely book on this matter. May it help to bring the Ethiopians, Somalis and Eritreans the freedom and justice they so rightly deserve.

It will be a test of the justice and integrity of the United Nations —a responsibility which none can shirk with impunity.

INTRODUCTION

In the following pages I have traced the almost unknown history of the Italian Somaliland Colony. I have endeavoured to portray the appallingly harsh conditions of its unheeded people, whose case against Italy before the United Nations has suffered most gravely by reason of their isolation and the lack of information concerning them.

The Wal Wal incident, Italy's pretext for mobilisation against Ethiopia, which was developed from her Somaliland Colony in 1934, Italy's poison gas invasion of Ethiopia, which followed in 1935, the swift East African campaign of 1941, the Mogadishu riot, the visit of the Four-Power Commission, were but flashes in the darkness, each of which for an instant illuminated the obscurity wherein these people, toiling in silent hardship, have been hidden from the western mind.

To the people of the British Commonwealth, who were welcomed as liberators and whose call to the Somaliland people to join in a common fight for freedom aroused their profound hopes and desires, the fate of the territory must not be indifferent.

To Ethiopia, three times invaded by Italy and for five years occupied by Italian forces, the future of this former Italian colony is of vital significance. It was anciently her own seaboard, and only in 1908 was the major portion of it severed from her by Treaty.

The material used in compiling this volume is drawn, in the main, from Italian and other official sources, Treaties and Ministerial Declarations in the Italian Parliament, Reports of official Italian Enquiries, conducted in the territory on account of the scandals and tragedies which developed there, British official reports of the conditions found in the colony at the time of the Italian collapse, the evidence presented to the Four-Power Commission, and other authentic sources.

The various stages of the Italian occupation of the Somaliland colony are traced: the acquisition of the coast and the later encroachments into the interior, the Treaty obligations in relation to the Slave Trade and the Arms Traffic which the Italian Government assumed in taking over the territory from Britain and the Sultan of Zanzibar, Treaties continuously and scandalously violated.

In order to remove the cost of the colony from the Italian Exchequer, it was passed over first to one, then to another Chartered Company. It is shown that both under the Government and under the Companies the slave trade was protected, and slavery even legalised; Italian officials took part in the traffic.

I have presented here Italian evidence recording the driving of the native population from the best of the land bordering the rivers, which is monopolised by the Italians to this day. The attempts which were made to popularise in Italy the acquisition of the colony and the subsequent conquest of its people, by fantastic accounts of its value as a field for Italian settlement, and as a source of raw material for Italian factories, I have described from Italian sources and compared with the meagre reality. In fact the colony was never self-supporting; it imposed an ever-increasing burden on the Italian State. Climatically and economically, the territory proved unsuited to Italian settlement; and Italian labour was early rejected as too expensive. The long impecunious neglect of the colony, under the " Liberal democratic " Governments of Italy, and their thesis, "Italy has no money to waste in Africa," was succeeded by the bubble expansion of Fascism, with its crescendo of Racism, intensification of forced labour and brutal cruelties, with the period of further subjection, expropriation and terror, called "the reconquest" of the colony by De Vecchi, leading up to the Ethiopian war.

I have sought to analyse and describe the present position of the colony, from its social, economic and political aspects, the needs of the people, the climatic and geographical possibilities of the territory in relation to the Ethiopian interior.

I venture to make a plea for dispassionate consideration of the facts here marshalled, and of the realities concerning this territory and its people in their situation on the Horn of Africa.

E. SYLVIA PANKHURST.

I

HOW THE COAST WAS ACQUIRED

Filonardi Active Among the Local Chiefs

In May, 1889, Italy induced the newly proclaimed Ethiopian Emperor, Menelik II, to assent to the notorious Treaty of Uccialli, Article xvii of which was seized upon by Italy as a pretext for attempting the conquest of Ethiopia. This reckless attempt was ventured unsuccessfully, and met with an utterly crushing defeat at Adowa and elsewhere in 1896.

Article xvii appeared in two different versions, the Amharic and the Italian. The Amharic version stated that the Emperor, if he found it convenient, might avail himself of Italian diplomatic representatives abroad for the transaction of his business with other governments. During the negotiations for the Treaty this article was urged upon him as providing a friendly offer of service which he might accept or reject on any occasion, as he thought fit. Thus article xvii in the Amharic version of the Treaty appeared as an optional arrangement.

The Italian version, however, stated that the Emperor consented to the transaction through Italy of all Ethiopia's affairs with other Powers and governments. That any King and government would hand over their country to another Power in so casual a phrase is, of course, unthinkable!

Here is a translation of the Italian version which appears in Hertslet's "Map of Africa by Treaty," a fully reliable semi-official work; it is a literal translation from the official Italian Green book:

> *Art. XVII. His Majesty the King of Kings of Ethiopia consents to avail himself of the Italian Government for any negotiations which he may enter into with other Powers or Governments (per tutte le trattazioni di affari che avesse con altre potenze o governi).*

A clause with an ostensibly similar object had been inserted, at Italian suggestion, in a Treaty Menelik had made with the Italians when he was King of Shoa, without any untoward results.

The Emperor Menelik and his advisers were far from imagining that a claim to possession of Ethiopia would result from the Treaty of Uccialli, but so it happened. The various negotiations between Italy and Ethiopia arising from the Treaty were not yet fully concluded when the Italian Government notified the Powers that Italy had established a protectorate over Ethiopia within the meaning of the General Act of the Conference of Berlin, of February, 1885. It will be remembered that under the above-mentioned General Act the Powers agreed to notify each other of their acquisitions in Africa; such a notification, unless another Power objected on the ground of a prior claim, was in effect sufficient to establish ownership so far as the European Powers were concerned.

Having notified the claim, which was virtually a claim to possession of Ethiopia, the Italian Government looked around to establish securely the boundaries of the Empire they hoped they had been obtaining by a facile trick. Presuming on the pretence of the Ethiopian Emperor's agreement to an Italian protectorate the Italian King, and the Foreign Minister Crispi, induced the British Government to enter into boundary protocols with them on this basis in March and April, 1891, and May, 1894.

On the seaboard to the north the territory now termed Eritrea had been annexed by a sly combination of force and cunning, particularly the latter. The seaboard to the south was occupied by similar means. Scientific exploration, the promotion of trade, friendly protection of the coast from hostile slave-raiders, promises to introduce modern education and western mechanical and scientific technique, and to act in accord with truly Christian principles were the cards repeatedly played by the various Italian official representatives and by the Government in Rome in dealing with the ardent modernist reformer, Menelik II.

Whilst Menelik and his counsellors were engaged in rebutting the Roman Government's claim to control all Ethiopia, Signor Filonardi, the Italian Consul at Zanzibar, had been entering into relations of ostensible friendship with the local chiefs, called Sultans, along the coast of the Red Sea, from Cape Guardafui to the Juba River. In May, 1889, he notified the Italian Government that he had induced the Sultan of all the Mijjerteins and the Sultan of Obbia to accept the protection of Italy. The Government at once notified the Powers of this new protectorate. Thus Italian possessions appeared to extend across the Horn of Africa, from the Red Sea to the Indian Ocean—provided, of course, the claim to a protectorate over Ethiopia could be successfully maintained. At that time Ethiopia's victory was still to win, and the possibility that any State situated in Africa could vanquish the onslaught of a European Power was not conceived in Europe, unless it might be among some knowledgable persons who were familiar with Ethiopia and her people.

Italian " protection " of the Ethiopian coast of the Indian Ocean was not, however, complete; the Sultan of Zanzibar held an important part of that coast, including the ports of Kismayu, Brava, Merka and Mogadishu, which lay to the south of the territories of Obbia and the Mijjerteins.

Taking time by the forelock, in order to profit by the fiction that an Italian protectorate over Ethiopia was actually in being, the Italian Government entered into negotiations to secure these ports, in order to provide adequate outlets to the Indian Ocean, as well as to the Red Sea, for the Ethiopian Empire which they fondly hoped they had acquired. We may pause here to emphasise that the ports the Italians sagely considered necessary for Ethiopia under their rule are equally necessary for her well-being under her own self-government. Negotiations had for some time been carried on and were about to be concluded between the Sultan of Zanzibar, H. H. Seyyid Khalifa-bin-Said, and the British Government, for the cession to the British East Africa Company of the ports of Brava, Merka, and Mogadishu, with a land radius about them of 10 sea miles, and of Warsheikh with a land radius of 5 sea miles. The Italians most adroitly persuaded the British Government to surrender the concession for these ports to them as soon as it was obtained from the Sultan, whilst the Port of Kismayu was to be jointly occupied. The arrangement was, of course, part of the division of the African coast between European Powers, each of the bigger ones getting a proportion, by agreement, in order to avoid fighting among themselves. This had been the purpose of the Congress of Berlin.

Britain, it should again be emphasised, was disposed at that time to favour concessions to Italy, assuming that she would be peaceful and loyal, in view of the rivalry which then existed between Britain and France, and between Germany and the other Powers.

Before proceeding with the history of Italy's possessions on the Indian Ocean coast it is well to cast a brief glance over the history of that area. It was anciently a part of Ethiopia, and, as such, as we know, it is mentioned on the famous inscriptions at Axum.

This Indian Ocean coast of Ethiopia had been familiar to the people of the adjacent Southern Arabia from early times. With the rise of Islam Arabian settlements were formed in the ports on this coast consisting of traders, emigrants and exiles from the strife of rival Arabian religious factions. These settlers did not penetrate the interior, but traded peacefully with the people of the hinterland who brought their wares to the ports.

After the discovery of the route to India by the Cape, Portuguese influence reached the east coast of Africa. From 1500 onwards Cabral, da Gama, D'Albuquerque, and Navasco were successively despatched from Portugal to establish control of that coast, including the Ethiopian sector. The decline of Portuguese power was already under way before the close of the sixteenth century and by the middle of the seventeenth century it had sunk to a low ebb. The Arabian Sultans of Muscat, the lords of Oman, replaced the Portuguese, but movements for independence from the Muscat rulers grew up among the seaport towns whose Arab settlers had intermarried with the native peoples.

We have seen that the Sultan of Zanzibar, His Highness Seyyid Khalifa-bin-Said, agreed to transfer to the British East Africa Company certain ports on the Ethiopian coast of the Indian Ocean, a part of the coast termed the Benadir, in the year 1889. At the same time, with the assent of the Sultan, the United Kingdom Government arranged that these ports should be transferred to the Italian Government. This was part of a larger transfer by the Sultan and covered also ports south of the Benadir, from the mouth of the Juba River, where the Italian concession terminated, to the mouth of the Wanga or Umba River.

We shall now examine the title of the Sultan of Zanzibar to the ownership of these African ports. At the close of the seventeenth century Sultan Sef, of the Arabian State of Oman, frequently called Sultan of Muscat after the capital of that State, sent a fleet to the East African coast and with the help of the people of the ports and islands finally expelled the Portuguese. The ports and islands, even Mogadishu, which had retained its independence under the Portuguese, now became nominally subject to Oman, but they made many declarations of independence and were in fact virtually independent, the lords of Oman having too much to occupy them in the Arabian conflicts to be able to enforce their authority so far afield. Sultan Said Said * of Oman (Sultan Said), who became the Imam of Muscat in 1806, then engaged in the task of bringing the East African ports and islands under subjection, an effort which was not yet fully accomplished when, in November, 1843, Dr. Krapf, of the London "Church Missionary Society," sailed slowly down the coast in an Arab vessel. The lead in resistance to the Sultans was taken by the islanders of Mombasa, termed Mwita in the Swahili language spoken along that coast. Dr. Krapf, who spent seven years in that area investigating the languages and customs of the people, states that Mombasa was then inhabited by the Kabila tribe of the Wamwita, who had populated the island from early times, with the remnants of eleven other tribes both Arabian and local, which had been dispersed or destroyed in the course of time, particularly during the rule of the Portuguese.

The rest of the coast and the neighbouring islands were doubtless similarly populated; the descendants of Arabian and Perso-Arabian settlers, Gallas, Somalis and others from Ethiopia, with remnants of the Bantu people who were extending from their original home but mainly spreading southwards, and Calicut Banyan traders. When Vasco da Gama visited Mombasa in 1498 numerous "Oriental Christians" were resident there. The people of the ports and islands had revolted many times against the Portuguese and were unwilling to submit to further conquerors.

---

* SULTAN SAID was an ancestor of Sultan Seyyid Khalifa-bin-Said, referred to above, who became Sultan in 1888.

The Governorship of Mombasa had become hereditary to the tribe of the Masarue (or Msara), believed to have been of Persian origin. At their head were three brothers, Abdullah Ben Akhmed, Mbarak and Salem. When Abdullah succeeded to the Governorship he determined to free Mombasa from the rule of Muscat and accordingly sent to Sultan Said, instead of the customary heavy tribute, some powder and shot, a shirt of mail and a small measure of corn. The Sultan understood this to be a declaration of independence, he made no comment but bided his time.

Abdullah Ben Akhmed journeyed to Bombay and asked the aid of the British Government in the coming struggle with the Sultan. He was cordially received, but no help was vouchsafed. Abdullah maintained the independence of Mombasa till his death in 1822, and gave assistance also to the other ports and islands. Patta, Brava, Lamu, Pemba and Zanzibar held out for some time, but Sultan Said conquered them at last. In 1823 he prepared to attack Mombasa where the aged Solim Ben Ali, who had succeeded Abdullah Ben Akhmed, was ill-fitted to conduct the defence. An appeal was accordingly made to a British naval force, which, under Captain (afterwards Admiral) Owen, was at the time exploring those waters. Mbarak, accompanied by the foremost citizens of the island, went aboard H.M.S. Baracouta and persuaded its commander, Captain Vidal, to permit the British flag to be hoisted in the fortress and the town. When the Sultan's commander arrived to bombard Mombasa, he retired on seeing the British flag.

Captain Owen, in February, 1824, made a convention with the islanders that Mombasa and all the ports and islands between Malindi and the River Pangani were to be under British protection, a British representative was to reside in Mombasa, half the public revenues were to be paid to the British, the other half to the Msara. The English were to be allowed to trade with the interior and the slave trade was to be abolished.

The charge for protection, half the revenue, would certainly have proved onerous and prejudicial to local development. The meaning which "protection" by a European Power came to have in Africa was evidently far from being anticipated by the people of Mombasa, who seem to have regarded the arrangement as a mere protection against enemies in return for an annual payment, no political control by the protecting Power being involved.

The convention of Captain Owen was, of course, subject to ratification in London. British Residents and some soldiers were stationed in Mombasa and Pemba for some time, but official British ratification was eventually refused.

When the British had withdrawn Sultan Said immediately took steps to deal with "contumacious" Mombasa. Having demanded unconditional submission he refused to deal with the envoys who journeyed from the island to make terms with him, and sailed in person to compel obedience with 2,000 soldiers, a warship, the Liverpool, of seventy-four guns, a frigate with sixty-four guns, two corvettes and seven smaller vessels, all of modern British or European build, a most formidable array. Nevertheless his demand for submission was again rejected. Mbarak was now dead, but Salem, the last of the three brave brothers, conducted the defence. Only after a terrific bombardment of the town and fortress did Sultan Said secure a compromise: The fortress was to be surrendered; the Sultan was to place there fifty soldiers; he was to have half the revenue, but Salem was to remain governor and his heirs were to succeed him. Sultan Said broke the agreement a few days later, by introducing further soldiers in order to reduce the governor to a position of military inferiority; but an attempt to overthrow Salem only resulted in Mombasa breaking free again. His Admiral having failed to take the island, Sultan Said himself made two further unsuccessful attempts.

Only after the death of Salem were members of another tribe induced by liberal bribery to assist the secret landing of troops from Muscat. Even then the Sultan judged it wisest to proceed by stealth. He sent his son in a warship to make a secret attempt to seize the chiefs of the Msara. Twenty-five of them were captured by surprise in a single night and removed in chains to Zanzibar, where the Sultan had now built himself a Palace. From thence they were conveyed in their chains to Muscat, where most of them died from the rigours of their captivity.

Those of the Msara who escaped capture fled the same night from the island with their wives and children, leaving behind all their property. They took refuge in the Wanika-land and afterwards settled at Takaunga, near Malindi, and at Gassi further south.

Soon after these events, on December 28, 1843, Dr. Krapf arrived at Takaunga with his wife, being obliged to wait there for a ship to take them on to Zanzibar. The inhabitants treated them most hospitably and lent them the only stone house in the village. They complained, however, very sorely that " the English had left the Msara in the lurch and had not protected them against the Imam of Muscat. They inveighed bitterly against him for his treacherous behaviour to their chief men, averring that the English had done wrong in giving over the people of Mombasa to his rule."

Dr. Krapf was embarrassed at receiving these complaints; he replied that his mission was religious and that he had no concern with politics.

Having subdued Mombasa Sultan Said Said transferred his residence from Muscat to Zanzibar in 1840. The United States Government had already established a Consulate there; Britain followed suit in 1843 and France in 1847.

The ports and islands off the East African coast had not yet been brought fully under subjection by His Highness the Sultan when they were transferred to the British East Africa Company and the Benadir coast was handed to the Italian Government.

British, French and German Recognition of the Sultan of Zanzibar's Right to Ethiopian South Coast Ports First Extended Only Within Town Walls

As we have seen, the Agreement concluded between the British Government and the Sultan of Zanzibar, that the Sultan should transfer certain ports on the Benadir coast of Ethiopia to the British East Africa Company, which would transfer them to the Italian Government, restricted the concession to a radius of 10 sea miles on the landward side around each of three seaport towns and but five sea miles around the village of Warsheikh. It is interesting to observe that by a Procès-Verbal, which had been signed at Zanzibar, on June 9, 1886, delegates of Great Britain, France, and Germany had unanimously agreed that the sovereign rights of the Sultan of Zanzibar on the Benadir coast covered only the actual ports of Kismayu, Brava, Merka and Mogadishu, and that "the territory belonging to the Sultan does not extend beyond the walls of those towns." We must conclude from this and other documentary evidence that the rights of the Sultan on the Benadir coast were shadowy, and, at most, extended only to the ports. The European Powers took a somewhat larger view of the rights possessed by the Sultan when they began the process of inducing him to transfer his rights to themselves. Nevertheless, Italy's possessions on the Benadir coast were at first narrowly restricted to the immediate neighbourhood of a village and four towns, one of which, Kismayu, she was to share on equal terms with Britain.

British Support for Italian Aspirations—Good and Bad

Formal British Government approval was stipulated as an essential part of the Agreement by which the British East Africa Company transferred to the Italian Government the Benadir Ports, received by the company from the Sultan. This approval being accorded, the Agreement was signed by representatives of the two Governments on August 12, 1892. To refute the latter-day propaganda, particularly in Fascist and post-Fascist times, that Britain is Italy's "traditional enemy," we need not go back so far as the period of Italy's struggle for national unity, when the assistance of William Ewart Gladstone, Lord John Russell and many other lesser-known people in Britain and the warm acclamation and agitation of the British public on behalf of Italian freedom advanced the Italian cause. That support should be proudly remembered by Britain and by Italy. British support for Italian colonial expansion is a less creditable record. As on the Red Sea, so on the shores of the Indian Ocean, British support, and British support alone, made possible the existence of the Italian colonies—more is the pity and the regret! Now that the colonial era is closing, we must express regret that Britain facilitated what proved to be a particularly evil phase of it in East Africa, an area where colonialism was least justified, because the expansion of the European Powers there was at the expense of the progressive Government of an ancient State, which had attained a high civilisation, and had maintained independence across the centuries, despite the assaults of many invaders from overseas.

Very significant is the following letter from the Sultan of Zanzibar, Hammed-Bin-Thwain, to Mr. Rennell Rodd, Her Britannic Majesty's Acting Diplomatic Agent and Consul-General, who conducted some of the negotiations concerning the occupation of the Benadir Ports by Italy:

THE SULTAN OF ZANZIBAR TO MR. RODD.
(*Translation.*) ZANZIBAR, *May* 14, 1893.

(*After compliments.*) *As to the wishes of our friends the Italians regarding the Benadir ports, I hereby appoint you and give you full power in that matter to do what may seem good to you, and it is better to have this matter settled by your Honour. I have faith in you that you will do nothing but good for us.*

Written by his order by his slave,
SALEM-BIN-MAHOMED.

About three years before the date of the above letter, on June 14, 1890, the Sultan of Zanzibar, Seyyid Ali-Bin-Said, had accepted a British protectorate over his dominions. His concessions to Italy were, in consequence, fully dependent upon British approval.

Government of Benadir Ports Transferred to Italian Company

The Italian Government were given power to transfer the administration and all the extensive rights conferred upon them by the Treaty to an Italian Company then in process of formation, which would administer " in the name of the Sultan and under his flag," on the responsibility of the Italian Government. The extensive rights thus conferred upon the Company included the sole authority to purchase or deal with public lands, all forts, buildings and proprietary rights, the power to appoint all officials and officers, to establish Courts of Justice, the exclusive right to levy taxes, tributes, dues, tolls, export and import duties, to regulate trade and commerce, to establish banks, issue currency, maintain troops, and take any measures they thought fit.

These extensive rights over the ports and their populations were granted to the Italian Government, and through them to the projected Company, for 25 years, renewable, if so willed by the Italian Government, for a further 25 years. The ethics of nineteenth century European Government did not preclude the bartering of the liberty and happiness of distant peoples and their transfer to the arbitrary rule of mere commercial enterprises.

Rule of the Benadir Ports and the territories of Obbia and the Mijjerteins by the Company created by Filonardi, who had engineered Italian " protection " of the two last-named territories, proved unacceptable. Administration was transferred in 1898 to the Benadir Company, but it proved so tragic and scandalous that, in response to public and Parliamentary outcries, the Italian Government was goaded into holding an enquiry; this revealed an appalling condition of misrule under which revenue was actually levied upon the slave trade. The Company was reconstituted, but iniquitous conditions still prevailed in respect of which a fuller description will be given later.

Italian Payments to Sultan of Zanzibar

In return for control of the **Benadir Ports the** Italian Government undertook to pay the Sultan of Zanzibar a premium of 40,000 rupees, and a further 160,000 rupees per annum, payable in four quarterly instalments. It seems the Italian Government found difficulty in meeting these obligations, for on May 15, 1893, they secured a deferment for three years of the 40,000 rupees premium, by a curious expedient: a supplementary Agreement, which provided that Italian administration of the ports, for the first three years, should be merely provisional. At the expiration of that period the Italian Government would pay the premium unless they should decide to evacuate the ports.

Most obviously the Italian Government intended no such evacuation. On the contrary, they were then actively manoeuvring, as we know, to secure the whole of Ethiopia, for whose southern commerce the Benadir Ports were essential.

II

THE ADVANCE INLAND: NEGOTIATIONS WITH THE EMPEROR MENELIK II

Having obtained the southern ports, the Italians at once began pressing inland from the south, as they were doing already from the north. In 1893 an Italian agent, Captain Bottego, penetrated as far as Lugh, on the left bank of the Juba, a fertile, populous area, well watered from the river, a market for trade with the Ethiopian interior as far as Shoa, particularly with the rich Boran province. In December, 1895, the attention of the Emperor Menelik and his generals was desperately engaged with the Italian attack from the north; the battles of Amba Alagi and Makalle were being fought. No thought could be spared for Captain Bottego, who, accompanied by an armed force, and an assistant, Ferrandi, again appeared at Lugh. These invaders erected a small fort; Ferrandi was left to hold it, with 42 Ascaris and a store of ammunition and provisions, while Bottego "continued his journey," as Tittoni[*], the Italian Minister of Foreign Affairs, subsequently stated. Ferrandi remained at the fort for sixteen months, and claimed that in December, 1896, he repulsed an attempt to dislodge him by an Ethiopian Commander, Wolde Gabriel. Apparently for this reason, the Italians added Ferrandi's name to the place, and called it henceforth, "Lugh Ferrandi"; glory was readily granted in those times for any petty skirmish undertaken in the interests of Italian expansion in Africa. The subsequent struggle to retain Lugh, and to snatch a southern colony, clearly demonstrates how little sincerity there was on the Italian side in the declaration of "perpetual friendship" embodied in the Peace Treaty, which had terminated Italy's war of aggression against Ethiopia only two months before.

---

[*] Speech to the Italian Chamber of Deputies on February 13, 1908. See authorised translation of the speeches of Senator Tommaso Tittoni, by Baron Quaranta, page 283 (London, Smith Elder).

The Emperor MENELIK II of ETHIOPIA
From a painting by the late G. F. Harris

Italy Tries Again; Obtains Vast Extension of Territory, But Still Unsatisfied

Undeterred either by defeat of their forces in the field, or by the promises of friendship they had made, both personally and by Treaty, the Italian Government proceeded, without a pause, to plan and manoeuvre for the conquest of Ethiopia by other means.

So early as March 28, 1897, according to the account given by Tittoni to the Italian Chamber of Deputies*, Major Nerazzini was sent to Ethiopia with instructions to regulate the Somaliland frontier. He returned to Italy in June of the same year with a map by Habernicht (Spezial Karte von Afrika, Sektion Abissinien, 6). Thereon the Emperor Menelik had traced a line representing the frontier he was willing to accept, and had affixed to it his seal. Major Nerazzini thus described the frontier Menelik had indicated:

"As to the border line on the side of the Indian Ocean, I obtained a demarcation which gave us, starting from the point of intersection of our frontier with the English one in the land of the Somalis, a zone of absolute possession parallel to the coast, of the depth of about 180 miles from the coast itself, and which reaches the course of the Juba at that point in which the cataracts of Von der Decken are marked. According to this frontier line, the station of Lugh would be excluded from our possessions, and I deemed it my duty to insist very strongly upon this point."

It was unfortunate, however, from the Italian standpoint, as Nerazzini observed, that the local Sultan of Lugh, though Captain Bottego had induced him to sign a Treaty, had bound himself by a written agreement with Menelik, and a declaration that he was an Ethiopian subject. Nerazzini continued:

"Menelik refuses to recognise the absolute possession of Lugh by Italy, but undertakes to recognise the establishment of Italian commerce in that station, engaging himself to protect it from raids on the part of the Amhara."

By "the Amhara" Nerazzini apparently meant the forces of the Ethiopian State.

An Easy Prize

Despite the exclusion of Lugh from the area Menelik had agreed to allow to Italy, a large territory would be secured without a blow; the entire coast, on which the Benadir Ports, leased from the Sultan of Zanzibar, were situated, to a depth of 180 miles would now be held by Italy, in place of the mere radius of 10 sea miles around the ports. Moreover, the agreements, of doubtful value, which Filonardi had made with the local Sultans of Obbia and the Mijjerteins, would be replaced by a Treaty officially signed by the Emperor on behalf of himself, his heirs and assigns, extending Italian territory on the Indian Ocean coast to a depth of 180 miles right up to its northern extremity at Cape Guardafui.

---

* Speech to the Chamber of Deputies, February 13, 1908. See Storia Diplomatica Dell' Etiopia, Carlo Rossetti, S.T.E.N., Torino.

This was, of course, a wonderful stroke of luck for Italy. The Italian President of the Council and the Ministers for War and Foreign Affairs telegraphed direct to the Emperor on September 3, 1897, accepting his proposal.

The Emperor replied:

"*Telegram of September 3rd received. Very glad of the ratification of Treaty of commerce and of Agreement upon new frontier; hope in friendly relations between ourselves and Italy.*"

The Emperor's satisfaction was short-lived; Italian rapacity immediately advanced a further claim. The Italian Government were determined to accept no fixed boundary; their policy was to keep the frontier moving, in accordance with an ever advancing colonisation.

This view was expressed by Foreign Minister, Tittoni,* to the Italian Chamber of Deputies:—

"*The Hon. Canetta has insisted that the question of the frontier between Italian Somaliland and Ethiopia be speedily defined; but, frankly, I do not see the urgency and necessity of such delimitation. Between the Benadir proper and Ethiopia there is a very vast region which belongs no one knows exactly to whom . . . . Let us leave, therefore, to time the solution of problems such as this.*"

The story that territory the Italian Government desired to annex belonged to no one was of course convenient to the Italian Government and was used by Italian Foreign Affairs Ministers in dealing with their Parliamentary critics. Yet they recognised the territory as part of Ethiopia in negotiating with the Emperor of Ethiopia to allow them a share of it.

Moreover Tittoni himself, in a speech to the Chamber of Deputies on May 16, 1908, clearly admitted that the territory was not no-man's land but belonged to Ethiopia in these words:—

"*It was difficult to contest the right of Ethiopia and to confute the logic of the Negus.*"

Ethiopian Boundaries

Before King Victor Emmanuel of Italy and his Prime Minister Crispi made war to secure a protectorate over Ethiopia, and whilst they were still declaring that Italy was Ethiopia's only true friend in Europe, the Italian negotiator, Pietro Antonelli, had been instructed by the Italian Foreign Minister to induce the Emperor Menelik to address a circular letter to the Powers defining the boundaries of Ethiopia. A letter written by Antonelli from Aden, on March 26, 1891, to the Italian Foreign Affairs Minister in Rome,

---

* Italy's foreign and Colonial Policy speeches of Senator Tommaso Tittoni, authorised English Translation (Smith Elder), page 270.

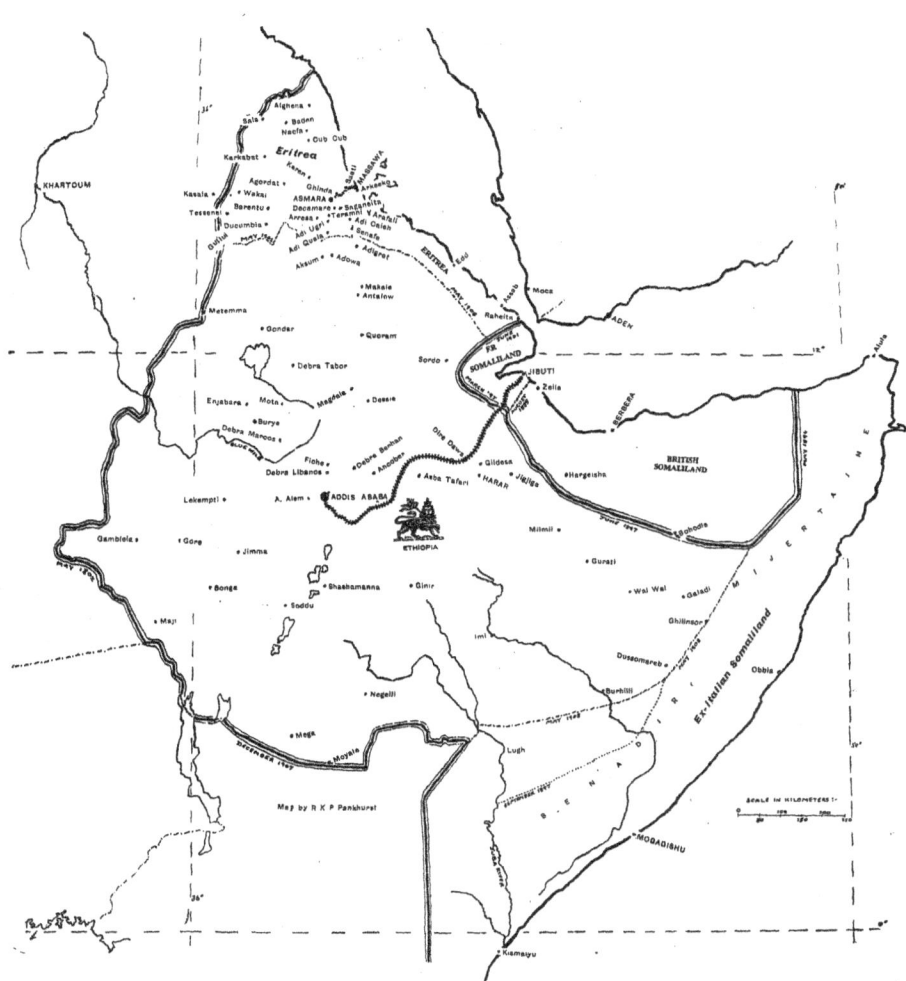

Map of Ethiopia and the surrounding European colonies and the boundaries fixed by treaties between Ethiopia, Britain, France and Italy as given by Carlo Rossetti in "Storia Diplomatica dell' Etiopia Durante Il Regno Menelik II (S.T.E.N., Turin).

states that the draft for this circular which Antonelli had submitted to the Emperor was discussed at length. The Emperor was not satisfied with the draft, and protested that Lake Stefanie and Lake Rudolf were included within the Ethiopian boundaries. Antonelli's draft has been reproduced in part along with his letter to the Minister in Rossetti's "Storia Diplomatica."* The draft is vague and somewhat jumbled; it appears to have been prepared by one who was not very familiar with the geography of South Eastern Ethiopia. It states, however, definitely that the Ethiopian Empire includes the whole of the Ogaden and the lands inhabited to the south and east by the Gallas and Somalis, some of whose tribes it names. Though the draft includes within Ethiopia the Somalilands, except the portions already annexed by Britain and France, the Italian Foreign Ministers, Visconti Venosta and Tittoni, subseqently alleged to the Italian Chamber of Deputies that only the Galla lands were included and that the Emperor Menelik had made no claim to territories inhabited by the Somalis until after the Italian defeat at Adowa. There is much evidence to prove this allegation incorrect.

From the King downwards, viscounts, marquesses and commoners, all the Italian negotiators who were concerned in dealing with Ethiopia were as one in their determination to cheat the guileless Ethiopian and rob him of his ancient patrimony.

On September 13, 1897, the Italian Government had telegraphed to the Emperor Menelik accepting the Somaliland frontier he had offered them, which gave them "a zone of absolute possession" in an area covering 1,000 miles of coast to a depth of 180 miles. This was an amazingly handsome gift from a sovereign whom the Italian Government had so recently tricked, and against whom they had waged aggressive war. Less than a month after receiving the donation of this large territory which had neither been conquered, nor, for the most part, even explored by Italy, Visconti Venosta instructed Major Ciccodicóla, Italy's representative in Addis Ababa, to confirm the acceptance of what Menelik had offered, and to press for more.

From Bardera to Lugh

Beyond the frontier of the big territory thus obtained stood the little fort Captain Bottégo had built at Lugh. Menelik had consented to guarantee it as an Italian commercial station, but it was regarded by the Italian Government as a pawn they had been able to advance beyond the rest of the new colony; they were determined to bring the entire frontier into line with it—and then to advance further.

On October 19, 1897, Visconti Venosta instructed Major Ciccodicóla:—

" The recognition of the establishment of an Italian commercial station at Lugh is not sufficient to guarantee the

---

* Carlo Rossetti, " Storia Diplomatica " dell' Etiopia Durante il Regno di Menelik II.

> *station. You will have to propose for Lugh a real and proper commercial convention, which guarantees both the station and the roads communicating with the coast.*
>
> *" You must also insist with the Negus in order to obtain the inclusion of Lugh in Italian territory."**

Menelik Protests: Why Re-open Frontier Question?

The Emperor being unwilling to assent to further Italian inroads, Visconti Venosta telegraphed on January 6, 1898, ordering Ciccodicóla to insist on the inclusion of Lugh within Italian territory.

> *" Why," Menelik protested, " should we wish to begin again to talk of the boundary at the moment when, thank God, it is all settled? The Government of His Majesty the King of Italy accepted the frontier I proposed for their consideration. If after that we return again to talk of the frontier, then the question renews itself and we shall have no end to it."*

Successively the Italian Ministers Capelli in 1898, Morin in 1903, Tittoni in 1905, San Giuliano in 1906, renewed the same instructions to the ubiquitous Major Ciccodicóla who was always there in Addis Ababa pressing for Italian ownership of the little fort at Lugh, which was to draw into line with it a vast new territory. Guicciardini, in March, 1906, hazarded a more subtle method of approach to the desired end by suggesting the establishment of a neutral zone, " without talking of the demarcation of frontiers."

"The Frontier is at Bardera"

In June, 1906, Tommaso Tittoni, who again occupied the Foreign Ministry, sent Martini, the Governor of Eritrea, to discuss with Menelik a neutral zone at Lugh. The Emperor protested: " The frontier is at Bardera!" and stated that he could show to Martini the Italian Government's acceptance of that frontier. Captain Colli was now instructed to keep the negotiations going. In telegrams of September, October and November, he reported renewed assurances of the Emperor that the Italians could retain their so-called commercial station at Lugh, but the Italians were not satisfied with that.

Frontier Conflicts

There were frequent frontier incidents. The Italians made sallies from the fort at Lugh. The local population bitterly opposed them. On May 16, 1908, Tittoni told the Italian Parliament that his policy throughout this period had been to prevent any action by Ethiopia south of the British Somali Protectorate, whereas the Emperor Menelik contended that Ethiopian sovereignty extended southward as far as the border of the territory

---

* Quoted by Tittoni. See Quaranta's translation (Smith Elder), page 285, and Carlo Rossetti " Storia Diplomatica," p.p. 405-6.

he had agreed to cede to Italy in 1897 with the frontier at Bardera which the Italian Government had accepted.

Tittoni complained in his speech to the Chamber* that the population of the territory Italy most coveted in the neighbourhood of the Juba and Webbi Shebeli rivers, was of "bellicose character," disposed to rebellion and easily led to follow Ethiopian policy.

Menelik, he asserted, was following a system of pacific propaganda among the Somali tribes to ensure their loyalty to Ethiopian sovereignty. Three Rahanuin chiefs who had been arrested by Ethiopian officials had been affably received by the Emperor who had assured them of his protection. These chiefs had returned from Addis Ababa to their tribes wearing the ceremonial dress which it was customary for the Emperor to present to loyal and meritorious subjects. Moreover, the Emperor had sent to administer the Somali territories a Muslim chief, who, by his appeal to their own religious feelings, would give major value to his assurances of peace and security. "We cannot escape," said Tittoni, "from the importance and danger of this Ethiopian policy. It is more civilised than the ancient system," but "little by little it will lead to the disappearance among the Somalis of their old dislike of the Amhara." He emphasised that local opposition would thus be more and more directed against the Italians.

"The voluntary recognition of the Ethiopian Government by the Somali tribes will irremediably prejudice our aspirations and will stabilise the right and the fact of Ethiopian rule in those territories."

This speech of Tittoni is immensely important to an understanding of Italian policy towards Ethiopia, which was characterised by efforts to cause disaffection and disruption inside Ethiopia by the suborning of chiefs by bribes of money and arms, the setting of tribe against tribe, the arming of irregular bands who were encouraged to raid across the frontiers for loot. The difficulties created for the Ethiopian Government by a Power operating such a policy on the frontier may be partially realised by Europeans who were neighbours of Germany during the period of Nazi expansion. More ruthless methods could be employed, and were employed, in East Africa remote from observation by Press and other critics.

Again the question arises why, after the defeat of Italy at Adowa, the Emperor Menelik assented to the occupation of any further Ethiopian territory by that Power whose successive administrations had dealt with him so unscrupulously. To comprehend his policy we must again recall that Italy was Britain's protégé and had continual support from her. We must realise too the overwhelming nature of European expansion in Africa which overcame every native State there, save Ethiopia alone.

---

* Speech of Foreign Affairs Minister, Tommaso Tittoni, to the Chamber of Deputies, May 16, 1908, quoted by Rossetti "Storia Diplomatica," from the official Atti Parlamentari. "Storia Diplomatica," pp. 409-10.

Menelik knew he could not hold the coast; he strove to save the interior. He hoped the coast would some day be regained if the independence of the more populous and fertile interior could be maintained.

Rendered anxious by the continual efforts of Italy to advance further inland, distressed by the hardship to the local population caused by the continual Italian raids from the fort at Lugh, he insisted in 1908 that the frontier question should be settled by a formal treaty. Therefore, much as the Italians desired to keep the frontier open, Tittoni informed the Chamber of Deputies "it was no longer possible to protract a solution."

Anglo-Ethiopian Boundary

The British also had been thrusting north from the coast they had obtained from the Sultan of Zanzibar. In February, 1908, Sir Thomas Holer induced the Emperor Menelik to grant a frontier starting from the junction of the river Dawa with the river Ganale to form the Juba river near Dolo, and thence westward, past the lowest creek of Lake Stefanie, and cutting off the end of Lake Rudolf, taking the greater part of that lake into British East Africa. (subsequently Kenya colony).

From Lugh to Dolo

This treaty between Ethiopia and Britain, Tittoni informed the Italian Chamber of Deputies, was dangerous for the commerce of the Italian Benadir, which might be diverted to the coast through British territory. At the same time the British Treaty which brought the Kenya frontier almost to Dolo on the Juba a good many miles north of Lugh, encouraged the Italians to advance their claim. They now demanded, and obtained by a Treaty of May 16, 1908, a frontier extending from Dolo on the Juba to the Webbi Shebeli, where it joined the line of frontier agreed in 1907. The wedge of territory thus secured by advancing the frontier from Bardera to Dolo gave them 50,000 kilometres of territory more than the 1907 line would have given them, an area, as Tittoni boasted to the Chamber, twice the size of Sicily.

Ethiopian Opposition to Enlargement of Italian Colony

Count Colli di Felizzano, as Tittoni further declared, affirmed that this line was the maximum obtainable owing to " the precedents of Ethiopian right and of fact " in that region, and " the general obstinate opposition " to the Italian occupation on the part of all the Ethiopian chiefs (Capi Abissini). This opposition had in part been stated in writing. Therefore, he added, the announcement of the conclusion of the Treaty was received with astonishment in Addis Ababa.

Three million Italian lire had been paid to the Ethiopian Emperor as compensation for this cession of territory; as Tittoni observed: " Not an exaggerated sum if one knows how to value the importance of the territory secured."

The Importance of the New Territory

The new acquisition, he explained, included the district of Baidoa, an agricultural zone of no little importance which Captain Bottégo had described when he first discovered it as follows:—

" *We are in the centre of Baidoa. Who has not visited this region, called the granary of Somaliland, cannot imagine how, after long reaches of arid steppes, appears almost by magic a land so fertile. The contrast between the green, populous farms, which render the country pleasant and cheerful, and the deserted thorn bush and burning sands of the coastal region, produces in the mind of the traveller the most agreeable surprise. To have an idea of such fertility one must think of the rich cultivation of our own country.*"*

Such descriptions of the territory the Italians discovered in East Africa when they first set foot there are important as a corrective to their subsequent claims that they turned barren wastes into fertile farms and taught savage peoples the art of cultivation. A testimony to the ability of the local population of Baidoa as agriculturalists, herdsmen and merchants was given by Tittoni, who told his Parliament that with the new Treaty, Italy had acquired possession of all the lands inhabited by the Rahanuin Somalis, whom he described as a population "difficult, but laborious, who practise, with equal activity and ability, agriculture, stock raising and commerce."

As we shall presently show, it was the policy of the Italian Government to dispossess these people of their land and to compel them to work as labourers for Italian proprietors.

Italy now possessed, Tittoni explained, the caravan routes between the coast and the basin of the Juba river. A commercial agreement with Ethiopia had been obtained which guaranteed Italian action between the Benadir and the Galla and Arussi areas, Jam Jam, and the Boran, in order that Lugh might recover its ancient position as the market between the Galla districts and the Benadir. Tittoni did not indicate how Lugh had come to lose that ancient position, but we may conclude that the presence of armed Italians there, and the fighting initiated by them had deterred many peaceful merchants from resorting there.

By an exchange of notes between the Emperor Menelik and the Italian Minister in Addis Ababa the Italian Somaliland colony was assured the same conditions in regard to commerce, customs, etc., as were enjoyed by the French and British colonies. Italian merchants from the Benadir colony on entering Ethiopia were assured of protection by the Ethiopian authorities and the same treatment as Ethiopian merchants, and were permitted to establish agencies and depots of merchandise in Ethiopia and to engage in commerce there.

---

* Quoted by Tittoni from " L'Omo," page 66, etc.; see also Carlo Rossetti " Storia Diplomatica " S.T.E.N. Torino, page 412.

Benadir Ports: Full Ownership Transferred to Italy

When the Italians began their efforts to obtain a colony in Somaliland, they operated, as we have seen, from the Benadir ports, which were leased to them for 50 years by the Sultan of Zanzibar, by favour of the British Government, who had induced the Sultan to accept British management of his dominions. The lease of the ports to Italy was due to terminate in August, 1942, when the Sultan, had he been permitted, might have given the Italians notice to quit. Again the British Government befriended Italian colonisation by arranging in 1905 for the Sultan to give Italy absolute possession of the ports on payment of a mere £144,000!

Kismayu and Jubaland Ceded to Italy

In 1905 also, Britain leased land near the Port of Kismayu to Italy. In 1924 bitter Italian complaints that their country had received less than a fair share of the spoils of the first World War (as promised by the Treaty of London, 1915), caused Britain to offer appeasement by ceding to Italy the 36,000 square miles of Kenya adjacent to Italian Somaliland called Jubaland, thus giving Italy the coveted fertile land on the right bank of the river Juba, which had formed the frontier between the two territories, and also the Port of Kismayu.

This concession did not at all satisfy Italian ambitions. Italian Somaliland thus included an area of 194,000 square miles, whilst British Somaliland had 68,000 square miles, French Somaliland, 8,492 square miles, and Ethiopian Somaliland had been reduced by the colonisation of the three Powers to 100,000 square miles.

SOMALI FISHERMEN, circa 1920.

THE MULLAH'S STRONGHOLD AT TALE, built in 1913; destroyed with explosives by a British demolition force, a company of the Camel Corps, in 1920. It consisted of a main walled enclosure of stone, 12-14 feet thick at base, 6 feet thick at top, surmounted by 13 forts. Within the enclosure were numerous stone granaries and ample space for many hundred head of stock. Three covering forts at a distance of 200 yards were not less than 50 to 60 feet high.

III

THE RISE OF THE MULLAH: "ITALY HAS NO MONEY TO WASTE"

During the years when Italy was acquiring the Somali colony, Tittoni frequently declared that no steps could be taken to occupy the colony until the revolt of the Mullah had been liquidated.

These words of his were typical: "The Chamber does not want that, at a time when very serious economic problems call for our attention in Italy, we should waste money elsewhere."

"We could not possibly adventure ourselves in any expedition against the Mullah," Tittoni said, on May 14, 1904, "nor occupy the hinterland of Somaliland, because such a course would have cost us no less than it has cost England, who, according to the declarations made in the House of Commons by Mr. Arnold Foster, has spent sixty million lire, without counting the sums which will be charged to the Indian Budget."

In short, the Italian Government stood aside and waited for the old British benefactor to accomplish the task and pay the bill.

It is not our purpose to make any assessment of the personal character of Mohammed bin Abdullah who styled himself "The Mullah," and was called by his opponents the "Mad Mullah." We refer to the events of which he was the centre only in so far as they have a bearing upon Italian rule in Somaliland. No fair judgment of him can be obtained from the writings of members of the foreign administrations against whom he fought; the defeated rebel receives no laurels. Douglas Jardine,* Secretary of the British Somaliland Protectorate during the Mullah's campaigns, has published a letter from the Sheikh of Mecca to the Mullah which appears to be an authentic document. Therein the Sheikh reproaches the Mullah for licentious and cruel treatment of his own people and orders him no longer to style himself Seyyid, Mahdi or anything of the sort. Yet the Mullah appears to have begun his career as a religious leader preaching austerity and purity of life and faith. His fight, whether for personal power, or to free his country from the European Governments, was conditioned by the country and the enemy he had to face. He could not success-

---

* "The Mad Mullah of Somaliland," by Douglas Jardine, O.B.E. (Herbert Jenkins).

fully engage European troops in their fortified towns on the coast but must rely on ambushing small forces on the march. He seems to have relied for the maintenance of his armies on the stock he could capture from the tribes who refused to join him. His warfare caused appalling distress and famine; but the rebel who takes up arms to expel a foreign government from his native land has always been counted a hero when the liberation of his country has been effected.

That the Mullah displayed both daring and able strategy, and that he secured a considerable following, was admitted by his British adversaries, who were surprised by the great stone fortresses erected under his auspices, particularly that of Tale which had walls 12 to 14 feet thick at the base, and forts 60 feet high.

We may here fitly quote Jardine, who, writing after the death of the Mullah, had only hard words for him, and yet was not wholly blind to some of the matters the Mullah and his supporters resented:—

> "Has the Somali so very much to be grateful for? Those who know the country can best answer this question for themselves, bearing in mind that it has taken thirty-six years of British government to establish peace and order, that the real wealth of the country is no greater than in 1884; that no system of education has been established; that agriculture and industries are still almost as non-existent as when we first took charge; and that taxation is already very high, having regard to the poverty of the people and the low stage of development in Somaliland."

Mullah Alternates Between British and Italian Territory, Seizes Illig

The activities of the Mullah commenced in the remote south-eastern corner of the British Somaliland Protectorate, near the border of Italian Somaliland, where he repeatedly took refuge when attacked, for the Italian colony was mainly unoccupied and uncharted. Moreover, without Italian permission the British forces could not pursue him there. He operated often in the Nogal Valley, which lay half in the British Protectorate, half in the Italian colony. He was frequently in the Italian colony and occupied and fortified there the seaport village of Illig, on the Indian Ocean, where he received supplies of arms from Arabia.

There was at first little real force to oppose the Mullah. British garrisons were manned by a few dozen officers and a few hundred African or Indian soldiers. The tribes had been disarmed in the area under British administration and promised British protection; under the Pax Britannica the tribes had grown unused to war.

First and Second British Expeditions Against the Mullah

The Mullah succeeded in eluding four successive expeditions which were organised to capture him. The first two, in 1900 and 1901-2, consisted of Somali volunteers who enlisted in large numbers under British officers. The third and fourth expeditions, in 1903 and 1903-4, were composed of regular forces from India, South Africa and the Sudan, and latterly also from England. The first expedition was rendered abortive by the retreat of the Mullah into Italian territory. The British commander consulted the Italian Consul-General who was eager for the British to follow the disturbing rebel into the Italian colony to apprehend him, but the London Government refused permission.

The second expedition terminated with the flight of the Mullah into waterless, unexplored bush in the Italian colony.

Third and Fourth Expeditions: Italy Strikes a Bargain to let British Forces Pass

For the third expedition the British were desirous of effecting a pincer movement starting from bases at Berbera on the Gulf of Aden and Obbia on the Indian Ocean. For permission to land troops at the latter port the Italian Government was approached through diplomatic channels, but the Italian politicians proved reluctant. They finally consented to a conference at which, amongst other matters, they stipulated the following conditions which were conveyed to the British commander by instructions from Field Marshall Earl Roberts and were subsequently published by Jardine in his book on these campaigns:—

(1). British forces must prevent the Mullah going south to the Webbi Shebeli and the Benadir coast in order to avoid disturbance of the trade which provided revenue for the Italian-held Benadir ports.

(2). An Italian political officer must accompany the British forces from Illig to Mudug which (if the British were successful in disposing of the troublesome Mullah) the Italian Government hoped to fortify and hold, as they had held Lugh to form an outpost from which further advances into the interior would be made.

This Italian scheme was frustrated because the Mullah eluded the British pincer action. So far from being disposed of, he presently succeeded in ambushing and almost annihilating a small British force at Gumburu, the nine British officers of this contingent all being killed.

The third British expedition terminated with the decision to send a fourth, and stronger force.

Mullah Escapes Across Border: Italy's Tardy Permission to Follow

After several defeats with great losses, inflicted by the fourth expedition, the Mullah again escaped across the Italian border, but permission to follow him was not granted till April 7, 1904, ten days too late Jardine declared. The Mullah now entered fortifications which he had erected at Illig, where the British commander had for some time been asking Italian permission to land. This was granted at last on condition that the landing was made in the presence of an Italian warship, but on this occasion also the Mullah escaped capture.

All the British campaigns against him had therefore proved abortive, except that the last campaign had greatly shattered and demoralised his forces and driven him out of the British protectorate to seek safety elsewhere, at least for a time. The third and fourth campaigns had cost more than five million pounds sterling and many British lives. The United Kingdom Government were unwilling to incur further expenditure on chasing the Mullah.

Ethiopian Collaboration to Protect Peaceful Cultivators

The Ethiopian Government had been asked to collaborate with all four British expeditions by establishing a barrier to prevent hostilities from spreading to the fertile cultivated regions of the Webbi Shebeli and Juba rivers, a precaution desired by Italy for her own interests, as well as being a protection to peaceful farmers. Ethiopian forces discharged this task with efficiency, courage and success.

Italian Prestige and Self-Interest: Prevarications of Tittoni

The question whether Italy's dignity and prestige required her participation in the conflict against the Mullah was many times debated in the Italian Parliament. Tittoni, with his crabbed face and narrow, drooping-lidded eyes, invariably protested that the national exchequer could not support the cost of a military expedition. When challenged in the Senate, he claimed that the disorders of the Mullah concerned only the British as the Mullah only operated in British territory, his headquarters in the Nogal valley being inside British territory. This statement was, of course, entirely untrue, for, as we know, the Mullah was often fighting in Italian territory, and even on the Indian Ocean coast itself. Whilst repudiating all responsibility, Tittoni claimed credit for having permitted British forces to pass through Italian territory, pompously declaring: "If we had been egotistical we should have said to England: The Mullah is in your own territory; this conflict is not our business. You must fight it out with him." On the contrary the British had been permitted to pass through Italian territory "because we recognised the duties imposed upon us by the solidarity of civilised peoples, solidarity to which our ancient friendship with England has given greater efficacy."

"A Duty of Friendship" to Permit the British to Prevent the Mullah from Troubling Italy

A few days later the troubled Minister was accused in the Chamber of Deputies of being too compliant and yielding to England in having granted permission for British troops to pass through Italian territory. "What does England do for you in return for the support you give her?" hotly demanded jealous patriots. Tittoni now reversed his geographical standpoint, and insisted that so far from the Mullah's field of operations being entirely in the British protectorate, as he had told the Senate, the border between British and Italian territory actually ran through the Nogal Valley, where the Mullah was then conducting his campaign, sometimes on the British side of the valley, sometimes on the Italian. "If in her action against the Mullah," he urged, "England had been obliged rigorously to respect this imaginary line drawn between the two possessions, her operations would evidently have been fruitless. It was therefore our duty, without associating ourselves with her war (and we have never done so), to give the English all those facilities which would permit their preventing the Mullah from making our territory the base of his operations. This was the duty of friendship, and it was a duty we felt all the more inasmuch as it would be in no way possible for the Italian Government to adopt an unfriendly attitude towards England in Africa, and expect England to reciprocate with a friendly one in Europe. The problem is a complex one.

" The Hon. Chiesi has said that I am content with the news given out by the British headquarters. Really, this is not correct; we have precise news, which comes to us direct, because an able officer of our Army is stopping at the British headquarters, follows the war operations, and informs us of them. There is reason to hope that the campaign against the Mullah may come satisfactorily to an end in the near future. In spite of this hope we are not only not satisfied, but decidedly dissatisfied. In this region we have a protectorate which has remained purely nominal; we have confined ourselves to paying an annuity to the two Sultans of Obbia and the Mijjerteins and to sending some battleships to exercise a repressive action.

" If we want to do something more in the midst of fanatical and rebellious populations, which are kept in a constant state of unrest by the Mullah's agitation, we should have to have recourse to one of those expeditions which cause the Hon. De Andreis so much anxiety. We have done nothing of the kind; we have not landed a single man.

" The Hon. Chiesi has added, ' What does England give you in return for the support you have given her? . . . . It is precisely our loyal and friendly relations with England that are permitting us to enter into negotiations concerning the settlement of some questions that are vital for our possession of the Benadir and the question of the port of Kismayu."

A Bargain Counter Policy

The result of the negotiations with the British Government here referred to by Tittoni, have already been described: they resulted in the conversion of Italy's fifty years lease of the Benadir ports into absolute ownership, and gave her a landing at the port of Kismayu, which could be used all the year round, and therefore was valuable when the monsoon made the Benadir ports unusable; Italy's foreign policy was always much of a bargain counter.

The "sacred egoism," so loudly boasted by her official spokesman, and which so greatly disgusted President Wilson during the peace negotiations following the first World War, 1914-18, was already highly developed in the first decade of the 20th century, of which we are treating at this point. In addition to the material advantages in the Benadir and Kismayu, above mentioned, Tittoni managed to secure public expressions of thanks in the British House of Lords from the Foreign Secretary, Lord Landsdowne, and from

Lord Percy, in the Commons, for the permission to pass, which, Jardine has told us, came too late. Said Tittoni:—

"*England has declared herself to be most grateful to us for this permission to operate in our territory under certain conditions. Lord Landsdowne recently made himself the mouthpiece of these sentiments in the House of Lords, and the following day Lord Percy declared in the House of Commons that Italy's decision not to enter into any action with troops on land had been previously notified to the British Government, but that fact did not lessen the value of the service to England by the Italian Government in giving her free access to their territories for military operations which could not otherwise have been carried out.*"

Attitude of Ethiopia and Italy Contrasted

Ethiopia who (not for the first or the last time) had put her forces into the field at Britain's request may have received some compliments and thanks but her Government neither demanded nor were offered in return for their active assistance such material rewards as were accorded to Italy, along with the compliments for her mere permission to pass!

Tittoni again averred: " In this territory, which is not occupied by us, we exercise a purely nominal Protectorate. England could reasonably have answered our declaration of neutrality by demanding that whenever the Mullah passed from his own territory to ours he should have been disarmed and his followers driven back. We were not in a position to do this." Nevertheless the Minister declared he had telegraphed to the Minister of Marine to instruct the Italian commander at Aden to send a ship to co-operate with the British at Illig in action from the sea against the Mullah. This declaration was made in response to Parliamentary protests that Italy was humiliated because her ship had been present at an action in which she took no part. We have learnt from Jardine that the presence of the Italian ship was merely an assertion of Italy's sovereignty on the coast and that no action was either taken or intended. Tittoni's own statement a little later concerning Illig renders the whole affair entirely ludicrous.

" Is it a town? No, because the huts of the natives are erected along the shore when they choose to do so, and in time of war, when battleships approach, they are taken into the interior out of reach of the guns. Therefore, as a matter of fact, if we had not made peace with the Mullah, he would have stayed at Illig even without our consent."

An offer of collaboration from the sea alone was thus from Tittoni's own showing of little value, even on the impossible assumption that the British Naval contingent which operated off Illig required Italian aid.

The Mullah Becomes an Italian Protégé
Hard Terms

The British Government were not now disposed to find either men or money to continue the fight against the Mullah. British operations in Somaliland were henceforth rigidly restricted. A few years later (in November, 1909) complete withdrawal to the coast, after distributing arms to the tribes of the interior for their own self-defence, was the decision made in Whitehall.

The Italian Government, having become aware of the trend of British policy, understood that, for the time being at least, all hope that the British would rid them of the Mullah must be abandoned. Cavaliere Pestalozza, the Italian Consul-General in Zanzibar, was therefore instructed to open peace negotiations with the Mullah, offering him a portion of the waterless plains of Northern Somaliland and the port of Illig, which he had already re-occupied. The land and the port assigned to him lay in the territory of the Mijjertein tribes, a part of it under Sultan Osman Mahmoud of the Northern Mijjerteins, and a part under Sultan Jussuf Ali of Obbia of the Southern Mijjerteins.

An Agreement was drawn up, to which the approval of the British Government and of the two Sultans was obtained, containing the following provisions:

(1) There was to be peace between the Mullah " Seyyid Mohammed bin Abdulla with all the Dervishes dependent on him and the Government of Italy and all their dependents, the Somali Mijjerteins and others."

" In view of this, and in relation thereto," there was to be peace between the Mullah and the British Government and their dependents, and with the Ethiopian Government and their dependents. Some of the phrases were curious. For instance:

"The Italian Government guarantee and pledge themselves on behalf of their dependents, as also on behalf of the British Government. Every disagreement between the Seyyid and his people and the dependents of the Italian Government, or those for whom the Government have pledged themselves, as, for example, the English and their dependents, shall be settled in a peaceful and friendly manner by means of an ergo, or envoys from the two parties under the presidency of an Italian delegate, and also in the presence of an English envoy, whenever British interests are concerned."

It will be noticed that the Italians pledged themselves for the English, without mentioning the Ethiopians. The remaining clauses were of vital importance to the Mullah:

(2) He was " authorised by the Italian Government to establish for himself and his people a fixed residence," between Ras Garad and Ras Gabbe, with the approval of Sultans Yussuf Ali and Osman Mahmoud."

The territory assigned to him, with all its inhabitants, was to be " under the protection of the Italian Government and under their flag."

The Italian Government when they thought fit would " install there a representative of Italian or other nationality as Governor, with soldiers and custom-house, or tithes."

The Mullah was to "help and support the Italian Government in all matters," and to be "their procurator" until they appointed a representative of their own.

The government of the tribes subject to the Mullah was to remain in his hands, but was to be exercised "with justice and equity."

The Mullah was to provide for the security of the roads and the safety of caravans in his district.

(3) Commerce was to be "free to all" in the Mullah's territory, "subject to the regulations and ordinances of the Italian Government."

The import of firearms and the cartridges, lead and powder required for them was prohibited. "A formal and complete pledge" by the Mullah and his people, and the declaration that they had taken an oath before God to prevent the traffic, importation and disembarkation of slaves and firearms, whether by sea or land, was embodied in the Agreement. It was added that "whoever shall infringe this Ordinance shall be liable to such punishment as shall be considered fitting by the Italian Government."

The territory assigned to the Mullah included Illig on the coast, the Nogal valley, and the Haud in Italian territory, with the use for grazing of the part of the Nogal valley in British Somaliland.

All differences between the Dervishes and their neighbours were to be "referred to the examination and decision of the Italian Government."

This Agreement placed the Mullah completely under Italian control if Italy chose to occupy the part of Somaliland assigned to him. Though nominally the Mullah had the rule of his own people, the Italian governor and his soldiers would be actually in command, particularly as the Mullah was precluded from importing arms. Moreover, the Mullah could scarcely raise any substantial revenue from recognised sources, as the Italians had monopolised the Customs House. The presence of the Italian governor and Italian soldiers altogether negated all question of a free territory under purely native control, to secure which the long fight of the Mullah had been directed. He does not seem to have been favoured with a subsidy like the Sultans of Obbia and the Northern Mijjerteins. On signing the Agreement (according to the copy supplied to the British) the Mullah wrote:—

> "I have read the above document and understand its entire contents. I have accepted it all in perfect sincerity, and have signed it—in fact Cavaliere Pestalozza knows my state."

These phrases contrast strongly with the bold and truculent style the Mullah habitually employed. If in fact the words were his own, and he actually understood the rigorous terms of the Agreement, it seems clear that either he counted on the continued inactivity of the Italian Government to afford him a freedom not granted by the Agreement, or the losses inflicted upon him were so serious that he was compelled to grasp any respite to recuperate.

Tittoni's Satisfaction
Mullah's Domain Famine-Stricken

Tittoni expressed great satisfaction with the Agreement. In the Chamber of Deputies* some doubts were raised, but he insisted, "the agreement has an enormous importance. I believe I may take one credit, that of having had from the first moment a true perception of the question. The first time I spoke about it, I said explicitly that the essential condition to the unfolding of our action in Somaliland was to make peace with the Mullah."

To Deputy Prinetti, who retorted, "Take care; you have granted him too much by allowing him a place on the coast at Illig!" Tittoni replied caustically: "What is Illig? Is it a port? No. it is a desert and inhospitable shore."

That the economic situation of the Mullah's new realm was in fact untenable became rapidly evident. Three years after its inception the population was so grievously hard pressed for food that, according to information received by British administrators, the Mullah had resolved to kill all his remaining stock before the Muslim fast of Ramadam, at the end of September. It was assumed correctly that he would then be compelled to quit his barren domain in Italian territory, and would assume the offensive to capture fresh herds in the British protectorate, where he had kept in touch with some of the tribes. He had written to the British Commissioner there, Captain Richard Cordeaux, complaining of the Italians, "Who pester, incite and annoy us, and curse us in every way. Being cursed is harder for us to bear than having our necks cut off." He protested that his dhows had been seized and their cargo stolen, his stock had been looted.

> When in November, 1908, the British withdrew to the coast, the tribes of the interior to whom they had distributed arms were less well supplied in this respect than the Mullah, who continued to receive fresh supplies from various sources.
>
> In March, 1914, forty men, assumed to be Dervishes, rode to the gates of Berbera, and fired into the native quarter. It was rumoured that a siege of the port was intended. The British Government thereupon decided to reoccupy the interior, but owing to the outbreak of the first world war a few months later, only modest forces were available, Reoccupation was, in consequence, gradual. The Mullah continued his struggle without much loss of power. In 1919 a final British expedition was organised. Viscount Milner† subsequently wrote that he was persuaded by Mr. Churchill and his advisers at the Air Ministry that with the help of the Air Force the objective could be more cheaply and quickly accomplished. He, in turn, persuaded Mr. Lloyd George, then Prime Minister. The campaign lasted three weeks, and cost £100,000. The Mullah was heavily defeated and fled across the Ethiopian frontier into the Ogaden, where he and many of his followers died of disease and famine. A tomb was erected over his remains.

---

* Sitting of Chamber of Deputies, June 9, 1905 (Quaranta's translation (Smith Elder, London)).

† "The Mad Mullah of Somaliland," by Douglas Jardine, with a foreword by Viscount Milner (Herbert Jenkins, London, 1923), page vii.

IV

GOVERNMENT OF THE COLONY: PARLIAMENTARY DISCLOSURES OF CHARTERED COMPANY MISRULE

Let us consider now how Italy was administrating the vast colony she had acquired in Somaliland, fronting the Indian Ocean.

The subject was often debated in the Italian Parliament. The speeches of Tommaso Tittoni, the Italian Foreign Affairs Minister, who was responsible also for the administration of the Colonies, clearly indicate that under the Benadir Chartered Company, to which the administration had been relegated, appalling misrule continued for a number of years. The company was permitted to select the Governor as well as to exercise all the prerogatives of government. The slave trade was openly maintained, there were slave markets in the ports and the Governor imposed a fiscal tax on the unfortunate human wares. Justice was not organised. The judges and interpreters were frequently bribed. Public order was confided to a body of Askaris, recruited in Arabia, who were wretchedly paid and ill-equipped. These strong assertions and the following detailed statements we take from the authorised translation of Tittoni's speeches by Baron Quaranta, which was published in London by Smith Elder in 1914. The selection from the Minister's speeches in that work was made with a view to enhancing the Minister's reputation, and in order to portray the Italian Government in a favourable light. Nevertheless, the statements of the Minister reveal most appalling and utter misrule in the Benadir colony, a truly outrageous condition of affairs. Tittoni admitted categorically that Italy had not yet occupied, nor did she even intend to occupy for a considerable period, the colony she had been so urgent to possess and to extend. He clearly asserted that the government lacked revenue even to administer, much less develop, the colony.

In respect of public order and the control of the slave trade, he said:—

"*We have no garrison in that territory, and the 'Benadir Company' is under obligation to maintain only 600 armed Askaris, who are a very meagre force for the very extensive territory they are supposed to police.*"

In the debate on the Budget of 1903-4, Senator Vitelleschi accused the Government of having neither the courage to abandon the Somaliland colony, nor the willingness to spend sufficient to make it fruitful.

Tittoni replied that Italy had "modestly participated in the colonial movement," but could not spare capital to transform Somaliland into a prosperous colony. The Government had announced the Conversion of the Public Debt; colonial enterprises must, therefore, be left in abeyance.

"*In the meantime we have a contract with the Benadir Company, to which we pay a subsidy, not by any means a conspicuous one, since more than half of it is paid to the Sultan of Zanzibar, and the balance is devoted to placing the Company in a position to fufil its obligations towards the State, which consist in keeping 600 Askaris, of providing a postal service, of enforcing the provisions of the Brussels Conference, and of providing also a navigation service.*"

The Company had recently undergone a transformation, Count Mercatelli, Italian Consul-General at Zanzibar, was on his way to the Benadir to investigate the work of the Company. The inhabitants of the coast, within range of the guns of Italian ships, had accepted and respected the Italian protectorate, said the Minister. but:

"*to render our protectorate effective among the tribes which inhabit the desert hinterland, it would be necessary to send an expedition, which would cost an enormous sum; in fact, it would mean unlimited expenditure, because one knows how these colonial wars begin, but not how they will end. . . . . If at the present moment we were to throw ourselves into an adventure we should be acting imprudently, and I am convinced the country would not follow us on this path.*"

Here was a clear indication that the alleged desire of the people concerned to receive the protection of Italy was non-existent.

"Putting the Matter on the Shelf"

On February 20, 1904, Tittoni was interrogated in the Senate by Odescalchi and made this striking admission of misrule:

"He has said (and I believe there is a good deal of truth in his statement), that the Charter granted to the Benadir Company was simply a way of putting the matter upon the shelf. In fact no one can think that the men, who stipulated that contract, could have believed they were thus solving the question. It is not with a meagre subsidy of a few hundreds of thousands of francs that one can expect to restore such a vast territory to order, and to enhance its value by causing agriculture and commerce to prosper in it. The Government did not want to spend much money on that Colony, and this way out of the difficulty was found as a means of keeping the Colony, while putting off the real solution of the problem to the distant future."

The Minister thus admitted that the rule of the Chartered Company was bad and could not be substantially improved, because the subsidy paid by the Italian Government to the Company was too meagre to cover the cost of government. Nevertheless, the Government was determined to continue this method, because it was the cheapest possible.

Revenue from the Slave Trade

Tittoni next referred to the question of slavery. The revelation that the administration of the Colony was partially sustained by a tax on the slave trade had caused an outcry in Italy and abroad:

"Our Consul-General in Zanzibar, who has gone to the Benadir and established himself at Mogadishu, has occupied himself with the question of slavery, which was a menace to the colony itself.

"This question has deeply stirred the feelings of Parliament, and has given rise to an enquiry carried on by the Consul-General and Commander Di Monale, the result of which has already been laid before Parliament.

"After that enquiry the Governor of the Colony was recalled.

"Another scandalous fact which came to light through the enquiry has also ceased to exist—that is to say the sale of slaves in the market, on which sale, without the Company's knowledge a fiscal tax was levied."

The Company, as Tittoni subsequently stated, had paid dividends to its shareholders in preference to providing a proper government, both objectives being more than could be attained. The Governor was made the scapegoat for the ills which resulted:

"*Senator Odescalchi,*" Tittoni continued, "*has spoken of the Askaris who are stationed in the Benadir; he is right in saying they are ill-paid and worse outfitted. I have seriously called the attention of the Company to the fulfilment of its obligations on this point, and it has sent arms, munitions and uniforms for these men. The Company, according to the Charter, is obliged to keep six hundred Askaris; as a matter of fact it keeps one thousand, but they fall very far short of what should be desired.*

"*They come from the coast of Arabia, are poorly paid, and must provide for their means of livelihood by engaging in some trade. They are therefore undisciplined, disorganised, and, in consequence, absolutely inefficient.*"

It would be necessary to continue to obtain Askaris from Arabia, Tittoni declared, but they must be selected with greater care and organised more efficiently. He added:—

"If the Company should fail in its duties and should not fulfil the engagements contracted by the Charter on May 25, 1898, the Government would not hesitate to declare the Charter revoked. It is well that this be known; because if there is any one who believes that the Company, thinking itself indispensable, may act as it pleases, and that the Government would hesitate to call it to the fulfilment of its obligations, that person would be very much mistaken, because if we were obliged to tolerate the unfulfilment of the conditions of the Charter we would sooner face the monetary difficulties which the direct administration of the Colony would entail.

"Having said this much, in order that it may be clear to all, I add that if the Company will carry out, as I am confident it will do, its obligations, it will be desirable and useful that it remain in existence and that the Charter continue to be in force."

It was clear that Chartered Company rule was thoroughly bad, and had been so ever since the creation of this Charter six years before. Tittoni himself had earlier stated that the subvention paid to the Company was far too small to ensure good government.

His protests were those of the weak Minister of a neglectful government, unwilling to undertake the cost of reform and seeking to place the blame on other shoulders.

On March 14, 1904, Tittoni was challenged, in regard to the Chartered Company's misrule, by Senator Santini, who charged the Company with slave dealing and other offences. Tittoni replied:—

"I am not called upon here to come to the Chartered Company's defence, nor to justify in any way the points in which it is in fault and which I myself will indicate.

"As to the very serious question of slavery it has been discussed at length in the Chamber, and, therefore, as regards the past, it is useless for me to return to the subject, as all the Hon. Members are acquainted with the Reports of Consul Pestalozza and Commander Di Monale, which have been published in a Green book.

"It is, therefore, superfluous to insist upon the responsibility of the Chartered Company and of Governor Dulio in what took place in the past; it is more important that I should speak of the actual state of affairs.

"The first measure which imposes itself is the reorganisation of the Corps of Askaris, apropos of which I also must pronounce severe words of condemnation. The organisation of this corps has been deplorable in every way. These Askaris are miserable men, ill-clothed, ill-fed, poorly paid, who carry on all sorts of trades and who are occasionally called to give service; when they must escort some caravan to the interior they are useless, because, being unaccustomed to handling a gun, they fire inconsiderately, wasting all their cartridges.

"The local Government and Consul-General Mercatelli have elaborate a scheme for the reorganisation of the Askaris, which would require an annual expenditure of about 230,000 lires. I will send this scheme to the Company asking it to act upon it at once, because this constitutes one of the obligations contracted by it in the Charter.

"It is necessary that the Company shall provide what is lacking in the Colony, not only at present, but also making up what has been wanting in the past, not through the Company's fault alone, but through everyone's fault, including the officials sent there, who, in many cases, proved themselves absolutely unfit for the task entrusted to them. An immediate reform is needed, and first of all it is necessary to proceed to the appointment of the Governor and to use greater caution in the choice.

"After the Company have submitted, to the Government's approval, the name of the Chief Executive of the Colony, it will have to fulfil all the conditions of the Charter.

"Apropos of this I wish to answer the question asked by the Hon. de Andreis, ' What will you do,' he asks, ' if the Company will not fulfil its obligations ? ' "

Most obviously it was evident after six years of Parliamentary wrangling the Chartered Company neither would, nor could, provide an adequate administration, and that if pressed to do more, the Company would renounce the Charter, and throw responsibility for the Colony back to the Government.

Tittoni knew this and replied to De Andreis in guarded terms:

"We will avail ourselves of all the means placed at our disposal by the law; but we must also examine the possibility that the Company should prefer to cease to exist. In this case it is evident we cannot find even in the law sufficient means to oblige it to live and operate.

"The only right we could exercise would be that of bringing an action against it for damages due to the unfulfilment of its obligations and endeavour to ascertain and fix the responsibility. We must, therefore, prepare ourselves also for the possibility of our having to assume the direct administration of the Colony."

Withdrawal of the Chartered Company

We have observed that the Italian Government, while constantly pressing for the enlargement of the Somaliland Colony, were unwilling to provide sufficient revenue to administer it adequately, still less to build roads, to develop irrigation from the rivers, or to effect any of the numerous improvements required to increase the prosperity of the vast area they had acquired. As the cheapest method of ridding the Government of the problem of administration and also to satisfy certain repacious interests, the Colony had been handed over to a Chartered Company*, which was given an inadequate subsidy and invested with all the powers of government.

Continually taunted on account of the Benadir Chartered Company's misrule, Tittoni declared that if the Company would not provide an improved administration the Italian Government would be compelled to assume control of the Colony, but he hoped the Government would not be obliged to do so.

"Certainly this is not the solution I would prefer; I should

---

* For further details concerning the Filonardi and Benadir Companies see Chapter V, From Inside the Colony.

always prefer the continuation of the Company's administration, and I will do all I can to keep it in existence; but I must declare that should it cease to exist we should not alarm ourselves unnecessarily, because it will not be a case of undertaking expeditions, wars, or conquests, but simply of administering efficiently the Benadir."

"Now I repeat that I will ask the Company to fulfil its obligations, that I will avail myself of all the means the law places at my disposal to make it work satisfactorily, that I sincerely hope the Company will place itself in a position to carry out a serious programme, but that I am also ready to contemplate with equanimity the possibility of the Government's having to undertake direct administration of the Colony."

On May 14, 1904, Tittoni disclosed that the Company would not continue to administer the Colony without a higher subsidy: The Government had refused to pay, and was therefore obliged to assume direct responsibility for the Colony.

In order to camouflage the ignominious position of the Government he prefaced this disclosure by a general denunciation of the Company rule he had been anxious to maintain:—

" I would have done everything possible to keep the Company in existence, such as it is, but it seems to me that after the latest reports from our Consul Mercatelli, after the publication of the results of the Chiesi-Travelli inquiry, if the Company may still be of service by transforming itself into a commercial concern it must renounce exercising functions of State, for which it has shown itself absolutely unfit.

" The speakers who have taken part in this discussion have already justly remarked that, in entrusting the Benadir to a private Company, the Government of the day had only one end in view, that of getting it off its hands at any cost. It entertained the most delusive idea that the administration of the Benadir by a private Company would have relieved it of every responsibility. To my mind the Hon. Scalini has justly remarked that the Convention signed with the Benadir Company contained the germs of all the evils which have since been deplored.

" The State very lightly caused the Company to assume serious engagements, without making sure that the latter had the means, the capacity, and possibility of fulfilling them, and the Company, with equal lightness, assumed them.

" The consequences are known to all, and are such as to require serious provision, and not merely expedients or palliatives. The idea of patching it up as is best possible, and in order to avoid trouble to the Government, to continue in the system of letting the Company exercise functions of State for which it has no aptitude would be, to my mind, a serious mistake."

Rapacity of Italian Company

" Italy must profit," said the Italian Minister, " not only by her own experience but also by that of other nations. We can learn much," he said, " from the example of the Imperial East Africa

Company, at the head of which figured the most prominent names of the British aristocracy.

"*In opposition to the course followed by the Benadir Company, which neglected the functions of State entrusted to it in order that the dividend due to the shareholders might be forthcoming, the British Company that obtained the administration of the vast possessions bordering upon our Benadir, devoted itself to a political action and assured to England a vast territory; but its commercial action was very deficient, and the results were disastrous for it, as in 1895 it was dissolved, turning over to the Government the administration of the Colony.*"

In other words the British Company had displayed some patriotism and public spirit, whilst the Benadir Company, rapacious and corrupt, had been animated wholly by desire for private gain.

It was but too clearly obvious that public complaints of the evil conditions in the Colony had compelled a reluctant Government to demand from the Benadir Chartered Company a better administration. Tittoni's own speeches had shown that he wished to retain the Company, and if the Company had been willing to continue at the old price, even a mere promise of reform would have been gladly accepted by the Government. Having raised its price, the Company must go.

" *In order to continue to exercise functions of State the Benadir Company would ask at present for a greater contribution from the Government.*

" *Now I believe no one, after what has taken place would dream of proposing, nor would Parliament be found willing, to vote a larger contribution to the Company.*"

In consequence, the Government would now take over the functions hitherto exercised by the Company. Tittoni was careful to add that this would not increase the burden upon the State finances, for though it would be necessary to spend something more on the Benadir than the Company's former meagre allowance, the extra sum required would be obtained from a surplus in the Budget for Eritrea.

An annuity of 600,000 lire, by which the Italian Treasury was reimbursed for a sum advanced when the frontier between Eritrea and Ethiopia was fixed, would now be transferred by the Treasury to the Budget for Somaliland. Moreover, 150,000 lire, which had been paid annually to the Pirelli Company for the construction of the submarine cable from Massawa to Assab, would shortly expire. These two annual payments together would aggregate 750,000 lire; they would now be added to the amount hitherto paid to the Benadir Company in order to furnish the Budget of the Somaliland Colony. The solution was perhaps a trifle like the dog eating his own tail.

Summing up the evils of Chartered Company rule, on March 14, 1904, Tittoni said justice had not been organised. " It is not known under what jurisdiction the whites of the Colony were placed. The Capitulations* in force in those stations when they belonged to the Sultan of Zanzibar cannot now be appealed to by us against our own Administration.

" Our Residents † have not been able to curb the arrogance and venality of judges; on account of their ignorance of the local languages they were obliged to resort to interpreters, and those who corrupted the judges corrupted the interpreters as well.

" The same thing must be said of the administrative and financial systems in which everything has to be reorganised.

" But beside this administrative disorder, there has also been a deficiency in the political direction, which has been the cause of serious consequences, as it has lowered the prestige of our Representatives and has caused the neighbouring tribes to become hostile to them on account of the alternating acts of arrogance and acts of weakness.

" It is a well-known fact that in the Colonies the tribes that are not subjugated are made friendly by giving them an annual subsidy. These subsidies have been granted also in the Benadir, but in so ridiculously small a measure that they do more harm than good."

---

* Under the capitulations citizens of European Powers were not subject to the jurisdiction of the country, cases affecting them being tried by the Representatives of such Powers in their own Legations.

† Italian representative exercising authority in the locality where he was stationed.

V

FROM INSIDE THE COLONY: CHIESI-TRAVELLI REVELATIONS

In the Italian Parliament, Tittoni, the Minister responsible for the administration of the Colonies, denounced the misrule of the Benadir Chartered Company. A study of the Report of Gustavo Chiesi and the lawyer, Ernesto Travelli* who were sent out to the Colony to investigate the state of affairs on the Chartered Company's behalf, reveals that, though the misdeeds of the Company were manifold, the Italian Government was much more culpable. This important Report reproduces many documents essential to a study of this question, and a wealth of evidence, which affords irrefutable testimony that while successive Italian Ministers were continually striving to extend the vast area of Italian possession, they were utterly callous in their neglect of the Colony and its inhabitants, and of their Treaty obligations in respect of it.

Obligations to Suppress Slavery and the Slave Trade

These Treaty obligations included the suppression of slavery and the slave trade, the protection of the inhabitants from unjust labour contracts, and the favouring of religious, scientific or charitable institutions without distinction of creed or nation. The Treaty obligations concerning slavery were flagrantly disregarded, as the Chiesi-Travelli Report demonstrated. Before considering the Report itself it is well to recapitulate what those Treaty obligations were and how they were contracted.

General Act of Berlin

Italy was a signatory to the General Act of Berlin, of February 26, 1885, and to the Brussels Act, of July 2, 1890. Under these Acts she bound herself to assist in the suppression of slavery and the slave trade.

The following quotations from these Acts are taken from " The Map of Africa by Treaty," by Sir Edward Hertslet, published by Her Majesty's Stationery Office, 1894.

---

* Le Questioni del Benadir, Atti e Relazione dei Commissari della Societá, Signori Gustavo Chiesi e Avv. Ernesto Travelli (Milano, P.B. Bellini, 1904).

Under the General Act of Berlin the signatory Powers expressly bound themselves to assist in the suppression of slavery and the slave trade in the following terms:—

Article VI. All the Powers exercising sovereign rights or influence in the aforesaid territories bind themselves to watch over the preservation of the native tribes, and to care for the improvement of the conditions of their moral and material well-being, and to help in suppressing slavery, and especially the slave trade.

Brussels Act

The General Act of the Brussels Conference of 1890 made detailed recommendations for the liquidation of slavery, and also imposed some binding obligations, which the signatory Powers, including Italy, undertook to fulfil. By Article III, the signatories undertook to devote themselves to the extermination of slavery. Leave was given by the Act to delegate to Chartered Companies the responsibility of Governments; nevertheless, these Governments pledged themselves to remain directly responsible for their engagements under the Brussels Act and expressly guaranteed to execute them. Here is the Article embodying these pledges:—

Article IV. The Powers exercising sovereignty or protectorates in Africa may, however, delegate to Chartered Companies all, or a portion of, the engagements which they assume in virtue of Article III. They remain, nevertheless, directly responsible for the engagements which they contract by the present General Act and guarantee the execution thereof.

By Article V the signatory States bound themselves to enact laws for the punishment of persons concerned in the capture and sale of human beings, the organisers and abettors of this traffic, and all carriers, transporters and dealers in slaves. Convoys of slaves were to be stopped, and the slaves liberated. Article VI provided that the liberated slaves should, if possible, be restored to their country of origin. Otherwise they must be helped to obtain means of subsistence, and, if they so desired, to settle on the spot. Provision must be made for the education of abandoned children.

Article VII directed:

" *Any fugitive slave claiming on the Continent the protection of the Signatory Powers shall obtain it, and shall be received in the camps and stations officially established by them, or on government vessels plying on the lakes and rivers.*"

By Article XVI the Powers pledged themselves to establish posts on the coast and at the intersection of the principal caravan routes for the interception of slave convoys and the liberation of laves. By Article XVII the Powers undertook that strict supervision should be exercised by the local authorities at the ports, and in the territories adjacent to the ports, to prevent the sale and shipment of slaves, or the passage into the interior of man-hunters and slave-dealers, as well as the inspection of caravans passing to and from the interior.

By Article LXXXVI the Signatory Powers undertook to establish such offices or institutions as were sufficient for the freeing and protection of slaves. Article LXXXVII provided that these institutions or the Authorities charged with this service should " deliver letters of freedom and keep a register thereof." On receiving notice of slave trading or illegal detention all necessary diligence was to be used to secure liberation of the slaves and the punishment of the offenders. Article LXXXVIII provided that the signatory Powers should encourage the foundation in their possessions of establishments of refuge for women, and education for liberated children.

Article LXXXIX directed:—

" Whoever shall have used fraud or violence to deprive a liberated slave of his letters of freedom or of his liberty shall be considered as a slave-dealer."

No heed to these large obligations was paid by the Italian Government in taking over the ports or in their subsequent advance inland.

Italy's Treaty Pledges Concerning Slavery in the Benadir.

In acquiring the Benadir Ports, by the assistance of Great Britain, the Government of Italy agreed to take over the Treaty obligations concerning slavery and the slave trade, which the British Government had induced the Sultan of Zanzibar to accept. Moreover, a formal pledge was exacted from the Italians to fulfil the obligations of the Berlin and Brussels Acts, which Italy had already signed.

It will be remembered that the Benadir Ports were ceded by the Sultan of Zanzibar to the British East Africa Company, and that the Italian Government had induced the British Government to arrange for the British Company to surrender the ports and for the Sultan to lease them to Italy. The gift of the ports, by Britain, to Italy, for a gift in effect it was known to be, was, according to the ethics of those times when the European " scramble for Africa " took little account of pre-existing rights, a very generous act by the British Government. The Italian Ministers pressed for the gift on account of their alleged protectorate over Ethiopia, which proved to be non-existent, but to which, had it existed, ports would have been required, just as they are in fact required by Ethiopia to-day! Treaties between the three parties having been signed at each stage, the Act of Concession* by the Sultan to the King of Italy was

---

* Concession of Benadir Ports granted by the Government of His Highness the Sultan of Zanzibar to the Government of His Majesty the King of Italy, August 12, 1892. See Hertslet, page 950, 1894 Edition.

signed, not by the Sultan who was under British protection, but by representatives of the British and Italian Governments, (G. H. Portal and P. Cottoni) under the stipulation that the Concession must be ratified by the British Government.

Article IV of the Concession, having set forth the powers of Italian Government in the ports, stipulated:—

"But it is clearly understood that the exercise of these rights and privileges shall be in conformity with the Treaties existing between the Zanzibar Sultanate and foreign Powers and with the obligations which are or could be imposed by adhesion to the General Act of Berlin, 1885, and to the General Act of the Brussels Conference, 1890."

In Article II of the Concession the Italian Government was " authorised " to concede to an Italian Company the administration of the towns and ports included in the Concession, " *but always on the responsibility of the Government of His Majesty the King of Italy.*"

These pledges were given by the Italian Government repeatedly; the phrases used in the Agreement between the British East Africa Company and the Italian Government on August 3, 1889, are particularly emphatic:—

" The Italian Company shall comply with all obligations undertaken herein by the Italian Government who will themselves remain responsible for the strict compliance with the obligations herein contained. This Agreement to be construed according to English law."

Zanzibar Anti-Slavery Treaties Taken Over By Italy

The obligations which the Sultan of Zanzibar had undertaken in Treaties contracted with Britain for the abolition of slavery and the slave trade, for which the Italian Government had now become responsible, must next be considered.

Italy's Obligations Under Treaties with Britain and Zanzibar

Arising from the efforts of the British Government to destroy slavery and the slave trade in the dominions of Zanzibar, no less than fifteen Decrees and Treaties, between Britain and successive Sultans, were made in the twenty-five years from June 5, 1873, to October 17, 1898. Here is a list of the most important of these engagements, and those which applied specifically to the Benadir ports:—

June 5, 1873: Treaty between Britain and the Sultan of Zanzibar to abolish the slave trade.

January 15, 1876: Decree of the Sultan abolishing slavery in Kismayo and the Benadir.

April 18, 1876 : Decree abolishing caravans of slaves in the interior.

November 8, 1886: The Sultan signed the General Act of the Brussels Conference concerning slavery and the slave trade.

The slave trade was thus declared unlawful, and the legal status of slavery was abolished in Kismayu and the Benadir ports, subsequently transferred to Italy.

A more gradual policy was adopted for the rest of the Zanzibar Sultanate by the following measures; the first of which prohibited the introduction of further slaves into the dominions of Zanzibar, and limited slavery in those dominions to the life of existing slaves:

September 13, 1889: Sultan Seyid Khalifa Bin Said authorises British and German naval ships to visit all Zanzibar and Arab vessels, and declares free all slaves who enter his dominions after November 1, 1889, or are born in his dominions after January 1, 1890.

August 1, 1890: the Sultan confirmed and enforced all previous Decrees, and made regulations for the amelioration of the lot of existing slaves. Exchange, sale or purchase of slaves was strictly prohibited; any person found in possession of a new slave was subject to severe penalties and to be deprived of all slaves. Slaves might only pass to the legitimate children of a deceased owner; in default of such heirs they must be liberated.

Every slave was given the right to claim liberty in the Kadi Court on payment of a "reasonable and just price," to be fixed, in the words of the Decree, "between ourselves and our Arab subjects." The slave was to pay this price to the master in presence of the Kadi, who would thereupon immediately hand to the slave his certificate of freedom.

The Sultan had placed his dominions under British protection earlier in the same year; the price of the slave's ransom was, therefore, of course, fixed in conjunction with the British authorities, who made a practice of paying it in order to liquidate slavery as soon as possible.

A Decree of April 6, 1897, tightened up this procedure; all cases between slaves and their owners were to be brought before the Kadi Courts, but these Courts were to refer to the local governor all claims to the possession of slaves, or to the payment derived from the labour of slaves whom the master allowed to work for other employers. The damages which the owner would suffer by the loss of the slave being thus assessed, were paid by the British authorities, and the slave freed. This last Decree of 1897 was not binding upon Italy, but, both to the British Government and the Sultan of Zanzibar, the Italian Government had given explicit Treaty pledges to fulfil all the former Decrees, which applied to the Benadir ports. In fact, the Italian Government were bound by the Decree of 1876 to abolish slavery, as well as the slave trade, in the Benadir ports, and to stop all conveyance of slaves to and from the interior. The milder regulations, above cited, referred, as we have noticed, to other parts of the Sultan's dominions, and not to the Benadir; but even these milder regulations the Italian administrations utterly failed to execute.

To sum up: the Italian Government were bound by the strict Treaties with the Sultan of Zanzibar and the British Government in respect of the Benadir ports. For all their colonial dominions, including the Benadir ports, they were bound by the General Acts of Berlin and Brussels.

The Treaty obligations of the Italian Government, in regard to these pacts, were clear and strict. Whilst slavery, and the traffic in arms and spirituous liquors were the subject of international intervention, other aspects of administration, for which the Italian Government had assumed responsibility, were of not less vital importance, and were fundamentally essential to adequate administration.

For the discharge of all these obligations, to say nothing of Italy's so called "civilising mission," the Italian Government first turned over the Colony to a Chartered Company, formed by Vincenzo Filonardi, who assumed control as manager of the Company in 1893. Filonardi had furthered substantially the Italian Government's colonial ambitions. As their Consul-General in Zanzibar, he had visited the northern Somaliland coast and made contact with the chiefs. In February, 1889, escorted by the warships Staffeta, Rapido and Dogali, he had hoisted the Italian flag, and notified his government that he had procured from the Sultan of Obbia a request for Italian protection. Thereupon, the Italian Chargé d'Affairs in London had notified Lord Salisbury, then British Foreign Secretary, that " the Sultan of Oppia (or Obbia) on the East Coast of Africa " had made this request " through a Special Mission." He added the Italian Government had ascertained on the spot that " neither a Foreign Power, nor any private Company, depending on a Foreign Power," had taken possession, or established a Protectorate. An Italian Man of War had hoisted the Italian flag, and declared a Protectorate, by means of a Treaty with the Sultan, on behalf of his successors and the chiefs under his sway. This notice was communicated to Lord Salisbury, and to the Foreign Ministers of all the Powers which had signed the General Act of the 1885 Conference of Berlin, in accordance with Article XXXIV,* an Article which the Italian Government adopted with a zeal not shown by them in respect of other parts of the Berlin Act. A right welcome Article it was, and most pleasantly accordant with Italian Government intentions; it secured the unhindered possession of a large colony in Africa, by a mere circular letter to the Powers, without the least trouble or expense ! No matter that the area of the new territory was not yet known exactly; it was notified as extending from 5° 30' north latitude on the north, to 3° 40' north

---

* Article XXXIV.—" Any Power which henceforth takes possession of a tract of land on the coasts of the African Continent outside of its present possessions, or which, being hitherto without such possessions, shall acquire them, as well as the Power which assumes a Protectorate there, shall accompany the respective acts with a notification thereof, addressed to the other Signatory Powers of the present Act, in order to enable them, if need be, to make good any claims of their own."

latitude on the south; a subsequent communication extended the Royal Government's claim to 2° 30′of north latitude on the south to 5° 53″ of north latitude on the north. By the latter communication was notified also a further Protectorate over the domain of the Sultan of the Mijjerteins, extending from those of Oppia to 8° 3′of north latitude.

The Short-Lived Filonardi Company

Filonardi's activities had given him a claim on the gratitude of the Italian Government, for, at very small cost to the Exchequer, he had done what was necessary to enable the government to claim this extensive Protectorate on the northern part of the Indian Ocean Somaliland coast. When the Benadir ports further south were added, the privilege and responsiblity of governing the whole long strip was readily passed over to him by a Sovereign and a government whose aim was to secure the glory of an Empire without the cost of maintaining it. Had Filonardi been other than rash and impulsive he would not have accepted a flimsy contract for three years only. Most obviously he could not hope to induce prudent investors to risk their capital on the security of so brief a contract, even had the territory not been remote and little explored, even had there not been a strong reluctance among Italians to venture into African Colonial investment, as the Government had discovered when endeavouring to raise loans for Eritrea even though backed by a government guarantee. Filonardi succeeded in raising only a meagre capital The contribution of the government towards the vast undertaking was paltry in the extreme. Their subsidy of 300,000 Italian lire per annum, to be paid in quarterly instalments, was mortgaged by the obligation to pay to the Sultan of Zanzibar an annuity of 160,000 rupees, valued at 220,000 lire. This left the Company only 80,000 Italian lire for all the needs of the administration. Out of which, 3,600 silver Maria Theresa dollars, had to be paid to the Sultan of Obbia ! Other less important chiefs had also to receive stipends. This information is contained in the Chiesi-Travelli Report.*

The Filonardi Company was to take complete control of the colony, to maintain the police and soldiers, the authorities in the ports, the officers and officials of every rank, the Kadis, who administered justice according to the laws of Zanzibar in the native courts, the Italians who administered Italian law for the few Europeans. The Company had also the full responsibility for discharging Italy's onerous Treaty obligations.

The Italian Government, in a letter† to Filonardi, which formed the basis of their contract with his Company, V. Filonardi and Co.,

---

* Handbook No. 128 prepared under the Direction of the Historical Section of the Foreign Office (H.M. Stationery Office 1920) states that Filonardi received from the Italian Government only sufficient to pay the Sultan. It may be that the 80,000 lire which appears to be a balance towards the administration was in fact absorbed by other subsidies.

† Published in the Chiesi-Travelli Report.

had promised to permit the Company to purchase arms and munitions at cost price from government stores, "possibly from Massawa." It was also understood that an Italian warship would be maintained near the Benadir coast to give aid in case of need. The promise regarding arms and munitions was not fulfilled. The assistance of the frigate, Staffetta, was granted from September, 1903, to January, 1904, only.

Filonardi took up his charge under tempestuous auspices. None knew better than he that though the Sultans of Obbia and the Mijjerteins might have been induced to sign some document relative to Italian protection, they had no intention of accepting Italian Government. Their people were totally opposed to foreign interference. Had Filonardi not refrained from suggesting that the Protectorate would involve any compulsion it would have been refused. He arrived aboard the Staffetta in September, 1893; his contract having commenced on July 16 of the same year. His proclamation that an Italian Protectorate would be operated by his Company, joined as it was by the issue of regulations and the exercise of authority in the ports, was greeted with smouldering resentment. At his official assumption of control at Merka in October, a naval lieutenant, who had been present at the ceremony, was assassinated, whilst re-embarking, by a Somali who had mingled with the porters and sailors. The assassin was immediately slaughtered by the Askaris in attendance on Filonardi, who, not content with this summary vengeance, rashly ordered the bombardment of the town. His policy of duplicity, and now of aggression, intensified the difficulties inevitable to a vast and grossly ill-provided enterprise. His correspondence published in the Chiesi-Travelli Report reveals that in April, 1894, little more than six months after his arrival, he was miserably complaining to Antonio Cecchi, who had replaced him as Italy's Consul-General at Zanzibar, of the Government's refusal to supply even "a few hundred" of the promised muskets, the withdrawal of the warship, which was to have remained off the coast in case of need, the rejection of the appeal of his Filonardi Company for an advance of half a year's subsidy to meet the expense of "sanguinary conflicts," which had forced his Company to build a wall round Mogadishu and to fortify and provision the town. These refusals, Filonardi protested, had put his Company in the power of the Somalis, whom they had "severely punished in the name of Italy" the previous October. The Askaris of the Company had been promised Italian muskets before the closing of the coast by the monsoon from May to October. To break that pledge to provide arms would cause loss of Italian prestige, perhaps a revolt. He had never thought the Government would leave him without arms for defence; they were not ignorant of his Company's limited financial resources! It was impossible to raise important sums for a country so distant, with only a three years' contract. The Company had accepted responsibility, believing the Government would keep their promises. The refusal of a mere advance had compelled the Company to raise 150,000 lire in the course of a few days, an operation which had entailed much sacrifice and grave damage to the Company's credit.

"A Company," he urged, "which has to govern a vast territory for the benefit of the fatherland cannot live without the support of the Government. The simplicity of the contract, and its scope so vast and complex, amply prove that the Company assumed the obligation as a co-operator with the Government, and not otherwise. If the contract between the Government and the Company is not to be understood in that light, one is led to the far from alluring conclusion that the Authorities have taken advantage of the weak mind of a poor madman. The Company, which the Government have honoured with so much confidence as to leave to them the administration—with the most ample powers—of an Italian territory, have made every sacrifice to maintain the burden."

He must sorrowfully hold the Government responsible for the Company's losses.

The Italian Government had no intention of accepting that responsibility; they had passed the control of the Colony to Filonardi simply in order to avoid expense. The inability of his Company to raise sufficient means to finance the administration was not in their opinion a reason for assisting his Company; on the contrary they were already negotiating the formation of another Commercial Company, able to command greater financial support. To clear Filonardi's Company out of the way, Cecchi, who had been employed in the creation of the new concern, was instructed to inform Filonardi that the Government wished a friendly termination of their contract with his Company, which had still nearly two years out of three to run. If he agreed to abandon the shareholders of his Company in this manner, the Government were prepared to offer him the post of manager to a new Company at a salary of 30,000 lire per annum, but there would be no guarantee as to the duration of the engagement as the Consul-General pleasantly explained: "The duration of your new functions will depend on the zeal with which you execute the instructions of the Royal Government, which your experience of the locality, and your personal influence with the Arab functionaries and the native chiefs will render easy for you." Cecchi added that the offer was also made in recognition of Filonardi's former services, and that it would afford the most favourable solution for him, as the Government had no intention of renewing the contract with his Company. Filonardi had served the Government in securing their Protectorate, but his sense of honour was more live towards his compatriots. He replied, not without dignity, that he could not consider accepting a salary for himself until the Government had decided to repay the sums expended on the Colony by the Filonardi Company. He had pledged his good name for the disbursement in excess of the Government subsidy of about three hundred thousand lire. "It is my duty," he wrote, "to think of liquidating the debts I have contracted before thinking of my own future position." The wall and the four forts encircling Mogadishu, which his Company had constructed, were worth more to the Government, he asserted, than the 300,000 lire paid to the Company; he could not believe the Government would replace the Filonardi Company without repaying what had been spent on the Colony by a "group of good citizens," who, having faith in him, "and in the rectitude of the Government" had risked their capital "for the grandeur of our Italy."

The Government, preoccupied by financial embarrassment at home and by other imperial ambitions, for which they seriously lacked sufficient capital, turned a deaf ear to such pleading. They merely awaited the expiry of their contract with the Filonardi Company, whilst negotiating its successor.

War of Conquest in Ethiopia Disturbs Plan for New Chartered Company to Administer Somaliland; Government Takes Charge for Three Years

In 1895 the new Benadir Commercial Company, for which Cecchi, as agent of the Italian Government, had secured the support of substantial business interests in Milan, awaited only the demise of Filonardi's ill-fated venture. A contract between the Government and the new enterprise was ready for submission to the Chamber of Deputies; but disastrous reverses in the war of conquest Italy was waging in Northern Ethiopia compelled the postponement of any commercial project in East Africa.

The financial embarrassment of the Italian Government, who, unable to raise adequate revenue for home affairs, were venturing inadequate sums for war abroad, revealed itself in every debate in the Italian Parliament, and was the predominant subject of all official correspondence. G. F. H. Berkeley, in "The Campaign of Adowa,"* gives excerpts from letters of General Baratieri, who was conducting the war in Ethiopia, and the Government's replies. Baratieri was demanding a further 13,000,000 lire for the war; Baron Blanc, in apologetic terms, replied for the Treasury that no more than 8,000,000 could be found:

"*It goes to my heart to have to say that the Country regards above all other things the question of expense, and the financial overbalance, from which abyss we have only just been delivered.*"

Prime Minister Crispi telegraphed in reply to Baratieri's further insistence:

"*In order to save Erythrea in Parliament we must keep within these limits; we do not wish to risk the fate of Italy for the sake of a financial error committed in Africa.*"

Conquered Ethiopian Territories too Much Exhausted to Supply Furthur Contributions for More War

Pressed further, Crispi retorted that if Baratieri required to retain so many Italian soldiers, he must find means in the locality to maintain them. He added ruthlessly:

"*Napoleon I made war with the money of the conquered!*"

---

* The Campaign of Adowa, by G. F. H. Berkeley (Constable, 1902), p.p. 97-100.

Baratieri replied that the Ethiopian territories he had conquered were now too much exhausted to supply any further contributions. This is a significant admission of the terrible impoverishment which the local population suffered by Italy's Colonial warfare.*

Baratieri now offered his resignation, and suggested that a successor not compromised by aggression, as he was, might abandon the war policy of which he had been the instrument and establish good relations with Ethiopia. "I understand," he wrote, "how much public opinion is alarmed, and that the Government must take steps to calm it, at the supreme moment of the elections, on which depend the interests of the country."

The Crispi Government pressed on with the war until they fell, not heeding the General's mild advice, which, has a monitory ring for Italy to-day.

Since King and Government would have war, Baratieri got his 13,000,000 lire, and advanced for further conquests; but his forces were heavily defeated on the frowning heights of Amba Alagi in December, 1895, which forty-six years later were to witness the surrender of the Duke of Aosta to British and Ethiopian troops.

Amid outcries of revenge for that first crushing defeat at Amba Alagi the Italian Parliament voted a further 20,000,000 lire; but only defeat resulted. After further reverses in several small skirmishes an Italian garrison surrendered at Makalle. The Emperor Menelik permitted the Italians to depart unharmed, to prove Ethiopia's Christian forbearance, and even provided them with mules to transport their belongings and an escort in charge of the chivalrous Ras Makonnen.

Despite these reverses, Baratieri wrote to his Government that he was still confident. "But," he insisted, " a campaign of conquest of Abyssinia requires means that cannot be improvised in a country devastated by wars, and by the hordes that have lived there so long."

Again we have Baratieri's evidence of the impoverishment suffered by the population of the conquered territories who were compelled to maintain the Italian forces.

The failure to make headway with the desired conquest led to Crispi's notorious cable of February 25, 1896:—

"This is a military phthisis, not a war .... We are ready for any sacrifice in order to save the honour of the Army and the prestige of the Monarchy !"

Thus admonished, the Italian forces advanced to the disastrous battle of Adowa, on March 1, 1896. Vainly attempting to secure victory by stealth, they crept up close to the Ethiopian camp during the night, under cover of an armistice for negotiations. General Baratieri had written only a few hours before, asking that negotiations might continue. Suspecting no treachery, numbers of the

---

* When Berkeley wrote the original edition of his book he was sympathetic to Italy's imperialist aims; he only occasionally cited facts so damaging.

Ethiopian soldiers were away at the old city of Axum* attending a religious festival. Though the sound of the cannon warned them to return in haste they could not reach Adowa till some hours after the battle had begun. Despite their wretched stratagem the Italians suffered overwhelming defeat; they withdrew in utter rout.

Crispi, in fear of losing the whole colony of Eritrea, initiated peace negotiations, then resigned amid a storm of Italian indignation. On March 17, 1896, the Marquis Di Rudini announced to the Chamber of Deputies that the new administration would continue peace negotiations. All claims to an Italian Protectorate of Ethiopia and to the annexations Baratieri had attempted in the Tigré province would be abandoned.

Governor Dulio

Against this background of disastrous war in the north, Italy's southern colony drifted penuriously. On May 11, 1896, Filonardi received a reminder from Consul-General Cecchi that the contract of his company would terminate on July 15. Cecchi stated that the territory would then be administered directly by the Government. By that time, however, the coast would be closed and Cecchi would accordingly be unable to be present to take possession of the colony on behalf of the Italian State. The Government had therefore instructed him to appeal to Filonardi " not to abandon the coast," but to accept the position of Royal Commissioner, from July to September, when the Consul-General would arrive.

The correspondence which was published by Chiesi and Travelli makes no mention of a salary for the Royal Commissioner, and as Filonardi had previously written that his conscience would not permit him to accept a salary from the Government till his shareholders were reimbursed, it would seem that it was an honorary office.

Filonardi was further requested, whilst awaiting the termination of his contract, to receive, as the substitute of Consul-General Cecchi, a certain Dr. Emilio Dulio who would be accompanied by Filippo Quirighetti, a surveyor, to make use of their services and to guide and instruct them in all matters concerning the colony.

On July 15, Dr. Dulio assumed the management of the colony, with Quirighetti as customs officer. Filonardi, having surrendered all documents and direction to these newcomers, remained in the melancholy, if decorative, position of Royal Commissioner, till a letter from Cecchi in September informed him that the arrival of the Consul-General in Mogadishu, had finally brought to an end his own equivocal office of Royal Commissioner. From the casual " Caro Filonardi " of the Consul-General's earlier letters he was honoured by being addressed as "Al Pregiatissimo Signor Cavaliere Vincenzo Filonardi, Egregio Cavaliere," and was informed that his patriotism would be an example to his successors in the administra-

---

* " Modern Abyssinia," by A. B. Wylde, formerly British Vice-Consul for Red Sea (Methuen, 1901), p.p. 204, 208.

tion of the colony which Italy owed, as the Consul-General's letter averred, "in large measure" to his "work" and to his "cleverness." Cecchi's attempt to conceal that another commercial company was to replace him did not deceive Filonardi, for he had received from the Benadir Company an offer of employment in the venture, which he had declined on the same ground of solidarity with his shareholders which had prompted him to reject the Government's prior offer. Moreover in August he had been thanked by San Severino, the President of the Benadir Company, for the assistance he had given to the Company's Dr. Dulio.

This glimpse of Italian official method at the period is interesting. The fiction that the southern colony would produce great wealth for those who had the good fortune to exploit it was being vigorously propagated in official circles, as a counterbalance to the disappointing meagreness of Eritrea and the failure to capture Ethiopia.

Disaster at Lafole

Peace with Ethiopia was signed on October 20, 1896; the way appeared clear for the Benadir Commercial Company to take control. An unforeseen fatality again disturbed confidence in the commercial success of the venture. Towards the end of November, Consul-General Cecchi and sixteen other Italians, all well armed, with an escort of 70 native soldiers set out to explore the fertile area on the west bank of the Webbe Shebeli river. The party were attacked at Lafolé by the inhabitants who believed, as later enquiries revealed, that the party had been organised to seize for Italian settlement the fertile land cultivated by the people in that area, as well as to tax the wares sold in the local market which was a centre for the exchange of produce from the interior and imported goods. This was in fact the ultimate object of the Italian expedition though its immediate purpose was merely to explore the ground.

Consul-General Cecchi and thirteen other Italians were killed in the fight. When the news of this fatality reached the administration in Mogadishu, a number of Somalis and Arabs were arrested on suspicion. The interpreter of the departed Filonardi, who had been much in his confidence, was particularly suspected as he was believed to resent the supersession of his employer. When arrested he proved to be a native of Zanzibar, and claimed British protection. He was transported by an Italian warship first to Zanzibar, then to Aden, for interrogation by the Consuls. No conviction being obtained, the Italian Government shipped him, quite illegally, to Eritrea, where, along with a supposed accomplice, he was incarcerated at Keren and remained there eight years until liberated by the approaches to the Italian Government of Chiesi and Travelli.

A considerable time after the fight at Lafolé, three companies of Askaris were sent from Eritrea to burn and devastate villages and farms, and to shoot a number of their inhabitants, in order to vindicate Italian prestige. Chiesi and Travelli asserted, after investigating the facts, that the victims suffered vicariously, as they were not the people who had killed the Consul-General and his companions.

Under Dulio and Sorrentino Fugitive Slaves Imprisoned and Chastised

After the death of the Consul-General the administration of the colony was confided by Viscount Venosta, the then Foreign Minister, to Commander Sorrentino of the battleship, Elba, as Royal Commissioner, and to Dr. Dulio, who was then termed Royal Civil Commissioner.

Chiesi and Travelli report that the archives of the Administration during this period of direct Government control were scanty and in disorder. The functions of Commander Sorrentino became " every day more nominal and decorative." His reports to the Ministry for December, 1896, suggested that the best policy for the colony was to temporise and to " wait and see." Above all, nothing must be done which would reduce the receipts of the customs and "this became the principal care of the Administration of the colony under the direct control of the State."

So far from improving conditions in the colony as they had existed under the Filonardi Company, Chiesi and Travelli declare that the management provided by the State caused a grave deterioration. Their report makes the following accusations:—

No improvements were effected in the ports.

No roads were made to the interior, nor was there any clearing of the woods which impeded the passage to the coast of caravans bringing produce from the fertile, cultivated regions near the rivers and from Ethiopia.

No betterment was effected in the rudimentary military organisation of the Askaris under Filonardi.

The obligations of the Government under the General Acts of Berlin and Brussels, and the Treaties with the Sultan of Zanzibar and with the British Government were disregarded.

The practice initiated by Filonardi was changed only for the worse.

Before becoming governor, Filonardi had promised that there would be no interference with the possession of slaves within the colony, which was, of course, a violation of the Treaties above cited. On taking over the management of the colony he issued a proclamation that the slave trade was prohibited, and that special regulations would be issued for the gradual abolition of domestic slavery. In practice he did not interfere with slavery inside the colony, and even returned fugitive slaves to their owners.

" The administration operated by Dulio and Sorrentino handed fugitive slaves from the interior to those who claimed to own them, and sometimes with cruelty (mal modo), imprisoning and chastising

them before consigning them to those who came to claim them—in open contravention of the explicit directions of the Brussels Act."

It was found convenient to call Slavery "domestic."

"Records of the purchase and sale of slaves, their succession to new owners, their transfer, mortgage and pawning were inscribed in the records of the Kadi Courts.

"All this was done without the Government in Rome, the Royal Commissioner, Sorrentino who navigated between the Benadir and Zanzibar and the Royal Civil Commissioner Dulio, appearing to know anything about the Decrees of the Sultan of Zanzibar, which the British were vigorously applying in Zanzibar, Pemba and Mombasa."

The neglectful evasion of duty and responsibility, which was painfully evident in the Government's administration of the colony, from September 20, 1896, to December 31, 1899, continued under the same director, Dr. Emilio Dulio, when the Benadir Chartered Company assumed the management of the colony.

The Benadir Commercial Company Assumes Control

On January 1, 1900, the Italian Commercial Company for the Benadir assumed the management of the company with a share capital of 1,000,000 Italian lire, of which 300,000 lire had been paid up. It was far too small, far too uncertain a provision for so vast an undertaking entailing such tremendous responsibilities.

From the Government the Benadir Company was to receive a subsidy of 400,000 Italian lire (as compared with the 300,000 lire accorded to Filonardi). In July, 1894, this sum had been worth 300,000 gold francs, but the disastrous Ethiopian war had intervened. Out of the 400,000 lire the Company had to pay 120,000 rupees to the Sultan of Zanzibar, which was worth 204,000 to 210,000 according to the rate of exchange in Zanzibar, and 3,000 thalers to the Sultans of Obbia and Alula. The net subsidy received by the Company only amounted to from 180,000 to 190,000 lire per annum.

The contract between the Government and the Company, with additions made in the Italian Parliament, obliged the Company to administer the cities and towns of the Benadir and their hinterland, a vague term which failed to indicate whether the mere neighbourhood of the coast was indicated or the entire colony reaching to the boundary with Ethiopia, which the Italian Government still desired to advance further.

The Company was under obligation to conserve in good order all the property in buildings, etc., of the Government, to keep at least 600 guards for public security, an absurdly inadequate number, as well as to promote the commercial and general welfare of the colony and administer justice. The Company was precisely charged with the duty of "applying the General Act of Berlin and the General Act of Brussels."

Neither Government nor Company ever Intended to Fulfil Treaty Obligations—Open Traffic in Slaves

That there never was on the part of the Italian Government or on the part of the Benadir Company any intention to implement Italy's Treaty obligations respecting slavery is completely evident, a matter which is the more important because the question of slavery was subsequently used as a propaganda asset to employ with a wealth of false accusations and propaganda against her neighbour Ethiopia.

In July, 1901, Dr. Dulio, now Commendatore (a rank equivalent to Knight-Commander) returned to Italy to interview the Council of the Company and the Government and remained till March, 1902. Describing the first period of his administration as preparatory he presented to the Company and to the Ministry of Foreign Affairs a programme for the future government of the colony, in which he stated:—

"*It is not possible to think of abolishing domestic slavery and of liberating the 10,000 slaves who still live in the Benadir without having taught the natives how to substitute the labour of oxen for that of slaves. The abolition of slavery to-day would result in the almost complete abandonment of the cultivated land. Instead of succeeding in taking our Colony along the road of civilisation such a provision would reduce it to a barbarism much worse than at present.*

"*Owing to the conditions of agriculture in the Benadir the abolition of domestic slavery would lead to a revolt by almost all the Somali tribes which inhabit our Colony. Our regulations would be ineffective because no tribe would accept them without being reduced to submission by force.*"

This view of Governor Dulio was accepted by the Benadir Company and, what is more important, by the Italian Government.

Scandalous rumours concerning Italy's Somaliland Colony continually circulated and were repeatedly confirmed. Pietro Giorgi, inspired by enthusiasm for colonial development, journeyed to Mogadishu. He was tremendously disappointed with the backward conditions he encountered, and was indignant at being forced to pay customs dues of 30 per cent. on merchandise he had brought with him, and even on his private baggage. He protested to the governor without success. Grain was taxed as high as 40 per cent. When the merchants of Merka augmented the price by 800 thalers above the charge in other ports the governor compelled restitution, but not to the customers—only to the coffers of the Benadir Company. Giorgi discovered, and this was subsequently confirmed by Chiesi and Travelli, that the Kadis, who gave judgment in the native courts, were paid no more than five to seven thalers a month, less than a domestic servant—a wage on which they could not live and were, therefore, compelled to demand money from the persons whose cases they tried, a most serious impediment to a fair trial. The Askaris were paid only three or four thalers a month (about nine Italian lire at the rate of the time) and in consequence were obliged to engage in trade and nefarious pratices.

Giorgi was shocked to discover an open traffic in slaves; he was shown several contracts for the sale of slaves and sent one of them to the veteran Socialist, Filippo Turati, who raised the question in the Chamber of Deputies. In view of these revelations the Italian Government instructed Consul Pestalozza and Commander Di Monale to investigate the management of the Colony. Their revelations were terrible in respect of every aspect of government. The traffic in slaves both inland and overseas was legalised by the official stamp of the Chartered Company, and the imposition of a tax. Consul Pestalozza declared that instead of facilitating the abolition of slavery the action of the Company was consolidating the institution. Commander Di Monale considered that:

> "*The condition of the slaves in the Benadir was not that of domestic servitude, but of true slavery, that liberation in many cases was impossible, that the Chartered Company instead of providing for the gradual abolition of slavery was perpetuating and aggravating it.*"

After these revelations the Foreign Affairs Minister, Tittoni, expressed deep regret for this evil state of affairs. He declared that the tax had been levied on the traffic in slaves without the knowledge of the Company, but actually, as reproduction of the records by Chiesi and Travelli prove, high officials of the Company—governors of the ports—stamped and signed these records, and the tax was in many cases paid at the official residence of the Governor of the Port.

The Benadir Company Demands an Explanation from Governor Dulio

In view of these events Cavaliere Carminati, the Administrator of the Company, and members of the Council in Milan informed Governor Dulio of the charges against him excitedly circulating throughout Italy, and urged him to send explanations which would placate public opinion. He replied in a confident manner that he observed "the Honourable Members of our Council have been vividly impressed by the polemics in the Press on the subject of slavery in the colony of Benadir." It would be useless to dwell on the past, for it was not to his honourable colleagues that he need draw "a lovely picture" of his work; it was sufficient to say that the affairs of the colony were always "better and better."

Realising that his post was in danger he endeavoured to turn the flank of the opposition by declaring that whilst slavery in the Interior was no concern of the Company because they had no control there, it would be " convenient, decorous and necessary " for the company to abolish domestic slavery in the ports. To accomplish this the slave owners must be compensated. He calculated it would cost 100,000 thalers (about 220,000 francs to liberate all the slaves in the ten stations occupied by the Company in the Benadir. He did not know whether the Council could do this without consulting the shareholders. Twenty thousand thalers could be raised in the colony. To show that the Governor could set an example he was disposed to give 10,000 lire himself, and he " authorised " the Administration to deduct this sum from his stipend at the rate of 2,000 lire per month. He would consider himself honoured if the Council would accept his modest contribution to the humanitarian work they had called for in the colony. This proposal had no placating effect. The Secretary's reply manifested the utmost irritation. He retorted: "Your proposal has found us totally unprepared; this is the first time we have had from you such expressions of old humanitarian sentiments." The Governor had made a totally opposite report little more than six months earlier, when he declared the impossibility of abolishing domestic slavery and the grave consequences which would follow even a modest step thereto. Before any such innovations could be attempted the Mad Mullah must be liquidated by the English; the Company's reserve in the matter of slavery was fully justified, but the Governor must understand "the immediate necessity of replying to the accusations with which you and the Company are assailed. Articles against you and the management of the colony contain the most grave and damaging accusations, particularly of having favoured slavery and profited by a tax on it." The General Assembly of shareholders of the Company had been called. The Governor must send a detailed report on the administration of the colony showing it to conform to the Berlin and Brussels Conventions regarding slavery. The Council had cabled to him: " Indispensable to protect ourselves. Telegraph the names of persons really dismissed." Evidently the Council desired some scapegoats.

Robecchi-Bricchetti Revelations

Robecchi-Bricchetti on behalf of the Anti-Slavery Society of Rome, visited Mogadishu, Brava and Merka, in April, 1903. He paid the tax to liberate two slaves and examined Court records concerning others and saw slaves bought and sold. On returning to Italy he protested against the open traffic in slaves in the " Sole " of Milan and other newspapers. At meetings of the Anti-Slavery Society, reported in " Il Secolo," he displayed fetters, chains and manacles, which he had removed from the bodies of slaves. This caused an uproar in Italy. Questions were being asked in Parliament. Robecchi-Bricchetti was accused of theatricality and sensationalism, but he was not the man to care for that. An experienced traveller, he had journeyed through the Libyan desert to the Oasis of Jupiter Ammon in 1885, dressed as a Bedouin Arab. In 1888 he had visited Harar, met Ras Makonnen, had been commissioned by him to build a church, and had made a vocabulary of the Somali language. In 1890 he had explored the Somali coast from Obbia to Aloula; he was fully informed and he refused to be silenced.

Chiesi and Travelli Revelations

It was on account of these revelations that Gustavo Chiesi and Ernesto Travelli were requested by the Council of the Benadir Company to serve as a commission to report on conditions in the colony. The Council, entrusted them with a letter of dismissal to present to Governor Dulio, who had failed to produce the report desired of him, exonerating himself, and acquitting the Company of all blame. Nevertheless, the Council greatly hoped the Commissioners would be able to present a report, which would refute at least the most adverse charges and would enable the administration of the Colony to continue without any substantial change. Above all the Council desired to be spared the cost and difficulty of liquidating slavery.

The Commissioners were instructed to confer the Governorship of the Colony on a Naval lieutenant, Cavaliere Igino Badolo, then Governor of Merka, who had already served as acting governor during the absence of Dulio. Consul-General Mercatelli at Zanzibar, to whom they disclosed the identity of the proposed Governor, protested most vigorously, stating that Badolo had had Somalis punished, without the least shadow of a trial, by being tied to a cannon and given fifty strokes of the curbasco, from which they invariably died. This exaggerated punishment had created a most adverse impressioin at Kismayu, in the neighbouring British Colony, where it was illegal to give more than 24 strokes. By regulations there a doctor had to be in attendance to examine the offender beforehand and remain during the punishment. Consul Mercatelli reported that the prisons of the Italian colony had so evil a reputation in the British colony that it was commonly said there, many of the living enter the prisons of the Benadir, but only the dead come out !

The Commissioners reported after studying voluminous evidence that while Governor of Merka, Badolo treated the inhabitants with terrible severity. He returned fugitive slaves to those who claimed them, and if no claimant appeared, would put them in prison and leave them there till they died.

"*This system of arresting people and leaving them to die, or having them killed in prison, adopted by Lieutenant Cavaliere Badolo while he was Governor of Merka, has put in the hearts of the population a dumb terror, mingled with a desire for revenge, which results in an overwhelming hatred of our domination, which we realised when we were in the Benadir.*" *

The Commissioners had traced about thirty persons imprisoned by Badolo in Merka without trial, who had died there. They asked: Did they succumb to calculated cruelty, to the neglect of the warders or from the deplorable condition of the prisons? " In the opinion of Chiesi and Travelli all three causes contributed to their sad end. What opinion, they asked, can the people of the colony have of Italian justice, if we cause people to die in prison or by beating.

---

* Vide Chiesi-Travelli Report, page 159.

without trial, without the least defence or equity toward the accused. Thus died the family of the Asheraf of Merka, the old Kadi, Sherif Osman, his two sons, his nephew and Shobla ben Sherif Duroba, his friend and confidant, arrested at Merka, and transferred for greater security to Mogadishu when Badolo was deputy Governor. They might have been tried, as was often done then, by the Italian Consul at Zanzibar, by a council of war on one of the Italian warships— in any case by Italian colonial functionaries, but they died without a trial.

Gay Orgies by Italian Officials

Gaiety was a characteristic of Badolo's deputy governorship. Large provision of wines and spirits was imported from Italy. There were contests to ascertain who could drink the most glasses. Almost every night there were drinking parties at the Governor's Residence. Women were brought in, and plied with intoxicants till they became unconscious. It was a habit with the Italian Governors of the coast towns to take or send the Askaris to take the most beautiful women in the locality, Somalis, Gallas, Arabs and others to give pleasure to their junior official colleagues. Such incidents had tragic repercussions; a girl of the Bimal tribe was shot at the town gate by her brother because she had passed the night at the official residence with Badolo.

"*All that contributed to alienating the population and to increase their suspicion and distrust of us, and to lower our prestige and our dignity in face of them.*"

" Badolo did not content himself with taking one woman, as in general most of the Residents did to employ for their use. He had pleasure in changing them often, and in Merka and Mogadishu he had women belonging to the chiefs and notable citizens likewise for his subordinates and colleagues, and to satisfy some of them paid as much as £4 sterling for a woman."

The utter neglect of duty by Governor Dulio encouraged the excesses of some of his subordinates; for months he scarcely left his house. He left his Muslim interpreter, Hagi Ahmed, to carry out most of his own duties.

The tolerance of Governor Dulio towards slavery appears in many documents. One of the most striking is his instruction of July 7, 1908, to Lieutenant Badolo, then on a Mission to Lugh.

" I recommended you, and you should recommend the two Residents of Bardera and Lugh to treat with the greatest possible tact, and to act with the greatest prudence in all questions concerning slavery, and not to be mistaken in regard to our duty to proceed little by little in this matter so as not to wound or damage the interests of populations unaccustomed to European rule, who have previously enjoyed limitless independence, and who are now put under submission to the Italian Government, and who consider slavery as one of the most important institutions of social life, equal to that of property and family. Do not make the mistake, except in some isolated and exceptional cases, of liberating the slaves. This can be done later on when we have the means to indemnify the masters."

On the following day, the Governor wrote further:—

" My recommendation on the question of slavery: Add yourself verbally what is not possible to put in writing and what you think necessary for the instruction of Cappello and Icheri in respect of whom reports leave me in some doubt.

" In conclusion, do not break the glass ! "

Subsequently, Cappello and Icheri, like Badolo, became very grave offenders in respect of the slave trade and used harsh cruelty towards the native people. Icheri executed Badolo's order to have tied to a cannon and beaten the Somali whose death occasioned adverse criticism in the adjacent British Colony.

Enrico Perducchi stated that when he was stationed in Mogadishu, he had met Pietro Giorgi, who told him of his disapproval of the Governor and the management of the Colony. Perducchi considered it his duty to warn the Governor of the hostile impressions which Giorgi was carrying back to Italy, and which might result in adverse propaganda there.

In the following February, the Governor sent for Perducchi and he was called into council with the Governor, and Monti, Marchini and Petrini. The Governor then declared that the civil engineer, Sala, had had published in an Italian newspaper an alleged bill of the sale of a slave in Mogadishu, which the Governor declared had never taken place. On this account he had imprisoned the Kadi and other natives, who had confessed during their encarceration that the document was a forgery. They had acted under the instigation of the engineer, Sala. The Governor then brought forth a regulation to the effect that the Governor was empowered to expel any official of the Company, or any European in the Colony, without giving any reason. He invited Perducchi to state his opinion as to the action to take regarding Sala. Perducchi, without hesitation, declared that Sala ought to be expelled. Later, however, on learning more of affairs in the Colony, he had grave doubts.

The same case was referred to by Lieut. Marchini, who stated that he had been called to this meeting very shortly after arriving in the Colony, where he had come with enthusiasm and hope. He believed the accusation against Sala, at the time, but later he found that the sale of slaves was a common practice, and that a tax was levied on the sale as a matter of course. He mentioned that Haji Ahmed, the Governor's interpreter, had purchased a woman brought from Lugh for 50 thalers, though she was worth 150 thalers, and what was worse she was a free woman and not a slave.

When appointed Resident in Brava, Marchini was determined to put an end to the slave trade, and gave orders that he was to be advised of any caravans approaching the town in order that he might arrange to arrest the slave owners and liberate the slaves.

His efforts had latterly been frustrated because caravans were accompanied by a letter from Cavaliere Cappello, the Resident at Lugh, stating that the numerous men and women slaves on the caravan belonged to one of the merchants of the locality, and therefore must not be intercepted.

The View of the Kadis:
Abolition of Slavery Could be Affected in Ten Years

The Commissioners interrogated the Kadis of Brava, the Chief Kadi Waliji ben Abdherrahman of the Bida Homran, stated that he had exercised the function of Kadi for about six years from the time when Lieut. Mamimi was Resident in the port. A much older Kadi, Mohamed ben Hagi Mai Omar of the Rer Faki tribe, had exercised this function in Brava from before the Italians took control, having been Kadi under the Administration of the Sultan of Zanzibar. Asked why some of the chief Kadis were dismissed by the Italians, he stated that he did not know for certain, but he understood they were dismissed because they had issued an order stating that the new Italian administration would not change the existing law, that agriculturalists should continue to attend to their land and the merchants to follow their calling as before. He could not say whether in Mamimi's time a change had taken place and the slave trade had been re-introduced in Brava, but under Lieut Cappello the trade became common, and at least once or twice a month, caravans brought many Galla slaves into the City, from the regions of Badera and Lugh. These, and others introduced into the City, were bought and sold, and some of them were used for cultivating the soil in the neighbourhood.

Whilst Cappello was Resident, and many slaves were brought in, there were naturally many bills of purchase, sale and exchange. When Lieut. Bossi became Governor, a case of a mortgage upon slaves was brought before the Kadi. Before agreeing to sanction the registration of this mortgage, the Kadi consulted Lieut. Bossi, who prohibited the transaction. Moreover, Lieut. Bossi decreed that in cases of succession, slaves could only be transferred to the immediate heir of the deceased slave owner. Lieut. Marchini, who became Governor after Bossi, exercised an active surveillance, and prohibited any bill of purchase, sale, exchange or mortgage, and posted an order to this effect on the door of the official residence.

Since the departure of Resident Marchini, the Court had registered many inventories of the property of deceased residents, wherein were included all together the animals, money and slaves which the deceased had possessed. These were transferred, sold or exchanged, and the Administration imposed a tax of one per cent. upon them. Signor Marchini had prohibited the inclusion of slaves in such inventories. The Kadis, he said, should be given greater respect and authority and removed from the temptation to accept bribes.

Asked whether in his opinion slavery could be abolished and

free labour substituted, the Kadi replied that he did not think it could be eradicated immediately as the soil would be left untilled; but the legal status of slavery could be immediately abolished, and the existence of slavery could be brought to an end after a fixed time, probably in ten years, which would give both slaves and masters an opportunity to make other arrangements. In the meantime, the Governor ought to regulate the obligations of both parties.

During the investigation of the Commission, the Resident at Merka requested their decision as to whether he should indemnify the owner of a fugitive slave, as had been done in the time of Governor Dulio, when it had been the custom either to return the fugitive slave to his master, or to adopt him and pay an indemnity. The Commissioners indignantly replied that to indemnify the master of an escaped slave would merely result in maintaining the practice. The owner would spend the indemnity in purchasing two other slaves, younger and stronger than the one he had lost.

Salem Maruasi, interpreter of the Residency in Brava, when interrogated by the Commission on October 15, 1903, stated that he had come to the Benadir in the service of Consul-General Cecchi, who had engaged him at Zanzibar as his interpreter. He stated that at that time no steps were taken to impede the trade in slaves, who were brought freely into the city by their owners, and sold and exchanged without any hindrance on the part of the authorities.

When Badolo was Resident, he imprisoned many people, amongst whom were four Asheraf, who were transferred to the prison in Mogadishu, where they remained five or six months, and then died.

An order having been issued prohibiting the natives from bringing into the city knives, lances and other weapons, under pain of 50 strokes of the Curbasco tied to a cannon, three Somalis who were found with arms were subjected to this punishment. One died the same day, and the others in prison a day or two afterwards.

Such cases made a great impression in the country, because the people were not used to such punishments. The notables of the town waited on Signor Badolo requesting that another type of punishment should be substituted, but he replied that this punishment had been decreed by the Governor and the Commander of the *Staffetta*, his superior. A short time afterwards, the brother of a Somali who had been killed in this way, entered the town and attempted to attack Signor Badolo but was immediately killed by the Askaris.

Chiesi and Travelli interrogated a number of the inhabitants who owned slaves and summed up these interviews by the following conversation:—

"When your brothers, the white men, began to buy our girls we did not think it wrong for us to buy or exchange slaves while no prohibition was published."

" But the white men," we replied, " buy women to free them."

"No! They buy them for their pleasure, to make them their concubines, and not to liberate them. Why don't they also buy the old and the destitute?"

The two commissioners summarised the responsibility of the Italian Government in these words:—

"*The responsibility of the Italian Government in the question of the Benadir and South Somaliland is of a political and moral order.*

"*The Government declared an Italian protectorate from Cape Guardafui to the Juba, and announced to the world its work of civilisation in this vast piece of Africa, but its work ended with the announcement of it.*

"*The condition of the Italian Exchequer, which did not permit the luxury of an active Colonial policy, more than justified the reluctance of the nation for African enterprise after the sorrows and disasters in Eritrea. The Government, therefore, sought a means of ridding itself of the responsibility involved in the protectorate.*"

Kadi Courts Records Reveal Traffic in Slaves

In the Chiesi-Travelli Report are reproduced some extracts from the Registers of the Kadi Courts, recording the sale of slaves, the price paid for them, and the tax paid to the Italian Government, or the Chartered Company, as the case might be. Here is a translation of one of these extracts:

Italian Somaliland,
   Mogadishu,
      N. 269.

In the name of God, clement and merciful—God be praised—Iasin ben Abdel El Moghir Tim has purchased from Nur Ali ben Mussa the woman called Ahboi for 80 Maria Theresa thalers. Sold and bought truly, with full agreement between the parties to the contract and the price:

(Here follow signatures of three witnesses).

Written in legal form by the Kadi Mohj Eddin ben Aseek Moharram, October 20, 1901.

Paid to the Government one thaler of tax.

                                                     BADOLO.

The Badolo who signed this contract was the same Naval Lieutenant Cavaliere Badolo, whose unsatisfactory conduct has already been described, and whom the Benadir Company had intended to appoint as Governor in place of Governor Dulio.

Registration No. 245, records the sale of the slave, Galla Khadiga, and his two sons, Jusuf and Mohammed, for 200 Maria Theresa thalers, on account of which a tax of two thalers was paid at the Residenza to Cavaliere Badolo. Another extract from the same Register records the sale, on September 7, 1902, of "two females, Aiscia and Hamaule, and a male, Modi" for 211 M.T. thalers. Three thalers were paid for the registration of this sale to the accountant of the Colony, Signor Guido Mazzuchelli.

On October 4, 1902, the sale of a slave, called Bilal, for 90 thalers was registered by Signor Mazzuchelli on payment of one thaler. On October 4, 1902, were also sold, "two individuals, Tanaccal and Ascia ben Tanaccal," for the price of 135 M.T. thalers. Two thalers were paid for the registration of the sale to Signor Guido Mazzuchelli. Other records revealed inclusion of slaves of deceased persons in the inventory of the possessions sold for the benefit of their heirs. In the Register of the Kadis of Brava it was recorded, on April 15, 1895, that 45 thalers, the proceeds of the sale of the slaves of a deceased owner, were divided among his three sisters. One thaler was paid to the Italian Residente.

On March 21 the Register of the Kadi of Brava records that 190 thalers, the proceeds of the sale of slaves who had belonged to a deceased woman were distributed as follows: two thalers for the Residente, five thalers for the funeral, one thaler and five-eighths for the town-crier, and the rest among the heirs.

On January 24, 1898, the sale of four slaves and a variety of goods of a deceased man were sold for 130 thalers. Of this sum two thalers were paid to the Italian Residente, 121 thalers and 44 docras were paid to sundry creditors, eight thalers and 56 docras remained for distribution to the heirs—four women and seven children.

Records of the pledging of slaves to guarantee debts of their owners were also reproduced in the Chiesi-Travelli Report.

On March 22, 1900, was registered the pledging of three of a "species of merchandise (slaves)," as a guarantee for the repayment of 50 silver thalers. One thaler was paid to the Residenza.

Sometimes the slaves were merely referred to as "species of merchandise." In a record of August 24, 1901, we find "species of merchandise" in a list of goods including cattle.

Records of cases concerning slaves which were tried before the Tribunal of Mogadishu included many applications for liberation, generally made by slaves on their own account, occasionally by others. The indemnity paid to secure liberation was usually about 50 dollars, rather more than slaves fetched when sold among the goods of deceased owners.

On June 27, 1903, a woman slave, Fecile Foiida Haidon, who had married a liberated slave, Hilole, claimed her freedom; she was freed on condition of paying 50 dollars, though according to the Sultan's Decrees she should have been freed automatically in any part of the Sultan's dominions on marriage to a free man. All the above transactions violated Italy's Treaty obligations.

On May 2, 1903, the slave woman, Mariam Hamed, was punished by three days' imprisonment for having refused to work during a religious holiday and for having replied insolently.

COMMISSIONERS CHIESI AND TRAVELLI INDICT THE ITALIAN GOVERNMENT

Chiesi and Travelli were pursuing their investigations in the colony, when Tittoni in the Chamber of Deputies in Rome, was denouncing the misdeeds of the Benadir Company, and declaring that his Government had taken active measures which had liquidated slavery and the slave trade in the Benadir coast towns, only domestic slavery now being permitted to exist there.

Chiesi and Travelli replied to the Minister in a letter of indignant protest addressed to the Italian Consul-General in Zanzibar, which they subsequently published in their Report. They showed by reference to documentary proof that the worst abuses had been perpetrated when the colony was under the administration of officials directly appointed by the Italian Government. They made clear that under the Government, as well as under the Company, fugitive slaves who had fled to the coast towns, instead of being aided and liberated, were returned by the officials of the Administration to those who claimed to own them, "an open defiance of the Brussels Act"

" The question of slavery " they declared," is becoming more and more grave and urgent. If the Government wishes to keep the colony, there must be combined action between the Government and the Company." It was the old demand of the Filonardi Company. In view of the Minister's strictures they declared :

" We cannot remain silent on reading the tardy reply of the Ministry of Foreign Affairs to the request of Ex-Governor Dulio, on April 22 of this year, for definite instructions, which he made at the very time when the revelations of the official Green Book, and the Parliamentary discussions about it had caused the most painful surprise and concern in Italy. The character of that tardy reply of the Ministry does not appear quite consonant with the explicit declaration to the Chamber of Deputies by the Minister of Foreign Affairs, which received the support of the entire national representation, wherein definite and prompt remedies and energetic action were promised to solve the problem of slavery, and to remove this shameful incubus, which weighs upon the Colony of the Benadir.

" Still less does the Minister's reply appear consonant with a communication on this matter by the Colonial Office, to which has been confided the task of applying the promised ' energetic measures' to combat slavery. What are the measures which it is claimed have been recently taken by the Ministry of Foreign Affairs? What are the energetic remedies applied by the Colonial Office?"

The Commissioners had not found in the official archives of the Governor in Mogadishu "any trace of remedies, either energetic or otherwise", which had been taken by the Italian Colonial Office to combat slavery. As Italians, they were mortified to be compelled to state that their government had given no serious instructions on this question. They had merely schemed to escape, once again, the duties and responsibilities rendered incumbent upon them by Italy's signature of the General Act of Brussels. The Ministry of Foreign Affairs in Rome could not, and ought not to ignore the truth that slavery in the Benadir was not a transitory domestic servitude, but was slavery properly speaking. It must not be ignored in Rome that along the rivers cultivation was exclusively done by slaves, "under conditions that it would be hypocrisy to speak of as domestic slavery". The slave population in the region of Mogadishu numbered ten or twelve thousand souls, without mentioning those in the hinterland of Merka, or the smaller numbers around Brava. These slaves were obliged to work to excess, wearing fetters to impede escape, and any attempt to do so was savagely punished.

"*The number of slaves is continually augmented by new acquisitions, obtained from the traffic with the north of the Colony, carried on with impunity in a region which is ostensibly owned and protected by the Italian Government, but which is open to the arms traffic and where no measure has been taken to repress slavery.*"

The traders who carried on their nefarious traffic unchecked in the colony were even penetrating British and Ethiopian territory to make their captures. The Commissioners had themselves seen fugitive slaves who had fled from the interior, still wearing the fetters imposed to restrain them.

Having been commissioned to investigate on the Company's behalf, Chiesi and Travelli complained strongly that since the recent scandals, Governor Dulio, instead of returning the fugitive slaves to the owners as heretofore, was now freeing the slaves and paying a ransom to their owners. This was imposing a heavy financial burden upon the Company which had not been contemplated when the contract between the Government and the Company had been made. On the company's account, the two investigators objected emphatically to this expense. On principle, they considered the procedure an ignominious recognition of slave owning, and a stimulus to the slave traffic. The compensation paid on behalf of the company was higher than the price of a slave in the interior. With the company's ransom, the owner could purchase two new slaves, younger and stronger than the one who had been freed.

The Commissioners insisted:

"*This is a decisive moment for the Government, as well as for the Company.*

"*The Government cannot shelter any longer behind mere platitudes. It must sincerely apply the Brussels Act, as ratified by the Italian Parliament.*

"*If the Government intend to rid themselves of their obligations again by mere pious expressions, ignoring the exorbitant (sic!) demands introduced by the Italian Parliament into the contract between the Company and the Government; if the Government mean to leave the Company to shoulder all the moral and material responsibility of the Government's Treaty obligations, we do not advise the Company to accept.*

"*We consider it our duty to express this opinion to you, and to request you to inform the Government.*

"*We are sending a copy of this letter to the Company in Milan.*"

The Commissioners thus uttered a very grave indictment of the Italian Government, the justice of which cannot be denied. The Government, not the Company, had signed the Treaties which had been violated. The Government had itself been violating the Treaties with Britain and the Sultan of Zanzibar, and the obligations of the Berlin and Brussels Acts before the Benadir Company was established in the colony. The Government had undertaken to "protect" the Somaliland population, and had thereby assumed grave responsibilities towards them. The ultimate duty and responsibility belonged to the Government, not to the Benadir Company, a mere commercial concern.

The Commissioners attached to this letter of protest the following official documents:

LETTER OF CONSUL-GENERAL CECCHI TO GOVERNOR DULIO

Zanzibar.
July 29, 1896.

"*If the slave is fleeing from his master for proved maltreatment which he has suffered, the authorities at the port should give him a letter of enfranchisement. Otherwise when it is proved that his master has treated him humanely, the slave must be returned to him. I am a partisan of unconditional liberation, and if this can be done without raising objections and protests from the proprietor, the noblest and most humanitarian solution is that of Article LXIV of the Brussels Act, which says:*

"'*All slaves arriving at the frontier of one of the Powers mentioned in Article LXII shall be declared free and shall have the right to call for letters of enfranchisement from the local authorities.*'

"*Naturally, in such cases it is necessary to act with much tact in order not to arouse the hostility of all the Muslim world of the coast and the interior.*

"*Domestic slavery in the Benadir should disappear little by little, after it has been abolished in Zanzibar and on the German coast.*"

It will be observed that the Italian Consul-General Cecchi, the responsible official representing the Italian Government, in this letter of instruction to the Governor of the Colony, refers to the Brussels Act, which the Italian Government had taken a solemn pledge to apply, as though it were merely a pious aspiration, for application only when convenient. Governor Dulio, in consequence, ignored the Brussels Act, as his instructions to his subordinate Badolo, and other evidence already cited, amply prove. As the Commissioners observe, the Governor informed his subordinates that only the slave trade by sea was to be checked; and that "the Brussels Act was in no way concerned with the traffic on land, the sanguinary raids on remote villages and on the weaker tribes for the purpose of capturing prisoners to be dragged along with the caravans and sold off at the markets."

The assumption of such an extreme degree of ignorance by Governor Dulio and his subordinates must be regarded in the light of the profits yielded by the slave traffic. Yet again, the Government must be regarded as the responsible authority, which refused to give effective supervision, or even to issue adequate instructions.

Dulio pleads ignorance of the Sultan's decrees against slavery which the Company was under obligation to enforce

The outcry which was raging in Italy having aroused anxiety in the breast of Governor Dulio, he wrote, as the Commissioners show, to Italian Consul-General Pestalozza in Zanzibar, requesting him for a copy of the Decrees on slavery of the Sultan of Zanzibar, for which the Italian Government had assumed responsibility. The Consul-General did not possess such copies; he was obliged to obtain them from the British. On receipt of these copies, Governor Dulio replied to the Consul-General, stating that hitherto he had been ignorant of these obligations, and expressing surprise that during the many years in which he had governed the Colony, he had not been informed of them. Here is his letter:

GOVERNOR DULIO TO ITALIAN CONSUL-GENERAL PESTALOZZA AT ZANZIBAR

"*Signor Consul-General,*

"*Thank you for the Copies of the Decrees of the Sultan of Zanzibar.*

"*I confess sincerely that I was ignorant of the existence of these Decrees.*

"*What appears grave is that, as I affirm, they were never communicated to me, either when I came to the Benadir and was installed as Governing functionary or subsequently.*"

Frantic Last-minute Efforts to Remove Bad Impressions

On account of the outcry in Italy, and only on that account, Governor Dulio now issued announcements, and had them posted on the doors of the "Residencies", on the lines of the Sultan's Decrees, that buying and selling of slaves was prohibited, that they might not be introduced into the Benadir, that on the death of an owner, his slaves could pass only to his wife and children, and in default of such heirs must be liberated, that slaves under thirteen years of age must all be freed, that slaves desirous of liberation were entitled to ransom at a fair price.

An important provision was that the earnings of a slave by trade or his own labour were his absolute possession, and that his master was not to be entitled to claim from him any portion of his earnings.

This very moderate amelioration was almost immediately overthrown by the explicit decision of Tittoni, the Minister responsible for the colonies, as we shall presently see. All the new rules were in fact practically dead letters.

Governor Asks Definite Instructions
Must All Slaves Claiming Freedom be Liberated?
Who Will Pay the Ransom?

On April 22, 1903, Governor Dulio wrote to the Italian Consul-General in Zanzibar, enclosing the above published letter he had had from Consul-General Cecchi in July, 1896.* The Governor complained that the new regulations were causing numbers of slaves, demanding their freedom to seek refuge in the coast towns. He therefore asked Consul-General Pestalozza to obtain from the Government in Rome definite instructions as to whether all fugitive slaves should be liberated in Mogadishu, and other coast towns, particularly Merka. The instructions he had received in 1896 from Consul-General Cecchi should, he urged, " be confirmed, abrogated, or modified."

He desired further to know whether compensation should, or should not, be paid to the slave owners when a slave was liberated, and if compensation were paid, whether it was to be charged to the Company, or who would pay it? It would probably aggregate a substantial sum in view of the increasing demand of slaves for liberation.

Tardy Reply: The Government Will Pay Nothing

It was not until October 31, 1903, that Governor Dulio's request for instructions received any response from Italian Government sources. By that time, he had been dismissed from the service of the Company, and the two Commissioners, Chiesi and Travelli, had assumed temporary responsibility for the affairs of the colony. It was to them that Consul-General Mercatelli, who had succeeded Pestalozza, made the belated Government reply. It contained these passages which were referred to in the above-quoted protest of the Commissioners:

Zanzibar.
October 31, 1903.

"*My predecessor did not fail to make to the superior Ministry the communication of Commendatore Dulio, in his letter of April 22 last, and his more recent report of September 25. The Ministry, replying to this Consulate, in June last, could give no other instructions about the abolition of the slave trade and the gradual disappearance of domestic slavery than to request the Benadir Company to apply the terms of the General Act of Brussels with such caution as the conditions of the locality and the nature of the population require, in order to avoid giving rise to turbulence.*

---

* See page 73.

"Because Commendatore Dulio also raised the question of expense the Ministry added that in any case no expense could be put to the charge of the Government for measures in connection with slavery.

"The Communication of Commendatore Dulio had not any character of urgency, as it treated only of measures and questions at large, and not specific facts. I reserved my examination of the matter till my arrival. Now, in view of Commendatore Dulio's notification of his departure, I hasten to make known to you the above reported instructions of the Government.

"I should add my personal opinion that the forcible restitution of slaves who have emancipated themselves seems to me in open contravention of the spirit of the Brussels Act and to the more evolved conception of domestic slavery as a transitory institution, which should lead to complete liberation, presupposing the tacit acquiescence of the slave in his lot, and rejecting any violence which might make domestic slavery degenerate into slavery true and proper."

Thus, as on all previous occasions, the Italian Government, in the so-called Liberal Democratic period, made a categorical refusal to incur expense, and having done so withdrew with pious platitudes, leaving the responsibility to the Chartered Company.

VI

ITALIAN GOVERNMENT LEGALISES SLAVERY

In 1911, two years after an alleged "spontaneous awakening" of Italy's " national energies " towards the Somaliland colony, there were still only a mere 14 hardy grantees who had been willing to take up concessions of free land there. Amid the many deterrents there were locusts, malaria-bearing mosquitoes, and the tsetse fly in some areas, but the unwillingness of the native inhabitants to serve the new colonists for whom they had been evicted from the lands near the rivers presented the greatest difficulty. Prestige was still cited against importing Italian workers, but the cost of bringing them and the unanimous preference of Italian emigrants for Europe and America were more insuperable obstacles. Only the concession held by Signor Carpanetti on behalf of the Somaliland Cotton Company was partly worked by Italian labour. Chinese labour and Tamil labour, which might be obtained by arrangement with the Indian Government, were considered as possible expedients but nothing came of either proposal. According to a handbook prepared by the Historical Section of the British Foreign Office* and published by His Majesty's Stationery Office in 1920, alleged escaped slaves, and slaves freed from their masters, by force or purchase, were the only sources from which the Italian Government could obtain labour for road construction, and from which Italian grantees could get labour for their concessions; but attempts to free a number of slaves had created too much disturbance. Governor Dulio's injunction to Lieut. Badolo: "Do not break the glass," may be recalled. Chiesi and Travelli stated in their report that the attitude of the inhabitants towards foreigners had altered greatly for the worse since Filonardi first journeyed from the coast to Bardera, accompanied by his wife.

Since then the Italians had established themselves on the coast, and had attempted to assert their authority at certain spots in the river areas. Filonardi had bombarded Merka and commandeered labour for building the wall and forts around Merka. As Pestalozza and Di Monali, Chiesi and Travelli, and numerous other

---

* Handbooks prepared under the direction of the Historical Section of the Foreign Office—No. 128, **Italian Somaliland.** (His Majesty's Stationery Office, 1920).

witnesses testified, the conduct of many Italian officials was such as to create acute tension among the people of the land. Governor Dulio's somnolent inactivity, which evinced solicitude mainly for the customs, in some respects tended towards detent, but rapacious customs exactions caused hardship. Dulio established four Bezas per day as the rate payable by a slave to his master if he undertook paid employment for someone else when his master did not require his services.

Reference is frequently made by the Chiesi-Travelli and other contemporary reports to slaves of the interior; it should be explained that slavery did not exist in the northern part of the Italian colony, nor in the greater part of Somaliland. As is made clear by works of writers familiar with that area before and during the period immediately under review, while slavery had no part in the typical Somali economy, certain tribes which to-day number about two per cent., are described by European observers as low caste tribes, the Midgans, Yebirs and Tomals, who, like the Gipsies have a language of their own which is not usually imparted to others. They are not unlike other Somalis in appearance, but tend to be somewhat shorter. Like the Gipsies the Yebirs deal in charms and omens; they attend births and marriages. The Tomals are craftsmen in metal and produce knives, hatchets, swords and spears. The Midgans, who are the most numerous are workers in leather, making saddles, shoes, wallets and prayer mats; they are hardy fighters with bows and arrows, skilled hunters and trappers, employing cleverly trained dogs. They live among the pastoral tribes who are rich in flocks and herds. The position of these craftsmen is not at all that of serfs, though some Midgans may work as hewers of wood and drawers of water for the herdsman whose own function is to care for their animals. Most of the drudgery, both heavy and light, in the pastoral tribes is traditionally performed by the wives of the proud nomadic herdsmen. Burton, in his famous " First Steps in East Africa," describes a couple of these gallant damsels who accompanied his caravan and performed hard work of every type. He expresses his admiration for their cheerful zeal for all needful labour. Seeing, as one may do to-day, a group of slender Somali women, charmingly robed in draperies of harmonious colours, gracefully reclining in the shade at noonday, one could not imagine them bearing heavy burdens.

The leather and metal work of the Midgans and Tomal craftsmen are essential to the pastoral population and are part of the distribution of functions, which, in one form or another, has been developed by peoples all over the world at some stage in their evolution.

Though slavery had no part in the northern Somaliland economy, the slave trade existed in Italian Somaliland in its complete and unregenerate form. On page 31 of the Chiesi-Travelli Report, Lieut. Badolo is quoted thus:—

" *Everyone knew that Lugh and Bardera were veritable markets for slaves, that almost all the askaris of the district had them, and that the caravans escorted by Signor Icheri from Gesira to Mogadishu transported as much white ivory as there was black."*

Here is a clear indication of the existence of the classic slave trade in which the African people were bought and sold; slaves were habitually described as "black ivory," and we have this statement of the Assistant Governor of the colony that an official of the Chartered Company escorted these caravans.

In the classic African slave trade, "the African heart disease," as Henry Drummond well described it when it was at its height more than fifty years ago, slaves, ivory and guns were inseparable; guns to effect captures, slaves to carry ivory on the long march to the coast, and then if they survived the terrible ordeals of the journey, to be sold with the ivory for shipment overseas. The small local craft, the dhows, drawing shallow water only, could put out to sea where the vigilant watchers on naval ships could not observe them.

The phrase, "there is a considerable transit trade via Lugh and Bardera on the Juba, which is chiefly concerned with the products of big game hunting," obviously covered much—of all the products of big game hunting, none could compare with ivory; of all the big game hunted, none could compare with man. The Chiesi-Travelli Report quotes a statement that the profits of the slave traffic were 25 per cent. but they may have been much greater.

In the South Eastern corner of Italian Somaliland in the cultivated areas along the banks of the Juba and Webbi Shebeli which are irrigated from the river, some 44,000 people are now engaged in agriculture, a proportion of whom speak a Bantu language, whilst others have adopted the Somali dialect of their neighbours. In the comparatively fertile area between the rivers, which is dependent on rainfall irrigation, being too far from the rivers to receive water from them, is a population of about 292,000 people who are engaged in mixed farming. They speak Sab, which is closely allied to Somali.

What the conditions were in these areas when the Italians began to establish their colony has been obscured by the many diverse statements made by the Government, the officials of the Chartered Companies, and by their various employees in the colony, when enquiries were held. The following statements by Enrico Perducchi, Italian Resident in the Lower Juba under the Benadir Company, to the Chiesi-Travelli Commission, and reproduced in their report, appear to be substantially correct. Perducchi was regarded by the two Commissioners as one of the most trustworthy men employed by the Benadir Company. The Commissioners therefore appointed him as provisional Assistant Governor under Ugo Ferrandi, when Governor Dulio and his assistant, Lieut. Badolo, were dismissed for maladministration. Perducchi stated that an agricultural population of about 35,000 occupied the entire length of the east bank of the Juba, to the width of a mile inside the Italian colony, the west bank being then held by the British. The fact that only about 44,000 of these so-called Negroid people inhabit both banks to-day suggests a fall in population. Though it has been suggested that they were brought from further south in the course of the slave trade, it is more probable that these river bank people established themselves on the Juba and also on the Webbi Shebeli where they are to-day, at an early period. Their ancestors may have lived and worked there before the ancestors of the Somalis arrived from Arabia. They may have occupied the whole of the area between the Juba and the Webbi Shebeli in former times, or even a much larger area.

All this is, of course, mere speculation. To-day the perpetuation of differences between them and their neighbours could only interest the anthropologist.

Perducchi described the river bank cultivators as " mostly free." This appears to refute other statements that slavery existed in this area when the Italians arrived. If anywhere in the Italian colonies servitude disappeared this was not due to humanitarian action by Italian Governments as Italian Ministers repeatedly stated that they would not attempt to abolish " domestic slavery."

Perducchi said these river bank people were careful not to go far from their homes owing to their fear of being captured and sold at the markets of Audegle and Maublen, in the region of Merka.

Perducchi reported that the Sab people in the area between the rivers were in the habit of hiring the river bank agriculturalists to work for them. To ensure that the river people should be permitted to return home at the end of the season for cultivation in the Sab area, he used to commandeer some of the herds of the Sab people, as hostages.

It was in the coast towns and in the agricultural and mixed farming area near the coast, that " domestic " slavery was entrenched. If the reports concerning it by numerous witnesses can be held to be true, the only sense in which it could be described as " domestic " was that its victims were not just then being shipped abroad. They were alleged to be working under tragic conditions, wearing manacles and fetters.

Having described what was being done by the several European States to abolish slavery and the slave trade in various parts of Africa, the Chiesi-Travelli Report paid a tribute to British efforts: " England, be it said to her glory, holds the first place in the world, and is far beyond other nations in the fight against barbarism and slavery."

The Report then adds:

"*The localities in which the question of slavery is of greatest importance to us Italians are those of Zanzibar and Pemba, because they were till recent years under the Zanzibar administration, like our Benadir, because of their near vicinity to it, and by their ties of tradition, race and family with it. Fifteen years ago Zanzibar and Pemba were the greatest centres for furnishing slaves to Arabia and the Persian Gulf.*"

Since Zanzibar and Pemba came under British protection, however, the status of slavery was abolished there. In the five years 1897-1901, 4,379 slaves were liberated by the Government on the island of Zanzibar and 9,492 on the island of Pemba, a total of 13,811. A further 3,776 were voluntarily freed by their owners, this meant 17.587 slaves were freed on the two islands in five years.

Italian Government Legalises and Whitewashes Slavery

The strong reports presented by the Italian Government's own Pestalozza Di Monali Commission and the Benadir Company's Chiesi-Travelli Commission appeared to call urgently for drastic reforms. The response of the Italian Government was surprisingly ineffective. Tittoni, the Minister responsible for the administration of the Colonies, on March 14, 1904, laid before the Chamber of Deputies the proposals of his Ministry for dealing with the problem of slavery in the Somaliland Colony. He declared that the vigilance of his government had entirely suppressed the trade in slaves, and that in the coast towns "slavery real and proper" had disappeared. This was untrue, for no action had yet been taken. He further claimed that only what he termed, "domestic slaves," now existed in the coast towns. Such slaves, he said, could not be bought and sold, though they were obliged to work for their masters, and when they worked elsewhere they had to pay the master on account of their earnings. He hoped to reduce this payment.

Where slavery in the old form still existed the efforts of the Italian Government would be directed towards transforming it into "domestic" slavery, as a step towards gradual abolition. He was totally opposed to immediate abolition, and declared:

"*It would be contrary to every principle of wisdom suddenly to abolish slavery in the interior; slaves would hasten to escape to the coast, and would create a serious economic disturbance, throwing into the walls of the cities of the coast thousands of persons unaccustomed to provide for themselves, and at the mercy of their bad inclinations.*"

The question he considered "very delicate."

Consul-General Mercatelli had been given power to negotiate with the chiefs of the Bimal tribes to establish regulations which would lead to the gradual transformation of regular slavery into domestic slavery. The slaves attached to the tribes of the interior were to be:—

"*Considered domestic servants, bound to their masters by a uniform contract of labour, by which the servant's work is paid by board and lodging in ordinary circumstances, as well as in sickness, and old age.*"

The children of slaves were not to be bound by the contract which bound their fathers and mothers; they were to have their own labour contracts.

The masters were to treat their slaves humanely, and grant them liberty to work some days on their own account, whereby they might be able to put together something towards their ransom. Domestic slaves were not to be passed from one master to another.

"*Thus*," *remarked the Minister with satisfaction*, "*this serious question may be said to be on its way towards a solution that will answer to every humanitarian, political and economic interest.*"

The modest ameliorations, so pleasing to the Ministry, were unfortunately accompanied by provisions to prevent slaves from obtaining freedom by escape, as they had formerly done:

"*In the case of a servant escaping towards the coast, he will no longer obtain unconditional freedom, but only after the decision of an Italian Tribunal, purposely established, that will examine the reasons of the fugitive slave, and those of his master. If the latter should prove guilty of cruel treatment, or of any other infraction of the regulations agreed upon, the former will be immediately released from every obligation towards his master, and declared free, whereas if the servant should prove to have escaped without any justifiable motive, he will be returned to his master, and obliged to pay him a fair indemnity.*"

Thus the Italian Government formally approved the existence of slavery, gave it a legal status in Italian Colonial law, and provided for the punishment of a slave who attempted to escape from the master, unless the slave could satisfy an Italian tribunal that his master had been guilty of excessive cruelty. The odds against the slave in such cases were usually overwhelming. Thus slavery continued in Italy's Somaliland Colony.

In 1935, when preparing war against Ethiopia, the Italian Government raised a hue and cry throughout the world that slavery existed in Ethiopia. On this account it was claimed that Italy's civilising mission compelled her to make war on that ancient African State.

At the very time when this outcry was raised to beat up propaganda for the forthcoming war of conquest, the Italian Government made the following communication, dated May 1, 1935, to the Secretary-General of the League of Nations, relative to domestic servitude in the Italian Colonies. The terms are, of course, guarded, but the facts are clear.

CYRENAICA

"In zones controlled by us it was not possible, however, to extirpate the residual form of slavery that subsisted—essentially slavery of a domestic character. The old slaves continued to live in the families in which they already are, some of them refusing to leave their former masters, and even asking our authorities to intervene.

"The present situation as regards domestic servitude is uniform throughtout the colony There is no need to recapitulate the special features of this kind of servitude: but it may be mentioned that every well-to-do Arab-Berber family includes not only one or more families of masters, but also one or more negro families, who have been living with their masters for a more or less long period of time..

"When these negroes reach marriageable age, the masters themselves make arrangements for their marriage with slaves belonging to the same family or to friendly families, and defray the marriage expenses. This is, in short, a form of voluntary servitude which will eventually die out owing to lack of new blood; at the moment, however, it cannot be eradicated because the serfs accept it willingly. If the law required the negroes to be removed from their masters' families, they would soon come back and ask their former masters for employment.

"Furthermore, as these negroes have had no opportunity of learning any trade, if they were removed from their families they would be reduced to the most squalid poverty and would have no hope of earning a living."

TRIPOLITANIA

"The status of the different groups of slave origin is now roughly as follows:—

"**Abid.**—There are frequent cases of men and their families, who have remained with their former masters under the old condition of servitude, either because they are unable to make a living in any other way, or because they are attached to their masters' families. These are cases of domestic serfdom (domestic servants, guards, watchmen, etc.), or agricultural serfdom (cultivating, sowing, ploughing) or serfdom as shepherds, the sole remuneration being maintenance.

"**Shuashena.**—Here again we find old slaves who have remained with the families of their former masters for similar reasons to those mentioned above. A few individuals or families are also still in a state of servitude on account of old debts; this is not a case of slavery, but merely of working off the debt year by year until it is extinguished."

"**Atara.**—The position of these groups in the communities to which they belong is undoubtedly one of inferiority; but it is not, strictly speaking, one of servitude.

"We must, however, regard as being clearly remnants of a former state of servitude the by no means small number of serfs who have remained in that condition of their own free will, with the families of their former masters."

ERITREA

"There are some natives whom the people call slaves, but they are no longer slaves, since they live of their own free will in that state of **domestic servitude which is wisely permitted by the Brussels Act, and which it would be neither just nor expedient to disturb** by an exaggerated and restricted interpretation of the intention of the law.

"The conditions of these serfs is perhaps better than that of many completely free natives. **The excessive zeal of certain officials has caused what was actually domestic servitude to be regarded as a condition of slavery.**"

Slavery in the Interior of the Colony

"Certain forms of agricultural serfdom, where they survive, present no feature resembling those of slavery, and are free of all essential elements of that institution; such serfs or dependents of the 'nobleman' are remunerated for the work they do, and can leave the family with which they are living whenever they wish to go to another family, or, if they prefer it, can change their occupation and residence.

"**This condition of labour is not offensive to Western morality nor subversive of public order:** these local authorities have never had occasion to intervene in these relations of employer and employed, which are established between the parties by free and mutual consent."

SOMALILAND

"Domestic serfdom also, although it should be tolerated under the laws in force, no longer exists in any compulsive form restricting individual liberty."

[The Parliamentary statements by the Italian Minister, Tommaso Tittoni, quoted in this and the following chapter are from the authorised English translation of his speeches, "Italy's Foreign and Colonial Policy," published by Smith Elder in 1914.]

VII

HOW THE COLONY WAS CONQUERED

Having made peace with the Mullah, and disposed of the Chartered Company, the Italian Government considered the time had come to conquer the Somaliland Colony, in order that its supposed great riches might be exploited for Italy.

Revenue to devote to the Colony was grievously lacking; a barracks had been built for the Askaris, and a couple of infirmaries, to serve the vast territory of 150,000 sq. miles. The Minister hoped to raise six million lire for public works by conventions with commercial companies, spread over a decade—quite an ingenious scheme for a poor government to devise, but it does not seem to have been realised.

To encourage the Deputies to face the future certainty of unpleasant warfare and unwelcome expenditure, the Minister offered them many engaging prospects of prosperity, and rosy hopes of great achievements, with small expenditure, some of them not even yet accomplished though forty years have passed. Amongst these was an all-the-year round port to overcome the Monsoon, to be constructed for a mere 800,000 lire, under the auspices of Signor Albertazzi, the engineer. The re-opening of the Gofka Canal, which was alleged to have been flowing till only thirty years before, when the Bimal tribes had obstructed it, had been promised by the Ministry year after year, a work which these poor tribesmen had inconveniently effected had thus far proved too much for the Italian Great Power to repair. Tittoni himself had advocated the re-opening as a necessary measure to increase fertility; but now he abandoned the project as too difficult. The canal, he argued, had become a mere trench, its level was higher than the river; there were matters of greater importance; the entire " hydraulic system of the Webbi Shebeli river must be studied." The necessary works, he assured the Deputies, would not be costly, as in Eritrea; they would be " easy and entail but small expenditure." He was eloquent on the value of the colony; its future prosperity; its suitability to accommodate " a stream of Italian emigrants." The fertility of the soil between the Juba and the Webbi Shebeli, so often described as an argument for acquiring and retaining the Colony, he extolled with enthusiasm; it was " flat and free from gravel "; it had " the characteristics of the Lombardy Plain "; even under the " rudimentary " methods of native cultivation it gave three harvests a year. Cotton, sesame, corn, tobacco, sugar-cane and rubber could be cultivated successfully. When security had been established, the progress of this zone would be "not a dream but a certainty upon which we may congratulate ourselves." Cattle, goat and camel skins, butter and camel grease were at present the main exports, but all the great tropical products could be grown and exported. Cattle could not survive in Zanzibar and the Seychelles; meat had to be imported there. The Benadir, with over 2,000,000 head of cattle, could supply it. True, the export of that commodity was falling; this would be remedied.

Better Cotton from the Benadir than from Egypt, U.S.A. and Australia

"Cotton would prosper in this region, which should in fact be preferred to all others." Better cotton, cheaper cotton, could be grown in the Benadir than in Egypt. Experiments had demonstrated that a greater weight of cotton per hectare was obtainable in the Benadir than in Egypt, America or Australia. The Benadir would supply the needs of Italian cotton factories, as well as those of other flourishing industries. The Benadir was in "the fortunate position that all the products of the Ogaden and of a part of the rest of Ethiopia must necessarily find their outlet on this coast." "Therefore, its commercial importance could not possibly be in doubt." Moreover, it was healthy; it was considered by the natives "the climatic station of Eastern Africa."

On the other hand, the supporters of a greater colonial expansion must not regret that modest steps must be taken within the means at the Government's disposal.

A road from the Coast to Bardera and Lugh, the famous Lugh Ferrandi, which had provided the excuse for the acquisition of so much territory, had frequently been urged in the Italian Parliament. In 1904, Tittoni had discouraged the project. "It is a very costly enterprise, which cannot be carried out in a few years." In 1908, he emphasised the need for it. "There exist only few and very bad caravan routes, along which the goods are carried on camels' backs in difficult conditions . . ." "Our not being yet established on the Webbi Shebeli seriously harms the development of the Colony's commerce, as the exchange of goods wholesale is carried on along the Shebeli, where the price of the merchandise is fixed."

On February 13, 1908, Tittoni explained to the Chamber of Deputies his plans for the conquest. He led up to the question of taking possession of the fertile land gradually, being solicitous not to present so bitter a subject in a manner which would give too much handle to opposition propaganda, or provoke public anxiety and humanitarian reproaches. He began by emphasising the insecurity of the caravan routes from the coast to the interior, especially to Lugh, which was an important centre for the imports and exports of Southern Ethiopia. "Only few, very bad, very narrow caravan routes" existed; goods were carried on camel back under extremely difficult conditions. Moreover, whilst the Italians had established themselves at some points on the Juba, they had not yet any foothold at all on the Webbi Shebeli, a not less vital route for Ethiopian trade. To be absent from that river meant losing a substantial source of gain. It was prejudicial to Italian interests not to be there, for the wholesale exchange of goods took place along the river; the prices were fixed there; the coast had to submit to what was arranged on the river. Therefore the river must be occupied by Italy.

Moreover, the Bimal and Wadan tribes must be conquered and forced to submit to Italian authority. This might be done "gradually, profiting by any favourable conditions which might present themselves," or " suddenly, by a rapid advancing movement, breaking down all resistence," as General Baldissera had recommended. Tittoni preferred the gradual method.

Gilib, on the coast, had already been occupied by Italian forces, he told the Chamber; possession would next be taken of Danane and the wells to which the Bimals resorted with their cattle in the dry season. Seizure of the water would give the government the whip hand, above all in a country of that type. Kaitoy, on the Webbi Shebeli, would then be seized, and afterwards Afgoy and Gheledi, opposite Mogadishu.

To accomplish these military operations the force of Askaris, which at that time numbered 2,442 with 30 Italian officers, must be increased to 3,400 with 46 Italian officers. Thereby it would be possible to strengthen the garrisons, and to establish a moving column, which could proceed rapidly wherever needed. The occupation of the area from Merka to the Webbi Shebeli would be easy, for the distance was only 20 kilometres, and no thick forests intervened, but from Mogadishu to the same river the distance was double, and the region covered with dense woods, " which lend themselves to ambuscades."

" Bloody Conflicts " but no " Heavy Expenditure."

The Minister warned the Deputies that they must not be squeamish about the results of the military measures required for these conquests:—

" It is not impossible that, in spite of the gradual and pacific character of the occupation, there may be some bloody conflicts. Well, if this should happen, we must be ready to receive the news of it with equanimity, because we are not going in for an action which can lead us into unexpected adventures, or entail heavy expenditure."

It would not be wise, Tittoni argued, to delay military action, for that would give time for the tribes along the river to obtain arms for their defence, and to come to an understanding with the Mullah, whose future remained for Italy "a dark point." Rather than wait, and possibly have to deal at the same time with the Bimals and the Mullah, despite the agreement with him, which was known to be untenable, it would be better to begin by solving the much easier question of the subjection of the Bimal tribe.

The quality of the Askaris, who would be used for the fighting, had been greatly improved, he declared, since the days of the Benadir Company. " The Company recruited them everywhere, among Somalis, Eritreans, Swahilis and Arabs." To-day 95 per cent. were " recruited in Arabia, in Yemen, and in Hadramaut."

Having begun by suggesting a peaceful operation in which nevertheless, "some bloody conflicts" might take place, the Minister in order to eulogise the " intrepidity in battle " of the soldiers recruited in Arabia, revealed that stern warfare was in progress. He read the following extract of a report from Commander Cerrina of " the Denane encounter " :—

" The troops in their turn, so well directed, behaved always splendidly, be it for individual courage, collective discipline, calm precision of range. This has been obtained through the assiduous work of all the Officers in command of the companies. Those same elements who, at the time of the Company's administration, had inspired in all quarters so little confidence, have been transformed into very good soldiers."

Soldiers' Low Pay Under Italy: Effort to Induce Other Governments to Come Down to Italy's Low Level

These "very good soldiers " were paid seven Maria Theresa Thalers a month, in British currency 14s., about 204 lire per annum. This was no mere pocket money; they had to live on it. Under the Company, Tittoni recalled, they had received only from 144 to 180 lire. Despite the somewhat higher scale:

" We must admit," he added, " that even the actual pay is very small; it constitutes one of the essential difficulties in recruiting.

" Certainly it will not be possible to maintain the present conditions, which clash with those of the adjoining Colonies where the Colonial troops are better paid. I propose to study the opportunity of a Colonial understanding among the States which have possessions adjoining ours to establish a common medium scale of pay."

It will be recalled that the Minister had explained, in denouncing the Chartered Company, that the Askaris were so miserably remunerated that they could not exist on the pittance paid them, and that they were compelled to resort to trade as a means of obtaining a living. Tittoni's proposal to induce Britain and France to reduce the pay of their Colonial soldiers was ingenious, rather than generous!

The hoped for Colonial understanding to keep the pay of all Colonial soldiers down to a level Italy could afford to reach was not realised. On June 25 of the following year Tittoni announced that recruiting in the Yemen had proved difficult. Like the Chartered Company, he also had resorted to Eritrea, and even to Somaliland itself to recruit Askaris. He had condemned the Company for this practice, stating that the Eritreans were a source of discord in Somaliland, and that the Somalis had " shown little courage." In fact they had absconded when expected to fight their own people.

Now that the Government had become the paymaster the matter was regarded from another aspect. By recruiting in Italy's own colonies, the Government avoided the competition of richer governments, which had to be faced in Arabia. They could pay what they chose in their position of authority. The practice of raising troops in one colony to coerce the people of another colony soon became fully established. To popularise this policy the Minister eulogised highly the " resistance, discipline, and dash of Eritreans," and declared that " the young Askaris of the Benadir." who were being tried, had " proved themselves worthy."

An active military campaign was indicated by declaring that " fame " had been won in combats at Gilib, Egalla, Danane, Dongad and Mellet. Days had been spent in " marching and fighting," for 10, 12 and 13 hours at a stretch. There had been " nightly alarms," and the troops had been increased to 3,689, with 230 police, and irregular forces in addition. The tribes, who had been promised " protection," friendship and trade, were taken unaware and by superior arms and were overcome, district by district. Neither the Hague Rules, nor any other international convention designed to mitigate the barbarism of war was applied in their case. Defence of their homes and farms was punished as rebellion to a government in regard to whose advent they had not been consulted. The term " protectorate " has been used in Africa to cover the most ruthless types of warfare, and the most arbitrary forms of government.

Forced Labour to Clear the Jungles: The Conquered Forced to Make Roads to Facilitate Further Conquests

As the tribes were conquered they were forced to the arduous labour of clearing roads through the jungle and bush.

Forced labour was a continuous feature of Italian rule in Somaliland, from the early days of the occupation until the Italian defeat in 1941.

Tittoni recorded the work already accomplished and the programme immediately projected:

"*I believe it will interest the Chamber to know what has been done. The labour of clearing has been imposed as a punishment upon the rebellious tribes which have been subjugated. At the middle of last March the clearing had been executed along the paths which adjoin the following localities:—*

"*(1) Mogadishu-Afgoy, with the understanding that the passage already cleared be widened in as brief a space of time as possible, which is already being done on the Afgoy side, the work being executed by the Wadan tribe.*

"*(2) Afgoy-Barire, a clearing of sufficient width, executed by the people of Merere, and of unquestionable utility for communications and for the rapid concentration of the two garrisons on the river.*

" (3) *Barire-Danane, a clearing also of sufficient width (in some places of about 50 metres).*

" (4) *Merka, front of Kaitoy, recently begun and carried on with alacrity under the vigilant care of our Resident at Merka.*

" The following clearings are decided upon and will be shortly carried out:—

" (a) *Mogadishu-Darerta-Ghet-Faki-Balad.*
" (b) *Jesiria-Derdif-Adadle-Afgoy.*
" (c) *Kaitoy-Mallable.*
" (d) *Brava-Havai (for a certain distance)."*

There was infinite tragedy in this Colonial war to obtain the markets and the fertile land which had been occupied by industrious cultivators for centuries. The cheerful farms and villages, which had given so much pleasure to the first explorers, were now devastated, the crops trampled, the humble dwellings reduced to smoking ashes. In place of the friendly, light-hearted, folk, who had welcomed the missionaries and travellers, were the dead and the dying, whilst the unfortunate survivors were driven in forced labour gangs under compulsion of whip and gun to the stupendous, unpaid work of jungle clearing. So Italian colonisation proceeded.

Only the Italians have written the story of their conquest of Somaliland. The agonies suffered by the conquered people in defence of the fertile lands they had cultivated from generation to generation, have not been chronicled; their dead and their exiled are unrecorded.

VIII

LAND SEIZURES AND CONCESSIONS

Hopes of Large-scale Italian Settlement Dashed

The conquest of the Somaliland Colony being now under way, the Foreign Affairs Minister announced to the Chamber of Deputies, on February 13, 1908, that exploitation of its alleged immense resources could forthwith begin. For years he had repeated that Eritrea could not support a numerous Italian population. The barren wastes in the northern part of the newer Somaliland colony he had described as still less suited for colonisation, but he had continually insisted that the southern part of that colony, both the Benadir coast and the interior, were eminently suited for large-scale Italian settlement; he repudiated all contrary suggestions.

In declaring the utilisation of the colony now imminent, Tittoni overthrew all the hopes he had built up for years that a large outlet for Italy's landless unemployed could be found in Somaliland. He still extolled the climate of the southern part; the health of Europeans residing there was "excellent," "their activity" was "not subjected to the exhaustion of tropical climates." Nevertheless the Chamber must not hope for large-scale emigration there.

Master Race Must Not Work

It was not any shortage of land which would preclude Italian settlers; on the contrary, though the "density of population" was "considerable in the agricultural areas," vast tracts of land "would always be at Italian disposal," because under Italian direction, he claimed, "the reservations to be left to the natives would be rendered more fertile by rational methods of cultivation." This was a euphemism for what was in fact actually intended: to deprive the natives of ownership of the land and to compel them to work for the Italian concession holders who were to replace them.

The necessity of upholding Italian prestige would, however, render impolitic the settlement of Italian peasants and labourers in the new colony. The Italians must appear as a master race who do not deign to labour in the field.

"*We must remember,*" he urged, "*that in those regions work is looked down upon, and is left to inferior races, and to slaves. Therefore the Italian agricultural population would be lacking in the eyes of the Somalis in that prestige which is necessary to the European, in order to impress himself upon the numerically superior native element. This fact would, moreover, have an unfavourable influence upon the security of the inhabitants of the colony.*"

It will be observed that the view expressed by Tittoni, which was the general opinion of the Italian professional politician of the time, differed greatly from the opinion and practice of Dr. Krapf and his fellow missionaries who half a century earlier had built their dwellings, dispensaries and workshops and raised their food from the soil of Eastern Africa with their own hands, and thereby had won the devoted affection of the native inhabitants.

Cheap Native Labour More Convenient

But Tittoni had another, and to his mind, equally important objection to the advent of Italian labourers; the Somaliland native would always be cheaper than the Italian, even though the Italian was accustomed to very sparse living in his home surroundings:—

"*Nor must we overlook the economical side of the question. Emigration promoted by the commercial enterprises started in the Colony would not thrive for several reasons, which can be easily guessed. The employment of the labour of natives, and of the inferor Suaheli race, will always be much less costly and more convenient.*"

No Money to Establish Poor Settlers

Tittoni further argued that Italian peasants desirous of emigrating to Africa to cultivate the soil on their own account would be unable to find the necessary capital, nor could the Italian Government afford to subsidise them. In the neighbouring British colonies £750 (18.750 lire) was considered necessary for the settler to establish himself there. Even were this amount reduced in accordance with the smaller requirements of the poor Italian peasants, who were accustomed to a lower standard of life than that of British labourers, Italian settlers would be unable to find the cost of travel and settlement; assistance from the Italian Emigration Fund would be necessary.

Nevertheless the Minister would not extinguish all hope of the desired outlet for surplus poor people; not now, but at some future undetermined date, he would be disposed to favour investment of the Emigration Fund in the colony; in time Italian colonisation would be possible, but the necessary favourable conditions must be prepared.

At present the Government desired to promote large-scale occupation of land by persons who could supply substantial capital. Large concessions of land for cotton growing would be granted for 99 years (afterwards reduced to 60 years). The concessionaire would be expected to make a survey of the land granted to him. Thus a Colonial Register of the Survey of Lands would be provided without expense to the Government. The concessions would cover 1,000 hectares, to be extended to 5,000 hectares, if the concessionaire had cleared and cultivated 400 acres in the first three years.

Having declared that native labour must be used on these large-scale concessions on account of its cheapness, and that Italians must refrain from labour in the interests of Italian prestige, the Minister made an effort to assuage disappointment by the promise that the period of five years exemption from taxation accorded for the encouragement of concessionaires would be extended to ten years, if a number of Italian families, including not less than fifteen able-bodied men, were employed. "White labour being more costly than native labour we intend to favour the grantee who thus starts Italian colonisation in that region," Tittoni said. This would be in fact a very modest beginning; as each concession was intended to cover 5,000 hectares the scheme would provide a tiny proportion of Italian workers.

No Government or Private Capital for Colonial Investment

To stimulate the development of the colony which was alleged to contain so much potential wealth, several members of the Chamber of Deputies suggested various forms of colonial credits, loans, banks, etc. Tittoni discountenanced all such projects on the ground that no capital was available. He protested impatiently:—

"*That the actual conditions of capital in Italy are such as to discourage the floating of a loan with any probability of success is an affirmation that does not need much demonstration. In fact, the difficulties encountered by the Bank of Italy in order to place at the disposal of the Eritrean Government the sum of 17,000,000 lire —though this would constitute a loan guaranteed by the State for public works required in the Colony in accordance with the law of 1903—are well known.*"

This was the settled state of affairs in relation to the colonies; neither the Italian Government nor Italian investors were willing to provide capital for their development. The failure of two successive Chartered Companies had probably destroyed all faith in such investments.

The New Concessions : Native Cultivators Evicted

To overcome this difficulty Tittoni had decided to grant colonial concessions on the emphyteutic system: the grantee who was accorded 5,000 acres of land in the colony would have to guarantee to cultivate all the land within ten years, and to expend 500,000 lire upon it. He would pay nothing for the concession, only a tax after five years, or ten years if he employed 15 Italian men. The land would revert to the State at the end of sixty years.

Announcing to the Chamber of Deputies, in February, 1908, that a first concession under this system had been granted to Signor Carpanetti, the Minister observed guardedly that the concession had only " a provisional character," and before making it final " the land regime of the colony " would have to be " established." This,

Tittoni stated blandly, should, of course, have been done before making any concession of land; but he added, with truly blatant insincerity:—

"*We were in the presence of this dilemma; either solve at once the land problem, that is to say, precipitately, and without knowledge of the de facto conditions existing in the Benadir, or lose the opportunity of encouraging this private initiative, which is an expression of the country's interest in the Colony, an interest that it is necessary to foster.*"

The Carpanetti concession, and three others virtually granted, would assist in solving the land problem, because the grantees were under obligation to make a survey of their land which would form the basis for the Colonial Land Register.

"*The relations between the grantees and the natives, he said, "will give us the most exact criteria for the demarcation of the Crown lands, according to the modifications made to Mussulman Law by local habits and customs, and will allow us to fix with greater certainty the vacant territories and the rights and reservations of the natives.*"

That this was mere prevarication is but too painfully obvious, since Italian forces were even then engaged in warfare to destroy the rights of the native people by dispossessing them of their fertile, cultivated lands, and were compelling the conquered to forced labour. Moreover, it is evident that to appoint the new Italian grantees who had taken up concessions, as arbiters of the rights of the native people, was the very height of injustice.

Italian public opinion being at that time not wholly devoid of a sense of justice and humanity, protests were raised in the Italian Press.

When the Somaliland colony was again discussed in the Chamber, on June 25, 1909, Chiesi* severely criticised the conduct of the Minister. Tittoni excused himself by declaring that his speech of the previous year had been followed by "a spontaneous awakening of our national energies towards our colonies"; he had not wished to discourage it or to delay the productivity of the colony. Eleven grantees had taken up each 5,000 hectares in Gosha, two others had taken 500 acres in the Jumbo vicinity, one had taken 800 acres near Brava. He had been desirous of providing "the best possible conditions" for these grantees, for, he asserted, "the whole future of the colony would rest on their success, given the impressionability of Italian public opinion." Thus the Minister excused the fact that he had given the Italian grantees the right to decide what, if any, land or other rights should be given to the natives.

He added with amazing sang-froid and tortuous subtlety, that the Government would in no case assume any responsibility for the disposal of any rights of third parties which might exist on the new concessions until after

---

* Gustavo Chiesi, who with the lawyer Travelli, had visited the Colony to report on conditions there in 1904.

the area had been surveyed and the Crown lands demarcated. This declaration had to be made, he explained, because of "*the political necessities in which the Government might find itself in relation to the native proprietors. The grantees have been informed of this; it has not discouraged them, and they have strongly insisted upon receiving the concessions of land.*"

This was tantamount to saying to the Italian grantee: We give you this parcel of land for sixty years. You must make a survey of it and decide whether any part of it is to be allowed to the natives. We reserve, however, the right to reverse your decision and to take back part of the land we have given you, if we subsequently find ourselves in difficulties because we have deprived the native people of their land.

The grantees, as Tittoni observed, were not at all deterred by this bit of camouflage; they were particularly confident of their position because the Italian forces were vigorously engaged in reducing the former native owners to subjection.

Proceeding with his story the Minister remarked that the Land Survey Register would be gradually prepared by the grantees themselves. They would have concluded it before they had cultivated more than a few hectares of land. It was highly improbable that rights which had escaped the previous "accurate examination of titles" would refer "to those very pieces of land." Therefore the clause in question "while juridically and politically necessary to scrupulous entertaining of title in demarcating the land, cannot form a serious obstacle to cultivation." The cruel absurdity of this argument is revealed by reference to the Minister's former speeches. On April 8, 1905, Tittoni had spoken of this very region of Gosha as one in which "the conditions of security are normal." On February 13, 1908, he said it belonged to the Banke race "which is peaceful and devoted to agriculture" and "inhabited by the freed men of Gosha."

It was, of course, impossible that in this Gosha area, then densely populated and cultivated, 55,000 hectares on the river bank could be transferred to European grantees without displacing the indigenous cultivators. Tittoni had replied to questions in the Chamber that he had given instructions that to prevent the first Italian grantees taking up all the river bank to the detriment of subsequent Italian grantees, only one side of the square of 5,000 hectares would be allowed them actually on the bank of the river. In the case of the first six land grants of 5,000 hectares this had not been possible because the cultivable land was narrow, the concessions had thus been made long and narrow, with one long side on the river bank.

For the key to this problem one can but turn back to Tittoni's warning of February 13, 1908:—

"**In spite of the gradual and pacific character of the occupation, there may be some bloody conflicts. Well, if this should happen we must be ready to receive the news of it with equanimity.**"

The bloody conflicts, as he had himself made known, were proceeding, but members of the Italian Parliament were doubtless content to have a little soothing dust cast in their eyes.

The Minister went on to observe that the grantees were taking up land along the banks of the Juba, and that the government retained the right to dig canals between the concessions to irrigate lands to the rear. He then praised the discipline and dash "of the Askaris who had occupied the lower Shebeli. In this manner was the " scrupulous ascertainment of title " carried out.

Such were the subtleties of Italian Parliamentary Government during the creation of Italy's Colonial Empire! That the Italian grantees failed to fulfil their obligations, to invest capital in the lands which had been torn from the native people, and that much of the land went out of cultivation in consequence, that the supposed Somaliland El Dorado became merely another costly drain on the Italian exchequer, are historical facts which should not be forgotten.

IX

THE FASCIST ERA

The hope that the Somaliland Colony would prove a vast source of wealth for Italy and the Italians, and a rich storehouse of raw materials for Italian industries failed utterly.

That the territory would afford little outlet for Italian emigrants was already known whilst the Italian Government was pressing the Emperor Menelik to agree to its enlargement.

The Colony was always a financial burden to the Italian Exchequer. For the year 1908-9 a deficit of 1,935,000 lire was anticipated, but this proved too optimistic a forecast; a further 3,000,000 lire had to be voted to balance the accounts. The following estimates for the year 1912-13 are a typical budget for the early years:

Revenue	Lire
Customs	530,000
Posts and telegraphs	56,000
Various taxes	45,000
Fines and legal dues	15,000
Divers Receipts	45,000
State Contribution	3,629,000
Extraordinary Revenue from the Italian Treasury	2,611,000
	6,931,000

This total was equivalent to £277,240 sterling at the time.

Expenditure	Lire
Government and Civil administration	
Ordinary	1,499,400
Extraordinary	1,671,459
Military	2,896,700
Expenditure common to civil and military	638,441
Special expenditure for Northern Somaliland	225,000
	6,931,000

The drain on the Italian Exchequer is obvious; that the Colony was mainly a military outpost is made evident by the character of the expenditure.

Imports from the colonies had proved a heavy disappointment; high hopes had been placed on the production of sugar cane, but in the years 1921-23 only 3 hectares were under this crop. In 1925 seven hectares were grown, but no information regarding the yield of these crops was published then, or for eight years afterwards. The yield of cotton, too, was negligible; Tittoni in 1908 had hoped the Somaliland Colony would produce the 1,650,691 quintals Italy then imported for her mills, but only 14,219 quintals were produced in the Colony in 1935, and after that the yield fell to 9,000, 6,000 4,000, 3,000 in subsequent years.

The export of cotton from the colony was in consequence negligible. Moreover its cost was so exorbitant that high protective tariffs were necessary to make possible its sale in Italy. Production of sugar was disappointingly unimportant. Hopes of rubber failed entirely. The colony was always an importer of agricultural foodstuffs.

Imports from the colonies having failed to realise expectations it was insisted that they must at least afford markets for Italian goods; by preferential tariffs it was found possible to drive up the import of Italian goods by the Somaliland Colony from £9,000 sterling in 1898, to £97,000 in 1912-13. The imports from Italy were mainly unbleached cotton piece goods, and this was far from beneficial to the Somalis, because cotton goods which were their main import could have been obtained much more cheaply from India and Japan, but for the tariffs. In the years 1923 and 1924, exports to Italy valued 2,000,000 lire and 5,000,000 lire respectively; imports from Italy were 16,000,000 and 19,000,000 in the same years. Trade with Italy was 25.3 per cent. of the total trade of the Colony in 1923, and 25.5 per cent. in 1924. This counted little in the volume of Italian trade. Every year the trade of the Somaliland Colony showed an adverse balance. In 1889 the imports had valued £112,000, the exports £62,000; in 1914-15 the imports were £286,000, the exports only £64,000, which was actually a decrease of £20,000 on the 1912-13 export.

Passing over the period of the first World War, 1914-18, we find in 1919 onwards a rising deficit, as the following figures show:

1919:—imports, 13,768,702 lire; exports, 7,556,846 lire; adverse balance, 6,211,856 lire.

1920:—imports, 39,411,372 lire; exports, 17,623,110 lire; adverse balance, 21,788,162 lire.

1921:—imports, 71,112,002 lire; exports, 12,129,065 lire. The adverse balance was now 58,982,937 lire, four times as much as the total exports.

In the following years the adverse balance dropped slightly, being 39,900,000 lire odd in 1922; 40,700,000 lire odd in 1923; 42,600,000 lire odd in 1924.

Fascist "Reconquest" by De Vecchi

The adverse balance leapt to 47,000,000 lire in 1925; 100,000,000 lire in 1926; 130,000,000 lire in 1927. This was the period of the so-called Fascist "reconquest of the Empire," which was effected in Somalia by the notorious Fascist, Count De Vecchi. He commenced his ruthless campaign in 1925, and completed it in 1928. He had been a man of terrible deeds in the civil war by which Fascism rose to power in Italy. It will be understood that he used no gentler methods in an African dependency.

Italy's New Treaty of Peace and Friendship with Ethiopia in 1928

In that year, 1928, a Treaty of perpetual peace and friendship was signed between Italy and Ethiopia, on August 2:

"*(1) There shall be constant peace and perpetual friendship between Italy and Ethiopia.*

"*(2) Each Government undertakes not to engage under any pretext in action calculated to injure or prejudice the independence of the other; the two Governments undertake to safeguard the interests of their respective countries.*

"*(5) Both Governments undertake to submit to a procedure of conciliation and arbitration disputes which may arise between them, and which it may not have been possible to settle by ordinary diplomatic methods without having recourse to armed force. Notes shall be exchanged by common agreement between the two Governments regarding the manner of appointing arbitrators.*

"*(6) The present Treaty must be registered at the League of Nations. It must be ratified and the exchange of ratifications must take place in Addis Ababa as soon as possible.*

"*(7) The duration of the present Treaty shall be twenty years, to date from the exchange of ratifications. At the expiration of this period it shall be renewed from year to year.*"

The last article stating that this Treaty pledging "constant peace and perpetual friendship" is to last for twenty years only, and thereafter is to be renewed from year to year is curious and indeed incongruous. It was destined to continue only seven years.

Italian Pressure on Ogaden Frontier

The Ogaden Province of Ethiopia, from which Italian Somaliland was detached, consists for the most part of scrub-land, with only occasional wells, and is mainly inhabited by nomads, wandering with their flocks and herds, which feed on the scant herbage. It was the custom of the Ethiopian Government of the Ogaden province to make an occasional military surveillance of the frontiers of this vast area. This was a necessary precaution, for, despite the Treaty fixing the frontier upon which the Emperor Menelik had insisted, the policy of keeping the frontier moving onward and of penetrating further into Ethiopia had never been abandoned by Italy.

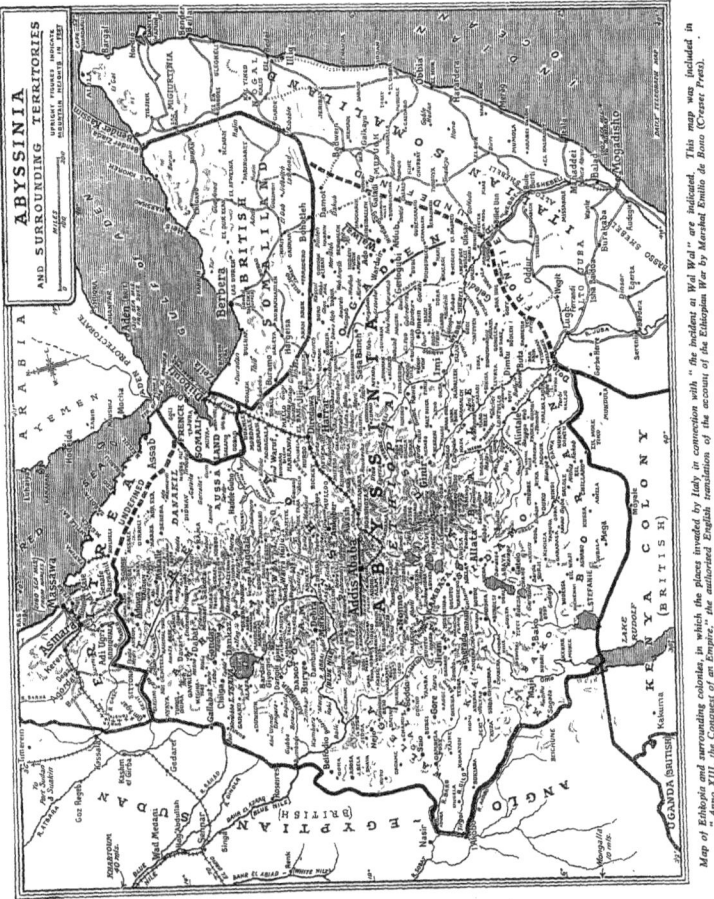

Map of Ethiopia and surrounding colonies, in which the places invaded by Italy in connection with "the incidents at Wal Wal" are indicated. This map was included in "Anno XIII, the Conquest of an Empire," the authorized English translation of the account of the Ethiopian War by Marshal Emilio de Bono (Cresser Press).

X

THE WAL WAL INCIDENT

After the rise to power of Fascism Italian pressure on the frontier was intensive. It was operated by Italian officers, assisted by so-called " native irregulars," paid a mere pittance, but provided with arms and ammunition.. They wore the usual turban and white cotton shirt of the area, being supplied with no uniform, save belts of divers colours, to indicate their regiment.

De Vecchi employed the Banda during his " reconquest " of Italian Somaliland; they were African "Squadristi" in the service of Fascism there, like the Blackshirt formations in Italy.

The policy operated by the Banda's Italian command was to advance, as and when possible, from the Italian Colony into Ethiopia, travelling up into the heart of Ethiopia, through the lands traversed by the Webbi Shebeli to the Arussi country, pointing directly to Addis Ababa, and by the river Fafan, leading up towards Harar, Jigjiga and Dire Dawa on the railway. The Banda were to proceed from water point to water point, in the dry lands of the Ogaden, thus occupying the inhabited areas, and to fortify and maintain themselves there if they could, as earlier Italian emissaries had done at Lugh. In 1922 and 1923 considerable Ethiopian forces were required to dislodge the Italians. Between 1925 and 1928 all Italian forces available in Somalia were occupied with the " reconquest " of the Colony itself; not invading hired Banda, but escaping Somali fugitives, came over the Ethiopian border, seeking asylum. In 1931 the Banda commanders, under instructions from Rome, were led across the frontier to occupy Moustahill, on the Webbi Shebeli, and also the water line of wells from Wal Wal, Wardair, Gerlogubi, Gorahai and Gabridihari on the Fafan, whilst others in Italian pay occupied the habitable places on the Webbi Shebeli as far north as Imi on the edge of the Bale province of Ethiopia.

This was now an invasion of a formidable portion of Ethiopia, though loosely held by irregulars. Were it allowed to continue, a claim to permanent ownership would be made by the Italian Government, for this was how Italian colonisation proceeded.

Dedjazmatch Gabre Mariam, Governor of Harar, with 1,500 Ethiopian troops and Fitaurari Shefera, Governor of Jigjiga, with

3,000 men, accordingly joined forces and marched south to clear the Italian Banda out of the Ogaden.. As the Ethiopian forces approached, the water points were vacated. An Ethiopian garrison was established at Tafera Katama, near Moustahill and at Gabridihari. All such events were represented in Italian propaganda as aggressive Ethiopian attacks on Italian territory, although they took place on Ethiopian soil far into Ethiopia. This procedure was, of course, typical of the method of the Rome-Berlin Axis; both Dictators openly declared that a lie repeated sufficiently and with sufficient emphasis comes finally to be accepted as truth. Moreover a careful examination of Italian tactics in dealing with Ethiopia, from the commencement of relations between the two countries, indicates clearly that the Italian Monarchy and the Ministers of the Crown maintained from first to last the intention of obtaining possession of Ethiopia, and that in pursuit of this objective any ruse was considered admissible, any trap which Italian statesmanship could successfully set for the Ethiopian was held to be praiseworthy. Marshal De Bono, the organiser of Italy's war of aggression in 1935, and Mussolini's co-adjutor in that and many other dark and terrible deeds, states in his book on the war in Ethiopia*: " The Libyan war showed us that Abyssinia had no desire to create difficulties." Nevertheless, the propaganda pamphlets, published in Rome, with which Europe was deluged in the course of Italy's political preparation for the war of 1935 and for the subsequent recognition of the resultant conquest, declared that " the Ethiopian Government promoted and supported a bitter campaign against Italy " during the Libyan war, and " an attempt was made to take advantage of the Italo-Turkish hostilities to attack the Italian Colony of Eritrea." These statements were totally false as the words of De Bono completely prove. On the other hand, if, as alleged, the Ethiopian Press had expressed disapproval of Italy's war in Libya, it should be recalled that in Italy itself there was great opposition to that war. Mussolini was actually imprisoned for urging the people to tear up the railway lines to prevent the Italian troops from being sent off to the war. This was the man who alleged Ethiopian opposition to an Italian war in Libya in 1911-12, as one of the pretexts for Italian preparations to make war against Ethiopia in 1934 !

Political Preparation for War

It happens that the British Press was almost unanimous in denouncing Italian atrocities towards the Libyan population in the war of 1911-12. De Bono, in his above mentioned book, describes with amazing frankness, Italy's so-called " political preparation " for the war of 1935:

"*Only one kind of political action is possible and practical,*" *he writes,* "*when one sees in the background a possibility of conflict . . . One must foster ambitions and dissensions, and spend money—a great deal of money.*"

---

* Anno XIII, by Emilio De Bono with an introduction by Benito Mussolini (Cresset Press), page 44-46.

De Bono records that as early as July, 1925, Mussolini was considering the war of aggression in Ethiopia. On this account, to use De Bono's cynical but entirely revealing phrase, the Duce called on the Italian Minister of the Colonies, the Prince of Scalea, to improve the "defences" of Eritrea. In March, 1932, De Bono asserts without subterfuge that he was himself sent to Eritrea to ascertain what would be required there in preparation for the war to conquer Ethiopia. On his return "guided by the directions" of Mussolini, he drew up a "definite programme." 1933 was the year, De Bono tells us, in which the practical measures for the war were decided, and in which Mussolini granted his request for "the honour of conducting the campaign." "From this moment the Duce was definitely of opinion that the matter would have to be settled no later than 1936," writes De Bono, on page 13 of his book. In the autumn of the same year he discussed with Mussolini his plans for causing political disruption in Ethiopia, which he hoped would make it easier "to go right in with the intention of making a complete job of it." "Money will be needed, Chief; lots of money," said the old conspirator; Mussolini replied, "There will be no lack of money."

With Eritrea as their base, various incidents were organised in northern Ethiopia by the instrumentality of the governor of the Colony, Senator Gasparini, Baron Franchetti, who busied himself to and fro between Ethiopia and the Colony, under the pretext of conducting his own private business undertakings, and Colonel Ruggero (of the Bersaglieri), head of the political bureau. The purpose of several manufactured "incidents" was two-fold: (1) to secure pretexts for sending greatly increased forces into Eritrea without producing defensive precautions by Ethiopia, or measures by the League of Nations to obstruct the intended aggression. (2) to build up among Governments and individuals the impression that Ethiopia was turbulent and disorganised and that the Ethiopian Government was either weak and ineffective or ill-disposed.

The Wal Wal Incident

In Somaliland the Governor, Rava, co-operated with De Bono in nefarious "political preparation" and measures for the coming war. The Banda Commander, Captain Roberto Cimmaruta, a wild and ruthless adventurer and daring cattle-raider, was a willing tool in aggression.

The assumption of the Italian Government was that any Ethiopian territory occupied by an Italian force became automatically Italian territory. They were determined to sustain this assumption without regard to the Italo-Ethiopian Treaty of May 16, 1908, defining the boundary of the Italian Colony, which had cost the Emperor Menelik II so much hard bargaining, without regard to the Treaty of 1896 recognising Ethiopian sovereignty, and the numerous Treaties and pledges of friendship which had followed.

In August, 1934, or thereabouts, the Italian Banda crept into the Ogaden and established themselves at Wardair and at Wal Wal, where in the course of a couple of weeks or so they erected a rough little fort with some material which was lying about there, and had been used for a similar purpose in former times.

Wal Wal, as shown by the maps in use throughout the world, was sixty miles within the Ethiopian frontier, according to the Italo-Ethiopian Treaty of 1908. After the famous incident Italian maps showing the boundary were withdrawn from circulation, but numbers of them were available for comparison.

In November, 1934, an Anglo-Ethiopian Boundary Commission, consisting of representatives of both Governments, arrived at Wal Wal. They had completed the demarcation on the spot of the frontier between British Somaliland and Ethiopia, and were in the course of a joint survey of the Ogaden pastoral areas, which are frequented at certain seasons of the year by tribes who are ordinarily resident in the British protectorate, and are recognised by both governments as under British protection. This survey was made in accordance with the Anglo-Ethiopian Treaty of May, 1897. By an annexe to that Treaty it was provided that free access to the wells and the pastures must be open to tribes living on both sides of the frontier. In the course of their investigations the Commission had trekked from Dagah-Bur to Ado and on the morning of November 23 they arrived at Wal Wal. They had been preceded the previous evening by an Ethiopian escort under the Governor of Jigjiga, Fitaurari Shefera. They were confronted by some 250 armed Italian Banda. A short distance further south a small fort was discerned on an eminence from which flew the Italian flag. A Somali petty officer in charge of the Banda ordered the Boundary Commission to withdraw. It had been only with difficulty that the Ethiopian escort had been able to get to the wells, the water being an absolute essential for men and animals after their long journey through dry land.

During the morning a Somali petty officer in the Ethiopian escort was seized and made prisoner by the Banda, a note couched in far from courteous terms arrived from Captain Cimmaruta warning the heads of the Ethiopian escort not to cause an incident with the Banda, and stating that in case they desired to communicate with him they should write to him at Wardair, where he lived. Wardair was in Ethiopia, as already observed.

Lieutenant Colonel Clifford, head of the British Boundary Commission, and the head of the Ethiopian Commission, Dedjazmatch Tessemma Bante, sent a written protest to Captain Cimmaruta against the interference to which they had been subjected by Italian forces on Ethiopian soil and for the seizure by the Banda of the Somali officer. Captain Cimmaruta replied that to avoid trouble between his forces and the escort of the Commission both sides should take care that their troops did not advance beyond their present positions, and that a line should be marked between them on the trunks of the trees. Next morning he visited the camp of the Boundary Commission and endeavoured to secure agreement to this extraordinary proposal. It was naturally rejected by the Ethiopian Commissioners, who could not thus casually agree to the establishment of any territorial rights for Italy on Ethiopian soil. Captain Cimmaruta's attitude was entirely truculent and authoritative; he refused even to withdraw his Banda a short distance so that the Ethiopian escort might freely circulate among the wells to secure sufficient water for their needs. He was willing only to allow the Ethiopians to pass behind his lines to draw water under his control, an offer which the Ethiopian escort most obviously could not accept from a body of armed trespassers.

Becoming more and more aggressive Captain Cimmaruta threatened to summon reinforcements. While the discussion proceeded two Italian military aeroplanes appeared circling and plunging, and training their guns on the British and Ethiopian camps and their national flags at low altitude. This menacing demonstration raised the patriotic wrath of Captain Taylor, Lieutenant Collingwood, Mr. Curl and Corporal Griffiths, who were witnesses of the scene, as well as the Ethiopians present. The Commissioners protested to Captain Cimmaruta, who was totally unconcerned by their reproaches.

Attempts to Annex by Occupation; A Violation of Treaties and of The Covenant of the League of Nations

In fact Captain Cimmaruta was acting under the orders of Rava, the Governor of the Italian Somaliland Colony, who had in fact sent the two aeroplanes to Wal Wal. The Governor was fully informed of all that was happening and was in constant telegraphic communication with the Italian Minister of the Colonies in Rome, as his telegrams, subsequently published, reveal. Governor Rava took his stand on the contention that Wardair, Wal Wal, and all the neighbouring area in that part of Ethiopia, were Italian territory for the sole reason, apparently, that Italy had sent the Banda irregulars there. That the Italian Government were fully cognisant of the fact that they were completely unjustified in this territorial claim is most clearly evident, because in the subsequent arbitration under the auspices of the League of Nations, the Italian representatives refused to have the fact that Wal Wal and neighbourhood were in Ethiopia submitted to the Arbitration Tribunal. They insisted that the location of Wal Wal in relation to the frontier should not be discussed at all. It seems that at one time the Italian Government considered setting up a claim to an extensive part of the Ogaden by simply declaring an Italian protectorate there, using the procedure of the General Act of Berlin; but the fact that Ethiopia was a member of the League of Nations doomed to failure any such attempt. The truculent assertion that the territory was Italian was adopted.

In his telegram to the Italian Government on November 22, 1934, Governor Rava referred to the trespassing Banda at Wardair as "the Italian Authorities." He stated that he had sent reinforcements to Wardair and Wal Wal consisting of a squadron of three aeroplanes and a squadron of machine guns. "The normal forces at Wardair and Wal Wal were 257 and 180 men respectively, with four guns at Wardair." These he had " adequately reinforced."

In a telegram to Rome, on December 2, Governor Rava reported the arrival of the Commission and stated that the Banda and the Ethiopian escort faced each other in opposing lines, the distance between the two lines varying from two metres at some points to from five or six metres at the most. " Captain Cimmaruta declared himself ready to furnish them with all the water they could need, but, he added, this water would be furnished under our surveillance because it was in our territory."

There was thus a clear attempt to annex territory simply by occupying it, thus reverting to the old method of annexation, in direct violation of the obligations of Italy's Treaties with Ethiopia, and with the obligations of the Covenant of the League of Nations, which Italy had freely signed. In his telegrams of November 29 and December 2 to the Ministry of the Colonies in Rome, Governor Rava complained of 270 armed Ethiopians at Gerlogubi and about 500 at Ado, an indication that those localities would also presently be claimed as Italian. Gerlogubi had in fact been occupied by the Banda in 1931. The small Ethiopian forces here referred to were sent to reinforce Gerlogubi and other points under the orders of Gerazmatch Afewerk, Director of Jigjiga, in view of the advances of the Italians from their Colony into Ethiopian territory.

Lt. Col. Clifford's Protest

After the hostile demonstration by the aeroplanes sent by Governor Rava, Colonel Clifford, as head of the British Boundary Commission, despatched a letter of protest to Captain Cimmaruta, stating that owing to the provocative attitude of the Italian authorities, the presence of the Anglo-Ethiopian Boundary Commission at Wal Wal involved grave risk of a regrettable international incident. In order to avoid complicating the situation for the Ethiopian authorities, Colonel Clifford added that he had decided to withdraw the joint Boundary Commission to Ado in Ethiopia, some distance further from the frontier. The Commission would wait there the response of the Italian Government to the joint protest which the British and Ethiopian Commissioners had made. Colonel Clifford was sending copies of the protest to the British and Ethiopian Governments.

Captain Cimmaruta replied in haughty style:

" (1) *The locality being near the frontier and the contact which the British Authorities have with the local Dolbahanta population, the British Authorities could not be ignorant of the fact that we are in garrison in the Zone of Wal Wal and Wardair.*

" (2) *No notification had reached the Italian Authorities of the presence of the British Commissioners, or any even indirect news of their intention to come here. Moreover, in approaching our lines the British Authorities did not even take the trouble to send a message in advance to inform us of their arrival.*"

Following up this ingenious subterfuge, which arrogantly maintained the claim of Italy to occupy Ethiopian territory, the Captain averred that his warplanes were engaged in surveying the territory on account of notorious brigands in the hinterland—evidently the Ethiopian forces of Gerazmatch, Afewerk. The Italian authorities at Wal Wal and Wardair being he re-asserted, unaware that British functionaries had arrived in the Wal Wal zone, the planes coming from Mogadishu could obviously know even less of them.

The British and Ethiopian Commissioners replied that as they were certainly in Ethiopian territory, as recognised by the Treaty of 1908, there had been no occasion for them to announce their arrival to the Italian authorities since they had no intention of entering Italian territory and their mission was concerned only with the Ethiopian Ogaden and the movement of British protected tribes. The joint Commission had no official cognisance of the Italian occupation of the Wal Wal-Wardair region.

Governor Rava in a telegram to the Italian Government stated that he had given instructions that if the Ethiopians desired to discuss the frontier they would be given an escort to Galadi, in the Italian Colony, to interview an Italian Commissioner there. This information was now brusquely conveyed by Captain Cimmaruta to Fitaurari Shefara, the head of the Ethiopian escort, in the course of a highly insulting letter in which he referred to an officer of the Ethiopian escort as "one of your brigand chiefs."

Boundary Commission Withdrawn: Ethiopian Escort Attacked

The Boundary Commission had by this time been withdrawn to Ado in accordance with Colonel Clifford's announcement in his letter of November 24. There never was any concealment of the fact that the withdrawal was made with the utmost reluctance on the part of the British members of the Commission, who acted under direct telegraphic instructions from the Foreign Office. They felt their honour blemished by thus leaving the Ethiopians to face the act of aggression with vastly superior arms, which they were certain the Italians intended to launch as soon as the British Officers were out of the way. The Commission were accompanied on their withdrawal by a part of the Ethiopian escort and a contingent of the British Somaliland Camel Corps.

The Italian Attack at Wal Wal

The Ethiopian force left to maintain their country's territorial right against the Italian invasion of the Ogaden consisted of local guards, in the main, elderly men, and all slenderly armed. Theirs was a force, not intended for war, at most for police duties, which had been mustered mainly as a courtesy escort to the joint Boundary Commission.

On December 4 a letter was received from Captain Cimmaruta, addressed to the Ethiopian head of the Boundary Commission, Dedjazmatch Tessema Bante, and the head of the escort, in which the

Captain stated that he had news of a very strong concentration of armed men in the Ethiopian line facing Wal Wal. He further alleged, quite falsely, that these armed men had attempted to force their way through the Italian lines during the previous night. He threatened that any attempt to force the line, on any pretext, or to pass into the territory occupied by the Italians would be considered as directed against the territory of His Majesty the King of Italy and would be repelled by force.

Thus the bluff was maintained.

On December 5, at 3.30 p.m., the Italian force attacked the Ethiopian line, suddenly and without warning, in response to a command given in Italian. Aeroplanes, bombs, tanks, cannons and machine guns were employed in a devastating onslaught. The Ethiopian escort, despite the paucity of their equipment bravely withstood the attack until 11 p.m., when in view of the heavy casualties, including 107 killed and 45 severely wounded, the Ethiopian commander, Shefera Balcha, ordered a retreat towards Ado.

On December 8, the joint Boundary Commission left Ado for Haradiguit, their departure being watched by Italian military planes, which were surveying the area to ascertain their movements. The baggage of the Commission, which was to follow later, was left in charge of an Ethiopian officer, Ali Nur, and some Ethiopian soldiers under his command. When the Boundary Commission was well on its way, the Italian planes discharged five bombs over this small Ethiopian guard, who fortunately escaped injury. The Italians had probably failed to observe the presence of Lieutenant Collingwood who, with twenty-five members of the British Somaliland camel corps, had remained behind with Ali Nur and his guard. The Lieutenant, already thoroughly disgusted by the whole procedure of the Italians throughout the incident, was rendered still more indignant by this further cowardly attack. He had with him a small film camera, and was able to record a part of the events at Wal Wal and Ado. His film afforded valuable evidence of the aggression, and was seen with great interest by London audiences when he came home on leave shortly afterwards.

The Italian bombing planes passed on to Gerlogubi, where they bombed an Ethiopian camp, destroying six tents out of ten. *

This account of the Wal Wal aggression, and the events which arose from it, is based upon the voluminous documentation published by A. de La Pradelle, reproducing the full text of all the official statements, letters and telegrams, which passed between the Governments concerned and were laid before the League of Nations and the Arbitration Tribunal.

---

*LE CONFLIT ITALO—ETHIOPIEN; by A. de la Pradelle (Les Editions Internationales, Paris), 1936.

ETHIOPIAN GOVERNMENT PROTESTS
ITALIAN GOVERNMENT DEMANDS COMPENSATION

On learning of the Italian aggression at Wal Wal the Ethiopian Minister for Foreign Affairs, Blatten Gueta Herouy, the venerable Ethiopian author and educationist, addressed both a verbal and written protest to Signor Mombelli, the Italian Chargé d'Affaires in Addis Ababa. The Chargé d'Affaires replied curtly that the fault lay with the Ethiopian escort, that the Italian force had lost thirty men and that the Italian Government demanded apologies and compensation.

The Ethiopian Government protested that the Italian occupation of Ethiopian territory at Wal Wal and Wardair contravened the fundamental principles of the Covenant of the League of Nations as well as those of the Italo-Ethiopian Treaty of Friendship, Conciliation and Arbitration of August 2, 1928. The Ethiopian Government proposed to submit the dispute to arbitration, as provided by the Treaty of 1928. Repeated through the Ethiopian Representative in Rome, the proposal was ignored there; Mombelli presented a Note which was calculated to create profound consternation in Ethiopia on December 11, 1934:

"*The Italian Government demands solemn apologies by the Ethiopian Government, and reparations corresponding to the gravity of the losses and the damages suffered by us.*"

The following extraordinary demands were then set forth:

"(1) *Dedjazmatch Gabre Mariam, Governor of Harar, must present himself at Wal Wal, where he will offer, in the name of the Ethiopian Government, formal apologies to the Commandant of the Italian Garrison. At the same time an Ethiopian force must render honours to the Italian flag.*

"(2) *The Ethiopian Government must pay to the Royal Legation of Italy, the sum of* 200,000 *Maria Theresa dollars (approximately* £20,000) *as an indemnity for the numerous losses in dead and wounded suffered by our troops, as reparations for the damage to our forts, and to reimburse the expenditure that the Government of Somaliland has been obliged to incur as a result of the aggression.*

" (3) *Those responsible for the attack must be arrested and deprived of their respective commands; after having taken part in honours rendered to the Italian flag in conformity with local usages, they must be adequately punished without delay.*"

To accept these conditions would have been to cede the Ethiopian territory occupied by the Italians, in the most ignominious manner possible, and to invite the Italians to annex further territory, as and when convenient to them.

The Ethiopian Minister for Foreign Affairs replied patiently, and with great courtesy, reiterating the proposal for arbitration, which the Italian Government now rejected, on the ground that an unprovoked aggression against an Italian garrison was not a fit subject for arbitration.

Appeal to the League of Nations

The Ethiopian Government had no other alternative than to appeal to the League of Nations. Accordingly, on December 14, a Note was addressed to the Secretary-General of the League calling the attention of the League Council to the gravity of the situation. The Italian Government retorted denying the Ethiopian account of the events at Wal Wal, and rejecting renewed requests for arbitration.

On December 24, 1934, the Ethiopian Government telegraphed to the League that Italian forces were advancing further into Ethiopia, that they had occupied Afdub and were making a road towards Ado and Gerlogubi.

The Italian Government replied that Afdub belonged to Italian territory and denied any advance into Ethiopia.

On January 3, 1935, the Ethiopian Government notified the League that the Italians had advanced to Gerlogubi, and called for measures in accordance with the League Covenant to prevent a breach of the peace.

On January 17, the Council of the League of Nations decided to place the Italo-Ethiopian dispute on the Agenda for discussion.

The Italian Government replied, with blatant duplicity, that the dispute was under discussion between themselves and the Ethiopian Government; they did not think it one which could affect the peaceful relations of the two countries, who could settle their differences by the procedure indicated by their mutual Treaty of Arbitration of 1928; in the meantime measures would be taken to avoid further incidents.

The Ethiopian Government accepted this Italian offer, but on March 17 they were constrained to appeal again to the League of Nations, on account of the continual arrival in Eritrea and Italian Somaliland, of troops, war workers and munitions, the vast preparations for war being made in those Colonies and the vociferous war propaganda in Italy. Moreover, the Italian Government had refused all negotiations, and had repeated their demands for apologies and reparations before entertaining any discussion of the dispute. To the Ethiopian proposal for arbitration by a third Power the Italian Government had responded by mobilising a further class and accelerating the despatch of troops and war material.

Marshal De Bono was feverishly engaged in enlarging docks, erecting warehouses and building roads through Eritrea to the Ethiopian frontier.

The Italian Government replied to the Secretary-General of the League on March 22, 1933, professing a desire for arbitration. The Ethiopian Government proposed that within 30 days the two Governments should select arbitrators, otherwise the League of Nations should appoint them.

On April 10 the Italian Government informed the Secretary-General of the League that they did not regard negotiations through ordinary diplomatic channels as having failed and did not therefore consider resort to arbitration necessary. There were long Conferences between the Emperor and his Ministers, who took their stand always on international justice and the League of Nations Covenant; long Conferences also with the Foreign Advisers Everett Colson, the American, General Virgin, the Swede, and Maître Auberson, the Swiss lawyer. Truculent, aggressive, the Italians persisted in their demand. Count Vinci, the Italian Minister, a strange, sinister figure, offered occasional provocations. The Ethiopian Government notified the League that 4,000 war workers had been imported from Egypt into Italian Eritrea. Every day produced some hostile incident.

On April 15 the League Council was convoked, on the request of the French Government, to consider the menace to France of German rearmament. The Secretary-General announced also the Ethiopian protest, but after hearing the views of the Italian and Ethiopian Delegations the President of the Council declared that as both parties to the dispute avowed peaceful intentions, and desired to settle their differences in accordance with their mutual Treaty of Arbitration, he did not consider the Council should intervene at that stage. It was therefore agreed to place the dispute on the Agenda of the Council in May.

The Great Powers on the League Council desired to avoid adopting any definite attitude on the Ethiopian dispute. The French Foreign Minister, Pierre Laval, had newly made a Pact with Italy in Rome and his actions throughout the dispute were affected by it. France had made a concession of the northern corner of her Somaliland Colony to Italy in January, 1935.

Count Vinci proposed a neutral zone in the Ethiopian Ogaden, ostensibly to avoid the possibility of further incidents, but actually because Governor Maurizio Rava had to report that the Italian Colony was not yet in a material or moral condition to resist an Ethiopian attack, as General Virgin, Swedish Military adviser to the Ethiopian Government, has recorded.*

On May 25 the Council of the League adopted resolutions favouring arbitration of the Italo-Ethiopian dispute, during which procedure Italy was to abstain from further preparations for war.

The Arbitration

The Italian Government appointed as arbitrators Count Luigi Aldrovandi, formerly Italian Ambassador in Berlin, and Councillor of State Raffaele Montagna. Ethiopia appointed two well-known professors of international law, Professor A. de Geouffre de La Pradelle, Professor of Law in the University of Paris, and Professor Pittman B. Potter, of New Jersey, Professor of International Organisation at the Institut des Hautes Etudes Internationales of Geneva.

The Sessions of the Commission were opened in Milan on June 6, where a Secretariat was appointed, consisting of three Italians: Enrico Cerulli, then Director in the Italian Ministry of

---

* "The Abyssinia I Knew," by General Virgin (MacMillan), 1936.

the Colonies and subsequently Assistant Governor-General in Ethiopia during the Italian usurpation of that country, Guarnaschelli, Italian Director of African Affairs, and Captain Zanchi with Raymond de Geouffre de La Pradelle, son of the Professor, to represent Ethiopia.

On June 25 the Commission arrived in Scheveningen, in Holland, where they were joined by Professor Lessona, of the University of Florence, who was designated "Agent of the Italian Government," and a number of other Italians. Professor Gaston Jèze, of the University of Paris, was then appointed Agent of the Ethiopian Government. His Excellency Takle Hawariat, Ethiopian Minister in Paris, was deputed to represent his country.

The first Session was held on July 4, when Professor Lessona presented the case for Italy. Professor Jèze commenced to put the Ethiopian case, but as soon as he sought to prove that Wal Wal was in Ethiopia, Professor Lessona objected to any discussion of this point. The two Italian arbitrators upheld his objection. Professors de La Pradelle and Pittman B. Potter refused to essent to the utter stultification of the Arbitration which would result from the exclusion of the most material fact. The Commission was thus at a deadlock.

Geneva Again

The case had again to be taken to Geneva. On July 31 the Council of the League of Nations again discussed the arbitration. Provision was made for a fifth arbitrator, whose casting vote could terminate a further deadlock. The Ethiopian Delegation were persuaded to permit the fact that Wal Wal was in Ethiopia to be ignored by the Arbitration Tribunal; they accepted, with hope, the decision of the League Council to meet on September 4 to consider the whole problem of Italo-Ethiopian relations.

M. Pierre Laval, then Foreign Minister of France, declared that, once again, the Council of the League had "fulfilled its high and noble mission."

The sorry farce continued: to make a show of doing something Britain and other Powers imposed an embargo on the import of manufactured arms by both Italy and Ethiopia, but not on raw material; Ethiopia had no arms factories; Italian arms factories were working at top speed. The embargo did not hinder the transport of Italian arms to the Italian Colonies, the bases from which Ethiopia was invaded!

Three Power Negotiations in Paris

The pretence that the Wal Wal arbitration had any relation to the war Italy was threatening grew even more shadowy—Mr. Eden, during a visit to Rome in June, had offered to make a gift of the Port of Zeila, in British Somaliland, to Ethiopia if this would facilitate the surrender to Italy of further Ethiopian territory in Somaliland. Mussolini rejected this truly unfortunate attempt to appease him.

On August 16 a Conference was held in Paris, between Mr. Eden, Pierre Laval and Baron Aloisi, the Italian Minister in

Geneva, in the effort to arrange a compromise to satisfy Mussolini in the interests of European harmony. The Italian demand for a military occupation and protectorate over the greater part of Ethiopia was rejected by Mr. Eden as too extreme to be acceptable to British public opinion.

The Arbitration Tribunal resumed their Sessions and sat on through August in Berne and in Paris. On August 27 they again came to a deadlock. M. Politis, the Greek Minister in Paris, was called to serve as fifth Arbitrator.

On September 3 the Arbitrators gave this verdict: "The incident at Wal Wal was an accident for which no blame could be attributed to either side. The Italian and Ethiopian Authorities both believed Wal Wal to be in their own territory. The subsequent bombing and other offences were purely minor events, quite ordinary in the region where they occurred, and of no international importance."

The Arbitration was ended—Italian war preparations were near completion.

The Italian forces crossed the Ethiopian frontiers in October.

The events of the war, the Geneva manoeuvres, the failure of Sanctions, Italian bombing of the Red Cross and use of poison gas, the five years occupation of Ethiopia, its massacres and sorrows, the collapse of the League of Nations, Ethiopia's long, brave, lonely struggle, and final liberation in the course of the second World War, belong to the general history of Ethiopia, the League of Nations, the world struggle for International Peace and Justice. They cannot be dealt with in these pages. The effort to assess them must be left to a further volume.

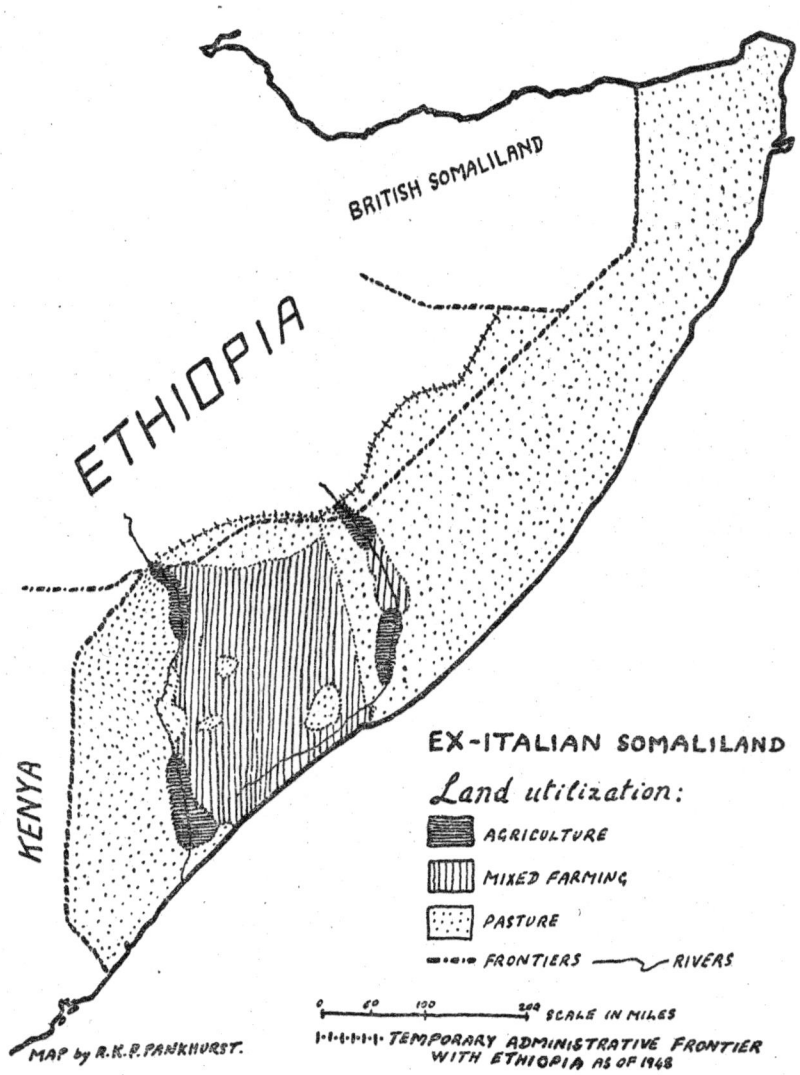

XI

THE COLONY AS A BASE FOR WAR

Graziani Makes the Road

The Somaliland Colony had made little economic progress up to the time when it began to attract some international notice during the preparations for the Ethiopian war. The agricultural station, founded by the Duke of the Abruzzi in 1921, was still its only considerable agricultural enterprise.

Geoffrey Harmsworth* who was commissioned to report the Italo-Ethiopian war for his uncle Rothermere's "Daily Mail," arrived at Mogadishu in April, 1934, first among all the world journalists. He reported that Graziani's predecessors at Mogadishu had overlooked the paramount necessity of communications. Governor Rava had evidently been too much occupied with the Banda penetrations into Ethiopia, to think of such a matter. Until the date of the war was decided and had become imminent, roads in Somaliland were considered of little importance.

Graziani immediately summoned road experts from Italy, England and America. It was going to be an "engineers' war." Mr. Harmsworth went out with a Maltese engineer, to see the latter's experimental road which a few days later brought him a handsome contract from the Italian Government. Soft soil, great heat, heavy rainfall, rendered a difficult problem the construction of roads able to withstand all these and enormously heavy loads. The Maltese accomplished the task—a victory for wonderful Italian enterprise, in the Fascist parlance of those days.

Graziani refused to be interviewed, but he offered to send the youthful reporter and his friend, Evans, on a trip to the Juba River, to Lugh and to Iscia Baidoa, and granted them an interpreter and a military lorry.

"*A car would have been out of the question,*" wrote Mr. Harmsworth, "*for, with the exception of the coast road to Brava, and the road to Iscia Baidoa, the only way of getting from place to place in Italian Somaliland is by lorry.*"

This estimate of road facilities in the Colony proved too high in the author's maturer judgment. When the lorry was on its way he adjusted:

---

* "Abyssinian Adventure," by Geoffrey Harmsworth (Hutchinson), 1935, p.p. 73-133.

MARSHAL GRAZIANI

who commanded the Southern Army which invaded Ethiopia from the Somaliland Colony in 1935. Graziani was known by the victims of his ferocity as " the Hyena of Libya," and " the Butcher of Addis Ababa." He was appointed Viceroy of Ethiopia after Marshal Badoglio resigned that office.

The Juba River in 1935

"*I use the word road a little hesitatingly because, strictly speaking, no road (as recently as June of this year, 1935), in the European sense of the word, exists in Italian Somaliland outside Mogadishu.*

"For that reason it was essential to take our long trek by lorry and not by car.

"We were jolted, jerked, bumped, rocked, pitched, tossed and shaken until we felt we had developed floating kidneys, housemaid's elbows, shingles and St. Vitus's Dance all at once. It was all very well for a few hours—but for a week ... it came near to martyrdom."

This, be it noted, was the approach to Lugh and to Iscia Baidoa, once regarded as marvellous sources of raw material for Italian industry; they had grown to be so little regarded that a quarter of a century after their conquest "no road in the European sense" had yet been made to them!

In the coast towns, except Mogadishu, Italian occupation had made few apparent changes: they appeared as they were when the Arabs built them. "The architecture of Merca," Mr. Harmsworth wrote, "is definitely Arabian, like all the towns along this coast."

At the hotel, the author and his friend Evans were introduced by the interpreter, Lieutenant Di Mottola, as "important persons." All three "were shown up to an indescribably dirty bedroom with three beds. There was every indication that the last occupants had only just vacated the room. It was this, or sleeping on the beach."

They were still on the coast road to Brava, but they made a slight detour to visit Awai, where there was "a large banana plantation and a few acres of maize, which supported a small community of Somalis, and a hunting box for big game enthusiasts. A year or two before, King Victor Emmanuel had planned to come here and a special road had been built from Awai to a spot some ten miles away much frequented by elephant. The authorities had not been able to control the rains and the Royal visit had to be abandoned. If we had waited two weeks it would have been impossible for us to reach Awai."

No All-Weather Roads

Thus there was no all-weather road in Italy's Somaliland Colony.

There were five European inhabitants only, three wireless operators and two overseers at Awai.

Mr. Harmsworth, his friend Evans, their interpreter, the Commissioner of Brava and an Italian Marquis set off on the road prepared for the King of Italy. It was the first time a lorry had passed there. An overhanging branch almost demolished the upper framework of the lorry. Progress at more than ten miles an hour was impossible, the utter wildness of the scene is well described, with the swarms of mosquitoes and the barrage of tsetse flies.

Brava was even more Arabic in architecture and atmosphere than Merca; the people there, partly of Arabian, partly of Somali descent, were artistic; the reporter regretted he could not carry away one of their beautifully carved doors.

The Italian Commissioner lived in what might have been a Sultan's Palace; his nails were the longest the reporter had ever seen " on any man or woman, not excepting the Chinese, pointed and extending fully an inch beyond the tips of the fingers." Such an evidence of abstention from labour must surely have sustained Italian prestige!

At Jelib the influence of the Juba made the country greener. The life of the Italian representative was lonely, for there were only two or three Europeans in the district, " but I gathered," writes the reporter, " that the madame system was the order of the day here too."

"The road to Bardera was, if anything, worse than the others." It was " little more than a dried-up water course." "Occasionally a few natives would leave their herds of goats and camels to peer at the strangers. Only once in a month or six weeks does a lorry penetrate into the territory of these remote people." At Bardera, where the frontier had been fixed by Emperor Menelik, the only Europeans were the Resident, the doctor and two wireless operators.

The imminence of the rain prevented continuing the journey to the object of the long diplomatic frontier contest, Lugh Ferrandi.

The travellers turned back towards Iscia Baidoa, which Captain Bottego once ecstatically described. They succeeded in reaching it, despite " trench holes " in the road, which threatened to break the lorry's axle. Here, for the first time, they discovered " a neat little European township," with a church and a number of houses, where the Government Officials lived. A considerable military force was being concentrated. There was to be a full-dress Fascist dinner that night.

As he reviewed it later from a Leopard Moth 'plane, the Colony appeared to the reporter " mere scrub and sand, broken only once by the model village and plantation founded by the late Duke of the Abruzzi."

The tragic war waged by Italy in Ethiopia, for which Graziani had prepared the road, and which was launched simultaneously from the Somaliland Colony and from Eritrea on October 3rd, 1935, cannot here be described. It is well, however, to recall that a considerable number of Somalis from the Italian Colony in 1935 crossed the border into Ethiopia to take up arms on her behalf despite the long separation from Ethiopia, the persistent efforts of the Italians to sow suspicion and dislike of the people over the border, the terrible penalties awaiting the deserter who had the misfortune to be caught, and the fact that they were going to assist a cause which might well have seemed at that time to be utterly lost. They were not ignorant of the huge armament massed against Ethiopia; they knew but too well the odds which those who fought for her must face.

The following list of these brave warriors has been preserved:*

Desertion of Somalis During the War of 1935-36
Chiefs

Dejazmatch Oumer Sematar (subsequently Governor of Jig Jiga in Ethiopia, 1945).
Dejazmatch Hirsi Oumer.
Dejazmatch Aydded Oumer.
Dejazmatch Bechir Oumer.
Dejazmatch Moussa Oumer.
Dejazmatch Mohammed Oumer.
Dejazmatch Gogal Yousuf.
Dejazmatch Gelam Mohammed.
Dejazmatch Abdullahi Boure.
Dejazmatch Ali Abchir.
Dejazmatch Hussein Mohammed.
Dejazmatch Deuryou Oumer.
Dejazmatch Jama Oursoma.
Dejazmatch Ali Kurhan.
Dejazmatch Sahl Ibrahim.
Dejazmatch Sougel Mohammed.
Dejazmatch Hussein Terra.
Dejazmatch Cherif Abrahim.
Dejazmatch Ougaz Nour.
Dejazmatch Ibrahim Mohammed.
Dejazmatch Abdullahi Mohammed.
Dejazmatch Atted Mohammed.
Other ranks supporting these important leaders are known to have numbered more than 2,000.

---

* Memorandum of the Ethiopian Government presented to the Paris Conference, July, 1946.

XII

THE ITALIAN COLLAPSE: THE SLAVES DESERT

Somali Opinion

The Italian collapse throughout East Africa was primarily the result of desertion by their African conscript forces. Their own poor morale, which was a strong contributory factor, arose from numerous origins imbedded in their own history. Amongst them the uppermost and most compelling was in the character of Fascism itself, with its corruption and bombast, its slavish adulation of Fascist leaders, often secretly hated for their arbitrary, arrogant misrule by the very men who fawned on them, and the fertile crop of grievances concerning pay and working conditions among Italians themselves. The habit of cruelty towards the African people was boasted, praised and rewarded under Fascism, and was an outgrowth, accentuated in brutality, of the original terrorism which accompanied the capture of State Power in Italy by Mussolini and his gang. Recollections, terrible recollections, of the tortures they had exuberantly perpetrated on the dark-skinned people, returned ominously to Italian officers and soldiers, when they saw that their African conscripts were disappearing, and that an air of aloofness, a lack of attention to orders was rapidly developing among the thinning ranks of coloured troops.

It is true that since the time of the Ethiopian invasion, rather more consideration had been shown to the natives of Somaliland and Eritrea for, with Arabs imported from Libya, their assistance was required against the patriotic resistance in Ethiopia. Mussolini had decreed that the natives of Italy's two oldest colonies should be officially termed Eritreans and Somalis, not merely " subjects," the designation applied to the people of Ethiopia, who were relegated to a still lower social category. Yet Eritreans and Somalis were also " subjects," rigidly distinguished from " Italian citizens " to indicate whom the term " citizens " was sufficient, they being " the Master Race," whose status and conditions no African, no Semite, no non-European was ever to be permitted to approach. Official Decree Laws, even elementary prudence, might order a less contemptuous

THE COLLAPSE OF ITALIAN MORALE
Some of the evidence that an abundantly equipped Italian Army surrendered in Somaliland with scarcely a fight. Photograph reproduced in "The Abyssinian Campaigns" (His Majesty's Stationery Office) shows a British soldier checking Italian ammunition abandoned at Mogadishu.

One of the colossal effigies of Mussolini which were placed, by his orders, along the Strada Imperiale from the Colony into Ethiopia, prepared by Graziani for the war of invasion. All these effigies were deliberately defaced during the war by Somalis in revolt and by the Forces of Liberation.

and kinder treatment of the inhabitants of the old colonies than was meted to the resisting Ethiopian population. Colonial conscripts might be eulogised for their services and permitted to share some of the flocks and herds looted from Ethiopian patriots. Yet even though some of the evanescent artificial prosperity produced by the Ethiopian war and occupation might seep through to the Somalis, old habits of Italian arrogance were not discarded. Moreover, the reality of economic and political subjection of the inhabitants of the colony to Italy was unaltered; forced labour, with wretchedly inadequate payment and cruel punishments, and other fundamental evils continued. When 1,000 Ethiopian prisoners were employed in forced labour on the Italian estates at Genale, there might be some easement for the Somali population who had formerly borne the full brunt of the forced labour required there, but the fundamental subjection and frustration were unchanged.

The urge for liberation, democracy and progress, which is stirring throughout the world, and is the expression in our time of the striving towards improvement, always the fundamental quality of the human mind, was stimulated in Italy's Somaliland colony by the appeals to join the world struggle for liberation which were disseminated by radio broadcast, by leaflets showered by the R.A.F., and other means. The news that Emperor Haile Sellassie had reached the border of Ethiopia with British support and co-operation, that the Ethiopian patriots, who had never given up their fight for freedom, were rallying to join him, aroused a surge of hope and expectation beyond the Ethiopian borders.

Somali tribesmen of the Ethiopian Ogaden had resisted the Italians at Wal Wal in 1934, and had played their part in the defence of the country against the Italian invasion of 1935. During the five years of the Italian usurpation they had taken part in the guerilla warfare against the invaders. They had ambushed motor convoys and left the lorries blazing, held up trains on the Jibuti-Addis Ababa railway, served as protectors and guides to messengers carrying news of the patriotic struggle in all parts of Ethiopia to the Ethiopian Legation in Jibuti, for transmission to the Emperor in London.

The movement seething among the Somalis of the Ogaden was felt also across the border in the Italian Colony.

Their enthusiastic welcome to British forces, and the utter collapse of Italian morale, due in large measure to the desertion and hostility of their African troops, are outstanding features of the lightning Southern Campaign of 1941. Jubaland was conquered between January 24 and February 14, the rest of the Italian Somaliland Colony between February 14 and February 25, when Mogadishu surrendered, after which the flight of Italian forces to refuge in Ethiopia was merely a rout and all fortified positions surrendered without a fight.

Already in the period of stalemate from September, 1940, when East, West and South African Brigades were mustered to defend the Kenya frontier against a possible Italian attack from the Somaliland Colony, small bodies of Somalis were enlisting with the British as irregular forces to operate against the native Banda irregulars of Italy.

Somalis of Kismayu Welcome British Liberators

The arrival of the King's African Rifles in Kismayu on February 16, 1941, was greeted with enthusiasm by the Somali people. " All the populace were out in the streets to welcome us, clapping their hands," wrote a British Officer, whose description of the British capture of Kismayu is included in the anthology of war impressions collected by Kenneth Gandar Dower.*

George Steer† in, " The official story of the conquest of Italian East Africa," tells us :

"*Kismayu proved to be a dusty, untidy town, vigorously and pettily, though unscientifically, sabotaged. The whole white population had been evacuated and the ice factory had been destroyed, but three of the 4.9 defence guns, and 10 of the 16 anti-aircraft guns had not been damaged beyond repair.*

"*The Somalis and Arabs gave our men an enthusiastic reception. A great crowd assembled in the square, and we encountered the remarkable friendliness, which all through the campaign was displayed by the alleged enemy peoples.*"

Collapse of Italian Morale

The captured diary of an Italian officer, from which Gandar Dower has quoted, describes the ignominious retreat from Kismayu, a well fortified town which, had it been defended, would have cost the British heavy losses. He complains that the command was the first to leave the sinking ship, and expresses a melancholy surprise that "such instincts of bestial destruction can suddenly seize upon a man." He and his fellow officers, being ordered to sink the Italian ship, Casaregis, amused themselves by firing at it with a single gun till their poor target was full of holes. The forces assigned to withdraw first from Kismayu sacked the quarters of their fellow Italians before departing, and left them so completely wrecked as to suggest that " Attila had passed that way. "

At Jumbo, where forces evacuated from Kismayu halted, there was indescribable confusion. Soldiers sleeping on the ground, baggage and market produce, weapons cast away by the roadside, groups of fugitives who had lost their units. A soldier desiring a lift in a passing lorry flings a hand-grenade at the driver.

At Jelib, the confusion was still more terrible. A soldier was guarding a truck load of officers' suit cases. It had been previously filled with guns and ammunition, but when, in obedience to orders, the soldier drove it round to the Military Headquarters, he was ordered to sling out the war materials, and load up with the officers' cases:

---

* "Abyssinian Patchwork." An anthology by Kenneth Gandar Dower, Ministry of Information representative attached to Lieut-General Sir Alan Cunningham: London, Frederick Muller.

† " The Abyssinian Campaigns." The official story of the conquest of Italian East Africa: H.M. Stationery Office.

"*So the guns and ammunition, including that belonging to other batteries, are all left behind in Mogadishu!*" the diarist wrote, "*and we are here, 500 men out of 1,000 who left the original position, without a cartridge or a gun!*"

The British made immense advances with little opposition. They encountered more serious resistance on approaching the Juba river. At Bulo Erillo, the Gold Coast Regiment had to contend with land mines, tank traps and dense bush, alive with machine gun posts, through which the Italian armoured cars charged down specially prepared lanes. The Gold Coasters lost practically all their white personnel but they pushed the attack home and captured the objective, taking quantities of war material, including a 65 mm. battery and five armoured cars. The Italians fired the bush before they fled. The Gold Coast Brigade fought with the flames to rescue the Italian wounded lying in the blazing undergrowth, and were shelled by Italian guns from Jelib in the course of this stern humanitarian effort. Black stood out nobly against white on that occasion.*

Near Jelib, the South Africans also had a stiff fight, having to cross the Juba, which was 850 feet wide at that point, by pontoon bridge under fire.

The plight of the Italians, their moral collapse and panic, deserted as they were by the native forces they had conscripted, is graphically described in some of their own diaries, which fell into British hands. In one of these revealing documents, quoted by Gandar Dower, an officer writes:

"*I am put in charge of 190 Askaris. The following day they have shrunk to 130, and the day after that to 80. They get away during the night, either to the British lines, or into the bush . . . .*

"*I see Troia running up to me, rifle in hand. He asks, 'Did you see an Askari running this way?' I reply, 'What's wrong with you? Askaris are running all the time!*'"

"*22nd February, 1941.*

"*I send a runner to Command, asking for instructions having noted that the 75th Colonial Infantry Regiment is retreating from Mansur to Jelib. The reply comes, 'Beware of armoured cars.'*"

An exploding shell hits Captain Nolli, the diarist's "personal friend from Mogadishu." To get his friend to hospital he hails a passing lorry—

"*The driver refuses to stop; I have to pull out my pistol and hold it to him . . . . British armoured cars are everywhere; from Jelib one can hear the rattle of machine-gun fire, without reply from our own troops.*"

Refusal even to listen to orders had become general; the Italian debacle was complete. In company with some sailors whom he had encountered in his flight, the diarist aims to reach a post on the Mogadishu Road where he hopes to find some lorries in which to escape faster and further.

---

* "It's a Long Way to Addis." By Carel Birkby: Frederick Muller, p. 161

They slept by the roadside, "not having fed for forty-eight hours." Next morning they discovered a wounded medical lieutenant who had taken refuge in a native hut. They also would have sheltered there, but the diarist records bitterly, " The local inhabitants invite us to remove ourselves as rapidly as possible."

The Italians had become friendless and homeless in Somaliland; the colony was already lost to them; the long-oppressed native people had no longer any regard for the former masters who had lost the power to coerce them. They struggled on, impeded by the wounded medical lieutenant. At last, only four of them left now —the others had apparently hastened on—they sat in the shade of some straggling bushes and waited till a South African patrol found them—" Our suffering is ended," the Italian officer wrote.

The boasted Colonial Empire meant little to the Italians whose diaries and letters have been published, when their personal safety was at stake. Their happiness at being taken into safe custody by British forces contrasts strangely with the stern determination of the Ethiopian people to fight on when the Italians had forced their way through to Addis Ababa by aerial bombardment and poison gas five years before. The attitude of the Italians differed greatly also from that of the British and African soldiers, who, outnumbered and out-armed, broke in and vanquished, by determination and courage, larger and better equipped enemy forces.

Somalis Befriend a British Airman

Strikingly different from the story told by this Italian diarist was the experience recorded by G. Kinnear in the "East African Standard," of a South African pilot whose 'plane crashed amid the arid sand and thorn bush of Jubaland. He and his crew forced their way through the trackless bush under the burning sun for seven days, almost without food, for their emergency rations served only for a single meal, and for days and days without drink, for their single water tin was damaged in the crash.

They suffered so acutely that when on the eighth day they discovered a waterhole, it was agreed that the pilot, being less exhausted than the others, should leave them at the water and go on alone to seek help in the direction they thought most likely to lead to a British post.

He was overtaken by some Somalis, who, seeing that he was British, lavished on him the utmost kindness. They conducted him to their village, fed him with the best they had, tenderly washed his hands and feet, which were blistered and torn by the thorn bushes. Two of them set off with a note to obtain British assistance for his friends, a third became his guide. When he fell worn out by the way, this Somali guide walked a day and night long without a pause, twenty-five miles to his village and twenty-five miles back to bring water and food to the British airman.

Under the title "Come Abbiamo Diffeso L'Impero,"* an Italian author, Raffaele Di Lauro, has attempted to rebut the account of the

---

* Raffaele Di Lauro, "Come Abbiamo Diffeso L'Impero." Roma, 1949. Edizioni L'Arnia, pp. 217-233.

"Italian collapse" in Somaliland, given in the British story of the War in East Africa ("The Abyssinian Campaigns"). He alleges the British forces under General Cunningham were superior in numbers and equipment to those of Italy, in Somaliland a claim widely known to be untenable. In other respects, his version largely supports those of British observers. He declares General Pesenti was removed from the command of Somaliland for gross incompetence, his defensive preparations were " puerile ", revealing " ignorance of the principles of modern war ". General Simone, who replaced him, Di Lauro accuses of " technical incompetence, professional ineptitude," and " lack of confidence in victory." One of the first to flee from the Juba, says Di Lauro, was General Brunelli, who was therefore summoned by the Viceroy for trial by the Military Court. Many other Italian Generals " mortified " the spirit of their troops. There was " evident incapacity " in the Italian command. The Italian Air Force rarely appeared.

Once the British had succeeded in passing the Juba, the Somali soldiers " sought to get back to their homes." The Italians, " deserted " by their Commanders, " waited at their posts, saddened by the hard destiny of becoming prisoners." " One should not speak of the conquest of Somaliland, but of the pacific and bloodless occupation of places like Brava, Merka and Mogadishu." Some little groups of Blackshirts near Vittoria d'Africa fired a few shots at some motor lorries and at a few South Africans; then escaped into the bush.

The Bloodless Capture of Mogadishu

Mogadishu, described by Captain Willis as " a hot, odoriferous port," was captured without resistance. Declared an open town, it had escaped both bomb and shell.

When the Nigerian Brigade entered they were confronted by great slogans posted on the walls: " Victory is meant for the Italian people! " "Fight! Believe! Obey! "

The British had captured in Somaliland, up to this point, " 250,000 square miles of territory, 20,000 prisoners, 350,000 gallons of petrol, rations to feed 10,000 men for six months, weapons and stores of every kind in perfect condition."* The Italians were retreating frantically, leaving great stores of war material behind them.

The Nigerian Brigade had covered 275 miles, from 6 a.m. on February 23 when they started from Mbungo, to 5 p.m. on February 25, when they reached Mogadishu. The heat was intense and they had had little water on the way, though normally accustomed to drink much; they had no "comforts" for a month, Captain Willis tells us, but they were very cheerful. But they were "losing faith in the Italians; would they never turn to fight? Why did they never blow up any bridges, or do anything to hinder us? " The famous Italian roads, too, had thus far proved a disappointment.

---

* " The Abyssinian Campaigns." The official story of the conquest of Italian East Africa: H. M. Stationery Office, 1942. Page 85 says 30,000 prisoners.

On the road to Mogadishu, British Staff Officers met "a group of armed Italians who put up their hands and asked to be taken prisoner. The Staff Officers were willing to assist, but there were complaints from the column of transport behind that the advance was being delayed. The prisoners had politely co-operated by piling their arms at the roadside, but the Staff Officers had not room in their cars for such a large number of rifles, even though they had signal vans behind to take some. Eventually they told the prisoners that they would find food and water twenty miles ahead if they cared to walk, and would they please take their rifles with them. The Italians smiled their gratitude, and set out walking at a smart pace."

Carel Birkby* of the South African Press Association entered Mogadishu with Captain Philip Percival before the surrender. They found it a silent city, with terrified faces at the upper storey windows. A policeman with a tommy gun, the magazine of which contained forty rounds, was stationed at every hundred yards, civilians wearing brassards acting as special police for fear of a native insurrection. The high Fascist officials, and the Governor and Military Commander of the Colony, General Simone, had fled inland with the troops, except those who had demobilised into civilian clothes, and were mostly discovered and rounded up later.

The city came to life after the Nigerians marched in. The Fascist "Podestà," the chief official of the city, and other municipal officials had remained to hand over Mogadishu to the British. Some three hundred nervous Italians, Birkby tells us, had locked themselves up in a cage they had themselves constructed, and were waiting there for the British to arrive. During the afternoon, upwards of 5,000 Italian prisoners poured into hastily constructed cages. A party of Italian officers desired to surrender the same evening, with 1,000 troops who were waiting outside the town. The British officer who was consulted asked whether they had food and water, and on learning that they had, replied "We can't be bothered with these men in town this evening, tell the officers to go back to their troops and bring them in to-morrow morning." The Italians gave thanks and came in with their force next day.

At that time there were only about 1,000 British troops in Mogadishu.

287 persons, 197 of them British, whose ships had been sunk by a Nazi commerce raider, were interned on a lonely part of the coast. Ninety seven had to be taken to hospital.

The utter neglect of sanitation in Mogadishu and other towns, the forced labour under slave conditions on the Italian estates, the wretched state of the hospitals, the filth and cruelty in the prisons are revealed in chapter XIV by extracts from the official reports of British officers who had the duty of liquidating these evils as far as possible.

Food Shortage in Mogadishu

The Italians had fled from their estates, and were throwing themselves on the mercy of British troops to save them from the

---
* "It's a Long Way to Addis," by Carel Birkby; Frederick Muller.

vengeance of the natives whom they had compelled to labour as slaves. The Somalis had refused to bring meat and vegetables into Mogadishu; the city was short of food. The people had been disillusioned by the sight of the truck-loads of food the high Fascist officials took with them when they decamped before the British arrival as well as by their flight after the brave boasts of stern resistance they had made.

The Italians were amazed, Carel Birkby tells us, that the British insisted on setting aside sufficient bread and meat for the civil population before the needs of the victorious army were considered.

Causes of the Italian Collapse

The dirt and neglect in the towns, the utter collapse of Italian morale, Italian terror and eagerness to surrender, are mentioned with surprise by all who have recorded first-hand impressions of the brief hostilities, and the spontaneous abandonment of the struggle. These phenomena, which occurred throughout the colony, had doubtless common origins. The native inhabitants had been the workers who had kept the cities clean, removed the garbage, swept the roads, performed the menial work everywhere, marched in the ranks of the army. The native workers of the colony, and the native forces, whether from Somalia itself, or from Eritrea, were in revolt. The slaves—for labour being compulsory, they were in fact slaves—had largely withdrawn their labour. The conscript soldiers were also withdrawing from service in a war of which they disapproved.

Carel Birkby emphasises the dependence of the Italians upon their native levies.

"*Everywhere the Italians were plentifully equipped with field-pieces, quick-firing anti-aircraft Bredas which could be used at low elevation, anti-tank guns, heavy machine guns and a wealth of light automatic weapons. They had large stocks of shells of all calibres and countless dumps of small arms ammunition. They had all the equipment a foe needed to put up a stern fight, except determination.*"

On the other hand, the native troops had left the Italians and also had turned against them. Birkby continues:

"*Without their native levies the Italians seem to have been unable even to contemplate fighting it out alone, as our men would have done.*"

"Askaris were Deserting and Firing on us"—Diary of an Italian Officer

The following extract from an Italian officer's diary, indicates that the Italians faced not only the desertion of their former native troops, but active attack by them, and that this happened not in Ethiopia alone, but in the former colonies:

"*All who came from Mogadishu were fleeing in terror, without knowing where they were going, caring nothing except to keep moving, and to get as far away as possible from the British tanks, of which they told fabulous stories.*

" On the evening of March 20, the entire 38th Battalion deserted en masse, leaving the Commandant and the Officers to defend the pass alone.

" The 39th Battalion was moved and posted to the Babile zone, which was our second line of defence. The days we spent at Babile were really terrible. The lives of the Officers were in danger every night; every night more Askaris were deserting, and then firing on us, in the hope of terrorising us to the point where they would be able to get away with the battalion's arms and equipment.

" We were ordered to withdraw towards Karsa. . . . When we started the companies consisted of 30 to 40 men each, most of whom were Eritrean N.C.O.s, whom we thought were still faithful to us, but during the march the Askaris were going along firing and throwing grenades constantly. It was impossible to stay on one's mule, because bullets were whistling round our ears on every side. The orders and reproof of the Officers were ignored, and it was now clear that we were faced with complete and irreparable collapse. When one sees one's authority going in this way, one falls into a feeling of utter despair . . . .

" At Assako we were met by volleys of rifle fire from all sides, and were attacked very heavily by the rebels for a whole day. General Santini had no idea what to do. He was in command of the column, which now consisted of Officers and Italian Other Ranks who had joined up with us to save themselves from the Abyssinians, and of Eritrean N.C.O.s (about 400 men in all).

" It was decided to make an attempt, moving only at night, to find our way back to the main road and give ourselves up to the British. I was given the task of going ahead with a white flag to parley with the English.

" On the 10th April, near Aba, 25 kilometres from Awash, I finally discovered a South African Officer, to whom I reported the object of my mission. . . . This British Officer was very good to us, and his first concern was to give us something to eat when he saw what poor physical condition we were in."

Though the Italians were deserted by their native levies, their forces outnumbered British Commonwealth and Allied troops of all races in East Africa.

The British official story of the war, " The East African Campaigns," declares Italy had 300,000 troops in East Africa. Lord Rennell, in " British Military Administration in Africa, 1941-47 ",* which is based on official documents, and was prepared with the permission of the Army Council, makes the same statement. "The Abyssinian Campaigns"† states that Italy had 33,000 troops in the Somaliland Colony, of whom 21,000 were taken prisoner or voluntarily surrendered to British forces. These would be all of Italian race.

---

* " British Military Administration of Occupied Territories in Africa, 1941-47," by Rennell of Rodd. K.B.E., C.B., His Majesty's Stationery Office.

† " The Abyssinian Campaigns." The official story of the conquest of Italian East Africa: H.M. Stationery Office.

Moreover, in addition to the troops, labour battalions were drilled and armed. For a number of years, Italian boys of all classes, both in Italy and the colonies, had received military training from an early age; they were obliged to pass through the various stages of military training before joining the Fascist Party as practically all the men and youths of the Italian colonies did. Thus, even when engaged in civilian employment, practically every Italian man and youth in East Africa had been trained as a soldier.

Numbers of the British, on the other hand, had gone to war from the office stool, the shop counter, the journalist's chair, with only the briefest training.

An order of the day of Major-General Fowkes, commander of the 22nd East African Infantry Brigade, issued on July 7, 1941, gives a revealing picture of the war in East Africa, though the figures there quoted do not record so remarkable a contrast in the numbers of the rival forces engaged as can be quoted in other cases. Nevertheless, the discrepancy is striking. In offering " warmest thanks and appreciation" to the units and sub-units which formed "Fowcol", General Fowkes said:

" *We have captured about* 25,000 *prisoners,* 85 *guns,* 11 *tanks, and innumerable machine-guns, rifles, etc. Our bag has included* 12 *generals, some complete with their staffs, and many other senior officers. It would probably be safe to estimate the casualties we have inflicted at nearly* 1,000. *At no time was ' Fowcol' more than* 6,000 *strong, and our own casualties were under* 100."

In short, the outstanding feature of all the East African campaigns was that in every area thousands of Italians were surrendering to a few British officers with African forces very much inferior in number to the Italians whom they were taking into custody.

The rot in moral fibre which caused masses of Italians to be tyrants and brutal sadists in dealing with unarmed Africans, but feeble cowards when confronted by white soldiers, had been promoted by Fascism, for which Mussolini himself, in one of his moments of arrogant frankness, had accepted the designation " a criminal conspiracy."

The Somaliland colonists were alarmed by Hitler's declaration of war in 1939, for many feared that Mussolini would immediately follow suit. They were relieved and delighted by his announcement of Non-Belligerency and jubilantly declared that as neutrals they would grow rich at the expense of the countries at war. Whilst the belligerents exhausted themselves, Italy would become the greatest nation in Europe. Even the bankrupt Empire would flourish.

It is true some anxiety was felt, lest Britain, though it was proper for every true Fascist to call her decadent, might prove, after all, a tough antagonist, but this was an opinion too unpleasant to be freely expressed. In any case, no one in the Somaliland colony desired to fight; to make war in that area was declared entirely futile, mere useless bloodshed; the war would be won when Hitler invaded

Britain—and that, it was insisted, would happen soon. The most prominent Fascists were most determined to remain in civil life.

There was in fact, no need of troop reinforcements, or of further military equipment, but there was moral unpreparedness, and in consequence, military unreadiness. No one prepared seriously for hostilities. General Pesenti was sent out to take command in the colony, but on learning the state of affairs there, he resigned the commission. Generals Simone and Santini replaced him. The occupation of British Somaliland, which was effected by an Italian army of 25,000 men, outnumbering the defence by upwards of ten to one, rejoiced the Italians and gave new confidence to the wavering spirits in the Somaliland colony. But they wished to preserve a safe course. Mombassa must not be bombed, lest Mogadishu be bombed also; moreover, it was well to save petrol. The shore batteries must not be used against British ships.

When the colony was at last invaded by British Commonwealth troops, the main resistance was made on the Juba River. Even to this key position the Fascist officials in Mogadishu refused proper supplies of the food reserves which filled the military stores there.

The officers on the Juba were deprived for many days of the macaroni, cigarettes and wine which they considered essential to their fighting spirit. The knowledge of this selfish corruption on the part of the Fascist officials, who finally decamped with the stores, gave rise to mutual recriminations among the volatile Italian population.

Italian Officer's View of the Italian Defeat in Somaliland

An Italian officer's analysis of the causes which led to the collapse of Italian resistance in Somaliland are in some respects as severe a condemnation of the Italian Colonial regime as any which has been uttered from non-Italian sources. He emphasises that general belief in an easy victory which would require no effort or sacrifice on behalf of the Italians in Somaliland was stimulated by exaggerated and false reports emanating from Rome. On August 8, 1940, Count Carlo Tosti* Commander of the 14th Colonial Brigade, announced: " Malta has been occupied. Graziani's troops are only 26 kilometres from Port Said; Gibraltar and Haifa have asked for terms of surrender!" Then followed "news" of Churchill's resignation, and a landing carried out by German troops and Italian Bersaglieri on the English coast.

The result was a general conviction that there was no point in fighting, or preparing to fight, because an armistice was to be expected at any moment.

General Wavell's victories in Libya, however, aroused uneasiness, and in December rumours of a British offensive with well armed forces began to spread. Prices soared. Corruption, always rife under Fascism, became utterly "shameless." "To get permission to transport salt, or other goods into the interior, considerable sums had to be paid to the high officials of the Fascist Party through the 'pompadours,' who acted as intermediaries."

---
* " Abyssinian Patchwork," by Kenneth Gandar Dower (Frederick Muller).

As the threat of a British invasion became more evident, the Fascist officials summoned meetings of their Party, and of the population at large, and delivered "flowery" speeches declaring that they would never permit themselves to be taken prisoner; to their bold spirits death would be preferable. In the unlikely event of an invasion, they would take to the bush and maintain a " terrible guerilla war."

This bold talk which already seemed to foretell defeat and failure could not reassure the majority of the Italians, nor could it preserve the morale of the speakers. The officer adds this crushing indictment of his compatriots:

" *The majority of the Italians were like lost men; they lived in a stunned condition, surrounded by gossip, believing it impossible to overcome the economic difficulties which faced them. The stoppage of imports, the almost total limitation of transport due to the rigid rationing of fuel, the suspension of public works, swelled the long list of dissatisfied people. Life was dominated by a strange atmosphere of waiting, and a general psychology of helplessness. The dominating sentiments were uneasiness, uncertainty. Something was about to happen, people felt; some solution was necessary. . . ."*

Now follows the Italian officer's epitome of the mental condition of his compatriots in the colony:

" *To their weak spirits, so much attached to material life, so lacking in spiritual force, without which one cannot resist or fight, the British Army brought that solution."*

A pregnant factor in the failure of Italian morale thus described in Italian words was the attitude of the native people; not alone in Ethiopia was their hostility felt as a dreaded menace; even in the Somaliland colony, the same Italian officer records their manifest aversion:

" The mistrust of the natives was clearly shown by their refusal to accept our currency. They would only part with grain, coffee, etc., in exchange for other goods; they refused Italian money."

It should be recognised that the British war effort in the Somaliland colony was based upon African forces to a greater extent than that of Italy. The outstanding difference between the African forces of the opposing armies was that those of Britain gave whole-hearted service, whereas the African conscripts of Italy ranged themselves to a large extent against the Italian masters when the hour of trial came.

It is a factor of our time that the soldier, the common man, in Africa as elsewhere, has gained political consciousness; he cannot successfully be either hired or conscripted to fight for a cause which conflicts with his natural sympathies and loyalties, and which outrages his sense of justice and righteousness. Moreover, his social conscience and his political awareness are alike wider than in former times. They are no longer confined to his family, or his village. He is developing world interests.

African owned newspapers, written by Africans both in English and in African languages, have made great strides in the past twenty years as observers of local and world politics and as enunciators of policy.

The British Government realised the wisdom of addressing African opinion, which Italy had flouted. Radio broadcasting extended and elaborated the propaganda addressed to the soldiers of all armies. Instead of a mere impromptu exhortation by the commander to acquit themselves as brave men for the honour of their regiment they were subjected to systematic and carefully prepared propaganda. Speakers of their own race and country were engaged to address them in their own language to provide the requisite stimulus to enthusiasm.

In the contest of argument all the facts were against Italy, whose exuberant propaganda of racial inferiority, and whose "racist" laws, which imposed a more ruthless discrimination and oppression against Africans than had hitherto been applied anywhere, inevitably turned African opinion against her. The brutal conquest of Ethiopia, the use of poison gas, bombing of the Red Cross, slaughter of prisoners and wanton massacre of defenceless Ethiopian villagers were not forgotten.

The "New Times and Ethiopia News," from its first publication in May, 1936, onward, had a considerable circulation in Africa, and was widely quoted in the African Press. Funds were collected by Africans in the British Colonies and Protectorates for the fund organised by Dr. Warqneh Martin, the Ethiopian Minister in London, to assist the Ethiopian cause. Many Africans from all parts of the continent expressed their desire to fight for Ethiopian independence in 1935-6.

African soldiers in British ranks declared the conviction that a victory for Italy in East Africa would enable Mussolini and his Axis partner to advance their conquests into other parts of Africa, everywhere oppressing the African peoples and subjecting them to the horrors of Belsen and Buchenwald, and destroying all possibility of progress.

If the African soldiers of Italy were induced to imbibe more facts about the Nazi crimes in Europe than about the massacre perpetrated by Marshal Graziani in Addis Ababa, and other Italian atrocities in Africa, this was not accidental.

The outcome of the known facts within their recollection and of the able propaganda of the B.B.C. African Service and other agencies was that the British command in East Africa had the willing service, not of mere African mercenaries, but of troops whose sympathies were warmly engaged in the struggle. This was an invaluable asset, which might not have been available in the same abundant measure had the policy and record of Italy and her German partner been other than it was. This is a fact worthy of profound consideration.

"In every situation they have distinguished themselves. Their spirit, their efficiency, and their high courage are admired by all," wrote the Commanding Officer of a body of Colonial troops, quoted by a Ministry of Information Press " hand out " in August, 1941. For many months after Italy's entry into the war, the King's African Rifles of East Africa bore the brunt of the desert campaign. The Gold Coast troops at El Wak, on the Western borders of Jubaland, in December, 1940, struck the first effective blow at Italy's Southern Colony. They captured 150 prisoners and 15 guns, and completely destroyed the Italian base. They established a moral ascendancy over the Italians, which was maintained throughout the Somaliland campaign. The King's African Rifles captured Afmadu, the first important objective gained inside the Somaliland Colony. The speed of their advance caused the Italians to evacuate Kismayu without a fight. The Nigerians captured Brava, Merka, and Mogadishu, and led the swift advance through the Colony into Ethiopia, as far as Dire Dawa.

The same British Ministry of Information Press " hand-out " of August, 1941, stated that British forces on all fronts in East Africa when Mussolini declared war in 1940 numbered a mere 25,000, only 5,000 of whom were white, a fact which manifests the greatness of Britain's war debt to the soldiers of Africa and India. Subsequent reinforcements were largely drawn from India and from South, West, and British East Africa, as well as from Ethiopia. Recruits also came from the ex-Italian Colonies.

The Ministry of Information adds that Italy entered the war in East Africa with 325,000 soldiers, 125,000 of them Italian Metropolitan and 200,000 African. Of these soldiers " nearly 100,000 Italians are our prisoners, 6,000 are still at large, and the rest are dead." "Of the 200,000 native troops, some 60,000 are prisoners, the rest have deserted, and many have turned against Italy and are fighting for Haile Sellassie." That was in August, 1941.

The British by that time had captured 800 Italian great guns, many thousands of machine guns, 150 tanks, thousands of motor vehicles. At Asmara, in one depot alone, were captured 1,500,000 shells, 300,000 rounds of rifle ammunition, at Iscia Baidoa, in the Somaliland Colony, 3,500,000 rounds. The Italian Air Force in East Africa began the war with 212 aerodromes and hundreds of 'planes. "The British Air Force was hopelessly outnumbered, and was not of modern type," but " parity was soon established by the small British force, a single squadron of which, between January 19th and April 7th, destroyed 42 Italian bombers, 28 fighters, and damaged others in battle and on the ground." The official " Abyssinian Campaigns " mentions the exploits of the South African airman, Captain Jack Frost, " who single-handed shot down three Italian bombers and one of their two escorting fighters, in the course of a few minutes." After that event, the Italian Air Force reserved themselves for moonlight bombing, which made possible the advance of British forces by daylight, thereby speeding the pace of victory.

In view of these facts, Signor Di Lauro's sad complaint that " blonde giants " from South Africa, " armed at every point " were resisted only by " the lean and bony, ill-armed coloured soldiers " of Italy, can be regarded in its perspective.

XIII

HOW THE BRITISH FOUND IT

Extracts from:—
"THE FIRST TO BE FREED"
The Record of British Military Administration in Eritrea and Somalia, 1941-1943.

Issued by the Ministry of Information, London: His Majesty's Stationery Office, 1944.

Somalia, like Eritrea, is a desert, but of a more normal kind. Eritrea is small, spectacular, and vertical. Somalia is vast, dreary and flat. Of all its 274,000 square miles, only in certain small portions of the South-Eastern Province can it be called productive. For the rest, it is a featureless expanse of nothing in particular. There is not a single farm in the thousands of square miles of Mudug Province which, in the words of one political officer who had cause to know it well, is " a worthless desert of sand and low scrub which does not grow to the height of more than about three feet. In general the view of any part of it, as from the bridge of a ship at sea, is perfectly flat—a featureless plain with an equidistant horizon in all directions. Great numbers of stock subsist on the scrub, and on the stock subsist the people, their diet being confined to milk and meat." The North-West Province is much the same, save that here the ground rises slowly to the Ethiopian border, while the remote red mountains of the North-Eastern Province stretch interminably to the lighthouse of Gardafui. Apart from the wandering tribesmen, no one lives there now save a handful of political and gendarmerie officers, whose duty it is to keep order. These men are practically cut off from their fellows, for Dante, for instance, lies far from Mogadishu at the end of 1,200 miles of boulder-strewn roads, covered twelve inches deep in friable dust in the dry weather and impassable during the rains.

Of Somalia's four main rivers, only the Juba flows all the year round or contrives to find the sea. The Webbi Shebeli, after a promising start, loses its sense of purpose, runs parallel to the coastal dunes for the last 150 miles of its curious course, and just fails to reach either the Indian Ocean or the Juba. It is along these rivers that the only cultivable part of Somalia lies, with the exception of the Iscia Baidoa area, a country of many natural springs and the centre of native millet production.

For the rest Somalia is a land of distances and heat, wells and camels and gathering desiccation, of interest only to the policeman and the administrator. No one, however much of an eye he has for grandeur, will say "magnificent" and anyone industrially minded will still say "what a hole."

At Mogadishu, and on the Webbi Shebeli plantations, and later on the Juba river, which was ceded to Italy after the last war, 250 colonists lived for many years quiet, unpolitical, unostentatious lives.

It was not until 1930 drew near that expansion fever came over these two deserts.

* * *

The Labour had Run Away

In Somalia conditions were similar to those of Eritrea in the main, though different in detail. True, Mogadishu had never suffered from the elephantiasis that had overtaken Asmara. True, the Italian population of the colony was only one-tenth of that of Eritrea; but they were more violently Fascist, incorrigibly corrupt, and cordially hated by the Somali, who is difficult to deal with even at his friendliest. Here in Somalia there was some agricultural development, but the crops grown had always been uneconomic and were practically useless save for export to protected monopolistic markets. In any case, production had broken down, for the labour had run away, and the farmers seemed unwilling to help either themselves or each other.

* * * *

The first Deputy Chief Political Officer for Somalia was appointed on February 11, 1941, while the armies were tearing their way through Jubaland. Four days later he flew to Kismayu, the little Indian Ocean port. It had been captured only the day before. He found everything in chaos. The Italians had fled before the British came, sanitary services had broken down. He appointed a Senior Political Officer who had previous experience of Somalis in Kenya's Northern Frontier Province, and then returned to Nairobi to organise. Almost before he got there, Mogadishu had fallen and the army was racing for the Ethiopian border. Vast new tracts of country were conquered from day to day, and were duly handed over to the Administration. The D.C.P.O. returned forthwith with such assistants as he was able immediately to muster. A few of these were flown direct to Mogadishu but the main party of sixteen British officers, three British other ranks and twenty-nine motor vehicles, left Nairobi by road on March 7 and after a thousand miles of hard driving reached the capital in a week.

These new Political Officers were distributed as rapidly as might be through the vast square mileage of Somalia's less barren wastes. Here, isolated from the world and from each other, often unaided by so much as a native clerk (the average Somali being ignorant alike of English and of typing), each wrestled with the particular brand of chaos he found in his own allotted district.

Administrative duties were not the only tasks that fell to these officers in the early days. The army had advanced so swiftly into Ethiopia that it had left behind it whole tracts of untouched country, especially to the north-east between the Mogadishu-Jigjiga road and the Cape of Gardafui. These vast, desolate stretches of rock and sand might have given scope for prolonged resistance in the hands of a more determined enemy; as it was, they were swiftly reduced to order by a handful of Political Officers.

Thus the occupation of the greater part of Somalia had been completed with the use of the fewest possible troops, and the British officials had to settle down to less exciting days: to thinking out what was to be done with the wrecked tunny fishery at Bender Cassim and the always uneconomic £3,000,000 salt works at Dante.

* * * *

Italian Officials had to be Removed After Five Months' Trial

In Somalia, though the European civilian population was less than 7,000, both international law and common sense demanded that the Administration should as far as possible work in with the Italian authorities. Such a policy would keep both the native and European population in employment, would reduce the danger to security, and reduce to a minimum the British staff which it was necessary to employ. Here, however, the Italians proved less unreservedly co-operative, more Fascist and more corrupt, than those of Eritrea. In Mogadishu immediate co-operation of a kind was obtained from the municipio, whose mayor, despite pronounced Fascist sympathies for which he later had to be interned, saw the necessity for organising relief. The staffs of the various government departments, who had already received three months' pay in advance, found it difficult to make up their minds. In the end two parties emerged—a Fascist minority which consisted of the more recent immigrants, minor officials and a few hot-headed, diehard leaders, and the government party, including the civil servants and residents of long standing, who recognised that co-operation was in the best interests of their country.

In the end, however, even their assistance proved more trouble than it was worth. To quote from a contemporary report, " the Italian officials we have retained in office pursue their corrupt and idle course. They do little and care less for the welfare of their fellow countrymen. Italians in difficulties inevitably come to British officers for help and advice, and openly expressed contempt for Italian officialdom is growing in volume." In the end, after five months' trial, the experiment had to be abandoned and the majority were removed.

* * * *

Somalis had a Positive Hatred of Former Masters

In Somalia at the time of the occupation, there were only 6,000 to 7,000 Italians compared with 55,000 in Eritrea, but they were more violently Fascist, more corrupt, and quite a number had criminal records. Somalia's 1,500,000 natives had a positive hatred for their ex-masters.

* * * *

Inefficiency of Italian Police

In March, 1941, the General Officer Commanding gave authority to raise a force of 1,500 men, to be known as the Somalia Gendarmerie.

In Mogadishu security suffered less from the turbulence of the Somalis than from the inefficiency and extreme Fascism of the Italian police. For some weeks after the occupation these men had to be left at their posts, for there was no means by which they could be replaced. During this time they proved themselves to be a useless body, ineffective, given to intrigue, and corrupt in their dealings both with natives and fellow Italians. Soon their attitude deterioriated even towards the British. On April 16 they all had to be interned.

* * * *

Prison Conditions Intolerable
Sadist Cruelties

Just as in Eritrea, so in Somalia the Administration found the prisons in a condition which no British authorities could tolerate. In the main jail at Mogadishu 400 prisoners were confined in overcrowded cells and wards, of which the walls had been periodically whitewashed until they were inches deep in half-concealed filth. The sanitation was such that the prison could be smelt 200 yards away; a senior official of the Administration who inspected it was promptly and literally sick. The prisoners were supposed to wash, but no washing water was provided. The regulations prescribed a shower-bath every day, but the key could not be found when a British officer asked for it, and the condition of the lock made it clear that it had not been used for months. The prisoners were supposed to have breakfast, and a midday meal of stew; but no breakfast was served, and the midday meal consisted of a bowl of watery rice. Health conditions were shocking, as was only to be expected, and most of the inmates suffered from running sores.

The warders were the merest turnkeys, despised, despising, illiterate and somewhat sadistic. They dispensed with normal disciplinary routine, yet there were stocks in which the ankles of victims had been fastened for days at a time. One prisoner was still under treatment for wounds inflicted on his chest; he had been held down and jumped on with long-nailed climbing boots.

Many of the 400 men in Mogadishu jail were political prisoners from Ethiopia. An attempt was made to investigate all cases. It emerged that some seventy of the inmates had not been tried at all, while others had completed their sentences some time ago and were awaiting repatriation. But in more cases than not it proved quite impossible to ascertain the facts at all. No proper records had been kept of the crimes for which prisoners had been sentenced. Upcountry commissioners and residents, it seemed, had frequently conducted cases in the most arbitrary manner, merely writing a letter to the director of the jail asking him to imprison natives for various terms. Convicts were not told that there was any right of appeal, and often did not know that it existed. In some cases neither the crime nor the punishment was recorded; where both were known it was clear that sentences had been vicious. Ten years for failing to hand in arms was as light a sentence as most of the Ethiopians had received. Of twenty men committed in 1940 for taking part in a tribal fight in which two men had been killed by unknown hands, the majority had been sentenced for life, and none for less than seven years. It is an illuminating comment on the conduct of the prison that by the spring of 1941 two of these twenty men had died, three were in hospital, and eight had escaped.

Despite the difficulty in obtaining an accurate account of cases, the Administration had no hesitation in releasing a considerable number of prisoners on the spot and in greatly reducing the majority of the remaining sentences. Undoubtedly some genuine criminals were released; in the circumstances it was better to lean on the side of generosity.

60 out of 100 Died

As in Eritrea the faults of one prison were found in most of the others. At Kismayu and Iscia Baidoa the jails were little more than lock-ups, while Denane, a few miles down the coast from Mogadishu, had been planned to rival the notorious Nocra. Occasionally investigation revealed the existence of a humaner regime; the Resident at Dante had asked Rome for permission to issue sun-glasses to native prisoners working in the blinding glare of the salt-mines. But the stocks at Villaggio told a more normal tale. To this prison had been sent one hundred Ethiopian political prisoners of whom only forty were still alive when the British arrived; the rest, the Administration learned, had died of " malaria."

To-day in Somalia's prisons everything is changed. Reasonable standards of sanitation have been attained. Juveniles have been segregated from adults, and sent to the reformatory started at Afgoi. Prisoners are properly fed. They no longer spend their time drearily milling round in a central court-yard, but take regular exercise and work at a variety of prison industries ranging from the hard labour of building askari lines or stone-breaking to the lighter tasks of making soap, cloth, brushes, brooms and more recently, sandals for the gendarmerie. Almost all the old warders have been dismissed; their successors are of a better type, and their salaries are high by previous standards.

On the occupation of Somalia it was intended that the Italian courts should continue to function, as in Eritrea; in the first proclamation of the General Officer Commanding they were invited to do so. It seemed best that the civil courts should reopen as soon as conditions became more settled while the criminal courts should resume duty at once. Before they could do so, however, inquiry revealed a situation as intolerable as the condition of the prisons. The examination of the records showed that at the worst prisoners were convicted without trial, and that at the best they were tried according to principles repugnant to British conceptions of justice. To the Fascist judges of Somalia, a prisoner who was an Italian was regarded as guilty unless he could prove himself innocent; if he was a native, he was convicted anyway, merely receiving a lighter sentence if he did not happen to be guilty.

It also became clear that the non-Italian population, and especially the Somalis, would not willingly submit to the continuation of Italian jurisdiction in any form, either judicial or administrative, and that attempts to make them submit would simply puzzle them. The original scheme was, therefore, abandoned. Offences against proclamations were tried by the military courts of the Administration, while the native courts of the Cadis were re-established to deal with those cases relating to marriage, inheritance and personal status which it was customary for such Moslem courts to try. There is an appeal from these courts to Sharia tribunals, and in the last resort to the Chief Administrator, who takes advice from the Legal Adviser.

The court of the Italian civil judge re-opened in October, 1941, but relations with the Italian law department staff have never been as harmonious as in Eritrea. The present chief Italian judge was number four on his departmental list at the time the British arrived, number one being in Italy while numbers two and three had immediately to be interned. Though the penal code has still to be enforced by British military courts, it is possible for Italian civil cases to be tried by him under Italian law, purged of Fascist conceptions and in certain respects simplified. Even so, procedure was at first much too dilatory by British standards. Only six cases out of twenty-two had been finished by the end of 1941, and though improvements have been effected the position has never been entirely satisfactory.

Agriculture Abandoned

Of the 274,000 square miles of Somalia almost all is desert, but along the meandering course of the Webbi Shebeli, on either side of the Juba, and around the springs of Iscia Baidoa there are rich areas capable of being made to bloom. Iscia Baidoa is the centre of native millet production. On the lower Juba and especially at four points on the Webbi Shebeli, the Fascist Government had set to work with irrigation and machinery and had achieved impressive and nearly useful results.

The chief products were cotton, bananas and sugar. True, the bananas could be made to pay only by selling them as a monopoly in Italy at four times the world price, and the cotton made to pay only by selling it similarly at twelve times the world price; true, the sugar was so expensive that while it was possible to export it to the State-provided market in Italy, Somalia found it cheaper to import sugar for its own consumption from Yugoslavia. During the war none of the crops grown could be of use even for export and only sugar for local consumption. But all the same the canals had been dug, the fields were watered, and in these areas lay the only hope of making Somalia self-supporting.

Unfortunately, when political officers first visited the farms soon after the occupation, they found a state of chaos. Most of the farmers had fled to the towns and were unwilling to return. Only a handful of brave men, regardless alike of Somali revolt and Fascist instruction, had refused to leave their land and had successfully protected their property from the orgy of looting. Elsewhere destruction was so great that compensation claims were filed to the total of 25,000 000 lire (probably an exaggerated figure).

A tour of inspection revealed that the least collapsed of the Italian concessions was the Società Agricola Italo Somala plantation at Villaggio. It had been founded as long ago as 1920, had plenty of skilled labour, and having probably treated its manual labour better than other farms was suffering less acutely from lack of manpower. Elsewhere the picture was not encouraging. At Afgoi, of fifteen holdings totalling 2,000 hectares, only nine were being worked at all and only three intensively. At Genale, where a main irrigation canal had been dug as early as 1926 and 27,000 hectares had been fertilised, thirty-two of the 136 holdings were totally abandoned, thirty-six others were idle, on thirteen a moderate amount of work was being done, and only on six was there extensive cultivation. Worst of all was the situation on the Juba where, in an area of 10,000 hectares, five of the thirty-four concessions were working well, five more were kept going only on the basis of partnership with natives, and the rest were abandoned or idle. Here the president of the Consorzio was living in a state of unbelievable squalor, while many of the farmers had settled down most philosophically to do absolutely nothing, had grown no vegetables, and had allowed houses and machinery to fall into disrepair.

Only 500 out of 8,000 Labourers Report for Work

It was decided that the best thing to do was to get the farms going again by hook or by crook. Apart from many other considerations, it was better both for security and Italian self-respect that farmers should be supporting themselves, even uneconomically, than that they should be drawing relief in Mogadishu. Yet the difficulties were immense. The customary crops were useless under existing conditions. Even after some weeks' effort at Genale, only 500 of the required 8,000 labourers were reporting for work. Much of the machinery had been wantonly damaged. It appeared that if production was to begin again petrol and lubricants would have to be supplied for transport and for the irrigation pumps at special rates below cost. Lastly, many of the farmers were afraid to return.

Conditions of Slavery; Cruel Punishments

Agricultural Societies have been switched over almost entirely to sugar cane; though they are working at only half capacity, they are able to supply Somalia with the sugar it requires. Five thousand hectares at Genale and 2,500 on the Juba produce useful crops such as maize, sesame, groundnuts and beans, while Afgoi concentrates on fresh vegetables for Mogadishu.

This labour shortage, which at one time threatened to stop production altogether, was caused by the wholesale refusal of the Somalis to continue to work for the Italians. This was hardly surprising. For when the circumstances under which labour had been recruited were investigated, a situation was disclosed even less tolerable than the state of Mogadishu jail. Under the " colonia " system men, women and children had been taken by force from remote places and condemned to an indefinite period of servitude on Italian farms. To quote from an official report, " rations were grossly inadequate both in quality and quantity, and pay varied from one to three lire a day. Bachelors were forced to marry women who had been born and bred on the estate. Punishment, inflicted by the resident on the ex-parte representations of the employer, was brutal and excessive. For a first offence of disobedience or indiscipline fifty lashes with a hippopotamus-hide whip was a common award, and for a second offence the victim was strung up for several hours on a gallows, with his toes just clear of the ground, suspended by chains attached to wooden billets under his armpits, and with his hands handcuffed behind his back. It is not unnatural that the native labouring population regarded our coming as a deliverance from their Italian oppressors and that they resolutely and determinedly refused to return to work for them, in spite of our efforts to persuade them to do so." They had had enough of slavery.

Somali Agriculture Brighter

This labour problem is still only partly solved. There is still an immense natural hostility to the Italians to be overcome; secondly, the Somalis are more interested in the development of their own native agriculture, which it is also the policy of the Administration to encourage. Fortunately the picture of native agriculture is brighter. Many of the natives, particularly the Goshas of the Juba valley, are good farmers; the millet growers of Iscia Baidoa are doing well, and some of the Italian concessions are being worked by natives on various agreements. This is, of course, true only of the riverine tribes.

British Relief for Italians

Under the Italian administration, industry had been neglected. The six or seven thousand Italian civilians were mostly loyal but unwanted Fascists who swelled the numbers of the civil service. With the British occupation, it was clear that the number likely to come on relief, while absolutely fewer than those in Eritrea, would be relatively higher.

The problem of European poverty was tackled in much the same way as in Eritrea and a similar relief organisation was set up. The medical authorities worked out a scale of diet, a number of other items such as clothing and rent were taken into consideration, and in the end forty-five shillings a month was arrived at as a reasonable payment. This has since risen in partial conformity with the cost of living index. Owing to the comparative smallness of

Somalia's Italian population, there have never been more than 1,400 on public assistance; the vast majority of these were the wives and families of prisoners of war. To-day, with the repatriation of colonists and the start of industries, the number receiving relief has shrunk to the moderate total of 380.

Housing was a problem in the early days though it was never as acute as in Asmara, for Mogadishu was almost the only part of Somalia where Europeans had lived in any numbers. The shortage was dealt with by various measures, including rent restriction.

Food supplies were soon supplemented by Somalia's agricultural drive. By June, 1941, Italians living in and around Mogadishu were rationed on a basis that ensured them adequate supplies of fresh vegetables, fruit and milk, while the ending of the salt monopoly had reduced the price of this commodity. To-day they receive bread, pasta, rice, flour, sugar, coffee, olive oil, tea, jam, alcohol and wood. Food is more plentiful and better distributed than before the occupation. A tale is still told in Mogadishu of how in the old days a doctor, unable to get milk for the hospital, wrote a letter exposing the scandal and was held in prison until he had retracted—this at a time when a prominent administrator was getting 35 lb. of grapes flown out to him from Italy. In 1940 the Italian population lived largely on black bread; nowadays consignments of flour are imported from Ethiopia.

Concerning one of these an illuminating story is told. Doubting its quality, the Administration had samples taken for analysis; doubting the quality of the Italian analyst, the Administration doctored some of the samples, introducing in one instance fifty per cent. of soda. The result was declared by the analyst to consist of practically pure, unadulterated flour, containing only a small percentage of rice flour, and to be fit for the consumption of his fellow Italians.

Appalling Neglect of Sanitation

The medical problems encountered in Somalia were nearly as shocking as those of Eritrea. When Mogadishu was declared an open town, the mayor came out to meet the advancing British troops and announced that public services were continuing as usual. This statement, unfortunately, was literally true. Water-borne sanitation had broken down, and the accumulation of many months' refuse lay piled between the houses. One hundred tons of dust-bin rubbish were removed by the British hygiene staff from the dock area alone; even the well-equipped Italian hospital had disposed of its garbage and the soiled dressings of 400 patients by throwing them over its boundary wall. Flies swarmed through the streets and buildings of the town.

Even worse conditions had been encountered in Kismayu. Practically every town in Somalia was found in the condition of either Mogadishu or Kismayu.

Medical achievements in Somalia, though not so spectacular as in Eritrea, have not been insignificant. In Mogadishu, as in Massawa, the campaign against the aedes mosquito has resulted in the practical elimination of dengue fever. The greater part of the fly population has met with an overdue fate, and a sanitary market has replaced the square of sand on which natives sat and sold their wares. Water supply has proved a considerable worry, as the three excellent but elderly distilleries which the Italians had constructed are beginning to break down. The discovery and development of a new supply, four kilometres out on the Afgoi road, has greatly eased the situation, however.

The Malaria Scourge

All over the country similar improvements in hygiene have been made wherever they were possible. The remark of the Italian doctor who declared of Villaggio D'Abruzzi, in which he had lived eight years, that " the native village is cleaner now than it ever was " is equally true of most small towns and villages throughout Somalia. No answer has yet been found, however, to the scourge of malaria. Mogadishu and the little coastal ports derive an immunity from the sandy soil of Somalia's narrow line of dunes, but it will be many decades before this disease can be eradicated from the Juba valley, the springs of Iscia Baidoa and, above all, from the canals and waterways of the Genale settlements.

Education

Native education had been deliberately neglected in Italian times. A government school was built in 1939, but it was soon closed down as a matter of policy. Here, therefore, it was necessary for the Administration to innovate. Two schools were started—an Arab school, attended by 300 children, and a Somali school, where 220 learn to read and write in Roman as well as in Arabic characters. Perhaps, as in many Moslem schools, too much emphasis is laid on religious teaching, for the Arabs and Somalis learn to read and write solely from the Koran. The headmaster has been imported from Mombasa; the assistant masters are local.

Co-operation with the Italian administration has been attempted everywhere and achieved where possible. The multitudinous Italian government servants have been reduced in numbers, and there has been some simplification of the machinery of government, which was unnecessarily complicated. But co-operation has always continued, partly through lack of British staff, primarily because international law demands that, where possible, the Occupying Power must make use of existing administrative machinery.

Much of this may have read like an indictment of Italian incompetence in East Africa between 1935 and 1941. But Eritrea and Somalia were in many ways little developed according to British standards not because Italians tried and failed, but because they did not try. They were far more interested in another purpose, which plays little part in British administration—the development of these territories as a base for war.

Similarly, in describing the Italian attitude to natives, this book does not intend to give the impression that Italians were without exception brutal. There were disgraceful abuses, certainly, especially in Somalia. Such were the status of agricultural labourers, the condition of the prisons, and the administration of justice.

The book of Lord Rennell of Rodd, " British Military Administration in Africa 1941-47," adds further details to those reproduced in the fore going ten pages. The following quotations* are drawn from Lord Rennell's account :

" Thanks to this hastily created force,† a degree of security prevailed throughout 1942 and 1943 which, though by no means perfect, had probably never been equalled in the history of the country in spite of the savage repression and punishments backed by large military and police establishments, which were the rule under the Italian regime.

" Throughout the period of British Military Administration under review no British officer lost his life at the hands of a Somali."

PRISON CONDITIONS DEPLORABLE: MUCH EVIDENCE OF BRUTALITY

" Prison conditions in Somalia were found to be deplorable in every way. Much evidence of brutality towards the native population was found, not only in the prisons, but by the Italian political and police officers all over the country The central prison at Mogadishu was put under the Commandant of the Gendarmerie, and the necessary reforms were instituted.

" The whole of the Italian provincial administration had disappeared, collapsed or been swept away during 1941. But the same general line was followed in Mogadishu as in Eritrea of maintaining in employment as much as usefully could be kept of the Italian civil service. It was, however, impossible to employ all.

" In spite of the number of Italian officers who had been closely associated with, and were believed to have enjoyed some esteem and influence among the Somali tribes, and had provided the personnel of the Italian Somali ' Banda' (irregular formations), few of them made any attempt to wage guerilla warfare or lead parties of Somalis. Such parties might have caused a great deal of trouble during the active military phase of the occupation in so vast a country where our political and police officers were few and far between. The early period of the occupation was full of rumours and stories of such bands, and of Italians who had taken to the bush. As time went on, most of the potential Italian guerilla leaders were accounted for as captured or killed, with only a few in hiding under assumed names. The alleged Somali loyalty to the Italian irregular leaders was as evanescent as a summer mist."

COUNTRY UNSUITED TO EUROPEAN OCCUPATION

" The problem of the Italian population in a country unsuitable for permanent European colonisation, and without any hill station or convalescent area when the Harrar Plateau was no longer available, was more one of morale than of political or even economic conditions. The unemployed male, and more especially the female and child population in the families, whose male elements were interned as civil or military prisoners, presented greater difficulties than in Eritrea, where a good deal of occupation and distraction and a congenial climate had made exile from the homeland supportable.

" In Somalia there was no known method of providing employment for everyone or a healthy climate for the sick and stale. There was in consequence a good deal of neurosis in all classes.

" It was decided to evacuate as many women and children and invalid men as possible in the third flight of Italian ships sent to fetch the balance of evacuees from Ethiopia in 1943. In July, 1943, some 2,300 persons were evacuated from and through Mogadishu by Italian steamers without mishap, in spite of the fact that embarkation took place during the monsoon season. A total Italian population of some 4,500 remained, and as a consequence of the evacuation, the number in receipt of public assistance at the end of 1943 fell to below 400."

---

* British Military Administration of occupied territories in Africa, during the years 1941-1947, by Lord Rennell of Rodd, His Majesty's Stationery Office, 1948.

† The Somalia Gendarmerie, see page 135, ibid.

"Some 900 Ethiopian political prisoners, interned by the Italians prior to March, 1941, in a beastly penal settlement at Danane, were sent home by motor transport convoys. One such convoy of 350 Ethiopians was conducted by a single British officer and a few Gendarmerie ranks, and handed over for dispersal to the British Political Officer at Diredawa.

SEVERE LABOUR POLICY
Indistinguishable from Slavery

"During the last thirty years of Italian occupation, considerable attempts had been made by the Italians, at first very largely on the initiative of H.R.H. The Duke of Abruzzi, a member of the Italian Royal Family, to develop modern agriculture by utilising the perennial waters of the Juba and Webbi Shebeli rivers. This initiative was strongly supported and extended under the Fascist Government in conformity with the policy of rendering Italy, with her colonial possessions, economically self-sufficient. Irrigated agriculture in several forms had been developed along the Webbi Shebeli at Afgoi, Genale and Vittoria, on the lower Juba, and in a substantial enterprise some forty miles from Mogadishu, named after its founder, Villagio Duca degli Abruzzi.

"But all these agricultural enterprises were run by, and for the benefit of, Italians, and depended on native labour being available to the Italian concessionaires.

"They were not essentially of the type of family farm-holdings which the Fascist Government had set up in extensive areas in Tripolitania, Cyrenaica, and, later, Ethiopia, where the Italian family was intended to be the sole labour unit working a peasant holding.

"The Villaggio Duca degli Abruzzi property was a concession managed and administered by the Italian employees of the company—the Italo-Somali Agricultural Company. In addition to some 16,000 acres under potential cultivation, the company owned quite extensive housing and mechanical equipment, including irrigation and pumping machinery, agricultural machinery, Decauville railway plant and a sugar mill with a theoretical capacity of several thousand tons a year."

"The Genale-Vittoria farm area was on the other hand a pump irrigation enterprise, with Italian colonists settled on plots and employing forced native labour on a minimum basic wage and with compulsory domicile. The Juba irrigated lands, depending on pump and gravity irrigation, were likewise settler-colonists enterprises dependent on native labour. During recent years these Italian agricultural enterprises had been turned over to producing crops, which were generally speaking uneconomic in world markets, but desirable from the point of view of an Italian metropolitan regime, which was involved in heavy military and other expenditure for which insufficient foreign exchange was available."

"The Somalia enterprises had been devoted to growing many sorts of crops for which they and the climate were not necessarily well suited, and which contributed little or nothing to a local balance in food production, either for the Italian or the native population. Much emphasis had, for instance, been placed on the production of cotton, oilseed, bananas, etc., and little on local grains and edible oils.

"Moreover, nothing much was done to stimulate native agriculture production. This was presumably because the large majority of the population was well content with a pastoral existence, which produced a fair quantity of skins, hides, gum, incense, etc., from the vegetation of the country, and the remainder was conscripted to work on Italian farms.

"The conception of these agricultural enterprises as 'exploitation concessions' engendered under the Fascist regime a labour policy of considerable severity in theory, and actual brutality in practice. It was, in fact, indistinguishable from slavery."

"Since it was obviously desirable to maintain as much cultivation as possible, the Military Administrator himself took over at once a large tract of land at Afgoi as a market garden to produce vegetables for the British community at Mogadishu, while at Villaggio Duca degli Abruzzi, a British Political officer took charge and with proper control of the Company's activities secured at last some continuity of cultivation; the production of sugar cane from the refinery was on a scale which from the outset nearly sufficed for local needs.

"In 1942, 3,650 acres under cultivation of the Società Agricola Italo-Somali estates were as to 88 per cent. under sugar cane. In the later period of occupation, sugar production was in fact stepped up to take care of all local needs. But the disappearance of native labour, the flight of Italian settlers to the nearest inhabited centres and a scarcity of petroleum products for the pumping machinery led to the initial abandonment of the whole Genale-Vittoria enterprise and most of the Juba farms.

DIFFICULT TO INDUCE LABOURERS TO RETURN

"In 1942 such steps as were possible were taken to reclaim at least some of the farms which had gone derelict. This involved not only inducing the Italian settlers to return to work, but also securing native labourers to work, under new conditions, for their old employees—an exceedingly difficult undertaking in any event, and more particularly so in dealing with Somalis. By 1942, 8,000 acres were, however, under cultivation as to 80 per cent. by natives as tenants of the Italian settlers.

"But it was not until 1943 that any real rehabilitation of the Italian agricultural enterprises, other than at Villaggio Duca degli Abruzzi, became possible. 1942 had seen growing scarcity in East Africa of primary agricultural products, including maize on which Somalia might have to depend for the normal deficiency in local production of the settled communities. At the beginning of 1943, the food shortage in East Africa generally had become really serious. It was, therefore, of paramount importance to make Somalia self-supporting. The Administration was accordingly directed to assume the financial risks involved in agricultural development, even when this was uneconomic.

"A policy of agricultural re-settlement, begun on the Juba in May, 1942, was extended to the Genale area. But whereas the Juba farmers had welcomed the agricultural policy of the Military Administration, those from Genale raised considerable objections, mainly on the grounds of inadequacy of capital and the derelict condition of the enterprises.

"The Administration intervened to assist in canal clearance and the provision of fuel oil for tractors and pumps. Cash advances were made for strictly farming activities."

"The Chief of the dominant local tribe was persuaded to provide native labour, on the understanding that his people were permitted to cultivate with the Administration's assistance a large area of land which had been alienated from them.

"90 per cent. of the native cultivation was in maize and the remainder in sesame. The tribesmen were also persuaded to agree to hand over to the Administration a portion of the yield from their cultivation in return for assistance in ploughing. On the Juba, native cultivation was also successfully encouraged in some areas on former Italian land, which had been abandoned, or could not be worked by Italians.

"At the end of 1942 only 1,120 acres out of a possible 4,000 were being worked. But by the end of 1943 most of the reasonably fertile Italian farms were in cultivation, under food crops, mainly maize, either by Italians or Somalis. The yield was much below expectations, mainly owing to the abnormal behaviour of the two rivers. Nevertheless, advances not recovered, but largely recoverable, amounted to only £29,000

The cost of production of food-stuffs under European cultivation was high, and in world markets, uneconomic, mainly owing to the high cost of petroleum products.

SOMALI LABOURERS DISAPPEARED

"With the defeat of the Italians and the commencement of the British occupation, all the native labour employed on the farms, except at Villaggio Duca degli Abruzzi, disappeared, and in the latter was so drastically reduced that the acreage which could be cultivated had to be severely curtailed,

A notorious Italian punishment employed in Italy by the fascists against their political opponents, and exported to the African Empire.

The victim is tied to a motor lorry, which is set going at full speed till the body of the prisoner is broken up.

One of the many photographs taken by the Italians themselves, and later discovered at the time of their defeat in 1941.

Italian armed labour battalion in Mogadishu marching to their daily work. Photograph reproduced from Lavoro Italiano nell'Impero, by Davide Fossa (A. Mondadori, Milan).

Italian armed labour battalion parading before the Viceroy at Mogadishu —from Lavoro Italiano nell'Impero, by Davide Fossa (A. Mondadori, Milan)

CONDITIONS IN DANANE CAMP, ITALIAN SOMALILAND

The following extracts are drawn from Documents on Italian War Crimes, submitted to the United Nations War Crimes Commission by the Imperial Ethiopian Government, Vol. 1. (Ministry of Justice, Addis Ababa, 1949.)

Extract from an Affidavit Made by Blatta Bekele Hapte Michael, Judge at the High Court of Ethiopia, Addis Ababa

(Translated from the Amharic)

8. When we arrived at Mogadishu we were put directly into the central prison there, and next morning we were taken to Danane. There we were put among 200 war prisoners, who were captured on Ras Desta's front. The Italian commander who brought us from Mogadishu handed us over to the commander of the Danane prison camp. We assumed that they were going to put us among the captives, but contrary to our expectations we were put among criminal murderers. The food which the Italians gave us was very bad for our health. The food was rotten biscuits with many worms in them and we also got tea or coffee alternatively.

As we were not accustomed to what they used to give us for food we all became sick because of unsuitable food. When we were imprisoned in the criminal jail, the commander of the jail was Brigadier Leyopadel Baroni. We repeatedly complained to him about the food, but he said he could not do anything about it, because it was ordered by his superiors. Even if we possessed a small amount of money we were forbidden to buy any kind of food from the neighbourhood.

9. Soon after the attempt on Graziani's life the Italians brought about a thousand Ethiopians to Danane and confined them in the concentration camp specially prepared for the confinement of Ethiopians near the criminal prison where we were imprisoned. Before the said thousand Ethiopians came, the concentration camp was occupied by sixty Ethiopians, who were brought from Harar and Addis Ababa; and we were also taken out of the criminal prison camp and put in confinement with them. Afterwards we were put with the rest of the confined Ethiopians. The food conditions were even worse than before. As I mentioned above we were about a thousand Ethiopians, who were confined in that camp; and because of the lack of sufficient latrines, the filthy conditions and the lack of suitable food in the camp, many persons got sick, and the death rate was four to five persons daily.

10. When relatives were ill in the prison camp, wives were forbidden to nurse their husbands, and the husbands to nurse their wives, and relatives to nurse a relative.

Extract from an affidavit made by Michael Tessema, employee at the Ministry of Justice, Addis Ababa (translated from the Amharic)

(9) I stayed three years and three months in Danane prison. The conditions in this prison were as follows :

(a) Three prisoners used to live in a little tent provided for one soldier. The prisoners were not given any kind of cloth, blanket or carpet to sleep on.

(b) At first, the food was four hard biscuits (Galete) in a day.

(c) As we used to drink sea water, the daily death rate was between six and thirty persons, who died from dysentery. A total of 3,175 persons died. I was able to know this, because while I was a prisoner myself there, I was given a job as a medical assistant, and so records of the sick persons and obituary notes were kept by me. Up to the end, the Italian authorities never provided potable water to Danane prisoners.

(d) From 6,500 persons, who were at Danane, 3,175 died. The reason why not all of them perished was because the prisoners used to receive some money from their relatives and bought 'acqua minerale' which was brought from Italy in sealed bottles, and churned milk from Somalia. For food, after about a year, we were given bread, macaroni, rice, tea and meat once a week. For the sick ones there was also some improvement. The administrator of the Danane prison was Colonel Mazeketi. The paymaster was Captain Rossi and the medical officer was Captain Antonio. I cannot recollect the other names, but the staff included a total of about sixty Europeans.

(e) From among the Italians who were there, Brigadier Baroni, Sergeant Tosato, and a marshal of carabinieri, whose name I have forgotten, used to whip prisoners, saying that the prisoners did not salute them, or that they did not work hard enough. The sort of work which the prisoners used to do, was to clean away dirt, to go to a place called Ganale* and work in the garden, to collect and fetch firewood and build roads.

(f) Those females and males who were tired and refused to work were tied by their hands behind their backs and hanged on the wall for seven days without their feet touching the ground. Because of this cause, the arms of two persons swelled up and were amputated.

(g) When prisoners became very sick, Captain Antonio used to say it is better for them to die and killed them by giving them injections of arsenic and strychnine. Also when some of them came for treatment, he used to tie them down by force and perform operations against their will.

---

* See references to Ganale in extracts from, " The First to be Freed," Chapter XV.

XIV

BRITISH MILITARY ADMINISTRATION AND SOMALI ASPIRATIONS

British Commonwealth forces had been welcomed as liberators by the Somali people; the Italian slave-drivers had fled, the prisons were opened. But the situation could not remain static; a new era of liberty and progress had been promised, hopes of self-government had been unleashed; either these hopes and promises must be realised, or the glamour of victory would fade to frustration.

A detailed description of British Military Administration in the former Italian territories in Africa, has been given by Lord Rennell of Rodd in the semi-official work, " British Military Administration of occupied territories in Africa during the years 1941-47," * which was prepared by permission of the Army Council. The " conclusions, inferences and opinions " contained in it are those of Lord Rennell, but the facts concerning the machinery and personnel of the British ·administrations in the various territories are given from official sources. Lord Rennell's official position in relation to these territories enables him to describe with authority the principles and motives which directed them.

We learn from him of the decision of the British War Cabinet, on February 20, 1941, "that the War Office must be responsible for the Italian territories conquered and occupied by British troops because the Foreign Office was not suitably equipped," and " if the Colonial office were in charge of any enemy territories, we should be suspected of seeking to incorporate them in our Empire."

Lord Wavell (General Wavell, as he was then) was informed of the decision on February 23, and at the same time a section of the Directorate of Military Operations called M.O.11 was created in the War Office to deal with Military Government   A

---

* British Military Administration in Africa, 1941-7, by Lord Rennell of Rodd (His Majesty's Stationery Office).

Financial Department, the F.5, was established to deal with economic questions concerning the occupied territories, including finance and currency. The War Office, with the world war to win, was facing its greatest task of all time. The Lord Privy Seal had written on February 19, "the War Office will need the help of several other Government Departments." "A Standing Inter-Departmental Committee on the Administration of Occupied Enemy Territory" was formed on March 26, the India Office and the Colonial Office being included. Officials drawn from these services, and particularly from the British Colonial territories in East Africa, were appointed to administer the occupied Italian territories. Many of these Colonial officials had had military experience; the personnel of the two services were always closely related.

Sir Philip F. Mitchell, Governor of Uganda till the outbreak of war, and Deputy Chairman of the East African Governors' Conference, was appointed Chief Political Officer to advise the Commander-in-Chief Middle East, and to organise the administration of the conquered territories. Sir Philip Mitchell had served during the first World War in the East African Campaign against Germany; he had occupied an official position in the administration of the former German Colony of Tanganyika, when it was governed as occupied enemy territory, and had seen it pass to the position of British territory under Mandate from the League of Nations. Mr. (subsequently Sir) R. Hone, Attorney-General of Uganda, was appointed Chief Legal advisor. Major-General the Hon. Francis Rodd, subsequently Lord Rennell of Rodd, and the author of the volume under reference, was made controller of finance. He had had experience of administration in Syria in 1918, in the Diplomatic Service from 1918-1924, in the Bank of England, and as Manager of the Bank of International Settlement. These three gentlemen were all given military rank, and subsequently all received the title of Major-General.

The remarkably swift advance of British forces into the Somaliland colony had not been foreseen. The Military Plan of Campaign was only to occupy Jubaland in the early months of 1941, with a possible thrust as far as Mogadishu before the summer rains. Therefore, Sir Philip Mitchell appointed only a small staff to assist Mr. W. E. H. Scupham, the Administrative Secretary of Tanganyika, whom he now appointed Deputy Chief Political Officer for Somaliland. It was intended for some time to administer from Nairobi the small part of the Italian colony which it was hoped might be occupied in the spring, and to set up only a provincial branch office at Kismayu.

British forces having reached Mogadishu on February 25, and the entire Somaliland colony, from the Juba in the South, to Cape Guardafui in the extreme North, having fallen swiftly into British hands, the scheme for its administration had perforce to be expanded. Moreover, the fleeing Italians had vacated the Ethiopian Ogaden and the British Somaliland Protectorate had also been re-taken by March 24.

The whole vast area of Somaliland, with the exception of the small French colony, was now under British control.

Those lands have a romantic charm—an ever-changing landscape, the earth itself black, or brown in some areas, in others, for great distances, a splendid red, an opulent hue, recalling, but richer and ruddier, above all under that powerful sunlight, the rocks at Plymouth Hoe, a wonderful setting for birds of all imaginable colours, for flaming cacti, for shrubs, leafless but laden with brilliant yellow or pink-white blossoms. Here and there the way lies through fine green foliage. There is the area of the extinct volcanoes, numbers and numbers of them; one can see still their dried-up streams of lava fanning out like fringes of stone seaweed, the later eruptions crossing the earlier with intricacies of patterning now fixed in stone. Or one passes into a strange pale fairyland of miniature trees, decked-out with spiky fruit, cold, purple-gray and white. With the bare ground almost devoid of grey-green grass, they seem like decorated Christmas trees, despite the heat.

There is life everywhere, herds of goats, dainty and slender, reaching to nibble the branches, flocks of sheep browsing on scanty herbage, occasionally a Somali tribe with their camels, the men wearing long robes and turbans, the slender women draped in their many coloured muslins. For those who look deeper there is much of pathos; these people are leading spare, hard lives, always wandering for a bare sustenance for themselves and their herds.

Burton, the enthusiastic traveller and lover of men, and other enthusiasts for the ancient cultures, have found much to learn from these nomads, their devout Muslim faith, attuned to the desert, their poets whose verse graces weddings and victories, their schools of poetry, bards, famous and esteemed. Their songs, their stories and legends, their games, dances, festivals have attracted students from the western life of towns so largely stereotyped and commercialised. The vigorous Dibaltiq, a song and dance on horseback given in honour of some personage, one of their own chiefs or a British officer who seated in a chair with his retinue around him hears his praises sung by Somali warriors, is typical.

This great wilderness with its life of riding is irresistible to many; it has endless resources for the naturalist and the hunter; lion, leopard, rhinoceros, and elephant are there still, though the great shots with fine European guns have played great havoc with them, giraffe, buffalo, zebra, wart-hog, an amazing fellow with those humorous curled tusks, baboons, monkeys—their human appearance deterring more tender-hearted hunters—antelopes innumerable, from the Koodoo, thirteen hands high and the swift, glossy hartebeest, to the delicate klipspringer, and the tiny dik-dik, weighing less than an English hare, ostriches, eagles, vultures, great storks with yellow bills, four feet high. There are birds, too, for the pot, guineafowl, partridges, grouse and the rare bustard.

Great Somaliland

The idea of a great Somaliland, administered entirely as a British protectorate, had long been entertained in certain British official circles.

The campaign against the Mullah, who had so often escaped across the Italian frontier, where he could not be followed until Italian government permission had been obtained—in each case too late—was irksome to the British command. Escape across the frontier was the natural impulse of any law-breaker. A single administration would destroy that means of escaping the law. Cattle raiding was the most prevalent form of law-breaking in that area where cattle are the main source of wealth. The British administration believed they could deal more effectively with this offence if the whole Somali area were under their control.

Moreover, it was commonly considered by British administrators that British administration is the best existing, and that all the Somalilands would benefit by coming under the same rule as the British Somaliland Protectorate, which had changed little since the protectorate was established. British rule there did not involve any large-scale confiscation of land, only sufficient for the bare needs of the administration, or any substantial changes in the way of life which had existed for centuries before the British advent; to maintain order, to punish law-breakers, to protect the territory against invasion were conceived to be the main duty of the protecting power, though historically this had not always been accomplished. As we have seen, the hinterland had been evacuated in face of the Mullah and the entire territory had been speedily lost to the Italians in 1940.

For much of the period of British administration, there had not been a single government school. In 1938, Lord Rennell informs us on page 479 of his book, the Director of Education was stoned out of the only existing government school. The people were mainly illiterate, there was no bank, the territory was held at a loss, and was dependent on a subsidy from the British Exchequer. The native-produced exports were such as they had been for centuries, mainly hides and gums. The commerce through the ports had declined seriously after the Emperor Menelik II of Ethiopia inaugurated that modern innovation, the Franco-Ethiopian railway, which diverted Ethiopian trade to the port of Jibuti in the French colony. The Ethiopian trade had been the main source of prosperity for the protectorate, where all remained static and no effort to open up new sources of development was attempted. The last Report of the Governor of the Protectorate issued before World War II, stated that there was not a single hotel, and that the only all-weather road was that which had been made to the Ethiopian frontier, in conformity with the " Gentlemen's Agreement " with Italy following the Italian occupation of Ethiopia.

On the other hand, there was high financial probity among the British officials, who were zealous in training the Somali Camel Corps, of whose smartness on parade and obedience to orders they were particularly proud, and also the armed police, called Illaloes.

Lord Rennell in one of the Press controversies which raged after the second World War concerning the future of the Somalilands, expressed the desire for a great Somaliland wherein the Somali would forever "roam and hunt and fight." This yearning to hold back the processes of evolution is far from being shared by the young Somali; it can find support only among a fast dwindling section of old folk in Somalia as elsewhere.

<h2 style="text-align:center">Anglo-Ethiopian Agreement 1942
permits
Temporary British Administration of Great Somalia</h2>

The United Kingdom Government in London and the British Military Officials in East Africa were insistent to retain British Military Administration of the large area of Ethiopian Somaliland when the rest of the country returned to Ethiopian self-government. The World War was still raging, the French colony with Jibuti was still held by the German dominated Vichy administration of Pétain and Laval; its frontier with Ethiopia must be held, its coast was subject to blockade. British negotiators urged that to facilitate transference of men and arms between the Red Sea and the Indian Ocean, the Military Command must hold not only the British and Italian territories on both coasts but the Ethiopian Ogaden which lay between.

The negotiations which finally resulted in the Anglo-Ethiopian Agreement and Military convention of January 31, 1942, whereby the British Government terminated the "occupied enemy territory administration" of Ethiopia and handed the government back to the Emperor, were greatly protracted by this British demand, which the Ethiopians finally conceded with much reluctance, in response to the British plea of War strategy, in the following terms:—

ARTICLE V

"His Majesty the Emperor agrees that the part of the territory of the Ogaden which was included in the former Italian Colonial Government of Somalia shall, during the currency of this convention, remain under British Military Administration of Somalia."

The reserved areas were defined by a schedule attached to the Military Convention:

SCHEDULE

1. A continuous belt of Ethiopian territory 25 miles wide contiguous to the frontier of French Somaliland running from the frontier of Eritrea to the Franco-Ethiopian Railway. Thence South-west along the railways to the bridge at Haraua. Thence South and South-east, excluding Gildessa, to the North-east extremity of the Garais Mountains, and along the crest of the ridge of these mountains to their intersection of the former Italian Colony of Somaliland. Thence along the frontier to its junction with the frontier of British Somaliland.

2. All land within Ethiopia occupied by the Franco-Ethiopian Railway and its appurtenances.

The reserved area, it will be observed, included Ethiopia's one railway and the adjacent land, extending from the French colony to Addis Ababa. It included also the important railway town, Dire

Dawa* built by the French technicians of the Jibuti-Addis Ababa railway in the time of Menelik II. Posted on the walls there, the order of the former Italian Invaders, "out of bounds for natives," was still seen two years later under British Military Administration.

How obtuse in such matters we British often proved in dealing with our gallant Allies of Ethiopia, whose assistance in the battlefield had been vital but a few months before!

"The Cantonments and Reserved Areas were in practice restricted in number and scope to a greater extent than was at one time anticipated," says Lord Rennell. †

Nevertheless, on February 25, 1942, in fact 25 days after the signing of the Anglo-Ethiopian Agreement with the long and hardly negotiated acceptance of the British Military Occupation of the Ogaden and Reserved Area, General Platt issued a "Reserved Areas Notice," whereby he added further reserved areas under British Military Administration, viz.: Addis Ababa, Adama, Jimma, Hawash, Gondar, Dire Dawa, Debat, Harar, Adi Arcai, Adowa, Dalle, Adigrat, Neghelli, Quiha, Yavello, Gombolsha, Mega, Sardo, Mojo. These towns—the main urban centres of Ethiopia—were termed "British Cantonments." So long as they were "reserved areas," they were regarded as "occupied enemy territory." All legislative, executive, administrative and judicial powers there remained outside the sovereignty of the Emperor and were vested in the British General Officer Commanding in Chief (General Platt), who now delegated his powers to the Chief Political Officer, Sir Philip Mitchell.

This occupation of many important administrative centres, particularly the capital, Addis Ababa, and the important towns of Harar and Dire Dawa, presented many difficulties, but with the exception of Dire Dawa they were restored to Ethiopian administration before the termination of the Anglo-Ethiopian Agreement, 1942.

It is useful to depart here from the chronological order of events in the Somalilands to explain that the Ogaden was retained under British Military Administration after the expiration of the Anglo-Ethiopian Agreement, and in fact, until after the conclusion of the World War.

---

* It is of interest to observe that the Foreign Office at that time endeavoured to preserve also the new boundary the Italians had established for their colony of Eritrea, which took in a considerable portion of the Ethiopian Province of the Tigre, moving the boundary South from the Mareb to the Takazzee, and including the historic Ethiopian towns of Axum, Adowa and Makalle. This proposal could not be carried into effect, owing to strong resistance on the Ethiopian side. Nevertheless, the project was pressed by British negotiators for some time. Official instructions to British Officials on the spot, which Lord Rennell has been permitted to publish, suggested that the various new provincial boundaries created by the Italians might conveniently be retained on account of the administrative machinery, office files, and what not, which had for some years been established on that basis. There was, however, a difference of emphasis regarding the external boundaries.

† British Military Administration in Africa, 1941-7, page 194.

Anglo-Ethiopian Agreement, 1944, Prolongs British Administration but Safeguards Ethiopian Sovereignty in the Ogaden

On December 9, 1944, a further Anglo-Ethiopian Agreement was signed, which restored the town of Dire Dawa to Ethiopian Administration. It also provided for the British evacuation of the Jibuti-Addis Ababa railway when the Ethiopian Government had made satisfactory arrangements for running it, which, in fact, meant, and was intended to mean, the restoration of the Franco-Ethiopian railway company.

Article VII safeguarded Ethiopian sovereignty in the Ogaden in a clause drafted by Lord De La Warr, leader of the British delegation, when the negotiations were on the point of breaking down owing to Ethiopian resistance to the British demand to prolong their occupation of the Ogaden.

Article VII

" In order as an Ally to contribute to the effective prosecution of the war, and without prejudice to their underlying sovereignty, the Imperial Ethiopian Government hereby agree that, for the duration of this Agreement, the territories designated as the Reserved Area and the Ogaden, as set forth in the attached schedule, shall be under British Military Administration."

The Agreement further provided that on all Government buildings in the Ogaden, the British and Ethiopian flags must be flown ; on the other hand the Agreement completely excluded the Ethiopian authorities from the area under British control.

The Schedule attached to the 1944 Agreement was exceedingly elaborate, so meticulously indeed was the boundary of the territory to remain under British Administration defined that British officials in Addis Ababa at the time declared the United Kingdom Government intended British Administration of the area to become permanent; it would never be relinquished. Lord De La Warr, however, held otherwise; he stated his conviction to the present writer at the time that the Ogaden would be restored to Ethiopia. He also believed Ethiopia would regain her lost province, Eritrea.

SCHEDULE.

" 1. Reserved Area.

" A continuous belt of Ethiopian territory bounded by a line starting at the point where the French Somaliland and British Somaliland boundaries meet, thence in a westerly direction along the French Somaliland boundary to the point where it cuts the Franco-Ethiopian railway, thence along the eastern limit of the railway zone, in a south-westerly direction as far as the railway bridge at Haraua, thence in a south-easterly direction to the gorge of the Hullo River, thence following the Hullo River bed to a point at Haramakale, where it is crossed by the Dire Dawa-Jibuti motor road at 45 km. from Dire Dawa, thence in a south-easterly direction to the summit of Burta Amare, thence to the south-western summit of Gara Okhaya, thence to the north-eastern summit of Dagale, thence to the summit of Gara Digli, thence in a direct line to the summit of Mount Goreis, thence along the crest of the Goreis range to the top of the Marda Pass, thence following along the crest of the Goreis range over the following summits: Burfik, Boledit, Burkulul, Dibba, Hagogani, Nig Niga, Kabalkabat, Dandi, Karabedi, Konyo and Adadi, until it intercepts the ninth parallel of latitude at a point approximately three miles south of Burta Adadi, thence due eastward along the ninth parallel of latitude to the point where it meets the British Somaliland boundary, thence following the British Somaliland boundary in a north-westerly direction to the starting point.

· Note.—Map Reference; East Africa 1; 500,000 leaf, No. 552.

" 2. Ogaden.

"The area of Ethiopia which is at present being administered by the British Military Administration of Somalia."

Thus the entire area of the Somalilands from Red Sea to Indian Ocean, was to remain, for some time at least, under British Military Government.

How were these vast lands administered? The table below indicates the bald framework of the departments and their direction, as they had been developed up to December 31, 1945, nearly four years after British Military Administration was established throughout these areas.

The Somalilands Under British Military Administration

CIVIL AFFAIRS ORGANISATION CHART, as at 31st December, 1945.
General Officer Commanding East Africa Command
Chief Civil Affairs Staff Office
Civil Affairs Branch, Nairobi (21)
Locust Control Pool (12)

BRITISH SOMALILAND	SOMALIA	RESERVED AREAS OF ETHIOPIA
HQ (Hargeisa) (11)	HQ (Mogadishu) (7)	HQ (Dire Dawa) (3)
District Administration	*Provincial Administration*	*District Administration*
Berbera (1)	Ogaden (5)	Jigjiga (2)
Burao (2)	Upper Juba (6)	Dire Dawa (1)
Erigavo (1)	Mijjertein (5)	
Hargeisa (3)	Mudugh (5)	
Borama/Zeilah (1)	Benadir (12)	
Las Anod (1)		

	Departments	*Departments*	*Departments*
Finance, Revenue & A/cs.	(8)	(17)	(1)
Customs and Excise	—	—	—
Trade and Supplies	(2)	(with Transport)	—
Education	(3)	(3)	—
Legal	(4)	(3)	—
Agriculture	(5)	(3)	—
Printing and Information	—	(1)	—
Veterinary	(1)	(2)	—
Medical and Public Health	(13)	(11)	—
Public Works	(5)	(9)	—
Labour	—	—	—
Transport (Road and Rail)	—	(5)	—
Ports, Lights and Marine	—	—	—
Post and Telegraphs	(1)	(6)	(1)
Custody of Enemy Property	—	(1)	—
Antiquities	—	—	—
Survey	(1)		
	Police (16)	Somalia Gendarmerie (86) (86)	*Police* (4)
Total War Establishment	138	322	17
Total strength	95	223	15

(Figures on the chart in brackets, thus ( ), show actual strength and deployment of *officers* only).

At the first glance it will be observed that the number of officers was extremely small, particularly in the Reserved Area of Ethiopia, where there was a total of only 17 officers though the important towns of Dire Dawa and Jigjiga were included in this area. As the Administration was a Military one every British official, medical practitioner, teacher or technician would be given military rank. The full number of all such persons is therefore comprised in the figures given in the table, which is reproduced from the book of Lord Rennell, " British Military Administration in Africa 1941-7," and is based on official War Office information.

It will be noticed that in the Reserved Area of Ethiopia the only departments of Government were those of finance, posts and telegraphs (mainly for official use) and police. Education and Public Health, Public Works, Agriculture, Veterinary, Transport, Labour, Law, Information, Trade, which to-day are almost everywhere held to be normally and necessarily within the scope of Government, were absent in the part of Ethiopia under British Military control.

The General Officer Commanding the troops in East Africa, as indicated on the table, was responsible for the military control and defence of the entire area. He was also Governor of the British Somaliland Protectorate. Brigadier A. R. Chater, of the Royal Marines, who had commanded the Somaliland Camel Corps in the Protectorate before the war, was appointed to this post in April, 1941. He established his headquarters at the port of Hargeisa in the British Protectorate. He was responsible to Sir Philip Mitchell, the Chief Political Officer of the Commander-in-Chief, whose headquarters were in Nairobi, for the Civil Administration of British Somaliland. For the Military control of all the Somalilands he was responsible to the General Officer Commanding East Africa*, at that time General Cunningham.

Ex-Italian Somaliland and Ogaden Administered Together

Ex-Italian Somaliland and the Ethiopian Ogaden were placed under the same administration. The Italians had made one province of their former Somaliland colony and the Ethiopian Ogaden and had administered them together under the designation Somalia. This procedure was followed by the British Administration under the general instruction issued in January, 1941, by the Chief Political Officer, Sir Philip Mitchell, with the agreement of the Government in London—it followed the lines of Italian provincial administration. To follow the plan of the brief 5 years Italian usurpation, disregarding the pre-war boundaries, was a curious procedure, which regarded in retrospect and from an independent view, would be difficult to defend.

Public Order

The King's African Rifles and the Somaliland Camel Corps were under the military command of Brigadier Chater for the whole

---

* This arrangement continued until 1948 when the Somaliland Protectorate was restored to Colonial Office administration.

of the Somalilands. Internal public order in the British Somaliland Protectorate was in part confided to the Camel Corps, which in pre-war times and now for some years onward, performed both military and police functions. There were also Somaliland irregulars, Somaliland Scouts, and armed police called Illaloes, who later were equipped with armoured vehicles. The King's African Rifles and Camel Corps had the duty of defending the whole of Somaliland from sea to sea. With the Illaloes and the Somaliland Scouts they were also used at times for purposes of internal order in all the Somalilands. In addition to their work in the British Protectorate, they operated particularly in the Reserved Area of Ethiopia, but they were also used at times in the Ogaden and the former Italian Colony.

The Ogaden and the former Italian Colony, as explained above, were administered from Mogadishu as a single province. As in the case of the Reserved Area of Ethiopia the administration of the Ogaden was of a rudimentary order.

The Ogaden and the ex-Italian Somaliland Colony were policed by the Somalia Gendarmerie.

As the table on page 154 indicates, the British members of the Administration, in other words the educated, trained and qualified members of the British Military Administration of the vast Somaliland area were excessively few. Lord Rennell records: " In 1943 the total officer strength of the Administration, including the Somalia Gendarmerie, was 177. In 1944 matters improved somewhat, and the figure rose to 219, but by the end of the year the staff position had again become ' most serious '."

Popular Disappointment

The first task of the British Military Administration, which took over the Somaliland territories at the time of the Italian defeat, is stated by Lord Rennell as follows:

" It was first of all necessary to make clear to the disorientated populations who had lost their government, that another was there at hand, and ready to take its place."

The British War Cabinet now decided that despite the promises made during the hostilities, the future of the conquered Italian colonies should not be determined till after the war.

" *Italian law and regulations, territorial and municipal,*" *would be in the meantime retained* " *as far as possible,*" *and if Italian Judges and Magistrates were* " *willing to remain in office,*" *they should be* " *permitted to function, with such safeguards as might appear desirable.*"

Operating under these stipulations, the British Military Administration could not in any event have satisfied the ardent desire for self-government and reform which was surging among the Somalis of the Italian Colony. Conditions, as they were found by the British forces who entered the Colony, have been extensively described by the British Ministry of Information pamphlet, " The First to be Freed," and by Lord Rennell's "British Military Administration in Africa, 1941-7," both published by His Majesty's Stationery Office. Important extracts from these works are reproduced in Chapter XV.

It is stated in "The First to be Freed" that among the Somalis "there was danger of a Jehad," which seems to indicate a fear on the part of the Administration that the people of the Somaliland Colony and the adjacent Ogaden might take steps to realise for themselves and by their own efforts the freedom talked of on the radio. "Everywhere," says "The First to be Freed," "the advent of the British is welcomed, but that is not to say that the Somalis are prepared to obey our orders."

A large number of rifles and light automatic weapons had been abandoned by the Italians all over the country, moreover they had had ammunition dumps as reserve depots hidden in the bush, of which the Somalis were aware. The "Banda," whom the Italians had enlisted as irregular soldiers, were also in possession of arms, and, according to Lord Rennell, "remained together as raiding bands, seeking whom they might devour." In Mogadishu, says "The First to be Freed," "security suffered less from the turbulence of the Somalis, than from the inefficiency and extreme Fascism of the Italian police." Their unreliability and indiscipline caused the decision to disband and intern them as prisoners of war, and to form a Somali Gendarmerie to replace them. A hundred Tanganyika native police formed the nucleus of the urban division of the new force, with the 1st and 2nd Irregular Companies of Somalis, who had been trained for the war by British officers under General Cunningham. Some assistance on the line of communications with Harar was given by detachments of the King's African Rifles, for a short period. In April, the Gendarmerie, with the addition of some casual recruits, numbered 1,300, with no more than fifteen British officers. The force was sent out to the task of disarming the population without preliminary police training. By the end of August, 1941, they had collected 14,000 Italian rifles and 6,000,000 rounds of ammunition. By the close of 1943 the force numbered 3,070 Somali and African ranks and 120 British officers. The Gendarmerie had now the task, not only of maintaining order in the vast territory, but also of defending it against "possible Japanese invasion." British Commonwealth forces having been withdrawn for war service elsewhere, only a small mobile field force was retained for all the Somalilands, the British Protectorate, the Ethiopian Ogaden and the former Italian Colony. This military force was under the command of the Governor of the British Somaliland Protectorate, who was also termed "Officer Commanding the troops in Somaliland."

The officers of the British Military Administration became exceedingly proud of their "Somali Gendarmerie," their intelligence, "smartness on parade" and keen attention to orders. Lord Rennell declares:

"Thanks to this hastily created force, a degree of security prevailed throughout 1942 and 1943, which, though by no means perfect, had probably never been equalled in the history of the country in spite of the savage repression and punishments backed by large military and police establishments which were the rule under the Italian regime."

Nevertheless the hasty recruitment of the Gendarmerie, the use of forces brought in from other parts of Africa who did not know the language of the population, the lack of "training, and scanty supervision by experienced officers, undoubtedly created difficulties and abuses." Confusion arose from the use of five languages by the Gendarmerie, Somali, Swahili, Italian, Arabic and Chinyanja.

"The First to be Freed" states:—

"*It was realised from the first that the Administration had neither the time nor the means to create a fully trained police, such as existed in neighbouring British territories.*"

The same official publication adds:

"*The first hundred men had to be recruited from Mogadishu gaol. The subsequent behaviour of some of them proved that their imprisonment had not in all cases served merely a political purpose; they were familiar enough with Somali looting but less so with loyalty or esprit de corps. Once when a guard was placed on the Italian police garage, a patrol found donkey carts drawn up at 3 a.m. in front of the building, large-scale looting taking place, and the gendarmerie assisting their friends to load the carts.*"

In the evidence of the British Administration before the Four Power Commission of Investigation it was stated that the Italians had destroyed the prison records. The compiler of the Ministry of Information Pamphlet, "The First to be Freed," considered "no proper records had been kept." He adds: "Undoubtedly some genuine criminals were released; it was better to err on the side of generosity." One may agree to that wholeheartedly, but in the absence of reliable records it would seem rash and even naïve to enlist the armed police force among the prison population!

"The First to be Freed" declares that such misdeeds of the Gendarmerie, as above recorded, "did not continue long. Undesirables were quickly weeded out; the arrival of 500 Nyasas and 40 Uganda police raised the standard, and before long the force was doing useful work."

An effort was made to overcome linguistic difficulties by concentrating on Italian and Swahili, but this proved inconvenient, and the decision was made to teach English to all the Gendarmerie. This proved popular and effective. Enterprising young men were eager to enlist in order to profit by the instruction in reading and writing, which was given along with English and other subjects, as five months preliminary training was now provided for all new entrants, together with other educational opportunities. When the Gendarmerie was first constituted, recruits were drawn as far as possible, from all the tribes, but later the Darot tribe appeared to have predominated, which resulted in a tendency to antagonism on the part of other tribes. This became more noticeable when political parties were formed shortly after the visit of the Four Power Commission of Investigation was announced. It would hardly have been possible to avoid some resentment towards the new Gendarmerie on the part of men who had been employed in the " Banda " and other native forces of Italy, if they were refused admission to the Gendarmerie, and were now unemployed and poverty-stricken. The policy of the Administration tended to exclude them, on the ground, stated in " The First to be Freed," that " men who had served for any length of time under the Italians were idle, dirty and undisciplined." In fact they had frequently been employed for raids against the people of the Ogaden and other parts of Ethiopia, and encouraged to looting and terrorism.

Collective Punishments

The system of collective punishment, under which the whole tribe is punished by seizure of its cattle and destruction of its dwellings on account of some theft or act of violence by one or more of its members, has remained since the early days of Colonisation. It is an anachronism which has long outlived its time. It is regarded with horror in Ethiopia, where the law punishes the individual offender for his own misdeeds, not his neighbours or tribesmen. Fines of five hundred or more camels may have a gravely impoverishing effect on a tribe. Lord Rennell mentions a fine of 1,700 camels[*]

The employment of the Gendarmerie in collective punishments, including picketing of the wells, tended to cause the force and its members to be disliked, as was evident in some localities when the Four Power Commission of Investigation made their enquiries in 1948. The employment of the Somali Gendarmerie, in conjunction with the Somaliland Camel Corps from the British Protectorate, in the imposition of collective punishments and the officially termed " sweeps " for arms, which continued for a number of years, caused the members of the force to be distrusted. The Somali Youth League, an organisation originated by progressive young Somalis, which is dealt with more fully in a subsequent chapter, was largely an outgrowth of the Somalia Gendarmerie. Whereas in Eritrea the police were forbidden to join political parties or to express political opinions, the British Military Administration of Somaliland made no such restriction. The Somali Youth League was approved by the Administration and so large a proportion of the Gendarmerie belonged to it that the two organisations were declared by many to be synonymous.

The Four Power Commission of Investigation were told at Afgoy: "The people who make things shameful for the British are the Somali Youth League." Throughout the territory two

---

[*] British Military Administration in Africa, page 180. "1,700 camels were duly collected, the individual offenders punished and a large collective fine imposed."

complaints were made to the Commission: the imposition of forced labour in the time of Italian rule, and intimidation and violence by the Gendarmerie and Somali Youth League since the Italian defeat. At Buracaba representatives of the Elai tribe told the Commission, "We do not want the Italians back; they took us as slaves" They were unanimous in opposition to the return of the Italians, but equally opposed to the Somali Youth League and the Gendarmerie, whom they declared belonged to the League. Some suggested that if the Askaris were better paid they would not disturb the people.

The decision to treat as Occupied Enemy Territory the ex-colonies, whose inhabitants had been promised liberation, profoundly affected the populations of all these areas. They had to share the disabilities and restrictions imposed upon their former masters, who had treated them so ill, and in whose downfall they had played their part.

The requisitioning of cattle for the use of the military without effecting payment, the methods employed in disarming the population, the dismantling of Italian industrial plant which caused unemployment among the Somali people, the removal of agricultural machinery which imposed a check on the desire of Somali agriculturalists to increase food production, the fixing of the Italian lire at 480 to the £ sterling, were felt as unmerited hardships. The colony was conquered enemy territory; it was considered just in London that the enemy should be made to contribute to the needs of the nations whom they had wantonly attacked; but the Somali population, who had welcomed and assisted as far as they could the allied forces, did not feel that they also should be obliged to suffer.

In June, 1942, a Public Works organisation was established in the colony; its first task, as stated by Lord Rennell,* was to rehabilitate operational airfields and to dismantle materials required for other theatres of war.

"*This included the dismantling and removal of oil storage plant, an oil-seed crushing plant at Mogadishu, 4,500 tons of Decauville material, seventy miles of narrow-gauge railway track; five Diesel locomotives, rail-cars, coaches, etc., for use in the Middle East. In the following year machinery of all sorts, including electric generating plant, lighters and cable, were removed from the elaborate salt works at Dante (Ras Hafun), near Cape Guardafui —also for military use in other theatres in connection with the Arabian long-distance air route to India.*"*

Lord Rennell added:

"*The Tosi-Marelli power plants from Hordio, near Dante, were put into use in Kenya. Numerous workshops were equipped with electric motor and power-driven tools from the salt works; speed boats, a tug and surplus oil and cargo-lighters were distri-*

---

* British Military Administration in Africa 1941-7, by Lord Rennell of Rodd, pages 169-170.

buted among R.A.F. installations, squadrons, the Royal Navy, and harbour construction at Kilindini. 1,000 tons of Diesel fuel were removed for naval use, and the oil storage installations at Mogadishu were dismantled for re-erection as forward operational storage in the Middle East."*

" The Administration was able to spare eighty-six tractors from Somalia for military and civil (agricultural) use in Kenya, to make good deficiencies, or save imports into that country." †

The decision that all overseas imports and exports of the Somaliland colony must pass through Kenya was felt to be an economic hardship, particularly in respect of cotton goods, the largest import of the Somali people. The increased cost of imports owing to world war conditions occasioned suffering. At the same time the efforts of the British Administration to reduce the cost of the colony to the heavily burdened British Exchequer led to increased taxation. Direct taxation on the dwellings of urbanised Somalis was reimposed.

The closing of the salt works was cited as a cause of hardship to the native people of the Mijjertein province. A communication strongly complaining of conditions under the British Administration was received by the Four Power Commission, ostensibly from headsmen of the Mijjertein, but the Commission were unable to ascertain its origin; it is possible it was concocted by the Italians. It alleged that at the time of the British occupation, 200,000 camels and 500,000 goats and sheep were looted by British troops, commanded by Colonel R. H. Smith, later Brigadier and Chief Administrator of the former Italian colony. This document further alleged that Somalis had been killed without due process of law, that 60 dhows and their cargoes had been confiscated, women outraged and huts set on fire. Memories of these war-time incidents, it was declared, still rankled. Owing to the removal of the industrial plant at Bender Kassim, Hafun, etc., Somalis who worked there were still unemployed, still suffering deeply, though the war had ended. Similar allegations have been made from numerous other sources. The accounts of Lord Rennell of slenderly officered forces of Gendarmerie and Camel Corps operating in " sweeps " for arms and against alleged cattle raiders indicate actions nearly approximating to warfare, and suggest only too clearly the probability of arbitrary and reckless action.

" On the 4th May " (1941), Lord Rennell records, " one company of the camel corps set off to deal with Mijjertein raiders and the whole formation, with only 15 per cent. of its officer establishment and 15 per cent. of its establishment of British N.C.O.s, was

---

* British Military Administration in Africa 1941-7, by Lord Rennell of Rodd, page 436.

† British Military Administration in Africa 1941-7, by Lord Rennell of Rodd, page 165.

in active employment, armed with Italian weapons and a miscellaneous collection of equipment."

The need to improve food production in view of the difficulty of import owing to war conditions, as well as the desire to get the Italians off the British relief list, caused the British Administration to make great efforts to induce the Somali labourers to return to work on the Italian estates from which they had fled. The wretchedly low pay, coupled with memories of the cruelties formerly practised by the Italians under the regime of forced labour, caused a general unwillingness to go back to the old masters. Moreover, the Somalis were eager to farm on their own account. At length, expedients to find workers for the Italian farms having failed to produce sufficient response, the British Administration introduced a quota system, which was a form of forced labour.

In December, 1946, Mr. Abdul Kader Sakhawadeen, a native of the Somaliland Colony, addressed an open letter to Mr. Attlee, and requested publication of it in " New Times and Ethiopia News." He protested that the Somalis were not the enemies of the Allies; it was their misfortune that the Italians had occupied their country fifty years before. He entered a plea against collective punishment and forced labour in the following poignant terms:

OPEN LETTER TO MR. ATTLEE

"Your Excellency,—I have taken the liberty to draw your attention to the afflictions with which the Somali people are burdened under your Government, which is represented by the British Military Administration.

"We have heard and believed that Great Britain had sacrificed the blood and lives of her sons and daughters, and devoted all her resources of wealth and manpower, in the fight against the Axis Powers in order to make the world safe for Freedom and Democracy.

"The Somalis were not the enemy of the Allies. It was their misfortune that your enemy—the Italians—forcibly occupied and subjected our country fifty years ago. We are, therefore, among the enslaved and oppressed to whom Freedom and Democracy was promised.

"To the people of Somaliland the five years since the day of our 'liberation' have been conspicuous in their lack of humane considerations and the brutal suppression of democratic rights. To-day the British Military Administration is almost as feared and disliked as the tyrannical Fascist Rule.

Racial discrimination exists in Somaliland, notably at Mogadishu.

---

* British Military Administration of Africa 1941-7, by Lord Rennell of Rodd, page 180.

"*Collective Punishment Laws have been enacted and are enforced. They are the means of spreading terror and want among the people. For instance, some Askaris recently deserted. The livestock of their innocent tribesmen was seized. The criminals had not taken refuge with the tribesmen. The incident had taken place very many miles away from the tribal area. No livestock of the deserters was in the hands of the tribesmen. The milk of livestock is the staple food of the people. Seizure of livestock is all the more detestable in that it deprives the women and children of their means of sustenance, through no fault of their own.*

"*Collective punishment is also the root cause of the majority of killings in Somaliland, for when the ignorant tribesmen get excited at such a tyrannical act and protest against it by stone-throwing or the futile brandishing of sticks, they are shot down for rioting.*

"*Conscription for slave-labour exists. The poor wretches thus collected are parcelled out by the British Military Administration among the agricultural concessions at Genale, along the Juba River and the area held by the S.A.I.S. (Societa Agricola Italo-Somalo). The slave-labourers are compelled to work in these areas under conditions which are a living mockery of Democracy and the ideals of human rights. The workers are brutally flogged in public for routine offences.*

"*Some officers of the Administration flagrantly violate one of the foremost of human rights—the sanctity of the person. Elders and respected Somalis are bullied and struck in offices by them or on their orders at any show of spirit.*

"*The laws and policy under which our country is administered were forged mainly by the Italians and Fascist statesmen for their own vile ends. The application of this tyrannical law by a Democratic Power is not only a great wrong but is causing the gravest miscarriage of justice.*

"*We recall to you the ideals and principles for which the heroes of England and the Allied countries gave their lives, and beg of you to send a disinterested and competent Commission or Mission to examine our complaints and make recommendations for the speedy relief of the causes of misrule.*

"*I have the honour to be, Sir, your obedient servant,*

"*ABDUL KADER SAKHAWADEEN (a Somali).*"

Mr. Sakhawadeen's protest resulted in questions on the floor of the House of Commons concerning forced labour in the Somaliland colony and the subsequent abolition of the quota system.

It must not be thought that the hated collective punishment was not the rule under Italian Colonial Government; it was in fact most ruthlessly practised in an extreme form. It was the continued imposition of collective punishment after the winning of the war of liberation which caused bitter disillusion. The reimposition of forced labour to benefit Italians, instead of throwing open the river-irrigated land to Somalis, was also deeply resented, but many Somalis declared warm appeciation of the partial reforms effected under British Caretaker Government.

British Military Administration of the Ethiopian Ogaden

The exclusion of the Ogaden from Ethiopian Administration under the 1942 Agreement was deplored by the Somalis of that province; the extension of the exclusion under the 1944 Agreement was more bitterly resented, for it was felt that the danger of enemy invasion in that area had entirely passed. " We fought against the Italians; we suffered under the Italians; we fought for liberation like the rest of Ethiopia; why are we not also liberated ?" * protested the loyal chiefs of the Ogaden.

Throughout the period of British Military Administration, the people of the Ogaden complained they were left without a government to protect them. They were disarmed by the British Military Authorities whilst the tribes of the British Protectorate were permitted to carry arms when they entered the Ogaden, as they did annually for grazing. This gave an advantage to the seasonal visitor in any dispute. If a scuffle arose as to which tribe should be first to draw from the rare water-holes or any other matter, Ethiopian Somalis complained that the British officers always took the part of the British protected tribes, without enquiry, and the people of the Ogaden, after being worsted by the outsiders because the latter were in possession of arms, were obliged also to submit to punishment for resistance to the intruders by the confiscation of the best of their herds. They were thus becoming grievously impoverished.

The Anglo-Ethiopian Agreement of 1897, between the Emperor Menelik II and Queen Victoria, wherein the boundary between the British Somali protectorate and Ethiopia was defined, provided for the free passage of the frontier by the Somalis on either side of the line, for trade, grazing or water, according to their immemorial custom, centuries before the advent of European colonies had destroyed the ancient unity of that area. The 1897 Agreement stipulated that the tribes on passing the frontier must obey the Governor of the territory in which they were for the time being. This was not pleasing to the British Somaliland Administration, who arranged, in May, 1941, that the British protected tribes, on passing into the Ogaden should still be under the administration of political officers from the Protectorate, enforced by the armed Illaloes. The result was prejudicial to the permanent residents of the Ogaden. According to Lord Rennell in his " British Military Administration 1941-7," page 182:

> "It was found that the British Somali tribes were over-grazing and exhausting the Ogaden Grounds and wells to the detriment of the Ogaden Somalis, who were dependent on them for their existence all the year round, and not only during the periods immediately after the

---

* cf., British Policy in Eastern Ethiopia, the Ogaden and the Reserved Area by E. Sylvia Pankhurst (New Times and Ethiopia News, 1945).

rains, when the British Isaak and Dolbahanta tribes had been using the Haud grazing. Eventually a new agreement was reached in June, 1943, which left the administration of the immigrant tribes in the hands of their own Political Officers, but control of the wells and grazing periods was undertaken by the Somalia administration. The real and practical solution was found in the co-operation engendered by more meetings (i.e. of the two British Administrations in Somaliland) and the single control under the Chief Political Officer in Nairobi of both Administrations."

The agreement above described is more fully* dealt with on pages 488-9 of Lord Rennel's "British Military Administration in Africa."

* " Early in 1943 the Chief Administrator of Somalia had drawn attention to the fact that, while in the past it had been the habit of the Isaak and Dolbahanta to migrate to the Haud during and after the two main rains when standing pools enabled their herds to enjoy the rich pastures, and to return to British Somaliland when these pools dried up, there had in recent seasons, since the British occupation of Somalia, been a marked tendency for the British tribes to remain in the Haud after the pools had dried up in the vicinity of the wells in the Wal Wal-Wardair area. This tendency was in his opinion to be deprecated, because it placed undue strain on the wells; furthermore, it involved overgrazing the area in the vicinity of the wells. To overcome these difficulties and to avoid increasing the anxiety of the Ogaden tribes, the Chief Administrator proposed to cancel the agreement come to between the two administrations in Burao in 1941, whereby the British Somaliland Administration was accorded permission to establish Illalo (tribal police) posts in the Haud and to be generally responsible for the administration of the British tribes during their sojourn there. The Chief Administrator now proposed to assume full administrative responsibility for all the Somalis in the Haud, whether they were British or Ogaden tribesmen. This proposal had to be modified, mainly because it seemed undesirable to deprive the British Somaliland Government of its right to administer a large proportion of its male population for approximately half the year.

The arrangements finally agreed to at a meeting between the heads of the two Administrations at Hargeisa in June, 1943, maintained the rights of the British Somaliland authorities to administer their tribes while in the Haud, but left the control of the wells in the hands of the Somalia Administration. It was also agreed, in the interests of all, that pressure should be applied to the British tribes, to leave the Haud when the pools were drying up so as to conserve the grazing in the vicinity. The arrangement, thanks to the co-operation of the officers of both Administrations, on the whole worked well and was thought to provide the best solution possible.

Few incidents took place in the Haud during 1944-1945, but in March, 1946, the situation in the grazing areas again became complicated when a party of Isaak tribesmen from British Somaliland crossed the Aware-Wardair road, defying patrols of Somali Gendarmerie and Illaloes. On the 23rd April the Chief Administrator of Somalia and the Military Governor of British Somaliland, with their respective advisers, again met at Mogadishu. After a preliminary discussion it was decided to hold a joint Durbar at Harardighet in the Ogaden Haud in the middle of June, at which representatives of both Ogaden and Isaak tribes were to be present. This was to be treated as a joint Durbar convened by the Military Administrator, in which the Military Governor was invited to participate so as to emphasize ceremonially the fact that the political and administrative policy, followed in the Haud, was one that was agreed to and approved by both Administrators. The Durbar took place on the 14th June, twenty-two officers being present, including the Commander of the Somalilands Sub-Area and the Commanding Officers of the Somalia Gendarmerie and of the Somaliland Scouts, whose units provided a combined guard of honour for the two principal officers. Representatives attended from all the Isaak and Ogaden Septs concerned.

A joint speech, drawn up by the Chief Administrator and the Military Governor was read."

The Agreement between the two British Military Administrations was obviously a violation of the Anglo-Ethiopian Treaty of 1897. The new Agreement of 1943 between the two British Administrations also violated the Treaty and did little to mitigate the hardships of the residents of the Ethiopian Ogaden.

The Ogaden people suffered both morally and materially by their separation from Ethiopia. The maintenance of law and order was given to forces from other parts of Africa, the King's African Rifles, officered as we have seen very sparsely by residents of Kenya and other colonies, many of them with a distinct bias against African self-government. The people bitterly complained against the conduct of these imported troops—particularly towards their women—a complaint invariably made when bodies of foreign troops are imported into any territory and retained for a number of years, instead of enlisting a police force from the people of the country. The raising of a native police force was not attempted in the Ogaden and the Reserved Area; it was known that whatever their outward relations with the British Administration might be, the people objected to rule by a foreign Government, and were eagerly awaiting the resumption of their former position inside Ethiopia.

Whilst they suffered economically by separation from Ethiopia, their cultural losses were not less felt. They were eager to share in the educational advance which they knew to be going forward over the border. They had no education in the Ogaden other than that provided by their local Muslim religious leaders. The much-prized modern Ethiopian schools were denied to them. In 1945 an Ethiopian Government school was at length re-opened in Jigjiga by agreement with the British Government, but it was inadequately housed. The former premises, with all the other main buildings, had been taken over by the British Military Administration. Boys from the Ogaden had formerly attended Ethiopian Government schools in Harar, Dire Dawa and Addis Ababa, where Arabic and Khoranic instruction were provided, as well as a general curriculum. The British Administration deprecated such attendance and it was rendered difficult. The son of Balambaras Abdulhai Farah, who was at school in Addis Ababa, on returning to his home at Dagabur, was ordered to remove the lion badge of his school, and on his refusal it was plucked from his uniform by order of a British officer. The father of this boy of thirteen years is a notable Somali of great repute among his people, who had lived all his life among them in Dagabur till they chose him to represent them in the Ethiopian Parliament.

Hospital accommodation and medical treatment were greatly lacking in the Ogaden, the cost of cereals and of cotton cloth, which the people mainly used for their clothing, was appallingly high, in fact prohibitive. Above all they complained that they had no Government of their own to care for their needs and to protect them from looting and cruelty by foreign soldiers.

Disarmament of the Tribes: Machine Guns Round the Wells

Disarmament of the Ogaden people was not effected without hardship and protest. It had been customary for tribes to carry a few old guns to protect their herds and the weaker members of the tribe from attack by lions, leopards and other carnivora, and also for hunting.

The expedient of placing troops with machine guns round the wells, in order to compel the handing in of arms was deeply resented in all the Somalilands. It was regarded by the Administration as the easiest and most economical method, but the Somalis protested bitterly. In the Ogaden they declared they had not got all the weapons the British estimated were in their possession. They told the present writer when in the Ogaden and stated in petitions to the Emperor Haile Sellassie, copies of which they showed to the present writer, that to procure the arms demanded they had sent some of their men into British Somaliland to purchase arms from their clansmen there, in order to induce the British officers at the wells to permit water to be drawn. Even then they were reproached for not having brought in all the arms they had; some it was said must be still hidden away; therefore only some of their cattle were allowed to drink; the rest were shot. They alleged, with great bitterness, that women, children, aged people and animals had died for lack of water, on account of this " convenient " method of gathering in the arms supposed to be at large.

Requisitioning of Animals: Failure to Pay

The failure of British officers to pay for the animals requisitioned for feeding their troops was also a bitter grievance. In such cases a receipt would generally be given, and the owner would be instructed to present it, in applying for payment, in a given locality where the army was at the time stationed. By the time the tribe arrived at the place indicated, British forces had vacated it —in consequence payment was not received. One of these unpaid receipts, a very casually* executed document was handed to the present writer. It reads:

> Payment for Fresh Meat.
> Ration "D" (M.I.) Coy. IMI Det.
> I certify I have to-day received
> 15 Camels,
> 33 Sheep.
> No payment has yet been made in above.
> Signature.
> 30/12/43. Capt.

A photograph of this scrap of paper is reproduced facing Page 146.

---

* This chit was sent by the present writer to the War Office for inspection in the hope that the recipient might be paid for the stock which had been requisitioned, but the reply by the War Office was that the signature would be impossible to identify.

As an Appendix to this chapter is reproduced the speech in the Ethiopian Parliament of Balambaras Abdulahi Farah on the continuation of British Administration in his native province, and letters and petitions of the Ogaden people. If the statements in these documents be discounted by half, enough remains to show the suffering of their unfortunate authors under a Military Administration, not so ruthless as that of Italy, but which included collective punishments of tribes for the actions of individuals, involving confiscation of cattle and destruction of villages by armed raiding parties, carried out without trial by process of law.

In Ethiopia, it must be emphasised, the individual accused is brought to trial before a duly constituted civil court by a procedure not differing greatly from that which obtains in Britain. Where the barrier is so great between the Government and the governed as to allow of the continuance from generation to generation of collective punishment by punitive raids, it is impossible to speak of preparing the population for self-government.

Education

Education which was a foremost demand among the progressive Somalis received some genuine support from the British Administration, but on a very tiny scale. It accounted for only one-half per cent of the expenditure including the education of both Italian and Somali children, a total cost of 73,102 East African shillings (roughly £3,650) in the period 1941-48.

In July, 1944, Lord Rennell reports: " A qualified and experienced British officer was appointed as superintendent of Education and six Zanzibar instructors were later seconded from the East Africa Army Education Corps for duty with the Somalia Education Department."

" The Somalis," Lord Rennell adds, " had a real desire for educational facilities." The facilities provided were, however, much restricted. In 1944 209 Arabs and 190 Somalis attended the schools provided for them where English was taught. " The provision of teachers became a serious problem" as time went on adds Lord Rennell; the provision of staff for what was regarded as a backwater was always a difficulty. In 1945 a nine months teachers' course was started, an inadequate makeshift *faute de mieux*. A new native school was built at Galkayu; buildings at Merka, Afgoi and Lugh were adapted for school premises. Girls were admitted to the Hamarwein school.

The Four Power Commission of Investigation reported that in 1947 there were 17 elementary schools for the Somali and Arab population, with a total of 1,040 scholars, 539 Arab, 501 Somali, 54 of whom were girls. There was a Teachers' Training School with 50 Somali and Arab students. There were three private schools, one for Indians, two for Somalis. In these schools were 52 teachers, of whom 25 were Somalis, 22 Arabs and

5 from Kenya and Zanzibar. Of these teachers five had completed the "War Course" for teachers at Nairobi. The Commission reported, "of the remainder few have any recognised qu'alifications."

The Commission added:

"No large or radical reforms in education have been carried out."

Members of the Commission visited a native school and the Teachers' Training School in Mogadishu and found the standard of education extremely low. There was little here to satisfy the Somali yearning for an efficient modern education which would fit the native people of the territory to administer a progressive democratic state and man its technical services. There was nothing comparable to the education provided by the administration of self-governing Ethiopia.

Appendix to Chapter XV.

SPEECH BY BALAMBARAS ABDULAHI FARAH, DEPUTY OF OGADEN IN THE ETHIOPIAN CHAMBER OF DEPUTIES 20th DECEMBER 1944

Ministers and Dignitaries to-day assembled in this Parliament,

On behalf of all the people of the Ogaden, I beg to state the condition of Ogaden:

We have not heard previously of people who ill-treat those entrusted to their care by God except Fascists. It does not give any shame to state that the British Military Authorities have committed crimes in Ogaden which have never even been done by Fascists.

Proof of this:

The Fascists used to kill a man, but until they killed him they never deprived him of water. But the British Authorities surrounded the wells and the cattle for about seven days, depriving them of water, and people suffered death owing to thirst.

After seven days they permitted some of the cattle to drink water and machine-gunned the rest.

When these events took place the British Somalis were permitted to draw water and their cattle were given natural treatment.

The British proclaimed punishment against those who supplied water to any Ogaden people, and those who intermingled through marriage or in case of relationship.

The English during their occpation of the Reserved Areas and the Ogaden did not consider Ethiopia as an Allied people; on the contrary they killed the educated persons and impoverished the rich. They misled the uneducated with false reports so as to separate them from their Emperor and their brothers, the Ethiopians.

I believe that you who are assembled here have only a superficial knowledge of the ill-treatment of the people of the Ogaden.

Four years after the restoration of the Ethiopian Government the Ogaden people were still hopeful that their Ethiopian brothers would help them to partake of the freedom they are enjoying.

After suffering and torture were brought on the Ogaden people the matter was brought to the notice of His Imperial Majesty. It is very sad to learn that the problem of the Ogaden will only be settled after two more years.

To-day the people of the Ogaden are not enjoying their normal life; their position is like that of a man who is on the point of death and whose grave is ready.

I therefore beg to remind your Excellencies that God has created one powerful and the other weak; when the powerful man ill-treats the weak one has nothing else to do than to cry to God. Therefore I beg you to pray for us in the Churches and wherever you are assembled together.

As he concluded the Deputy for the Ogaden broke down and wept.

PETITIONS FROM PEOPLE AND CHIEFS OF THE OGADEN PLEADING TO BE RESTORED TO ETHIOPIAN GOVERNMENT PROTESTS AGAINST COLLECTIVE PUNISHMENTS

PETITION TO HIS IMPERIAL MAJESTY

Your Imperial Majesty,

We have so far informed and explained to the Authorities all our sufferings and those of our tribes.

Now we most respectfully and humbly repeat the same to Your Imperial Majesty.

Your Majesty,

It is our last hope that this our petition will be listened to.

It is obviously true that when a man's one eye is sore, the other eye will weep, and naturally we are weeping when we see the continual suffering of our tribes and brothers.

The British Government has cruelly treated us, your people, in a manner not done by any considerate Government.

1. Our daughters and wives are forcibly taken by them and raped.
2. Our cattle are machine-gunned.
3. Without any crime having been committed they came to our village at Fik, and burned our houses.
4. On the pretext of gathering in rifles they have killed many of our brothers who were found with rifles. By this system many of our brothers have been killed.
5. Without even an allegation of crime they imposed fines on any man of from 300 to 400 camels, and did not tell him the reason.
6. They have separated mothers from children, wives from husbands and they cannot see each other.
7. They also come to our camp and kill many of our innocent brothers.
8. They come in the night and rob the clothes and ornaments of our wives, with the result that our wives go naked.
9. They take our cattle from the pasture land without any reason.
10. When a man commits an offence, instead of punishing the offender legally they burn four or five villages.
11. They cause us to quarrel among ourselves so that we kill one another.
12. They are also asking Your Imperial Majesty's subjects who are on the Ethiopian border to come to them, and when they refuse they abuse them.
13. They claim that the Ethiopian Government was restored by them and they say that Ethiopia is in their hands.

We give in detail the ill-treatment which was inflicted on one clan. Not a single individual has escaped the ill-treatment.

The ill-treatment inflicted on the clan called Amaden Adenkere

1. In the village called Daudid, eleven months ago, at 5 o'clock in the evening, one South African * called Lt. Degader, as he is called by the local Somalis, robbed 500 camels and burnt our village. The reason is not known to us.
2. Nine months ago, at 5 o'clock, Captain Magg headed 25 soldiers and came and looted 200 camels from us.
3. Fifteen men from our clan and fifteen from another had a clash, and our clan took from the other clan 200 camels, the British obliged us to give them back. After these had been returned they imposed on us a fine and we paid 551 camels. In this case the fifteen men should have been punished, and not all the clan, which is against human law.
4. A year ago, on a mountain called Chiko, our camels were grazing and just at 12 o'clock of the day they bombed our camels and killed 100 of them and wounded 70.
5. In the month of December, the British soldiers pretended to buy cows, and killed two cows, following this they fired on the village. And they gave false reason that it was the natives who fired, because of this they made them pay 100 cattle as a fine. They said that in case they did not pay these cattle within ten days the fine would be increased to 200 cattle. But as they could not pay at such short notice they asked for more days.
6. 25 days ago, in villages called Nejaha and Addeyo, four English soldiers came and wounded a 12-year-old girl, killed 17 sheep, took 11 camels and burnt 30 houses.

Your Majesty,

About handing over our arms, in pursuance of the order of the Government, we began to do that. Soon after the British permitted the natives to buy rifles, and therefore the people hid them.

---

* " South Africa " was often used by the Somalis to denote Kenya.

A month and a half ago in the village called Jilawer Inba, those who hid rifles took 180 camels from those who had handed over their rifles.

The above mentioned ill-treatment has been inflicted repeatedly on us and our brothers, we therefore beg that your Imperial Majesty will liberate us from this yoke.

We submitted our application in 1936* in the month of June on the same subject, when your Imperial Majesty promised us that our case would be dealt with in a short time, but time is passing and we, your people, are suffering.

We, your subjects, most humbly beg you to return us to our old state of freedom and enable us to see our brothers who are separated from us by force.

THE PEOPLE OF OGADEN.

Tribe.	Name and father's name.	Position.	Thumb print Sign. of Applicant.
Malingur	Ayub Guledo	L. Chief	
Rer Hirsi Jirif	Abdul Khen Mohamed	Represent.	
	Shiek Ismael Gure	Shiek	
	Mohamed Budul	Elder	
	Mohamed Aden	Elder	
Maligur Farah Semeter	Shiek Ibrahim Bedi	Shiek	
	Ahemed Mohamed	Elder	
Malingur	Au Hussen Mohamed	L. Chief	
Rer Werfaguled	Au Ummer Nur Hure	Elder	
Rer Saad	Yusuf Ran	Represent.	
Rer Saad	Au Arah Jebril	Elder	
Rer Saad	Au Ali Au Hussen	Elder	
Rer Saad	Adoua Au Abdi	Elder	
Rer Delel	Aden Abdi	L. Chief	
Rer Delel	Hussen Adem	Elder	
Rer Delel	Beshir Au Ali	Elder	
Hirsi Semeter	Serhaye Ali	L. Chief	
Amaden	Shiek Tahir Abdi Salam	Elder	
Bah Haber Eli	Shiek Ahemed Siraj	Shiek	
Bah Haber Eli	Hussen Nuh	Elder	
Bah Haber Eli	Ummer Mealin	Elder	
Bah Haber Eli	Au Aden Mohamed	Elder	
Bah Galad	Bedel Diss	L. Chief	
Adem Bedir	Ummer Abdi	L. Chief	
Mekahil	Shiek Abdelrahman Ibrahim	Kadi of Fik	

CLAIM
TO HIS IMPERIAL MAJESTY.

Your Majesty,

We, the undersigned Tribes of Ethiopian Somali, namely the Chiefs and Elders, petition your Majesty as follows:—

For the sake of our pride and liberty we demonstrated our hatred of the Italian enemy, and have struggled as much as we could for our freedom before the enemy overran our country. Further, after the occupation of our country by the enemy, we helped as much as we could by means of correspondence.

---

* 1943, according to the European Calendar.

Four years ago the British Army, which we accepted with great joy, came and cleaned out our enemies from our country.

Later on, Your Majesty gave over temporarily the district of Ogaden to the British Military Army, as a military cantonment, and when the event took place and your Majesty's order was sent regarding the same, some of us were in Addis Ababa.

As soon as two years elapsed we waited anxiously for the British to move away, so that we could be under the protection and guidance of our King of Kings as before, but on the contrary, time passed and our suffering became more and more acute.

We are forbidden from visiting our brothers, who are dwelling nearby.

Enmity is created in such a successful manner that it became possible for brother to kill brother, and because of such bloodshed we were forced to consider one another as enemies.

Owing to lack of justice we were beaten and flogged to death. Our wives are always being taken by force by the British soldiers and raped. Our cattle are machine-gunned and killed with thirst. The ill-treatment which we cannot show in writing is continually inflicted on us.

With open hands and broken hearts we beg Your Imperial Majesty to take pity on your people and free us from prison. Your Imperial Majesty not expecting that such ill-treatment will befall your people temporarily lent us as a temporary cantonment. Now the loaned thing is spoiled, tortured and misused, therefore if Your Majesty will not take the necessary steps to take us back, it is clear and true that we shall all completely be tortured to death.

In the cantonment given them for a short time they are compelling us to hand over our rifles and ammunition, and we have done this. Nevertheless, they are still compelling us, and our cattle are machine-gunned and some of them have suffered death with thirst. Because of our affections we have bought rifles from our clansmen existing in the British Colony and have handed them over to the British. There is no reason why we should hand over to them our arms. They should be made to leave this cantonment.

We, your people, have fulfilled what Your Imperial Majesty required of us. Therefore we must humbly beg that Your Majesty may remember us.

After the restoration of Ethiopia's freedom we have become so unfortunate that we have lived under tyranny for four years. We therefore beg Your Imperial Majesty to put an end to our sufferings and send us Your Majesty's representative.

Tribe.	Position.	Name and father's name.	Thumb print of applicant.
1. Shekash	Khadi	Shiek Ibrahim Haji	
2.	Mislene	Bedi Abdi	
3.	Demina	Amenja Jegol	
4.	Demina	Usman Ummer	
5. Habar Awal	Represent.	Kesse Farah	
6.	Demina	Ali Kedah	
7.	Demina	Seid Aden	
8.	Demina	Akli Dembil	
9. Gedeburssi	Represent.	Yusuf Ugaz Roble	
10.	Represent.	Maid Meidene	
11. Ogaden	Represent.	Kelif Shewal	
12.	Demina	Mussa Ibrahim Debeker	
13.		Ismael Mummin	

Jigjiga, January 17, 1945.

KENYAZMATCH ABEBA
Let peace rest on the Empire of Ethiopia.

We thank our Lord God who restored the freedom of Ethiopia so that she may live in her large territories with her liberty. We further thank Him for having broken the strength of her enemy.

Our will is to be under the Ethiopian Government in loyalty. Great harm has befallen us under the British administration. Life has not remained for us. We have been looted of our cattle and property. Some of our men have been killed, others arrested.

We like the Ethiopian Government because we were under it before and in addition our colour and skin are the same. We read in our sacred records that the Ethiopian Government is permanent in the world and will exist until the end.

We pray to our Lord to keep our Government and to crush our enemy.

In the letter which you have forwarded to us we are informed of your coming and we are awaiting it with pleasure. If we come to you the English will arrest our wives and children.

We have not received a reply to the letter we sent you. We beg you to write us everything in detail. I also beg to convey my best wishes to the Governor of Harar Province. Please write to us and tell us everything.

I am sending this letter by the hand of my brother. I could not come personally for fear of the English. My brother will explain to you the condition of my country.

(Signed)
SHIEK ABDUL UHAB SHIEK YUSUF,
Clan of Rer Abduli Chief Shiek.

I address this letter to the generous and peace-loving Governor Dedjazmatch Tassou Walalou. (Vice-Governor of Harar Province).

Let not peace depart from you as long as the world lasts.

I have desired for some time past to come to see you in Harar, and I have a desire that you take me before the Emperor.

You know that there was a solemn oath between my father and the Emperor. I desire there will be the same kind of oath between you and me. I have heard that you are labouring to ameliorate the lot of the people living in these parts.

I am ill in bed, and I and my people who are with me are in great difficulty. I have been strictly forbidden to come to see you and I am afraid you will have returned to Harar before I recover.

I have heard that you have enhanced the prestige of the Ethiopian flag. It is my earnest prayer that you and the great Emperor will be strengthened.

Send me a reply to this letter. You will know that my state is as described above.

We desire strongly to live united with you.

This is my letter and I am expecting a reply to it.

(Signed)
UGAZ MOHAMED UGAZ OMER.

XV

SOMALI YOUTH LEAGUE

The first news of a Somali political movement to pass the frontiers of the colony was a Press agency communication that a " Somali Youth Club " had been formed on the fifth of May, 1943. The Club had obtained an interview with the Chief British Administrator, Brigadier Wickham, and had demanded union to Ethiopia " claiming the Emperor Haile Sellassie as their King." The fifth of May, 1943, was a significant date, being the second anniversary of Ethiopian liberation. Though the Emperor Haile Sellassie had re-entered Addis Ababa on May 5, 1941, Ethiopian Government had not been resumed until February, 1942. Hence it was only by the second anniversary of the actual re-entry to the capital that news of the educational and other reforms rapidly being developed in Ethiopia could reach Italian Somaliland. The interview with the Chief Administrator was reported in the Press telegrams as having resulted from a demonstration of unrest arising from economic hardship, which had been brought to a point of crisis by the rumour that new taxation was about to be imposed by the British Military Administration. There was an element of stone throwing, and the possibility of more serious turbulence. The Chief Administrator had received the demonstrators and pacification had followed.

Apparently there were changes in the policy and purpose of the Youth Club. Moreover the formal foundation of the Club was subsequently claimed to have been effected on May 15, ten days after the first demonstration. The organisation was reconstituted on April 1, 1947, as the Somali Youth League.

Starting as a movement of Youth the organisation seems to have represented a spontaneous response by the long-oppressed people of the Somaliland colony to the widespread propaganda of liberation for the peoples of the former Italian Empire, which had been industriously disseminated by British war propaganda in 1940-41. This movement of the Somalis was not purely political; it represented an urge for education and progress and the status of a free people. Its statutes did not make any formal reference to the future of the Colony. Its aims were defined thus:

(1) *To unite all Somalis, particularly the youth, and to eradicate harmful prejudices which cause communal and tribal friction.*

(2) *To educate the youth in modern ideas and civilisation by schools and cultural circles.*

The Club made swift progress. When it was reconstituted as the Somali Youth League two further aims were added:

(3) *To eliminate by constitutional means any situation prejudicial to Somali interests.*

(4) *To adopt one Somali language, and to put into use the existing script known as " Osmania."*

The script, Osmania, had been initiated some thirty years before, but the Italian Government had strongly opposed it; any Somali found using it was imprisoned, as was stated by the Somali Youth League deputation to the Four Power Commission of Investigation.

The Youth League gained steadily in membership among Somalis of all ages. When testifying before the Commission in January, 1948, they claimed an active membership of 93,000, supported by 300,000 relatives, dependents and followers of members, and 79 branches outside Mogadishu. They explained that the Central Committee consisted of thirteen members, who elect from their number a President, Vice-President, Secretary-General, General Treasurer, two Financial Controllers, and two paid inspectors. The Central Committee had to meet at least once a week. There were local committees elected for six months by the local members. A Committee of Appeal of seven members was elected by the Central Committee. The President, Vice-President, Secretary-General and General Treasurer formed a Central Direction who formed the executive of the League, preparing the Agenda of the Central Committee and putting it into execution.

The General Assembly consisted of all members of the League in Mogadishu and representatives of local committees.

Membership was open to all Somalis and "assimilated Africans" not less than fifteen, or more than sixty years of age; persons over sixty might be elected as honorary members. All members must be of good character, without criminal convictions; they might not belong to other Somali organisations. The membership fee was 1s. per month, with 5s. entrance fee. For breach of rules, or behaviour prejudicial to the League, a member might be expelled, reprimanded or fined up to 100s. (£5). Appeal against such punishments might be made to an Appeal Committee. After expulsion a member if permitted to rejoin had to pay 50s. A member who voluntarily withdrew had to pay 100s. before being allowed to rejoin.

Members suffering financial or other difficulties might appeal for aid to the League.

It will be observed that the League had an exceedingly elaborate constitution, democratic in form, but of an authoritative trend, that it exercised a strong discipline over its members and imposed onerous penalties, which must have borne hardly on the small means of any who incurred them. The founders of the League regarded its work as immensely important.

The swift growth of the organisation, its early success in overcoming some tribal feuds apparently was greatly surprising to many British Administrators with long experience of Somaliland.

By 1947 the Youth League had a hundred full-time employees and was engaging actively in several aspects of Somali welfare:

(1) The League had intervened to secure ameliorations in the slave conditions of the indigenous labourers on the Italian estates at Genale and in other districts, and had succeeded in procuring some concessions.

(2) Two commercial and agricultural companies had been promoted by the League, the "Società Anonima Agricola Somali," founded in February, 1947, and the "Società Anonima la Somali" founded in May, 1947. The League claimed that the stimulus given to Somali agriculture by the first of these companies had doubled the area under indigenous cultivation by the end of the year.

(3) An anti-Tuberculosis Board had also been promoted by the Youth League, which had raised considerable sums for the work of the Board.

(4) The League claimed to have established and maintained without assistance from the British Administration, either in funds or material, six evening classes in Arabic, two in English, held regularly in Mogadishu, and a further eleven classes in English and seven in Arabic in the following centres: Beletwen, Bulo Burto, Baidoa, Bur Hakaba, Merka, Margherita, Kismayu, Brava, Galkayu, Gardo, Bender, Kassim, Villagio.

The maintenance of such classes is a praiseworthy activity, no small achievement on the part of a voluntary organisation of people with small incomes, in a period of economic depression; it indicates devotion and ability on the part of the organisers, and a keen desire for education by the students—a resilience and eagerness for advance in a long-oppressed people, which reveals them worthy of a better fate than to be thrust again under the old tyranny and exploitation.

The Somali Youth League received great encouragement from the British Military Administration. A speech of Brigadier Brigham, expressing sympathy with the League, was reported in the official organ of the British Administration. "The Somalia Courier," on May 21, 1947. In giving thanks for being invited to take part in the anniversary celebration the Chief Administrator said:—

"*The development and expansion of the Somali Youth League during the past four years has been a very remarkable achievement and reflects the greatest credit not only on those who have organised it, but on the large numbers of Somalis who are ready to devote their money and their services to the improvement of the conditions of their countrymen.*

"*The aims you have expressed to-day, and which are embodied in your constitution, are worthy of the highest praise, and you may be confident that during the short time which remains to them, the British Military Administration will afford all possible co-operation in attaining them."*

In Eritrea the police and other government employees were strictly prohibited from joining the Party of Reunion to Ethiopia. The British Military Administration in the Somaliland Colony, however, saw no objection to either police or other officials joining the League. This was declared on behalf of the Administration to the Four Power Commission of Enquiry. It was alleged by all witnesses opposing the League and the Administration, that the League was so highly favoured by the Administration that the great majority of police and other government employees joined it because not to belong to it was a drawback in obtaining government employment.

The striking difference between the attitude of the Administration towards the Youth League and towards the Eritrean reunion to Ethiopia Party can be explained in some measure by the fact that the former organisation devoted itself in the first years of its existence to charitable and educational purposes; it did not formally declare a political policy concerning the future government of the territory until after the forthcoming visit of the Four Power Commission to ascertain the views of the local population had been announced in the Press and by the Chief Administrator. The matter, however, went deeper. The first object stated in the Youth League constitution was the Unity of all Somalis; there was no statement that the Unity would be of a political character, or by what means it would be achieved, but the League's desire for the Unity of the Somalilands accorded with the policy of the British Administration. Here was a broad basis of agreement. There was no indication that the Youth League would adopt an attitude of opposition to the unity being effected under British Trusteeship. In short Somali Unity was regarded as sound policy for Somalis; therefore the Youth League could be safely encouraged.

The Unionist Party of Eritrea on the other hand was opposing the policy of the British Military Administration of that territory which favoured a British Trusteeship of the territory with the addition, if possible, of a portion of the neighbouring Ethiopian Tigré. Brigadier Stephen Longrigg*, for four years British Administrator of Eritrea, had been a particularly active protagonist of this policy, and had guided the views of his colleagues into this channel. Thus whilst the big popular Party in Ex-Italian Somaliland was considered a legitimate manifestation of the local population, and a body which the British Administration could usefully encourage, the big popular Reunion to Ethiopia Party of Eritrea, a spontaneous movement, answering to the long-held and deeply rooted aspirations of the people, was regarded by the Administration with disfavour, as inimical to official policy, a body which might in certain eventualities cause difficulties.

---

* See " A Short History of Eritrea," by Brigadier Stephen Longrigg (Oxford University Press).

It would be unfair towards the members of the British Administration not to recognise that many of them were animated by a sincere and wholly disinterested sense of justice in their sympathy for the struggle of the Somali people against the return of Italy. Notably the few soldiers still in Somaliland who had enlisted from non-official circles for the war emergency, and having helped to clear out the worst iniquities of Italian rule, were genuinely impressed by the brave efforts for education and public welfare made by the oppressed people to a large extent under the leadership of the Somali Youth League.

The years which had intervened since the Italian defeat in Somaliland, coupled with Press reports that the Council of Foreign Ministers was inclined to favour Italian Trusteeship in that area, had caused the exuberant war-time confidence in ultimate liberation and progress to flag sadly. Mr. Bevin's statement to the Council of Foreign Ministers, in April, 1946, favouring the union of British, Ethiopian and former Italian Somaliland under British Trusteeship, " in order to give the Somalis the chance of a decent life," was grasped as a life-line offering escape from the dreaded return of Italian rule. The ideal of the Youth League was an administration much more dynamically progressive than that of the British Somaliland Protectorate; they desired extensive opportunities of education and expanding experience of administration to prepare the people for self-rule, such as had not hitherto existed under British rule in Somaliland. Nevertheless, Mr. Bevin's words seemed to promise that Somali welfare was now to be considered in discussing the future of their homeland, moreover his proposal seemed to give weight to the advocacy of a united Somaliland by officials of the British Military Administration, and their predictions that it was destined to be established as part of the peace settlement.

These confident assertions, and continued Press discussions of Mr. Bevin's proposal, obscured in a measure the fact that the British Foreign Secretary had himself abandoned the project because of the lack of support for it in the Council of Foreign Ministers, and still more because of Ethiopia's refusal to surrender the Ogaden.

The discussion of the Italian Peace Treaty by the Paris Conference, from July 29 to October 15, 1946, was keenly followed by the Youth League leaders. The decision of the Conference that Italy must renounce all title to her former Colonies aroused new hope, despite the disappointing failure to decide what was eventually to happen to these territories, the agreement to give the Council of Foreign Ministers still another year to reach a solution—and the painful hint that, even yet, Italian rule might possibly be restored.

The announcement by Press and Radio, and by the Chief Administrator of the Colony, Brigadier R. H. Smith, that a Commission of Investigation would visit the Colony to ascertain the views of the local population aroused both hope and anxiety.

Though the opposition of the people to Italian rule was general, the Italians now bestirred themselves with tremendous activity to win over a show of support from their Somali employees in the various enterprises of the Colony and particularly in the former Italian native soldiery and police, most of all their ex-" Banda " irregulars, who under British Administration to a large extent lacked employment.

Somali Youth League Programme: Unity of all Somalilands

For the leaders of the Somali Youth League it was imperative to formulate a policy for the future government of the ex-Colony and to obtain the acceptance of their members to it.

They declared for the union of all the Somalilands under a ten years United Nations Trusteeship administered by the Four Powers who had assumed the right to determine their fate: Britain, France, the Soviet Union and the United States.

The brief temporary trusteeship was reluctantly admitted to be necessary owing to the illiteracy and lack of administrative experience among the Somali people.

The demand for Four Power Trusteeship was obvious enough; Mr. Bevin had abandoned the British claim on the score of Ethiopia's refusal to surrender the Ogaden. It was hoped to win the support of all Four Powers for Somali unity by requesting a Trusteeship of them all. Moreover, the four together, it was hoped, might check each other's desire to retain the territory permanently and the cost of progressive development would be shared.

British Administrators who had given their approval to the Youth League were not estranged from it by the appeal for a Four Power instead of a British Trusteeship. They were not at all disturbed by the proposal; if the principle of a " Great Somaliland " under a single administration were adopted by the Council of Foreign Ministers, the United Kingdom Government, having the British Protectorate to offer to the scheme, being actually in possession of the whole area, and having conquered it from Italy, would be in a strong position to claim the Trusteeship—always provided no more practical solution could gain acceptance. Many British Administrators throughout East Africa were under the influence of propagandists like Brigadier Stephen Longrigg,* who was strenuously campaigning to create a new British Trust Territory by a combination of ex-Italian Eritrea and the Ethiopian Tigré Province. They were inclined to think in terms of a reduced Ethiopian Empire, rather than of any extension of Ethiopian territory. The continued British occupation of the Ethiopian Ogaden, which had substantially out-lasted World War hostilities in East Africa, lent colour to the belief, then widely current among British

---

* Cf. e.g., Stephen H. Longrigg, A Short History of Eritrea (Oxford, 1945), also letter to the " Spectator," " I favour the proposed United Somalia . . . in no event should I approve the attachment of the Muslim Ogaden to Ethiopia," also letters to the " Times," etc.

officials in East Africa, that British Administration of Ethiopian Somaliland was destined to be permanent. They were not disposed to follow the Foreign Secretary in his tacit abandonment of the plan for a single administration on the ground of Ethiopia's refusal. To them this was merely a phase in the course of rendering permanent a British Administration which was already in being.

Aspiration for Unity

The aspiration of the Somali Youth League for the unity of the Somali territories was a natural extension of their desire for unity among the Somali people, and the abolition of tribal feuds, which they had been endeavouring to effect within the Somaliland Colony. To achieve that unity they were prepared to expend all sorts of effort and persuasion to overcome reactionary influences among their own people and the narrow tribal mentality, which in some cases, was disposed to regard almost as foreigners the Somalis of another tribe, or another area.

Mr. Bevin's protest against the artificial frontiers which divide British, Ethiopian and Italian Somaliland required no emphasis to the Somalis. Created by European Colonisation in the late nineteenth century, these barriers were so inimical to the roving life of the Somali people that provisions had to be included in all the boundary agreements between Ethiopia and the Colonial Powers who had occupied the coasts, providing for the Somali tribes to pass and repass the frontiers to and from their long accustomed seasonal grazing areas. The difficulty of dealing with divers governments, each using a different official language, was also felt, but the abolition of these inconveniences was far from comprising all their desires for the new era of liberation in which they had been led to hope.

In their claim to the union of the Somalilands they did not content themselves, like Mr. Bevin, with the proposal to unify British, Ethiopian and ex-Italian Somaliland; they added also French Somaliland to their claim.

They did not realise that this merely made their project for unity still more visionary, and that as matters stood it lacked all possibility of realisation, because France and Ethiopia * were both unwilling to cede their Somali territories, and the United Nations Charter expressly prohibits placing under Trusteeship territory belonging to States which are members of the United Nations Organisation. Here is the relevant Clause of the Charter:

---

* " Ethiopia could not admit that any question should arise concerning the return to her of territories comprising the Ethiopian Ogaden province, which were as a purely war-time measure contributed as an ally and without compensation to the effective prosecution of the war and should no more fall within the scope of the Peace Conference than similar war-time contributions of territories made by other allies."—Emperor Haile Sellassie in a Press interview.

Article 78, Chapter 12

"The trusteeship system shall not apply to territories which have become members of the United Nations, relationship among which shall be based on respect for the principle of sovereign equality."

People of the Ogaden Unwilling to Lose Ethiopian Citizenship

In their demand for Somali unity through a "Somali State" under Four Power Trusteeship, the Youth Club of the ex-Colony ignored the wishes and the interests of the Somalis of the Ogaden, who were appealing urgently to be restored to Ethiopian administration.

The proposed trusteeship was manifestly unacceptable to the people of the Ogaden, for it invited them to abandon their status as citizens of an independent self-governing nation for the greatly inferior position of a subject people under a foreign trustee, with the added disability of complete uncertainty as to how, or by what Power or Powers the Trusteeship would be administered.

Even had the people of the Ethiopian Ogaden and the Government in Addis Ababa been willing to accept the proposed surrender of Ethiopian territory, a course against which they were completely determined, the project to which the Youth Club of the Italian Colony had committed themselves was remote and doubtful in the extreme. Neither Mr. Bevin, nor any other member of the Council of Foreign Ministers, had foreshadowed any possibility of the early establishment of an independent Somali State, or mentioned any terms for the proposed Trusteeship. Mr. Bevin had quite clearly emphasised what he conceived to be the benefits of a British administration which would "organise things" for these poor nomads. His offer to add the British Protectorate to the scheme was entirely conditional upon the whole area being placed under British Trusteeship.

Moreover, even were the creation of an independent Somali State within a few years a probability, it could offer to the people of the Ogaden no inducement comparable to the great losses they would sustain if they were deprived thereby of Ethiopian citizenship. They would be impoverished, both economically and culturally, if divided from the prosperous, well-watered and temperate Ethiopian highlands, whence they obtain cereals and other commodities which the Somalilands do not produce in sufficient quantities, if at all. The Muslim schools and culture of Harar, Dire Dawa, and particularly Addis Ababa, are valued throughout the Ogaden. The view of Mohammed Abubaker El Morgani, supreme leader of the Muslim Church in Eritrea, that the welfare of his people lies in unity with Ethiopia, is shared by Muslims throughout Ethiopia.

A Wiser Plan

The wisdom of seeking union with the Somalis of the Ogaden without demanding their severance from the rest of Ethiopia, the strength and prosperity to be achieved by unity also with Ethiopia, was obscured by propaganda and short-term personal self-interest.

The Youth League did not realise their only means of securing unity with the Ogaden was by uniting the ex-Italian Colony to the Ethiopian State to which the Ogaden is attached. Lacking administrative experience and economic knowledge, they did not know that the ex-Italian Colony had no prospect of becoming a prosperous independent State, and that the British Government, having combined with it the Ogaden and the British Protectorate, had been obliged to subsidise each of these areas during the seven years of their administration, despite the rigid economies and stern efforts to balance expenditure and revenue, which had caused both hardship and complaint. Even the temporary Four Power Trusteeship the Youth League were demanding might, in the shifting temper of European policies, give place to Italian rule again, when after a few years the poor territory still failed to become economically solvent.

The Youth Club did not realise that the Ten Years' Trusteeship, which they reluctantly admitted to be necessary, owing to the abject condition of ignorance and subjection in which Italian colonisation had kept the Somali population, would be obviated by union to Ethiopia, where a stable and progressive Government could immediately provide the necessary administration, and would at once proceed to train the local population to share the privileges and responsibilities of a self-governing people.

It was not known to the leaders of the Youth League that the policy of detaching all Somalis from Ethiopia, to unite them under British or other European administration, had been paralleled, only a little earlier, in respect of the Gallas, who had failed to respond to the proposal of a Galla State, because they have become far too completely integrated with the whole Ethiopian population to be influenced at all by separatist propaganda. Nor did the Somalis of the ex-Colony know that even at that very time, an unsuccessful attempt was being made to detach from Ethiopia the Christian Tigrinya-speaking people of the northern Tigré, to join them with the population of ex-Italian Eritrea, in order to create another little subject people under trusteeship.

Italian rule had always aimed at dividing the people of East Africa into discordant segments. Colonial policy and distance combined to render the Ethiopian Capital inaccessible to the inhabitants of the Somaliland Colony.

Following the Italian defeat, the British Military Administration of all the Somalilands, with the policy of rigid maintenance of the temporary frontier with the rest of Ethiopia, imposed a formidable obstacle which almost prevented visits by the Somalis of Italy's former Colony to the Ethiopian Capital. The status of Muslims in Ethiopia and their relations with the administration were, in consequence, virtually unknown to the mass of the Youth League membership.

The Somali Youth League, who had taken the lead among the people of the Colony, were in the tragic position of putting before the Commission of Investigation, and subsequently before the United Nations, a demand which had no chance of realisation. The League had no alternative to offer. The unfortunate separation from Ethiopia, which the continuance of British Military Administration of the Ogaden had imposed, had perpetuated the artificial aloofness from Addis Ababa created by Italian colonisation, and had thereby prevented the friendly negotiations with the Government in Addis Ababa, and the relations of mutual confidence and co-operation which would have given the policy of the young, energetic and progressive Somalis another orientation and would have opened to them the possibility of the desired new era of happiness and liberty. That the way was, as yet, obscured was largely due to the protracted British Military Administration of the Ogaden, which had created a belief in the possibility of a separate Somali State.

" The atmosphere of intimidation which oppressed the colony, the economic pressure amid Somali poverty made a genuine and truly frank expression of Somali public opinion impossible. The Somali Youth League leaders were employees of the British Military Administration; they had their jobs to consider. Their opponents, who later gained courage to display themselves, were mainly employees, or former employees of the Italians. The two strong opposing forces: The British Administration, and the Italians, landowners, employers and still important officials under the British, created the view that there could be but two alternatives for the future of the Colony: the British plan, or the Italian plan. A Somali who held another opinion would be without support from either force—an outcast."

XVI

CONTEMPORARY SOMALILAND

POPULATION

There has never been a census of population in Ex-Italian Somaliland; only estimates of population have been attempted.

The British Military Administration estimate was approximately 971,000 in 1947, though as regards the nomadic population the estimate was considered by the Administration as subject to error up to 20 per cent.

Of the above total population estimate, 940,000 were judged to be indigenous. The remainder, living mainly in the seaport towns, were estimated as 25,000 Arabs, 1,000 Indians, 3,744 Italians.

Nomadic Tribes

Of the native inhabitants, the largest section, approximately 560,000, belong to the three main Somali tribal groups: the Darot, Hawiye and Dir. Within these are sub-tribes, sections and rers, which last term is equivalent to family, but it may be used to apply not only to the small unit of parents and children, but to a much more extended relationship.

The majority of these three main tribal groups, some 350,000 or thereabouts, live in the eastern and western pastoral areas of the Benadir and Upper Juba Provinces, the remainder comprise the majority in the sparsely populated Mijjertein and Mudugh. They are mainly nomadic, being compelled to this manner of life by their surroundings, and accustomed to it by long tradition, but the Dir and a few of the Hawiye have taken to mixed farming.

The members of the tribe are united by descent from a common ancestor. They settle their affairs in the tribal council, the "Shir," where all tribesmen are entitled to attend and speak, as in Saxon England. The chiefs and headmen are chosen by their tribes and sub-tribes. The greater chiefs are usually hereditary, but the succession is subject to the consent of the tribe. Important decisions by the chiefs are submitted to the Shir.

The tribes own no land, but certain wells are recognised as belonging to each tribe.

The Sab Tribes

The Sab tribes are estimated to number about 292,000. They speak Sab, a dialect closely related to Somali, and are considered to be of similar racial stock to the Somali speaking tribes.

They are engaged in mixed farming in the semi-fertile area between the rivers, in the Benadir and Upper Juba Provinces.

Though their organisation is tribal, they live in settled communities. They also hold their tribal councils and elect their chiefs, who are assisted by councils of elders. As settled communities they have more diverse business to transact than the nomads : the distribution of land, the care and cleaning of artificial reservoirs in which all tribesmen are expected to share, the control of water supplies and other matters.

Land is owned by the tribe, not by the individual. Land is allotted for cultivation, but it remains the property of the tribe.

The River Bank Population

Some 44,000 people, classed by the British Administration as " negroid " (who have come perhaps from further south, or, more probably, are the remnant of an older settlement), speak either a Bantu dialect, or the language of their neighbours.

They live by agriculture alone and are settled in villages. They have headmen and councils elected by themselves.

Craft Tribes

About 17,000 people belong to the so-called " low caste " tribes, but they should more properly be termed craftsmen's tribes; they are engaged in weaving, metal and leather work, as well as hunting and trapping. They have a language of their own, not imparted to others. They live scattered throughout the territory among the other inhabitants, who require the products of their crafts.

Somali-Arabs

Some 19,000 people were classed by the British Administration as Somali-Arabs; they are the fruit of the union of the two races who have for many centuries lived on this coast. They live almost entirely in the Benadir coast towns.

A further 8,000 people do not belong to any of the above groups.

Contact of the Administration with the People

Under Italian rule the appointment of all tribal chiefs and headmen was subject to the approval of the Italian Government of the Colony. The chiefs have functions in the internal administration of the tribe; they represent the tribe in dealing with the Administration; they act as agents of the Administration to the tribe in collecting tribute and other matters. The more important chiefs receive a small salary from the Administration.

Chiefs who failed to conform to Italian official policy were removed. The Italians sometimes made chiefs of their own nominees, as a reward for war service or other cause. The people in several cases approached the British Military Administration asking for the removal of chiefs thus imposed upon them by the former Italian Government.

The British Military Administration also have made the appointment of chiefs subject to their official confirmation, and also pay a small salary in respect of the services performed by the more important chiefs, as the Italians did before them.

As in the British Somaliland Protectorate, the British Administration sought to preserve the tribal structure of Somali society, to emphasise tribal authority and to punish the tribe for the offences of its members. To this aspect we shall refer later.

Urban Population

The urban population was estimated by the British Administration at 170,000, of whom 74,000 live in Mogadishu. 140,000 were judged as being of indigenous origin, 20,000 or 30,000 of them being employed in agriculture or fishing. 75,000 are considered to be of the Darot, Hawiye and Dir, 38,000 of the Sab, 9,000 from the river population, 3,000 of the so-called "low caste" or artisan tribes, 17,000 Somali-Arabs, sprung from the marriage of both races.

Map shows present-day Ethiopia surrounded by thousand-mile radius concentric circles based on the Ethiopian capital, Addis Ababa. Dotted are the former Italian colonies, Libya, Eritrea and Somalia; Ethiopia claims the restoration of the last two.

The indigenous population permanently resident in the towns is de-tribalised. The Administration must deal with them as individuals, whether for taxation, law-breaking or any other matter. They live and support themselves and their families as individuals, though members of their own tribe may perhaps feel special sympathy for them and may aid them in case of distress.

Some 20,000 or 30,000 native dwellers in the towns are estimated as engaged in fishing, or in agriculture outside the town. Others are employed in unskilled labour for private firms, or have work in the Government or Municipality, in the Gendarmerie and other Departments, in transport, trade and the peddling of water, milk, vegetables and other wares.

That water was still an object of street sale in the capital of the Somaliland colony, as it was also in Asmara, the capital of Eritrea, under Italian rule, is evidence that public amenities were still in a relatively primitive state in the Italian Empire.

ADMINISTRATIVE DIVISIONS.

The Somaliland Colony was divided by the British Military Administration, for Administrative purposes, into four Provinces, which roughly follow the natural geographical divisions of the country. The administrative divisions formerly established by the Italians were more numerous and required a larger personnel to operate them than is available under the present administration, but they conformed to the same geographical and climatic factors.

The four administrative provinces under British Military Administration are:

The Mijjertein in the north, which is divided into four districts: Bender Kassim, Alula, Iskushuban and Gardo, and consists of mountainous, semi-desert country, affording but scanty grazing and no organised agriculture. The people subsist by their flocks and herds, the scant pastures necessitating a nomadic existence, by the products of aromatic gum trees which have been famous in the service of religion from ancient times, or by fishing. A number were employed in the salt works established by the Italians at Hordio, but this was closed at the time of the Italian defeat.

Mudugh comes next to the south and is divided into the districts of Galkayu and El Bur. This area is entirely pastoral, but grazing is better than in the Mijjertein. There are numbers of cattle and the ghee and clarified butter produced from their milk is one of the more important exports.

Upper Juba includes Baidoa, Lugh, Bardera, Hodur and Belet Wen, districts frequently referred to in earlier pages. This includes a large agricultural area between the two rivers, the Webbi Shebeli and the Juba, and also a good pastoral area west of the Juba. The products include grain, sorghum, oil seeds, livestock, ghee and aromatic gums from the area around Lugh.

The Benadir. This province includes the coast and seaports and the rich area watered by the Lower Juba and the Lower Webbi

Shebeli, which turns on approaching Mogadishu and flows parallel with the coast till it goes to earth without reaching the sea. It includes the districts of Mogadishu, Villabruzzi, Afgoi, Merka, Brava, Margherita and Kismayu.

The products are maize, sorghum, cotton, bananas, groundnuts, sugar from the Italian-owned estate at Villabruzzi, and livestock. This is geographically by far the richest and most desirable of the provinces and here are to be found most of the Italian concessions which occupy the river-irrigated areas.

NATURAL RESOURCES OF ITALIAN SOMALILAND

The natural resources of Italian Somaliland, its rivers and rainfall, land arable and pastoral, livestock, forests, minerals and fisheries, have never as yet been fully exploited, but there is little doubt that as a separate territory divided from Ethiopia it cannot become self-supporting with a modern administration and ways of life. Its essential function is to provide ports and sea products for Southern and South-eastern Ethiopia. This opinion, expressed by Italian economists, is undoubtedly sound.

Half the Total Area Waste-land

At the present time it is estimated that one-half the total area of this former colony consists of waste-land. 80 per cent. of the other half is pasturage and three-quarters of the population are engaged in stockraising. Only about 10 per cent. of the whole ex-colony is arable land, and even of this only from 1 to 5 per cent. is actually cultivated.

Italians Occupy River-irrigated Land

The best of the arable land, which has been mainly taken up by Italians, is adjacent to the rivers. It profits by the fertilising sediment carried by the river floodwater at the time of the rains, as well as by artificial irrigation from the river.

Native Farmers Forced to Depend on Deficient Rainfall

The land more distant from the rivers, which has been left to native cultivators, depends upon rainfall, which occurs in two rainy seasons: (1) from the beginning of March to the beginning of June, (2) from the middle of August to the middle of November. It should be observed that only on an average of two years out of ten is there sufficient rainfall for agricultural purposes in this rain-irrigated land. In consequence much seed is destroyed by drought.

In addition to the lack of moisture in the areas under native cultivation, there is also exhaustion of the soil, through lack of rehabilitating manure. Consequently the practice of the natives is to cultivate for about two or three years and to allow land to lie fallow for seven or eight years, during which time it is put under pasturage, in order that it may profit by the droppings of the animals, but owing to the prevalence of tsetse fly in certain areas, only camel can be grazed there, as the tsetse has a devastating effect on cattle.

Land Increasingly Impoverished
Italy's Long Neglect of Scientific Measures

The area under cultivation varies from year to year in response to variation of prices and weather forecasts, but the yield of the soil as a whole is falling. Where records have been kept, it is found that the fall has been continuous. A hectare of land under maize, for instance, fell from 15 quintals in 1931 to 9.2 quintals in 1940. Between 1945 and 1947 the yield dropped from 9.7 quintals to 5 quintals. This unfortunate condition is explained by the exhaustion of the soil. It applies, of course, much more seriously to the area under native cultivation where fertilisation from the river is absent, than to the European holdings.

One cannot refrain from commenting that, during fifty years of Italian colonisation, efforts should have been made to decrease the area of wasteland and increase the area under cultivation, by the many means known to modern scientific agriculture. Care should also have been taken to increase the meagre area of forest land. Systematic planting would have done much to improve the colony.

Land Tenure
Native and Foreign

The land surface of the colony was officially divided by the Italians into Waste Lands, (Italian) State Lands, (Italian) Private Lands, (Italian) Church Lands and (Native) Communal Lands.

The Italian Government, as we have seen, permitted the rights of native owners to be determined by the new Italian concessionaires.

By an Italian Royal decree of June 8, 1911, the right to the land of the various occupants, Communal, Private and State, the boundaries of which the Italian concessionaires themselves had determined, were confirmed. No subsequent changes in ownership could be effected without the consent of the Government. Italian legislation officially precluded the indigenous population from acquiring property in land. A Governor's Decree of August 26, 1926, introduced a system of yearly licences for the cultivation of strips of land, called " Shambas." Applicants for such licences had to pay stamp duty of 4 lire for the original grant, and for the renewal of the licence each year. This placed the native cultivator, whether an individual or a tribe, under perpetual uncertainty as to whether the new licence would be granted at the end of the year.

Italian legislation officially precluded the native people from owning land, even though it had been recognised as having belonged to certain tribes for centuries under customary law. The system of licences tended to work against the old system of communal ownership by the tribe.

It will be remembered that the Italian Government, in the year 1909, offered to Italians only concessions of land of 5,000 hectares for a period of sixty years, subject to certain conditions of clearance and cultivation and a stipulated expenditure on the land. These conditions were not fulfilled by the concessionaires. Therefore on September 3, 1930, the Fascist Dictatorship having been established, a new Act reduced the period of the concession to nine years in all, and fixed the area of the concessions at 5,000 acres for irrigated and 10,000 hectares for non-irrigated land. Only from the third year after entering into possession was the grantee expected to pay rent, which was usually about 10 lire per hectare. He was under obligation to make certain improvements on the land. Non-fulfilment of these obligations empowered the Government to annul the concession at any time; fulfilment enabled the grantee to become the owner of the land, with the right to sell, mortgage, grant or bequeath it and with no rent to pay.

50,420 hectares of State land actually held under concession are not yet legally recorded as having finally passed into private ownership.

Well Watered Land Reserved for Italians But Much of it Unused

It is necessary to realise that though the areas of the State lands and Private lands in Italian possession cover much less ground than the Communal lands, they include the richest areas. The so-called Communal lands, which remain to the native people, are divided as follows:—

Arable land (rain irrigated)	7,862,510
Scrub, forest and pastures	27,000,000
Total	34,862,510

The waste lands, half the total area of the Ex-Colony, are partially used for pasture in rainy years when sufficient grass is produced to feed the cattle.

The State lands are divided thus:—

	Hectares
Arable land	35,037
Forests	64,000
Pastures	350
Mines	20
Total	99,407

The arable land of the Colony is divided thus:—

	Hectares
State lands	35,037
Church lands	278
Communal lands	7,862,510
Private lands	37,805
Total	7,935,630

Again, however, we must remember that the Communal arable land is irrigated by the insufficient rain, the State and Private lands are river-irrigated. According to the Italian Chamber of Commerce the Italian concessions in 1940 consisted of 38,696 hectares in the river irrigated areas of Genale, Juba and Afgoi; these, with 35,037 hectares of State arable land, gave 73,733 hectares of river-irrigated land in Italian hands. The British Military Administration estimated the area as 72,842 in 1947, approximately the same.

Prior to the Fascist regime, little was done to cultivate either the State or the private river-irrigated lands from which the ancient cultivators of the soil had been dislodged. When the militarist trend of Fascist policy was intensified, and " self-sufficiency ' became a slogan, somewhat more was done. From 1934, when the conquest of Ethopia was in full preparation, until the Italian entry into the second World War in 1940, there was an increase in the area under cultivation as follows:—

	Area of Cultivated Land
1934	18,700 Hectares
1935	20,505 ,,
1936	23,121 ,,
1937	24,192 ,,
1938	26,000 ,,
1939	27,812 ,,
1940	28,221 ,,

This gives an average for the seven years of 24,079 under cultivation—a meagre proportion of the well-watered, arable land.

The " Società Agricola Italo-Somalo " (S.A.I.S.) at Villagio, founded by the Duke of the Abruzzi, has a vast concession of 25,000 hectares of best arable land. Only 5,700 hectares, however, were cultivated in 1935, 4,600 hectares in 1939, and 3,000 hectares in 1947. This monopoly of 20,000 acres of well-watered, unused land, in a country where such land is scarce is a tragic crime against the population.

The private and State owned lands held by Italians and other non-indigenous people are distributed as follows: —

Private owners	Hectares
175 Italians	72,842
1,016 Arabs	15,000
1 Indian	5
	87,847

The Arabs, old residents, are thus poorly placed compared with the Italians.

Slave Labour on Italian Estates

The lands of Italian concessionaires were worked, as far as possible, by native labour. This labour was slave labour, workers being forcibly constrained to toil on the estates, kidnapped and brought from long distances for the purpose. *

With all the hue and cry the Italians raised concerning slavery, it was never eradicated from Italy's Somaliland Colony, forced labour remaining a continual grievance with the inhabitants throughout the period of Italian rule.

Machinery was employed on some of the Italian farms. When unable to obtain adequate machinery or labour, Italians sometimes let out the poorer part of the land to native cultivators.

Types of Irrigation Ancient and Modern

Simple forms of irrigation of the land by conveying water to it from the rivers had been carried on by indigenous cultivators from ancient times. The Italians, having seized the land it was possible to irrigate from the river, continued to employ the existing methods in some areas and introduced pumping machinery for use in others.

At Villaggio, irrigation was carried out by a system of dams and canals, at Afgoi by pumps, at Genale by canals and dams. On the lower Juba irrigation was by pumps, and also by an old indigenous method, called " deshek," which consists in breaking down the river bank and distributing the escaping water on patches of land below the level of the river bed.

Somalis Refuse to Work for the Old Masters

When in 1941 the Italian forces fled or surrendered *en masse* as the British entered the Italian Somaliland Colony from the South, the Italian concessionaires also decamped. There was a general refusal by the Somalis to work for the former Italian masters when the masters gained courage to return.

The British Administration was unwilling to reintroduce the forced labour of Italian times. Great efforts were made to persuade the Somalis to return to work in view of the great shortage of foodstuffs which, owing to war conditions, developed in 1942, and became acute in 1943. 8,000 acres were put under cultivation by Somalis as tenants of the Italians. Lord Rennell states that in the Genale area " the chief of the dominant local tribe " was induced to provide workers " on the understanding that his people would be permitted to cultivate with the assistance of the Administration a large area of land which had been taken from them."

Later, under the war-time pressure of need for food production, a quota system, which was a form of forced labour, was permitted to provide workers for the Italian farms in Genale, Juba and Villabruzzi, but was subsequently dropped. The Italians, who had been responsible for permanent conditions of forced labour, readily made capital out of this concession to their requirements.

---

* See the British Ministry of Information pamphlet, " The First to be Freed," extracts from which are reproduced in chapter XIV.

Cultivation was gradually re-established as follows:—

Years	Area of Cultivated Land Hectares
1941	7,021
1942	7,800
1943	9,980
1944	12,000
1945	12,550
1946	13,010
1947	15,740

An average of 11,157 for the seven years—not yet half the acreage under cultivation during the Italian regime, which was, at best, wretchedly poor.

The Church lands are the property of the Vicariato Apostolico of Mogadishu. These lands were tilled under the Italian Administration, but under the British Occupation only 20 hectares were under cultivation in 1947.

Indigenous cultivation is principally by the hoe—an ancient implement some 18 inches long, with an iron tip 5 inches in length and 2 inches wide. The land is thereby tilled only to a depth of a few inches. By the use of artificial manure and the plough it has been claimed that the yield of the land can be doubled, but under Italian administration the Somali cultivator was unable to obtain such facilities. Though under British Administration a proportion of Somalis have been enabled to use agricultural machinery, only approximately 5 per cent. of the native agricultural population have yet become accustomed to modern methods of cultivation and the use of machinery, which they now borrow when possible. This knowledge is steadily spreading, though owing to restricted opportunities progress is slow. The Italians hitherto opposed all such progress by the native people. The difficulties of agriculture, whether by Italians or Somalis, have been increased by the removal of agricultural machinery from the Colony by the British Military Authorities for use in Kenya. According to the British Administration the best machinery was taken, and the poor balance left for Somaliland is now in very bad condition. The territory has been seriously impoverished on account of Italy's aggression.

The Italians claim that the indigenous population cannot replace them so far as to restore the degree of efficiency which agriculture had reached under Italian rule. The British administrators are not of this opinion. There is no doubt that if adequate machinery were provided, modern methods could be applied to the whole area under native cultivation. The Somali cultivators are operating without the special assistance by which Italy formerly protected Italian cultivation in the Colony for reasons of prestige; fuel oil for their machines imported duty free and protective tariffs to enable Somaliland produce to be sold in Italy at exorbitant rates.

Somali agriculturalists, with tractor and disc harrow, bring back into cultivation the fertile lands at Genale which, under Italian owners, had been cultivated by forced labour. Photograph from "The First to be Freed," issued by the British Ministry of Information (His Majesty's Stationery Office), 1944.

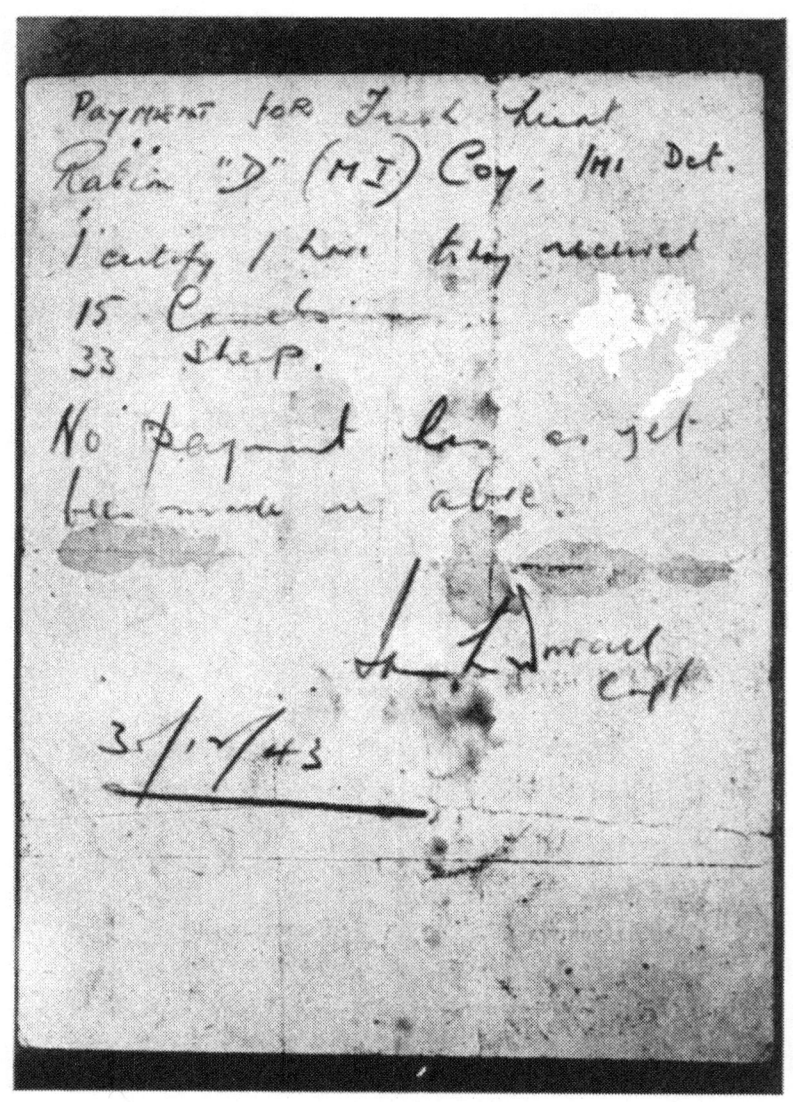

Receipt for animals not paid for, see text on page 167.

RECORDS DESTROYED BY ITALIAN OFFICIALS

In order to present a comprehensive picture of contemporary conditions in the Somaliland Colony, it is well to anticipate here the findings of the Four Power Commission of Investigation, who visited the Colony from January 6 to February 22, 1948. The Commission were handicapped in all their investigations by lack of time and means to verify the statements made to them by the various persons and interests.

The Four Power Commission were handicapped in all their investigations by lack of time and means to verify the statements made to them by the various persons and interests.

In everything pertaining to the administration and to economic conditions, the Commission were placed under serious disabilities by the destruction of official records, deliberately perpetrated by the Italian officials. The decision to retain the Italian staffs as far as possible, in accordance with the Hague Rules, pending a decision concerning the future of the colony gave the Italian officials a power to execute this mischief. The fact that they took advantage of the trust reposed in them to destroy official evidence of conditions under Italian rule makes clear that any evidence they subsequently gave to the Commission, and any statements they may henceforth make should be received with very great reserve.

Fortunately, some records were saved by the British Military Administration before the intended destruction had been completed. These remnants can be partially supplemented by reference to statistical and other information published by the Italian Government in Rome during the years before the Italian defeat. It has been recognised by international statisticians, as well as by numerous candid Italian critics, that the official publications of the Fascist regime were far from fully reliable; statistics were often distorted, or even falsified in order to present a more favourable appearance than the facts warranted. There were no freely elected Members of Parliament, no Parliamentary opposition to exercise supervision over the Government, as in democratic countries.

EXPENDITURE BY ITALIAN ADMINISTRATION
55 Per Cent. on Military; 1 Per Cent. on Education

Nevertheless the annual reports and other publications produced by the Ministry of the Colonies in Rome during the Fascist period, give a truer picture of Italian Colonial rule than the roseate visions conjured now in the effort to recover control of the territories renounced under the Peace Treaty.

The Four Power Commission, like other investigators, had recourse to such Italian Government publications of former years as well as to the branches of Italian Banks to discover as much as possible about conditions under Italian administration. Valuable information is available in an official memorandum on the economic and financial situation of the Italian territories in Africa, published in Rome in 1946. The expenditure of the Somaliland Colony administration in the years 1931/6 and 1936/40 is thus found to have been as follows:

Expenditure*	1931/36 Lire	%	1936/40 Lire	%
Administration	48,627,000	13	67,449,400	15
Social	21,367,200	6	28,448,400	6
Educational	3,336,800	1	4,429,000	1
Economics	11,391,400	3	14,572,900	2
Grants	2,230,000	½	2,500,000	½
Military	144,639,500	39	259,302,000	55
Other Ordinary Expenditure	75,275,800	20	93,583,000	18
Extraordinary Expenditure	60,827,300	17½	23,932,100	2½
Total Expenditure	367,695,000	100	494,217,100	100
Average Annual Expenditure	73,539,000	100	123,554,275	100

The first of these tables of expenditure deals with the period prior to and including the Italian war of conquest in Ethiopia. The Wal Wal incident of 1934, and the earlier raids of the Banda into Ethiopia are included in this period, during which Governor Rava's expenditure would include considerable purchases of arms and ammunition and payments to the native Banda and their Italian officers. The sum of 60,827,300 lire for "extraordinary expenditure", amounting to 17½ per cent. of the total, is doubtless war expenditure in excess of the budget incurred by Marshal Graziani when he came to take over control of the major invasion of Ethiopia from the south. The addition of this extraordinary expenditure to the sum ascribed to military expenditure, would give a total of 205,466,800 lire for military expenditure, 56½ per cent. of the total expenditure.

What is even more grave from the standpoint of civilised peacetime administration is that after the Italian Government had officially declared the war in Ethiopia terminated, and the country "pacified," military expenditure by the Colonial Government of Somaliland did not fall. On the contrary it rose from 144 million lire to 259 million lire, and accounted for no less than 55 per cent. of the total expenditure. Contrasted with the one per cent. devoted to education, the expenditure of more than half the total income of the colony on the military forces presents a truly gruesome picture of the Italian colonial system.

Statements of Italian witnesses from the Political Parties, and the Chamber of Commerce that only modest forces were used to maintain order under Italian rule are discounted by such figures.

* From Memorandum on the economic and financial situation in the Italian Colonies (Rome, 1946), quoted in Report of Four Power Commission Report.

REVENUE UNDER ITALIAN ADMINISTRATION
Subsidy from Rome Provides 64 Per Cent. of Total Revenue

Italian official information concerning the revenue of the colony is only available up to 1936, because later the revenue of the colonies was included with that of Ethiopia, making a combined total for the whole of East Africa. A sum of a thousand million lire had been reserved by the Italian Government to meet the East African deficit in the year 1939-40.

The following table gives the Revenue of the Italian Somaliland colony during the years 1931-36.

Revenue* 1931-6

	Lire	%
Customs and Excise	86,900,000	23
Port Dues	—	—
Licences and Taxes	14,200,000	4
Post and Telegraphs	6,000,000	1½
Receipts for Specific Services	2,500,000	½
Miscellaneous	4,100,000	1
Extraordinary Revenue	21,405,000	6
Total Revenue	135,105,000	36
Grant-in-Aid	232,590,000	64
Total	367,695,000	100
Average Annual Revenue	27,020,400	36
Average Grant-in-Aid	46,518,600	64
	73,539,000	100

Colonies a Deadweight—Maurizio Rava

It will be observed that the grant-in-aid from the Italian Government in Rome amounted to no less than 64 per cent. of the total income. Extraordinary revenue, 6 per cent. of the total, probably covered another grant, to meet a further deficit, unforeseen when the Budget was compiled, bringing the grant-in-aid from Rome to 70 per cent. of the Revenue.

Recalling the continuous drain on Italian resources of the unprofitable colonies Maurizio Rava, Governer of ex-Italian Somaliland, wrote after the conquest of Ethiopia which he had helped to organise:

" *It seemed that these colonies must be a dead weight, a cause of impoverishment. In a word, they were less than useless . . . . It appeared that henceforth they had a poor future, reduced almost to the condition of islands without their advantages, deprived of any commercial outlet by the latent hostility of the Ethiopians and*

---

* From Memorandum on the economic and financial situation in the Italian Colonies (Rome, 1946), quoted in Report of Four Power Commission.

the competition of neighbouring colonies . . . . In short, it might seem that the two colonies of East Africa, and particularly Eritrea, must be preserved for the sake of principle, of national unity, or so that others might not occupy them to our disadvantage, rather than because of any hope of a fruitful result in the future. To-day the two colonies are becoming what they should always have been, the two main outlets of the Empire. Eritrea not only comprises the two important ports of Massawa and Assab, it is also the big market for Ethiopia, and particularly Northern Ethiopia. Moreover, Eritrea and Somaliland, particularly, of course, Eritrea, are also the outlets to Arabia for the products of Ethiopia."

Customs and Excise made by far the largest contribution to the revenue actually raised in the colony. They form 23 per cent. of the total revenue, but 64 per cent. of the revenue raised in the colony itself. Indirect taxation is always recognised as bearing most hardly on the poorest classes of the community—in this case, the native people. In the period covered by the table before the Ethiopian war, the European population of the Somaliland Colony numbered less than a thousand persons. At present, with a European population (mainly Italian) of nearly four thousand, and a Somali population of 971,000, the total imports, according to British Administration statistics, are divided almost equally between native and European requirements. This denotes an extremely small use of imported goods by the Somali people; yet they were, and still are, largely dependent on imported cereals for food, and on imported cotton piece goods for their clothing.

One may assume that the native population paid, and still pay, approximately half the customs dues. In 1926, the Italian Government introduced a hut tax for Somalis who established themselves in settled communities, building with their own hands their small dwellings instead of keeping on the move throughout the year.

No Income Tax Under Italian Rule

Under the Italian administration, there was no income tax. A law establishing it was only introduced in 1938, and even then not enforced.

Whilst favoured by low taxation, the Italians received numerous benefits; they now complain bitterly of the loss of some of these privileges in which the native people, the ancient masters of the land, had little or no share. Not the least of the advantages was the supply of forced labour.

Somalis Forbidden by Decree to Participate in Overseas Trade

It will be observed from the table of Revenue 1931-6 that no port dues were levied. This benefited only the Italians and other foreigners, as the native inhabitants were forbidden by Decree to participate in the import-export trade.

During the early years of Italian possession, such revenue as the colony provided was obtained by the dues charged on native products and the modest native imports, and by the traffic in slaves. It was not until after the Italian conquest of Ethiopia that any serious attempt was made to apply Italian capital to the development of the Somaliland colony, along with the rest of the Italian East African Empire, of which it was now a part. The huge failure of that Empire and the gross waste of the vast expenditure lavished upon it has never been sufficiently exposed, except to a limited number of careful investigators. Yet in 1938 the poor exports from that Empire, including Ethiopia and the two former colonies, were given in an article of proud eulogy, in the officially controlled publication, "Rassegna Sociale dell'Africa Italiana" as follows:

	Lire
Coffee	9,600,000
Pineapples and Bananas	62,300,000
Undressed Skins	32,900,000
Others	31,200,000
Total	136,000,000

As stated in the same publication the imports totalled 1,816,600,000.

The import of wine, which amounted to no less than 85,200,000 lire, exceeded in value any of the export items the Italian authorities considered large enough to mention in a condensed list of main items.

During the years 1931 to 1940, in which the bubble of Italian glory was blown, advances by Italian banks to Italian firms in the colony are alleged to have amounted to 1,014,139,910 lire, 22 per cent. for agricultural, and 78 per cent. for other purposes. It must be recalled that the lire had fallen greatly owing to the astronomical budget deficits of that period. Moreover, the figures are not necessarily correct. One may presume, however, that there was a marked lavishness as compared with the financial stringency of the pre-Fascist period. These loans were not made without Government control, which was all-embracing under the totalitarian regime.

Little information is to hand concerning direct loans by the Italian Government to Italian concerns, but some 80 million lire seems to have been lent to the Società delle Saline e Industria della Somalia, and 33 million lire to the Società Agricola e Industria Somalia, known as S.A.I.S. The latter firm benefited by the expenditure under the head of Public Works, and from the public revenue by 18 million lire on the construction of a railway from its works to Mogadishu for the transport of the produce and the employees of the Company. This represented 12 per cent. of the total expenditure on Public Works in the period 1913-37. Grants to the same Railway totalled 3,730,000 lire in the period 1931-40. Sixty million lire (40 per cent. of the total spent on public works in the years 1913-37) was devoted to land reclamation, mainly for Italian concessions, which occupied the best of the land.

S.A.I.S. was a greatly favoured concern, having tariff preferences to protect its products in Italy, and a supply of slave labour.

It operated an oil seed crushing plant, and started a sugar factory and an alcohol refinery. Tobacco was made an Italian State Monopoly in 1936.

After the Ethiopian War, numerous para-Statal and private monopolies were established:

The supply of petroleum Azienda Generale Italiana Petrolio had the exclusive right to import and sell petroleum products.

Transport. Italiana Transporti Africa Orientale had the sole right to operate passenger services, and in some areas controlled all motor services.

Mining. The Compagnia Mineraria Etiopia, founded in 1937, held 24 out of 27 mineral concessions. All mining was reserved for Italian nationals in Somaliland, and throughout East Africa under the Empire, but very little was accomplished in this direction.

Bananas. In 1935 the Regia Azienda Monopoli Banane was established as a State Monoply for the transport and sale of bananas produced by two Italian companies in the Colony. The entire capital was provided by the Italian Government.

There were concessions for salt production, fisheries and canning. The tendency was for every form of production which could render a profit to pass into the hands of Italian para-State monopolies.

In all this, there could be no place for the native people.

Despite all the huge propaganda of Italian colonial development, and the numerous subsidies to promote Italian enterprise in the colony, the Four Power Commission unanimously reported:

Deficit Economy

"The overwhelming predominance of pasture (almost 90 per cent.) over agricultural land is indicative of the primitive character of the country, where nomadic animal husbandry and nomadic agriculture constitute the predominant forms of economic activity."

"The economic structure of Italian Somaliland has been characterised, up to the present time, by the impossibility of the territory meeting its elementary requirements from its own resources."

"Essential products which cannot be provided from internal sources and must be imported are textiles, representing about one-third of the total value of imports, foodstuffs, such as wheat and wheat products, coffee, tea and dates, petroleum products, motor vehicles and accessories, and tobacco. Total imports are approximately equally divided between native and European requirements. These imports are paid for by exports only to the extent of one-half of their value."

Unbalanced Budgets

"The budget throughout the years has been unbalanced, and in each year expenditure has considerably exceeded revenue."

External Trade

"Records of external trade show a consistent passive trade balance. During the period 1919-1938 the value of exports rep-

resented only 20 *per cent. of the value of imports, the adverse trade balance totalling* 2,417 *million lire, or an average of* 121 *million lire annually."*

Industry

" Apart from the sugar factory at Villabruzzi, and the salt works at Dante, there has never been any major manufacturing enterprise in the territory."

EX-ITALIAN SOMALILAND: VALUE OF EXTERNAL TRADE
1919-1939 *

	Imports	Exports	Adverse Balance
1919	13,768,702	7,556,846	6,211,856
1920	39,411,272	17,623,110	21,788,162
1921	71,112,002	12,129,065	58,982,937
1922	50,960,537	10,988,358	39,972,179
1923	52,957,923	12,235,806	40,722,167
1924	59,404,494	16,780,231	42,624,263
1925	75,712,191	28,519,339	47,192,853
1926	129,441,852	29,033,366	100,408,486
1927	156,246,673	25,300,950	130,945,723
1928	134,158,489	42,330,517	91,827,972
1929	143,906,526	49,980,699	93,925,827
1930	136,122,369	47,955,546	88,166,823
1931	128,789,227	78,823,060	49,966,167
1932	55,546,920	24,053,440	31,493,480
1933	58,662,580	30,252,670	28,409,910
1934	59,190,960	30,390,290	28,800,670
1935	440,807,000	23,550,000	417,257,000
1936	510,334,000	19,225,000	491,109,000
1937	378,817,000	40,676,000	338,141,000
1938	337,906,000	68,000,000	269,906,000
1939	151,261,000	62,625,000	88,636,000
(ten months)			

Incidence of Taxation
Italians and Somalis

During the period of Italian rule, such modest imports as were used by the native people were paid for either by the export of hides and skins, dried fish, clarified butter (ghee), gums and incense, which were produced by them, or by the transit trade with Ethiopia. This had been the case, of course, before the Italians obtained the ports, for it must be recalled that before the advent of Italian administration, there was a favourable balance of trade on the Benadir coast.

The subsidies from Italy, which were needed to maintain Italian consumption and Italian enterprises, did not embellish or amplify the lives of the mass of the Somali population. They remained illiterate and unskilled; their dwellings were poor huts of mud and sticks erected by themselves, or portable basketwork structures of grass and wands, made and carried by the nomads. The Four Power Commission made clear the facts :

---

* Compiled from " Somalia Italiana," by Guido Corni, " Annuario Africa Italiana," and from figures compiled by Somaliland Chamber of Commerce.

"*As the economy of the territory is basically pastoral, the demands of the indigenous population are extremely simple, their essential requirements from outside sources being confined almost entirely to cotton piece goods and certain foodstuffs, which together make up about 50 per cent. of the imports.*

"*Exports of livestock, hides and skins, dried fish, ghee, gums and incense have normally provided them with the means of purchasing their foreign needs.*

"*On the other hand, practically all the necessities of life of the European population of the territory have to be met from foreign sources, the main exceptions being primary building material, vegetables, meat, leather goods and some simple furniture.*"

Thus, despite the subsidies from Italy for the promotion of European enterprises, throughout Italian times the most important export continued to be hides and skins, produced by the indigenous Somali people, and the native people alone provided sufficient produce for export to balance their import needs.

Customs, as we have observed, provided the main source of revenue; fifty per cent. of import dues were raised from the Somalis and more than fifty per cent of the export dues were levied on their produce.

No Income Tax till the British Occupation

Under Italian administration, the Italian colonists were taxed much more lightly than their compatriots in Italy. They wholly escaped the income tax they would have been obliged to pay at home.

Under the British Military Administration no drastic change in the relative status of the Italian and Somali inhabitants of the colony was attempted. Yet there was an effort in some respects to secure a measure of greater equality and fairness.

Income tax was introduced by the British Military Administration on all incomes over £120 per annum on a sliding scale, rising from 6 per cent. to $33\frac{1}{3}$ per cent. This automatically exempted the majority of the poor Somalis, a fact which should be interesting to the relatively prosperous working class wage-earners of Western Europe.

Under the British administration, taxation in 1945-46, both direct and indirect, was estimated by the administration at roughly £25 per head for the European population, which is almost entirely Italian, and for the indigenous people, 5.17 shillings per head, and 8.33 per head in the Benadir, where the principal markets, the ports and main towns are situated.

The total revenue from taxation, including export contribution for the whole territory, was £429,671 in the year 1945-6. The Italian population of the colony numbered 4,822 in July, 1945, and 3,963 in July, 1946. Giving them the benefit of the larger figure, the total contribution to revenue made by the Italian population at £25 per head, amounted to £120,550, leaving £309,121 to be found by the Somalis, the Arabs and the Indians !

Moreover the Italians, whilst making but a modest contribution to the revenue, occupied still the privileged position in all matters: they had the best of the land, and a number of monopolies. Loans were made to them by the British Military Administration between 1942 and 1948, amounting to a total of £342,932, nearly three times as much as they paid annually in taxation. In the years 1941-47, the British administration provided £94,152 in relief and settlement assistance for needy Italians, whereas the unemployed Somalis were left to rely mainly on the succour afforded by their own people. Italian children received free education under British administration; the Somalis have to pay a fee of 2/- a month, unless the fee is specially waived on account of poverty, or the local Somali community raises means to support the school; 2/- a month per child for a parent who earns less than 2/-, perhaps only eightpence a day is not a small matter. Moreover, the total cost of educating the Italian children is higher than the total expenditure on the education of Somali and Arab children, amongst whom only a small minority can obtain places in government schools.

Forced Labour Under Slave Conditions

Documents concerning conditions of work in the colony under Italian administration were amongst those destroyed by the Italian officials at the time of the Italian defeat in 1941. The reason of this particular holocaust is obvious enough, for in the Shakespearian phase, " Conscience makes cowards of us all. " Wages ranging from 1 to 3 lire a day, when wages were paid at all, and a regime of floggings, imprisonments and cruel punishments amounting to torture, are not affairs to boast of.

The British Ministry of Information pamphlet, " The First to be Freed," describing forced labour as it was discovered in the colony at the time of the Italian defeat in 1941, has already been quoted. It reveals that slavery in an extremely bad form was practised under Italian administration until the overthrow of Italian rule.

Throughout the colony, complaints of forced labour were made to the Four Power Commission of Investigation. The Italians defended this wretched institution. The Commissioners unanimously stated :

"*A great many natives complained to the Commission about the system of forced labour for the agricultural concessions in Italian times, and the brutality with which it was enforced.*"

The Commissioners added,

"*The Italians claimed that the system of forced labour was made necessary after serfdom was abolished, in view of the reluctance of the natives to remain employed for a long time in the same enterprise, and of the necessity to promote, in the general interest, the economic development of the country.*

"*They also claim that this regime was not inhuman, but beneficial to the workers themselves.*"

Such excuses are a warning that there has been no change of attitude by the Italian colonists, on whose behalf Italian trusteeship is claimed.

In practice, after serfdom to provide labour for other masters had been abolished, it still continued for the convenience of the Italian " master race."

British Proclamation to Mitigate the Worst Abuses in Labour Conditions

In 1943 a proclamation entitled, " Masters and Servants," was issued by the British Military Administration, which aimed at abolishing forced labour, exacted by the Italians without payment, and other abuses. This proclamation made the following stipulations:

1. **Onus upon employer to prove payment of wages.**
2. **No discharge without due notice.**
3. **Pay to continue for 30 days during sickness.**
4. **Right of complaint to the Court through civil or police authorities.**
5. **Workers forbidden to leave their work if they had received advances of wages before advances worked off.**

In 1947, the British administration gave permission to Italians and Somalis to form trade unions.

Under Italian administration the Somalis were not permitted to form trade unions.

Italian workers were all obliged to belong to Armed Labour Battalions, controlled by the Fascist Party. Strikes were forbidden.

There was no age limit or special protection for child labour, no legislation concerning industrial accidents, medical inspection or hours of labour.

Wages 2/- to 60 cents per day

Wages were stated by the British administration on the basis of Italian standards, to have risen in the towns by 50 per cent between 1941 and 1947. In 1947 they were as follows:

An Italian worker of medium skill, £15 to £25 per month.

A native worker who has been employed by a firm for several years, 2/- a day.

Urban Workers

Between five and six thousand native women workers are employed in Mogadishu alone; they are paid less than men, but no rate is given.

Native children, 60 cents a day.

Native Workers in Rural Areas

Men, 80 cents a day.

Women and children, 60 cents.

Sometimes, some food is added to the small wage of rural workers and they may be given an allotment (Shamba) to grow food for themselves, but frequently have to pay rent for that. The cost of living is considered by the British administration to have risen 100 per cent since 1941, owing to war conditions.

The Italian workers in Africa were organised in a " corporative structure " under direct control of the Fascist Party. There were no Fascist Trade Unions, such as existed in Italy. In the colonies a more direct control by the Fascist Party was considered necessary. In fact, the Party exercised a greater control over the entire administration in Africa, even than in Italy.

The so-called "Fascist Voluntary Militia for National Security" organised "legions" of Italian workers, with the result, as stated in an Italian Official Volume, specially prepared for the enlightenment of Vichy France,* that not a single Italian worker was "refractory" or disaffected. The Fascist Militia, declares the same volume, had solved the problems created by bringing 100,000 Italian workers to the Empire. These workers lived in barracks; they were drilled and armed and marched to their work in military formation; it was officially stated they must always be prepared to exchange their working tools for a rifle. While work proceeded a guard was set and the guns were stacked in readiness to resist attack by the native people. This was the case in the colonies, as well as in occupied Ethiopia. The official Fascist publication, "Lavoro Italiano nell'Impero," reproduces photographs of these armed legions of Italian workers in Somalia and in Eritrea. Two of them, taken in Mogadishu, are reproduced facing page 195.

The condition of the Italian workers was often wretched in the extreme, but that of the native workers was still more deplorable.

Their condition was described in a letter of the Somali Youth League to the Governments of the Great Powers, on August 3, 1949:—

> "The past is very strong with us; we can never erase the bitter memory of Italian policy in our country. We see the ill-effects around us in the economic, political, social, educational and cultural spheres, where we lie miserably down and low. Fifty years of oppression, torture, slave-labour, confiscation of land and brutal massacres cannot be brushed aside."

Vehement Italian official propaganda of "racism" and vilification of African peoples among Italians of all classes in the colony could not fail to worsen the conditions of the native people and their treatment both by Italian employers and Italian workers. A typical article in an official monthly magazine "Etiopia," by G. M. Angioi, argued that the laws of the conqueror must assume a "divine character" to the conquered people. The idyllic notion of the "little black face," propagated for the conquest, must now be put aside. Treatment of the native with "much condescension and without severity" was not a method adapted "to enforce the conception of the divinity of the white race" which the Italian conquest had confirmed. Italian workers "landing in the Empire with innocent curiosity" had adopted an attitude of "confidence and friendship" towards the native, who had not recognised the "benevolent divinity, and condescension of the white as a superior being, but had imagined him a man like himself." Consequently, grave lesions had occurred in Italian prestige : "firm and even hard

---

* La Civilisation Fasciste en Afrique Orientale Italienne: l'Institut National pour les Relations Culturelles avec l'étranger: Novissima, Rome, 1943, pages 181-2,

measures" were now necessary. "History always teaches us that the preventive shooting of twenty often saves the lives of thousands."

There must be a speedy education of the masses arriving from Italy : little brochures must explain to them such essential principles; there must be conferences on the matter by the "dopolavoro." The races must be absolutely segregated. The native must feel "his life is regulated by the white," and "there is a force above him to guide and punish."

SOCIAL SECURITY ORGANISATIONS

No insurance against accident, sickness or unemployment for Somali workers existed under Italian administration. It was only in 1935, when thousands of Italian workers were recruited for public works in preparation for the war against Ethiopia, that the National Fascist Institute of Insurance Against Labour Accidents was established for Italians.

A "National Institute of Social Welfare" was also founded in 1935, and in 1936 followed a "Workers' Sick Fund in Italian Africa"; both these were for Italians only. In 1938 the Italians were further endowed by a "National Fascist Institute of Social Insurance," but this seems to have proved too expensive a venture to put into actual operation, for no information regarding its activities is available, nor could the Four Power Commission of Investigation discover any trace of them. The Italian Representative Committee, formed to put the Italian case before the Commission, would certainly have supplied any favourable facts, had they existed.

After Italian Defeat, Italians in Need Relieved from British Funds

Under the auspices of the British Military Administration an Italian Relief Committee was established at the time of the Italian defeat in 1941. This committee was furnished with British Government funds, which were disbursed with the approval of the British Administration. In the period 1941-1947 a total of £94,152 14s. 6d. was paid by the British Government for Italian relief and settlement. On July 1, in the following years, the Italians on the British dole numbered 855 in 1941, 1,488 in 1942, 1,470 in 1943, 326 in 1944, 266 in 1945, 231 in 1946 and 54 in 1947. During the whole of the year 1947, 82 persons were relieved, of whom 14 were between 40 and 50 years of age, and 19 between 30 and 40. 21 were half-caste children abandoned by their Italian fathers. This was, of course, fully in conformity with Fascist racial laws, which prohibited the support by an Italian *"citizen"* of his child by an Italian "subject," the term *subject* being applied to the natives of Italian Africa. It was decreed that the full maintenance of a half-caste child must be borne by the African parent.

British Aid Famine-Stricken Somalis

Not only the Italians have suffered from the prevailing condition of stagnation in the Colony, the Somalis have suffered greatly; for them there has been no dole system, but a camp described, not too generously, as for "Vagrants," was established in Mogadishu, where 1,560 destitute Somalis were given food and shelter in 1946 and 1947. It is noticeable that the people preferred starvation to work on the Italian concessions.

The failure of the grain harvest in 1946 and 1947, and the high cost of imported cereals, rendered necessary a free distribution by the British Administration of grain to the value of £7,403, in the Mijjertein Province, where stock raising and gum and incense gathering are the main occupations, the salt works at Hordio being closed down since the war. Moreover, in view of the uncertainty of the rain-irrigated agriculture of the colony, the British Government has found it necessary to purchase and store grain for use in case of future emergencies.

Somali Welfare Associations

It should be emphasised that Somalis living in tribal or village communities suffer famine only when the whole tribe or village suffers. Those who have left the tribe or village community to work for Italian or other employers in the towns are thrown on their own resources when unemployment comes. Whilst the Italian administration provided no social insurance for these urbanised Somalis, they were forbidden in Italian times to form any organisations; even clubs for mutual aid and welfare were forbidden.

Under British Military Administration a Native Betterment Committee was formed in 1942, with a Committee of seven Somali philanthropists, presided over by the British Civil Affairs Officer of Mogadishu. Funds were raised by a premium on sugar sold to coffee shops, which in 1947 amounted to 100,000 East African shillings (£5,000). The Committee was supporting, in 1947, an orphanage housing 65 orphans, and plans had been made for a larger orphanage and school.

A Centre for feeding the destitute, called the Suss * kitchen, was started in September, 1946, by a group of charitable Somalis and Arabs, and was continued till June, 1947, when a good crop of maize, available at low cost, rendered this relief unnecessary. 17,000 East African shillings (£850) were raised by public subscription. The Suss kitchen is ready to reopen should need arise.

The Anti-Tuberculosis Committee was formed by the Somali Youth League and is mainly, but not entirely, supported by the Youth League. Its aim is to support a tuberculosis ward in the Infectious Diseases Hospital of Mogadishu, and to assist the rehabilitation of patients on their discharge from hospital. In 1947 it had raised 4,000 East African shillings, (£200).

These and other charitable efforts, spontaneously organised by the Somali people to relieve their compatriots in distress, indicate, that, despite their long oppression, they are not wholly unprepared for the duties and responsibilities of citizenship.

---

* Suss—a measure in the local language.

FASCIST RACIAL LAWS
Oppressed Half-castes

In many Italian official publications the racial laws established in the Italian Colonial Empire to maintain the supremacy of the Italian Empire were eulogised thus :

" The protection of the dominant race is at once the corollary and the crown of Fascist policy. To prevent the formation in the African territories, subject to the might of Italy, of a line of hybrids, engendered by this people of poets, artists and heroes, saints, navigators, and emigrants." *

The imposition of this policy was much too late to prevent the creation of the hybrids who had been produced with all possible energy by Italian Colonists since they began establishing themselves in Africa towards the close of the nineteenth century when every Italian took a woman of the land to act as wife and servant, an arrangement termed the Madame system, to which numerous European writers have referred.

A. B. Wylde, † British Vice-Consul for the Red Sea area, wrote sympathetically of these unions, and praised the new race he saw growing up from them, stating that the children were handsome and intelligent.

Herbert Matthews, an American writer, who accompanied the armies of Marshal Badoglio, and supported the Italian side throughout, being evidently prejudiced against Ethiopia by a colour complex, nevertheless, gives this revealing glimpse of the manners of the Italian masters towards the girl children of the former Italian colonies at that time :

" Coffee, which tasted like nectar (it was one of the few good things in Africa), was served by the Italian, who ran the store with the aid of a pleasant little native girl, whom he had brought up from the age of nine, and who now being thirteen, had been his mistress for some time . . .

" His system was more or less to rob the cradle, teach the infant habits of cleanliness, devotion and respect, and when the proper time came he had a mistress made to order. At what period he considered their usefulness ended he did not say."‡

When in 1934 and 1935, the Italians were being mustered in Italy for the Ethiopian conquest, sex allure was plentifully used to popularise the war. Highly coloured photographs of nude and semi-nude African women were distributed to the troops, copies of which are in my possession; a lady who travelled from London to visit a relative in Rome was astonished to see the life-size photograph of a nude African woman displayed in the window of a recruiting office.

Dr. Chachka, the Hungarian Physician who spent some years in Ethiopia before the Italian war and practised in Addis Ababa for

---

* " La Civilisation Fasciste en Afrique Orientale Italienne," (Novissima), Rome.
† " Modern Abyssinia," by Augustus B. Wylde (Methuen), 1901.
‡ " Eyewitness in Abyssinia with Marshal Badoglio's Forces to Addis Ababa," by Herbert Matthews (Martin Secker and Warburg), 1937.

two years under Italian rule, has described appalling licentiousness on the part of the Italians and the sad results which followed to the detriment of Ethiopian women who were treated with utmost cruelty and disrespect, and to the injury also of Italian youth.

The racial laws, imposing severe penalties and rigid restrictions which were introduced in 1937, may at first appear to conflict strongly with the promiscuity which had been officially encouraged, but on fuller consideration, both of their contents and the conditions which continued after their introduction, the fact becomes obvious that their main purpose was to maintain the supremacy of Italian rule, and to prevent any such fraternisation by Italians with the African people as would produce any tendency among Italians to treat the African as a friend and an equal, or to resent or deplore any of the miseries and cruelties to which the native people were subjected. The aim of the Fascist racial laws was not to suppress rape, but to prevent marriage.

Italians were henceforth to be known in the Empire as Citizens, the native inhabitants as Subjects.

By no means could a subject rise to the position of an Italian citizen. "The legislature does not mean to encourage bizarreries of this sort, which it considers alien to the fundamental principles of Fascist Imperial policy."

Five Years Imprisonment for Italo-African conjugal Relations

The first of the Fascist racial laws, dated April 19, 1937, punished up to five years imprisonment, an Italian Citizen, who established conjugal relations with a Subject. The "Royal Decree-Law" of November 17, 1938, rendered impossible any legal marriage between the citizen and the subject. Both parties to conjugal relations, in such a case, were liable to five years imprisonment.

Citizens and subjects were alike punished for any act prejudicial to "the prestige of the Italian race in view of the African natives."

All so called "Aryans" of non-Italian nationality and "non-Aryan" foreigners were expected to conform to Fascist racial laws. They could not be punished with impunity if they were subjects of the Great Powers, or persons protected by Great Powers; in such a case they were liable to expulsion from the Italian Empire if they failed to conform to the Italian racial laws.

For citizens to frequent public or private resorts reserved for subjects, or for subjects to frequent those reserved for citizens was punishable by six months imprisonment and a fine of 2,000 lire.

A citizen who gave regular employment to a subject without the Governor-General's general or special authorisation in writing was liable to a fine of 5,000 lire.

It was forbidden to allow subjects to travel in the same motor 'bus as citizens, or to allow subjects to travel in motor cars which plied for public hire.

A subject who committed an offence against a citizen was liable to the augmentation of the legal punishment for the offence up to one-third more, if it were shown that the crime had been committed to offend the citizen as an Italian, out of hatred for the Italian race, or to blemish the prestige of the Italian race.

Oppression of Half-Caste Children

Italian citizens were forbidden to recognise their children by subjects, or to contribute to their maintenance or education. The half-caste must not bear the Italian parent's name.

It was a fundamental principle of Fascist policy that the half-caste must be considered a native subject and share the status of the native parent. It was thus sought to ensure an absolute separation between the white and the half-caste and to prevent any native woman deriving profit from union with an Italian.

Italian citizens were forbidden to adopt or affiliate half-castes or natives, and any European or other national who did so was liable to expulsion from the Italian Colonial Empire.

Simultaneously with the promulgation of the Fascist racial laws, a flood of racist publications began to appear; these contained photographs of unfortunate children alleged to be half-castes with hair-lips, withered arms and legs, and the many types of bone malformation associated with rickets, a common disease of malnutrition in childhood, a common indication of inadequate feeding.

The photographs of these child victims of an inhuman system, reproduced in numerous expensively elaborate magazines, some pseudo-scientific, some blatantly propagandist, remain to testify to one of the most flagrant crimes of Italian colonial rule. These innocent offspring of two races, unrecognised by the father, were in numbers of cases doubly orphaned. Their mothers who had often been forcibly removed from the tribe or village, could live but wretchedly when the master had done with them, and all too often met a violent end.

NO EDUCATION FOR SELF-GOVERNMENT

Efficient Public Education, with wide facilities for higher education, to fit a suffucent number of people for service in administrative and technical work, the liberal professions, and the fine arts, are a necessity of progressive and prosperous self-governing States in the world to-day. Such education as was provided for a small minority of the native youth in Italian Africa had no such aim. Its object was purely to train docile assistants for whatever subordinate work might be required by the Italian "master race." "La Civilisation Fasciste en Afrique Orientale Italienne" officially published for the Fascist Government by the "Institut pour les Relations Culturelles avec L'etranger," describes the rôle of the native school: it must not abstract itself from necessities, but must afford a practical elementary instruction to mould the young native for the work required in the locality, whether manual or agricultural.

Fascist writers continually insisted that the creation of "a native intelligentsia" was a folly of Britain, which Italy must avoid. The eulogies of the present Italian Government of "Italy's Action in Ethiopia" and of "Italy's work of colonisation in Africa" indicate that no marked change of view has been developed in Italian official quarters. When the British forces entered the Somaliland Colony any schools which may have existed there were so little in evidence that the Military officials who took control of the Administration of the Colony discovered no trace of them. "The First to be Freed," which reported conditions as the British Administration found them, states that not a single school for the native people existed at that time, and that though one such school had formerly been opened, it had been closed for reasons of policy.

The Italians claimed before the Four Power Commission of Investigation that a number of Roman Catholic Mission schools had existed in the territory at the time of their defeat in 1939. The list they presented to the Commission comprised 6 schools described as "Somali day schools," 3 described as "Somali schools," 3 "Somali evening schools," 4 "Somali evening classes" and 1 Askari "evening class." Twenty-two nuns were listed as the teachers of these nine schools and eight classes. The teaching was doubtless primarily religious. The scholars in all these day schools and evening classes are claimed to have aggregated 1,772, a figure which need not be taken too literally, in view of other exaggerations. Certainly the education provided by these schools was not such as would prepare the Somalis for the successful administration of their territory.

The Italians claimed that they provided also a school for the sons of Chiefs, an arts and crafts school and an agricultural school, but this was strongly denied by Somalis and no evidence of the existence of such schools seems to have been found. The Four Power Commission took the view that "under the Italian regime Catholic Missions had almost entire charge of education." The Commissioners quoted further the statement of the British Military Administration that "the influence of the only Mission at present working in the country, the Catholic Mission under the Bishop of Mogadishu, is small. Its work is chiefly among Italians and half-castes. Its chief work among natives is the conduct of orphanages for half-caste children abandoned by their relatives." This work has been subsidised by the British Administration.

Expulsion of the Swedish Mission

In the Italian East African Colonies the Swedish Mission schools alone provided for Africans an education approaching the European elementary standard. The Swedish Mission in Eritrea was expelled soon after Fascism obtained power in Italy in 1922.

The Swedish Evangelical Missionary Society had been established in Jubaland when that territory was under British administration before it was ceded to Italy as part of the price of her entry into the first World War on the side of Britain and the

Allies. The Mission had built churches and schools at Kismayu, Yorte, Mofi, near Margherita, and at Alessandria. Work at these centres was continued after Jubaland was ceded to Italy, but in 1935 the Mission was unceremoniously expelled at extremely short notice. The property of the Mission was taken over by the Italian Government. No compensation was ever paid. The Mission House at Kismayu was used by the Italian Government as a naval mess, and the church as an observation post. The church at Yorte was turned into a factory for ginning cotton. The church at Alessandria became the farm building of the Italian Government experimental farm. The Mission buildings at Mofi were left untenanted to fall into decay. The expulsion of the Swedish Mission from the Colonies and of several Missions from Ethiopia, during the Italian occupation, was a breach of the Act of Brussels for which Italy has never been seriously called to account.

EDUCATION POLICY

The racist policy of the regime in relation to education is well expressed in the following official Italian correspondence. It is taken from Volume I of the Ethiopian Government's Green Book,* "Documents on Italian War Crimes" which contains captured Italian telegrams and circulars.

It will be noted that the first of the two telegrams quoted was sent to the administration of the six regions into which the Italian Empire had been sub-divided, as well as to the Ministry of Italian Africa and the Director-General of Civil Affairs in Rome.

Governo Generale dell'Africa Orientale Italiana.
Direzione Superiore degli Affari Civili.
Addis Abeba, li 26 ottobre 1939 Anno XVII.
N. 78602 di prot.

Oggetto: Programmi di insegnamento delle scuole per sudditi coloniali. (Subject: Educational program of schools for colonial natives.)

Al Governo dell'Eritrea,	Asmara.
Al Governo della Somalia,	Mogadiscio.
Al Governo dell'Amara,	Gondar.
Al Governo del Harar,	Harar.
Al Governo dei Galla e Sidama,	Gimma.
Al Governo dello Scioa,	Sede.

p.c.

Al Ministro dell'Africa Italiana.
Direzione Generale degli Affari Civili, Roma.

At the last meeting of the Governors full assent was given to the principle determining the directions issued several times from this Government General, that the schools of all kinds established for

* Documents on Italian War Crimes submitted to the United Nations War Crimes Commission by the Imperial Ethiopian Government. Vol. 1 Italian Telegrams and Circulars. Ministry of Justice, Addis Ababa, 1949.

the subject peoples of Italian East Africa ought above all to aim at this goal: to train the pupils in the cultivation of the soil or to become qualified workers (not specialised) in order to create gradually native skilled craftsmen for all fields of labour where, for reasons of climate, surroundings or race prestige, the use of Italian labour is not admissible or convenient, and for the purpose of reducing the cost of labour and production in general by making use of native labour.

Consequently, it is important that the respective Governors, taking into account the special conditions of their own territories, the native attitude to work, and the demands of the local industries, should organise the schools for colonial natives, assigning to each of them specialisation that will most easily lead to the goal indicated above,

It is also understood that, with the exception of the schools for agricultural instruction, where the greater the number of pupils is, the greater will be the economic and social advantages derived from these schools, for all the others, vocational schools and the " cultural schools " reserved for the sons of native notabilities, the number of students should be decided, year by year, with regard to the employment possibilities in the industries and local occupations that can be held out to the students leaving each school.

However, it is considered that as an experiment and with the adaptations that each Government finds suitable, the study programs that this Government General has arranged and sent for approval to each Government, should be adopted for the scholastic year 1939-40.

To the training planned in those programs, should be added gymnastic-military exercises, in the form, and with the teaching staff that each Government judges most convenient.

At the end of the school year, and in all cases not later than July 31st next year, the Governments are to send in a full report, in which should be set forth the possible modifications to be made in the programs and proposals for the establishment of other types of schools, called for by the special demands of local industries.

In that way the Government General will have all the details necessary for the final organisation of the schools for colonial natives which was applied as an experiment during the school year 1939-40 and will be submitted to the Ministry for definite action.

Il Governatore Generale,
A. Di Savoia.

Governo Generale A.O.I.

DE-NATIONALISATION AND RESTRICTION OF EDUCATION

Subject: DIRECTIONS FOR THE EDUCATION OF NATIVES

R. Governo del Harar.

Direzione Affari Civili Politici—Sezione Politica. Riservata. Personale.

N. 25767 di prot. Politici. Harar 5 giugno 1938-XVI. Oggetto: Indirizzo per l'istruzione degli indigeni.

A Tutti I Commissari, Residenti, Vice Residenti, Tenenti Carabinieri.

On my visits, and from this bulletin, I continue to notice that Commissars and Residents have above all an ambition to extend elementary education for natives, and to teach our language to as many children as possible.

This is a fundamental political mistake that tends to put individuals out of their class who, solely because they possess a veneer of education, will refuse to work in the fields, as we know by our own colonial experience and by that of other countries. They are attracted to the towns, ask for Government employment, compete with the nationals in trades that should be reserved for the latter, forming a class of discontented, or even worse, of rebellious people.

As I have already said on other occasions, we should reserve the strictly necessary education for the sons of chiefs and more important notabilities only, because these can later on succeed to the duties of their fathers, serve us as interpreters and hold modest positions in offices.

However, while for obvious reasons we cannot altogether close the door of public education for the youth of the lower social classes, we can and we ought to close tightly the door to special courses, e.g., those for interpreters; and in general we should avoid propaganda and, still worse, pressure on families to send their sons to the Italian schools.

This principle, which can be absolute in the country, ought of course for obvious reasons to be subject to many exceptions in the larger towns (Harar and Dire Dawa).

Also, with regard to native orphans it is a mistaken policy, for the same reasons as mentioned above, to establish orphanages, because there, in the end, you will always give them habits that do not belong to their race or their social class.

Instead, these derelicts should be cared for by entrusting them to relatives, or at any rate to native families, who under our control and for a modest monthly sum can bring them up in the very surroundings in which they afterwards will have to live and work.

It is superfluous to add that the present directive is of a very secret character, and should be applied without divulging the real motives.

Il Governatore

(Gen. Guglielmo Nasi.)

Governo del Harar,
Segreteria particolare di S.E. il Governatore.

XVII

THE COLONY IN SUSPENSE

United Nations Create a Trusteeship Council

The future of the Somaliland colony, in common with that of the other territories Italy possessed in Africa, remained in suspense.

The control of their destinies still lay provisionally in the hands of the British Prime Minister, the United States President, and the Generalissimo of the Soviet Union, who together controlled the Allied war effort.

The formation of the United Nations Organisation to replace the virtually defunct League of Nations, had been announced by Mr. Churchill and the late President Roosevelt. The world war being obviously drawing to a close, the invitations to a conference for the inauguration of the new international body were issued by Britain, the United States, the Soviet Union and China as the sponsoring Powers.

The failure of the League of Nations through the defection of the United States, a blow delivered almost at the birth of the new institution, and the unwillingness of other Powers to shoulder their responsibilities under the Covenant when faced with the deliberate aggression of Italy, Germany and Japan, caused extreme solicitude that in the second attempt to create an international organisation the United States should have no reason for dissatisfaction, and that none of the major victorious Powers should have cause for withdrawal. Hence the Security Council on which Britain, the United States, the Soviet Union, China and France predominated, was given authority in certain vital matters above that of the General Assembly. Hence the veto, which was the prerogative of these Powers and precluded any decision to which any one of them objected.

The opinion was expressed in many high quarters, particularly among the prominent advocates of the League of Nations and its Covenant who most deplored its untimely demise, that the League had been damaged in prestige and efficacy as a peace-preserver by its responsibility for the Treaties between the victorious Powers and their enemies which succeeded World War I, with their punitive provisions, territorial transfers, reparations payments, Control Commissions, and all their errors and blemishes. It was claimed that the United Nations should arise free of all such commitments in order to gain universal confidence as the impartial bulwark of peace and international understanding.

This opinion coincided with the view that at all costs the victorious Great Powers must all be induced to accept responsibility for the maintenance of peace, and also with the view of the statesmen of those Powers, that the terms of the Peace Treaties should be decided by them, and afterwards ratified by the lesser Allies and the Parliaments concerned. The making of the Peace which was to follow World War II would thus be much more narrowly restricted than the great assize of Versailles, which attracted delegations, spectators and journalists from every corner of the globe under the auspices of President Wilson and David Lloyd George.

The United Nations Organisation, which was formally established at San Francisco between May 25 and June 25, 1945, had therefore no mandate to decide the fate of the ex-colonies, but it loomed in the background as a possible arbiter should the four Great Powers fail to agree on the disposal of these forlorn territories. Moreover the Charter of the United Nations prescribed the creation of a Trusteeship Council which might assume control of the ex-colonies. Trusteeship under the Charter might be applied to:—

1. Territories held under Mandate (the Colonies forfeited by the enemy States at the close of World War I.)

2. Territories which may be detached from enemy States as a result of World War II.

3. Territories which may be voluntarily placed under the trusteeship system by States responsible for their administration.

These provisions aroused considerable anxiety among the peoples of the former Italian colonies. Trusteeship was regarded in Eritrea as an altogether unacceptable substitute for the reunion to the motherland promised during the war. In Libya it was equally repudiated. The suggestion that Trusteeship should be applied to them was spurned with indignation by the vocal sections of the population of those territories.

In the more isolated population of the Somaliland colony there was also anxiety, but some were encouraged to believe that United Nations Trusteeship would afford an escape from the return of Italy and would bring prosperity and liberation.

POTSDAM CONFERENCE

Council of Foreign Ministers to Prepare the Peace Treaties

Following the creation of the United Nations, Mr. Churchill, who withdrew to make way for Mr. Attlee when the result of the British General Election became known, with President Truman and Generalissimo Stalin, met as victors at Potsdam, the Germans having surrendered in May whilst the victors were still occupied at San Francisco.

The three Statesmen decided to form a council of Foreign Ministers, adding representatives of France and China to the conclave, and charging the Council of five with the duty of drawing up the Peace Treaty with Italy and the satellite States, Bulgaria, Finland, Hungary and Rumania.

Council of Foreign Ministers Meet in London

Much activity was displayed in respect of the former colonies. The Italian Government had sent a memorandum to the Potsdam Conference, declaring colonies vitally necessary to Italy.

On August 28, the Emperor Haile Sellassie received the British United States, and Soviet Ministers in Addis Ababa, and stated that as the first victim of Italian aggression, Ethiopia attached special importance to the consideration of her claims by the Council of Foreign Ministers.

The Council of Foreign Ministers met in London on September 14. Mr. James Byrnes, the American Secretary of State, advocated collective trusteeship by the United Nations for all the ex-colonies. M. Molotov, on the contrary, advocated individual trusteeship by the Great Powers. He claimed the trusteeship of Tripolitania for Russia, and expressed Russian interest also in Eritrea.*

On September 18, Signor de Gasperi and Dr. Kardelj were permitted to plead the claims of their respective countries. Australia, Canada, New Zealand, South Africa and India were also invited to attend, but neither Ethiopia, nor the people of the former colonies were heard.

On September 21, the Emperor Haile Sellassie gave an interview to "Reuter" in Addis Ababa, and stated that a memorandum had been sent by the Ethiopian Government to London, urging that Eritrea and ex-Italian Somaliland should not be returned to Italy but handed to Ethiopia, "not as recompense for 10 years struggle against the Axis, but as territories incontestably belonging to the Ethiopian Empire since before the Christian era, and stolen through Italian aggression." He protested that Ethiopia had twice asked to be represented at the discussion of the former colonies by the Council of Foreign Ministers, but had been allowed only to submit written statements, whereas the enemy was given full opportunities of representation and discussion. This Ethiopia considered unjust.

The London Conference ended in a deadlock, the Foreign Ministers being unable to reach agreement. Their deputies, permanent officials in the respective Foreign Offices, were deputed to continue the discussions in the hope of reaching a compromise.

Paris Conference of Foreign Ministers, April-May, 1946

The Council of Foreign Ministers assembled again in Paris on April 25, their differences still unsolved. For the Italian colonies, four schemes were proposed:

1. BRITISH PLAN
 1. Immediate independence for a United Libya including both Tripolitania and Cyrenaica.
 2. A United Somalia under British Trusteeship, consisting of British and Italian Somaliland, plus the Ogaden region of Ethiopia, that country to obtain compensation in Eritrea.

---

* "New York Herald Tribune" report and Press Conference given by M. Molotov at Soviet Embassy in London, September 18; also Mr. James Byrnes in "Speaking Frankly."

Satisfactory to the people of Libya, this plan was wholly unacceptable to Ethiopia. It was in direct conflict with the Charter of the United Nations, which expressly provides that the territory of Member States of the United Nations cannot be placed under trusteeship.

Ethiopia was naturally unwilling to barter her Ogaden province in exchange for Eritrea, which she claimed as rightfully her own as well as the formerly Italian Somaliland colony. The Emperor's Coronation pledges debarred him from ceding any part of Ethiopia's national territory. Moreover, at that very time the people of the Ogaden were pleading and agitating to be restored to Ethiopian administration.

2. UNITED STATES PLAN

Collective United Nations Trusteeship for all the former Italian Colonies, with a promise of independence for Libya within ten years.

3. FRENCH PLAN.

Italian Trusteeship of all the former Italian Colonies, subject to United Nations supervision.

4. SOVIET UNION PLAN.

Collective Trusteeship, as in the American plan, but special regimes would be established:—

(a) Tripolitania would be governed by a Soviet Administrator and an Italian Deputy Administrator, supported by a Commission of British, American, French and Arab members.

(b) Cyrenaica would be governed by a British or American Administrator, with an Italian Deputy, supported by a Commission of British, American, Russian, French and Arab members.

Mr. Bevin opposed Italian trusteeship; Libya was of great strategic importance. Italy had used it to pour German troops into Africa; British troops had conquered North Africa in a campaign which had been one of the turning points of World War II. Moreover Britain was determined to keep her pledges to the Senussi, who had suffered greatly by Italian rule.

On May 10, M. Molotov announced the willingness of the Soviet Union to support the French proposal of Italian trusteeship of all the former colonies. Mr. Bevin expressed willingness to assent to Italian trusteeship of Tripolitania provided Britain received trusteeship of Cyrenaica.

The right of Ethiopia and of the people of the ex-colonies was as yet little regarded. Theirs was a cause which still had to win its way.

No agreement was reached; it was agreed to disagree on the most controversial matters; the disposal of the ex-colonies and the frontier between Italy and Yugoslavia; the deputies were instructed to prepare the draft Treaties for submission to a Paris meeting of the Foreign Ministers leaving those clauses blank.

Mr. Bevin's United Somaliland Proposal

Mr. Bevin in the House of Commons on June 4, 1946, explained his proposal for Somaliland, in respect of which Mr. Molotov had charged him with endeavouring " to expand the British Empire at the expense of Italy and Ethiopia, and to consolidate the monopolistic position of Great Britain in the Mediterranean and Red Sea."

Mr. Bevin urged that the Ethiopian Ogaden "is the grazing ground for nearly half the nomads of British Somaliland for six months of the year. Similarly the nomads of Italian Somaliland must cross the existing frontiers in search of grass." He added:

" In all innocence, therefore, we proposed that British Somaliland and the adjacent part of Ethiopia, if Ethiopia agreed, should be lumped together as a trust territory, so that the nomads should lead their frugal existence with the least possible hindrance, and there might be a real chance of a decent economic life, as understood in that territory. All I want is to give these poor nomads a chance to live; we are paying £1,000,000 a year out of our Budget to help to support them. We do not ask anything; but to have all these constant bothers on the frontier, when one can organise the thing decently—well, after all, it is to nobody's interest to stop these poor people and cattle there getting a decent living. That is all there is to it."

Mr. Bevin was no doubt sincere, but he had no personal knowledge of the territories. As we know the difficulties of the Somaliland people had not been liquidated by five years of British Military Administration covering the whole of Somaliland. More was required to promote prosperity than a mere policing of the territory. Mr. Bevin did not hear the sad complaints of impoverishment of the people of the Ogaden. He observed, however, that his proposal depended on the proviso " If Ethiopia agreed."

Paris Conference of 21 Powers

At a further meeting in Paris on June 14, 1946, the Council of Foreign Ministers resolved to call a conference of representatives of 21 belligerent Powers on July 29, also in Paris, to consider the drafts for the Peace Treaties which the Foreign Ministers had prepared. This conference would be purely advisory, but the Foreign Ministers declared their willingness to take into consideration any resolution passed by the 21 Powers by a two-thirds majority.

Being unable to agree on the disposal of the former colonies, they adopted a draft article enforcing a renunciation of the colonies by Italy, but adroitly postponing any effective decision by the following provisions:

a. Italy to renounce all right to her former colonies.

b. These territories to remain under British Military Administration pending their final disposal.

c. Their future to be decided by the Council of Four Foreign Ministers within a year of the signing of the Peace Treaty.

The Conference of 21 Powers assembled in the ornate Luxembourg Palace and debated at length the draft treaties with Italy and the Satellite States. The Italian Government was permitted to send a delegation to address the assembly and the Commission.

The adviser on the colonial questions to the Italian delegation was Enrico Cerulli, Vice-Governor-General of Ethiopia under the Mussolini regime, an administrator much feared by Ethiopians during his term of office there and also in the Somaliland colony, where he was first stationed.

Signor De Gasperi was willing to wait a year for a decision, provided Italy was not obliged to sign away her right to the colonies. He wanted to send there "tens of thousands of Italians" whom he declared had lived in Eritrea, Somaliland and Libya, and to retain the Italian officials in the administration of those territories. Signor Bonomi demanded trusteeship for Italy of all her colonies.

The Ethiopian delegates, Ato Aklilou Hapte Wold, Foreign Affairs Minister and leader of the delegation, Blatten Gueta Lorenso Taezaz, Ethiopian Minister in Moscow, Blatta Ephrem Medhen, Ethiopian Minister in London, stoutly upheld Ethiopia's claims.

Mr. Gladwyn Jebb on behalf of the United Kindom Government expressed sympathy with Ethiopia's claim to Eritrea.

Strong pleas were made to the Conference by the Council of Foreign Ministers to accept the compromise they had arrived at, not to vary in any material matter the drafts they had made. They promised that if within the year specified in the draft agreement with Italy they could not arrive at an agreement on the colonies they would refer the problem to the Assembly of the United Nations and would abide by the Assembly's decision of this matter. This proposal was eventually accepted by the Paris Conference.

A joint declaration issued by the Four Foreign Ministers announced that the final disposal of the ex-colonies was to be made in accordance with the wishes of the inhabitants of the territories and other interested governments. It might comprise:

i Independence.
ii Incorporation in neighbouring territories.
iii Trusteeship exercised by the United Nations as a whole, or by any one of them, or by Italy.

Commission of Investigation Appointed

At a meeting of the Council of Foreign Ministers in New York, from November 3 to December 12, 1946, the Council of Foreign Ministers appointed a Commission to investigate opinion in the former colonies.

Italian Treaty Signed

The Italian Peace Treaty was signed in Washington, London, Paris and Moscow during January and February, 1947. The Italian Government sent Marchese Lupi De Soragna to sign the treaty in Paris, on February 10. On the same day, Count Sforza, the Italian Foreign Minister, sent a peremptory note to the Allied Signatory Powers, declaring that Italy looked forward to the revision of the Treaty, and calling on the Powers " to review their attitude and dealings with the Italian People."

Ethiopian Minister to Enquiry Commission

In November, 1947, the Enquiry Commission appointed by the Council of Foreign Ministers, meeting in London, invited representatives of Ethiopia and Italy to state their views on the former colonies.

Ato Aklilou Hapte Wold, the Ethiopian Foreign Minister, described the ancient racial, historic, religious and economic affinities between the former Somaliland colony and Ethiopia. He stated that "one may pass, more or less imperceptibly from regions of Southern and South Eastern Ethiopia without finding racial or other differences among the Somali and Galla peoples of these regions. For many centuries Ethiopia included the entire Horn of Africa."

He emphasised the value of the Indian Ocean ports of the Somaliland colony to the commerce of Southern Ethiopia and the benefit to the colony of the foodstuffs it should derive from Ethiopia without an intervening frontier. As so often in the case of Eritrea, he emphasised the deficit economy of this poor strip of territory divided unnaturally from Ethiopia.

The colony lacking the means to be self-supporting whilst divided from Ethiopia, lacks the economic possibility to become a self-supporting independent territory.

He traced the long history of Italian misrule in the Somaliland colony, the scandals of Chartered Company rule, the slavery under the Fascist Regime which had ended only in 1941. The evil record was sufficient to exclude Italy from consideration as a possible trustee.

The danger to Ethiopia of Somaliland being again used by Italy as a base of aggression, he urged, is of prime importance. Continual Italian encroachments upon Ethiopian territory from their Somaliland colony had culminated in the Wal Wal incident of 1934 and the war of 1935. By her unprovoked aggression against Ethiopia, Italy had forfeited all claim to the Somaliland colony.

He claimed that the Italian inhabitants of the colony had amounted to only one-tenth of one per cent. of the population of the colony.

Somalia—A Strategic Area

Were trusteeship granted to Italy, she might probably declare the colony, by reason of its position on the coast of the Indian Ocean, a strategic area within the meaning of the United Nations Charter, which would involve the withdrawal of the area from all surveillance by the United Nations General Assembly and the Trusteeship Council. This was a very shrewd forecast.

When the interested Governments had been heard, the Commission of Investigation set off to visit the former colonies, Eritrea, Somaliland, Cyrenaica and Tripolitania.

XVIII

FOUR POWER COMMISSION OF INVESTIGATION

THE RIOT IN MOGADISHU
January 11, 1948

The investigations of the Four Power Commission in the former Italian Somaliland colony were rendered sombre and depressed by the tragic riot which occurred in the capital of the colony, Mogadishu, on January 11, five days after the Commission arrived on January 6, 1948.

Anticipation that their investigations would govern the decision of the future of the territory, had created high tension in popular feeling and probabilities of conflict between the population opposed to the return of Italy on the one hand, and on the other hand, the Italians, and a proportion of their native troops and employees who relied on their promises of back pay and balances due to them from former times.

The Italians were determined to impress the Commission with the importance of their following. They hung Italian flags out of windows, and on January 6, 7, and 8, organised processions of the motor buses and diesel lorries which they owned, driven by themselves and packed with their employees. These street demonstrations were held without any request to the British authorities for permission or even the bare notification requisite for obtaining police protection and the adjustment of traffic. That the British authorities were totally ignored in this matter was stated quite clearly with considerable self-righteousness by the Italian organisers in evidence before the Four Power Commission, though in every country the police are always at least consulted in respect of public processions.

That trouble was brewing was evident enough from the fact that on January 6 a bomb was thrown into the Nine Hundred Bar, and on January 7 a grenade was thrown into the Italia Bar. The authors of these deeds have never been made known.

It was therefore not totally without reason that on January 7 Brigadier Smith, the Chief Administrator, wrote to the Four Power Commission, urging that whilst demonstrations outside the capital would not constitute any grave threat to law and order, in Mogadishu itself this was far from being the case. There was a large floating population there, he wrote, ready to exploit any situation which could lead to looting. Processions and demonstrations would not be spontaneous expressions of popular desire, but the result of organisation, one procession would lead to another, with rising temper and risk of violent clashes. The Chief Administrator suggested that if the Commission decided not to view processions in the capital, tension would be eased and the risk of disorder much reduced. One must here emphasise that processions and interviews with self-appointed leaders and persons picked from the streets at random, is no proper substitute for a ballot vote of the population.

Had the Commission decided to refuse to view further processions in Mogadishu, as suggested by the Chief Administrator the advantage as regards street demonstrations would have been left with the Italians, only some minor impromptu counter-demonstrations having up to that time been held.

The Commission, however, replied that "within reason, political parties should be allowed to organise demonstrations as they wish."

Vain British Efforts to Stave off Conflict

Accordingly, the British Administration gave permission to the Somali Youth League to hold a procession on January 11, the secretary having first consulted the Commission in regard to a convenient place for the procession to be held.

It became known to the British Administration that the Italians intended to hold a procession of their own supporters simultaneously with that of the Somali Youth League. This was precisely what the Chief Administrator had suggested might occur. The British Civil Affairs Officer interviewed Dr. Vincenzo Calzia, the secretary of the municipality, and other prominent Italians, and endeavoured to persuade them to hold their own demonstration at some other time

On the face of it, any impartial person must admit that to insist on holding two opposing demonstrations at one time is unreasonable, and that in view of the high feeling on both sides, and the many disorders which had occurred in the town, the British Military Authorities would have been fully justified in deciding that the processions of the rival parties must be held at different times.

The weakness of the British authorities in this case appears to have been two-fold. On the one hand, it was made evident to them that the Italians would refuse to obey an official prohibition, that they would resist, and would call upon their followers to resist, any attempt to prevent them doing as they chose. To stop a procession by force would involve a conflict the administration desired to avoid.

On the other hand, the British Administration was anxious to fall in with the wishes of the Four Power Commission, and to act in a manner which the Commission would consider impartial. The Chief Administrator's appeal to the Commission to discountenance street processions in the city, had failed. Persuasion was therefore the only course open to the Military Administration, and that was unavailing.

Dr. Calzia, as he subsequently stated to the Four Power Commission, informed the British Civil Affairs Officer that the pro-Italy parties desired to demonstrate every day continuously, that they intended to demonstrate when the Somali Youth League did so, therefore there could be no compromise concerning the date.

British Official Account of the Riot

What followed was described by a communique issued by the British Military Administration, issued on January 11, gist of which was reproduced by the Press, as follows :

"The Four Power Commission finally assembled in Mogadishu on January 6, 1948. On that day and on the two succeeding days there were unauthorised demonstrations by natives mainly Diesel lorry-borne in buses driven by Italians displaying the Italian flag. Italian flags were also on show from a number of houses, etc. These processions were most clearly Italian organised.

"The Secretary of the Four Power Commission was sent a formal letter on January 7, 1948, by the Chief Administrator drawing attention to the danger . . . . The reply received on January 9 indicated that the Four Power Commission considered that processions should not be prevented and on the same day the Secretary made enquiries about the most suitable place for the Four Power Commission to view a Somali Youth League procession on the 11th, for which permission was then granted.

"On the morning of the 11th it was reported that 25 lorries, mainly Italian driven, had left Mogadishu to bring in Italian native supporters from the countryside, with a view to breaking up the Somali Youth League procession. At about 8-30 a.m. numerous bands of Italian supporters, many representatives of tribes and clubs known to be in receipt of Italian funds, started to enter the town. They were armed with clubs, bows and arrows and spears. It is said that arrows were fired at women and children outside the Somali Youth League Club building and casualties caused, and at the same time many native supporters of the Italians rushed through the streets throwing stones and attacking Somali Youth League lorries and individuals.

"It is known that the previous day sums of money had been disbursed to these supporters of the Italians. Within a short time the S.Y.L. * retaliated and the hooligans of the town, who were obviously awaiting this opportunity, commenced to loot extensively. Violent anti-Italian feeling was immediately aroused, which was fanned by Italians throwing hand grenades and firing shots. Shops and houses, particularly those displaying Italian flags, were looted, and individual Italians were attacked and in many cases killed . . . .

"The attitude of this Administration has been throughout that it should not repress exhibitions of political affiliation directed at the F.P.C. † It has equally considered it its duty to warn the Commission and the Political Parties concerned of the dangers of certain courses of conduct. That the warnings have been amply justified has been proved in the event and only the alerting of the Gendarmerie and King's African Rifles forces at the disposal of the Administration enabled a most violent uprising to be so quickly quelled, and prevented even greater losses of life and property amongst the Italian population.

> "(a) *On the 30th December the Commissario Straordinario was informed that the display of Italian flags on private buildings or by persons would not be officially prohibited during the period of the F.P.C., but that in the opinion of the Administration it would be most wise to discourage it for the personal safety of Italians.*

---

* S.Y.L. = Somali Youth League.
† F.P.C. = Four Power Commission.

"(b) On the 31st December the Chief Administrator personally warned the Commissario Straordinario, the Judge of the Colony, the President of the Chamber of Commerce and Dr. Calzia, Secretary of the Municipality, who was himself the leading protagonist of the Italian propaganda party, that any attempt to introduce country tribespeople into Mogadishu could only result in disorder, of which Italians would be the likely victims.

"**Police who had already been alerted had extinguished the main trouble by 1-30 p.m.. The King's African Rifles, who had been standing by, were called into the town immediately the disturbances started.**

"**A curfew has been imposed from 6 p.m. to-day.**

"**Arrangements are being made for Italian evacuees who had to be taken from their homes under Police protection.**

"**The following steps had previously been taken by this Administration:**

"(c) On three occasions during November and December the Commissario Straordinario * had been formally advised that the propaganda of the Italians would, in the opinion of the Administration, produce an inevitable reaction dangerous to Italian life and property."

What had happened appears evident. The Italians believed that with the support they had mustered, they could easily drive their opponents from the streets by shooting a few of them at the first onslaught. They had gravely miscalculated the temper of their Somali opponents, who turned against them in overwhelming numbers.

The conduct of the Italians had been so inexcusably provocative and so defiant towards the Administration that the British officers in charge were not prepared to open fire on the people whom the Italians had attacked.

ITALIANS AND SOMALIS KILLED AND WOUNDED
Causes of Injury

Later, it transpired that 51 Italians had been killed, and 51 wounded.

Somali losses were not so great, being 14 killed, and 48 wounded.

One of the British personnel was wounded.

The British Military Authorities gave a list of the injuries suffered by the wounded Italians, and by the wounded civilian Somalis. The cause of the injury of the wounded Somalia Gendarmerie, was not included in the list. Though consequently incomplete, the causes of injury of the wounded on the two conflicting sides is worthy of consideration.

Of the Italian wounded, none had been shot, 4 had been injured by bomb splinters, 28 had been stabbed, the remainder had been injured "by various clubbing instruments", which presumably means any heavy weapon.

---

* The Italian Administration still functioning under British rule.

Of the Somali civilian wounded, 16 had been shot, 9 were injured by blows from sticks, 7 by knives, 3 by iron bars, 7 by arrows, 1 by a spear.

These causes of injury bear out the British account, which stated the Italians had brought into Mogadishu, from the country, people with bows and arrows, and spears, to attack the Somali Youth League procession—after the fight, it was thus found that Somalis alone had been injured by arrows, and only one Somali had been wounded by a spear.

The Somalis alone, and none of the Italians, were injured by bullets; this indicates that the Italians carried firearms to the procession, to attack their opponents. The Somalis, however, did not carry firearms; therefore, no Italians were shot. Four Italians were wounded by bomb splinters.

Knives were used on both sides; they might have been carried habitually, and brought out for self-defence when the attack developed. Sticks and other weapons used for striking assailants might have been caught up from the shops, or anywhere available when the fighting began. The most significant injuries are those created by bullets and arrows.

177 Italian-occupied houses were looted, and the Italian Mission Press was damaged by fire.

Italians and Somalis Arrested

Dr. Calzia and four other Italians and five Somalis were subsequently arrested by the British Military Authorities, on the ground that the former were guilty of conduct prejudicial to public order, and the latter had accepted cash from the Italians as an inducement to create disorder on January 11. The British Military Authorities declared they were in possession of ample evidence to prove these charges.

Attack on Evacuated Italian Farms at Genale and Merka

News of the reverse the Italian attackers had suffered in Mogadishu, and the overwhelming retaliation of the population against them, spread rapidly to Italian concessions at Genale, and in the Merka area. The Italians fled from their farms. In their absence, though standing crops were untouched, their houses, stores and machinery were destroyed.

The King's African Rifles were sent to the Italian estate at Villaggio, to prevent destruction there.

BRITISH ADMINISTRATION VILIFIED
Italian Government Protests
COURT OF ENQUIRY ESTABLISHED

The British Military Authorities in East Africa immediately strengthened the forces in the colony, further troops were marched into Mogadishu. A Court of Enquiry by high British Officials from outside the colony was established to investigate the cause of the riots and the handling of the affair by the officers on the spot. Unfortunately, the findings of this court have not been published. The existence of the court rendered the question *sub judice*. The British Military Administration were therefore precluded from furnishing the Four Power Commission with the detailed particulars regarding what was termed the " pogrom," which were peremptorily demanded by the Commission.

In Italy there arose a storm of indignation. The Italian Government made diplomatic and public protests alleging failure by the British Military Administration to provide adequate protection for Italian citizens. Memorial services for the Italian "Martyrs" were held in all Italian Churches. Anti-British and anti-African propaganda ran mad. The Italian press published drawings of imaginary innocent Italians, attacked by imaginary black men. In

GENTLEMEN'S AGREEMENT   NEMMENO LA LIBERTA' DI LA' VORAREI

The cartoon on the Mogadishu riot of January 11, 1948, referred to above, which appeared in the Italian newspaper " Figaro."

one case the Italians were represented as streaming into Church, and assaulted by black men with swords. In a series of cartoons, John Bull was shown giving a dagger to a primitive black person, armed with a spear and bow and arrows, with the caption, " Gentlemen's Agreement." An Italian, industriously digging, had a large knife sticking in his back, with the caption, " Not even liberty to work."

Allegations that officers of the British Administration had been actively concerned in an unprovoked attack on the blameless Italians travelled even as far as the *Manchester Guardian*.

A series of conflicting statements were made to the Four Power Commission by 11 Italians, and 5 Somalis, and were published in their Report. According to some of these statements, "Askaris were killing Italians"; according to others, they were protecting them. It is interesting to observe that the majority of the Italians who made charges against the Askaris, admitted they had themselves been onveyed to hospital or to places of safety in the lorries of the Askaris. Four witnesses charged the British with direct participa-.ion in the riots by hand grenade throwing, firing revolvers, and loot-ng; others made vague general charges. Many of these complainants finished up their account by describing how they had finally been taken to hospital or some other place of safety in British lorries. Some witnesses had seen processions of pro-Italians with sticks, swords and lances. One of the wounded Askaris said he had been shot by an Italian, and stabbed by a Somali carrying an Italian flag.

Whilst the charges flew round, members of the British Military Administration had perforce to remain in stony silence; the whole affair was *sub judice;* they could make no answer to the charges diffused against them.

In some curious way the defeated Italians, who had themselves deliberately created the riot, were permitted to become the accusers of the British Military Administration, and of the Somali Police Force. Their losses secured for their accusations a grave and sympathetic hearing by the Four Power Commission of Investigation, particularly from the French and Soviet members, who reported on most questions in favour of Italian claims in accordance with the policy of their Governments at that stage.

On account of the Italian dead and wounded, the British Government in Whitehall, the British Military Administration in the colony, and the British Press, expressed condolences, and most tolerantly refrained from reproaches.

It is said the findings of the Commission of Enquiry were kept private at the request of the Italian Government, who appealed to British generosity, not to disclose the misdeeds of the Italian colonists, in order to spare the feelings of innocent Italians at home in Italy, whose relatives had been killed.

In view of the Italian allegations, it is much to be regretted that the findings of the judicial enquiry have not been published. The apparent assent of the British, United States, and French Governments to Italian Trusteeship of the Somaliland colony, which had formerly been favoured also by the Soviet Union, along with the Italian losses in the riot they had themselves created, and stern British orders from Whitehall to protect the Italian population at all costs, produced a considerable change in the atmosphere of Mogadishu. The Somali Gendarmerie were no longer the main force preserving law and order, other troops patrolled the streets. A curfew was imposed. The Somali Youth League had lost official favour.

HEARING OF THE SOMALI YOUTH LEAGUE

At their hearing by the Commission of Investigation, the Somali Youth League were asked : " Why do you want a trusteeship of Four Powers, not of one nation ? "

They replied:

"*We have been under one Government, and have little to show in the way of progress.*"

They expressed the belief that if the Administering Powers would do their utmost "to train the people of the ex-colony, they would be able to administer their internal affairs within ten years. Our second desire is education, but even if we were promised the very best education in every line within the next ten years, but were excluded from unity with other Somalis, we would not agree."

" It was stated that Mr. Bevin advocates the establishment of a greater Somalia. When we saw this utterance by the Foreign Minister of a great Power we were very happy because it is one of our aims. If you want us to live and progress, we can get it only by the unity of Somalia. This is a matter we put above all other questions."

Education

Mr. Abdulla Issa, the secretary and chief spokesman of the League, stated " we had no elementary education in the time of the Italians. Since British Military Administration came, elementary education has been organised. This education was mainly to get men available to be of assistance in the service of the administration, to be of service to the various departments, and to have a chance of earning a living in posts not open to them before."

Asked how many technical schools were opened to prepare the Somalis for expert professional employment, Mr. Issa said: "There is no technical school in the real sense of the word, but there is a departmental training school run by the police for the police force, there is a medical training class which was in existence at the time of the Italian occupation, but the standard has since been improved for the Somalis."

It should here be interpolated that such training is not medical training in the European sense, it is purely the training of medical orderlies, or "dressers." An idea of the standard may be gathered from the information by Lord Rennell,* that Somalis, thus trained

---

* British Military Administration of Occupied Territories in Africa.

for hospital service in the British Somaliland Protectorate, were paid 2/- per day.

Economic Development and Subsidies were all in Italian Interests

The development of the country whether by capital or technicians, was formerly all in the interests of the Italians, and not for the benefit of the Somalis, the same applies to the subsidies provided to maintain the colony.

If encouragement and assistance were given to the Somali people, there would be great improvement.

The encouragement of Somali agriculturalists by the British Administration had increased the production of foodstuffs.

"Under the Italian Administration, no Somali was permitted to export or import goods."

"No Somali owned land of any value which he could cultivate in his own interests,"

"There was restriction of movement; if a Somali wanted to go from Mogadishu to a neighbouring place, Brava, for instance, he had to get permission."

Racial Discrimination, No Freedom of Speech

"It was an order of the Italian Government that any Somali meeting a white man should salute him.

"We had no freedom of speech, no clubs, no associations, no bodies in which we could express our opinion.

"What freedom of speech we ever got, we got under the British Military Administration, not before."

Tribal Distinctions

"During the Italian occupation, tribal distinctions were emphasised. Tribal feuds in the interior are very limited. The Somalis understand the meaning of brotherhood.

"The feuds are chiefly around Mogadishu. The main cause is the money used by the Italians to have people under their hands."

"Osmania"

Osmania, a script for the Somali language previously unwritten, was invented thirty years before by Osman Yusuf. Under the Italians anyone caught using it was imprisoned. Its use has begun again since the Italians were defeated, but it has not made the desired progress for lack of books, printing presses and other facilities.

Attacks on the Somali Youth League by Italians, Pro-Italians and Individual Somalis

At the hearings of deputations from the various Somali organisations by the Commission of Investigation in Mogadishu, and the interviews with groups and individuals sought by the Commission in other areas, the Somali Youth League was attacked by its opponents on various grounds. It was charged with being dominated by "foreigners," a term which was elastic enough to cover Somalis from the Mijjertein in the north of the colony when used by Somalis in the south, and in particular Somalis from the British Protectorate or any other distant Somali area. The League was further accused of unwelcome interference in tribal matters, and of intimidation and violence towards other parties, the removal of their badges and tearing down of their flags. Not unnaturally, the Youth League regarded the supporters of Italy as traitors to their country.

On the other hand, the Somali Youth League member, Hagi Mohamed Hussein, informed the Commission, " Pro-Italian people are in danger of being beaten up by the population." He added that Somali notables who received communications from the Italians soliciting support sent these communications to the League. The gravamen of the case against the Youth League was that the police and Gendarmerie were to a large extent members of the League, and made use of their weapons and authority in defence of its interests against their political opponents, and sometimes brought about their arrest. It was alleged by the Italians and their supporters that membership of the Youth League and of the Gendarmerie was synonymous, and that to obtain employment of any sort under the British Military Administration it was necessary to belong to the Somali Youth League. Nevertheless, it is noteworthy that many persons who made this allegation were themselves actually employees of the British Administration at the time. When their attention was drawn by Mr. Stafford, the British member of the Commission, to the fact that they and several of their Party colleagues were employed by the Administration, they protested that they were mere exceptions.

It must be observed that persons who by defective work or unwillingness to execute instructions, revealed themselves unsatisfactory employees, hostile to the Administration, would be weeded out of employment and that those who considered their interests better served by service to the Italians would not apply for positions under the Administration. On the other hand, the members of the Somali Youth League being exceedingly numerous, eager to learn, and willing to work under the British Administration would inevitably obtain and retain many posts. Nevertheless the fact remains significant that in Eritrea the police and other employees were not permitted to join the big Union with Ethiopia Party and were obliged to make a formal declaration that they were not members of a political party and would not even express a political opinion whilst in ex-Italian Somaliland. The Administration, as stated before the Commission of Investigation, made no objection to gendarmerie, police and other employees of the Administration becoming members of a political party.

The French and Soviet members of the Commission accepted the charges against the Somali Youth League and inserted the gist of them in the Commission's Report. The British and United States Commissioners observed with greater caution and more friendliness towards the League, which they recognised as " active and progressive ":

" It seems probable, in view of the many complaints, that the numerous adherents of the Somali Youth League among the employees of the Administration used their position to advance the interests of their party and to bring pressure on their opponents, but the extent to which this was done could not be determined by the Commission.

" It should be noted that many of the complaints were obviously exaggerated."

The United Kingdom Delegation further protested against the inclusion in the Report of " unsupported allegations by political parties and others for the purpose of vilifying their opponents. The Commission has not investigated them, and they do not assist in a serious consideration of the question under report." The Commission obviously could not, with any degree of fullness, investigate, in their brief visit to the ex-colony, the charges of parties and individuals against their opponents. A vote by ballot could be the only means of ascertaining the majority opinion of the population.

YOUTH LEAGUE SCHEME FOR FUTURE SOMALI GOVERNMENT

The scheme for the future Government of Somaliland presented by the Youth League to the members of the Four Power Commission of Investigation was condemned by the Soviet representative as " a primitive document " having " many contradictions " which " cannot be considered serious." The British and Americans decribed it as " elaborate."

The suggestion was repeatedly made that perhaps the scheme had been drafted under foreign, and probably British influence. Such phrases as: " that the Judiciary be separated from the executive " would appear to suggest British influence. On the other hand, the English text was declared by the League spokesmen to have been written by two Somalis of the League who have had foreign education, Mr. Alex J. Saloloh, a lawyer, and Mr. Michael Mariano, who had lived in Aden and British Somaliland. These gentlemen had admittedly been consulted in the drafting of the scheme. The Youth League clearly stated that League membership was not restricted to Somalis of the ex-Italian colony. Though travel was sternly prevented, as far as possible, by the Italian administration and though education was mainly absent also in the British Protectorate, the British Administration had imposed no barrier to travel and a number of Somalis there obtained work on the ships or by other means left the colony, and thereby obtained a knowledge of events abroad.

The following points illustrate the general scope of the Youth League programme for the desired government:

"There shall be a constitutional means by which the people can make their will apparent."

A uniform system of law and administration; no racial discrimination.

"The judiciary to be separated from the Executive; qualified judges in higher courts."

The interests of the inhabitants to be paramount; no privileges, rights, or concessions to be granted which would affect the state ownership of land, or hamper the future political or economic development of the country.

The exploitation of the natural resources of the territory will be in the form of Government and private concessions, in which Europeans will be the employers and Somalis will be the labourers."

The above phrase strikes a note strangely acquiescent in the state of affairs which had always existed in the colony; it is here that one feels the suggestion of foreign drafting, or perhaps of the overpowering character of tradition which has caused the oppressed aspirants to political liberty to assent to the continued existence of an economic subordination of the Somalis without even a phrase to suggest that some day the old conditions will be changed. Such words could not have been written in Ethiopia. Though foreign firms exist there which employ Ethiopian labourers, the Ethiopian nation never accepted the principle that Ethiopian industry should fall into foreign hands. An Ethiopian share of the management and invested capital has always been stipulated in large enterprises. This was provided by the Emperor Menelik in his concession to the Franco-Ethiopian railway. The principle of Ethiopian participation has been even more fully safeguarded in recent concessions.

No More Slave Labour : " The Horrors of Genale "

In view of the stated position that "Europeans will be the employers and Somalis will be the labourers" the draftsmen continued:

"Thus a labour office will be required to safeguard the rights and liberties of the labourers, and make it impossible for the slave and forced labour of by-gone times ever to return to this land of ours.

"Labourers were treated as chattels during the Italian period and the horrors of Genale must not be repeated.

"The Labour Office shall be controlled by a Labour Officer, assisted by labour inspectors who shall visit all industrial and agricultural concerns where labour is employed.

" A 54 hours working week in factories.

" A 36 hours working week in offices."

The proposals for the standard of life of the unfortunate Somali labourer in the desired new era are so modest as to be painful to Western ideas, and indicate but too tragically the abject misery he and his have suffered hitherto:

"The worker shall receive the minimum wage that is compatible with a decent human life, giving the labourer the bare necessities of life, such as two square meals a day, enough clothes to cover and protect his body and a tolerable human habitation."

Then follow claims to:

The right to form Trade Unions.

14 days a year paid holiday.

Sick leave on pay for thirty days.

Half pay for two months. Compensation for injury at work.

Medical services for workers both preventive and curative. Dispensaries to be maintained by the employers for their workpeople.

Compensation for injury and death of workers.

Clubs for sport, libraries and evening classes for workers.

A juvenile affairs board consisting of employers, workers and educationists.

Rural schools for training of farmers and agriculturalists to be maintained by the government.

Investigation into Italian Activities and Responsibilities Demanded

The Youth League bitterly stigmatised the political activities of the Italians, and the so-called "pro-Italian" parties they had created among the Somali population in order to further Italian aims. The Youth League called for investigation into Italian economic exploitation of the people and the natural resources of the territory, and further declared that the Italians had evaded their due contribution to the revenue of the territory, as follows:

"*The Italian nationals are determined to stage a come-back for their Government, by hook or by crook, using to the full the administrative and economic hold they have, and the advantage their wealth and Press give them. They are led by the foremost Italian nationals in commerce and in the British Military Administration.*

"*The most active officials of the Italian Party are also officials of the Administration. They are Baron Beretelli, Dr. Vincenzo Calzia, Major Decina.*

"*The Somali pro-Italian faction are mostly people who have been bribed by the Italians, Chiefs and ex-Italian Government employees who have been promised arrears of pay for the past seven years.*

"*All the pro-Italian Parties have been founded and directed by Italians. They have done nothing of national value, and have no following except in places where there are Italians to support them.*

"*We have proof of unfair methods used by the Italians to influence and deceive the Somalis by pressure and bribery.*

"*The Italians are flooding Mogadishu with statements published in their Press which make it appear a foregone conclusion that the Italian Government is returning to Somalia. They have even written articles giving quotations which make it seem that the Four Big Powers favour the return of Somalia to Italy, and that this will undoubtedly be confirmed when the Commission of Investigation see the wealth and position of the Italians here. This is a deliberate attempt to kill opposition and to intimidate the public."*

The Youth League protested indignantly, and with a sense of outraged justice, against these attempts to intimidate opponents of Italian rule in order that they might be induced to express a view favourable to the Italians in fear of reprisals after the Italian return:

For an interested and prejudiced alien body, with powerful resources and facilities, to try, by fair and foul means, to deceive and influence a poor, ignorant, backward people is in itself contrary to the principles of democracy and fair play. It becomes downright wickedness when done at a time when the people are called upon to make a free choice of what they want for the future of their country, and the future generations of Somalis to come."

The Youth League made the following urgent demands:

Annulment of all Italian law incompatible with the principles of democracy and the rights of the inhabitants.

Removal of Italians from the Administration.

A Commission to investigate the Italian concessions, their contribution to the economic life of the colony, the profits of the shareholders, the exploitation of the Somali workers.

A court of inquiry to investigate claims against the Italian Government concerning savings bank deposits, arrears of pay to ex-Italian employees and arrears of pay, gratuities, pensions, etc., due to ex-Askaris.

Promotion of Adult Education.

The British Military Administration to remove restrictions upon trade with the outside world.

In the Report of the Inquiry Commission, the British and United States representatives commented on the Somali Youth League thuswise: " In the last five years a nationalist movement led by the Somali Youth League, has rapidly spread through the country, embracing most of the urban classes wherever located, and, through the influence of the chiefs and elders, almost all the tribes except those in the Sab Confederacy and a few others. This movement is well organised, possesses relatively competent leadership, and may well be the major force in Somali politics for some time to come.

" The other political parties have developed in opposition to the Somali Youth League, and, with one exception, are of recent growth. Their influence is slight."

The French and Russian representatives added the comment: " This development has sharpened relations between the tribes and contributes to the general feeling of insecurity."

THE HAMAR YOUTH CLUB

The Hamar Youth Club shared the aims of the Somali Youth League; it claimed a membership of 8,000; its activities were confined to Mogadishu.

The British Military Administration had provided teachers for educational classes held by the Club. In addressing thte Commission of Investigation they spoke with simple humility, " All things are in your hands, you Big Four; we want you to show us the way to independence. We want you to help us. We want to have a chance in the world."

THE SOMALIA CONFERENZA

In the Somalia Conferenza were combined all the elements in the colony which could be mustered to support the Italian claim to Trusteeship by the United Nations. The effort was supported by the Italian Press of the colony and by broadcasts of the Italian Minister of the Colonies in Italy, making lavish pledges of reform, by the pressure of Italian employers in the colony, by promises of pay and pensions to former soldiers of the Italian native forces and by payments to a number of individuals.

To muster a favourable vote by the Conferenza it was necessary to embody in it stipulations that Italian Trusteeship would be of a temporary character, giving place to early self-government and being accompanied by many beneficent reforms, which were embodied in twenty-three conditions.

Italian Trusteeship for Thirty Years

One must observe at the outset that this programme was purely a mirage.

There was some difficulty in proposing to the Conferenza thirty years trusteeship by Italy, in contrast to the ten years trusteeship of the Four Powers, during which the population would be trained to take over the administration which the Somali Youth League was advocating. The Italian Government, desirous of a trusteeship without any limit, would not consent to the mention of any briefer period than thirty years on the part of the Somali pro-Italian Parties of the Colony, which were operating under Italian auspices.

The ex-soldiers of Italy's native forces and other former employees of the Italian administration were by far the most numerous class prepared to accept a temporary trusteeship by Italy. Their motive was merely to recover sums due to them by the Italian Government, but they were not willing to accept more than ten or twelve years of Italian Government to secure them.

To overcome such reluctance it was emphasised that during the thirty years trusteeship the Somalis would take a continually increasing part in the government of the territory, both as administrators within the Government and by their own assemblies, which, beginning as advisory bodies, would steadily exercise more power, until at the end of the thirty years' probation they would assume the full functions of a democratic legislature.

Thus the trusteeship would gradually expire; from the moment of its inception the surrender of its functions to the growing government of the Somali people would begin.

To safeguard this conception of a temporary trusteeship, and to ensure that Italy would be obliged genuinely to accept a temporary charge and to prepare the people for self-government, the following 23 points were set forth as conditions governing the acceptance by the Somalia Conferenza of Italian trusteeship.

A careful perusal of these points indicates firstly that taken as a whole they do not envisage the Italian position in Somaliland, which is demanded by Italian propaganda inside Italy, where the colony is claimed as an outlet for Italian unemployed. Secondly, these conditions would involve exceedingly substantial expenditure by Italy for the benefit of the Somalis, and in the matter of education, more liberal provision for them than Italy has found for Italians at home.

Somalia Conferenza Demands

Mr. Islau Mahalle, President of the Somalia Conferenza, who is a typist in the office of the Italian Judge, informed the Four Power Commission that the Conferenza had been formed because the British Military Administration was assisting the Somali Youth League, and the promoters of the Conferenza hoped the Commission would see the present position of the Colony. The initiative was taken by Salah Sheik Omar.

The following demands were adopted at a meeting of the Conferenza:—

(1) Full independence and admission on equal terms to the comity of free peoples.

(2) Recognising that this is not immediately possible, socially, politically or economically, they asked for sincere and disinterested guidance by a European nation, to enable them to govern themselves within 30 years.

(3) An independent state conforming to the principles of the Muslim religion, but allowing the practice of any other religion.

(4) Parity of right and duty between the Somalis and the subjects of the Trustee Nation.

(5) Schools on European lines with Islamic teaching for the Somalis, and the right to enter any other schools.

(6) The greatest possible impulse to be given to Education in every branch.

(7) Increased participation of the Somalis in the Government to be assured.

(8) Gradual admission into the public administration of Somalis possessing the necessary qualifications and capacity, on equal terms with Europeans, especially in the local administration which will be autonomous.

(9) Somalis to be admitted to all grades of the civil administration, the army and the police.

(10) Somalis to be admitted to the Universities and assisted by Government grants during their studies.

(11) Existing Islamic schools to be maintained.

(12) An Upper Islamic school to be established for Somalis who should be sent to attend the El-Azhar courses.

(13) All school and other questions of interest to the Somalis to be studied jointly between them and the Government.

(14) Professional and commercial education shall also be provided.

(15) Central and local assemblies to be established, at first consultative but exercising increasing powers until the Central Assembly becomes a true legislative Chamber.

(16) Liberty of association, Press and opinion.

(17) Development of Public Health and Sanitation facilities.

(18) Liberty to select and engage in any employment or profession.

(19) The right to reside anywhere in the territory, except in any special areas restricted by law.

(20) Liberty of sojourn for study, business or other matters in the territory of European nations.

(21) Development of rural economy and veterinary assistance.

(22) Liberty of sojourn in European countries for study, business and other matters.

(23) Respect for Somali religion and customs.

(24) Assistance to orphan children, invalids and foundlings.

(25) The Trusteeship of the former Italian Colony to go to Italy.

(26) Security for the realisation of the above demands to be given by Italy.

(27) All pending claims for payment by Italy's former military and civil employees to be settled and all damages arising from the last war to be paid by Italy.

(28) Italy to " warrant that no revenge or retaliation will be perpetrated against the Somali people for their behaviour during and after the war up to the cessation of the present administration, and that the territory will be democratically governed and administered."

(29) No racial discrimination to be practised; in this connection the Italian Government should give the largest warranty.

The above are known as the " Twenty-Three Points," although in the English translation, as will be observed, the arrangement is such that there are more.

HEARING OF THE SOMALIA CONFERENZA

When a deputation from the Somalia Conferenza was heard by the Four Power Commission, Islau Mahalle, the president of the

Conferenza, said naively, "We believe that Italy civilised the world, and we think in a period of thirty years she can give us a government."

Asked whether the Somalia Conferenza would accept Italy on any conditions without Italian acceptance of the points they had enumerated, Islau Mahalle replied:

"*No, we would not accept Italy if she did not accept the 23 points.*"

Sheck Mohamed said: "We were hating the Italian Government, and were saying, ' May God bring the British Administration! We were hearing the British Administration was a justice giver and peacemaker.' " He proceeded to make a strong attack upon the Administration and the Askaris, the effect of which was undermined by exaggerations such as: "There is not any Somali in this territory who has not been looted or killed."

The veracity of the president, Islau Mahalle, was rendered doubtful by his conflicting statements on the outstanding question of forced labour. He alleged, "With Italy there was freedom of work and of agriculture."

The Soviet representative intervened: " Several of the representatives who have spoken before us have stated that there was forced agricultural labour during the Italian administration."

Mr. Islau Mahalle retorted: "Those who say that are Somali Youth League, no one else in Mogadishu."

Later, however, Islau Mahalle remarked that the imposition of compulsory labour was "the only error" committed by Italian Government.

Hillo Mahomed, of the Conferenza, made a complaint which showed clearly enough that the progressive element among the Somalis of the ex-Colony were opposed to that body and would make no compromise in their determination to be rid of the Italians; he said:

"*All the population of Sab Somali are included in the Somali Youth League because these people have gathered in order to have education. They are school boys. All Somali Youth League are gathered there, and they are from many tribes, having gathered in order to have education.*"

The Youth League could ask no finer tribute, the more so as this description of its members came from one who was styled an adviser of the opposing body, the Somalia Conferenza, which had appeared before the Four Power Commission to oppose the ideals of the League and to ask for a further period of Italian rule.

PATRIOTIC BENEFICENCE UNION

The Patriotic Beneficence Union was one of the Parties included in the Somalia Conferenza formed to support Italian interests.

They claimed a membership of 80,788, mainly of Abgal Somalis, including Yuzbashi and others of the Italian native forces and about 500 Arabs.

Like other parties represented in the Somalia Conferenza the Union was given also an individual hearing, a procedure which in the Report of the Commission tended to give to the parties influenced by Italy a disproportionate importance, since the parties opposing Italy, although considerably larger, numbered only three and one of them did not appear before the Commission.

The President of the Patriotic Beneficence Union, Salah Omar, had acted as Chairman of the Somalia Conferenza when its programme was drawn up.

Salah Omar complained to the Commission of hardship in the Colony, shops were closed, people unemployed. Many had to sell their property and spend their savings in order to live. Six months after the British came, the people decided they were worse off under Britain than they had been before the war.

Workers were paid only from 1s. to 1s. 6d. a day as a maximum. They needed more than £1 a week to live decently. They asked for the return of Italy on the 23 conditions adopted by the Somalia Conferenza. They complained of intimidation by the Askaris and suppression of their views by the Government. 9 of their members were under arrest, 4 had been deported. They had only been allowed to form an organisation in June, 1947. Despite these charges, Salah Omar, the President, was himself employed by the British Military Administration. He had been working for the Italians when the British came and they retained him. He complained he had suffered under British Administration, but afterwards admitted "from the point of view of my work I have nothing to suffer, but from outside, from the Askaris, I always suffered."

The Patriotic Beneficence Association claimed to maintain four schools and to give charity to poor members; this was the object of the society. When anyone died in hospital the organisation arranged the funeral. The activities of the organisation had been carried on by members' subscriptions. Salah Omar admitted that it had also received financial assistance from the British Government.

In a written statement the Union had declared: " They acknowledge that the British Military Administration during these difficult years has allowed them to express their opinions and at last to state their wishes to the Commission freely. For this they are grateful to the B.M.A."

Salah Omar, when questioned about this statement, which contradicted the whole of his testimony, was evasive. He ended by requesting the Commission to leave a representative in the Colony " to secure our safety."

HIDAITA UL ISLAM

The Sab Io Somali had formed seven parties, one of which, the Hidaita Ul Islam, appeared before the Four Power Commission. They explained that Hidaita Ul Islam means, " this land is ours." They had formed their organisation to defend their land. They belonged to the Conferenza. Their motives in joining it appeared to be a traditional conflict with the nomadic herdsman tribes of old standing, and the more immediate fact that numbers of their people were unemployed owing to the closing down of Italian enterprises. They spoke of persecution, though several of them were employees of the British Military Administration. Abuker Hussein, the Vice-President, said: " Wherever there is a British Officer, next to him is a Somali Youth League member, either as a boy, a personal servant, or as an interpreter, and that is why we have troubles." Material inducements obviously played a prevailing part in such support as could be mustered for Italian claims.

Amush Maalim said that the Askaris and interpreters who worked in the British Administration had informed the people that the Commission was coming " to settle Africa and ask the tribes what Government they want." The Somali Youth League then tried " to make an agreement between ourselves to ask for a government of the Four Powers. We did not wish to accept because their own land is not here; this land is ours."

Amush Maalim stated, and his colleagues held the same view, that:

" Beyond Galkayu, as far as we are concerned, it is Hargeisa, Jibuti and Addis Ababa. Beyond Galkayu, we consider them foreigners."

Asked by the United States Representative, Mr. Utter, to give any of the 23 points of the Somalia Conferenza programme, and again pressed to give even one point, the Hidaita Ul Islam Delegation were unable to reply.

Their statements were a sad evidence of the lack of education and enlightenment in which the people of the ex-Colony had been retained for half-a-century.

WAR VETERANS OF THE ITALIAN NATIVE FORCES

Six war veterans of the Italian Native Army, two of them Eritreans, came before the Commission to plead their poverty and, as they said, to apply for their rights. They claimed to represent thirteen others and to speak for 25,000 war veterans, of whom 7,000 were wounded, and also for 5,000 families of the men who had been killed. They had no organisation and were not regularly appointed, but a meeting of veterans had been held. There was no claim to public policy in their case; it was a case of misery which begs relief:

" We are all Italian military veterans. Italy left us in despair, owing to losses, owing to death. We have been waiting long years after the war before the Commission came to this place. We were soldiers, and therefore supplied with everything we needed. Since Italy left us we have been waiting seven years. We had been working for twenty or thirty years. We had only one profession, that of soldiers, and we have lost completely everything. We were left in the open air. That is why we were waiting for the Commission.

"What we want is to save our own things. Thank God the Commission is here. Those who died left wives and sons. The old veterans were so old that they could not work. Our prayer is, do not leave this country without helping those who have been abandoned by Italy.

"Some of us have not got our pay for the last year of the war. Sometimes the Askaris were taking their pay and depositing it with the Commanding Officer. The Commanding Officer was saving their accounts with the Post Office. Then there are all the people dead who left sons and wives. These people lack assistance and have not received what the deceased earned during the war.

"For the last seven years we have been, as it were, in a prison. We had been working for twenty or thirty years and nobody recognises this work. We have come here to claim our rights."

Asked whether they were under the impression that the Commission had come to settle their claims against the Italian Government they replied: "Yes, that is our desire." When it was explained to them that the Commission had not come for that purpose but to ascertain the wishes of the population respecting the future government they protested: "We have come here to claim our rights, since we were working in the Italian Guard."

That was the substance of such support as existed among the Somali population for the return of Italian Government.

Mohamed Ali, one of the six veterans, who was a member of the Abgal tribe, complained that his people were "without work and without clothes;" they lived in the bush and only wore goatskins. He worked in Mogadishu, but was paid only 1s. to 1s. 6d. a day to keep himself and his family of seven. This was not enough 5s. a day was the necessary minimum. They had only one meal of millet per day; he saw meat only once a week.

When they at last understood that the Commission had not come to grant them pay and pensions, these veterans asked for a twelve year Trusteeship by the Italian Government. Mohamed Ramadan, a Muslim of Eritrea, stated that he was a former Yubashi (an African non-commissioned officer in the Italian army). He had resided in the Somaliland Colony since 1910 and had fought for the Italians in Tripolitania and Cyrenaica.

THE DIGHIL MIRIFLE

Sheik Abdulahi, the President of the Dighil Mirifle, who reside in Mogadishu and from Afgoi to Iscia Baidoa, informed the Commission that they had been summoned to a meeting of the Somalia Conferenza. They were "not satisfied with the programme, and thought harm would come of their decisions" and that "they might make even worse decisions." They told the Commission: "We want the Four Powers, we do not want any more of those of before." They observed that there was forced labour under Italy.

In the course of the interrogation by the Commission it transpired that the letter sent by the Dighil Mirifle to the Commission had been altered by the Italian translator. Abikar Kassim, the Vice-President, who was a member of their delegation, had written the letter in Arabic. The Italian who had been paid to translate it, had inserted a phrase stating that they were afraid of reprisals. "I did not write those words, I did not even know they were being written!" Abikar Kassim explained. Such were the methods employed to conceal truth and bolster up a bad case.

YOUNG ABGALS

The Young Abgals also were represented in the Somali Conferenza. They complained that their Chief is detained in the Mijjertein area. "The Askaris come every night to prevent us defending our rights before the Commission."

They claimed to have 30,000 members, 25,000 in Mogadishu, from 12 to 60 years of age. They are a section of the "Comitato Progresso Somalia" and receive orders from the committee of that body. Sheik Mohamed Ahmed, their spokesman added that their business is dealt with by the Somalia Conferenza. In reply to a question whether the Imam Mohamed Abdul, chairman of the Comitato had joined the Somali Youth League on January 11, the day of the riot, he replied. "The Imam is finished, because he undertook another law. A king cannot be a king without his people." Evidently there had been a split as a result of the riot.

The spokesman of the Young Abgals asked for Italian trusteeship for 30 years under the 23 conditions of the Conferenza. Their spokesman said: "If the Italian Government do not fulfil the conditions, you Four Powers are responsible to see the Italian Government do so."

They stated that two or three chiefs of the Abgals are in their Party, five are with the Somali Youth League. Members of the Young Abgals club had been fined about 500/- (£25) they alleged for holding Italian flags. Nine Abgal chiefs were in prison, and four interned. These were evidently the same people mentioned by the Patriotic Beneficence Union, the majority of whose members were Abgals.

They complained that since the formation of political parties, those who had assistance from the police had been able to loot with impunity. Most of these internments and imprisonments resulted from the riots.

They demanded a Democratic Government which would not put people in prison. "The present position is really bad." They urged the Commission to "do something," saying: "You have our lives and deaths in your hands." Sheik Mohamed declared that for wearing the badge of the Young Abgals and carrying a stick, an

Askari will put a man in gaol, because the Askaris belong to the Somali Youth League; the Government will hear the complaint of the police, but not of the people who complain of them. " The nation which is in charge of this territory to-day does not treat people with an equal law. Lootings are done because there is no work, and because there is no work people steal at night."

The Young Abgals were not satisfied with the education under Italy but if the Italian Government would do as the Young Abgals had said, the Young Abgals would be satisfied!

ARAB COMMUNITY

A deputation waited on the Commission from the 25,000 Arabs of the ex-colony who live mainly in Mogadishu.

For the most part they have resided in the territory many years, but they come and go between Somaliland and the Arab countries. They stated that they would not accept nationality of the country, they would remain aliens, even were a Somali State established.

They complained of lack of security under British administration, but stated that in some matters the administration has improved.

Restrictions had been imposed by the Italians on Arab trade from the time of the beginning of the Ethiopian war. Thenceforward, hampering restrictions had been imposed on the export of currency and the import of goods from foreign countries. Under the British Military Administration there had been an improvement in the education and in the rights granted to Arabs who are now treated as Asians, not as natives of the colony.

SOMALI REPRESENTATIVE DENOUNCES ITALIAN RULE

The Chamber of Commerce of the Colony consisted, in 1947, of 220 members, 120 of whom represented Italian firms, 45 Indian, 22 Somali, 18 Arab, 2 British, 2 Jewish and 1 Eritrean.

A Memorandum for presentation to the Four Power Commission was drawn up by the Italian members of the Chamber, and submitted for the assent of a Committee, consisting of four Italian, two Indian, one Arab, one British and one Somali member. The Memorandum was accepted with some reservations by all except the Somali member, Haji Dirie Hersi, the one spokesman of the indigenous people, who repudiated it completely.

After consultation with the Somali group in the Chamber who were in complete accord with him, he stated he had not been invited to share in the compilation of the Memorandum and that it had been submitted to him too late for him to prepare a detailed reply in time for it to be laid before the Commission. He therefore wrote a brief protest insisting that he and the other Somali members of the Chamber refused to approve the Memorandum, which they considered " not in agreement with the real facts." He added the following comment on statements contained in the

Memorandum, declaring that these were but a few out of many objections which should be raised:

ASSERTION: That the employment of Somali labourers on Italian concessions contributed to the moral and material welfare of the Somalis.

REPLY: *"The labourers were slaves, therefore such a form of employment could not be a source of welfare for the Somali, or of material profit. 50 per cent. of those cultivators were destined to die of malaria, owing to the fact that no measures of prevention or treatment existed on their behalf."*

ASSERTION: There was a technical school for Somalis.

REPLY: *"No school of this sort ever existed in Somalia for the Somali.*

"Further, the following facts are personally known to me:

"Native cultivation by the Somali has increased 100 per cent. during the period of the British Military Administration.

"About ten transport companies and companies for export-import activities have been created under the British Military Administration."

When representatives of the Chamber of Commerce appeared before the Four Power Commission, Haji Dirie Hersi stoutly maintained his position. In reply to the statement that the Italian Government gave assistance to Somali farmers he protested:

"This is altogether false. No farming machinery or any other assistance benefiting the Somali was ever available to a Somali."

Asked how many agricultural schools existed for the native people and where they were located, he bluntly declared:

"Nothing has been done by the Italian Government in favour of us. They have only damaged our cultivation. There were no such schools where we could learn how to cultivate and sow. They did not give any machines we could use in our concessions. When the Sultan Oredine came out from Ethiopia to Belet Wen, near the border, he was given a pump by the Italian Government, but that had nothing to do with Somalia. It was a political matter. When he did his service against the Ethiopians the Italians gave him this machine. Now this machine has been sold to an Arab."

Before the Italians came, he said, there were many free Somali agriculturalists at Genale and on the Juba.

"When the Italians came to Villaggio and Genale the people who used to work their own land were pushed out, and made to cultivate the land on behalf of others."

Rebutting the Italian complaints that bananas had been subsituated by other crops, Haji Dirie Hersi declared:

"Before the British occupation all such commodities as oil, millet, and grain were obtained from Mombasa, Egypt, or even Italy. Since the British occupation they have been produced in the

Colony. *Previously the people ate flour and pasta, now they eat grain!"*

He produced an Italian Vice-Regal Decree prohibiting the export of goods by Somalis and handed it to the Commissioners, telling them that now the Italian Government was overthrown 200 Somalis were engaged in the export-import trade, 80 of them in Mogadishu.

SOMALILAND CHAMBER OF COMMERCE
Morbid Longing for Mussolini's Vanished Empire

A morbid longing for the vanished Italian Empire, created by the conquest of Ethiopia, disclosed itself in the report of the Somaliland Chamber of Commerce, prepared by the Italian members and presented to the Four Power Commission of Investigation. In the verbal statements of the Italian members of the Chamber to the Commission, the same dangerous attitude was evident.

In discussing the possibilities of increased prosperity for the colony and the illusive hope that it might be rendered economically self-supporting, Signor Rossi, the Vice-President of the Chamber, gave foremost importance to revival of the transit trade with Ethiopia. He argued that the Southern Provinces of Ethiopia could be better served through the Somaliland ports than any others. The colony was not getting the benefit of transit trade in southern Ethiopia's requirements. Only part of the wheat and macaroni the colony imported came from Ethiopia; the only materials sent to Ethiopia through Somaliland, were varnishes, locally produced, tanned skins, and spare parts for motor cars which came from overseas. The transit trade with Ethiopia " should be the most interesting part." In other words, he desired to obtain for the colony, customs and transit dues on all the goods imported or exported by southern Ethiopia.

At the same time, Signor Rossi and all his colleagues were exceedingly dissatisfied by the disability they suffered by reason of the fact that under the British Military Administration, the imports and exports of the colony, were through the British colony, Kenya, owing to war and post-war currency control.

That Ethiopia had reason to resent the subjection of her exports and imports to the toll of foreign powers on her seaboard instead of being able to use her own ports was a point evidently not considered.

The Chamber of Commerce report recorded that until 1934, the Ethiopian transit trade through the colony was practically non-existent. Southern Ethiopia preferred to deal through Kenya; only an occasional caravan appeared at the Belet Wen and Lugh Ferrandi markets while Eastern Ethiopia preferred Jibuti or Berbera in British Somaliland. Obviously, the estrangement caused by Italy's hostile and aggressive tactics of penetration, disruption and intrigue, and the consequent danger to Ethiopian merchants incurred by entering the Italian colony, inevitably led to a preference for other ports.

THE CONQUEST OF ETHIOPIA
Commerce " A la Hauteur "

With the conquest of Ethiopia, all was changed:

"*Commerce and internal trade," says the Chamber of Commerce, " got á la Hauteur, figures reached vertiginous heights, from 15,190,960 lire in 1934 to over 400,000,000 lire in 1936. The war, the public works carried out, the workshops and other new businesses created, changed the face of the country, and by raising the standard of living raised also the index of consumption.*"

" Bartering," continued the report, " was replaced by money transactions. The Italian firms obtained the success which had failed them in the previous years. They rose in number from 52 in 1934, to 895 in 1939. 600 kilometres of roads were asphalted. The transit trade with Ethiopia increased hugely, it was 47,750,000 lire in 1938; 44,000,000 in the first month alone of 1939; eventually, Somalia would have served entirely the Neghelly, which hitherto had dealt with the adjacent Kenya, and the area across the upper Shebeli, which had formally traded through Berbera and Jibuti The Somali dhows now numbered 400, diesel motors were imported for road transit. Air lines were established, with landings at Bender Kassim, Rocca Littorio, Belet Wen, etc. Three Italian banks opened branches in the colony. There was perfect efficiency; perfect order and consequently safety was ensured by the police in the full sense of the word ! (sic !)."

With 55 per cent. of the revenue devoted to the military, it might have been expected that the regular forces could have maintained order. Nevertheless, a voluntary Fascist militia was found necessary for national security. Moreover, the Italian workers were formed into armed legions, they marched to and from their labour shouldering their rifles, which were stationed beside them during their toil, while sentries kept a look-out !

When the Italian Empire collapsed, the transit trade between Ethiopia and Italy's lost Somaliland colony at once dwindled; the formerly preferred markets were again found more convenient; Jibuti and Berbera for eastern Ethiopia, while Neghelly, most naturally, went direct to Kenya instead of round about through Somaliland.

The Chamber of Commerce alleged failure of the British administration to keep the roads in good condition and to maintain public order, and exorbitant customs charges by Ethiopia as responsible for the loss of transit trade.

The old assumption of the right to insist that Ethiopian policy shall conform to Italian interests is still apparent. It arises from the never surrendered claim to the exclusive economic exploitation of Ethiopia by Italy—a claim which Ethiopia has never countenanced in any respect. The glorification by the Italian members of the Chamber of Commerce of the period of the Fascist conquest reveals a state of mind among the Italian colonists which would preclude even tolerably good relations with their Ethiopian neighbours. The report of the Italian members of the Chamber refers to the Fascist conquest of Ethiopia simply as " Italian times," comparing those "times" as if they were the normal times, the period of British occupation being the period of abnormality and disaster.

Comparisons cited by the Italian report to prove that " Italian times " were better than British times for the colony, were all based on the conditions existing when the former colony was part of the Italian Empire—rejoined to Ethiopia by the Italian conquest.

Nevertheless even at that time the colony was an immense loss, and had a vastly unfavourable balance of trade, agreeing in these respects with the Fascist Empire itself which was a huge total loss.

Could the Colony become Self-Supporting?

Asked by the Four Power Commission, how the colony could be made self-supporting, Signor Rossi contended this could be achieved by undertaking no more public works, and abolishing the conscription of the Somalis for the forces; thus, they could all be engaged in agriculture and production could be increased.

Mr. Ivrai Uscemboy, the Indian representative, however, replied with melancholy fatalism : " This is a very poor country, If God does not help us Somalia itself cannot stand on its own feet."

Mr. Goldsmit, the Jewish representative, spoke cautiously: " It is a very controversial, highly complex question. In my opinion, it depends firstly on what any future government thinks the standard of living of the native population should be; secondly, to what extent the future Government of this colony will be forced to keep a big or small administration in the colony.

"From the point of view purely of output and outgoing of capital, there has always been a gap both in Italian times, and under the British Military administration. The surplus of imports was mainly formed by the first necessities of life for the native population—food and clothing. Therefore I cannot see, without lowering the standard of living of the native population, that there would be a balance of payment reached."

Mr. Goldsmit added that the Somaliland products exported to Italy were produced at a relatively high cost, but Italy having at that time an autarchy economy, had an interest in purchasing the products of the colony, because foreign currency was not required to pay for them. Signor Forlani, one of the Italian members of the Chamber, explained that the bananas from Somaliland were absorbed into an Italian State monopoly, founded by the Fascist regime, and their import into Italy was " highly protected " by the Italian customs.

On the other hand, the colony had to import cotton piece goods from Italy, which were relatively expensive, but to ease the position customs duty was only charged on 25 per cent. of the cotton goods imported to the colony.

Impossible to Conduct Somaliland Business on 1936-1940 Imperial Scale

A paragraph in the annual report of the Chamber of Commerce expressed regret that:

"*Many Italian firms have started a policy of retrenchment by shipping machinery and materials to Italy. This is due to the belief that even if the territory is returned to Italy, it would not be possible to conduct business on the old pre-1939 scale, when circumstances were different.*"

Mr. Rossi endeavoured to evade the obvious fact that as a colony on the fringe of Ethiopia, the Somaliland colony is no longer the "Port of an Empire." He argued that the machinery sent to Italy consisted only of lorries; there had been 450 heavy lorries in the colony because "the weight of part of Ethiopia came on to Somalia."

ITALIAN COLONISTS OF TO-DAY
Their Political Parties and Claims
Complete Solidarity with Former Fascist Regime

The Italians in the former Somaliland Colony established in December, 1937, an Italian Representative Committee, to lay their claims before the Four Power Commission of Investigation. The Representative Committee consisted of the Italian Members of the Chamber of Commerce and of the small Italian Political Parties. The Christian Democratic Party, declared a membership of 65 only, but nevertheless were given also a separate hearing of their own by the Commission.

The obvious prevarications and falsehoods of the Italian representatives make a deplorable impression.

Two Members of the Italian Representative Committee expressed disapproval of Fascist racial discrimination, thereby finding an opportunity to praise the " present democratic Italian Government," and also themselves. Nevertheless, by their eulogies of the former Fascist administration the Committee identified themselves with that regime. The address of welcome prepared by the Italian Committee for presentation to the Four Power Commission is a most blatantly hypocritical document, in view of the appalling scandals and utter disregard of African rights and liberties, which disgraced the Fascist regime. The following phrases from this address must surely have caused a pang of shame to the least atrophied Italian consciences:

"*The Italians are conscious of the civilising work they have performed in this country, with so much love and in a spirit of sacrifice, and they trust, therefore, that they will be able to continue, in harmony with the life of Somalia's population in the new atmosphere of international co-operation, the common work for the prosperity and welfare of everybody.*"

THE ITALIAN THESIS
Charges Against the British Military Administration

The thesis urged by the Italian organisations before the Four Power Commission of Investigation contained these postulates:

(1) That 95 per cent. of the Somali population desired Italian Trusteeship, and that Somalis who expressed contrary wishes were either employed by the British Military Administration, and expresed the view desired by their employers, or were intimidated either by the British or by the Somali Gendarmerie acting under British influence.

(2) That the British administration was bad in every way and the police force was corrupt and inefficient.

(3) That the disorders on January 11 were deliberately created by the British Military Administration. Colonel X,* the Civil Affairs Officer, was accused of responsibility.

(4) That British Administration was in every respect inferior to Italian, that Italy had done great things for the territory and its population, and that the continuance of Italy's Civilising Mission there would render the territory prosperous and self-supporting.

Italian Claim to Trusteeship for an Indeterminate Period
Desire to Introduce " Large Italian Proletariat "

The Italian claim to trusteeship of the Colony for an indefinite period, was stated, on behalf of the Italian Representative Committee by Baron Beritelli, its president and founder, who was also the chief of the Mogadishu Municipality.

The Representative Committee stated in a written declaration:

" *The request of Italy to obtain the Trusteeship Administration must be considered only as a necessity of working of a large population working within narrow borders.*"

This assertion was the subject of much discussion and much prevarication. Baron Beritelli began by arguing that Italy has a large working class population, " a large African proletariat," desirous of employment in the former colonies.

The American Commissioner, however viewed with disfavour the idea that the 100,000 or more Italian workers, who had been engaged in war work or on labour contracts in Ethiopia or the ex-colonies during the Empire period, should now be admitted to the Colonies. Commissioners expressed the opinion that a large influx of Italian labourers would be prejudicial to the Somali people, and, therefore, would be out of harmony with the principles of the United Nations. Baron Beritelli, with the air of incomprehension to which he resorted in every dilemma, replied, " I do not believe so, because I believe one of the principles of the United

---

* The name of this Officer is not published, because he has not been given the opportunity to make a public reply to the Italian allegations against him.

Nations is the welfare of nations. The common work between Italians and Somalis would be useful to the wealth of the country." Finding the Baron's argument unsuccessful in gaining the sympathy of the Commission, his colleagues shifted the argument to the need of the Colony for Italian technicians.

The Innocence of Baron Beritelli

Baron Beritelli was asked whether the Italian political parties were subsidised from Rome, whether the Somali organisations formed to promote Italian trusteeship were financially assisted from Italian sources, and whether the Italians in the Colony were doing direct propaganda for Italian trusteeship. In replying, he prevaricated hugely, "It might have been some Italian servants, or some Italians themselves" who had "naturally created the atmosphere of enthusiasm"; propaganda had been made by "all the generations of Italians who passed through the territory for fifty years," and especially the workmen "who rolled up their sleeves and lived close to the Somalis to teach them every sort of trade."

Baron Beritelli ignored the fact that the poor Somalis were not taught "every sort of trade," and that racial laws precluded the employment of any native of Italian East Africa on any work which could be done by an Italian.

Still with bland assumption of innocence, he went on: "It may be the payment I give to the small boy running for my car; that sort of propaganda costs me several shillings a day." He could only answer for what was known to him personally; some chiefs had called at his office "to manifest their Italian sentiment . . . The natives always end their speeches by talking about backsheesh; you have to give them 5s. or 10s., which I did out of my own pocket."

Asked somewhat more sternly whether any active help or support had been given to the indigenous political parties by Italians, the Baron prevaricated: "Directly I do not know . . . I want to stress, as regards the native work, I never took an interest in it."

Subsequently the Baron admitted Italians had taken part in a so-called native demonstration, held on the night of the arrival of the Commission. He could not deny it, because the photographs taken during the demonstration displayed the Italians taking an active part in it. He also admitted the demonstrators had been supplied with Italian motor transport.

Baron Beritelli and his colleagues all agreed in asserting that the great majority of the Somalis desired Italian rule; they asserted that even the Somali Youth Club, who were in fact their most bitter opponents, were really desirous of having the Italians back, but, alas, were afraid to say so.

Dr. Falcone waxed eloquent: "Owing to my own profession, which is that of a veterinary, I live among the masses continuously, from the Juba borders up to the Mijjertein. I am an agriculturalist, a concessionaire, and I live among them with the labourers, and this puts me in a position to say this before the Commission, that 90 per cent. of the Somalis at least are in favour of an Italian Administration."

Despite this emphatic and categorical assertion, to a polite enquiry from the French Commissioner: " I understand you travel a great deal round the country on account of your job?" Dr. Falcone replied curtly: " No, my job is in Mogadishu; my colleagues travel around the country."

Law and Order

Baron Beritelli criticised the recruitment of the Somali Gendarmerie by the British Administration; under Italian rule, he said, the police were not recruited in the Colony, but consisted of Arabs with Italian officers and non-commissioned officers. His claim that the Italian Government had used foreign troops and police to maintain order is not, in fact, a matter to boast of. A Government which cannot rely on local police is not a popular, or a democratic Government!

The recruitment of forces from Arabia was part of the original plan for subduing the native people of the Somaliland Colony. For reasons of economy, forces were subsequently raised in the Colonies, but troops obtained in one territory were frequently transferred for service in another. For example, Eritreans were largely used in Libya, Libyans in Eritrea. Even when forces were raised for service in the same Colony they were not necessarily employed near their home, the tactics of employing tribe against tribe, religion against religion were closely studied in order to maintain a segmentation of the people, which would preclude any nationalist or other movement which would unite the subject people to strive for a higher status and improved conditions.

Italian representatives asserted to the Four Power Commission that by restoring the former efficient police organisation Italy would be able to maintain perfect order with a comparatively small force of police only, after a preliminary period in which a stronger force of police only, " nothing more," would be required. These Italian representatives ignored totally the fact that between 1936 and 1940 the Italian Administration spent 55 per cent. of the total revenue of the Somaliland Colony, including the grant from Italy, on the military forces of the colony. No comment on this appalling figure was made by the Commissioners. Nevertheless, it must be taken into account when considering the question of public security under the Italian regime, and the character of the regime itself. The regular establishment of an internal military force, which absorbs more than half the revenue, is a factor which should not be left out of account when attempting to assess the relations between Government and people.

Charges Against Police and British Civil Affairs Officer

Baron Beritelli declared that after the arrival of the Commission, rumours had circulated that he and Dr. Calzia, the Chief

Secretary of the Municipality, were to be murdered. He had asked, and obtained police protection on that account.

The Baron alleged that the riot of January 11 was deliberately prepared by the anti-Italian " minority " in the Colony. He accused the official forces of the Colony of deliberately murdering Italians. While the Askaris were killing the Italians their wives, who followed them, were looting.

Italian Charges Against British Civil Affairs Officers

Dr. Falcone charged the police and the Civil Affairs Officer, Lieut.-Colonel X,* with having assisted the Somali Youth League to bring people by lorry from the interior of the Colony to the coastal capital, Mogadishu, on the day of the riot, in order "to create such a situation" as would prove to the Four Power Commission "that every demonstration should be annulled."

After the riot, Baron Beritelli stated that he had headed a Commission, composed of the Bishop, the Judge of the Colony, and other " Italian Authorities," who had waited on the Chief British Administrator. Brigadier Smith had assured them that the lives and property of the citizens would be safeguarded. Baron Beritelli had seen troops arriving. On the surface the situation was much better but the population were still afraid, because, said the Baron, " they wonder whether the murderers have been arrested, whether measures have been taken against some responsible authorities."

Dr. Calzia Brought from Gaol

Dr. Vincenzo Calzia was brought to interview the Commission from Mogadishu gaol, where he had been detained since the riot of January 11 on the charge of instigating it. Dr. Calzia was determined to cast the responsibility for the riot on to the British Administration. He did so with emphasis. The Somali Gendarmerie had " known for a long time," he declared, that the events of January 11 would occur, and had " tolerated, if not assisted their organisation, and the carrying of them out." Lieutenant Colonel X * believed, said the doctor, that he, Dr. Calzia, was " the principal element of propaganda among Somalis," and in consequence had interviewed him several times, endeavouring to persuade him against the holding simultaneously of pro-and anti-Italian processions. Dr. Calzia declared: " He not only threatened me with personal reprisals, but in addition to that he threatened me with those acts which later occurred, masses of elements of the Somali Youth League attacking the Italians in their own houses."

This British officer was not heard by the Commission, and, so far as we know, he has never had an opportunity to reply to the charges the Italians made against him.

Two processions had been held on the 6th and 7th of January. Dr. Calzia declared they were pro-Italian processions, but that a

---

* The name of this British Officer is not published here because he has not been given an opportunity to make a public reply to the Italian allegations against him.

small number of the Somali Youth League also marched to demonstrate opposite opinions. Subsequently Colonel X informed Dr. Calzia that he had given official permission for the Somali Youth League to hold their procession on January 11. Colonel X requested Dr. Calzia to use his influence with the Italians and the pro-Italy parties to leave the streets to the Somali Youth League on that day. Dr. Calzia declared the pro-Italian parties had refused to agree. He insisted there was no reason to prevent the two processions taking place simultaneously, that no one objected to the two processions marching at the same time, and that " nothing would have happened if there had been no interference from third persons who intervened."

In short, Dr. Calzia charged Col. X with responsibility for the riot, and even charged him with having surrounded, with troops of the King's African Rifles, groups who would otherwise have protected the Italians from violence. He alleged that two thousand persons had been gathered from all over Somaliland for the Somali Youth League demonstration, and that the League had had the use of British Military Administration vehicles to bring them into Mogadishu. Colonel X, who was held responsible, has not been heard; the Colonel might perhaps have urged that delegates from a distance had no means of arriving in time, unless such transport was made available to them, and that only the pro-Italian parties could avail themselves of the motor vehicles possessed by Italian farmers and manufacturers which were used by them to beat up their employees to testify on their behalf.

Dr. Calzia went on to make the truly extravagant assertion that 75 per cent. of the Somali Youth League were pro-Italian, and that even those who dreamed of independence would willingly accept Italian trusteeship. He went so far as to allege that all members of the Somali Youth League, even members of the executive of the League who were arrested as a result of the riot, were pro-Italian; otherwise they would not have been arrested. Arrests he claimed to be an absolute evidence of Italian sympathy. Even members of the executive of the Youth League desired Italian trusteeship. Asked how it was that the Somali Youth League Memorandum took a strong and violently anti-Italian line, Dr. Calzia replied that the League was organised like the Fascist Party.

The Chief Administrator, Brigadier Smith, had informed the Commission that never at any time since the British Administration started had the Italians or pro-Italians been prohibited from organising political, economic, or social groups. Dr. Calzia, on the contrary, declared that the Italian parties " always had to work underground."

How little veracity there was in this statement, is evidenced by Dr. Calzia's own reply to the question: " Can you tell us whether any orders or proclamations have been issued, printed or by word of mouth, prohibiting pro-Italian propaganda." His reply to that question was, " No order."

British policy during the war was amazingly lenient towards Italian propaganda; the slogans of the Mussolini regime, " Believe, Obey, Fight ! " " Viva il Duce ! " and so forth were left in the streets until and unless the Italians themselves removed them.

Dr. Calzia's imprisonment temporarily deprived his compatriots of his assistance in preparing the vast stream of anti-British, anti-African, and pro-colonial propaganda which was developed in Italy on the basis of the riot; he did his best to promote the Italian thesis among the members of the Four Power Commission.

The Christian Democratic Party

The Christian Democratic Party numbered 65 members in the colony. Being, however, a branch of the party of the Government in Rome, it was able to publish the largest newspaper in the colony.

The Party presented to the Four Power Commission a Memorandum advocating Italian trusteeship, promising a programme of " development and betterment for Somalis ", which would entail " a vast expenditure ", and urging that the colony represents for Italy the land where surplus population may find work.

Association with the Government party in Italy, doubtless, evoked in the Christian Democrats the cautious refusal to promise that the Roman Government would provide the " vast expenditure " mentioned in the memorandum. Questioned as to where " the vast expenditure " would come from the spokesman of the party replied, " I do not think I wrote such a thing." When the statement was pressed as being in the Memorandum, contributions from the colony were suggested by the spokesman as the source frum which the expenditure could be raised :

" It would be easy to find some credit, particularly among the Arabs, Indians and so on.

" The fact is, considering how the Somali is anxious to learn, no doubt that education will cost large amounts of money, but it will be possible to find local contribution to education.

" We have many Italian firms working on export and import, not contributing to taxation."

These anticipations recall the expedients of the Tittoni period, when Government hopes were ineffectually launched that the colony might be developed by means of loans, provided by Italian commercial firms.

The Administrative Secretary of the Christian Democrats, Signor Biondi, when asked whether he " honestly " believed the colony could support a large-scale immigration from Italy, replied: " Not a large number, but several thousands." Asked whether these thousands would be " in the form of technicians and people of that sort," he replied :

" *More particularly specialists in labour, clerks, teachers, medical practitioners, persons employed in agriculture, mining technicians and all the staff of the fishing industry.*"

This reply is, of course, totally incompatible with the propaganda vociferously proclaimed among the destitute unemployed of Italy for the return of the colonies, as a means of providing prosperity for them, homes to shelter them, food to nourish them, clothes to cover them. Baron Beritelli's declaration that " Italy has a large African proletariat," is also out of harmony with the statement of the Christian Democratic Secretary.

The " Old Happy Stage "

Glimpses of the intentions of the present colonists, if the colony is returned to Italy, appeared in the Christian Democratic Memorandum, in its advocacy of restoring " the disciplinary measures existing under the Italian administration " and its reference to " The old happy stage." Questioned as to the period referred to as " the old happy stage," the party spokesman replied, " The period up to 1933, and 1934, and also the period up to the outbreak of the world war in 1939." No consciousness that this covered the period of Fascism appeared to cloud the Christian Democratic memories of " the old safe conditions " in this period. No reservations were mentioned concerning De Vecchi's savage repression of the Somalis. Governor Rava's penetration across the Ethiopian border, which culminated at Wal Wal, the Ethiopian war of 1935, the Fascist racial laws, " the horrors of Ganale and Danane ". No expression of regret or understanding of the miseries of the victims of these tragedies escaped the representatives of any Italian party.

The Christian Democratic Party President declared that there were no democratic institutions in Somalia; the Municipality was not elected; there were no Trade Unions.

As no democratic institutions had been permitted under Italy and as the British administration operated under the Hague Rules, this was to be expected. As in Italy, the towns were placed under a Podestà, appointed by the central dictatorship.

When asked what democratic institutions existed in the colony before the British occupation, the Italian complainant replied disingenuously : " In what meaning ? "

" In the same meaning that you said there were none here now," was naturally found embarrassing; the reply: " Social Insurance Organisations," was merely an evasion, these under Fascism, being autocratically governed.

Left Wing Parties

The Socialist, Communist and Azione Parties formed a combined Left Wing block. This block also presented a memorandum, advocating Italian trusteeship. They stated that a third of their membership consisted of former Fascists. Asked why their memorandum did not mention the wishes of the Somali population, they replied this was because in their opinion it was " impossible to ascertain what their wishes are." Nevertheless, they believed the population would accept an Italian trusteeship. They declared their opposition to the racial discrimination under Fascism. Nevertheless, they believed " a difference should exist between the pay of black and white workers, but the pay of the Somali is not sufficient to-day."

No Somali Artisans Exist

They stated there are no native workers with qualifications such as turner, lathe worker, or mechanic.

Here, alas, was the reply to the Baron Beritelli's story of the generations of Italian workers, who rolled up their sleeves to teach the Somali every sort of trade !

THE PRESS
Its Influence on the Political and Social Life of Former Italian Somaliland

The Four Power Commission of Investigation under-estimated greatly the influence of the Press in the Somaliland Colony. The Commission declared that the Press played " no rôle whatsoever in the political and social life of the native," and " a very small rôle in the political and social life of the alien communities."

It is true there was not, and never had been, a newspaper published by the Somalis.

As regards the Italians, it must be observed that they were not wholly restricted either to their own Colonial publications, or to the small daily sheet published by the British Administration ; they obtained newspapers and heard broadcasts from Italy; the newspapers produced by them in Somaliland were specially designed to keep them together as an Italian Community in the struggle to regain the Colony for Italy.

Moreover, as soon as it was announced that the Council of Foreign Ministers would appoint a Four Power Commission of Investigation to ascertain the wishes of the native people of the former Colonies, the Italian Press of the former Colonies began to devote itself to influencing the opinion of the local populations. In the Somaliland Colony the Italian newspapers, of which publication had been only occasional, began to appear more frequently. Articles written, or ostensibly written, by Somalis, former soldiers of Italy's Colonial forces and others, were published, advocating Italian Trusteeship. Much emphasis was devoted to the benefits which it was alleged Italian Trusteeship would confer. The promises broadcast from Rome by the Italian Minister of the Colonies, the Hon. Brusasca, were enlarged upon. Quotations were published from the statements of Ministers and political correspondents to create the belief that Italian Trusteeship was already decided, and that Somalis, Indians, Arabs, and others who desired to provide for their own best interests should put themselves in harmony with the coming Administration. The Italian newspapers used every endeavour to persuade the indigenous people that their position would improve under Italian Trusteeship, that the new democratic Italy would give them all they desired. Every drawback of the British Administration was, of course, accentuated. Every shortage, every difficulty, even though directly due to the war, was attributed to British mis-government.

It is true the influence of both British and Italian newspapers was largest in Mogadishu and the other coast towns, but the Italians spread their propaganda sheets among their agents in the interior, Chiefs who had been formerly in their pay, and particularly their former native soldiers, amongst whom, as in Eritrea, their propaganda made most headway, because of their promises of back pay, pensions and re-employment.

The Press Under Italian Rule

Under Italian rule the Press was not in any way intended for the use of the indigenous population. As in Italy and all Italian Colonies during the Fascist regime, all publications were under strict control by the Fascist Dictatorship; all journalists were obliged to belong to the Fascist journalists' organisation; anti-Fascist journalism was suppressed. A Decree of 1935 provided that a printer must submit to the authorities three copies of every publication. A Decree of 1939 provided that every newspaper and other publications must be licensed.

The publication of any matter " contrary to the interests of the social, political or economic organisation of the State, or offensive to natural feeling " was prohibited. This gave complete power to suppress the publication of any opinion disapproved by the Fascist Dictatorship in Rome, or by the Fascist Officials in the Colony. In short, there was no freedom of the Press, but this applied only to Italians, because for the native people there was no Press at all.

The Press Under British Military Administration

On the defeat of Italy in Somaliland the British Military Administration issued a Proclamation prohibiting the printing and circulation of any document or picture likely to cause unrest. During the war there was a censorship of publications but when the war terminated the censorship ceased to function and there was no further official restriction of the freedom of the Press. This, one must repeat, is entirely contrary to the Italian system, which maintained a strict censorship in peace and war.

The *Somalia Courier,* a daily newspaper, first published in September, 1944, under the auspices of the British Military Administration, was the only newspaper which had appeared regularly since the Italian defeat. It was printed by the Government Press. Of its four small pages, one was in English, two in Italian, one contained public notices and advertisements in English and Italian, with approximately half a column in Arabic. The circulation was 1,500, 1,300 copies being sold to Italians, and the remaining 200 to British, Indians, Somalis, Arabs and other readers.

The British Administration informed the Commission of Investigation that the *Somalia Courier* was non-political. We are fully prepared to accept the view that the "Courier" was exceedingly moderate as compared with the vehement propaganda sheets of the Italians, some samples of which ought to have been published in the Report of the Commission. Complete impartiality, is, however, another matter. An article published in the *Somalia Courier* during the visit of the Commission under the heading "Middle East Strategy," dealt with the disposal of Libya and developed the theme that the British and American Governments were preparing to control the Middle East by acquiring "striking bases in North Africa," by giving Libya to the Arabs and other measures. Its publication at that time evokes the question: have these military people begun to learn anything at all about politics? The article was bound to be to the Soviet representatives what a red flag is supposed to be to a bull, nor could it be pleasing to the French. It was, in fact, a syndicated article and was published in many other news sheets in other parts of the world at that time. The above article being complained of the British Administration replied that they had published matter expressing opposite views. The ineptitude of the editor is obvious.

The Commissioners expressed conflicting views; the British and American members considered the *Somalia Courier* impartial; the French and Russian members said it had published matter showing the good will of the British Administration to the Somali Youth League and conviction that the Colony would not return to Italy; the British and Americans replied that the newspaper had given space to other views.

The Italians, who had three newspapers of their own published in the Colony, in which they set forth Italian claims to the Colony, had no valid reason to expect their views to be represented also in the one newspaper published by the British Administration, which they alleged to have a smaller circulation than that of their own newspapers.

The Italian newspapers, which began to appear in 1946, after the world war ended, were *Il Popolo*, organ of the Colonial branch of the Italian Christian Democratic Party; *L'Italiano*, organ of the neo-Fascist Party, Uomo Qualunque; and *Bolletino del Movimento Sociale Italiano*, organ of the Italian Socialist movement. Their sponsors claimed that these sheets had circulations of 2,000, 1,000 and 500 respectively, the Italian population numbering only 3,774 men, women and children in December, 1947.

Editors of Italian Newspapers all Killed

It is a remarkable fact that the editors of these newspapers were all killed during the riot in Mogadishu, on January 11, during the visit of the Four Power Inquiry Commission. Were they murdered merely in the course of the mêlée, being all particularly active in the street conflict, or were they singled out for murder by their political opponents. In the latter case were they killed by their Italian political rivals, or by Somalis whose resentment their newspapers had aroused?

XIX

AT THE BAR OF THE UNITED NATIONS

The report of the Four Power Commission of Investigation was submitted to the Council of Foreign Ministers at their Paris meeting in September, 1948. The British, United States and French Ministers all agreed to place the former Italian Somaliland colony under Italian Trusteeship. Soviet representatives had hitherto favoured this solution for all the former colonies. Mr. Vyschinsky, however, now proposed to revert to a former American plan by which all the former colonies would be placed under direct United Nations trusteeship. As no action could be taken by the Council of Foreign Ministers, except by a unanimous decision, this Soviet change of front, for the time being at least, saved the Somali people from being forcibly returned to the Italian rule from which they had been ostensibly liberated in 1941!

The Council of Foreign Ministers finally decided on September 15 that they could not agree on the disposal of the ex-colonies. The year allowed them for decision since the signing of the Peace Treaty had now expired. Therefore, the question had now perforce to be transferred to the General Assembly of the United Nations which was to meet in Paris in October.

British Military Withdraw from Ogaden and Reserved Area of Ethiopia

The British evacuation of the Ogaden, which had been gradually effected during the summer and autumn of 1948, was announced in October. The long delay had been greatly unfortunate. The 1944 Anglo-Ethiopian Agreement had safeguarded Ethiopia's right to extract minerals from the subsoil of her territory during the British Military Occupation, and the Ethiopean Government had entered into a fifty years' contract with the Sinclair Company to extract oil in the Ogaden. Some small disturbances, worked up from the former Italian colony, had, however, caused damage to an aeroplane and machinery of the Company, and some minor injuries and annoyances to the personnel. The British Administration stated they were unable to afford guards to protect the Sinclair Company's installations, and boring for oil was suspended pending the withdrawal of the Military Administration. This check was most unfortunate in view of the acute world shortage of petroleum products, and the insufficiency of the quota allocated to Ethiopia and other Middle East countries.

More unfortunate still was the barrier imposed by the British Military Administration between Ethiopia and the Somaliland Colony.

There was great rejoicing in the Ogaden at the restoration of Ethiopian Administration. The Emperor Haile Sellassie received a heartfelt ovation on visiting the province, and was received with cheers in all localities. The " Ethiopia Herald " commented that the withdrawal of the British Military Administration marked the progressive fulfilment of agreements openly arrived at between two neighbour States.

The Ogaden having been evacuated by the British Military Administration, the British Colonial Secretary, Mr. Creech Jones, announced that the British Somaliland Protectorate would be restored to civil administration under the Colonial Office on November 15.

Emperor's Declaration : Eritrea and Somaliland Must be Restored

Whilst the United Nations Assembly still sat in Paris, the 17th session of the Ethiopian Parliament opened. The Emperor in his opening speech announced that the Ethiopian delegation to the Paris Assembly of the United Nations had been instructed to press for the restoration of both Eritrea and the former Italian Somaliland colony to the Ethiopian Mother-country. He recalled that Italy had used both there territories as bases for the invasion of Ethiopia. He expressed his hope for "fair and sympathetic consideration of Ethiopia's just claims " by her fellow members of the United Nations and a prompt settlement during the present Assembly.

As the Paris session of the United Nations Assembly was drawing towards its close, the following compromise proposal was agreed in private negotiation between the delegations of Britain, the United States and France: Eastern Eritrea to go to Ethiopia, Western Eritrea and Tripolitania to remain under British Military Administration for a further year, Cyrenaica to be put under British Trusteeship, the former Somaliland colony to be placed under Italian Trusteeship. The Assembly, however, rose without debating the future of the ex-colonies. The question was therefore postponed to the spring session of the United Nations to be held at Lake Success.

Again Somaliland was saved from Italian rule.

House of Commons Questions

The future of the Somaliland colony was now raised on several occasions in the British House of Commons. On November 21, 1948, Mr. Baldwin* urged that Jubaland should be restored to Kenya. Mr. Mayhew replied that Jubaland, having been ceded to Italy on July 15, 1924, was now part of the former Italian Somaliland, the disposal of which was to be considered by the United Nations.

Mr. Mayhew says Somali Organisations Not so Influential as they Claim to be

In the House of Commons on November 29, 1948, Mr. Skeffington asked the Secretary of State for Foreign Affairs:

---
* Unionist Member for Leominster.

Whether he is aware that it is the desire of the Somali populations of British and ex-Italian Somaliland that the two territories should be united, and that the Somali National League and the Somali Youth League have both expressed the wish that no part of Somalia should be placed under Italian administration, whether as a trust or otherwise; and what steps he is taking to meet these views.

Mr. Mayhew: *My right hon. Friend is aware that there is some support for a United Somalia amongst the Somalis, expressed principally through the two organisations mentioned by my hon. Friend, which are not, however, as influential as they claim to be.*

His Majesty's Government have in the past expressed the view that a United Somalia would be the best solution for these territories, but suggestions to this effect have not met with the support of the other Powers.

The most recent available information about Italian Somaliland is contained in the report of the Four Power Commission which visited Italian Somaliland early this year. This shows that a substantial portion of local opinion was not in agreement with the programme of the Somali Youth League, which includes opposition to a return of Italian administration.

His Majesty's Government are aware of the aspirations of the Somali people and would wish to promote them, but the matter is now one for the General Assembly, and not for His Majesty's Government to decide.

Somalis Allege they have been Bartered for Cyrenaica and Betrayed to Appease Italy

Mr. Abdul Rashid Ali retorted bitterly to Mr. Mayhew in an open letter, publication of which was requested in the "Manchester Guardian" and "New Times and Ethiopia News." The secretary of the Somali Youth League therein plainly accused the British Government of bartering Somaliland to Italy to secure British Trusteeship for Cyrenaica.

He declared the favour formerly shown to the Somali Youth League by the British Military Administration had disappeared with the change of official British policy. Now that the return of the colony to Italy was approved by the London Government, the League was suffering persecution. To recommend Italian Trusteeship for Somalia though the Four Power Commission had shown that 95 per. cent of the inhabitants were opposed to Italian rule, was to prove, he said, that the United Kingdom Government paid only lip-service to the principle that the wishes of the inhabitants are paramount.

"We Somalis will not acquiesce in Italian rule whether Italy claims to be democratic or not. We have had enough of Italy.

"Your Government has made a farce of the efforts of the Four Power Commission of Investigation when you think of appeasing Italy at the expense of us Somalis.

"You say: 'Our latest information suggests that there is no united hostility to Italy.' Yes, Sir, 5 per cent. of the Somalis desire Italian rule

THE OLD COLONIALS AT WORK
Two of many photographs taken by the Italians and left behind at the time of their defeat in 1941.

Homeless unemployed camp out in Rome.

The above photographs appeared in "La Voce dell'Africa," published by an Italian organisation working to regain the former African colonies. Propaganda in Italy to recover the ex-colonies as an outlet for Italian unemployed contrasts with the claim by Italian deputations to the Four-Power Commission of Investigation in Somaliland that immigration of only a few thousand experts was cont emplated.

and those Somalis are ex-ascaris and other ex-employees, who hope to receive back-pay on Italy's return. These stooges are financed by the local, as well as the official Italians."

'" In speaking about the Somali Youth League, you stated in Parliament: 'Our information is that this League is unrepresentative and that it has lost whatever influence it had.' This is one of the ways in which you wish to bluff the world. Your local Administration is endeavouring to muzzle the League. Some of the League leaders have been already clamped in jail without conviction before a Court of Law and merely on suspicion. Shambas are being taken back from Somali agriculturalists because they are nationalists, and believe in the League's programme."

" What will prove to you that the League is not what you are making others in Parliament believe? Will fighting, talking, and shouting anti-Italian slogans do the needful? The Administration does not permit all this. There is frequent parading of British troops and British tanks all over the town. Why all this show of force when you believe that the League 'has lost whatever influence it had?'"

"You may misguide the British people, but we Somalis can see through your crooked policy. You are keen on satisfying Italy, and for the purpose you are anxious to barter us and our sons and grandsons."

Strenuous efforts on the part of the Italian Government to secure the ex-colonies for Italy had been maintained, and were continued with ever greater energy when the question passed to the United Nations. Signor de Gasperi, Count Sforza, Signor Nenni, Signor Tarchiani and other leaders of divers Italian Parties and factions toured about Europe and America interviewing Foreign Ministers. In the time of Mussolini, the toleration of Italy's invasion and conquest of Ethiopia was urged as essential to prevent Italy from throwing herself into the arms of Germany. When she had done so, by forming the Rome-Berlin Axis, Mussolini must have the official recognition of his conquest by all the foremost Powers of Europe in order to induce him to persuade his Axis partner, Hitler, not to plunge the world into the most disastrous war of all time. To-day, the trusteeship of her former colonies was urged as essential to induce Italy not to pass " behind the iron curtain " and to make her and keep her a loyal and satisfied member of Western Union, a friend to the Western Powers in the Mediterranean.

During the recess between the two halves of the United Nations Assembly which began in the Autumn of 1948 in Paris and continued at Lake Success in the Spring of 1949 negotiations concerning the former colonies continued between the Governments of the Great Powers. At length, the efforts of the Italian Foreign Secretary, Count Sforza, were successful in winning Mr. Bevin's assent to a compromise plan which was eventually submitted to the United Nations as a British resolution as follows:

British Resolution Submitted to the United Nations

1 Libya, United Nations Trusteeship for ten years.

  A Cyrenaica to be administered by Britain.

  B Tripolitania to be administered by Italy.

2 Eritrea, the East to be united to Ethiopia and the West to the Sudan.

3 **Somaliland to remain indefinitely under Italian Trusteeship.**

Rioting immediately broke out in Tripoli when the introduction of the resolution was announced.

The resolution was referred to the Political Committee appointed by the General Assembly. The Committee invited representatives of the various parties among the inhabitants of the former colonies to express their views.

Mr. Issa of the Somali Youth League was heard on April 21st. He said, " The Italian Peace Treaty had seemed to mean ' the instrument of our liberation.' " If the Treaty meant anything it meant that Italy had been judged unfit to have anything more to do with the administration of her former colonies. The Somalis thought this just, natural and heartening.

Now it appeared that some governments considered the Treaty still left the way open to the return of Italian rule under the guise of United Nations trusteeship. His people would not see any difference between such trusteeship and the domination they had suffered formerly. Italian trusteeship would mean to them only that Italian rule was coming back, and that, he said, would be completely " contrary to the wishes and welfare of our people."

Experience had shown the Italians to be temperamentally unsuited to the administration of African peoples. The Somalis considered the aim of the Italian colonial policy was " to colonise and to exploit for the benefit of Italians, and to keep native peoples in a state of slavery."

Delegates had said Italy was the mother of civilisation. To the Somalis, Italy was the mother of brutality and tyranny. She had brought to their country " slavery, misery, suppression and oppression."

The Ethiopian Representative had called the Committee's attention to the presence in the Italian delegation here of a man who had been Governor of Ethiopia in 1937, when the Ethiopian people had been gassed and massacred. Mr. Issa said that this man, Enrico Cerulli, was also well known to the Somali people for his record of " cruelty and tyranny," and his part in organising forced labour during the time he was a high administrative official in Africa, before the Italian conquest of Ethiopia.

The Somalis cared nothing for the changes which had occurred in the Italian Government; to them, Italians were still Italians, whether they had doffed the black shirt or not.

Mr. Issa deplored and feared the tendency to discuss the future of his country on the basis of European politics. He appealed to the United Nations " not to sacrifice people on the altar of political expediency."

Henry F. Cooper (Liberia) asked in what way the Somali Youth League planned to " oppose " Italian trusteeship, as he had stated. " Would this opposition be physical, or warlike?" he asked.

Mr. Issa replied, " The Somalis prefer death to the return of Italy. Although they lack weapons, they would resist."

Dr. Wellington Koo (China) asked whether the representative of the Somali Youth League understood that under any trusteeship the United Nations would be the "supervisor," and that the aim of any trusteeship would be preparation for independence.

Mr. Issa repeated he was opposed to Italian trusteeship even supervised by the United Nations. Should the justified claims of the Somalis be ignored, they would have no faith in the United Nations.

Dr. Koo asked what were the preferences of the Somali people among the three possible types of trusteeship, by one nation, by several, or by the United Nations as a whole?

Mr. Issa said they would agree to any type of trusteeship provided administration by Italy was excluded.

The British Resolution (except the proposal to annex western Eritrea to the Sudan which was rejected) was accepted by the Sub-Committee of the Political Committee, which was not fully a representative cross-section of the United Nations. When the resolution was submitted to the Plenary Session of the General Assembly, strong opposition to Italian Trusteeship of Tripolitania and Somaliland became manifest. The proposal to unite Eastern Eritrea to Ethiopia was carried by 37 votes to 11—more than the two-thirds majority required for success.

On May 17, an amendment by the Egyptian delegation proposed United Nations Trusteeship for Somaliland, with Egypt, Ethiopia, France, Italy, Pakistan, the United Kingdom and the United States as a joint administering authority. This proposal was defeated on a show of hands by 40 against, 11 in favour, and six abstentions.

The Liberian delegation proposed to terminate the suggested Italian trusteeship of Somaliland after 15 years. An amendment moved by the delegates of Brazil and Peru would have increased Italy's trusteeship to 25 years, but was defeated in a roll-call* by 39 against, three in favour, 16 abstentions, and one absent.

The Liberian amendment itself was then rejected by a show of hands, 19 in favour, 23 against, with 9 abstentions and 1 absent.

The proposal of the Political Committee was then voted upon,

---

* The roll-call was as follows:—

In favour: Argentine, Brazil, Peru.

Against: Australia, Burma, Byelorussia, Canada, China, Colombia, Costa Rica, Cuba, Czechoslovakia, Denmark, Egypt, El-Salvador, Ethiopia, Guatemala, Iceland, India, Iraq, Israel, Lebanon, Liberia, Mexico, New Zealand, Nicaragua, Norway, Pakistan, Panama, Paraguay, Philippines, Poland, Saudi Arabia, Siam, Syria, Turkey, Ukraine, U.S.S.R., U.K., Venezuela, Yemen, Yugoslavia.

Abstentions: Belgium, Bolivia, Chile, Dominican Republic, Ecuador, France, Greece, Haiti, Honduras, Iran, Luxemburg, Netherlands, Sweden, South Africa, U.S., Uruguay.

Absent: Afghanistan.

and failed to obtain the two-thirds majority necessary for it to be effective.*

Italian trusteeship for Tripolitania was also voted down, a remarkable demonstration in defence of the people of the ex-colonies against a return of their old oppressor. The proposal to give western Eritrea to the Sudan also failed.

The Bevin-Sforza compromise was thus destroyed. The Argentine delegate called on the South American States to muster in support of Italy.

What was left of the Bevin-Sforza plan, as adopted by the Political Committee, minus the clauses defeated in the General Assembly, was then submitted to the vote of the Assembly; the compromise having been destroyed, the mutilated resolution failed to obtain the necessary two-thirds majority.

Eastern Eritrea was deprived of the hoped-for reunion to Ethiopia—Somaliland and Tripolitania were saved from the dreaded return of Italy.

All the former colonies were left to languish in economic stagnation under caretaker government.

The people of Cyrenaica refused to accept further postponement; the Emir Idris El Senussi notified the British Government that in accordance with the will of his people he intended to declare the independence of his country and call for immediate elections. The British Government assented to the decision by the Emir.

The situation in former Italian Somaliland and the other ex-colonies resembled that of the brooding overcharged atmosphere which precedes the storm.

In the two East African territories particularly, unemployment was considerable and the cost of living excessively high, conditions which were as favourable as possible to the efforts of the Italians to obtain from the weakest and least patriotic among the population a show of support by financial inducements and threats to dismiss all employees who refused to adhere to the Italian-sponsored parties.

To the Unionists of Eritrea, the intensification of economic misery merely accentuated desire for reunion to Ethiopia, for which they longed passionately, and wherein they saw the only possibility of escape from the insolvency of their territory, and of release from abject poverty and misery for themselves and their people. Their hope had been raised to a high pitch by the news that the Third

---

* IN FAVOUR: Argentina, Australia, Belgium, Bolivia, Brazil, Canada, Chile, Colombia, Costa Rica, Cuba, Denmark, Dominican Republic, Ecuador, El Salvador, France, Greece, Guatemala, Honduras, Iceland, Luxemburg, Mexico, Netherlands, New Zealand, Nicaragua, Norway, Panama, Paraguay, Peru, Siam, Turkey, South Africa, U.K., U.S., Uruguay, Venezuela.

AGAINST: Burma, Byelorussia, Czechoslovakia, Egypt, Ethiopia, Haiti, India, Iraq, Lebanon, Liberia, Pakistan, Philippines, Poland, Saudi Arabia, Syria, Ukraine. U.S.S.R., Yemen, Jugoslavia.

ABSENT: Afghanistan.

General Assembly had voted in favour of the return of Eastern Eritrea to Ethiopia by the majority of 37 votes to 11; their disappointment was correspondingly great when this vote was overthrown, and the Assembly again adjourned without reaching a solution. At the end of eight years of weary waiting for fulfilment of the war-time pledges, this third postponement by the General Assembly since the question of Eritrea's future had been referred to that body produced a sense of disillusion in the justice of the United Nations. There was an anxious suspicion that Italian diplomacy was making headway among the delegations to the detriment of the peoples formerly under Italian subjection who had been promised liberation.

It was at this time that attacks on Italian colonists and their indigenous supporters began to be made in Eritrea by a youth movement called " Andinet," which means " unity.' The British Administration suppressed " Andinet," closed its offices and confiscated its effects, but its activities continued, and were stimulated rather than deterred by persecution. " Andinet " shared the aspiration for reunion to Ethiopia of the Unionist Party, but whilst the Unionist Party preserved an orderly and peaceful course still hoping for a favourable decision by the United Nations, the impatient youth of " Andinet " drew inspiration for a more war-like policy from the events of the world war and particularly from the extraordinary success of the militant movement for Jewish nationhood. They had watched with intense interest the British withdrawal from Palestine and the creation of the State of Israel, the progress of the struggle for liberation in Indonesia had also its effect on them.

The position of the unfortunate Somaliland Colony had become even more bewildering than that of Eritrea. The leaders of the Somali Youth League, who headed the masses stirred by desire for liberation and progress, had induced their followers, under British guidance, to found all their hopes upon an independent development totally apart from Ethiopia. This solution was to be secured by British support and the aid of the United Nations. British support had been switched to Italy; the United Nations had carried a resolution for Italian Trusteeship; the proposal had only failed by a few votes to bring the majority up to the requisite two-thirds. In their consternation the Somalis had as yet formed no goal towards which to direct their efforts.

ITALY'S " INDEPENDENCE " POLICY

Before the Third Assembly rose, Count Sforza and his colleagues had adopted a new stalking horse—" independence "—for use in Libya and Eritrea, whilst retaining the claim for trusteeship in Somaliland. The pivot of the new compromise would be the Arab States and Pakistan plus the Governments of Latin

America, the two opposing groups whose differences had wrecked the Bevin-Sforza compromise. Italy and her friends of South America would permit the independence of all Libya, to satisfy the Arab States and Pakistan, who would reciprocate this concession by abandoning their unfortunate co-religionists in Somaliland to Italian Trusteeship with a promise of independence to follow.

The demand for independence would be raised also for Eritrea, but a solution might be postponed for a year, pending the visit of a Commission of investigation appointed by the General Assembly, which would visit the territory to discover the wishes of the population, and would present a report to the Fifth Assembly in the autumn of 1950, offering a solution for the future of the territory. This proposal was acceptable to the Arab States and Pakistan, who were led to believe both that their co-religionists formed the majority of the Eritrean population, and that the majority of Eritrean Muslims desired to establish an independent State. The parties to this compromise would work together to secure that the membership of the proposed Commission of investigation would be satisfactory to them.

If the objects of the new compromise could be achieved the claims of the Arab States, Pakistan and all Asian nations might be secured in Libya, their main objective. The Arabs might have a hope of drawing Somaliland and Eritrea into their own orbit eventually.

The Italian Government viewed the compromise from another angle. Trusteeship of Somaliland was essential to their plans. Apart from its own meagre possibilities, it was the southern gateway to Ethiopia; the desire to exploit that potentially wealthy Empire had never been abandoned.

Moreover, all, it was hoped, would not be lost for Italian aims by a nominal independence of Libya, and also of Eritrea. It mattered not that Italian diplomacy had persistently declared the populations concerned totally unfit for self-government, and that Count Sforza himself, on February 18, 1949, had unburdened his mind to the Anglo-American Press Association by a dramatic warning:

"*Gentlemen of Europe beware! You have lost Asia by your stupidity; see that you do not lose Africa also!*"

Consistency in official declarations was not considered necessary; Italian diplomacy, in order to win success, must adapt itself to the prevailing mode. The proud designation, "Empire," had already given place to "Trusteeship"; if a choice must be made between accepting the slogan, "Independence," and allowing any of the ex-Colonies to pass under the influence of some other European Power, still worse, if there were danger that Italy's so-called "first born" Colony of Eritrea might be united to Ethiopia, from whom Italy had torn the territory by painful and costly sacrifice, Italian diplomacy would unhesitatingly choose either the new slogan, "independence," or any other. Having ruled those lands for half a century, the Italians believed they would easily secure effective control of them, should they become nominally independent States. The British conquerors, particularly in Eritrea, had been most moderate and accommodating; they had not adopted the ruthless spoliation practised by Italy and her Axis partner. On the contrary Italian private properties—as distinct from State and para-Statal properties—had been preserved for their owners intact, Italians had been able to retain many key positions in the Administration. They knew all about the territories concerned; they had never lost touch. They occupied the best of the land; they were the owners and directors of industry and transport, and to a major extent of commerce. Apart from the Administration they were consequently the only large employers of labour. Their economic position, whether as owners or employers, was immensely superior to that of the subject people, particularly in Eritrea. With diplomatic support from Italy and her friends, the Italian colonists might obtain from the United Nations Municipal Charters and other "safeguards for the Italian minority," which would assure them special electoral and other privileges in controlling the administration of the new States. All these advantages, with their superior education and experience, and the financial support which the Italian Government would provide for development under Italian auspices, if and when high State policy required, would obtain for the local Italian communities—and for Italy—an overwhelming predominance in these economically deficient territories, which had never provided sufficient revenue to pay for their administration, and where the people of the country had been rigidly excluded by decree and custom from every sort of education or experience liable to fit them for any directive part in the administration.

Count Sforza and his colleagues having decided to adopt the "independence" slogan, the Eritreans who had been brought to Lake Success under Italian auspices to plead for Italian Trusteeship, and also those who had been mustered to ask plainly for Italian rule, were on May 12, 1949, hastily formed into a so-called "Independence Bloc." It was subsequently alleged that the originators of this Bloc thereupon cabled the news of its formation to their supporters in Eritrea who at once agreed to adopt the new policy of immediate "independence," and that a meeting of their adherents in Eritrea was subsequently convened and accepted the "independence" plan. On leaving Lake Success the "Independence Bloc" paid a visit to Rome on the way back to Eritrea. One of their members was finally despatched to Pakistan to address public meetings there!

In Somaliland all the groups forming the pro-Italian Somalia Conferenza displayed similar obedience to Count Sforza's policy by continuing to demand Italian Trusteeship, this being the action he desired of them.

XX
BACKGROUND

I.—ECONOMIC STRANGLEHOLD

The Italian Government had resorted to advocacy of a nominal independence for Eritrea and for Libya when, in the spring of 1949, a majority of the United Nations rejected Italian trusteeship of those territories. Adoption of the independence policy did not, however, mean the abandonment of the claim to special Italian privileges in the former Colonies, which might nullify true independence and maintain Italian predominance.

The proposal to retain the territories liberated from Italy under economic subjection to her recalls the long, persistent struggle of Italy to control Ethiopia's economy. In particular it brings to mind the tripartite Agreement of 1906, between Britain, France and Italy, by which the three Powers engaged to protect what they claimed to be each other's " interests " in Ethiopia, as follows:

1. *The interest of Great Britain in the affluents of the Blue Nile, which rise in Western Ethiopia and particularly derive from Lake Tana. This British " interest " was to be exercised with due respect for " local, and Italian interests." (Sic.).*

2. *The particular interests of Italy in regard to her colonies of Eritrea and Somalia, and " more especially in regard to the hinterland of her possessions, and the territorial union between them to the west of Addis Ababa." A glance at the map will indicate the magnitude of this tremendous claim.*

3. *The interests of France in the French Somaliland Protectorate and its hinterland, and the Addis Ababa-Jibuti Railway.*

This Agreement was negotiated between the three Powers without consulting Ethiopia. They notified the Emperor Menelik of its existence only after they had signed it; his reply indicated his refusal to recognise Agreements made between others concerning Ethiopia to which Ethiopia was not a party, and his assertion of Ethiopia's independent sovereignty within her own frontiers.

None of the so-called " interests " claimed in this Agreement of the three Powers could have any moral basis, except in so far as they had arisen from Treaties freely made with Ethiopia. The " interests " in free Ethiopian territory " in the hinterland " of their colonies which were claimed both by France and Italy in this Agreement were mere unjustified presumptions.

Still more unjustifiable was Italy's claim, firstly to build and possess a railway through Ethiopia, from Eritrea in the North to

Somaliland in the South East, which would make a detour west of Addis Ababa forming a large ellipse sweeping through the country, and to a great extent commanding it; secondly, the still more predaceous claim to "the territorial union between them."

Moreover, there was a further amazing feature of the Agreement: the three Powers pledged themselves to support the *status quo* in Ethiopia, which they deemed to be determined "by the existing state of affairs," and by the international arrangements they had made concerning Ethiopia; a list of these arrangements they inserted in this new Agreement. In this list the Foreign Minister, Tittoni, included three Anglo-Italian Protocols of 1891 and 1894, whereby Britain recognised the boundaries of a protectorate which Italy at that time falsely claimed to possess over Ethiopia. Italy's subsequent defeat at the battle of Adowa, in 1896, when she had taken arms to enforce the alleged protectorate, had been followed by the Peace Treaty in which Italy had recognised the completely independent sovereignty of Ethiopia and made a full renunciation of the claim to exercise a protectorate. This Peace Treaty of 1896 the Italian Foreign Minister, Tommaso Tittoni, most dishonestly omitted from the list, for though Italy had formally renounced the protectorate, she had not abandoned her ambition to possess and exploit Ethiopia. Therefore, Tittoni, as he subsequently explained to the Italian Parliament,* inserted the Anglo-Italian Boundary Protocols of 1901 and 1904 into the tripartite Agreement. The Protocols had no value he admitted, in relation to Ethiopia, because of the renunciation of the protectorate which Italy had made in the Peace Treaty and her recognition of Ethiopia as an independent State. He claimed, however, that between Britain and Italy the Protocols still held good. He further explained that as originally drafted the Agreement referred only to "communications" between the two Italian Colonies. The first text he said would have given to Italy "nothing but that fantastic railway," whereas the second text "clearly recognises the supreme interests which it was above all important for us to protect—and reserves for us in a more or less distant day the share which is due to us and is necessary to assure the future of the two colonies."

Could Mussolini have said more?

Thus Tittoni inserted the protocols recognising the boundaries of an Italian protectorate over Ethiopia which had never existed, whilst omitting the Peace Treaty whereby Italy had renounced all claims to that protectorate—a piece of sheer trickery!

Britain and France were fully aware through diplomatic and other channels of Italy's double-dealing in pursuing her predaceous aims after formally renouncing them in her Peace Treaty of 1896. Nevertheless, they completely accepted the Italian claims.

---

* *Italy's Foreign and Colonial Policy.* Speeches of the Italian Foreign Minister, Tommaso Tittoni (Smith Elder).

LLOYD GEORGE REJECTED ITALY'S PROPOSAL

The subtle working of this compact on the part of France, and particulary of Britain, the largest European investor abroad, to leave all share in Ethiopian development to Italy could not fail to lead to frictions and frustrations. France, Germany, Belgium, Holland or Switzerland, who at that period were all investing capital abroad, might have done something with the unrestricted field given to Italy; whereas Italy had not the means to make effective use of it. The Italians either lacked, or were unwilling to venture, capital to develop the colonies they had already obtained. Nevertheless, the appetite of the Italian Government for territory was insatiable. They knew the Ethiopian interior contained greater resources than the colonies they possessed on the coast; they hoped to find there the good fortune which had hitherto evaded their colonial adventures. They were continually complaining that owing to Ethiopia's obstinate unwillingness to assist them, the Tripartite Agreement they had made with France and Britain in 1906 had proved of little value to them. They were jealous that the Franco-Ethiopian railway from Addis Ababa to Jibuti carried the major share of Ethiopian commerce. Moreover, they had failed to secure from Ethiopia the concession for building the railway through Ethiopia, to which they had obtained the Agreement of France and Britain, but not of Ethiopia, in 1906.

THE TREATY OF LONDON, 1915

In 1915, when Britain and France were hard-pressed by German successes in the course of the first World War, Italy exacted from them the Treaty of London, as the price of her entry into the war beside them. When the Central Empires had been defeated, and the victorious Allies met to dictate the terms and divide the spoils, Italy fought bitterly to secure as much as possible from the Treaty of 1915. It is not surprising, in view of the restless ambition of her ruling elements to possess and to exploit Ethiopia, that the claims which had been made in the 1906 Tripartite Treaty were now advanced in a more concrete and imperative form. The Italian negotiators offered to lend Italy's friendly support for the purpose of inducing the Ethiopian Government to grant to Britain a concession to build a barrage on Lake Tana, in Ethiopia, for the regulation and utilisation of the waters of the Blue Nile which flow thence through the Sudan. In return for Italy's support for the barrage concession, Britain was to join in pressing the Ethiopian Government to give Italy a concession to build the desired railway; Britain would also support all Italy's demands for economic concessions in the zone Italy claimed; that is to say in all Ethiopia, except the immediate neighbourhood of the Franco-Ethiopian railway, and some area defined as " the hinterland " of the small French Somaliland Protectorate.

Had the British agreed to this proposal, there is little doubt the Italian Government would have followed up the compact with such military persuasion as had many times previously been applied in Africa. David Lloyd George, the British Prime Minister of 1919, curtly rejected the Italian proposals to strangle the liberty of a small nation; he probably considered they conflicted too flagrantly with the Charter of the League of Nations of which he and the American President Wilson were the foremost sponsors.

In fact the Charter of the League of Nations in Article 20 stated :—

"(1) *The Members of the League severally agree that this Covenant is accepted as abrogating all obligations or understandinge* inter se *which are inconsistent with the terms thereof, and solemnly undertake that they will not hereafter enter into any engagements inconsistent with the terms thereof.*

"(2) *In case any Member of the League, before becoming a member of the League, has undertaken any obligations inconsistent with the terms of this Covenant, it shall be the duty of such Member to take immediate steps to procure its release from such obligations."*

In 1925, when Mussolini was asserting himself as arbiter of European destinies, the 1919 proposals which Lloyd George had rejected were resurrected under the auspices of the Dictator of Italy and Sir Austen Chamberlain, then British Foreign Secretary. These proposals were even embodied in a formal Agreement, which was actually registered with the Secretary of the League of Nations under the terms of Article 18 of the Covenant directing that any Treaty or International Engagement should be so registered.

MUSSOLINI AND AUSTEN CHAMBERLAIN JOINT NOTE; ETHIOPIA PROTESTS TO LEAGUE OF NATIONS

The result was a Note signed by Sir R. Graham, British Ambassador in Rome, and Benito Mussolini to Ras Tafari Makonnen, Regent of Ethiopia (afterwards the Emperor Haile Sellassie I), informing him that the British and Italian Governments had entered into an Agreement to support each other, in conformity with the Anglo-Franco-Italian tripartite Agreement of 1906, in obtaining from the Ethiopian Government : for Britain a concession to build a barrage on Lake Tana and a road thence to the Sudan frontier; for Italy a concession to build and exploit a railway through Ethiopia to unite Eritrea and the Italian Somaliland Colony; this railway would pass west of Addis Ababa. Both the railway and the materials for its construction would be free to traverse the proposed British road from Lake Tana to the Sudan. Further, the Italian Government recognised the exclusive right of Britain to regulate the waters of Lake Tana and the British recognised the exclusive economic influence of Italy in the west of Ethiopia, and in the whole of the territory traversed by the proposed elliptical railway linking Eritrea and Somaliland—virtually, the whole of Ethiopia.

On receipt of this Note, Ras Tafari protested to the League of Nations* that pressure was being brought to bear on him, and that the freedom and self-government of Ethiopia, a member of the League of Nations, was thereby endangered. The British and Italian Governments replied that Ethiopia's liberty of action was not being assailed, but that the two Governments had agreed not to compete with each other in the matters in question.

Thus commenced the long struggle of Haile Sellassie I to maintain the independence of his country. Subsequently when the Ethiopian Government considered engaging the White Engineering Company of U.S.A. to build a barrage on Lake Tana and the extraction of petroleum from Ethiopian sources by a subsidiary company of the United States Standard Oil Company, diplomatic pressure was applied to nullify these projects by the three Powers who were the signatories of the Tripartite Agreement of 1906. Then followed the Italian invasion of Ethiopia.

From this summary of the series of events arising from the agreement by three Powers to reserve the greater part of Ethiopia for economic exploitation by one of their number, an agreement to which Ethiopia was never a party, it may be readily deduced that if an agreement were made to allow Italy the exclusive exploitation of any of the ex-Colonies, the latter would be faced with the impossibility of making contracts for public works and of obtaining capital investment except in Italy, a nation unable to export capital. The power to direct commerce which governments exercise through currency control and export and import licences would be used to prevent commerce except with or through Italy. Obviously the former Colony might become a dumping ground for inferior goods, whilst materials of self-defence might be found unobtainable, and there might be discrimination between the Italian and native purchasers of agricultural and industrial machinery and all articles in short supply.

---

* See official Anglo-Italian Agreement, registered with the Secretariat of the League of Nations, July 2, 1926. Journal of the League of Nations, November, 1926, pp. 1,518, 1,520, 1,523; also House of Commons Official Report, August 2, 1926. See also "Le Conflit Italo-Ethiopien," by A. de la Pradelle, 1936, pp. 111-138.

II—ITALIAN POLITICAL RETROSPECT

A member of the old political class of Italy from the deficiences of whose rule Italy slid under Fascist dictatorship, Count Sforza was a follower of the so-called Democratic Liberal, Giovanni Giolitti, for many years declared to be the "Master of Italian Politics." Don Sturzo has described Giolitti as "devoid of scruple as of idealism," adding that "by his long tenure of power and his ascendency over the political class, the harm he did to the public life of Italy was considerable." He reduced the political class to "a strong nucleus centring round himself, and upholding at all costs his disguised dictatorship; while he, in return, was strong in friendship and in enmity." Sforza, on the other hand, has eulogised his old leader.

The career of Giolitti reveals something of the turgid aspects of Italian politics. He was obliged to resign the premiership and to retire from political life for some years, on account of the support he had given, as Prime Minister and previously as Finance Minister, to Tanlongo, the Director-General of the Banca Romana, who had issued 62,500,000 lire of duplicate bank notes, beside heavily subsidising the Press and making considerable loans to Parliamentary Deputies and Ministers*. On regaining the premiership Giolitti waged the unprovoked war of conquest in Libya in which the Banca di Roma was heavily involved.

Sforza, in praising Giolitti, fully admits that his leader "welcomed" the appearance of Fascism "as a counterpoise to Socialism."† As a matter of fact Giolitti took the Fascists, who were then waging war on their political opponents, into his electorial bloc, and thus assured them an entry to Parliament which they could not otherwise have gained. Sforza did not himself, it seems, wholly disapprove of Fascism, for he asserts that in the beginning it was not lacking "in a certain idealistic passion for renovation,"‡ and also that it wished to be "generous."

Sforza, at the rise of Fascism, had been concerned with the Foreign Affairs of Italy for more than twenty years. He entered the diplomatic service in 1896, the year of Ethiopia's victory over Italian aggression at Adowa. He was Chargé d'Affaires in Turkey during the Italian naval demonstration of 1910 which led up to the unprovoked war of conquest in Libya, ruthlessly waged by Italy in 1911. After the World War he was successively High Commissioner in Turkey, Under-Secretary of State for Foreign Affairs,

---

* See Encyclopaedia Britannica, 1947, vol. 10, pp. 360-1, vol. 12, p. 797.
† "Makers of Modern Europe," Elkin Matthews and Marrot, p. 245.
‡ Idem, page 317.

1919-20, Minister for Foreign Affairs, 1920-21. His recollections of that period are given in his book, "Makers of Modern Europe," wherein he defends his own policy. We see him there obsessed by the constant ambition—"Italy a Great Power." He reveals himself as bitterly Anglophobe, bitterly antagonistic to Greece. "It was really not for a Great Power like Italy," he declared, "to have written Agreements to the effect that Greece should 'support' any essential point of Italian interest." *

We see him at Rapallo, determined "to impose on Belgrade Italy's amplest and most complete geographical frontier line," and to make Italy "the leading power in Central and Oriental Europe." He did "not agree with any of the so-called practical men" who thought that, "cost what it might, we must heal the gaping wound of the Adriatic question."

"Tittoni," he says, "had been ready to accept a frontier line only eight kilometres beyond Trieste; Scialoia, to share Istria." His leader, Giolitti, had "never been so optimistic" as to hope for all Sforza succeeded in gaining, which he described gleefully as :—

"*A frontier line more perfect than any under the Roman Empire, the whole of Istria, the islands of Lussin and Cherso, Zara, privileges for the Italians of Dalmatia*" (*which were not granted to the Slavs in the territories Italy was annexing*) "*independence to Fiume recognised as a free Italian town contiguous with the Italian boundaries; that is to say, Italian in practice, but with the autonomy traditional in its long history, which was better for its economic life than formal annexation.*"

Such untenable expedients were then in the air; the ill-fated Polish Corridor was a contemporary fabrication.

On Zara he was advised to compromise, he says, "from almost all Italian quarters." He tells us: "Signor Mussolini, whom I had received at length at the Foreign Office before my departure for Rapallo, had suggested Zara independent with Italian diplomatic representation."

Now that Fascism has long fallen and Mussolini is consigned to history's chamber of horrors it appears strange that the proud Count Sforza received the Fascist agitator in the exclusive sanctum of the Foreign Office, but the "Duce" of Fascism was at that time a coadjutor of Prime Minister Giolitti.

Though Giolitti telegraphed to him not to break off negotiations on account of Zara, Sforza was so determined to secure the port for Italy that he told the Yugoslavs his leader entirely supported his demand for it. He negotiated directly with the Yugoslavs in order to present the conference of the Powers with an accomplished fact, because in open conference he would have had to face the hostility of President Wilson, who was strongly opposed to Italian expansion into the Slav territories and along the Slav seaboard

---

* "Makers of Modern Europe," by Count Sforza, page 161.

just liberated from Austria, thus imposing a new foreign domination on their populations and a new stranglehold on their commerce.

Count Sforza does not mention that his negotiations concerning Fiume were facilitated by the Italian occupation of it under D'Annunzio, which Giolitti had permitted and allowed to continue until after the signature of the Treaty of Rapallo. Sforza tells, however, that he pressed his demands on the Yugoslavs by urging the danger of a Habsburg restoration and by promises binding only upon his own fugitive Government, which was soon to fall.

We see him as one of the three Allied High Commissioners in Turkey, during the Armistice of 1918, * with Admiral Calthorpe and Admiral Ahmet, his British and French counterparts, each of the three with his squadron. Sforza played a lone hand, endeavouring to get the whole of Turkey as " a market for Italian industries," and negotiating with the leader of the Senussi, who had fled from Italian rule in Libya, to induce him to acknowledge Italian sovereignty and to bind himself to favour Italy's political and economic interests in Benghazi and Tripoli. Sforza alleges that Mustapha Kemal Ataturk sent him this message:—

"*The maintenance of Turkish domination over the Arabs has been one of the causes of our decline. We do not want to hear any more about them. Let them settle matters with you as they please and as you please.*"

Sforza commended Kemal for daring " to renounce the noisy rhetorical legacies which the empty prestige policy of the previous régime had bequeathed to him."—" Makers of Modern Europe," page 365.

Sforza himself lacked that courage when he possessed the power to use it. When he wrote those words he was in what appeared might be a permanent exile from Government Office.

Vast political changes in great countries, prominent actors on the stage of contemporary history were, for him, all subordinate to his conception—Italy a Great Power. He writes of Kemal Ataturk, " The rubbish of most of his reforms," of Sun Yat-Sen, " his mental and cultural immaturity," " his empty Minn."— " Makers of Modern Europe," pages 5, 363, 386.

The Rise of Fascism

Thus decrying the heroes of other lands he endeavours to clothe with a mantle of greatness the old Giolitti, telling us that his leader knew by heart the whole of Dante's Divina Comedia, to discount the view that he was a mere political wire-puller, or a mere administrator. Nevertheless, Sforza makes some startling and terrible admissions concerning Giolitti's sombre political record and his cynical partnership with Fascism :

---

* " Makers of Modern Europe," p.p. 348-364.

"One day I came to see Giolitti while Buchanan was calling, and jokingly denounced his apprehensions to Giolitti, who looking out of a window, said: 'Do you see that olive tree, Sir George? You have never seen one in Russia, have you? 'Well, you will no more see Bolshevism in Italy than olive trees in Russia!'...."

"In 1920 there had been 1,881 strikes in the country (Italy); in 1921 the number fell to 1,045, with 720,000 strikers—very nearly the same figure as in 1915, the year of Italy's entry into the war. In short, there was the same curve of progress as there was in France and England.

"It was at this moment that Fascism, born as a revolutionary movement, had put itself more or less openly at the service of the employers to destroy the workers' unions. Giolitti welcomed it as a counterpoise to Socialism. But he was firmly convinced that the movement could easily be sobered into legality by Parliament. This is one of the reasons that decided him for a general election in 1921."—" Makers of Modern Europe," pages 244-5.

Don Sturzo, in his " Italy and Fascismo," a book which Count Sforza has greatly praised,* describes the connivance of Prime Minister Giolitti with Fascist violence:—

"Fascism made a noise, but did not increase the number of its adepts . . . . ; it lacked an outlet.

"And the outlet for its forces was opened by the old Giolitti. Towards the end of 1920 . . . . he thought it would be well to have other forces in hand which he could bring into play," against the Socialists, " without assuming direct responsibility" for the action of these forces. He could thus hope to bend the moderate section of Socialism towards collaboration (with his own party) " which he had hoped to do for a long time. For this purpose he could not lean on the Popolari,† whom he knew to be hostile to him" . . .

"Therefore, Giolitti thought to lean on the Fascisti, but his intention was to use them and at the opportune moment to get rid of them, after having gained the means of compromising their chiefs and neutralising their action should they rebel against him. With this plan, which corresponded to his well-known methods of government, he organised the national blocs for the Municipal Elections of the autumn of 1920, against the Socialists and against the Popolari . . .; the Fascisti in Upper and Central Italy took part not only with candidates and a very limited electoral contribution, but, and this was what counted, with armed bands which intimidated rural districts and towns. Part of their arms were those left over from D'Annunzio's expedition to Fiume, and part were secretly taken from the Military stores. The police

---

* Italy and Fascism which with its serenity seems more the work of a philosophic historian than of a political leader.—" Makers of Modern Europe," by Count Carlo Sforza, page 314.

† The Popolari, or Popular Party were a leftish Roman Catholic Party, led by Don Sturzo.

made a show of checking and pursuing lawless and violent actions, but they nearly always arrived too late and hardly ever found the responsible persons."—Pages 101-2.

Other writers have given more detailed information about Fascism in Italy and have exposed and criticised it more drastically than Don Sturzo. Professor Gaetano Salvemini has provided an invaluable store of irrefutable facts concerning it in a series of closely documented volumes: "The Fascist Dictatorship in Italy (1928)," "Mussolini Diplomate (1932)," "Under the Axe of Fascism (1936)," "Italian Fascism (1938)." Armando Borghi, Alceste De Ambris, Pietro Nenni, at one time Vice-Premier of Italy, have written with an intimate personal knowledge of the principal actors in the Fascist tragedy; scores of books have been written about Italy under Fascism. The book of Don Sturzo has been selected here for quotation because Count Sforza has himself praised it, because Don Sturzo, whose Party actually participated in Mussolini's Government at the commencement, gives the closest view of the failure of the old Italian political class, of which Count Sforza was a member.

At the time when Giolitti, as described by Don Sturzo and others, began to make use of Fascist violence, Count Sforza was Minister of Foreign Affairs in Giolitti's Government. Sforza at that time evidently did not foresee the destruction of his own Party which was destined to follow his leader's resort to violent aids; even in 1930 he wrote of that period. "The beginnings of Fascism were not lacking in a certain idealistic passion for renovation," but, "generous as it wished to be," it had not "the luck to find either the men or the occasions that might have made it useful, as it otherwise could have been."—"Makers of Modern Europe," page 318.

It appears truer to suggest that it was the Party of Giolitti who had not the "luck" to find in Mussolini and his Blackshirts a force compliant to their ends.

In the spring of 1921, Giolitti held a Parliamentary Election, for which he formed a National Bloc, consisting of his own adherents and those of Mussolini! The violence employed by the Fascists in the Municipal Elections was now intensified. In many constituencies the candidates of other Parties were unable even to appear; with their supporters they were beaten and even assassinated. Nevertheless, the Socialists obtained 123 seats, Don Sturzo's Popular Party 107. Don Sturzo tells that the Fascists, "who had come into the Chamber by the merits and will of Giolitti, at once took up a position against him, with the Nationalists, on the question of Rapallo." Mussolini, who had been elected to Parliament for the first time with about 30 of his Fascists, thus participated in the overthrow of Giolitti who had placed him there.

Confirmed as Prime Minister in May, Giolitti fell from power in June. He was replaced by Ivanoe Bonomi, who had been War Minister in his Cabinet when the Fascists obtained weapons from the arsenals of the State. Sforza had continued serving under Giolitti despite these tragic events; he lost the Foreign Secretaryship in July, 1921, when his leader fell, but was appointed Ambassador in Paris in February, 1922.

Giolitti soon withdrew his support from the Ministry of Bonomi, and thereby compelled his resignation. Bonomi was replaced by Luigi Facta, known as " Giolitti's friend." Count Sforza describes Facta scathingly, as a " pitiable little provincial lawyer, a nonentity assuming power for a few months while the leading actors arrange their troupe as they please and stage their re-entry." " Just because he was the arch-type of those who *mai non fur vivi* was he chosen to preside over a provisional Ministry that ought soon to have given way to a Giolitti cabinet, thought some; to a Cabinet of All the Talents, thought others." This is a striking picture of Italian politics in those days.

The Fascists were permitted to conduct a reign of increasing terror; Mayors and Councillors were driven from the Municipal buildings with firearms, towns were stormed and occupied. Mussolini's party held only 35 seats in a Parliament of 535 Members. Nevertheless, he ordered, and obtained the resignation of the Facta Government, and announced his " March on Rome." The King refused to sign a declaration of martial law, though Badoglio, as head of the Army, declared the Fascist rabble could be subdued in ten minutes with a whiff of shot. Mussolini was offered a place in a Government under Salandra, but replied that he would accept no office save the highest. The King then supinely invited him to Rome as Prime Minister.

Giolitti was meanwhile away in his country seat at Cavour. Count Sforza seeks to excuse his leader's connivance with Fascism on the plea that Giolitti believed it could be " sobered into legality by Parliament."

Don Sturzo, with much hesitation, offers the same excuse for the acceptance of seats in Mussolini's predominantly Fascist Cabinet by members of his Popular Party and the parties of the old political leaders, Giolitti, Orlando, Sonnino and Salandra—all the parties except the Socialists.

Mussolini faced the Chamber on November 15, 1922, " in the guise of a lion tamer," announcing that he could have made of that House the bivouac of his Black Shirts, and that he had the power to decide " whether it would live two days or two years." Despite that brutal challenge, the political parties of Italy, with the sole exception of the Socialists, slavishly passed a vote of confidence in Mussolini, and accorded him plenary powers to reform the administration, finance and the codes. Says Don Sturzo:—

" Both Senate and Chamber yielded up to him the legislature."

Count Sforza's Resignation

Mussolini had made opposition to the Treaty of Rapallo an important plank in Fascist propaganda and a crucial question in his opposition to the Giolitti Government when he and his little company of Blackshirt M.P.s reached Parliament by Giolitti's aid. The resignation of Count Sforza, who had negotiated the Treaty of Rapallo was, therefore, inevitable on the Fascist ascent to power. Sforza's opposition to Fascism was, nevertheless, not of such a character as to render him one of the numerous victims of Fascist violence. In his chapters on the Fascist regime, notably that on Mussolini himself and that on Giolitti, Sforza passes lightly over the sins of Fascism; he does not mention the murder of Matteotti, the courageous leader of the Parliamentary Opposition, an event which given a resolute leadership on the Opposition side might have overthrown the regime. He does not refer to the murderous assaults by Fascist gangs, which led to the death of Amendola, the Liberal leader, and other Parliamentary colleagues. Whilst deprecating dictatorship in principle, when he wrote in 1930, he did not want his readers to think hardly of Mussolini, urging that he had been " convinced in good faith " that all the problems could be easily solved. When he realised the truth he had become " a slave of the myth artificially created about him." " When comedy turned to tragedy one had to stay, cost what it might. Hence the complete transformation of the old romantic and revolutionary Fascism into an exact copy of France under Napoleon III."

So it would seem Sforza would have us believe there was little to be ashamed of in Italian Fascism; Italy had only repeated the errors of her greater Latin sister. He reminds us that Italy had had scant experience of freedom and democracy. That is truer still to-day.

The rise of Fascism Sforza ascribes to diplomatic, not to economic causes, nor to any misgovernment inside Italy. He puts the blame for the overthrow of democracy upon Baron Sonnino, the Foreign Minister, under whom he served in 1919-20, and whom he thus describes: " The son of a Scotch Presbyterian mother, and of an Italian Jew, he was obsessed by a puritanical and, seemingly pharasaical mania for thanking God that he was 'not as other men.' " In what Sforza terms " my tolerant Italian way," he has some bitter words for his former Chief, but excuses him somewhat on the ground that his " narrow honesty was outraged by the greeds and selfishness " which the representatives of other Powers " hid under the cloak of the new words " enunciated by President Wilson. Sforza had warned Sonnino of the need to adapt Italian diplomacy to the new model, but Sonnino lacked Sforza's adroitness. Unable to secure Dalmatia for Italy he made the mistake of allowing the Italian people to believe they had been cheated of their due proportion of the war spoils. Sforza, on the other hand, has always been at pains to assure everyone that Italy had gained by his own diplomacy "the most perfect natural boundary in the world," and that " no one has, in Europe, won the war as Italy has." The interpellation " in Europe," is worthy of note.

Don Sturzo has bitterly portrayed the non-Fascist Parties, refusing to cast a united vote to unseat the Fascist Government, in the period when the Parliamentary powers under which they might have done so still existed—refusing because of their own political differences and the utterly vain belief that it was possible to make the old leaders, Giolitti, Salandra and Orlando, " the centre of a new situation."

While the Fascists had still merely 35 seats in the Chamber every constitutional pass was sacrificed in turn.

The Fascist armed squads were transformed into one of the forces of the State, a voluntary militia under the personal orders of Mussolini for the protection of his regime.

A Bill to destroy the existing electoral system and facilitate the acquisition of a Parliamentary majority for Mussolini, if he could obtain a 25 per cent. poll, was passed into law because " the whole Opposition, except the Socialists, decided to abstain." Thus Don Sturzo tells us, on page 138 of his book, " The ' Totalitarian ' System of Mussolini " was " countersigned by all the men of the declining political class, represented by three names, Giolitti, Orlando and Salandra,"

The election contest of January, 1924, which followed, was disgraced by even more widespread and sanguinary violence than its predecessor. It opened with the murder of Piccinini, a candidate for Reggio Emila. The old Liberal and Democratic leaders, including Salandra and Orlando, agreed to add their names to Mussolini's List. Giolitti had a List of his own, limited to Piedmont, but declared this " did not signify hostility towards the Government. In point of fact it voted with the Government majority, and Mussolini was satisfied "—again we quote Don Sturzo's " Italy and Fascismo " (page 172). He adds: " The entry of the old men of Liberalism into the Fascist List " " widened the zone of confidence " in Mussolin's dictatorship.

Wherever the electors were able to record their votes without immediate coercion the results were very favourable to the Opposition Parties. In the South, owing to Fascist violence, " the majority of voters abstained and small Fascist groups voted in their stead, repeating the operation ten and twenty times." In spite of everything the Government had an unfavourable vote in Northern Italy; therefore, when the results were known, Opposition newspapers and organisations were punished by Fascist raids. Pope Pius XI sent half-a-million lire to repair the damage done by the Fascists on this occasion to the newspaper, " L'Azione Cattolica," at Brianza, in Lombardy.

Events were hastening towards the culminating tragedy, which was to precede the destruction of the Parliamentary constitution of Italy. Giacomo Matteotti, Secretary of the Socialist Parliamentary Group, by his courage and ability, was recognised as the leader of the Opposition to the Mussolini regime. On May 30,

1924, Matteotti delivered a precise, factual indictment of the corruption and violence which the Fascist Government had employed in the election campaign.

On June 10, Matteotti was suddenly seized on the Tiber embankment by five of Mussolini's associates, who dragged him into a motor car, murdered him, and buried his remains in the Quartarella, a wood in the Roman Campagna. There was an outburst of public feeling. Thousands of people flocked to the spot where Matteotti was kidnapped. The site was heaped with flowers, crowds of men and women knelt to pray. Fascists tore off their badges, it seemed the Fascist regime must fall.

Mussolini affected ignorance and consternation, he obtained from the Senate a vote of confidence. This was opposed by Senator Albertini, Editor of the "Corriere della Sera," from which position the Fascist regime would soon expel him. Count Sforza and Senator Abbiate also opposed. Nevertheless, Giolitti, Orlando and Salandra continued their support of the regime, which Giolitti had brought to power.

Revelations of Fascist Crimes

Startling facts irresistibly pointing to responsibility for the murder of Mussolini's close associates and Government colleagues —of Mussolini himself—began to leak out. Mussolini resigned from the Ministry of the Interior, which he held with other offices, and compelled the resignation of some of his colleagues who were implicated in the plot. One of these men, Finzi, the Under-Secretary of the Interior, believing Mussolini intended to make him a scapegoat, sent to the leaders of the Opposition an account of the Matteotti murder incriminating Mussolini. Rossi, the Chief of the Cabinet Press Bureau, disclosed the whole working of the Fascist murder gang, giving details of murders of prominent public men at Mussolini's behest.

These documents were laid before the King by the Liberal leader, Giovanni Amendola; the King took no action. Amendola, in consequence, was twice attacked by Fascist bullies and died at Cannes of the injuries thus suffered on account of his patriotic solicitude.

Professor Salvemini subsequently published the revelations of Finzi and Rossi in his important volume, "The Fascist Dictatorship in Italy."

The old Liberal leaders, despite the appalling disclosure concerning the crimes organised by Mussolini, whom Giolitti had raised to power, still gave their support and lent their prestige to his regime.

The Government majority in the Italian Parliament staged a commemoration of the man whom the Government had murdered, and whose mutilated remains were still undiscovered.

The Opposition Parties, disunited though they were, under Amendola's lead were nevertheless sufficiently drawn together to hold a public commemoration of Matteotti outside Parliament and to publish a manifesto demanding a return to constitutional liberty. The judicial proceedings then pending against De Bono and other prominent Fascists had revealed, they declared, an organisation " set up outside the law to execute sentence on political opponents," directed by persons in the confidence of the Head of the Government," a tangle of corruption and trafficking defiling the body public," and " a sinister association for the purpose of upholding, by all and every means, the positions of vantage and power which have been audaciously captured."

Nevertheless, the Opposition Parties, in view of these tragic facts, declared their protest " based solely on moral grounds." It was not their purpose to secure political power. Consequently their action was abortive; Mussolini's reign was unchallenged.

Having withdrawn from Parliament at this time, the Opposition Parties remained absent and held their own Assembly, termed the Aventine, but their unwillingness to assume the responsibility of forming a government robbed their movement of reality.

Fascist atrocities and Fascist defiance continued; it was not until November 15, 1924, two years after Mussolini was called so calamitously to power by a craven sovereign, that Giolitti openly broke with the Fascist Government. Orlando and Salandra followed suit two days later. Salandra was at that time Chairman of the Budget Commission and Representative, at Geneva, of the Fascist Government. These old Party leaders, long in government control, who during the two first crucial years of its existence supported Mussolini's Government and who aided him to power cannot be held guiltless of his misdeeds. Giolitti of all the old Ministers was the most responsible. The withdrawal of their support for him only came when Mussolini was beginning to place the Press and the law courts under Fascist control. In 1925 was inaugurated the policy of " all power to all Fascism," the " most Fascist laws " leading to the one Party State, the replacement of Parliament by the Corporations. Thus the time had come for the old fellow travellers with Fascism to pass into retirement—they could serve the dictatorship no more.

Giolitti, says Sforza, was " a great Liberal statesman of the nineteenth century; he firmly believed that all factions and all interests would find their compromise in Parliament. Indeed, he only broke openly with Fascism when it practically suppressed the right to vote." It is, however, clear that from the very commencement, the whole conception and practice of Fascism, with its squads of armed bullies, was a suppression of the right to vote, a suppression of the right of free choice, and of free expression of opinion in every aspect of corporate life. There can be no doubt that Giolitti had hoped to profit by fascism, that he broke with it only when he was forced to understand that Fascism would presently exclude him and his followers from the political life of Italy. He saw that the armed men he had brought to power, had destroyed, for the time being, the political conditions in which he and his like had operated.

FALL OF MUSSOLINI
THE EMIGRÉS RETURN

When Mussolini declared war on Britain and France in 1940, the Italian emigrés in the United States were divided between those who counted on a vast expansion of the Italian Empire, and those who began to speculate on the possibility of returning to a liberated country. When Britain was seen to have survived her darkest hour, and the United States entered the World War, in December, 1941, the Italian anti-Fascists abroad became more emphatic in their opinions; their numbers swelled considerably, and anti-Fascist sentiments became vociferant among some who had hitherto been prominent in support of the regime.

When the occupation of Sicily and a portion of the Italian mainland by the United Nations led to the resignation of Mussolini, King Victor Emmanuel of Italy appointed as Prime Minister Marshal Badoglio, who had conducted the war in Ethiopia (after the removal of De Bono) and had advanced his armies by the lavish use of poison gas. On September 8, 1943, it was announced that Badoglio's Government had surrendered to the United Nations and had pledged themselves to assist in expelling the German forces from Italian soil.

Count Sforza, on September 23, sent letters to Marshal Badoglio and to the United States Government, through Mr. Berle, declaring, " in my view, it now becomes the paramount duty of all Italians, irrespective of political and party differences, to support and assist in the struggle to crush the German armies, and to drive every German soldier from Italian soil, so long as Marshal Badoglio is engaged in that task, and is acceptable to the Allies. I consider it criminal to do anything to weaken his position. I am prepared to offer my full support, so long as he is thus engaged. Matters of internal politics can and should be adjourned for the period of the struggle, and the activities, military and political, of all Italians should be devoted to supporting the organised forces endeavouring to throw out the common enemy. I pledge my honour to do this myself, and to urge this course upon my many friends and associates."

On this understanding, facilities were given for Count Sforza to return to Italy. Mr. Churchill, who was not fully satisfied with Count Sforza's attitude, owing to statements of a different character which had been published, and also perhaps with memories of the negotiations which followed the First World War, interviewed Count Sforza as he passed through London, and went through the above letter which Sforza had written, almost line by line; Count Sforza assured him that this letter represented his most profound conviction.

Leaders of the various defunct political parties which had formerly existed, but which had been abolished under Fascism, were now invited to join a government under Marshal Badoglio.

They made the condition that the King must abdicate, but Count Sforza in a Press conference on September 2, expressed complete faith in Marshal Badoglio, who, he said, would make an " ideal Regent " for the young Prince of Naples, the King's grandson.

ABDICATION OF THE KING

On April 21, 1944, King Victor Emmanuel III announced: " I have decided to withdraw from public affairs, appointing my son, the Prince of Piedmont, to be Lieutenant-General of the Realm. This appointment will become effective by the formal transfer of power on the day on which the Allied troops enter Rome."

This statement satisfied the leaders of the resurrected political parties. They entered the Government of Badoglio, who held the positions of Prime Minister and Minister of Foreign Affairs, Count Sforza being appointed Minister without Portfolio.

On June 4, 1944, the Allies entered Rome. Badoglio then presented his resignation to Prince Humbert, the Lieutenant-General of the Realm, who commissioned him to form a new Government. On June 6, the political leaders unanimously voted a refusal to serve under Badoglio, on the ground of his association with Fascism. This accords most curiously with Sforza's declaration that Badoglio would make an " ideal Regent," and his proposal to Badoglio that he should be Regent, which Sforza recalled in a statement he issued on December 11, 1944.

In view of the refusal to serve under Badoglio a Government was now formed by Ivonoe Bonomi, the same who had served as War Minister under Giolitti in the period when the Fascists obtained arms from the arsenals of the Italian State. In Bonomi's administration Count Sforza served also as Minister without Portfolio.

On November 26, 1944, Bonomi's Government resigned. After two days negotiation, it was announced that Bonomi would form a new Government, with Count Sforza as Foreign Minister, but a notification was received from the British Minister in Rome that Count Sforza's appointment to that post would be unacceptable to the British Government.

Mr. Eden, in the House of Commons, on December 1, 1944, said: " In view of Italy's unconditional surrender, and her shameful record under Mussolini, His Majesty's Government were perfectly entitled to express their views about the appointment of any particular Italian statesman, especially in regard to the post of Foreign Minister. The Government does not feel that Count Sforza would be a particularly happy choice for that post. Before he returned to Italy, he told His Majesty's Government that he would pursue a certain course. Nevertheless, " he worked against the Italian Government and continued to work against the Bonomi Government. Count Sforza's record is not one that gives us confidence; that is the Government's view, and that is my view."

Mr. Churchill, on December 8, said: " We have not attempted to put our veto on the appointment of Count Sforza; all that we have to say about it is that we do not trust the man. We do not think he is a true and trustworthy man; nor do we put the slightest confidence in a government of which he is a dominating member. We are not avid of becoming deeply involved in the politics of the conquered or liberated countries; all that we require from them is a government which will guarantee us the necessary protection and facilities for the lines of communication from Naples to Ravenna and the north." He asked: " What is the Government's reason for objecting to Count Sforza ? Why is it that we, and I particularly, have no trust in him ? That we do not think he would be the sort of man we would like to do business with round the table ? " Mr. Churchill then read passages from Count Sforza's letter to Mr. Berle, and explained how he, in the presence of Mr. Law and Sir Alexander Cadogan, had particularly questioned Count Sforza in relation to this letter, and had obtained from him the assurance that it represented his " profound conviction "; yet, said Mr. Churchill, " no sooner had he got back to Italy than he began that long series of intrigues which ended in the expulsion of Marshal Badoglio from office. Many may be glad of this, but that is not the point I am considering. The point is whether he did not most completely, and without explanation, depart at a very early day from the solemn undertaking he gave." It was not Mr. Churchill's intention to defend Marshal Badoglio, though " we got from him the Italian fleet, which came over intact, except for the loss of one ship, and 17,000 men, and there was no moment in his tenure of office when he did not do his utmost to carry out his bond and help to drive the Germans from Italy. Presently, he fell a victim to Count Sforza's intrigues, and a Six Party Government was formed under Signor Bonomi. Six parties were in the Government, but none had the slightest electoral foundation. We did our best to help this new Government. I travelled to Italy and interviewed Signor Bonomi and others, and took the greatest trouble to draw up a series of mitigations in the treatment of Italy by the victorious Allies. Now Signor Bonomi has fallen, and I understand that he has formed another Government of four out of the previous six parties. We wish him well. We have no objection at all to his forming a Government of four parties." Count Sforza issued a statement on December 11 asserting that he had not written but only signed the letter to Mr. Berle, and that he had fullfilled all the engagements contained therein, a statement which seems hardly consistent with the facts.

The result of the British intervention, above recorded, was that Count Sforza was dropped from Bonomi's new Government, and obliged to remain outside the Italian administration until June 22, 1947, when he entered the Ministry of Signor Alcide De Casperi as Minister of Foreign Affairs.

XXI

COUNT SFORZA'S NEW COMPROMISE

Fourth Assembly of the United Nations
A Fateful Decision

When the Fourth General Assembly of the United Nations opened in September, 1949, it was evident that the disposal of the former Italian Colonies would be debated in an atmosphere radically changed by Count Sforza's new Asian-South-American compromise.

The Ethiopian Delegates were unprepared for the cruel blow which had been concerted against their country. They relied on the justice and equity of their case, and the assurances they had received from other governments, particularly those of Britain and the United States. The vote of the Third Assembly for the reunion of Eastern Eritrea to Ethiopia they believed to be conclusive for that territory. They hoped the solution Egypt had proposed for the Somaliland colony—a temporary Trusteeship of several Powers, including Ethiopia—would be successfully negotiated, with the support of the Arab States, Pakistan and others who had voted against Italian Trusteeship the previous session.

The warm friendliness, which from all sections of the Assembly had hitherto greeted the sober, well documented utterances of Ethiopia s representatives, in recognition of her heroic struggle against aggression and the justice of her claims, now gave place to a wintry coldness, or even to sharp hostility from those who were parties to the new compromise. The tables were turned; to the freeing of Tripoli along with all Libya, which had been defeated in the spring, not a dissentient voice was now raised; on the other hand the reunion of Eritrea to Ethiopia, which in the spring had secured an overwhelming majority, was now bitterly assailed.

Mr. Ernest Bevin

Mr. Bevin announced that his Government had assented to the establishment of an independent administration of Cyrenaica, under the Emir Sayyid Mohammed Idris el Senussi, and that the proposal of Italian Trusteeship for Tripoli, which Britain had supported in the spring, had become untenable; nothing short of independence for both Cyrenaica and Tripolitania, he declared, would meet the circumstances. As the Occupying Power, his Government would do everything possible in helping to reach a speedy solution. The British Delegation still supported Ethiopia's claim to Eritrea, except the Western Province. They still approved Italian Trusteeship for Somaliland. He made the following points*:

---

* United Nations General Assembly A/S.R.229, 27th September, 1949.

"*The Italian colonies had been under military occupation since 1943 and failure to arrive at a settlement had been a great handicap to the development of their political and economic needs.* The United Kingdom had had to operate a military occupation under the terms of the Hague Convention; it was unfair to the people living in those territories to handicap them further by failure to decide the issue.*

"*During the war a solemn pledge had been made to the Senussi and that pledge must be honoured. All would remember the great fight of the desert, and all would remember the period when the United Kingdom was largely alone. In order that internal affairs might be carried on (in Cyrenaica), a local administration had been established. That did not in any way prejudice the Assembly in dealing with the problem.*

"*With regard to Eritrea, it was the British Commonwealth which had liberated that country and Ethiopia. At the previous session of the General Assembly, after full consideration and study, the United Kingdom had made clear its attitude towards that problem, its position in principle remained the same. The United Kingdom Government supported Ethiopia's claim to Eritrea, except the Western Province.*

"*His delegation was firmly convinced that, provided proper protection was assured to the Italian minority, a great step could be made towards peace in that area. There had already been co-operation between the Italians and the Ethiopians in trade and development, and there was evidence that, if that was allowed to grow naturally, the whole community would benefit.*

"*For Italian Somaliland, the United Kingdom maintained the proposal it had put forward in the previous session of the Assembly for Italian Trusteeship.*

"*For Tripolitania, he wished once more to make it quite clear to the Assembly that the United Kingdom had no desire to remain in that territory. His Government was prepared to do anything it could as the Occupying Power in helping to reach a solution. The interests of the local inhabitants must be given full consideration, and it was greatly to be hoped that there would be no delay in producing a solution to the problem.*"

There was a difference in Mr. Bevin's emphasis on British support for Eritrean reunion and his support for the freedom of the Senussi, as there had been throughout the entire controversy on the former Italian Colonies, though British pledges to reunite Eritrea to Ethiopia were clear and incontrovertible.

Mr. Acheson, for the American Government, supported Independence for Libya, division of Eritrea between Ethiopia and the Sudan, the people of Somaliland to enjoy what he termed " the benefits of the Trusteeship system."

The Ethiopian Minister

Ato Aklilou Hapte Wold, the Ethiopian Foreign Minister, concurred in the hope of General Romulo, the President, that the Fourth Assembly might earn the title of the "Peace Assembly," but he shared also the anxiety of other delegates lest the United Nations, in multiplying its Committees and Commissions, might be tending to avoid its own responsibilities.

"Who among you," he asked, "have forgotten the dreary period during which the work and existence of the League of Nations gradually disappeared, when it sought to bolster itself with a multitude of subsidiary organisations, Commissions of Investigation and Sub-Commissions?

"For my part, I recall particularly the numerous commissions set up to deal with a question in itself extremely simple, namely, the Fascist aggression against Ethiopia. It was in large part due to the interminable references of that question to special commissions by the Assembly and the Council that the League of Nations failed in its duty to resolve that crucially urgent problem. It was as a result of that proliferation of meetings and commissions that the world accused the League of Nations of having practised "Spoliation by Procedure."

Of all the questions on the Agenda of the Fourth Assembly that of the former Italian Colonies he claimed had been studied most fully and was ripest for solution. It had been studied by the Council of Foreign Ministers, by the Conference of 21 interested States at the Paris Peace Conference of 1946, then again, for nearly a year, by the Council of Foreign Ministers and their deputies aided by the Commission of Inquiry the deputies had appointed. The interested States had been several times called to express their views to the Council of Foreign Ministers. The General Assembly of the United Nations had discussed the matter during the entire spring session; they had listened to the views of delegations from the territories, had heard reports and established Committees. Up to the present time no fewer than ten Commissions had discussed the problem. The Political Committee appointed by the Third General Assembly that spring had approved by a majority of six-sevenths the minimum claims of Ethiopia, but this partial solution had been suspended "for totally unrelated reasons of international politics." The Fourth Assembly had the duty of settling this urgent problem.

CASE OF EX-COLONIES REFERRED TO FIRST COMMITTEE

After the general debate the vexed question of the former Colonies was referred to the First Committee.

BRITISH POLICY.

Mr. Hector McNeil, M.P., British Minister of State, elaborated the policy Mr. Bevin had announced.

SOMALILAND.

Somaliland had been, jointly with Tripolitania, the scape-goat of the Bevin-Sforza compromise; it was now designated as the scape-goat both of the Anglo-American and of the Sforza-South American-Arab Pakistan compromises. Consequently, Mr. McNeil dismissed Somaliland and its people in a single sentence: " My delegation supports the proposal put forward at the last session of the Assembly for the placing of this territory under the international trusteeship system, with Italy as the Administering Power."

LIBYA: INDEPENDENCE, BUT ECONOMIC TIES TO ITALY

For Libya, Mr. McNeil said, the British Government no longer felt that trusteeship was " either applicable or warranted;" it was their view that full independence could be achieved in approximately three to five years. This would require " persistent and strenuous work by all concerned," for, said he:

" A generation of repressive and stultifying fascist rule robbed this community of its legitimate growth and political and intellectual habit and practice, and inevitably drove into exile many of its eminent sons. It is only now, since our occupation, that they have started to trickle back."

These remarks were, of course, applicable to all the territories Italy had ruled in Africa Moreover, as we have seen in earlier chapters, misrule was not confined to the Fascist period, though the ruthless ferocity practiced under Fascism was without parallel in modern times; being equipped with aircraft and modern weapons its cruelties were more terrible than those of the earlier tyrannies. It is unpleasantly remarkable that in none of the sessions of the United Nations where the question of the former Colonies was discussed, nor at the Paris Conference on the Peace Treaties, was there any admission by the official representatives of " the New Italy " that the Fascist regime in Africa had been grossly oppressive and cruel. On the contrary, Italian official representatives persistently declared that Italian rule in Africa was at all times beneficial to the populations concerned. " Italy always went hand-in-hand with the people of her colonies " was a cliché in habitual use, which found its way into numerous Italian official statements. Even more dismally ominous for the future was the fact that the Government of " the New Italy " were employing as their advisers on the colonial issue many of the men who had been high officials of the Fascist colonial regime, both in the Ministry of the Colonies in Rome where the policies of oppression and conquest originated and in the African territories where those policies were operated Foremost among these former Fascist officials was Dr. Cerulli, at one time Vice-Governor-General of Ethiopia under Marshal Graziani, and now listed by the United Nations War Crimes Commission, as a person presumed to be guilty of War Crimes. He had been highly placed in the Fascist Administration of Somaliland before the conquest of Ethiopia; and had held a directing position also in the Ministry of the Colonies in Rome. Despite the protests of the Ethiopian delegation that a War Criminal, guilty of illegal cruelties in Ethiopia, was amongst the Italian representatives, Dr. Cerulli continued as a member of all the delegations of " the New Italy."

TRUE INDEPENDENCE VERSUS FOREIGN ECONOMIC CONTROL.

Having briefly referred to the handicaps to the establishment of an independent administration in Libya which were the result of the Fascist regime, Mr. McNeil expressed the view that " the Union of the Libyan territories, Tripolitania and Cyrenaica, appeared " an historically inevitable development," but the form this unity would take " should be decided by the inhabitants of Libya themselves."

The imperfection of the method of consulting the views of the inhabitants of the former colonies which had been employed in the case of the Four Power Commission of Investigation might have occasioned some doubts as to how far the inhabitants of Libya would be permitted to make an unfettered decision.

It became evident in the course of the debate that though political independence and unity for Libya was at least nominally conceded, Italy's claim to control the economy of the Libyan State would be strongly asserted, and that French claims to economic control of the part of Libya named the Fezzan were not abated. Mr. McNeil proposed a formal Agreement tying the economy of Tripolitania to Italy:

> "*The association of Italy with Tripolitania in the past is well known. His Majesty's Government fully recognise the special position of the large Italian community in Tripolitania and the close economic and geographical ties which the territory has with Italy. I think it is also clear that this modern democratic Italy is peculiarly well placed to afford the territory the economic, and possibly the technical, assistance which undoubtedly the territory needs. My delegation consider that note of these facts should be taken in any resolution about the disposal of the territory that is adopted by this Assembly. In His Majesty's Government's view it would be in the economic and social interests of any future Tripolitanian or Libyan Government to conclude some form of agreement with Italy to formalise these ties. I would, however, emphasise here that this question is a matter for negotiation between Italy and the future Tripolitanian or Libyan Government.*"

This expression of British policy could not fail to sound sadly to the student of African economic and political history.

" Italy has no money to waste in Africa " was the ever-recurrent theme of Italian official utterances on the African colonies during the pre-Fascist period. During the Fascist regime expenditure was more lavish, but little of it was employed for highly productive installations. Not one of the African territories held by Italy was rendered profitable; they were all dependent on Italian State subsidies.

Italian statesmen continually protest that Italy is a poor country; so far from having surplus capital to invest abroad, Italy throughout the pre-Fascist period counted on the remittances of United States dollars and other foreign currencies sent by Italian emigrants abroad to their families in Italy. "Everyone knows," said the Minister, Tittoni, "that the numerous rivulets of gold which flow into Italy" from her emigrants "have greatly contributed in the last few years to render international exchanges favourable to us."*

Moreover, Italian Foreign Ministers frequently complained, as we have seen in earlier chapters, that Italian investors were reluctant to venture such modest liquid capital as they possessed in enterprises abroad; they were particularly shy of ventures in Africa. Again one may quote Tittoni:

> "*How often is it deplored that Italian money should not go to the countries where we hope to have a moral, commercial or political influence, and how often the Foreign Affairs Minister is called to task because he does not succeed in calling forth this reluctant capital? But when we reflect that right here in Italy, for the construction of public works and in the banking business itself, we have a noteworthy amount of foreign capital employed; and when we consider that in our own land and with such supreme interests at stake we have not been able to secure the employment of our own money alone, we cannot wonder that this great and useful idea of the exportation of Italian capital to foreign countries is for the present nothing but a dream . . . . These Italian capitalists willing to take into consideration such investments are not to be found, and if by chance one of them turns up who is prepared to risk his capital it is only upon condition that the Government guarantee the interest on the money invested.*"

It must be emphasised that historically economic predominance has been shown to lead to political predominance, and to loss of political independence and liberty by people whose countries have become spheres of economic exploitation by stronger nations.

The United Nations Organisation and its many auxiliaries should preserve all peoples from economic, as well as from political subjection. For this purpose the International Bank to provide "loans without political strings," and the various technical auxiliaries for promoting agricultural and industrial development have been created. The slave of a poor master has always been held to be particularly unfortunate; to place under economic slavery to Italy the new State of Libya, or any other among the ex-colonies

---

* Speech of Senator Tommaso Tittoni in the Italian Senate, February 20, 1904. See official English translation, *Italy's Foreign and Colonial Policy*, page 155 (Smith Elder).

who have been promised liberation, would be a most reactionary proceeding, unworthy of the United Nations ideal.

To-day, following her reverse in war, Italy is seeking not to invest capital abroad, but even more urgently than formerly to obtain capital from abroad for her own industries. Capital to develop latent natural resources, and thereby to raise the standard of living, is greatly needed by Libya, Somalia, Eritrea—the Middle East in general. Undeveloped in the modern sense, these cradles of ancient civilisations suffered by deforestation and destruction in past wars, the rise of trade routes which excluded them from world commerce, the competition of Western mechanised States. They now need large-scale planting and irrigation, the harnessing of their electric power resources, machinery for agriculture, industry and the extraction of minerals. Their peoples desire to effectuate such developments without putting themselves and their descendants in bondage to others. Mr. McNeil's indication that British policy would support the establishment by formal Agreement of economic ties binding Libyan economy to that of Italy offered to Libya a bleak prospect. Such an Agreement would tend to debar the new Libyan State from seeking capital, or placing contracts requiring capital, in the countries best able to provide it.

THE FEZZAN

Turning to the Fezzan, Mr. McNeil said the British Government recognised the special interest of the French Government in this part of Libya and would be glad to hear the view of " our French friends."

ERITREA

Mr. McNeil maintained the view that Central and Eastern Eritrea should be united to Ethiopia subject to safeguards for the Italian population and appropriate municipal charters for the city of Asmara.

Mr. McNeil did not state what form the proposed special safeguards or municipal charters would take. Italy never had municipal charters in her colonies. The Italians who remained in Ethiopia at the time of the Italian defeat, or had slipped over the border from Eritrea afterwards, had found life comfortable and prosperous in the Ethiopian realm. They had not felt a need of special safeguards; the difficulty had been to prevent more Italians from entering the country than the Ethiopian Government had desired to allow. The Italians had become prosperous, and had suffered no ill-usage or annoyance. As special safeguards for Italians not applicable to the rest of the population had not been required in Ethiopia, it did not appear that there would be any valid reason to establish them in Eritrea under Ethiopian administration. The popular animosity which had arisen against the Italians in Eritrea was a reaction caused by their own efforts to regain the territory for Italy, and the dubious methods they had employed. Had they refrained from active opposition to the reunion cause, they would still have been treated with the toleration extended to them in the early years following their defeat.

THE WESTERN PROVINCE

For the Western part of Eritrea, Mr. McNeil supported separation from the rest of the territory, and annexation by the Sudan. In support of this view he urged, "Most Colonial territories in Africa—and Eritrea is no exception—are not the product of organic political growth, but the legacy of the old Chartered merchant companies, of the hazard of last century colonial expansion."

This is well enough as a general description of colonial expansion in Africa but it cannot be held to apply precisely to Eritrea, which since before the opening of the Christian era was a part of the ancient Ethiopian realm, and maintained its identity as a part of that realm until the Italian conquest was accomplished in the years 1885-1896. Eritrea is, in fact, purely a strip of Ethiopia adjoining the sea, which was severed by foreign conquest.

Mr. McNeil went on to urge the division of Eritrea between Ethiopia and the Sudan on racial, religious and linguistic grounds. " Racially and religiously," he said, " Eritrea is mixed." No more concise and appropriate reply to Mr. McNeil's contention could, however, be found than the following passages drawn from an Italian Royal Commission Report of 1891 (*) on the Colony of Eritrea :

"*Münzinger, in his turn, defines the population between the Red Sea and Cassala in a synthetic phrase, applicable also to the Abyssinians, which comprehends their history and their physical and moral constitution, and reveals their future.*

"*They have, he says, Caucasian features, African colour, and Semitic speech—in fact, the Abyssinians well deserve their name (because Habesch means mixed†). The greater part of the inhabitants of our Colony (Danakil, Beduini Samhar, Habab, Begiuk, Beit-Takué, Beit Bidel, Marea, Mensa, Sabderat, Algheden, the greater part of Bogos, the Beni Amer, and the people of Massawa), have the same origin, the same original home, the same fundamental characteristics. They are but varieties of a single ethnic type.*

"*They are Semites, migrated from Asia to the high plateau of Ethiopia, and from there have spread to the lower slopes and plains.*"

This Italian view was expressed at a time when Italy's troops were still fighting to enlarge the newly acquired colony, and the facts concerning the territory and its people were too widely known to attempt to disguise them.

Mr. McNeil's support for the assumption that Eritrea should be divided, on the ground of religious diversity, was highly regrettable and impolitic. It is a most unworkable assumption for Africa,

---
* Relazione Generale della R. Commissione D'Inchiesta della Colonia Eritrea, Roma, Tipografia della Mantellate, 1891, pp. 40-41.
† This is an erroneous derivation.

where foreign missionaries of divers religions have long been active and have created innumerable religious communities, far too intricately interwoven to permit of any religious frontiers.

Moreover, the establishment of States on a theocratic basis is contrary to progressive modern ideas of government, and to the basic idea of the United Nations. Britain, in her island home, has succeeded in reconciling religious differences, and has established a common citizenship, irrespective of religion. Ethiopia has adopted the same wise and just course. It is, to say the least, inconsistent to suggest that Muslims who had existed as the subjects of Roman Catholic Italy would not tolerate reintegration into the citizenship of Ethiopia, where the Christian faith was established before the birth of Mohamed, the Prophet, and where there is also a large Muslim population who began to find a home there in the days when Mohamed himself praised Ethiopia as "the land of righteousness where no one is persecuted."

The proposal to unite Western Eritrea to the Sudan was a compromise proposal. In the opinion of some observers it was designed to appeal to the Muslim States and to detach them from the alliance with the South American friends of Italy; in the opinion of others it was an effort by Britain to secure control of Keren, the site of her hardest battle against Italy in East Africa, and also to put Western Eritrea with all the possibilities it might possess under the British Administration of the Sudan. The Gash River, which flows through Eritrea into the Sudan, was known to be a matter of interest to cotton growers in that area. Mr. McNeil's claim that the people of Western Eritrea and of the torrid Danakil coast to the east were some sort of Arabs, so far from recommending his project, tended to make it more unpalatable to Arab delegations.

Languages of Eritrea

Mr. McNeil's analysis of the languages and races of Eritrea, and his description of them as "Afa-Arab," "Beja-Arab," and so forth, has to be viewed in the light of the fact that all the Ethiopian people are held to be originally of Arab origin. The Beni Amer, whom he described as of "Beja-Arab" origin, are, of course, ancient inhabitants of Northern Ethiopia. It is true they are divided by the present frontier between the Sudan and Eritrea, which was pushed south-eastward, thus encroaching on Ethiopian territory in the time of Khedive Ismail. By far the greater part of the Beni Amer are, however, in Ethiopia.

On the question of language Mr. McNeil was badly briefed by the Foreign Office:

"*Linguistically,*" he said, "*the territory shows the same diversity as it does religiously and racially. There is no common language. The Coptic Christians speak Tigrinya, the same language as is spoken in the Tigrai province of Ethiopia. The Danakil speak Afar, a language completely of their own. The Saho Moslems also speak their own language. In the Western Province, on the other hand, the prevalent languages are Tigré (which I should explain, for I find this confusing myself, has nothing to do with the Ethiopian province of Tigrai or the language, Tigrinya), and Beja Arabic spoken by the people of the Western Province. Also spoken in the Western Province are Belein and Arabic and Baria and Baza by the semi-negroid tribes to whom I have already alluded."*

In reply to these contentions it must be stated that Tigrinya and Tigré, two closely allied Ethiopic languages, are the main languages of Eritrea. The latter is the spoken language nearest to the Gueze of the old Ethiopian literature, and is in fact almost pure Gueze. It is the main language of Western Eritrea.

It should be noted that Tigré and Tigrinya use the Gueze script, the old Ethiopic script descended from early times, in which all Ethiopian Semitic languages are written. Ethiopian Hamitic languages have no script. Of these the Afa of the Danakil, also spoken in Ethiopia, is closely allied, both to Saho and to Somali, whilst the Belein of Eritrea, is closely related to the Agau, which is spoken in the mountains of Lasta in Ethiopia; these are regarded by some philologists as the oldest languages of Ethiopia.

Arabic is the native language of only a small fraction of people, near the coast, on the western border of Eritrea. Again one may usefully turn to the Italian Royal Commission Report of 1891, to elucidate the point. We find there on pages 48 and 49:

"The language of the Okule-Kuzai, of the Hamasen and the Serae is the Tigrinya; the major part of the Muslim population subjected to us speak Tigré, which is allied to the ancient Gheez; here and there, especially among the Beni-Amer, Bedaunie is spoken, and Bilein survives still in the Bogos and the Takué.

"At Massawa all these languages are more or less spoken, and most of all the Tigré. Arabic is heard there, but its true domain commences beyond the western borders of our possessions."

This Italian account agrees substantially with the researches of philologists who have studied the languages spoken on the Horn of Africa, the ancient realm of the Ethiopian people.

Eritrea Objects to Partition

Mr. McNeil's claim that the British proposals were " the resolution into its component parts of a completely artificial unit " was, in short, based upon mistaken premises. He frankly admitted that the Four Power Commission of Investigation had reported an almost unanimous desire of the Eritreans for their territory to be dealt with as a whole, but he brushed the views of the population aside. The Christians wanted the whole territory reunited to Ethiopia, he said; whilst the Muslims hoped for an independent country, because they believed they would be able to control it. Thus the British representative discounted the whole plan of consulting the wishes of the population.

AMBASSADOR JESSUP, U.S.A.

Ambassador Philip C. Jessup, of the United States Delegation, declared that in the interests of the local inhabitants and of the overall peace settlement, a decision concerning the former colonies was urgently needed. The solution must "not only meet the three principles enunciated in Article XI of the Treaty of Peace with Italy—namely, regard for the wishes and welfare of the inhabitants, the interests of peace and security, and consideration of the views of interested Governments," but must "meet also the principles relating to non-self-governing territories of Chapter XI of the Charter." A sound and just solution "embracing the above principles" must be achieved.

Libya

The United States Government would support the establishment of an independent and unified Libya. The form of government should be worked out by the inhabitants of Libya. The State might be federal, unitary, or whatever form most acceptable to the inhabitants. Representatives of the inhabitants of Tripolitania, Cyrenaica, and the Fezzan should meet together to decide this. The British and French Administrations in Libya should co-operate in the formation of governmental institutions and in preparing the people for self-government, taking whatever steps the General Assembly of the United Nations deemed necessary. An Advisory Council should advise the British and French Administrations concerning measures to promote the future self-government on behalf of the United Nations, without interfering with the administration of the territories.

Eritrea

The United States Government would adhere to the same policy adopted by them in the previous session of the General Assembly, which coincided with that already enunciated by Mr. McNiel. The British and United States delegations appear to have been briefed from the same source. Ambassador Jessup argued:

"We are dealing here with an artificially created territory, whose inhabitants are almost equally divided between Coptic Christians and Moslems. The Eritrean plateau provinces are a continuation of the Ethiopian plateau, and the majority of the inhabitants of the entire plateau are related by language, race and religion. It is true that the port of Massawa, as well as the province of the same name, is predominantly Moslem, but it cannot be separated from the Eritrean plateau without economic disruption. Assab and the Danakil coast, which are part of the province of Massawa, have no lateral communication with the central provinces nor with the capital, Asmara. This area is geographically part of Ethiopia, and the Danakils who inhabit it are part of a tribe whose greatest numbers are within the borders of

Ethiopia. In our judgment, a substantial majority of the inhabitants of Eritrea, exclusive of the Western Province, favour union with Ethiopia.

"The majority of the inhabitants are Moslem, as are the people across the border in the Sudan. Three-fourths of the inhabitants of the Western Province are nomadic, or semi-nomadic, and follow a pastoral way of life quite different from the settled agriculturists on the central plateau of Eritrea. Climatically, the heat and aridity of most of the western and the coastal plain comprising this area resemble those of the Sudan. There is a religious tie with the Sudan through the adherence of certain tribes, such as the Beni Amer, in the Western Province, to the teachings of the Mazhani " Tariqa " or Confraternity, which is closely related to some 30,000 of its other members in the Sudan. The basis of social organisation for both nomad and sedentary peoples in Eritrea, as well as the Sudan, is the same : the Kinship group. Thus, social ties would be respected by changing the political orientation of the Western Province to the Sudan. The Western Province has few economic resources and cannot exist as an independent modern state.

"In brief, gentlemen, this Assembly is presented with an opportunity to make a long-term settlement of Eritrea, whose artificial borders were created in the era of colonial expansion in Africa; and it is our belief that the re-shaping of the map in the manner I have indicated will be a move toward an end we all seek—namely, to reunite racial, cultural, religious and linguistic groups separated by frontiers arbitrarily established in the 19th century."

The American Government's support for Ethiopia's claim to central and eastern Eritrea was gratifying. The proposal to join the western part to the Sudan was disappointing.

Ambassador Jessup's argument for this plan, like that of Mr. McNeil, entirely ignored the actual history of the territory, which the Italians named Eritrea in 1890. The evidence of stone inscriptions, is still extant, dating from the early centuries of the Christian era, that Eritrea was then part of a great Ethiopian realm, with its capital at Axum, to-day still in Ethiopia where traces of its ancient loveliness remain, and its famous seaport, Adulis, on the coast of what is now Eritrea. Much testimony is available in many libraries of European travellers who visited this territory, and knew it as Ethiopia. The important work of Francisco Alvarez, the Portuguese priest, who was a member of the first Mission from the King of Portugal to the Emperor of Ethiopia, first published at Coimbra in 1540, of which an English translation by Lord Stanley of Alderley appeared in 1890, must be readily found in United States libraries, as well as the works of several other Portuguese priests who wrote in the 16th century. The classic history of Ethiopia by the learned Ludolphus, (Frankfort 1681, English Edition, 1684), again reveals the same territory as part of Ethiopia. The French physician, C. J. Poncet, visited the territory and knew it as Ethiopia in the 18th century. His story, first published in Paris in 1713, can be read in both English and German translations. To James Bruce, the account of whose travels was published in 1768, 1773, and 1813, this territory was also part of Ethiopia. Lord Valentia's travels (1802-1806), and the magnificent works of his secretary, Henry Salt (1809-1814), show that though the Turks held Massawa and were ready to pounce upon foreign interference anywhere along the Red Sea coast, all that is known as Eritrea to-day was then Ethiopia.

From that time onward, until the advent of the Italians, who fought continuously to establish their colony from 1885 until 1895, the books of travellers from Britain, France, Italy, and many other nations, proving this was Ethiopia are too numerous to mention here. In 1834, the Protestant Missionary, Bishop Gobat, visited this part of Ethiopia, and wrote about it, as such, in 1847, and Isenberg and Krapf, who followed him, published their journals in 1843. To them present-day Eritrea was Ethiopia. Father Giuseppe Sapeto, an Italian Roman Catholic Missionary, was instrumental in purchasing a so-called coaling station for the Italian Rubattino Company in the Bay of Assab (at the peppercorn price of about £600) in 1869. He had reason to know the territory was Ethiopia, for an attempt which he and his fellow-missionary, Msgr. De Jacobis, made to get a part of the coast annexed by the French Emperor, Napoleon III, by means of an Ethiopian rebel, Negussie, who hailed from the Agau country, was checked by the Ethiopian imperial troops.

Most surprising of all was the total ignoring at Lake Success of the 19th century diplomatic correspondence, British, French, and Italian, concerning this part of Ethiopia, and the many inroads into what is now called the Western Province of Eritrea during the period of the Egyptian expansion under Khedive Ismail.* Successive British Foreign Secretaries—Lords Palmerston, Clarendon, and Russell—were constantly protesting against this raiding into Ethiopia. The French Consul at Massawa joined his British colleague in protesting against these raids into the part of Ethiopia now called Eritrea, both from Massawa and across the Sudan border. Father Stella, a Roman Catholic missionary, many times appealed for the assistance of the British consul to protect his Ethiopian congregation in Bogos (now in Western Eritrea). When a certain French Count de Bisson, in 1863, proposed to obtain some land in the part of Ethiopia (now Western Eritrea) called Bogos, the British Consul General in Cairo, Robert Colquhoun, on January 11th, 1864, wrote to Earl Russell:—

"I warned the Viceroy that there was no tribe of any kind who could legally transfer itself to any one; that all the country down to the Red Sea as far as a little above Sooakin was part of

---

*See specially "Abyssinia: Correspondence respecting Abyssinia 1846-1868, laid before Parliament, December 2 and 5, 1867, and February 20, 1868."

His Highness' dominions; that at that point the Egyptian Territories ran due south, with the exception of a narrow slip of land extending down to the sea-board, which was claimed and garrisoned by Turkey, to a point between the 16th and 17th degrees; that here the Tigré or Abyssinian territory commenced; the boundaries, it is true, being ill-defined, but that certainly none of the holders of the land could dispose of such territory."

In a firman of February 1841, 21° 05′ north latitude had been stated as the Egypt-Ethiopia boundary. (See Hertslet, page 260, 1894 edition.)

So fully was it recognised that the territory now called Eritrea was Ethiopia that on March 6th, 1856, the Earl of Clarendon, then British Foreign Secretary, wrote to the British Ambassador in Constantinople instructing him to advise the Government of Turkey to transfer Massawa to Ethiopia, in the following words:

"*I have received from Her Majesty's Agent and Consul-General in Egypt a copy of his despatch to your Excellency of the 16th ultimo, explaining the grounds on which he considers it is desirable that the Sultan should consent to transfer the port of Massowah to the Government of Abyssinia; and I have to instruct your Excellency to advise the Porte to enter into an arrangement for the transfer of Massowah, which appears to be of no importance to Turkey, and which she will not be able to protect in the event of the operation contemplated by the Rulers of Abyssinia being carried into effect.*"

When the part of Ethiopia called Bogos (now Western Eritrea) was invaded by Egypt, General Gordon, then employed by the Khedive as Governor-General of the Sudan, records that he wrote to Nubar Pasha on January 9th, 1879: "Provided Johannes does demand Bogos, and the lands we robbed him of, we must give them." Johannes was of course the Emperor of Ethiopia.

Eventually, in 1884, Britain and Egypt needed the assistance of the Ethiopian forces in relieving certain Egyptian garrisons which were besieged by the Dervishes in the Sudan. As so often has happened in history, under the pressure of need the injustice of a foreign occupation of the Ethiopian territory of Bogos (Western Eritrea) was recognised. Therefore, by a Treaty of May 5th, 1884, Egypt, and Britain as custodian of Egyptian affairs, agreed that Bogos should be "restored" to Ethiopia, and with the exception of a narrow neutral zone near Massawa (established to avoid possible friction), the whole of what is now called Eritrea was recognised as Ethiopia. The justice of Ethiopia's claim to the port of Massawa was tacitly recognised by the provision that Ethiopian exports and imports should pass through it freely, without the imposition of any dues or charges under British protection.

This Treaty the Italians ignored. The Ethiopian Northern Army, under Ras Aloula, Governor of Ethiopia's northern province, whose headquarters were at Asmara (now capital of Eritrea), departed to relieve the besieged Egyptian garrisons, as stipulated by the Treaty. In the absence of the Ethiopian Northern Army the Italians occupied the Port of Massawa, on the pretence of protecting it from the Dervishes.

The unsavoury manoeuvres by which Italy replaced Britain, who then held Massawa belong to a sad and deeply regrettable past, which has been aptly summed up by the British Vice-Consul, A. B. Wylde, who had participated in the negotiations for the above mentioned treaty: " Look at our behaviour to King Johannes from any point of view and it will not show one ray of honesty . . . . England made use of King Johannes as long as he was of any service and then threw him over to the tender mercies of Italy, who went to Massawa under our auspices with the intention of taking territory that belonged to our ally, and allowed them to destroy and break all the promises England had made to King Johannes after he had carried out his part of the agreement. The fact is not known to the British public and I wish it were not true for our credit's sake." *

The Italian occupation of the port was but the preliminary to a series of determined attempts to conquer the whole of Ethiopia. The conflict to annex the present colony of Eritrea involved a decade of sanguinary and continuous warfare.

Represented by a small deputation of grave men, the fine old Ethiopian nation, which for centuries maintained its culture and independence against the numerous conquerors to whom its neighbours succumbed, was now at the bar of the United Nations defending itself bravely against recalcitrant enemies, in an Assembly too lacking in historical erudition and practical day-to-day knowledge of the people and the country for full, or perhaps for even partial understanding of the conflict.

In reply to Ambassador Jessup's claim that the 300,000 Beni Amer of Western Eritrea are related to 30,000 of their tribe in the Sudan, it should again be recalled that the Egyptian conquests thrust the Sudan border into what was formerly Ethiopian territory. The Sudanese Prime Minister, Abdula Kalil Bey, recently informed a deputation of Eritreans that the Sudanese do not desire any part of Eritrea, on the contrary they are aware that a portion of Eritrea has been included in the Sudan, and should rightly be restored.

The diplomatic correspondence, to which reference has been made, records continual complaint during the period of nineteenth century Egyptian expansion that the Ethiopian border populations were being offered "the Khoran or the sword." Acceptance of the Khoran meant acceptance of Egyptian rule and payment of tribute to the nearest Egyptian administrator. Present-day Egypt cannot be held responsible for the barbarous practices of a barbarous time, in which the scramble for Africa was keenly practised by European Governments.

---

*A. B. Wylde, " Modern Abyssinia," 1901, page 39.

Touching the question of religion in Western Eritrea, we may again quote, with profit, the Italian Royal Commission Report of 1891, page 48:

"*For the rest, the Musulmans of our Colony are not fanatics; among the Bogos, the Beni Amer and others, who are converts to Islam of only one or two generations, it has not yet had time to temper and form their spirit, to extirpate the greater part of their former beliefs and customs and to substitute the Khoranic law for the Ethiopian law of Mogaresh. In Massawa and its environs, where the Islamic faith is fairly ancient, and relations with Egypt, Arabia, and the rest of the Muslim world are older, more permanent and manifold, the spirit of Islam has penetrated more deeply into the customs and the thought of the inhabitants.*"

British Consul Plowden, Consul Cameron and others, observed that many of the Muslims of the Ethiopian-Sudan border, had Ethiopian names which indicated that their fathers were Christian, as well as Ethiopian.

It should, moreover, be emphasised that Muslim citizens of Ethiopia form a third of the population, that they are patriots proud of their Ethiopian nationality.

It is evident that the annexation of Western Ethiopia to the Sudan would not, as Ambassador Jessup claimed, " reunite racial, cultural, religious and linguistic groups separated by frontiers arbitrarily established in the nineteenth century." On the contrary, if Western Eritrea were joined to the Sudan, new frontiers would be arbitrarily created by a vote at the United Nations by representatives of governments in all parts of the world, most of whom had no knowledge whatsoever of the territory in question. The failure of any section of the local population to assent to annexation by the Sudan was ignored.

SOMALILAND

Somalis Not Able To Determine What is Best For Them

For the former Italian Somaliland colony, the United States Government advocated Italian Trusteeship as before. Ambassador Jessup brushed aside the objections of the Somali people; they could hardly be expected to know by what means their aspirations could be fulfilled. He said :

"*The United States Government believes that the people of Italian Somaliland aspire to the status of independence and equality which will enable them to develop their culture and their country as a full member of the community of free nations. My Government believes that the people of Italian Somaliland should be assisted toward the goal of independence through the trusteeship system of the United Nations. We are convinced that such a solu-*

tion will best meet the requirements of the people, and will also provide a solution which will best guarantee the future security and stability of the area.

"Italian Somaliland is an area with undeveloped political institutions, the organisation of whose people is largely tribal and pastoral. We can hardly expect these people to be in a position to determine for themselves what means might best assure their achievement of self-government and independence, and the fulfilment of their national aspirations. It is therefore the view of my Government that the General Assembly has a special responsibility to assure that the solution which we recommend will in reality provide for the best interests of the inhabitants.

"If it is accepted that independence is the desired objective with respect to Italian Somaliland, and that a substantial period of trusteeship is needed to prepare the people of the territory for full self-government. We must next examine the type of trusteeship which will be best suited in the circumstances to achieve our desired goal. The First Committee last Spring carefully considered and discarded as impracticable, in the circumstances, both a direct United Nations trusteeship, and trusteeship with a multiple or joint administering authority. The problem now reduces itself to a choice of the most desirable single power to be the administering authority for Italian Somaliland.

The Italian Government Gave Formal Assurances

"During the many months and years which my Government has considered this problem, it has consistently been our view that the Italian Government is the best choice for the responsibility of administering a trusteeship of Italian Somaliland. This view was shared at the last Assembly by thirty-five Members. The Italian Government indicated its willingness to assume this responsibility, and gave formal assurance. that it would discharge such a task in accordance with the purposes and principles of the Charter of the United Nations and of the trusteeship system.

Objections Rejected

"The United States Government has carefully considered the objections to Italian trusteeship which have been voiced by certain elements of the population of Italian Somaliland. We have considered the reasons which have impelled these representatives to the position which they have taken, and we have considered the degree to which these spokesmen might actually represent the people of Italian Somaliland. We have also weighed contrary views, as well as other evidence, including the report of the Four-Power Commission with respect to this aspect of the problem.

"Having given full consideration to all of these factors, my Government has come to the conclusion that the Italian Government, under a trusteeship agreement approved by the General Assembly, can and will provide an administration which will effectively and promptly assist the people of Italian Somaliland in the economic, social and political development of their country, and will bring to fulfilment their desire for self-government and independence. The Italian Government has evidenced its deep interest in the United Nations and its devotion to the principles of the Charter.

"As the members of the Committee know, the United States has warmly supported Italy's application for membership in the United Nations. Indeed, Members of the United Nations have overwhelmingly agreed that Italy possesses all the qualifications for membership.

"The United States has full faith in the determination and ability of the democratic Italian Government and the hard-working Italian people to discharge faithfully this obligation toward the people of Italian Somaliland and toward the General Assembly of the United Nations."

Mr. James Byrnes, who was American Secretary of State and chief of the United States delegation to the Paris Conference on the Italian Peace Treaty in 1946, has recorded* that in the immediate post-war years it was official American policy to return to Italy all her former African colonies. Investigation of Italy's colonial record had, however, revealed its unsatisfactory nature and the unwisdom of re-establishing Italian colonial rule. American support for confiding the unfortunate Somalis to Italian trusteeship was, therefore, the last vestige of an almost abandoned American policy. Further knowledge might have resulted in American withdrawal also from this last vestige.

"The hard-working Italian people," to whom Ambassador Jessup referred, would, of course, have little part in discharging their Government's obligation in respect of the trusteeship. Their part would mainly be to support further taxation for the up-keep of the military occupation of the Somaliland territory.

M. COUVE DE MURVILLE, FRENCH DELEGATE

The leader of the French delegation, M. Couve de Murville, was the only spokesman of the Great Powers to have eyed the former colonies of which the destinies still hung in the balance. As a member of the Four Power Commission of 1947 he had had at least some glimpse of the squalid poverty, the sad suspense and conflict oppressing the populations of those forlorn territories. He emphasised the urgency of a settlement, the impossibility of attempting long-term projects for the betterment of the standard of life under a caretaker administration of uncertain term.

This said, M. Couve de Murville proceeded to express the policy of the French Government, which was actuated, he declared, by a spirit of "conciliation and realism."

---

* See "Speaking Frankly," by Ambassador James Byrnes.

Libya

He indicated the reluctance of the French Government to assent to the immediate independence and unity of Libya, but his expression of this view was modified by the knowledge that Count Sforza's new compromise had secured a majority for Libyan independence in the General Assembly. Nevertheless, the French delegate argued that " for peoples with no experience of political freedom independence does not necessarily work in favour of freedom itself." In the absence of maturity " de facto situations arise to the advantage of a few and to the detriment of the majority." He deplored that unwillingness to grant trusteeship to Italy on the part of a number of member States had resulted in the proposals for Libyan Trusteeship, wherein France and Britain were to share, which were discussed in the Fourth Assembly. In the interim the British grant of a government for Cyrenaica under the Emir Senussi, had " to some extent anticipated the decisions of the United Nations," and had caused trusteeship to be regarded as " outmoded." The French delegation would be delighted if means could be found " to spare the peoples concerned the risks of disorder, anarchy and poverty." But obviously he took a gloomy view of independence and would prefer the Fezzan, at least, to remain under French guidance.

Special care would have to be exercised, he urged, in the case of Tripolitania, in view of the large number of Italian residents and the " economic bonds " uniting the territory with Italy.

Eritrea

For Eritrea, the French delegate insisted " any decision must receive the agreement of both the Ethiopian and Italian Government." This was, of course, an impossibility, in view of Italy's refusal to abandon her efforts to dominate Eritrean affairs, and the determination of Ethiopia to free Eritrea from any form of Italian control. Insistence that both Governments must be satisfied would, therefore, inevitably involve a deadlock. The French delegate hoped for fruitful collaboration between two free countries, Italy " a member of the old European civilisation," and Ethiopia " also historically old, but economically under-developed." That Italy has large under-developed territories in her home peninsula and her adjacent islands, and that Italian capital for development there is not forthcoming was ignored in all these discussions.

Somaliland

For Somaliland the French delegate advocated Italian trusteeship as before.

COUNT SFORZA
Blandishments to Newly Liberated Asian States

Count Sforza sought and obtained leave for the Italian delegation to sit in the First Committee, without a vote but with freedom to take part in the discussion. The presence and arguments of subtle and determined Italian politicians exerted powerful influence on delegates of member States who lacked knowledge of those territories under review.

Count Sforza's long experience in political manoeuvres, his facility for humanitarian phrases, suggesting moderation and desire for peace and international understanding were brought into play.

Shadowed by memories of the long reign of Fascism in Italy, with Fascist cries again rising in the streets of Italy, now an old man of 76 years, he was back again as Foreign Minister.

No longer, as in 1920, among the victors imposing peace upon defeated nations, he still was animated by the old obsession, "Italy a Great Power." To that end he was striving to regain as much as possible of the African Empire Italy had forfeited.

Confident in the support of his South American and Muslim allies, his tone was truculent. Moreover, he adroitly played on the conflict between the Eastern and Western blocs:—

"*The cause of peace is served by truth and frankness,*" he said, "*rather than by comfortable oblivions. The Italian people have learned with increasing bitterness that another veto has once more prevented our coming here as a member. Not only in Italy, where the sense of justice is strong, as in all countries which have intensely suffered, but everywhere else in the world is recognised the full and judicial right on our part to enter the United Nations and the juridical and moral obligation on the part of the Four Big Powers to abide by the pledge taken in a solemn treaty to support our membership.*"

"*This pledge was the essential counterpart of the great sacrifice we made when we signed a Treaty of Peace that contained unjust clauses, mainly imposed by errors, perhaps inevitable in a period too near a terrible war. The Soviet Union has no right whatsoever to make our admission to the United Nations dependent upon conditions which do not concern us.* * *In respect to us the Soviet Union has one duty alone; that of carrying out the solemn commitment made in a Treaty, and of remembering that this Treaty has enabled her to demand to the very last pound of flesh the fulfilment of the heavy conditions which the United States, the United Kingdom and France—who have always favoured the admission of Italy to the United Nations—have generously waived.*"

Count Sforza's reference here was to the war reparations imposed upon Italy by the Peace Treaty. Many months later, however, the Soviet Government was complaining that Italy had defaulted in her commitments to the Soviet. To Ethiopia Italy had paid not a penny of the war reparations imposed by the Treaty, nor had she even returned the objects of artistic and historical

---

* This refers to the decision of the Soviet Union to veto the admission of Italy until the admission of Albania, Bulgaria, Hungary and Rumania was accepted by the Western Powers.

interest which she had looted from that country, and under the Peace Treaty she was under obligation to restore.

The attitude of arrogant self-righteousness which had been characteristic of Italian pronouncements under Mussolini was maintained. Cajolement was mingled with severity.

An attitude of suspicion towards Britain, who had proposed the re-union of Eritrea to Ethiopia and had initiated self-government for Cyrenaica, seemed to contrast with expressions of friendship for France and the United States, for which the Italian people "care so deeply."

He sought to impose the opinion that Italy could represent "strength" to the cause of international solidarity and peace. With an assumption of impeccable virtue, he challenged the United Nations in dealing with the territories he still called the Italian Colonies to show the world "they keep themselves above the cheap schemings and cruel bargainings of the old autocracies.' He lauded Italian colonisation, "Democratic Italy always regarded her colonies, not merely as Italian interests, but as Italian aspects of world interests. It is for this reason that Italy succeeded in contributing to the historical, economic, cultural and moral patrimony of the local populations."

The exclusive autarchy, the forced labour, the racists laws, the masses of abandoned half-caste children, the refusal of education, the stubborn attempts to conquer ancient Ethiopia which repeatedly stained the borderlands with innocent blood—all were blandly ignored. Alas the emptiness of this boasting was largely hidden from the delegates by their lack of first-hand information concerning the realities of Italian rule and the people of the territories the Italian Government was striving to regain.

In accordance with his new compromise, Sforza declared that in the previous April he had demanded Italian Trusteeship of the ex-Colonies, because Trusteeship then appeared "the most appropriate solution," and he could not admit that Italy should be unjustly refused "the performance of this international task." When the trend of opinion in favour of independence had revealed itself the Italian Government had adopted this solution as "the best way to guarantee Italy's national interests," and to secure the termination of British Military Administration.

It should be recalled that the Administration of Italy's Colonies had always been of a military character, in fact, if not in name. Nevertheless, Sforza deprecated military rule, on the grounds that it curbs initiative, paralyses trade, and spreads suspicion "by the tactics of the hateful *divide et impera*, practised by the old monarchies."

---

* Anno XIIII, the Conquest of an Empire, by Emilio De Bono, Chapter IV, Political Preparation (Cresset Press).

Italy, in the time of the Italian monarchy, had indeed practised the strategy of divide and rule; De Bono, * in his book on the war initiated in Ethiopia by Mussolini, makes clear that the policy of creating division in Ethiopia in preparation for war had been systematically pursued in Fascist times. Long before Fascism the Italian Royal Commission of 1891,* of which San Giuliano, subsequently Foreign Minister, was the relatore, declared it was most fortunate for Italy that her Colony of Eritrea contained both Christians and Muslims, because Italy could use the followers of one faith against the adherents of the other. The report also boasted that an ancient feud between the people of the Provinces of Okule-Kuzai and of Agamé had been re-opened by the Italian Command, in order to facilitate the conquest of more territory. During the whole period of the Italian penetration into Ethiopia from the Red Sea which was checked by the Ethiopian victory at the battle of Adowa, political intrigue to set Chief against Chief, and powerful Chiefs against the Sovereign, was the stock in trade of the Italian effort to obtain possession of Ethiopia. Penetration of Ethiopia from the Indian Ocean was advanced by the same method.

"GOOD OLD ITALIAN BANKS"

Continuing his attack on the British Administration of the former Colonies, Sforza exclaimed:—

" What civil administration would ever have thought of forbidding, year after year, the re-opening of the good old Italian banks which had been so generously and constructively helpful to the private interests of the Arabs and of the Italian settlers alike?"

There was no reply to this sally, as assuredly there would have been some years earlier; time had drawn a veil over the once widely known and hotly debated scandals of Italian banking and the connivance therein of Cabinet Ministers.

Mr. Francis McCullagh, in his account of the Italian conquest of Tripolitania, " Italy's War for a Desert," has some illuminating passages on the operations of the Banco di Roma in that territory, and the connivance with its unsavoury doings of Italian statesmen. The brother of Tittoni, the Foreign Minister of whom so much has been written in the earlier chapters of this book, was Vice-President of the Bank; its director was a friend of Baron Sonnino, the Conservative Minister under whom Count Sforza served in 1919 and 1920. The Bank was heavily subsidised by the Government, both for political penetration, and in its business speculations, which were of so reckless a character that the Italian occupation of the territory was urgently required to save it from disaster. On account of these revelations and his graphic accounts and photographs of the atrocities perpetrated by the Italians in

---

* Relazione Generale della R. Commissione d'Inchiesta della Colonia Eritrea, 1891 pp. 48 and 85.

Libya Mr. McCullagh was reviled in the Italian Press and by Italians in British and American newspapers of which he was correspondent.* The so-called "futurist" poet, Marinetti, who afterwards became prominent in Fascism, a "futurist" painter and an Italian whom he took to be the London correspondent of the Giornale d'Italia, sought out Mr. McCullagh in a lonely house on the Surrey downs where he was writing, challenged him to fight a duel and threatened him with violence. Recourse to action for libel against Mr. McCullagh, his editors and publisher, which was open to the statesmen and bankers whose doings he had exposed, would have been the obviously correct method for them to adopt had his charges been untrue.†

Italy's New Programme for the Former Colonies

Having developed his attack on the British Caretaker Administration of the former colonies with much subtlety, Count Sforza stated the Italian Government's revised programme in accordance

---

* The "New York World" and the "London Westminster Gazette and Daily News."

† The following passages are taken from "Italy's War for a Desert," by Francis McCullagh (Herbert and Daniel, 1912).

"For many years past the Banco di Roma has been pacifically penetrating Tripoli. It acquired enormous tracts of land; it established or financed corn mills and other industrial undertakings; it prospected for phosphates and minerals. The director of the Bank was a very able business man—Signor Pacelli, a friend of Baron Sonnino, the well-known Conservative leader and proprietor of an ultra-Catholic and ultra-jingoistic newspaper, the 'Giornale d'Italia.' Signor Pacelli has friends in every camp. He has friends even in the Government, for some members of the present Cabinet are financially interested in the Bank. The Italians bitterly complained of the obstacles thrown in its way by the Turks, but personally I cannot sympathise very much with the Italians in this matter, since the object of the Bank was undoubtedly to sap Turkish rule in Tripolitania and pave the way for the entry of the Italians."—Page 15.

"There is no doubt that it enjoyed the assistance of the Italian Government. When he was Minister of Foreign Affairs, Signor Tittoni had frequently denied that he had any interest in the Bank or any intention to acquire Tripolitania, but one assertion was probably as false as the other. Tittoni's own brother is vice-President of the Bank, and if that institution had had only its own resources to draw upon, it would have been bankrupt long ago. But the Government, that is, the unfortunate, overtaxed Italian people, were behind it.

"Various scandals indicated clearly the connection between the Bank and the Government. One was the granting to the Benghazi and Tripoli branches of the privilege of issuing postal orders in competition with the local Italian post-offices!

"It was decidedly lucky for the Banco di Roma that it had the Italian Treasury behind it, for all its business speculations turned out badly, and in this way it must have lost several millions. Then, the impresa diplomatica di penetrazione (diplomatic work of penetration) cost an enormous amount of money, but this was directly met, of course, by the Government. However, 'work of penetration,' is an elastic term, and I dare say many people feathered their nest by means of it and at the expense of the Italian taxpayer.

with the compact he had made with the South American and Muslim States as follows:—

Libya

For Libya he demanded the creation of three independent States, linked by a Federal Council. The events of war, he said, had bound Cyrenaica to Britain, and the Fezzan to France. In consequence these Powers must be entrusted with the task of guiding them to independence. "Italy fully appreciates the intentions of these Powers, and is ready to examine and accept their proposals, but we intend that the institutions which are being prepared for the said regions must come within the structure of a future federal unity of Libya, and that Tripolitania be granted full freedom to dispose of its future."

Tripolitania being the area of Libya with the greatest economic possibilities, was most coveted by Italy. Therefore, Count Sforza

---

"Meanwhile the fact that it was a kind of Government department instead of a commercial house made the place impossible from a business point of view.

"And, naturally, the Bank suffered on its business side. Its solicitor is said to have once confessed that the books were in such a state of confusion that he defied the best book-keeper in the world to make head or tail of them.

"Some shareholders, afraid that the institution would go to pieces, insisted from time to time on a reorganisation of the personnel in Tripoli. As a result of these complaints, the inspectors-general of the Bank came from Rome in May, 1911, in order to investigate matters; but just at that time Tripoli happened to be also invaded by a party of jingoist Italian journalists come *per intraprendere la campagna in favore dell' occupazione* (to open the campaign in favour of the occupation). The local director of the Bank accordingly made his excuses to the inspectors, saying that he really had to attend to the newspaper-men first. The inspectors acknowledged the justice of his excuse and returned to Rome without having examined his books."—Pp. 16—17.

"It started a steamship line with two vessels, for which it got a Government subsidy of 190,000 lire a year.

"Then the Bank lost an immense amount of money on the building of a flour-mill near Benghazi at a cost of 1,800,000 lire. The building operations should, at most, have cost no more than 300,000 lire."—Page 18.

"The Banco di Roma was much displeased with the Ottoman Government because that Government refused to grant it any monopolist concessions. To crown all, a German financial syndicate, headed by Herren Weickert and Encke, established in Tripoli a banking concern whose operations within a short time exceeded even those of the Banco di Roma. Signor Pacelli found himself very soon in difficulties. Clearly it was time to act. It was time for Signor Giolitti to declare that civilisation must be extended to Tripolitania.

"The last straw so far as Italy's patience was concerned, was the Banco di Roma's ruinous speculations in real estate. Always believing that the Italian occupation was at hand, the Bank had, since the beginning, bought up vast tracts of land in Tripolitania and in Cyrenaica, but especially in Cyrenaica. For this land it always paid at a very high rate.

"At the beginning of the year 1911, when serious doubts were entertained of the conquest ever coming off, a large portion of the Bank's Cyrenaica land, bought at 10 lire, was sold at the ridiculous price of 2 lire. The loss, of course, was heavy.

demanded "immediate independence" for Tripolitania, "free genuine" elections for a Constituent Assembly to be held within six months. This Assembly should immediately proceed to the appointment of the first Government of the country. It is at this time that British administration should cease."

Here was a peremptory order to quit by the conquered to the conqueror; Italy, in her own period of victory, had been far from submitting to such dictation. She had withdrawn from the League of Nations, and had raised a rigid barrier of military censorship around the country she had invaded, to conceal her doings from the outer world; missionaries and merchants of other nations had been expelled to make way for Italians; there had been wholesale expropriation of the Ethiopian people; the assets of the Ethiopian Government had been seized, and had been systematically sought and claimed even from banks abroad and in respect of payments due from the nationals of other Governments.

"The occupation saved the Bank from a disaster which could not have been otherwise delayed, and since it has in its possession nearly all the reclaimable land in Tripoli it is evident that its gains will be colossal and that those gains will save the situation so far as it is concerned . . .

". . . It is well known in Tripoli that the Banco di Roma purchased years ago the greater part of the reclaimable land in Tripolitania. By sanctioning those acquisitions, the Caneva decree will enable the Bank to compel the Government to buy in the near future, and at whatever price and on whatever conditions the Bank demands, the lands which private speculators will wish to get rid of owing to the fact that they are unsuitable for cultivation

"I have told how Signor Bresciani succeeded in the great work which the Bank entrusted him with when it originally sent him to open a branch in Tripolitania. That work was to drag Italy into the vilayet, so that the Italian name should serve as the instrument of his speculations, that the Italian flag should be his best commercial asset, and that any Italian who criticised his enterprise would only expose himself to the danger of being mobbed, spat upon, and denounced as 'unpatriotic.'

"Bresciani was the promoter of the Tripoli enterprise. At present he is practically the autocrat of the situation. The handful of his countrymen who supported him in his business now enjoy an unlimited credit at the Bank. Prominent among those lucky ones are Signori Baldari and Belli. Hence the common saying in Tripoli that Tripolitania is ruled by the three B's—Bresciani, Baldari, and Belli.

"These men, or the Bank which they represent, have had a monopoly of all Governmental work since the war began. They supplied the rafts and bridges used for the disembarkation of the troops, the animals, the food, the war material. They constructed barracks for the soldiers.

"To them or to the Bank every kind of contract is given—contracts for the supply of furniture, meat, flour, wheat, ice; in short, for all the innumerable things required by an enormous number of soldiers, 45,000 of whom are in Tripoli alone.

"Several independent Italian business men offered to do the work, but were refused, and the refusal was accompanied by the explicit statement that the Banco di Roma supplied everything which the army or navy or the civil Government required. They repeated their offer, pointing out, at the same time, that they would undertake to do the work cheaper. The answer was always the same: *Non importa. Ciò non ci commuove.* (No matter. That won't have any influence on us.)"—Pp. 19, 20, 21.

Sforza conceded that the British Administration might continue in Tripolitania until the elections he had demanded, but must not be permitted to control them:—

"In order that no doubt can be raised as to the way the elections are being conducted, it is absolutely necessary that this delicate electoral experiment, the first in the history of Libya, be organised and supervised by a Control Commission with an Italian member. Otherwise we would not be making history; we should be staging a comedy."

This was a plain indication that in his opinion the election would not be free and genuine if the British were permitted to control it. Confident that he could command the support of a majority in the First Committee, and in the General Assembly of the United Nations, he did not scruple to display an arrogantly aggressive bearing towards the British Government, who throughout the extraordinary bizarreries of the Italian political class, had displayed towards them a tolerance too often at variance with British interests and British conscience.

Pressing his point home, Sforza further insisted that should the formation of a Government for Tripolitania be delayed beyond six months, the international commission he had demanded for the elections must assume the character of an overall collaboration, failing which the occupying authority would be accused of seeking a mandatory authority.

Whilst delivering this further disparaging admonition to Britain, the Italian Minister was totally unembarrassed in asserting that free elections had not been held during the period of Italian rule, nor did he appear to conceive any inconsistency in the demand for the immediate independence of a territory which had hitherto been denied any measure of self-government whatsoever.

He urged there should be no delay; the independence of Tripoli was desired by the 45,000 Italian residents. Moreover, he declared:

"In Tripolitania there is a leading class ready to assume its responsibilities."

To those familiar with the history of Italian rule in Libya, the misfortunes it had brought upon the Arab population and their views concerning it Count Sforza's exuberant observations on the proposed new State are more than a little jarring.

"Italy's specific experience, which goes back half-a-century, allows us to assure you that such is the level of civilisation reached by the Arabs, and such the loyal co-operation of the Italian communities, that no possible doubt can be raised regarding the speedy elaboration of a constitution, and the building of the new State on solid foundations."

He added an intimation that Italy intended "the new State" to be under Italian influence:

" It is Italy's intention, once the Government of Tripolitania is established, to negotiate with it, on equal footing, appropriate agreements regulating the relations between the two countries, and adequately safeguarding Italian citizens and interests in Tripolitania."

If the Agreement Italy proposed to make with the Tripolitanian Government were overshadowed by a prior understanding that the Powers would allow Italy an exclusive economic influence in Tripolitania, obviously the parties to an Italo-Tripolitanian Agreement would not negotiate on an equal footing.

Eritrea

For Eritrea Sforza proposed independence. He disparaged the compromise he had been glad to make with Mr. Bevin in the previous year, and vaunted as a response to "a moral" duty his withdrawal from the Agreement he had made to accept the reunion of Eritrea to Ethiopia:

" The painful hesitancy I felt in accepting Mr. Bevin's point of view about Eritrea surely proved to him my keen desire to re-establish the old, cordial, mutual confidence between our two countries, shattered against the will of the Italian people. But in the course of history certain moral duties sometimes impose themselves on us, and have to prevail over any political consideration. When the London compromise did not materialise, what was natural for us to do was to assert the necessity of granting Eritrea an independence which—during the discussions on the compromise —had become popular, even with the Italians who have lived there for three generations, all the more so that the country has recently revealed a national sentiment which cannot be ignored. The Eritreans have proved conscious of their maturity, and determined to assert it. That the economic self-sufficiency of the country is possible is well proved by the existence of a flourishing industry and of well developed trade."

Some years hence the sums Italy expended for the rapid development of an Eritrean " national sentiment," which hitherto it had been her purpose to stifle, may be disclosed. The falsity of Count Sforza's pretence that Eritrea was economically self-sufficient is clearly demonstrated by Italian statistics.

Then followed an appeal to the pride of the small nations whose votes he desired to win:

" I have no doubt the small nations here represented," he urged, *" small in size, but often great in their contribution to civilisation, do realize how dangerous may be the objection that Eritrea is too small to be independent. Eritrea has vital forces within herself, that can hardly be measured in square miles."*

There is, of course, no similarity between colonies and self-governing States, however small, which have developed their own national institutions and have played an independent rôle in history. In the Colony of Eritrea the conquering Power, Italy, possessed itself of all sources of wealth and relegated the conquered people to the status of unskilled labourers, depriving them of all share in the administration of their native land. The "vital forces" within Eritrea so far as the Eritrean people were concerned had been imprisoned and stultified by the foreign domination.

Moreover, Eritrea was not a nation; its separation from Ethiopia was not a spontaneous development effected by the population of the territory, but the act of a foreign invader. Since Eritrea was separated from Ethiopia its population had never been permitted to exercise any form of self-government; it had always been a mere colony arbitrarily administered by a foreign Government.

There is no doubt about the tyranny of Italian rule in Eritrea, the tragic conditions of the numerous political prisoners discovered by British forces in 1941, as described in the Ministry of Information report, "The First to be Freed." There can be no denial that Eritrea was used as a base of war against Ethiopia or of the revelations of Italian methods contained in the Graziani telegrams and in the atrocity photographs taken by the Italians. The following boast of Count Sforza must be dismissed as utterly unrealistic:

"*Amongst the many titles which Italy has won in Eritrea, the establishment and maintenance of freedom, tolerance and religious peace is certainly not the last one.*"

An expression of regret for past misgovernment and aggression would have been more fitting from the representative of the Power which had acquired the poor territory, arbitrarily named Eritrea, by more than a decade of continuous warfare which had held it always under a stern military control, and had used it as a base of assembly for war on Ethiopia. To boast of having established freedom in a territory whose people had been subjected to the "racist" laws of Fascism was utterly grotesque. Apparently Count Sforza assumed the memories of the delegates to the United Nations, concerning Fascist ideology and practice, to be exceedingly defective and their knowledge of life in the former colonies of Italy to be nil. According to official Italian and British computation there were at that time upwards of 25,000 half-caste children in Eritrea whose Italian fathers had abandoned them in accordance with Fascist precepts, and whose Eritrean mothers were either dead or too destitute to support them.

But Count Sforza's boldest assertion was that his Government's opposition to the reunion of poor Eritrea and her Ethiopian motherland was conceived in Ethiopia's own interests:

"*An independent Eritrea,*" he averred solemnly, "*may be of great service also to Ethiopia; I hope their relations will be most cordial and fruitful, both in the economic and cultural fields. In* fact, it is also in the interests of Ethiopia that we desire the independence of Eritrea. We are convinced that Ethiopia will one day be able to give a precious contribution to the development of civilisation in Africa, but thaumaturgic gains of diplomatic origin have never proved useful in history—far from it."

This rodomontade by the spokesman of a Power which had so recently invaded and ravaged Ethiopia with poison gas and every species of atrocity, whilst systematically exterminating Ethiopians of superior education and experience, must have aroused strong and contemptuous disapproval in the Ethiopian delegation. If equally strong disapproval was not felt by other delegations also, one may explain this failure of perception by the truism that it is the wearer who knows where the shoe pinches.

The critic may suggest that Count Sforza's conviction—" one day Ethiopia will be able to make a precious contribution to civilisation in Africa "—was in reality a bright figment of his constant dream of Empire and arose from the cherished hope that " one day " the sons and daughters of Ethiopia might be again harnessed to the car of the Italian Empire, whereby, more patiently than on the former occasion, they might be used to serve Italian civilisation !

In his taunting phrase warning the sincere and deeply concerned Ethiopians against the attempt to achieve " thaumaturgic gains of diplomatic origin," the rusé old Italian politician was attributing to them the political sleight-of-hand which was his own habitual medium. Moreover, by this same taunt he was announcing to them in sardonic style his confident belief that he would triumph over them in that Assembly's round of their long, hard painful struggle for the reunion of the Ethiopian people; his Muslim-South American combination would outvote the support they would get by having accepted the Bevin proposal for Western Eritrea.

Somalia

For the former Somaliland Colony Sforza demanded Italian Trusteeship. Whilst giving lip service to the principle of ultimate independence, in order to retain the support of his Muslim allies, he insisted that Italian rule had been beneficial to the Somalis, and would continue to benefit them, a claim which can be judged from the material contained in the previous chapters, Sforza urged:

" *The development of Somalia has required a strenuous effort on the part of Italy. That effort could not be interrupted without serious damages and set-backs to the proper development of Somalia; a process still going on, and mainly due to our tenacious faith in the potentialities of the country, and our constant will to associate the Somalis in our Labour and Hopes.*

" *. . . . you will realise how useful it would be for the Somalis to go on benefiting by Italian collaboration until such time as the independence of that country is declared.*"

The Need for Capital
Sforza's Plea for an Extended Trusteeship

He interpolated an argument against a limited period of Trusteeship:

"*We have all of us to keep in mind that the development of Somalia requires the employment of considerable capital, Italian as well as foreign. Hardly any capital could be found unless a reasonable period of stability could be relied upon.*"

Sforza's plea that much capital is required for the development of the Somaliland ex-colony does not favour Italian trusteeship; on the contrary it argues the unsuitability of Italy as the agent for developing the territory. In the preceding pages it has been shown that even when Somaliland was regarded as a permanent possession the Italian Government constantly invoked the prior importance of home needs when proposals were made for colonial development and protested, "Italy has no money to waste in Africa!" Private investors were equally shy of risking their capital in the Italian colonies. Only for a few years under Fascism was there a burst of activity in the colonial field, and even that much advertised activity produced, as we have seen, but meagre results. Italy, following her losses in the Second World War, was not now in a position to furnish the equivalent of the capital expended in Africa during the period of Fascist imperialism.

The United Nations Organisation had not seriously faced the fact that Governments in general are not disposed to make large-scale expenditure to develop territories in Africa, without obtaining permanent advantages which would be apt to conflict with the future independence of the territories in question, and to mortgage their resources. This applies with special force in the case of Italy, economically weak, and having large areas of her own soil in need of development. As we have seen the Italians had already possessed themselves of the best resources of the Somaliland ex-colony.

"Italians Always Worked Hand-in-Hand with the Local Populations"

To dispel "the suspicions and doubts circulating—some of them in good faith—in this unstable world" Sforza found it "opportune" to explain how it was that the Italians, following the example set by Britain in other parts of the world, had become convinced that "they must actively seek the friendship of the new States coming into life in the territories where," he said, "we brought civilsation." Ignoring the "racist" laws came the habitual cliché:

"*Italians always lived and worked hand in hand with the local populations, even in the most difficult moments. Neither time nor events, still less extraneous influences, will succeed in obliterating their friendship, based as it is on memories, decades old, of fruitful work carried out together.*"

Yet the representatives of Italian workmen in Somaliland had testified before the Four Power Commission that not one of the Somalis in Italy's old colony had learnt to operate a lathe, or perform any other type of artisan work. The " racist " laws precluded their employment in such trades.

Turning to his Asian Allies in the compact to restore Italian rule in Somaliland, Count Sforza expressed the desire: —

" To come closer to the many noble peoples in Asia who have recently become independent, beginning with those nearer to our old Colonies, or bound to them by ties of race and religion."

Did any of the delegates of the " noble peoples " thus complimented recall Count Sforza's protest, uttered less than a year before: —

" Gentlemen of Europe; you have lost Asia by your stupidity; see that you do not lose Africa also ! "

There spoke the old imperialism of his youth, the old desire of European Governments to control as much as possible of the rest of the world, not totally overcome despite the existence of the United Nations. Had the Italian Government been in a position to determine the fate of the subject nations of Asia, there was small reason to believe independence would have been granted to " those noble peoples " at the present time.

An appeal for further United States assistance to Italy followed the plea for Italian Trusteeship of Somaliland: —

" We trust that President Truman's generous plan will soon open the way to solutions and transformations which will never threaten the principles of self-determination."

" President Truman's generous plan " was already being drawn upon to accumulate arms for use in holding down the Somali people in expectation of Italian Trusteeship in that area.

How much wiser, from every point of view, would have been a courageous decision to maintain the renunciation of the former Colonies which the Italian Government had signed in the Peace Treaty. Granted there would have been an outcry on the part of the old Fascists and other Imperialists; the Government who had acted thus in the true interests of their nation could have ignored all such shouting. They would have gained the gratitude and solid support of the majority of their people for having spared them the unwelcome burden of further fruitless losses in Africa. The respect of the world, which such an example of common sense and right feeling would have evoked, would have created a favourable atmosphere for United States and United Nations assistance in the development of Italy's own agricultural and industrial potential, so persistently ignored by former Italian Governments, whilst means were found for adventures in Africa—which all told, had produced only a bankrupt empire, depending for its existence on annual subsidies from the home Government.

Whilst battling to secure the return of the old conquered territories, Count Sforza claimed that his compatriots cared only for peace, an assertion which ignored the invasion by Italy of more than half-a-dozen countries in the course of a decade: —

" If we Italians believe only in peace," he said, " this is because people as full of industry and vitality as ours have everything to lose in a world polluted by hatred and iniquity, while we have everything to gain from peace and solidarity among free nations."

COUNT SFORZA'S ALLIES

Count Sforza's new and old allies struck out boldly for the new compromise. The strained situation in the Indian Sub-Continent between Hindu and Muslim, India and Pakistan, created in Sir Zafrullah Khan, the Pakistan representative, the belief that similar religious conflict existed also in Ethiopia, where Christian and Muslim lived peacefully together. Among the Arab States also there was much sensitiveness and unrest concerning the Arab-Jewish conflict in Palestine, and also regarding their own position in relation to the Great Powers.

Already in the General Assembly, Fayez El-Khouri Bey, the delegate of Syria, had voiced the desire to unite the vast Arab lands, of which he claimed Syria was only a part, not a State in the meaning which the West attached to the term. If their racial unity was not apparent in the distribution of the Arab States, Iraq, Jordan, Saudi Arabia, Lebanon, Egypt and North Africa, it was nevertheless a living reality in the souls and hearts of the inhabitants of those countries, whose faith was strong that sooner or later their unity would be realised. He complained that though during the first World War the Arabs had been promised liberation and unity, at the close of the war they had been divided into separate States under Mandate of the very Powers who had made this promise. The bitterness felt towards the Great Powers among some of the Arab States had produced an attitude of suspicion towards any proposal sponsored by them. There was also a suspicion that at least a good proportion of the inhabitants of Eritrea, as well as the inhabitants of Somaliland, might in fact be more closely related to the Arabs than to Ethiopia.

Mr. McNeil's faulty analysis of the racial composition of Eritrea had encouraged the mistaken belief that a part of the inhabitants of that territory were not akin to Ethiopia either in race or language. As we have seen, the majority of the Eritrean population speak dialects derived from the ancient Ethiopic, and they are historically old members of the Ethiopian community, whilst the Somalis also speak a branch of an old language widely diffused through Ethiopia, east and west, north and south.

In accordance with these policies, opposition to union to Ethiopia and separatist tendencies had been fostered by the British Administration or by some of its members. The Western Province had been created by combining the former provinces, Keren,

Agordat and Barentu, which were predominantly Muslim in population. The collection of native tribute, which carried with it a small stipend, had been removed by the British Administration from the former Chiefs who favoured union to Ethiopia, and placed in the hands of subordinates who were willing to support the policy of British Trusteeship and to oppose union to Ethiopia.

In the Somaliland ex-Colony, as we have seen, British Administration had been established at the time of the Italian defeat over the former Italian Colony and the Ethiopian Ogaden, and these territories had been unified with the British Somaliland Protectorate for administrative purposes, an arrangement maintained until 1947. As we have also seen, Somali nationalism had been fostered there by the British Administration, with a view to a permanent British Protectorate over the whole area. The Somali Youth League had been encouraged by the British Administration under the special care of Mr. S. O. Pearson, of Australia, who had assisted the Youth League to establish their organisation throughout the extensive territory. British transport lorries had been at the service of the Youth League organisers.

These efforts had had little effect in the Ogaden, but in the former Italian Colony, as we have seen, the Youth League obtained a predominant influence. It had representation in the Central Muslim League in Nairobi, thus emphasising the trend away from Ethiopia.

PAKISTAN DELEGATE ABANDONS OPPOSITION TO ITALIAN TRUSTEESHIP AND OPPOSES ETHIOPIAN CLAIMS

The fate of Somaliland seemed already settled from the commencement; the majority of delegations declared in favour of Italian Trusteeship; details only remained to be decided.

Sir Zahullah Khan, the Pakistan delegate, who had formerly opposed Italian Trusteeship for any of the former Colonies, and had defended the case of Somaliland against that solution, now turned his batteries against Ethiopia. He was not convinced that the economic deficiencies of Eritrea were any greater than the deficiencies of Ethiopia herself, and doubted whether Ethiopia had progressed further than Eritrea, even in political development.

He argued that ex-Italian Somaliland was only a segment of the Somalilands, which should all be united to form an independent political entity. This implied the annexation by some future Somali State of the Ethiopian Ogaden, as well as of the British Somaliland Protectorate and the small French Somaliland Colony.

In the meantime he would not oppose Italian trusteeship for the former Italian Colony. If on investigation it was found that the bulk or even a majority of the people of the territory would welcome, or at least not object to Italian trusteeship, the Pakistan Government had instructed its delegation to give sympathetic consideration to Italian claims.

ETHIOPIAN REPLY

A reply to this attack was given by Blatta Ephrem Tewelde Medhen, a member of the Ethiopian delegation, well known to the United Nations and to the elder statesmen present, from the time of the Italian invasion of his country. An Eritrean by birth, he had crossed the frontier as a youth to seek freedom in the ancient Motherland. Speaking with considerable emotion, he protested that Sir Zafrullah Khan's observations had come as "a rude surprise to a people who for centuries had maintained the closest bonds of friendship and sympathy with the people of Pakistan." He recalled that Eritrea, throughout the past fifty years, had had a deficit in foreign trade,* her imports exceeded her exports by 200 per cent. On the other hand, Ethiopia had always had a favourable balance of trade; she was a member of the International Monetary Fund; economic data concerning her trade balance was readily available. The suggestion that the economic situation might be worse in Ethiopia than in Eritrea was negated by the fact that so far from Ethiopia being obliged to import foodstuffs to keep her population alive, Ethiopia was a food exporter, and Eritrea had to import food from Ethiopia.

If he had any doubt that Ethiopia's economic stability was greater than that of Eritrea, the Pakistan delegate must assume that, like Eritrea, Ethiopia was supported by grants-in-aid from foreign sources. This was not the case; it was true that for the first three years after Ethiopia's liberation the United Kingdom had generously granted aid in the reconstruction of the country, but though an offer of continued assistance was most generously made, Ethiopia preferred to rely on her own resources, and in 1947 had also renounced all United Nations aid in favour of war-devastated countries. Ethiopia contributed her share to the United Nations Budget, not by any means the smallest, but not so large as it would have been had she not suffered a cruel invasion. Ethiopia had neither asked for, nor received Marshall Aid. The Pakistan delegate had evidently failed to observe that thousands of traders from his own country, Pakistan, found it profitable to do business in Ethiopia which he had mistakenly compared with derelict Eritrea.

Turning to the political aspect of Sir Zafrullah Khan's attack, Blatta Medhen protested that the Pakistan delegate would be the first to resent discussion of domestic matters in his own country, concerning the political regime and institutions, political and economic equality, selection of government officials and the democratic character of institutions. The Pakistan delegate had indicated his desire to ascertain the number of non-Amharic and non-Coptic persons in the higher ranks of the Government of Ethiopia. Blatta Medhen himself had for many years collaborated with many of those present, first at the League of Nations, latterly in the numerous organs of the United Nations. Thus he had not come there specially because he was, in the words of the Pakistan delegate, Eritrean and

---

* This was, of course, true in relation to Somaliland.

non-Coptic. The delegate of Ethiopia in the Fourth Committee of that Session, who had also been a delegate at the Second Session of the United Nations, was a Galla, non-Amharic and non-Coptic. Of the six Ethiopian delegates present only two were of the Coptic faith. After giving further detailed information, Blatta Medhen added, " Consideration might be given to the Muslim delegates in the Ethiopian Parliament which, to our amused astonishment, the delegation of Pakistan has now by fiat liquidated, in having stated that democratic institutions do not exist in my country." As to equality, he added, by far the richest merchant community in Ethiopia was Muslim, not Amharic and not Coptic. If more Ethiopian Muslims did not take part in the administration of their country, it was because they preferred to devote themselves to commerce.

Referring to the suggestion by the delegate of Pakistan, " that it would be profitable to carve up the territory of Ethiopia, as well as of some neighbours," Blatta Medhen observed, " Such a course is always easy to suggest, so long as one is not referring to one's own territory. In endorsing the principle of dismemberment of one of the United Nations he is proposing a novel precedent."

The Pakistan delegate, Blatta Medhen suggested, would not be content that the question of joining Kashmir to Pakistan should depend on a unanimous vote being recorded for it in the plebiscite to be taken on that question, " yet that would seem to be the position he had adopted, not for Pakistan, of course, but for Eritrea." A fine note of sarcasm crept into the grave tones of the Ethiopian delegate at this point.

To Sir Zafrullah Khan's suggestion that Eritrea's union with Ethiopia might jeopardise Ethiopia's own independence, the Ethiopian delegate replied, " Refusal of union would most definitely constitute a direct threat to the security of my country." He referred, in this connection, to the proposal to return Italy to the southern border of Ethiopia by giving her a trusteeship over Somaliland:

" *I declare here solemnly, in the name of my country, that the proposal to return Italy to Somaliland, and the refusal to satisfy Ethiopia's claim to Eritrea, take into account neither the desires nor the interests of the population, and abandon the interests of peace and security. They constitute a direct threat to the independence of Ethiopia. If this attempt should succeed, the United Nations Organisation would have lent itself to a greater injustice than that which Ethiopia suffered at the hands of the League of Nations. After all the sufferings Ethiopia has gone through, she will not allow herself to be sacrificed on the altar of the United Nations to appease Italy, as was done at the League of Nations. She will abandon all hope in justice from the United Nations, and will take all measures for legitimate self-defence, as provided in the Charter of the United Nations.*"

One can but comment sadly upon this utterance that, as all Ethiopia's natural ports are in the hands of foreign Powers, she might again be prevented from importing arms for self-defence should Italy again invade.

SOMALI YOUTH LEAGUE PROTESTS AGAINST ITALIAN TRUSTEESHIP

Hearings were given to representatives of divers organisations from the ex-Colonies, who had again journeyed to Lake Success, but they were not allowed the privilege accorded to Italy of sitting in the Committee and joining its discussions.

Mr. Abdullahi Issa, who represented the Somali Youth League, and the Hamar Youth Club, made a poignant appeal against Italian Trusteeship. He spoke with great bitterness of the considerable support given to the Bevin-Sforza Agreement in the previous United Nations Assembly. He and his fellow Somalis had come to Lake Success with faith and confidence in the United Nations; what they had seen and heard during the debate on their future was a complete and alarming contrast to their expectations.

Some Quislings had appeared claiming to represent non-existent or ineffective parties. These traitors were more interested in receiving the eight years back pay promised to them as ex-servicemen by Italy than in the welfare of Somaliland.

"Italy," he declared, "has issued a formal promise of eight years back pay to all ex-servicemen, in case she becomes again the ruler of Somaliland."

These traitors, who had been willing to accept Italian rule for an indefinite period, had made ridiculous statements that the Italian Government had opened universities and other higher educational institutions for the Somalis, and that more than 500 Somalis had obtained degrees. These false assertions proved them to be "traitors come to sell Somaliland and the Somalis." "Had the administration of Somaliland been in the hands of the people, our Quislings would have received the same justice as their colleagues in other parts of the world."

The Somali Youth League now asked for the "immediate independence of Somaliland," but if the United Nations Assembly considered the territory should be placed temporarily under the United Nations Trusteeship System, no objections would be raised, "provided the restoration of Italian administration in any form or guise, even as trustee under United Nations supervision, be completely excluded."

Proposals had been made to send a new Commission of Investigation to Eritrea; Mr. Issa urged that this should be done also for Somaliland, in order to give the people there a respite and a hope of reprieve from the calamity of Italian rule.

THE LATIN-AMERICAN COMPACT

He protested against the sacrifice of his people to political expediency, and quoted an article on the United Nations Assembly in the "New York Times" of October 7th, 1949, as follows:

"*The Latin-American delegations decided at a caucus this morning to link the question of independence for Libya with Italian Somaliland. Under the proposal, which was submitted by Mr. de Freitas-Valle, head of the Brazilian delegation, the Latin-American countries would not agree to independence for Libya unless the Assembly also agreed to the Latin-American proposal regarding Italian Somaliland.*"

Thus, declared Mr. Issa, the supporters of Italy's unjust claims were endeavouring to compel a group who strongly supported the independence and unity of Libya to sacrifice the Somali people to Italy. Some members had felt compelled to vote for Italian administration in Somaliland in order to obtain the support for other questions of the most powerful *bloc* in the General Assembly.

DEMONSTRATIONS AGAINST ITALY IN SOMALILAND : POLICE OPEN FIRE : MANY IMPRISONMENTS

Press reports of the many declarations in favour of an Italian trusteeship in Somaliland, which had resulted from Count Sforza's new compromise, evoked tumultuous repercussions among the desperately anxious population of the territory. On October 5th (1949) the Somali Youth League attempted a procession in Mogadishu, bearing banners expressing opposition to Italian trusteeship. The British Administration prohibited the demonstration. The police gave the people fifteen minutes to disperse. The crowd had stood their ground and had resisted what the Administration termed "normal police methods." Eventually the police opened fire. One man was shot dead and several were wounded. The crowd reassembled a few hours later. The military were summoned. Again one man was killed and several wounded, three of whom subsequently died.

Demonstrations were also held at Belet, Wen, Galkayu, Baidoa, Merka, Lugh, Dolo, Bur Hakaba, Afmedu, Bardera, Kismayu, Gelib, Margherita, Vilagio, Mahaddai, Genale, Dinsor, Hodduk, Shalanbot, Bulo Burti, El Bur, Dusamared, Obbia, Eil, Garoe, Gardo.

The British Administration ordered the closing of all political organisation offices, the imprisonment of numbers of Somali Sheiks and Chiefs, and the deportation of others to rural areas outside Mogadishu. These police measures were resisted in some areas, notably at Dolo, where two Somalis had been killed and many injured, and at Bardera, where two Somalis were shot by the Authorities, and a District Commissioner and several police were hurt by stones. A frigate was despatched to Mogadishu. R.A.F. planes were sent to reconnoitre.

In Mogadishu the following Chiefs were sentenced to imprisonment with hard labour: Haji Mohamed Abdullah, 12 months; Haji Musa Boghor, Vice-President of Mogadishu Town Council, 9 months,* Chief Jumali Barre, 9 months; Chief Farah Ali Farah, 6 months.

These events were brought before the Political Committee by Mr. Henry F. Cooper, the delegate of Liberia, who had been apprised of them by a letter from Mr. Abdullahi Issa, of the Somali Youth League. A resolution requesting the British Administration to permit free expression of Somali opinion was defeated by 20 votes to 16, with nine abstentions.

PRO-ITALIAN CONFERENZA

Highly exaggerated statements were made by the representatives of the Somalia Conferenza. Mr. Gassim, of the Conferenza, is quoted by the Provisional Summary Record of the UNO Secretariat as alleging that in the interior of the ex-Colony " all the doctors and heads of infirmaries were Somalis and possessed appropriate University qualifications; the same applied to other branches of the liberal professions." Further, that the highest legal functionaries in the country were Somali Muslims and that 3,000 Somalis were attending elementary and craft schools. When asked by the Pakistan representative for precise details, he replied that he did not know the precise figures, but in the school which he had

---

* Haji Musa Boghor is the hereditary Chief of the Mijjertein tribe. The nearest translation of Boghor (which is a title and not part of his name) is King.

The position of the Somali in relation to the European Administration, whether British or Italian, is clearly revealed by the fact that the Administration had arrested and sentenced to nine months imprisonment the hereditary ruler of an old Sultanate of the former Italian Somaliland, whose territory covered an immense area. It is also significant that permission had been refused for such a demonstration at a time when the future of Somaliland was under discussion.

The Town Council of Mogadishu, of which Musa Boghor was Vice-President, was an organisation formed by the British Administration. It consisted of 15 members, all of whom were natives of Somalia. Their chief functions were to advise the Provincial Commissioner of the Benadir Province on such subjects as taxation, education, cost of living, tribal complaints, social services, agricultural and water schemes, orphanages and similar questions. The members of the Town Council were, in the main, chiefs, headmen and influential traders. They met the Provincial Commissioner monthly at a regularly appointed meeting, but had access to him at any time they considered necessary or advisable. As a result of the usefulness of the Mogadishu Town Council and the work it did, District Commissioners in all other areas were authorised to form advisory councils in their own areas. The Mogadishu Town Council consisted of 9 pro-Somali Youth League members and 6 pro-Italian members, although they were not in fact selected on a political basis.

These councils, initiated by the British Administration, were the first attempts ever made to give the Somalis a minor share in the administration of their territory. Nothing of the sort existed in Italian times.

The sentences on Haji Musa Boghor, Haji Mohamed Abdullah Jumali Barre, headman of a sub-division of the Abgai tribe, and Farah Ali Farah, were all reduced by approximately three months, and all those who had been imprisoned as a result of the demonstration on October 6, 1949, were released before the British handover of April 1, 1950.

attended as a child there were 200 pupils. Interrogated concerning the profession of the members of his delegation he replied that he and another delegate were employed by the British Administration. He was a collector of revenue and Mr. Mohamed was a legal adviser to the Department of Justice. Mr. Clutton, of the United Kingdom delegation, retorted that none of the Conferenza delegation were employed by the British Administration. Mr. Mohamed was not an employee of the British Department of Justice, he was employed in the Court of one of the Italian judges. There were three separate kinds of courts in Somaliland: Khoranic Courts, Italian Courts and finally the Courts of the British Administration, which administered British law and British proclamations. In reply to a further question, Mr. Gassim declared that 30 per cent. of the Somaliland population were of similar education and social standing to those of his delegation. The Pakistan delegate hereupon retorted that the evidence of Mr. Gassim would seem to show Somaliland had reached a higher level of literacy than India and Pakistan had achieved when they obtained their independence. He therefore expressed surprise at the request for Trusteeship instead of immediate independence. Mr. Gassim replied that there were also economic obstacles and that the Somalis required to become fully ripe for self-Government. The representatives of the Conferenza further claimed to represent 95 per cent. of the population of Somaliland.

These poor tools were easy prey for the witty Minister of Pakistan; everyone laughed at their absurdities; nevertheless their claims would be quoted by delegations who intended to vote for Italian Trusteeship as evidence that the Somalis were not opposed to the return of Italy.

SOVIET RESOLUTION ON THE FUTURE OF THE EX-COLONIES

Whilst the debate in the First Committee proceeded several delegations tabled resolutions. The Soviet Union proposed to give independence to all the ex-Colonies: Libya immediately; Eritrea and Somaliland after five years, during which they would remain under United Nations Trusteeship, with an Administrator appointed by the Trusteeship Council and an Advisory Council composed of the five permanent members of the Security Council, Ethiopia, Italy, and two indigenous representatives appointed by the above-mentioned seven representatives.

An outlet to the sea through the small, undeveloped, shallow-water port of Assab, the Soviet was willing to concede to Ethiopia.

These proposals militated against the reunion of the Ethiopian people and would have left to the Trusteeship Council the decision on Italy's claims.

U.S.A. RESOLUTION

The United States delegation sponsored independence for Libya after three years; the reunion to Ethiopia of Eritrea, except the Western Province, which would be joined to the Sudan; Italian Trusteeship of Somaliland for an indefinite period.

PAKISTAN RESOLUTION

Pakistan, as a foremost Muslim State, proposed independence for Muslim Libya after three years; independence for Eritrea after three years, leaving Ethiopia an outlet to the sea through Assab; independence for Somaliland after ten years, "with a view to its incorporation into a United Somaliland," a proposal involving the cession of the Ethiopian Ogaden Province, as well as the British and French Somali Protectorates.

These proposals, based on the bargain with Count Sforza, were opposed by Ethiopia, the Eritreans and Somalis.

All resolutions were referred to a Sub-Committee,* in the hope of arriving at one agreed Resolution to be submitted to the General Assembly.

To produce an agreed solution from these conflicting proposals might well have appeared most difficult, but in fact the meticulously prepared compromise of Count Sforza went through with extreme ease.

Ethiopia was largely isolated. The sponsorship of the reunion of Eastern Eritrea to the motherland by the United States and Britain did not suffice to achieve that end; at best it might be said to have assisted in averting an adverse decision and securing a year's postponement instead; but for postponement Count Sforza and his allies were not unwilling; it is indeed possible that Italian strategy deliberately sought postponement, for after the Fourth Assembly had risen Count Sforza, ignoring his previous eloquent pleas and brusque demands for Eritrean independence, informed an international Press Conference that if the United Nations Organisation were "realistic" they would put Eritrea under ten years' Trusteeship.

Italian strategy would presently abandon the present demand for the immediate independence of Eritrea and substitute another effort to gain Trusteeship.

TO SELL A COAT TO A BUTTON

The witty Mr. Manuilsky, of the Ukrainian delegation, in support of the Soviet Resolution, delivered a number of sparkling sallies against his numerous political opponents. He stigmatised as "selling a coat to a button" the British proposal to annex Western Eritrea to the Sudan in order to unite the 300,000 members of the Beni Amir tribe in Eritrea to the 30,000 members of that tribe in the Sudan. Mr. Manuilsky had certainly the best of this particular

---

* This Sub-Committee consisted of Argentina, Australia, Brazil, Chile, China, Czechoslovakia, Denmark, Egypt, Ethiopia, France, Guatemala, India, Iraq, Liberia, Mexico, Pakistan, Poland, Union of South Africa, Union of Socialist Soviet Republic, United Kingdom and the United States of America.

argument, for the fathers of the Beni Amirs of the Sudan were certainly Ethiopians who were rendered Sudanese during the wars waged in the 19th century by the Egyptian Khedive, Ismail, the conqueror of the Sudan.

GREECE AND ERITREA

The Greek community in Ethiopia are ardent in their expressions of affection for their second motherland, in whose commerce and industry they play an important part. They were enthusiastic supporters of the reunion of Eritrea to Ethiopia, being fully aware of the benefit to the trade of the whole area which would result therefrom, and being also exceedingly desirous of promoting the security of Ethiopia against the possibility of a further Italian aggression. They had formed an active committee to work for the reunion of Ethiopia.

The Greek delegate, Mr. Pipinelis, supported the proposal for Libyan independence, but rejected that solution in the case of Eritrea, because it was a province of Ethiopia which had only been separated from the motherland in 1885. Eritrea should therefore be reintegrated into the framework of Ethiopia, rather than set up as a new and independent State. The previous General Assembly had approved the union of Eastern Eritrea with Ethiopia. The Greek delegation would vote as before for this proposal. They would do so not only because Ethiopia had been the victim of unjust aggression, but also because the Ethiopian nation had endeavoured valiantly to defend its independence in a grave crisis of its history. This was a factor to be born in mind, for in defending its own independence a nation defended not only its own dignity, but also the cause of world peace.

THE CHINA OF CHIANG KAI-SHEK

Dr. Tsung-Chi Yu, representing the Chiang Kai-shek Government of China, adopted a pro-Italian and anti-Ethiopian attitude. He said this delegation considered a conciliatory attitude should be adopted towards Italy; the United Nations should not allow itself to be influenced over-much by passion and the spirit of revenge. It was the business of the Assembly to settle the question of the colonies in accordance with the Charter, not to punish Italy, which had already paid the price of its error at the peace conference in 1946* The Chinese delegation considered the Assembly should not adjudicate rewards to certain nations.

---

* It should be noted that little of the punishment imposed upon Italy by the Peace Conference of 1946 had been carried into effect. The reparations to Britain and the United States had been waived and much financial assistance had been given instead. Little of the reparations to other states had been paid and none to Ethiopia. The Free State of Trieste had not been created and concessions had been promised to Italy. The treasures of art and history looted from Ethiopia had not been returned. The renunciation of the colonies was only formal and Italy was now engaged in a struggle to regain them.

"All the efforts of the United States, the United Kingdom, and the Chinese armies had contributed to a common victory; that was not a sufficient reason for granting territories to one particular nation; China would not consider it for a moment."*

This was a reference to the British resolution to restore Eritrea to Ethiopia and to annex Western Eritrea to the Anglo-Egyptian Sudan. Had the principle here urged by the Chinese delegate that Eritrea, which had been annexed from Ethiopia by Italy should be returned to the defeated aggressor, been applied to all conquered territories, the Chinese Government would have had no island of Formosa as a refuge when its hour of misfortune arrived. The time would come when Formosa, so lately recovered from Japan, would be the only foothold left to the Chiang Kai-shek Government, the only means by which it could retain a seat in the United Nations.

The Chinese representative declared that China had always been in favour of returning Somaliland to Italy. He agreed that Ethiopia, who had been the first victim of Italian Fascist aggression, as China had been of Japanese aggression, should have access to the sea; the territory to form an outlet to the sea should be in accordance with the will and aspirations of the inhabitants. The rest of Eritrea should be placed under international trusteeship leading to independence.

As Blatta Ephrem Medhen of the Ethiopian delegation rightly commented, no member of the United Nations had come into existence as the result of having been declared independent following enemy aggression. Independent nations had emerged from other states, not by foreign conquest, but through revolutions, or by agreement with nations to which they had formerly belonged.

YUGOSLAVIA

Mr. Bebler of Yugoslavia said his delegation in general favoured the independence of peoples and equality of rights, but the right of self-determination did not seem to them to militate in favour of an independent Eritrean state. It was obvious that the just application of the rights of peoples to self-determination could not here be expressed in any other way than by the incorporation of that territory into Ethiopia. National minorities, including those in cities and ports, would naturally have to share the destinies of the majority of people in the territories concerned. As to the Western Province, neither the findings of the Four Power Commission, nor the views expressed during the present debate proved that the province was capable of forming a new Arab nation. Nor was it found to form a part of the Sudanese nation. He advocated collective trusteeship for Somaliland.

---

* Provisional Summary Record, First Committee of the Fourth Assembly of the United Nations, 3rd October, 1949—A/C. 1/S.R. 280.

VENEZUELA

Mr. Stolk (Venezuela) declared that all things considered, the fate of the former Italian colonies could be decided only in the light of the Italian point of view and with the co-operation of Italy, and this represented the view of most of the South American supporters of Italy.

ISRAEL

It was surprising that the delegate of the new State of Israel, which the Jewish people had formed after their long dispersion, had not understood the yearning for reunion of the Ethiopian people who have been dispersed by European conquests. Mr. Eben, the Israeli delegate, totally ignored the claim of the Ethiopian delegation for reunion of the lost provinces and insisted, on the contrary, that the ex-colonies become independent states. He would not have quoted Hitler on the aspirations of the Jewish people, but he quoted the representative of Italy, who he said had spoken "from long experience," in relation to Eritrea. Ethiopian-Eritrean aspirations he dismissed by saying they should be the subject of negotiations between Ethiopia and the future Government or Administration of Eritrea, which would be derived from the decision of the United Nations.

Mr. De Freitas Valle, of Brazil, urged that members of the sub-committee "should not be prejudiced by any promises that member states might have given to the indigenous populations."

It was painfully evident from the outset that Ethiopia would have to take an almost lone stand, and that apart from her deeply felt struggle, such "fight" as there was in the Political Committee was mainly displayed by Count Sforza's Latin American-Arab-Pakistan-Muslim compromise coalition. In any case Britain, the United States and France had already pronounced in favour of Italian Trusteeship in Somaliland before the case went from the Council of Foreign Ministers to the United Nations.

Sub-Committee's Compromise Resolution

The Resolution which emerged from the "conciliation" Sub-Committee proposed: for all Libya independence after three years; for ex-Italian Somaliland, Italian Trusteeship, leading to independence in ten years unless the United Nations should decide otherwise at that time; for Eritrea postponement of all solution till the next Assembly, a Commission to visit the territory in the meantime.

Soviet Views

Mr. Arutiunian, of the Soviet Union, denounced the Sub-Committee's resolution as a "compromise between Colonial Powers." He alleged that Cyrenaica would remain under permanent

United Kingdom control, the Fezzan under the French, Tripolitania nominally under Italy, but actually under the United States. In short there would be a veiled partition of Libya.

In Somaliland the proposal for Italian trusteeship maintained the Bevin-Sforza proposal for this territory without any "beautification," though it had already been rejected by the General Assembly, and in spite of Somali opposition.

Italian trusteeship would be a temptation to rebuild the old empire which had collapsed as a result of World War II. The Somali people would " be justifiably suspicious that the Administering authority had no intention of preparing them for independence." These suspicions would not promote the normalisation of the situation in Somaliland.

The Committee should not ignore the statement of the Ethiopian delegate that the proposals for Eritrea and Somaliland would constitute a great threat to Ethiopian security. Mr. Arutiunian quoted a statement of the Italian Defence Minister, Signor Randolfo Pacciardi, in the Italian Senate, on October 8, 1948, that Italy's armed forces must be so organised as to create " a nation in arms." What this meant was well known to Ethiopia said the Soviet Representative. He asserted the Soviet proposals did not ignore the " interests " of the Italian people as such. They proposed that Italy be represented on the Advisory Councils in Somaliland and Eritrea; the " lawful interests " of Italy and the Italians would, therefore, be well safeguarded, but not at the expense of the indigenous inhabitants.*

It should here be recalled that at an earlier stage the Soviet Union had advocated returning to Italy all her pre-war colonies. Later generations will marvel that in the middle of the twentieth century colonial claims in Africa were so universally respected that even the Soviet Union, which was in general opposition to the claims of the bourgeois democracies and to western capitalist imperialism, admitted the existence of " lawful Italian interests " in the former colonies. The Soviet delegation proposed to hand the administration of the Somaliland people, who had been promised liberation, to a body of governments with whom the Soviet Government were in perpetual conflict. The aggressor, Italy, would be accorded the same representation as the victim of aggression, Ethiopia, who was, moreover, the ancient land from which Somaliland, and also Eritrea, had been torn. The native people of the territory would get but two members on an advisory council of ten, and even these so-called representatives would be nominated by the Great Powers of the Security Council. " Full executive powers " would be vested in a sole administrator, surely a most retrograde proceeding and lacking in the very essentials of democracy. This administrator would be appointed not even by the General Assembly of the United Nations Organisation, in which

---

* Vide United Nations Department of Public Information, Lake Success, Press Release G.A./P.S./303, November 7, 1949.

Russia formed an opposition minority, but by the Trusteeship Council, wherein no less than half the membership consisted of those very Colonial Powers with whom the Soviet was ever in embittered conflict. The Soviet resolution on the ex-colonies was thus manifestly inconsistent with the general trend of Soviet policy. It would seem the dictum that socialist policies evaporate when Africa is reached applies to the Soviet Government, as well as to many socialists of western Europe! One must hope for progress in this respect as in so many others!

Like the other delegations whose views on economic questions were so little approved in the U.S.S.R., the Soviet delegates omitted any effective analysis of the economic capacity of the Somaliland territory to lead a prosperous existence as an independent State in the absence of foreign subsidies.

Soviet Delegate on Eritrea

The Soviet proposals for Eritrea were identical with those for the Somaliland Colony. The Soviet delegate declared: "Only direct United Nations Trusteeship in Eritrea could safeguard all justifiable interests," a remark which revealed an unaccustomed faith in the United Nations Organisation as at present functioning. It appears to reveal some failure of realisation that the Ethiopians, and their compatriots across the artificially created border of Eritrea, have the same love of country and the same desire to manage their own affairs free of domination from abroad as the Soviet people.

It should be noted that the Ethiopians regard Mussolini and all previous invaders of their country as the Soviet people regard Hitler and his like.

The Soviet delegate further observed that Ethiopia demanded eastern Eritrea and claimed that independence for eastern Eritrea would be realised through union to Ethiopia. If that were so, he argued, an independent Eritrea would itself join Ethiopia. The question does not seem to have been posed as to whether the United Nations would permit that reversal of their decision. Nor was it inquired what step the United Nations would take if Italy were to intervene in a weak and defenceless Eritrea to prevent such reunion. The fact that Eritrea had only been divided from Ethiopia by Italian imperialist aggression, and that it was as much a part of Ethiopia as Manchuria of China, did not appear to have been grasped in Moscow.

The Soviet point of view was further elaborated by Mr. Voina, of the Ukranian Soviet Socialist Republic. He stated that his Government had hoped the former Italian Colonies might be placed under the administration of a democratic Italy freed from fascism. The present government of Italy, however, had delivered that country, bound hand and foot, into the hands of the capitalists. His government had therefore realised the impossibility of allowing

Italy to administer any of its former colonies. It was trying to protect war criminals from justice and was denying the principles which had guided the United Nations during the second World War. It was, therefore, not surprising that Ethiopia and other states were feeling deep anxiety concerning Italy.

ETHIOPIAN PROTEST

Protesting against the sub-committee's proposals, Ato Aklilou, Ethiopia, declared: " We feel profoundly the justice of our claim. Our claim is based on the principle of self-determination of peoples. If the peoples concerned wish to be reunited, union is not incompatible with the principle of self-determination. Italy should be the first to recognise that principle since she was constituted from a number of states which had been independent. The delegates of the Soviet Union who had most emphatically stressed the idea of independence should not gainsay the value of union, because the Soviet Union itself comprises a number of states. To put Italy again in Somaliland, we feel deeply, constitutes a threat to us. The decision to put Italy in Somaliland and, at the same time, to postpone Ethiopia's just claim to Eritrea would have a cumulative impact constituting a threat to the security of my country. A commission of investigation has been proposed for Eritrea, why do you refuse to apply the same solution in the case of Somaliland? We beg members to put themselves in our place.

" . . . The Italian Colonial Ministry has now been placed under the Foreign Ministry, but the colonial service uses personnel who have a record of being ardent fascists. They were intimately connected with the occupation of Ethiopia.

" Attached to the Italian colonial service are two former fascist officials who were intimately connected with the occupation of Ethiopia. One was the former Governor of Addis Ababa, the other was the director of native affairs in Addis Ababa. Regarding co-operation with Ethiopia Italy had yet to take the first step."

ITALIAN PROMISES

Signor Tarchiani, of the Italian delegation, declared that he could assure the Ethiopian Representative that the "old colonials" who were officials of the Colonial Department in Rome were employed only in routine matters devolving from Italy's past connection with the African territories, their task was to supervise the payment of pensions, provide aid for refugees and settle outstanding economic problems. They would never become the instruments of future aggressive expansion in Africa.

Signor Tarchiani assured the Committee that Italy would only send to Somaliland a small military force, " the minimum necessary for police purposes " which " would be utilized with the utmost moderation. Certainly the Italian Government had no thought whatever of establishing military bases." " The United Nations itself was Ethiopia's best guarantee of security. The Italian Government looked forward to co-operation with Ethiopia which would certainly offer the possibility of prosperity and advancement to the latter." *

LIBERIAN OBJECTIONS

Mr. Henry F. Cooper, Liberian delegate, protested that the only concern of the Sub-Committee had been to give " some kind of consolation to Italy, whether the Somalis like this or not." The definition of the word " democracy " must have appeared puzzling to many, particularly to the peoples of the former Italian Colonies present there. The Somalis knew human nature, even if they did not know so well the true meaning of high-sounding phrases such as "self-determination of peoples."

Mr. Cooper added that anti-Italian demonstrations had taken place all over Somaliland, according to the admission of the United Kingdom representative and according to his own information these demonstrations were continuing. " No fine phrases or grandiloquent words " about the " New Italy," he said, could obliterate from the minds of Ethiopians the fact that Somaliland had been a base for the Italian invasion and subjugation of their country. Under these circumstances there were bound to be border incidents, and in the view of Liberia, " any action taken by Ethiopia would be justified, even if it led to an occupation of Somaliland."†

The Liberian delegation urged that the United Nations Commission of Investigation which was to visit Eritrea should be sent also to Somaliland.

MR. MALIK OF LEBANON

Mr. Charles Malik, of Lebanon, who was both a delegate of his country and a member of the United Nations Secretariat, stated that his delegation could not accept the resolution on Somaliland. Some compromise must be effected. He favoured the sub-commission's recommendation of sending an inquiry commission to Eritrea and the committee's proposals on Libya. As the Somaliland proposals of the Committee were unlikely, in his view, to obtain a two-thirds majority, that part of the resolution might be

---

* The UNO Summary Report states: " It was worth mentioning, the Italian representative concluded, that after the events of October, 1947, and of January, 1948, the only political leaders who were arrested were those who opposed the League." On the contrary Mohamed Mohamud Aden was sentenced by the British Authorities to 21 years imprisonment, with hard labour, for having shot an Italian during this riot, although according to the British Authorities the Italians were entirely to blame as they had made an unprovoked attack on the Somali Youth League demonstration, which had been held by permission of the British Authorities.

† The above quoted statement of Mr. Henry Cooper and the entire account of the discussion by the General Assembly and its auxiliary bodies have been taken from the official reports of the United Nations.

rejected, and since the first committee wished its decisions concerning the three former colonies to stand or fall together, a compromise must be sought. The best proposal in his view was to place the territory under the trusteeship of three states, and if that were proposed again his delegation would support it. In view of their conviction, however, that a solution should be reached in the current session, the Lebanese delegation had decided to make a new proposal based on the following principles. In the first place Italy was entitled to receive some satisfaction from the settlement. The Lebanese delegation did not agree with those who considered Italy a threat to the security and freedom of certain nations. Italy was a great nation and many countries owed more to it than to any other nation. Italy should, therefore, be the administering authority. Nevertheless, the fears and reservations expressed by the representative of Ethiopia were genuine. Ethiopia had suffered under fascist aggression and was entitled to receive certain guarantees, although the new Italy could not be regarded as a danger to Ethiopia.

"The Lebanese delegation proposed, therefore, that an advisory council be set up composed of five members. If the members of that council were chosen wisely, it would represent a firm guarantee for Ethiopia, which was moreover championed by the countries of Asia. Fear of Italy need not, therefore, stand in the way of a solution of the problem of Somaliland.

"The Lebanese delegation had listened with great attention to the representatives of Somaliland; nevertheless, it was essential in the interests of the United Nations that a solution should be found during the current session. If some such formula as that suggested by the sub-committee was the only one likely to be accepted with regard to Somaliland, the statute of that territory, the activity of the trusteeship council, and the proposed advisory council, the influence of the Asian countries, the different character of present-day Italy, could be considered as sufficient guarantees both for the populations concerned and for Ethiopia."

Conflicting Views

The Ecuador representative accepted Mr. Malik's proposal for an advisory council for Somaliland. Mr. Azouni, Yemen, again emphasised the objection of the local population to an Italian trusteeship for Somaliland. He urged that a commission of investigation should be sent there as well as to Eritrea. If the Somaliland population was not mature enough for independence the United Nations should promote such maturity without imposing a state of affairs which might endanger peace and security. He opposed Italian trusteeship, but would be in favour of collective trusteeship by the United Nations for a period not exceeding ten years. He objected to tying up the future of the people of Libya with those of the Somalis and Eritreans. This had only been done to provide an opportunity for bargaining. Those who criticised the U.S.S.R.

in the matter of vetoing Italy's admission to the United Nations until other states were also admitted were adopting precisely the same tactics in this case. The Burmese delegate would regret the postponement of a settlement for Eritrea as the claims of Ethiopia were justified, and also her preoccupation with the question of her security. Italian trusteeship could be accepted provided it would lead to independence, additional safeguards should be effected by an advisory council or a collective trusteeship. He urged also another commission of investigation for Somaliland. Mr. Costa du Rels, Bolivia, considered that Somaliland, the poorest of the three former colonies, would be "scant compensation" to Italy for the loss of the other territories. Ethiopia required access to the sea. The compromise arrived at by the sub-committee he considered extremely precarious; he believed it would lead Libya into regrettable economic and political adventures. His delegation would agree to the resolution but without enthusiasm, it was based on bargaining and not on principles, he was not deceived by the demagogy surrounding the proposal.

Attempts were made by Ethiopia and other delegations to secure that the clauses dealing with the sub-committee's resolution covering Eritrea, Somaliland and Libya should be voted upon separately, but this was strongly opposed by the South American delegations despite the plea of Sir Mohamed Zafrullah Khan, of Pakistan, that the bargaining which resulted from the composite resolution might prove a most unfortunate precedent and become the rule in all subsequent Assemblies. His delegation was quite convinced that a large majority of the people of Somaliland were opposed to Italian trusteeship. Unless a compromise solution could be reached his delegation would be compelled to oppose the resolution on Somaliland. The delegates of Saudi-Arabia and Iraq expressed the same determination and declared they would not vote for a trusteeship of Somaliland by Italy alone. A formula must be found whereby the Italian administration would be helped by other states. Mr. Jamali, of Iraq, also urged that Ethiopia's special position must be recognised and that Ethiopia must be included in any new formula intended to supplement Italy's trusteeship over Somaliland. If Italy were to be trustee the trusteeship agreement must prevent the establishment of military bases in Somaliland.

Mr. Bebler, of Yugoslavia, declared that the Somali Youth League, which according to the Four-Power Commission represented the overwhelming part of the population, had absolutely opposed Italian trusteeship, nevertheless, the sub-committee had decided upon Italian trusteeship for ten years with a threat that it would be perpetuated thereafter.

Mr. Couve de Murville, France, understood the bitter feelings which the Ethiopian delegation were bound to entertain and their anxieties and fears regarding the security of their country. These fears would be largely overcome if satisfactory precautions were undertaken for Somaliland. Nevertheless, he supported the single trusteeship of Italy for that territory.

VOTING

The Somali Youth League begged leave to address the Committee before the voting on the resolution. But on a motion by Mr. Arce, of Argentina, it was decided by 25 votes to 19 with two abstentions that the Youth League might only submit its observations in writing.

At the request of the Soviet delegate the resolution of his delegation was taken before that of the Sub-Committee, but every clause of it was rejected by a mere show of hands and no roll call.

SUB-COMMITTEE RESOLUTION
Libya to be an Independent State

After a long discussion the first paragraph of the Sub-Committee's resolution was adopted by 51 votes to none with seven abstentions in the following form: that Libya comprising Cyrenaica, Tripolitania and the Fezzan shall be constituted an independent Sovereign State.*

A Polish amendment to render Libyan independence operative in January 1951 instead of 1952 as proposed by the Sub-Committee was defeated by 25 votes to 15 with 11 abstentions. The Sub-Committee's proposal for Libya was adopted on show of hands by 54 votes to none with two abstentions.

PROPOSAL TO SEND COMMISSION TO SOMALILAND REJECTED; WOULD " UPSET THE APPLE-CART "

The Liberian proposal that a Commission should be appointed to ascertain the wishes of the inhabitants of Somaliland was debated at some length. Mr. Arce, Argentine, adroitly declared that to allay all anxieties his delegation would accept the Lebanese proposal for an advisory council on which one Latin American and one Arab country should be represented. The power of Count Sforza's South American-Muslim alliance was again demonstrated. Mr. Sunde, of Norway, declared support for the Liberian amendment, as did Blatta Ephrem Medhen, the Ethiopian delegate, and Sir Zafrulah Khan, of Pakistan, who added that the fears of Somali opposition, from which might arise disastrous consequences even for the administering authority, might be exaggerated. Mr. Jamali, of Iraq, however, spoke against the Liberian amendment, as did the delegate of Peru. Mr. Malik, Lebanon, though he said he could not in principle oppose the desire to ascertain the true wishes of the population, regretted that to carry the Liberian proposal for a commission would " upset the apple-cart " which had been erected with difficulty; it was obvious that his remarks carried weight and that he had assumed a directing position in relation to the resolution. It was notable that Mr. Arutiunian, Soviet Union, also opposed the Liberian amendment, declaring his preference for that of Poland. Mr. Jessup, of the United States, expressed his agreement with the U.S.S.R.; a decision had to be reached during the current session. Mr. Pipinelis, Greece, would

---

* The abstentions comprised New Zealand, Sweden, the Soviet bloc and Yugoslavia.

oppose the Liberian amendment but claimed that logically the problem of Eritrea should also be settled that session. He considered Ethiopian claims were justified and would vote in support of them.

The Liberian amendment was voted down by 40 votes to 11 with eight abstentions.*

The Sub-Committee's proposal that Somaliland should be an independent State was adopted by 58 votes to none with one abstention, Sweden.

THE PHILIPPINES AMENDMENT: THE 10 YEARS LIMIT TO TRUSTEESHIP MAINTAINED

The Sub-Committee proposal to make this independence effective after 10 years " unless the General Assembly decide otherwise at that time," aroused opposition. Mr. Chanco, of the Philippines declared that the United Nations should not by unwarranted reservations lessen the effect of an action of high moral significance; to give and take back at the same time was a futile policy. He moved to delete the clause giving the Assembly power to decide that independence should not come into force after 10 years. The Polish and Byelo-Russian delegates supported this view whilst the Pakistan delegate ironically remarked that even the Somalia Conferenza, which was not asking for immediate independence and supported Italian trusteeship, had claimed that 500 posts in the higher Civil Service were occupied by Somalis, that there were hospitals, roads and schools in Somaliland, that 50 per cent. of the judges in the higher courts were Somalis. The answer given by these representatives had left one wondering what gaps the trusteeship arrangement would have to fill. If the views expressed by these pro-Italian delegates, which were presumably also the views of the Italians in Somaliland, corresponded with the facts, why should ten years elapse before Italian Somaliland would be ready for independence? It was precisely the statement of that group of delegates which had been taken as a basis for the conclusion that at least one large section of the population would give a favourable reception to Italian trusteeship. If the point of view of those opposed to Italian trusteeship was also taken into consideration, and if Italy was, nevertheless, given the trusteeship, it

---

* In favour: Yemen, Yugoslavia, Ethiopia, India, Iran, Iraq, Liberia, New Zealand, Norway, Pakistan, Philippines.
 Against: Union of South Africa, Union of Soviet Socialist Republics, United Kingdom of Great Britain and Northern Ireland, United States of America, Uruguay, Venezuela, Argentina, Australia, Belgium, Bolivia, Brazil, Byelo-Russian Soviet Socialist Republic, Canada, Chile, Colombia, Costa Rica, Cuba, Czechoslovakia, Denmark, Dominican Republic, Ecuador, El Salvador, France, Greece, Guatemala, Haiti, Honduras, Iceland, Lebanon, Luxembourg, Mexico, Netherlands, Nicaragua, Panama, Paraguay, Peru, Poland, Turkey, Ukrainian Soviet Socialist Republic.
 Abstaining: Afghanistan, Burma, Egypt, Israel, Saudi Arabia, Sweden, Syria, Siam.

would have to be established quite clearly that it was the intention of the General Assembly and the administering authority to enable the population to become independent as soon as possible.

Unfortunately the Pakistan delegate added that if the good faith of the United Nations and the administering authority was clearly established there were grounds for hoping that the part of the population opposed to Italian trusteeship would accept the proposed formula.

His delegation would vote for the Polish amendment to reduce the period of trusteeship to three years, if that was defeated he would vote for the Phillipines amendment.

The Polish amendment to reduce the trusteeship period to three years was then rejected by 35 votes to 18 with six abstentions.*

The Philippines amendment was next carried by 33 votes to 22 with four abstentions. This was an exceedingly remarkable success for the principle of liberation; the Philippines amendment was carried in spite of the opposition of the United States and all the west European States with the exception of Norway and Iceland who voted in favour, and Sweden who abstained.†

MORE ITALIAN PROMISES

As the vote on the question of Italy's trusteeship of Somaliland approached, Signor Tarchiani raised a further plea on Italy's behalf and protested against doubts of his Government's sincerity. He insisted that should the Italian Government obtain the trusteeship they would scrupulously observe the time limit established by the General Assembly, and on the appointed date would transfer

---

† In favour: Cuba, Czechoslovakia, Dominican Republic, Ecuador, Egypt, of Soviet Socialist Republics, Yemen, Yugoslavia, Afghanistan, Byelorussian Soviet Socialist Republic, Cuba, Czechoslovakia, Ethiopia, India, Iran, Iraq, Liberia, Pakistan, Philippines, Poland.

Against: Turkey, Union of South Africa, United Kingdom of Great Britain and Northern Ireland, United States of America, Uruguay, Venezuela, Argentina, Australia, Belgium, Bolivia, Brazil, Canada, Chile, China, Colombia, Costa Rica, Denmark, Dominican Republic, Ecuador, El Salvador, France, Greece, Guatemala, Haiti, Honduras, Iceland, Luxembourg, Mexico, Netherlands, New Zealand, Nicaragua, Norway, Panama, Paraguay, Peru.

Abstaining: Sweden, Thailand, Burma, Egypt, Israel, Lebanon.

** In favour: Cuba, Czechoslovakia, Dominican Republic, Ecuador, Egypt, Ethiopia, Haiti, Iceland, India, Iran Iraq, Israel, Lebanon, Liberia, Mexico, Nicaragua, Norway, Pakistan, Panama, Paraguay, Peru, Philippines, Poland, Saudi Arabia, Syria, Thailand, Ukranian Soviet Socialist Republic, Union of Soviet Socialist Republics, Yemen, Yugoslavia, Afghanistan, Burma, Byelorussian Soviet Socialist Republic.

Against: Colombia, Denmark, France, Greece, Guatemala, Honduras, Luxembourg, Netherlands, New Zealand, Turkey, Union of South Africa, United Kingdom of Great Britain and Northern Ireland, United States of America, Uruguay, Venezuela, Argentina, Australia, Belgium, Bolivia, Brazil, Canada, Chile.

Abstaining: China, Costa Rica, El Salvador, Sweden.

The Philippine amendment was adopted by 33 votes to 22, with 4 abstentions.

their powers to a duly constituted Somali Government. Mr. Arce, Argentine, again assisted the Italian case by bringing forward the proposal of the Advisory Council and suggesting that it should be voted upon before the question of the trusteeship.

The United Nations will enter Somaliland—Argentine delegate

He proceeded to make a most remarkable statement which would be recalled in the light of subsequent events:

"*The day on which Italy takes up the responsibility as an Administering Authority in Somaliland, that is to say if the General Assembly approves our draft resolution, it is the United Nations which will enter Somaliland. I repeat: the United Nations, and no power on earth—not just Italy—will be able to assume any attitude in discrepancy with the Charter and the purposes of the United Nations.*"*

THE ADVISORY COUNCIL

The composition of the advisory council now became a subject of urgent interest. Mr. Jamali, of Iraq, who was genuinely troubled by the prospect of allowing Italy to return, had already suggested as a necessary safeguard that Ethiopia should be a member of that council. Mr. Langenhove, Belgium, proposed the Union of South Africa as a member. Mr. Fawzie Bey, Egypt, proposed to omit the word " advisory."

The Polish delegate interposed here that his amendment putting Somaliland under direct trusteeship of the United Nations was closest to the spirit of the Charter. To put Somaliland under the trusteeship of a country which had previously oppressed the territory would cause a deterioration of the situation there. The Ethiopian people would not feel secure if Italy were granted trusteeship in Somaliland. They had been the first victims of fascism and could not forget. Mr. Belaunde, Peru, protested that the committee had no right to doubt the motives and ideals of the Italian Government since Italy would be assisted by an advisory council under the supervision of the General Assembly and the Trusteeship Council and there would be a Trusteeship agreement. The Polish amendment should not be considered. Mr. Belaunde was sure that Italy would apply the ideals of Christian democracy in any territory which the United Nations gave it to administer. The delegates of Iran and Burma, and Sir Benegal Rau, of India, said though they favoured direct United Nations trusteeship in general they would abstain from voting on the Polish amendment. The delegates of the Philippines and Israel and Sir Zaffrulah Kan, of Pakistan, also declared they would abstain. Again it was evident that Count Sforza's new compromise was working successfully.

---

* Verbatum Record A/pv. 520, page 56.

The Polish amendment was then defeated by 35 votes to 8 with 16 abstentions. Ethiopia, Liberia, Yugoslavia and the Soviet bloc voted in the affirmative.*

THE FUNCTIONS OF PROPOSED ADVISORY COUNCIL

Mr. Charles Malik, Lebanon, now made an urgent appeal for Italian trusteeship of Somaliland on the plea of explaining his proposal for an advisory council.

The Egyptian delegate endeavoured to secure the deletion of the word "Advisory" in relation to the council proposed by the Lebanese delegation, and urged that the council which was being proposed for Libya was not designated advisory. As the council proposed for Somaliland was offered as a guarantee to the Somalis the guarantee should not be weakened. Blatta Ephrem Medhen, the Ethiopian delegate, declared the Advisory Council would in no way diminish the threat to Ethiopia and would provide no guarantee. His delegation would decline nomination for the council. His delegation would, therefore, vote against it. Mr. Jordaan, Union of South Africa, was opposed to an advisory council, and still more to its participation in the administration, his delegation would nevertheless abstain, but the membership of the council should be reduced to a minimum. Whilst thanking the Belgian delegation for their nomination of South Africa, he could not accept unless the council were to consist of two members only. Mr. Couve de Murville, France, though French delegations had consistently stated that Ethiopia required guarantees, now declared the advisory council unnecessary. Nevertheless, he would not oppose on the ground that the council might allay some fears. It should be advisory only and consist of two or three members.

The advisory council was a device which was obviously overcoming the strong opposition to an Italian administration. Mr. Malik declared genuine guarantees were being provided against any abuse of the Somalis on the part of the administering authority. There was a prospect of definite independence after ten years. The Trusteeship Council would be able to include in its agreement with the administering power safeguards for fundamental human rights. The advisory council would be situated in Mogadishu. It would help and advise Italy " and would be collaborating in the administration." "The peoples of Somaliland could always

---

* In favour: : Poland, Ukranian Soviet Socialist Republic, Union of Soviet Socialist Republics, Yugoslavia, Byelorussian Soviet Socialist Republic, Czechoslovakia, Ethiopia, Liberia.

Against: Turkey, Union of South Africa, United Kingdom, United States of America, Uruguay, Venezuela, Argentina, Australia, Belgium, Bolivia, Brazil, Canada, Chile, China, Colombia, Costa Rica, Cuba, Denmark, Dominican Republic, Ecuador, El Salvador, France, Greece, Guatemala, Haiti, Honduras, Iceland, Lebanon, Luxembourg, Mexico, Netherlands, Nicaragua, Panama, Paraguay, Peru.

Abstaining: Philippines, Saudi Arabia, Sweden, Syria, Thailand, Yemen, Afghanistan, Burma, Egypt, India, Iran, Iraq, Israel, New Zealand, Norway, Pakistan.

appeal to the advisory council; they could always talk to the members of the council to make sure that no abuse had been exercised by adminstering authority upon the Somalis." It would have an intimate relationship with the administering authority and would have the interests of the people at heart.

Mr. McNeil, of the British delegation, interposed to protest against Mr. Malik's flattering remarks on the Advisory Council; that Council would have no share in the administration, the sole administrator would be Italy. Mr. McNeil also repudiated the talk by the Philippines delegation of a share in the administration for the Advisory Council. The Council would have no share in the administration. If the first committee attempted to extend its functions they would be deceiving themselves, creating a most ambiguous precedent and probably would end up with considerable legal difficulties on their hands if they were guilty of creating this confusion.*

This vehement lecture may be viewed in relation to the fact that the First Committee was merely engaged in preparing proposals to be considered and voted upon by the General Assmbly of the United Nations. The hyper-sensitive attitude towards the prerogatives of administering authorities displayed by the Powers wielding authority over subject peoples, here painfully displayed by the British Representative, was but a poor augury for any assistance which the Advisory Council would be permitted to render to the Somali people, unwillingly thrust again under Italian rule. Mr. Malik, of Lebanon, hastened to explain that it had never been his intention that the Advisory Council should " interfere in the actual administration of the territory." The Representative of the Phillipines, subsequently addressing the General Assembly, spoke up more stoutly declaring that unless the Advisory Council " had a much higher status than a mere group of observers " its presence would either be " a luxury or a pretence in which neither the States concerned nor the United Nations could afford to indulge." Just though that protest was, it was evident that the Advisory Council had been most deliberately restricted to offering advice alone.

Mr. Wierblowski, Poland, proposed that three representatives of the local population elected by the political organisations of the territory should be added to the proposed Advisory Council. This had been agreed to in the case of Libya and seemed even more advisable in the case of Somaliland if that territory would again be placed under Italian control. Mr. Malik replied it was unnecessary at the moment to consider the participation of the local population on an equal footing with the members of the United Nations. Mr. Malik also rejected a proposal by the Phillipines that the members of the Somaliland Advisory Council should have seats on the Trusteeship Council.

---

* United Nations, T/A.C. 18/L.2.9, January Working Paper by the Secretariat.

The amendment to place three representatives of the local population on the Advisory Council was rejected on a show of hands by 33 votes to nine with 17 abstentions.

The amendment to delete the word " advisory " in relation to the proposed council was defeated by 37 to 14 with eight abstentions.*

The amendment of Mr. Malik, Lebanon, to establish an Advisory Council composed of Colombia, Egypt and the Philippines was adopted by 48 votes to one—Ethiopia alone voting against. There were 10 abstentions.†

ITALIAN TRUSTEESHIP VOTED

The crucial question of Italian Trusteeship in Somaliland was now reached. Sir Mohamed Zaffrulah Khan, of Pakistan, announced that his delegation would abstain from voting on this point. They would have preferred collective United Nations Trusteeship administered by the Trusteeship Council, but as the majority of Member States considered the circumstances were not yet ripe for that kind of Trusteeship for any territory, his delegation had not insisted on a vote for that proposal. His delegation would not object to Italian Trusteeship of Somaliland. He appealed to all the Somali parties and groups which had hitherto protested again Italian Trusteeship to reconsider the proposal. The committee should try to convince them of the necessity of applying the proposals in such a way that they could be granted independence at the earliest possible date. The administering authority would be urged to avoid discrimination in favour of local political leaders who had supported Italian trusteeship. The Ethiopians entertained certain fears, but it must be hoped that when they had studied the proposals as a whole, both the Government of Ethiopia

---

† In favour: Dominican Republic, Ecuador, Egypt, El Salvador, France, Union of Soviet Socialist Republics, Yemen, Yugoslavia, Byelorussian Soviet Socialist Republic, Czechoslovakia, Egypt, Iraq, Israel, Liberia, Pakistan.
Against: Union of South Africa, United Kingdom of Great Britain and Northern Ireland, United States of America, Uruguay, Venezuela, Argentina, Australia, Belgium, Bolivia, Brazil, Burma, Canada, Chile, China, Colombia, Costa Rica, Cuba, Denmark, Dominican Republic, Ecuador, El Salvador, France, Greece, Guatemala, Haiti, Honduras, Iceland, Lebanon, Luxembourg, Mexico, Netherlands, New Zealand, Nicaragua, Norway, Panama, Paraguay, Peru.
Abstaining: Philippines, Sweden, Thailand, Turkey, Afghanistan, Ethiopia, India, Iran.

** In favour: Dominican Republic, Ecuador, Egypt, El Salvador, France, Greece, Guatemala, Haiti, Honduras, Iceland, India, Iran, Iraq, Israel, Lebanon, Liberia, Luxembourg, Mexico, Netherlands, Nicaragua, Norway, Pakistan, Panama, Paraguay, Peru, Philippines, Saudi Arabia, Syria, Thailand, Turkey, United Kingdom of Great Britain and Northern Ireland, United States of America, Uruguay, Venezuela, Yemen, Afghanistan, Argentina, Australia, Belgium, Bolivia, Brazil, Burma, Canada, Chile, Colombia, Costa Rica, Cuba.
Against: Ethiopia.
Abstaining: Czechoslovakia, Denmark, New Zealand, Poland, Sweden, Ukranian Soviet Socialist Republic, Union of South Africa, Union of Soviet Socialist Republics, Yugoslavia, Byelorussian Soviet Socialist Republic.

and the people of Somaliland would react favourably. His delegation would not object to the trusteeship of Somaliland being entrusted to Italy.

ANOTHER ITALIAN PLEDGE

Signor Tarchiani assured the Committee, on behalf of the Italian Government, that no discrimination of any sort would be exercised against Somalis who had opposed Italian trusteeship. On the contrary, their co-operation in the development and well being of Somaliland would be appreciated by Italy in the most friendly spirit.

A vote by roll-call was then taken on the question of Italian trusteeship, which was accepted by 48 votes to 7, with four abstentions. The seven who voted against the return of Italy were: Ethiopia, Yugoslavia and the Soviet bloc. The abstainers were: Liberia, New Zealand, Pakistan and Sweden.

THE INDIAN ANNEXURE

The Indian delegation now proposed an "annexure" containing suggested constitutional principles to be added to the resolution already adopted, as a guide to the trusteeship council and to the administering authority. Its intentions were doubtless, excellent, but its terms were exceedingly vague. The text of this annexe, together with the resolution on the disposal of the ex-colonies, as subsequently adopted by the General Assembly, will be found at the close of this chapter.

The Belgian delegate recalled that sub-committee 17 had not debated the Indian annexe, and he therefore doubted the competence of the First Committee to vote on the text. He thought it would be better to add it to the resolution without a vote. If the committee were to vote on the annexe this would be tantamount to approval, whereas the text had not been examined in detail either by the committee or by the sub-committee. It was finally agreed that the committee should submit the Indian annexe to the General Assembly without expressing any opinion upon it.

Blatta Ephrem Medhem, the Ethiopian delegate, again emphasised that his delegation considered the imposition of Italian trusteeship upon Somaliland constituted a threat to the independence and security of Ethiopia.

ERITREA: ANOTHER COMMISSION

The first committee then proceeded to debate the sub-committee's resolution, Section C, on Eritrea. Realising that in view of the success of Count Sforza's cleverly devised alliance, the only alternative to a decision dividing Eritrea from Ethiopia would be to agree to a postponement, Ethiopia decided to abstain from voting on that clause in the sub-committee's proposals. In the discussion on the proposed commission of inquiry to visit

Eritrea, Ato Aklilou Haptewold, Ethiopia, stated that he would abstain on the proposal of the establishment of the commission, but he would vote on its membership. He preferred absolutely neutral countries. The representative of Chile nominated Pakistan. Ato Aklilou protested that Pakistan was not neutral having strongly supported "independence" for Eritrea; he protested that Ethiopia should be included if interested nations were to have seats on the commission. The Philippines representative supported the Ethiopian view, but Mr. Santa Cruz, of Chile, declared Ato Aklilou's argument unacceptable and persisted in his nomination of Pakistan. The Burmese delegate, U So Nyong, nominated South Africa, Guatemala, Norway and Burma, and said he would leave it to the committee to decide between Egypt and Pakistan. The Polish delegate suggested an immediate vote by secret ballot. Mr. Santa Cruz declared that a secret ballot was correct in electing peoples not countries. Dr. Phillip C. Jessup, United States, declared that a secret ballot would result in "hopeless confusion." The Danish delegate observed that a secret ballot would hardly achieve the purpose the committee had in mind. It was clear that the organisers of the compromise were not convinced that the commission would be such as they desired if a secret ballot were taken. Mahmoud Fawzi Bey, Egypt, said his country would be very willing to serve on the commission. Egypt wanted "a real solution for a real situation." Ethiopia and Egypt knew the area and understood the people. Countries which knew something about Eritrea should serve on the commission. U So Nyong accepted Pakistan as the fifth member of the commission. New Zealand was nominated, but Sir Carl Berendsen, New Zealand, said he was very reluctant to be dragged into this dog-fight." This was a "perfectly ridiculous discussion"; to take a secret ballot was the simplest way out. The proposal for a secret vote was defeated by 23 votes to 24 An Iraqi proposal for a commission of seven including Egypt and Ethiopia was rejected by 21 to 11 with 24 abstentions. South Africa, Guatemala, Norway, Burma and Pakistan were then appointed by 40 votes to 6 with 9 abstentions.

The question whether the sub-committee's composite proposal should be dealt with in a single vote was still undecided. The South Americans demanded a single vote; the Arab States and Pakistan preferred each part of the resolution to be decided separately. The U.S.S.R. desired a single resolution. The proposal for 3 separate resolutions was rejected by 28 to 24 with 4 abstentions.

THE FRONTIER BETWEEN SOMALILAND AND ETHIOPIA

The question of the frontier alone remained to be decided. The following resolution was adopted by 23 votes to 10 with 23 abstentions:—

"*The General Assembly, considering the recommendation concerning the disposal of the former Italian colonies calls upon* the interim committee of the General Assembly to study the procedure to be adopted to delimit the boundaries of the former Italian colonies in so far as they are not already fixed by international agreement, and to report with conclusions to the Fifth Regular Session of the General Assembly."

The Argentine delegation then moved that Italy should be invited to undertake the "provisional administration" of Somaliland pending approval by the General Assembly. Dr. Arce argued that the United Kingdom Government would wish to terminate its administration as soon as possible, and the Trusteeship Agreement would probably take some time to negotiate and approve. Mr. Hector McNeil, United Kingdom, responded that some arrangement had to be made for "a quick and orderly transfer of power," the United Kingdom had been merely a caretaker and this was not enough from the point of view of the inhabitants.

Ato Aklilou, Ethiopia, protested that if the Argentine proposal were accepted, Italian rule would be imposed on Somaliland without safeguards. Italian interests would be met, while the claims of Ethiopia and the threats to his country's security were ignored.

The Soviet delegate doubted whether the Argentine proposal was legal. Dr. Santa Cruz, of Chile, to overcome this difficulty suggested that Italian administration should begin after a Draft Trusteeship Agreement had been negotiated by the Trusteeship Council and the Administering Authority. A proposal that Italian trusteeship should not start until after the Draft Trusteeship Agreement has been negotiated was then adopted by 38 votes to eight with ten abstentions.

The whole resolution was accepted by 49 votes in favour with eight abstentions, Ethiopia alone voting against.*

Dr. Arce, the Argentine delegate, lightly discounted any ground for anxiety by Ethiopia, insisting she had nothing to fear from " an army of Italian clerks armed with fountain pens."

Blatta Medhen retorted that the Italian newspaper, " Progresso Liberale," had reported that an expeditionary force of 16,000 was being made ready in Italy for Somaliland. Signor Alberto Tarchiani replied that he was not responsible for what was published in a Fascist paper.

---

* The voting on the various sections was as follows:—
Libya: 50 votes in favour, none against, 8 abstentions (Yugoslavia and the Soviet bloc).
Somaliland: Adopted by 47 votes in favour, 7 against (Byelorussian, Czechoslovakia, Ethiopia, Poland, Ukraine, U.S.S.R., Yugoslavia), with 4 abstentions (Liberia, New Zealand, Pakistan, Sweden).
Eritrea: Adopted by 47 votes in favour, 5 against (Byelorussia, Czechoslovakia, Poland, Ukraine, U.S.S.R.), with six abstentions (Ethiopia, Greece, Liberia, Philippines, Sweden, Yugoslavia).
The resolution as a whole was adopted by 49 votes in favour, 1 against (Ethiopia), 8 abstentions (Byelorussia, Czechoslovakia, New Zealand, Poland, Sweden, Ukraine, U.S.S.R., Yugoslavia).

In fact many other Italian newspapers had also published and declared the aforementioned fact.

In those days Italian newspapers were already announcing that the Italian Government had enrolled 16,000 military volunteers for Somaliland equipped with all the engines of modern war, a few weeks later the volunteers were said to be 70,000. It was announced that contingents of Italian volunteers were stationed at Naples waiting to sail for Somaliland. Signor Pacciardi, the Italian Minister of Defence, announced to the Chamber of Deputies that Italy was rearming; the cruisers, Luigi di Savoia and Duca degli Abruzzi, were being reconstructed, two anti-aircraft ships, six destroyers, a convoy escort, and a number of fast motor gunboats and coastal vessels would be built immediately. The Italian Government also revealed that they were negotiating for the purchase of jet fighters, that the standing army would be raised to 250,000 men. Infantry divisions would be immediately raised from eight divisions to twelve.

An Italian soldier of the Commando Company, 2nd Battalion, 9th Infantry Regiment, stationed at Piccia Barracks, wrote a letter to his parents which was sent by them to an Italian weekly. This letter recounted that the soldiers had been subjected to a rigorous medical examination because " Italy is going to reoccupy her former Colonies and they will send us there." The soldiers had been informed that those who would sign as volunteers "for an unknown destination " would be paid 40,000 lire monthly for two years; those who would not volunteer would get only 300 lire per month. All this and much more to similar effect concerning Italian military preparations reached the delegations at Lake Success during their discussions. Nevertheless, Mr. Arce, of Argentina, ridiculed the possibility of Italian aggression and asked the Ethiopian delegation whether they anticipated that a great Italian army furnished with penknives would invade their country.

Ground for anxiety to Ethiopia was given by the composition of the Commission of Inquiry which the Political Committee proposed to send to Eritrea; South Africa, since the Malan Government came to office, had been regarded as specially opposed to any form of African self-rule; Guatemala, one of Italy's Latin American allies, and Pakistan who had been active opposing the reunion of Eritrea to Ethiopia. Norway was the only one of the five who had been included among the 37 Delegations who had voted for the reunion cause in the Spring.

GENERAL ASSEMBLY RATIFIES RESOLUTION ON EX-COLONIES

The resolution of the First Committee on the disposal of Libya, Eritrea and Somalia were submitted for ratification by the Fourth General Assembly in plenary meeting on November 21, 1949. They were adopted without amendment or debate.

INDIAN ANNEXURE

General Romuli, of the Philippines, remarked that the "Indian annexure" would not be submitted to the vote but attention was called to it, as stated by the Rapporteur of the First Committee.

POLISH AMENDMENTS REJECTED

The Polish amendments on Libya were submitted first, and rejected. Polish amendments to render Somaliland independent in three years time, to add two Somali representatives to the Advisory Council for Somaliland, to instruct the Trusteeship Council to prepare the Draft Trusteeship Agreement instead of to negotiate it with the administering authority, were likewise voted down, as well as the various clauses to make Eritrea an independent Sovereign State.

FIRST COMMITTEE RESOLUTION

The resolution of the First Committee was then dealt with by a vote on each of its component parts:

A. Libya

Section A, making Libya an independent Sovereign State, was carried by 40 votes to none with nine abstentions, the only change being that France, having cast an affirmative vote in the First Committee, now abstained.

B. Somaliland

The provisions of Section B on Somaliland were carried by 48 votes to seven with three abstentions. Sir Zafrulla Khan, of Pakistan, who had abstained in the Committee cast the vote of his delegation for the Italian trusteeship of the Somali people. The opponents as before were Ethiopia and Yugoslavia, who had suffered Italian invasion, and the Soviet bloc, whose demand was for another formula of United Nations trusteeship which has already been explained. Liberia, New Zealand and Sweden were the only abstainers.

The Muslim delegations whom the Somalis hoped would preserve them from Italian trusteeship had abandoned them to Italy in accordance with Count Sforza's compromise plan.

C. Eritrea

The postponement of all solution for Eritrea, and the appointment of a United Nations Commission of Investigation for that territory, provided by Section C, were adopted by precisely the same voting as in the First Committee: 47 votes to five with six abstention. The abstainers, as before, were Ethiopia, Greece, Liberia, the Philippines, Sweden and Yugoslavia, the opponents, as before, were the Soviet bloc.

It is noteworthy that at that stage the Yugoslav delegation voted with the Soviet bloc on all points except on the question of Eritrea in respect of which they voted with Ethiopia.

The resolution as a whole, precisely as it had issued from the First Committee, was carried by the General Assembly by 48 votes to Ethiopia's sole negative. The abstainers had risen from eight to nine, for France, who had voted in favour of the whole resolution in the First Committee, now abstained.

All matters comprised in the resolutions of the First Committee on the disposal of the ex-Colonies having been accepted by the Assembly, the Soviet representative desired that a vote be taken also on his own resolution. Mr. Hector McNeil, however, protested that in what he termed "this rather happy moment," having just decided what to do with the former Colonies, it would be illogical to vote on a contrary proposal. By a vote of 17 to 16, with 18 abstentions, it was decided not to vote on the Soviet proposals.

Mr. McNeil ejaculated when the voting ended, "I am expecting great things of Italy!"

Blatta Medhen, of the Ethiopian delegation, rose up in stoic fortitude to make yet another protest. He urged that the area then occupied by the British in Somaliland, comprising as it did a part of the Ethiopian Ogaden, had been held since the war by Britain under agreement with the Ethiopian Government, and bore no relation to the limits of what was formerly the Italian Colony. It would be unthinkable, he declared, for the United Nations, or any of its organs, in studying and examining the problem to permit an occupation, even of the most limited kind, by Italian forces or authorities of territory claimed by Ethiopia.

In view of this problem it was impossible to imagine a State more interested in any trusteeship agreement concerning Somaliland than Ethiopia. Whatever might be the view as to whether the Four Great Powers to whom the recommendations of the General Assembly were to be submitted could be considered States directly interested in the future of Somaliland, Ethiopia was such a State. Article 79 of the United Nations Charter directed that Trusteeship Agreements must be agreed by the States directly concerned. Therefore, he found it necessary to intervene with reference of the projected work of the Trusteeship Council on Somaliland.

The President announced: "We have finished the question of the disposal of the former Italian colonies."

The representatives of the Somali Youth League and of the Eritrean Unionists were stricken with heavy disappointment by decisions which would cause sorrow and suffering to their people at home.

The reunion of Eritrea to Ethiopia, which had appeared so near, so certain in the Spring, was now postponed and beset by obstacles. This rendered more tragic the cruel abandonment of Somaliland to Italy by the defection of the Asian States whose votes had saved the Somalis from that unwelcome fate in the

Spring. The Somalis would be immediate sufferers by the decision but Ethiopia faced the possibility of being placed again between the pincers of Italy.

Two points only had been gained: Italian Trusteeship in Somaliland, instead of being without stated limit, as formerly proposed, or to continue for thirty years as Italy's Somali satellites in the Colony had requested, was scheduled for ten years only. The convenient handle for prolonging the Trusteeship, which had originally been attached to the agreed resolution, had been struck off by the deletion of the words: " unless at the end of that period the General Assembly decides otherwise."

RESOLUTION OF THE GENERAL ASSEMBLY OF THE UNITED NATIONS ORGANISATION ON THE DISPOSAL OF THE FORMER ITALIAN COLONIES.

A.

The General Assembly.

In accordance with Annexe XI, paragraph 3, of the Treaty of Peace with Italy, 1947, whereby the Powers concerned have agreed to accept the recommendation of the General Assembly on the disposal of the former Italian Colonies, and to take appropriate measures for giving effect to it,

Having taken note of the report of the Four Power Commission of Investigation, having heard spokesmen of organisations representing substantial sections of opinion in the territories concerned, and having taken into consideration the wishes and welfare of the inhabitants of the territories, the interests of peace and security, the views of the interested Governments and the relevant provisions of the Charter,

A. With respect to Libya, recommends:

1. That Libya, comprising Cyrenaica, Tripolitania and the Fezzan, shall be constituted an independent and sovereign State;

2. This independence shall become effective as soon as possible and in any case not later than January 1, 1952;

3. That a constitution for Libya, including the form of the government, be determined by representatives of the inhabitants of Cyrenaica, Tripolitania and the Fezzan meeting and consulting together in a National Assembly;

4. That, for the purpose of assisting the people of Libya in the formulation of the constitution and the establishment of an independent government, there shall be a United Nations Commissioner in Libya appointed by the General Assembly and a Council to aid and advise him;

5. The United Nations Commissioner, in consultation with the Council, shall submit to the Secretary-General an annual report and such other special reports as he may consider necessary. To these reports shall be added any memorandum or document that the United Nations Commissioner or a member of the Council may wish to bring to the attention of the United Nations;

6. That the Council shall consist of ten members, namely:—

(a) One representative nominated by the Government of each of the following countries: Egypt, France, Italy, Pakistan, the United Kingdom and the United States of America;

(b) One representative of the people of each of the three regions of Libya and one representative of the minorities in Libya;

7. That the United Nations Commissioner shall appoint the representatives mentioned in 6 (b), after consultation with the administering Powers, the representatives of the Governments mentioned in paragraph 6 (a), leading personalities and representatives of political parties and organisations in the territories concerned;

8. That, in the discharge of his functions, the United Nations Commissioner shall consult and be guided by the advice of the members of his Council, it being understood that he may call upon different members to advise him in respect of different regions or different subjects;

9. That the United Nations Commissioner may offer suggestions to the General Assembly, to the Economic and Social Council and to the Secretary-General as to the measures that the United Nations might adopt during the transitional period regarding the economic and social problems of Libya;

10. That the administering Powers in co-operation with the Commissioner:—

(a) Initiate immediately all necessary steps for the transfer of power to a duly constituted independent Government;

(b) Administer the territories for the purpose of assisting in the establishment of Libyan unity and independence, co-operate in the formation of governmental institutions and co-ordinate their activities to this end;

(c) Make an annual report to the General Assembly on the steps taken to implement these recommendations;

11. That upon its establishment as an independent State, Libya be admitted to the United Nations in accordance with Article 4 of the Charter.

B. With respect to Italian Somaliland, recommends:—

1. That Italian Somaliland shall be an independent sovereign State;

2. This independence shall become effective at the end of ten years from the date of the approval of the Trusteeship Agreement by the General Assembly;

3. During the period mentioned in paragraph 2, Italian Somaliland shall be placed under the International Trusteeship System with Italy as the Administering Authority;

4. The Administering Authority shall be aided and advised by an Advisory Council composed of representatives of the following States: **Colombia, Egypt and the Philippines.** The headquarters of the Advisory Council shall be Mogadishu. The precise terms of reference of the Advisory Council shall be determined in the Trusteeship Agreement and shall include a provision whereby the Trusteeship Council shall invite the States members of the Advisory Council, if they are not members of the Trusteeship Council, to participate without vote in the debates of the Trusteeship Council on any question relating to this territory;

5. That the Trusteeship Council negotiate with the Administering Authority the draft of a Trusteeship Agreement for submission to the General Assembly if possible during the present session, and in any case not later than the fifth regular session;

6. That the Trusteeship Agreement shall include an Annexe containing a declaration of constitutional principles guaranteeing the rights of the inhabitants of Somaliland and providing for institutions designed to ensure the inauguration, development and subsequent establishment of full self-government;

7. That in the drafting of this declaration the Trusteeship Council and the Administering Authority be guided by the annexed text proposed by the Indian **delegation;**

8. That Italy be invited to undertake provisional administration of the territory

    (a) At a time and pursuant to arrangements for the orderly transfer of administration agreed upon between Italy and the United Kingdom, after the Trusteeship Council and Italy have negotiated the Trusteeship Agreement;

    (b) On condition that Italy gives an undertaking to administer the territory in accordance with the provisions of the Charter relating to the International Trusteeship System and to the Trusteeship Agreement pending approval by the General Assembly of a Trusteeship Agreement for the territory;

9. That the Advisory Council shall commence the discharge of its functions when the Italian Government begins its provisional administration.

C. With respect to Eritrea, recommends:

1. That a Commission consisting of representatives of not more than five Member States, as follows, **Burma, Guatemala, Norway, Pakistan and the Union of South Africa,** be established to ascertain more fully the wishes and the best means of promoting the welfare of the inhabitants of Eritrea, to examine the question of the disposal of Eritrea, and to prepare a report for the General Assembly, together with such proposal or proposals as it may deem appropriate for the solution of the problem of Eritrea;

2. In carrying out its responsibilities the Commission shall ascertain all the relevant facts including written or oral information from the present administering Power, from representatives of the population of the territory, including minorities, from Governments, and from such organisations and individuals as it may deem necessary. In particular, the Commission shall take into account:

    (a) The wishes and welfare of the inhabitants of Eritrea, including the views of the various racial, religious and political groups of the provinces of the territory and the capacity of the people for self-government;

    (b) The interests of peace and security in East Africa;

    (c) The rights and claims of Ethiopia, based on geographical, historical, ethnic or economic reasons, including in particular Ethiopia's legitimate need for adequate access to the sea;

3. In considering its proposals the Commission shall take into account the various suggestions for the disposal of Eritrea submitted during the fourth regular session of the General Assembly;

4. The Commission shall assemble at the headquarters of the United Nations as soon as possible. It shall travel to Eritrea, and may visit such other places as in its judgment may be necessary in carrying out its responsibilities. The Commission shall adopt its own rules of procedure. Its report and proposal, or proposals shall be communicated to the Secretary-General not later than June 15, 1950, for distribution to Member States, so as to enable final consideration during the fifth regular session of the General Assembly. The Interim Committee of the General Assembly shall consider the report and proposal, or proposals, of the Commission and report, with conclusions, to the fifth regular session of the General Assembly.

D. With respect to the above provisions:

1. **Invites** the Secretary-General to request the necessary facilities from the competent authorities of each of the States in whose territory it may be neccessary for the Commission of Eritrea to meet or travel;

2. **Authorises** the Secretary-General, in accordance with established practice;

(a) To arrange for the payment of an appropriate remuneration to the United Nations Commissioner in Libya;

(b) To reimburse the travelling and subsistence expenses of the members of the Council for Libya, of one representative from each Government represented on the Advisory Council for Somaliland and of one representative and one alternate from each Government represented on the Commission for Eritrea;

(c) To assign to the United Nations Commissioner in Libya, to the Advisory Council for Somaliland, and to the United Nations Commission for Eritrea such staff, and to provide such facilities as the Secretary-General may consider necessary to carry out the terms of the present resolution.

THE INDIAN ANNEXURE

The Trusteeship Council of U.N.O. and the Administering Authority of the Somaliland Trusteeship were instructed to be guided by this annexure in drafting the Declaration of Constitutional Principles provided for in section B, paragraph 6 (see section B, paragraph 7).

The following constitution shall be annexed to and form part of the trusteeship agreement for any of the former Italian colonies that may be placed under the International Trusteeship System:

1. The sovereignty of the Trust Territory shall be vested in its people, and shall be exercised on their behalf by the authorities and in the manner prescribed herein.

2. The executive authority of the Trust Territory shall be exercised by an Administrator appointed by the Administering Authority.

3. To assist him in the discharge of his functions the Administrator shall appoint a Council consisting of five representatives of the principal political parties or organisations in the Trust Territory.

4. In matters relating to defence and foreign affairs, the Administrator shall be responsible to, and carry out the directions of the United Nations, acting through its appropriate organs. In all other matters, the Administrator shall consult, and be guided by the advice of his Council.

5. The legislative authority of the Trust Territory shall normally be exercised by the Administrator, with the consent of his Council enlarged by such additional representatives of the people as the Administrator may summon for the purpose. In exceptional circumstances, the Administrator may, subject to the control of the United Nations acting through its appropriate organs, make and promulgate such ordinances as, in his opinion, the circumstances demand.

6. The judicial authority of the Trust Territory shall be excercised by a Supreme Court and courts subordinate thereto. The judges of the Supreme Court shall be appointed by the Administrator but shall hold office during good behaviour and shall not be removable except with the consent of the United Nations acting through its appropriate organs.

7. All the authorities of the Trust Territory shall, in the exercise of their respective functions, respect human rights and fundamental freedoms for all without distinction as to race, sex, language and religion.

8. The United Nations, acting through its appropriate organs, may:

(a) Make rules to supplement this constitution;

(b) Review the administration periodically and amend this constitution so as to establish the Trust Territory as an independent State within a period not exceeding five years.

B.

The **General Assembly,** to assist it in making the appointment of the United Nations Commissioner in Libya,

Decides that a Committee composed of:

> the President of the General Assembly, two of the Vice-Presidents of the General Assembly (Brazil and Pakistan), the Chairman of the First Committee, and the Chairman of the **Ad Hoc** Political Committee

shall nominate a candidate or, if no agreement can be reached, three candidates.

C.

The General Assembly,

Considering its recommendations regarding the disposal of the former Italian colonies,

Calls upon the Interim Committee of the General Assembly to study the procedure to be adopted to delimit the boundaries of the former Italian colonies, in so far as they are not already fixed by international agreement, and report with conclusions to the fifth regular session of the General Assembly.

XXII

DRAFTING THE ITALIAN TRUSTEESHIP AGREEMENT

On December 5th, 1949, Ato Aklilou, as Ethiopian Minister of Foreign Affairs, addressed a letter to the Secretary-General of the United Nations, affirming the right of Ethiopia, under Article 79 of the United Nations Charter, to participate, as " a State directly concerned," in the preparation and approval of the Trusteeship Agreement for the former Somaliland colony. This right had already been invoked on Ethiopia's behalf by the Ethiopian Delegation on 31st November, when the General Assembly voted to place the ex-colony under Italian Trusteeship. Ato Aklilou claimed that under Article 79, unless the "interested States" had agreed to the Trusteeship proposals, such proposals could not be brought before the United Nations Assembly for approval. He requested the Secretary-General to ensure the application of Ethiopia's right under Article 79.

The right thus claimed for Ethiopia was brushed aside on December 9th, 1949; the Trusteeship Council, in appointing a special Somaliland Committee to draft the Trusteeship Agreement, did not include Ethiopia. The members selected for this special Committee represented the Dominican Republic, France, Iraq, the Philippines, Britain, and the U.S.A. Representatives of Egypt and Colombia were invited to attend, without votes, as members of the Advisory Council for Somaliland appointed by the United Nations Assembly. The third member of the Advisory Council, the representative of the Philippines, as a member of the Trusteeship Council, had also been appointed a member of the Somaliland Committee, as noted above.

Representatives appointed by Italy were invited to take part in the work of the Committee and to negotiate on Italy's behalf.

An invitation to send observers without the right to vote was also addressed to Ethiopia. This invitation was accepted, " pending a decision of Ethiopia's claim to participate with the right to vote." " it being understood that the fact of sending and receiving such observers " should " in no way prejudice the respective positions and legal rights and reservations involved."

The Ethiopian delegates, Ato Abbebe Retta, Ethiopian Ambassador in London, and Ato Tesfaie Teguegne, Minister in Paris and

Brussels, with Mr. John Spencer, therefore attended in that capacity. A representative of India, on account of the Indian annexure presented at Lake Success, was invited to attend such sessions of the Committee as dealt with the general principles of the constitution of the Trust Territory. A representative of the International Labour Office requested permission to attend, and after some discussion was permitted to do so, on the urgent appeal of the Philippines representative.*

The Committee were empowered to hear representatives of local parties and organisations in Somaliland, but no such representatives appeared, as is recorded by the Rapporteur of the Committee. Did this mean that the Somali Youth League, which had passionately opposed the Italian return, was unwilling to offer suggestions concerning a Trusteeship established in defiance of its desire? Did it indicate that none of the local population considered it wise to intervene now, in view of possible Italian action against persons who had made themselves prominent in such a matter? Did it mean that former backers were no longer willing to meet expenses? The Committee were left to draw what inference might seem most probable to them, in view of the strange fact that Somali organisations which had journeyed to Lake Success repeatedly did not appear at Geneva.

The Committee for Somaliland assembled at Geneva on January 9th, 1950, in the splendid white marble Palace of Peace, surrounded by spacious gardens, on the shore of beautiful Lake Léman. Erected to house the now defunct League of Nations, its foundations had been laid amid a chorus of Governments and peoples expressing hopes, so confident as to be well nigh certainty, in the attainment of Permanent Peace and International Justice assured by the Covenant of the League. Before the Palace of Peace was yet completed those hopes had begun to fade.

When at last they were opened for the use of the League and its organs, what cruel betrayals those magnificent halls witnessed! What intrigues were conducted in the luxuriously upholstered antechambers and corridors, where the emissaries of Mussolini developed the plots hatched in Rome and Berlin for the investment and conquest of Ethiopia, and the subsequent destruction of the League and its Charter. To-day a mere auxiliary European rendezvous for the subsidiary bodies of the United Nations based in America, this palace of the dead League was a mortuary of broken faith to the Ethiopian representatives now attending the Somaliland Committee. Again, as in 1934, 1935 and onward, they

---

* The Somaliland Committee was composed as follows: Chairman Mr. Henriques-Urena; Dominican Republic, Mr. Franco y Franco; France, Mr. Jurgensen; Iraq, Mr. Jamali; Philippines, Mr. Ingles; Britain, Mr. Fletcher-Cooke; U.S.A., Mr. Sayre; Columbia (without vote), Mr. Gabriel; Egypt (without vote), Mr. Amin Rostem; Ethiopia (without vote), Mr. Retta, Mr. Tesfaie Teguegne, Mr. John Spencer (Advisor to Ministry of Foreign Affairs); Italy (without vote), Mr. Brusasca, Mr. Cerulli; International Labour Office, Mr. Gavin (without vote).

had come to uphold their national cause against Italy, their old aggressor, who was advancing as before by no title of right or justice.

The Somaliland Committee were instructed by the Trusteeship Council to take into account a draft Trustee Agreement which the Italian Government had already submitted through the Secretary-General of the United Nations. Mr. Ingles, of the Philippines delegation also submitted a draft which was far in advance of that presented by Italy, and which influenced for the better the final draft adopted by the Committee. The Iraqi and Dominican Republic delegations also submitted suggestions.

ITALY'S OWN DRAFT AGREEMENT

The Italian Government had compiled their draft with some attention to precedent, having incorporated certain features common to other Trusteeship Agreements. In particular, there were references to the Charter of the United Nations, and provisions to prevent discrimination against nationals of any State member of the United Nations.* The Advisory Council already appointed by the United Nations was accepted as part of the scheme.

Only part of the Italian draft was finally incorporated in the text adopted by the Committee. The Italian draft is of special importance because, in some measure, it reveals the intentions of the Italian Government towards the territory and people they were again permitted to rule. It has therefore been reproduced in full at the end of this chapter, together with the draft finally adopted by the Trusteeship Council. In the annex appended to the Italian draft, ostensibly "for the purpose of solemnly guaranteeing the rights of the inhabitants of the territory and ensuring the realization of the objectives of trusteeship," one would expect to find the best the Italian Government was prepared to offer, thus indicating a breach with the Fascist past. A study of this annex, however, reveals that each guarantee contains a qualifying phrase. The cumulative effect of these several qualifications appears to indicate the obstinate intention to continue the Administration much as it was in former times, and to maintain the old racial restrictions. In the following clauses extracted from the Italian draft annex, the qualifying phrase has been *italicised*:

" The Administering Authority shall guarantee to all inhabitants of the Territory full civil and political rights *consistent, as regards the exercise of such rights, with the progressive political, social, economic and educational development of the inhabitants, and with the advancement of traditional institutions towards democratic representative systems.*"

It will be seen that the exercise of full civil rights was only to be assured in so far as they might be considered by the Italian

---

* Some escape clauses provided, however, that such equality of treatment must not prejudice the political, social and economic advancement of the inhabitants or prevent the establishment of monopolies.

Authority as consistent with the political, social, economic and educational development of the inhabitants. The people, because they are poor, uneducated, and socially ostracised, would consequently suffer reduction of civil rights. That appears to be the plain English of these phrases.

The annex continues:

> "In particular it shall guarantee to them: the preservation of their personal and successional status, and the civil advancement of the same: individual liberty, *which may be restricted only in the cases and according to the regulations established by law*: the inviolability of the domicile, *to which the competent authority may have access only by virtue of the law and in the manner prescribed in accordance with local customs;* the recognition and the guarantee of property, *except in cases of expropriation carried out in the general interest, and after payment of just compensation, and subject to other restrictions established by law.*"

As the "law" would consist only of the arbitrary decision of a foreign Administration appointed by a foreign Government, all these phrases are meaningless, and offer no reliable guarantee. The Italian Administration would be the judge as to whether expropriation of Somali native lands would be "in the general interest," and of what could be considered "just compensation."

> "The free exercise of professions, trades and economic activities, *in accordance with local customs, and in conformity with such regulations as shall be enacted*. The right to compete for public employment, *in conformity with regulations which shall be enacted, and which shall determine the particular conditions of eligibility*."

Having regard to the italicised passages, the above paragraph, so far from assuring freedoms, would in fact deny them. It indicates the intention of the Italian Government to restrict the exercise of professions and economic activities and the right to compete for public employment by regulations not to be inserted in the Agreement and as yet undisclosed. Great perspicacity is not required to discern that the regulations of the Italian Administrator would prove to be designed to protect Italian supremacy in trades and professions and economic activities. The frequently introduced term, "local customs," would afford no sort of amelioration, local customs having been built up during half-a century of Italian rule: the term "local customs," might be applied as aptly to Italian "racist" restrictions as to Muslim or other indigenous traditions. In any case, the progressive Somali to-day is not willing to assent to being obliged to follow the trade of his father simply because the Italian Administrator so orders. The right to emigrate and to travel might involve liberty to obtain education abroad and to escape from political persecution; the Italian draft offered:

> "The right to emigrate and to travel, *subject to the restrictions determined by law, for health and security reasons.*"

The closed frontier of Mussolini's regime, during which, even in Italy, men and women risked their lives in escaping abroad, is here suggested.

As a gesture, but no more than a gesture, towards the self-government for which the Italian Trusteeship was ostensibly to prepare the people of the Territory, the Italian draft proposed advisory councils appointed by the Italian Administrator:

"In particular, the Administering Authority shall provide, at its central, regional and municipal organs, for the establishment of appropriate *advisory councils, appointed by the Administrator, in which at least one half of the members shall be native inhabitants.* The functions of the councils shall be defined by law."

Again the qualifying phrases are *italicised*. The proposed councils, being advisory, could exercise no power. The members of these councils, being appointed by the Administrator, could not effectively oppose his policy; if they did, he could replace them.

In any case, the Italian draft suggests that these advisory, nominated bodies would be largely composed of Italians. The functions of these councils were to be defined, not by the Trusteeship Agreement, but by the Italian Administrator whose decrees would be "law." In short, the Administration foreshadowed by these regulations, despite some liberal phrases, suggests the strong probability that the Trusteeship Administration was intended by the Italian Government to differ little from the old Colonial regime.

It must further be noticed that, as subsequently agreed by the Committee, the term "indigenous person" is to include any person born in the Territory who accepts citizenship of the Territory. Among the Italian colonists a younger generation has, of course, grown up in half-a-century. These people could, and doubtless would, obtain citizenship of the Territory when arrangements for citizenship had been made, perhaps retaining also Italian citizenship.

Reference to the text of the Draft Agreement adopted by the Trusteeship Council for submission to the United Nations (which is appended to this chapter) reveals that it contains numerous improvements upon the Italian proposals. Full civil rights are guaranteed by the Trusteeship Council's draft, the provisions concerning political rights have been rendered more generous, but the exercise of professions, trades and occupations, and the right to compete for public employment, as well as liberty to emigrate, are still regrettably restricted. The old racist discrimination may still operate without difficulty under the terms of the draft Trusteeship Agreement.

ATTEMPT TO AVOID TEN YEARS LIMIT TO ITALY'S TRUSTEESHIP

A most unpleasant feature of the Italian draft was the omission of all mention that the United Nations had decided the Somaliland ex-colony should become an independent State, and had specifically limited to ten years the period during which the territory should remain under Italian Trusteeship. Had these material factors been omitted from the Trusteeship Agreement, the Italians would doubtless have claimed at the end of the ten years that the Trusteeship granted to them had not been restricted to any term, and that, consequently, they were no more bound to withdraw from the Administration at any specific time than any other Administering Power from any other territory.

The Committee for Somaliland proposed, and the Trusteeship Council subsequently accepted for the draft Trusteeship Agreement, the following precise declaration that the former colony was to become an independent sovereign State, and that Italian Trusteeship would terminate in ten years:

"*The territory shall be an independent and sovereign State: its independence shall become effective at the end of ten years* from the date of approval of the Trusteeship Agreement by the General Assembly."

THE PERILOUS BOUNDARY
ITALIAN ATTEMPT TO ADVANCE AGAIN TO WAL WAL

In Article I of the Italian draft, an attempt was also made to include under Italian Trusteeship the territory in the Ethiopian Ogaden which Italian forces had invaded at the time of the Wal Wal incident of 1934, and also the adjacent areas into which Italian forces subsequently advanced in the same year. Here are the passages in the Italian draft:

"The boundaries of the territory are those resulting from the Treaties and conventions concluded between the Italian Government and the adjoining States, *with effect from 1st January,* 1935."

The mischief is in the last phrase. It must be emphasised that despite Ethiopia's appeal to the League of Nations, and the Arbitration which resulted from the intervention of the League of Nations, the Italians did not withdraw from Wal Wal and the other parts of the Ethiopian Ogaden they had invaded, but clung on there during the many months of discussion which led up to their major invasion of Ethiopia, in 1935. Thus, on the 1st of January, 1935, Italy was a good deal more than sixty miles inside Ethiopia.

The Italian penetration through the Ethiopian Ogaden to Wal Wal; the Italian attack on the Ethiopian escort to an Anglo-Ethiopian Boundary Commission which arrived at that spot in 1944; the subsequent claim by Italy, the trespasser and aggressor, to be indemnified for the " incident "; the Italian assertion that the Ethiopian territory which Italian troops had invaded belonged to Italy, in defiance of the evidence of Italian and other maps; Ethiopia's appeal to the League of Nations; the arbitration, discussions and delays under the auspices of the League of Nations, which extended month after month, and under cover of which the

Italians mustered and equipped their forces for the invasion condemned by 51 States, members of the League of Nations, are described in Chapter X. The map facing page 99, by which the Italian penetration into Ethiopian territory at the time of Wal Wal may be traced, should be consulted here.

It was unpleasantly and most sadly ominous that in 1950, despite the lessons of Italy's defeat in the second World War, despite the fall of Mussolini and his Dictatorship, to find representatives of Signor De Gasperi's Government, there at Geneva, endeavouring to enclose under Italian Administration the very Ethiopian territory which the forces of Mussolini had invaded and used in 1934 as a preliminary base of aggression for the war of conquest in 1935.

It was still more disquieting that this amazing attempt was not immediately and fully repudiated by all the representatives of other nations present. Instead, there was a curious obtuseness, a hazy lack of knowledge in some quarters, or maybe a failure to remember the issues and the incidents which succeeded each other in a tragic sequence of crime and martyrdom in the years 1934 to 1941.

Being invited by members of the Somaliland Committee to express the Ethiopian view on the boundary, Mr. Abbebe Retta repeated with unequivocal directness the statement already made by the Ethiopian Delegation at the United Nations:

"*Ethiopia does not accept the idea of Italian Trusteeship of the former Italian Somaliland Colony, which spells a threat to Ethiopia, who has reserved her right under Article 79 of the Charter of the United Nations.*

"*Coming to the provisions of the first article of the Draft Agreement, I wish to indicate the significance to Ethiopia of the last phrase, which refers to the boundaries of 1935. Concerning that date, it is wise to remember the incident of 1934 at Wal Wal, in the very area under consideration, which led to the Italian full-scale invasion of Ethiopia in 1935 and 1936. The lack of a fixed boundary in that region served as the occasion for the incident. The Ethiopians view the establishing of Italy in that neighbourhood with misgivings. They cannot consider such a design with equanimity.*"

In response to the Italian representative's assertion that an agreement had existed with respect to the boundary, Mr. Retta replied, speaking for his country, that whatever agreement might have existed before 1935 had been rendered invalid by Italy's aggression. Therefore there existed no valid agreement. He added that to import into the Trusteeship Agreement any past international agreement concerning the ex-colony by which Italy had benefited would " contradict the words provisionally agreed to for inclusion in the Preamble, namely ' Italy renounces all right and title to the Italian territorial possessions in Africa."

The Dominican representative proposed that an annex, including a map showing the demarcation line of 1908, should be annexed to the Agreement. (See map facing page 22).

Mr. Fletcher-Cooke (United Kingdom) stated that in the opinion of his delegation, the boundary question was not one for consideration by that Committee, or by the Trusteeship Council. The question of the frontiers of former Italian Somaliland was " extremely difficult "; the line of demarcation between the territory of Ethiopia and the territory at present occupied by the British Military Administration was a provisional one, and would not necessarily coincide with the boundary of the Trust territory. He invited the Ethiopian representative to give further expression to his views on this thorny matter.

Thus appealed to, Mr. Retta admitted the existence of a temporary Agreement between the Ethiopian and United Kingdom Governments, a matter which, he declared, was subject to settlement only between the two Governments.

DISCLOSURE THAT BRITISH FORCES STILL OCCUPY ETHIOPIAN TERRITORY

These observations by the Ethiopian and British representatives drew world attention to the fact that the final withdrawal of British forces from Ethiopian territory, which it was generally believed had been fully effected in 1948, was not in fact complete. The *Manchester Guardian* now published an article by its Diplomatic Correspondent, containing the following inaccurate statement, and a map corresponding to that below :—

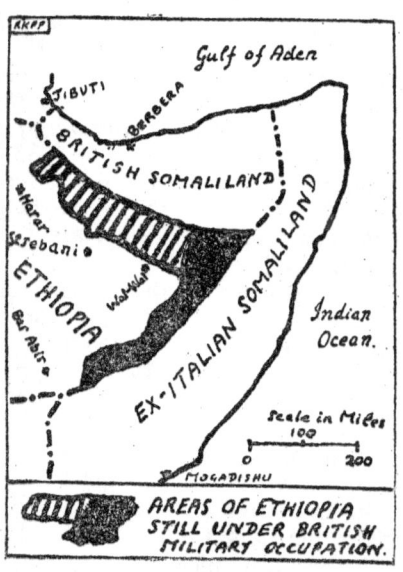

Map of Somaliland showing the Ethiopian territory still occupied by British Forces.

"*In 1948 Britain signed a protocol with the Ethiopian Government (the terms of which for some mysterious reason have never been made public), in which we agreed to withdraw from the Ogaden into Italian Somaliland to a boundary temporarily fixed without prejudice to the ultimate validity of another undemarcated boundary of 1908, to the west of which it ran for almost its entire length.*"

The " undemarcated boundary of 1908 " referred to by the *Manchester Guardian* was that embodied in the Treaty concluded between the Emperor Menelik II of Ethiopia and the Italian Government, after long and difficult negotiations, as described in Chapter II. The text of the Treaty appears at the end of this chapter. The frontier line fixed by the Treaty was marked, by agreement between the two parties, on a map of the period, as approximately indicated on the map facing page 26, which is based on that published in "Storia Diplomatica dell' Etiopia Durante il Regno de Menelik II,"* a volume compiled from official Italian sources.

During the discussions of the United Nations Assembly on the future of the Somaliland ex-colony, the British representative had claimed that for about 200 miles the border of the ex-colony was marked on the map and demarcated on the ground. From that point to where the frontier meets the British Somaliland border, not merely was the frontier not demarcated on the ground, but "it did not really exist, except as an imaginary line on any map."† The line on the map was nevertheless sufficiently exact and definite, if honourably respected, to preclude the large deviation of the Italians into Ethiopian territory involved by their advance to Wal Wal. The bulge into Ethiopian territory by the British Military Administration, which was the subject of the agreement referred to by the *Manchester Guardian*, was admittedly also a deviation from the "imaginary line on a map" of 1908, but the area which remained under British occupation through the latter deviation did not extend nearly so far into Ethiopian territory as Wal Wal. On the other hand the British were occupying Ethiopian territory, as the map reveals, but not, as in Italy's case, as a base for aggression!

In view of the above facts, it was obviously the duty of the British Government to withdraw to the 1908 boundary line before handing the ex-colony to Italian Trusteeship. The Ethiopian territory occupied by British forces by agreement with the Ethiopian Government could not rightly be transferred in defiance of Ethiopian wishes to a third party—least of all to the repeated aggressor, Italy, against whose return to her seaboard Ethiopia did not cease to protest. To evacuate Ethiopian territory to Italy would have been unjust on the part of the British Government. Moreover, unless a further Italian aggression were now to be openly condoned by the United Nations, the frontier could be no other than the line marked on the map by the 1908 Treaty; it could only safely be demarcated and the Ethiopian frontier posts established by British and Ethiopian agency, before British forces would hand over the former colony to Italian control. That haste in effecting the demarcation would now be necessary, and that the demarcation would take place in an atmosphere of tension and distress was due to nine years of procrastination by the London Government.

That the territory on Ethiopia's southern border, including the Indian Ocean coast, was to be handed back to Italy was a cruel

---

* Storia Diplomatica dell' Etiopia Durante il Regno di Menelik II, by Carlo Rossetti, Società Tipografico-Editrice-Nazionale, Torino, 1910.

† Committee for former Italian colony of Somaliland, Working Paper prepared by the Secretariat, T/AC.18/L2, 9th January, 1950.

blow to the much-wronged Ethiopian people. To leave them to struggle for their frontier with powerfully equipped and ruthlessly commanded Italian forces on the spot, and with truculent Italian diplomacy in Rome, would thrust them into a position of immediate peril.

The Geneva negotiations were befogged by the absence of a clear statement of British intentions concerning the frontier. Mr. Sayre (United States) appeared to know nothing of the history of Italy's aggressions on that frontier, or of Italian threats and browbeating of the Ethiopian Government, accompanied by further armed frontier violations which had vitiated all attempts to promote negotiations between the two States in 1934. As though all that had never happened, the American delegate declared the frontier must be settled between the Italian Administration of Somaliland and Ethiopia—a solution which would inevitably have cast Ethiopia back to the dilemma she faced at Wal Wal.

Through the mouth of the Rome correspondent of the *Manchester Guardian,* Italian diplomacy was meanwhile urging that until the United Nations had finally demarcated the frontier it would be an act of " generosity and statesmanship " on the part of the Ethiopian Government to agree to a " provisional " Italian occupation of the Ethiopian area in which British troops had remained! It would have been an act of great generosity certainly, but scarcely of statesmanship! Possession is always nine points of the law. There would have been no going back from any line occupied by the Italian forces, except by forcible eviction or the immediate certainty of such action.

Signor Cerulli, the Italian observer, argued that "in the interests of peace," a provisional administrative demarcation line should be adopted. Mr. Fletcher-Cooke agreed there must be a demarcation line, but argued that the Committee for Italian Somaliland was not competent to delimit the frontier; this task had already been entrusted to the Interim Committee of the United Nations. It was for the Governments of Ethiopia and of Somaliland "to settle their common frontier, and for the Interim Committee to co-operate with the two parties in delimiting the boundary as fixed." Thus, like his colleague of the United States, the British representative proposed to cast the frontier issue back to Ethiopia, for direct negotiation with Italy! In case of dispute—just as it was in 1935—Italy would have the Indian Ocean ports in her possession, through which she could import arms to enforce her will, whilst Ethiopia—still land-locked by European colonies—would only be permitted to bring in what the military Powers which encompass her might choose to allow. Their dictum again might prevent her from importing means of self-defence.

Terrible anxiety and sense of desertion must have been painfully intensified in the minds of the horrified Ethiopian Observers by the British Representative's further remarks, thus reported by the Secretariat:

"*Mr. Fletcher-Cooke (United Kingdom), returning to the text of Article I, provisionally adopted at the previous meeting, stated that he felt uneasy at the use of the phrase ' existing international agreements,' since, at a later stage, the point might possibly be raised that one or more of the agreements concerned might have been in some way abrogated by events during the past fifty years. He would be interested to hear the view of the Committee, and particularly of the representatives of Italy and Ethiopia on that point, and noted that the Italian draft, presumably foreseeing such a difficuly, had quoted a definite date. While that provided a possible solution to the delimitation, another alternative would be to insert a form of words, such as ' prior to the outbreak of hostilities in the area under consideration,' and there might be others."*

Mr. Fletcher-Cooke's suggestion appeared to be that the violation of a frontier fixed by International agreement might be recognised as an " abrogation by events," which might now permit the establishment of a new frontier, to the advantage of the aggressor. His proposal to put the frontier where it was at the outbreak of hostilities was tantamount of course to the Italian claim to have it as Italy stood at Wal Wal in 1935 !

(Was the spirit of the Conference of Berlin, where the European Powers agreed to ratify each other's African annexations, provided these did not infringe their own prior annexations, still alive despite the passage of two world wars for freedom and democracy and the successive creation of the League of Nations and the United Nations?)

Perhaps the Ethiopian Observers conveyed to Mr. Fletcher-Cooke some inkling of the dismay his utterance had caused them, or perhaps further reflection revealed to him its unwisdom. However it may have been, he subsequently notified the Secretariat that he wished to delete the words " prior to the outbreak of hostilities."

Mr. Cerulli suggested that as the date, January 1st, 1935, " had not proved agreeable to Ethiopia," January 1st, 1932, might be substituted. He was aware that even this earlier date could be turned to Italian advantage, for even in 1932 the Italians were already pushing across the frontier into the Ethiopian Ogaden, their native irregulars—the so-called " banda "*—under control of Italian officers. Ethiopian forces repeatedly had to expel them!

The Somaliland Committee wisely refrained from adopting either of these dates; the final form of Article I of the draft Trusteeship Agreement reads:—

"*The territory to which this Agreement applies is the territory formerly known as Italian Somaliland, hereinafter called*

---

* " The *bandas* were instructed simply to encroach, in obedience to the policy then reigning in Rome . . Great Britain enjoyed the same experience in the Sudan, at much the same time, when an Italian column occupied the oases of Kufra, far outside their frontier and within ours." From " Caesar in Abyssinia " by G. L. Steer (Hodder and Stoughton, 1936) p.p. 15, 16.

the Territory, bounded by the Somaliland Protectorate, Ethiopia, Kenya, the Gulf of Aden, and the Indian Ocean. Its boundaries shall be those fixed by International agreement, and in so far as they are not already delimited, shall be delimited in accordance with a procedure approved by the General Assembly."

"THE DISCUSSIONS HAVE NOT CHANGED THE POSITION; ETHIOPIA RESERVES HER RIGHT"

The Ethiopian Observer repeatedly expressed dissatisfaction: he could not accept the view that Italian aggression or penetration could determine the frontier of Ethiopia: he could not do other than repeat Ethiopia's refusal to assent to the return of her aggressor. On January 18th he protested:

"The discussions have not changed the position of the Ethiopian Government, as stated in their telegram to the Secretary General of the United Nations of December 31st, 1949, regarding the boundaries of Ethiopia; they do not feel they are in a position to agree with the provisions contained in the Draft Agreement.

"My statement in regard to the Treaty concerning the boundary between Ethiopia and former Italian Somaliland means that Ethiopia reserves her right in regard to the decision reached by this Committee. I wish to make it clear that I have not committed, and I cannot commit my Government in advance.

"The Ethiopian representatives are here, without being in the capacity of delegates, not being able to take part, or share in the proceedings. For the Ethiopian Government, the time has not yet come to give a considered view regarding the whole matter, and I must reiterate my Government's attitude regarding the boundary.

"I must reiterate again one point with regard to the understanding which exists between the Administering Authority in former Italian Somaliland and my Government. As I have already stated, that is a matter between the two Governments."

The British representative rejoined that in view of the Ethiopian observer's reservations, he also reserved the right of the British Delegation to revert to the matter again at a later stage.

The Italian determination to advance the border further into Ethiopia, if possible, was again revealed by Mr. Cerulli under cover of expressions of desire to serve the interests of the Somali people. He asked that the following statement on behalf of the Italian observer be added to the Report:

"On the question of boundaries, I have already explained the position of my Government. Our task in that question, and indeed in any future negotiation, shall be only in accordance with the aim of the Trusteeship we are accepting, the best

protection of the interests of the Somali people. The boundary between the future Somali independent State and Ethiopia shall be delimited in such a way as to ensure peaceful relationships between Somalia and Ethiopia. In that spirit, I associate myself with our distinguished colleague from the United Kingdom, whose reservations may be considered as done by the Italian delegate too."

THE FRONTIER AGAIN

The frontier question was obliquely raised again by the proposal:

"*The Administering Authority undertakes to maintain the application of any international agreements already existing.*"

Signor Cerulli, lynx-eyed for all chances to advance the border, proposed to substitute "*any international agreements which are at present in force in the territory.*" That possibly might be held to negate any specific undertaking by Italy to maintain the frontier Treaty she made with Emperor Menelik, because, British forces having sprawled across the border, the argument might be hazarded that the 1908 Treaty was no longer "in force."

The words Cerulli proposed were accepted immediately, but this phrase, thus slipped into the Trusteeship Agreement by the Italian observer, in a clause not referring to the boundary could scarcely effect his intention; an appeal to the International Court would assuredly sustain the 1908 Treaty, to which Italy was not merely a consenting but an urgently demanding party.

AIR, NAVAL, MILITARY AND POLICE FORCES

The forces which Italy would establish in Somaliland were, of course, intimately connected with Ethiopia's anxieties concerning her national security, now acutely aroused by the return of her old aggressor. The Italian draft Trusteeship Agreement claimed for Italy: "*Power to establish in the Territory whatever military, naval and air installations are necessary for the defence of the Territory, to maintain its own armed forces, and to raise volunteer contingents.*"

The Philippines draft, on the other hand, expressly declared that: "*unless authorised by the United Nations, acting through its appropriate organs, the Administering Authority shall not establish naval, military and air bases, or erect fortifications in the territory, or station and employ its own armed forces in the territory.*"

Moreover, the Philippines draft proposed only to give the Administering Authority power "to make use of voluntary forces, facilities and assistance from the Trust territory." If the Administering Authority desired to recruit police from outside the territory, the maximum strength of the whole police force must be subject to approval by the Trusteeship Council.

The proposals of the Philippines delegate were in fact based on the Charter of the United Nations, which authorises for Territories under Trusteeship only volunteer forces, facilities and assistance from the Territory itself (Article 84).

The provision in the United Nations Charter referred to in the above clause is Article 84, Chapter XII, of the Charter, which is devoted to the " International Trusteeship System. Article 84 reads:

> "*It shall be the duty of the Administering Authority to ensure that the Trust territory shall play its part in the maintenance of international peace and security. To this end, the Administering Authority may make use of volunteer forces, facilities and assistance from the Trust Territory in carrying out the obligations towards the Security Council undertaken in this regard by the Administering Authority, as well as for local defence and the maintenance of law and order within the Trust Territory.*"

It may be recalled here that under the Charter of the League of Nations, Colonies of States defeated in the first World War, 1814/18, were distributed among certain of the victors under Mandate, and that Article 22, Clause 6, of the League Charter expressly prohibited in the Mandated Territories " the establishment of fortifications, military and naval bases, and military training of the natives for other than police purposes and the defence of territory."

The Charter of the United Nations thus followed that of the League in restricting the forces to be used in the ex-enemy dependent territories to local volunteers.*

Mr. Jamali (Iraq) urged that voluteer forces recruited in the territory would suffice for legitimate needs. The question of external defence was unimportant, as there was no danger of aggression from the countries bordering the Territory; and it was not of strategic importance. " In the unlikely eventuality of an external threat to the Trust territory, the Administering Authority should appeal to the Trusteeship Council for special powers to

---

* Only if the Trusteeship Territory be designated " a strategic area," which thus far has not been done, may other than local volunteer forces be authorised. The whole question of the defence and administration of the Territory would then become extremely complicated. Responsibility for it then would be transferred from the General Assembly to the Security Council. The Security Council could, if it so desired, refer back the political, economic, social and educational matters to the Trusteeship Council, " subject to the Trusteeship agreements." In other words, these matters would go back to the original Administering Authority. In the case of Members of the United Nations, this provision would be subject to Agreements made under Article 43 of the Charter between the Security Council and members of the United Nations. Presumably, the Security Council would be responsible for defence, and as Italy is not a Member of the United Nations, it would appear the defence of the territory would appertain to the Security Council.

meet it, or call on the Security Council to take the necessary measures to defend the territory."

The French and Dominican Representatives, however, supported Italy's demand for freedom to establish military, naval and air bases, on the plea that "as a result of developments in the international situation," a threat to the security of Somaliland might arise.

STRANGE DICTUM THAT TO LEAVE DEFENCE TO UNITED NATIONS IS TO HAVE NO DEFENCE

Mr. Fletcher-Cooke uttered an amazing statement, which if publicly made on the authority of the British Foreign Secretary would assuredly evoke consternation in Britain, and also in the world at large. It amounted to a denial of all hope of collective security, and of any possibility of action by the United Nations to protect peoples threatened by aggression. Dissenting from the plea of the Iraqi representative that the Italian Government must be prevented from building up powerful armed forces in Somaliland, whereby they would have the power to threaten Ethiopian security, Mr. Fletcher-Cooke is reported as follows by the Summary Record* of the Somaliland Committee:

"*Mr. Fletcher-Cooke (United Kingdom) pointed out that if the Territory were to enjoy the normal privileges of an independent nation ten years hence, it would be necessary for the Administering Authority to lay at least the foundations of a system of national defence. To leave the question of the defence of the territory to either the Trusteeship Council or the Security Council would, in practice, mean that the Territory would have no defence at all.*"

If this declaration of Mr. Fletcher-Cooke may be taken to represent the true position, the whole basis of the United Nations Organisation, and of the Security Council which was "to put teeth in it," has disappeared. Instead of a strong fortress of defence against aggression there is merely a façade, in presence of which any unoffending small nation may be invaded and conquered and its very name erased from the world map, as happened to Ethiopia in 1936.

One would ask whether the statement of Mr. Fletcher-Cooke represents the views of His Majesty's Government in the United Kingdom, and of the Powers who are members of the Security Council. How does it accord with the war in Korea?

---

* United Nations Trusteeship Council, T/AC.18/SR.6. Committee for Somaliland, Summary Record of the Sixth Meeting, 12th January, 1950, page 4.

ITALIAN OBLIGATION TO CONSULT ADVISORY COUNCIL BEFORE ESTABLISHING FORCES

Mr. Retta, the Ethiopian Observer, suggested that it might be reassuring to the people of Somaliland if reference were made in the Trusteeship Agreement to "some sort of limit to the forces the Administering Authority might use for external defence purposes, and if mention were made in the Article of the need for consultation in relation to such forces on Italy's part." He pointed out that "the distinction between forces used for internal order and those used for external defence was rather artificial."

Mr. Cerulli, the Italian Observer, responded unctuously to these points. It was the task of Italy, he said, to prepare the former Colony for independence; to a certain extent this would be a liability, but it would prove an asset from one point of view, by providing Italy with an opportunity of demonstrating her friendship for the countries bordering on her territory.

"*Italy gave the formal undertaking,*" he said, "*that she had no intention of sending a larger metropolitan force to the Trust territory than that at present maintained by the British Military Administration in Somaliland; indeed, Italy would be happy to manage with less.*

"*His Government was also in agreement with the principle that any measure for defence of the Territory should be taken after consultation with the Advisory Council.*"*

Mr. Sayre (United States of America) commended this utterance, and, on his suggestion, it was agreed that the Italian Administering Authority must consult the Advisory Council before establishing installations for the defence of the territory, and even in regard to the progressive development of the Somali forces. The relevant article thus reads:

ARTICLE 6.

"*The Administering Authority may maintain police forces and raise volunteer contingents for the maintenance of peace and good order in the Territory.*

"*The Administering Authority, after consultation with the Advisory Council, may establish installations, and take all measures in the Territory, including the progressive development of Somali defence forces.*"

Unfortunately, the "consultation" thus stipulated with the Advisory Council might be merely perfunctory, since the Council was advisory and totally without power. The Philippines delegate made another effort to introduce more effective restraint, by the stipulation:

"*in matters relating to defence and foreign affairs, the Administrator shall be responsible to, and shall carry out the directions of the United Nations, acting through its appropriate organs.*"

---

* United Nations Trusteeship Council, T/AC.18/SR.6. 12th January Committee for Somaliland. Summary Record of Sixth Meeting, page 4.

Mr. Jurgensen (France) interposed to insist that the Italian Administrator would not be responsible to the United Nations, but to the Italian Government, the Administering Authority of the Territory. Mr. Sayre (United States) supported the French view. Mr. Ingles, of the Philippines, protested against this conception; he urged that if the Administering Authority could obtain sanction to establish installations and station troops by consultation with **the Advisory Council**, the United Nations ought to be in a position to supervise the measures adopted by Italy as a result of such consultation. Therefore, he urged the embodiment in the Trusteeship Agreement of the following stipulation contained in the Indian Annexure, which the Somaliland Committee had been instructed to use as a guide in framing the Agreement:

"In matters relating to defence and foreign affairs, the Administrator shall be responsible to, and carry out the directions of, the United Nations, acting through its appropriate organs."

Mr. Cerulli (Italy) rose at once to object. The responsibility of Italy, the Administering Authority, would have no meaning, he declared, without direct responsibility for defence. Moreover, the whole matter had been settled by giving Italy the power to establish bases and to station troops, after consultation with the Advisory Council.

That many on the Committee did not conceive such consultation would or should impose any effective restraint upon Italian action became increasingly clear as the discussion developed. Mr. Fletcher-Cooke (United Kingdom) supported Mr. Cerulli's objection to any interference with Italy's freedom in these matters. He argued that although the United Nations General Assembly had thought some supervision of the Administering Authority's defence measures desirable, "there could be no question of any such initiative by the United Nations in this matter, as was proposed by the Indian text." He added another most amazing dictum:

"*Nor should the United Nations at the present stage of development of international security, seek to give a non-member State directions which it was not yet competent to give to member States.*"

Here was evinced a complete refusal to recognise the fact that the Agreement under discussion related to the conditions by which an aggressor State, compelled by the Peace Treaty to renounce all right and title to the territory in question, should be permitted to resume control of it. To assert that safeguards which had not been imposed in the case of law-abiding member States should not, therefore, be imposed in respect of the aggressor, was a folly so wilfully perverse as to merit designation as a crime against the neighbours whom the aggressor had invaded, and against the principles of international peace. This amazing dictum had not been applied in Germany's case.

The fact that the return of Italy to Somaliland was an exceedingly precarious experiment, fraught with strong probabilities of injury to the Somali population and to Ethiopia, was most unfortunately ignored.

Mr. Jamali (Iraq) vainly joined the Philippines in endeavouring to make Italy responsible to the United Nations for the defence and foreign affairs of the Somaliland Territory, and to impose the obligation to carry out the directions of the appropriate United Nations organs. The Colonial Powers were determined to keep these matters out of the General Assembly. Mr. Jurgensen (France) was insistent to transfer the vital questions of defence and foreign affairs to the more lenient control of the Trusteeship Council, where fully half the membership consisting of fellow Administering Authorities, jealous for their prerogatives, would oppose any interference with those of their Italian colleague, except in the most extreme case. Though no harsh judgment of Italy's actions was to be anticipated from the Trusteeship Council, the United States and Dominican representatives deprecated any specific mention that Italy would be responsible to the Trusteeship Council in matters relating to foreign affairs and defence: the matter could be taken for granted. Mr. Cerulli grasped at Mr. Fletcher-Cooke's dictum that the obligations of Italy under the Trusteeship Agreement, because she was not yet admitted to the United Nations, should be slighter than those imposed on member States. Mr. Cerulli was prepared, however, on behalf of the Italian Government, to give the general undertaking to observe the provisions of the United Nations Charter which his Government had given in applying for membership of the United Nations, and acceptance of which was a condition of admission to the United Nations Organisation. These ingenious efforts to escape even a mention of the lenient supervision of the Trusteeship Council in relation to defence and foreign affairs, did not succeed; the following clause was inserted into the annex to the Trusteeship Agreement embodying Constitutional Principles:

ARTICLE 6 (ANNEX)

"*In matters relating to defence and foreign affairs, as in other matters, the Administering Authority shall be accountable to the Trusteeship Council, and shall take into account any recommendations which the Council may see fit to make.*"

Regrettable subterfuges, it will be observed, have been employed to give Italy a dangerously free hand to build up armaments in Somaliland and to impose obstacles tending to prevent information concerning aggression from that base being swiftly laid before the United Nations.

Nevertheless it must be emphasised that there is adequate authority in the Charter of the United Nations Organisation, and adequate collective power among the member States, to defeat aggression by Italy if the Governments concerned are so resolved. If aggression is again permitted to develop and to succeed, it will not be for lack of means, but for lack of will to prevent it.

FUNCTIONS OF THE ADVISORY COUNCIL

Article 6 of the Trusteeship Agreement stipulated, as we have seen, that only after consultation with the Advisory Council, consisting of Egypt, Colombia, and the Philippines, might Italy establish military installations and take defence measures. Yet such consultation could impose no real check upon Italian action. The Advisory Council was a body totally without power, as was repeatedly emphasised, both at Lake Success and during the Geneva Trusteeship negotiations. Its establishment had been a concession to the humanitarian and democratic sentiments held by some of the delegations at the United Nations, and by world public opinion, but the determined resistance of Governments responsible for the administration of Trust territories to any interference with their own freedom of action by the United Nations caused them to deny to the Advisory Council for Somaliland any effective authority. If a Council appointed by the United Nations were given power to interfere in Italy's Trusteeship Administration, or even to make an adverse report on it, a precedent might be established for interference with other Administering Authorities in other Trust territories. Consequently, Italy had the support of other Administering Authorities in restricting the powers of the Advisory Council.

The Philippines draft was taken as the basis of discussion when considering the functions of the Advisory Council. The proposal that the Italian Administrator should seek the advice of the Advisory Council concerning the annual budget of the territory, was immediately opposed by Mr. Cerulli, on Italy's behalf. Supported by France and the Dominican Republic, he easily obtained agreement that budgetary matters must be outside the sphere of the Advisory Council. The Council would not be permitted even to offer comments and recommendations regarding the scope and incidence of taxation, on the proportion of the revenue to be raised from the Somalis, the Italians and others, respectively, or on what proportion should be spent on Education, Public Health and other amenities in the interests of the native people, as compared with police, armaments, and any such public works as would mainly conduce to the prosperity of the Italian colonists. The Advisory Council being prohibited from advising on budgetary matters, their advice on economic development, education and other vital matters would tend to lack realism.

Even more astonishing was the defeat of a Philippines proposal that the Advisory Council should be free to "visit public institutions" and "to travel throughout the Trust territory," which was rejected in response to a protest from Mr. Cerulli, supported by Britain, France, and the Dominican Republic, that the Advisory Council was "not a supervisory body."

Mr. Sayre (United States) would have permitted reports by the Advisory Council to be included in the Annual Reports of the Administering Authority to the General Assembly of the United

Nations, but Signor Cerulli protested against having written into the Trusteeship Agreement any right of the Advisory Council to submit reports to the United Nations, even as proposed, through the agency of the Italian Authority. The Dominican Republic supported the Italian view, which was maintained also by the representatives of France and Britain, who, as Administering Powers would not brook interference in the Trust territories under their own authority. The Committee being evenly divided, Mr. Cerulli appealed to his friend of the Dominican Republic to hold informal conversations to arrange a compromise.

It was subsequently found possible to agree that when, periodically, the Trusteeship Council would be discussing the Somaliland Trust territory, the Advisory Council might attend such discussions and submit to the Trusteeship Council either oral or written reports. There would be nothing rapid in such an arrangement, however urgent the need of action might be.

Thus the Advisory Council were not only precluded from any power of interference with the Italian Administrator's freedom of action, they were also prevented from reporting direct to the United Nations any developments in the Trust Territory which they might consider harmful. Mr. Inglis, of the Philippines, protested in vain that without direct access to the General Assembly, the Advisory Council could not properly discharge their functions.

It was constantly ignored that in view of Italy's past record and the bitter opposition of the local people, Italian Trusteeship was a hazardous experiment. At the 1946 Paris Conference on the Peace Treaties, M. Bidault, the French representative, had said that none knew better than the French Government how Italy had misgoverned her colonies, both by using them as bases for attacking her neighbours and by maltreating the native peoples. Nevertheless, he advocated giving Italy " another chance " in Africa, but only under very " severe " restrictions and guarantees. The need for such precautions appeared to be little perceived by the French Delegation during the Geneva discussions of the Italian Trusteeship Agreement.

PROGRESS TOWARDS SELF-GOVERNMENT

Article 3 of the draft Trusteeship Agreement provides:

"*the Administering Authority shall foster the development of free political institutions and promote the development of the inhabitants of the Territory towards independence, and to this end shall give the inhabitants of the Territory a progressively increasing participation in the various organs of Government.*"

How does the Trusteeship Agreement provide for practical application of this article?

The only provision which the draft Trusteeship Agreement makes for any sort of participation in the administration is a consultative " Territorial Council," appointed by the Italian

Administrator. This provision will be found in Article 4 of the annex to the draft Agreement, which reads:

"*The Administrator shall appoint a Territorial Council composed of inhabitants of the territory and representative of its people.*"

Discussion of the practical measures for progressive self-government by the natives rapidly disclosed that the Italian Government had no intention of allowing even a purely consultative council, although nominated by the Italian Governor, to be composed wholly, or even mainly, of the indigenous people of the territory. The Italian draft for the Trusteeship Agreement proposed the appointment by the Administrator of a number of "appropriate advisory councils," central, regional and municipal, the functions of which were to be "defined by law"—the law of the Italian Administering Authority to be produced subsequently. For these Councils, with as yet undefined powers, the Italians proposed "at least one half the members shall be native inhabitants."

Even this proportion, however, is not definitely assured to the native people in the draft Agreement, as finally adopted for ratification by the United Nations.

Mr. Sayre (United States) proposed that at least half the members of the Territorial Council should be "indigenous inhabitants of the Territory." Mr. Jamali (Iraq) argued that the Council should be composed wholly of indigenous inhabitants. Mr. Cerulli, on behalf of the Italian Government, declared it would be "premature and impracticable to set up a council wholly composed of indigenous inhabitants" who lacked experience of administrative and financial matters and of parliamentary methods. Eventually it was agreed that the Territorial Council should represent all sections of the population, both indigenous and non-indigenous, no relative proportions being fixed. The selection of these representatives was left to the unfettered choice of the Italian Administrator. The Italian Government would thus have full power to decide whether the Territorial Council would be mainly an Italian assembly, dominated by the Italian colonists, and whether it would permit any free and genuine expression of opinion by the native people, the true indigenous population of the Territory. The fact that all its members would be appointed by the Governor would rule out any strong and sustained opposition to Italian official policy. Any persistent opponent would obviously be removed.

It is noteworthy that in general the draft Trusteeship Agreement and its annex refer broadly to the "inhabitants of the Territory"; only in the articles providing against alienation of land and natural resources and in one of the clauses relating to education is the term "*indigenous*" introduced. On the basis of the discussion, it may be assumed that when the words "persons" or "population" are used without the qualification *indigenous*, the intention is to include the Italians, and perhaps also the Arabs, Indians and other non-indigenous residents.

The Territorial Council established by the Agreement is consultative, and therefore without power. It might, however, be a valuable focus for the opinion of the people, if it were truly representative. Though powerless to act, it might be the means of directing popular influence upon the Administration if it were a freely elected representative body. Even though appointed, it might voice native popular opinion to some extent, or, on the other hand, it might be used as a means of misrepresenting majority opinion and desires. The character of the Territorial Council would largely depend on that of the Administrator, still more on the policy imposed upon him by the Italian Government.

The relationship of the Territorial Council to the Administrator was defined by the annex to the draft Trusteeship Agreement as follows:

"*In all matters other than defence and foreign affairs, the Administrator shall consult the Territorial Council.*

"*The legislative authority shall normally be exercised by the Administrator, after consultation with the Territorial Council, until such time as an elective legislature has been established.*

"*In exceptional circumstances, the Administrator may, after consultation with the Advisory Council, make and promulgate such ordinances as in his opinion the circumstances demand. These ordinances shall be laid before the Territorial Council as soon as may be practicable, and the Administering Authority shall include an account of all such ordinances in its annual report to the Trusteeship Council.*"

It should be observed that no stipulation was made concerning the meetings of the Council; it was left entirely to the Administrator to decide whether the Council should be a body sitting almost continuously, as Parliaments normally do, thus being able to offer constant suggestions upon administrative matters, or whether it would be summoned only occasionally to receive a statement by the Administrator.

The draft Agreement stipulates that the Administrator shall consult the Territorial Council in all matters other than defence and foreign affairs. The nature of such consultation was undefined; whether it would affect the character of the Administration or exercise any influence on the actions of the Administrator, whether it would enable the indigenous people to gain experience in administrative matters, was entirely problematical.

Yet these were urgent and vital questions, if the ostensible purpose of the Trusteeship—preparation of the indigenous population to administer their homeland in ten years time—were to be genuinely effected. One might hazard the opinion that the period of Trusteeship under Italy would be time lost for the indigenous people, in so far as concerned opportunities to gain administrative experience. It would be for the Trusteeship Council to insist upon "progressively increasing participation" in administration by the native population; but such insistence by the Trusteeship Council presupposes an assumption of compulsive authority which that body has not hitherto exercised, and which the terms of the draft Agreement and the discussion thereon, clearly indicate the majority of its members are unwilling for it to exercise. It presupposes an entirely new attitude towards the functions of the Trusteeship Council by the Administering Powers, who comprise half its members, and have hitherto resisted any sort of dictation by the United Nations Organisation and its auxiliary institutions.

TRANSFORMATION OF TRUSTEESHIP INTO SELF-GOVERNMENT

Nevertheless, in accordance with the decision of the United Nations Assembly, Article 24 of the draft Trusteeship Agreement provides that the Agreement must terminate ten years after its approval by the General Assembly of the United Nations; the Territory must then become an independent sovereign State.

In preparation for this event, Article 25 stipulates that eighteen months before the expiration of the Agreement, Italy must present to the Trusteeship Council " a plan for the orderly transfer of all functions of Government to a duly constituted independent Government of the Territory."

These must prove the most important articles in the Agreement, if actually carried out by the Italian Administering Authority (assuming that the Italian Trusteeship will last ten years, a matter on which certain indications evoke some doubts).

Assuming the Trusteeship were maintained for eight-and-a-half years, the following crucial questions would present themselves, and would become increasingly urgent during the final eighteen months of the ten-year term:

1. *Would the Italian Government voluntarily prepare to withdraw and present the necessary plan for the termination of their functions at the end of the term, without being subjected to political or military compulsion?*

2. *If the Italian Government proved unwilling to fulfil their undertakings, would the General Assembly of the United Nations effectively insist upon the termination of Italian Trusteeship and apply such moral or material pressure as might be necessary to secure obedience?*

3. *If at the end of eight-and-a-half years, the Italian Government signified willingness to withdraw from Somaliland and presented to the United Nations a plan for the future Government of the Territory, would this plan be worthy of acceptance by the United Nations? Would it confer genuine self-government on the native people? Or would it merely offer effective government by the Italian minority, the native people remaining still in subjection to them?*

Long before the termination of eight-and-a-half years, the actions of the Italian Government will reveal whether their intention is eventually to leave the people of Somaliland to the enjoyment of self-government and of such sustenance and comfort as they are able to obtain from the natural resources of their land, or whether, on the other hand, the intention of the old conquerors is to maintain their grip on the territory.

LAND AND NATURAL RESOURCES

Proposals to prevent the further passing into foreign hands, to the detriment of the Somali people, of the land and natural resources of their territory, were made by the United States, the Dominican Republic, and the Philippines representatives. The United Kingdom representative, Mr. Fletcher-Cooke, expressed his concurrence in this benevolent plan, "subject to the agreement of the Italian delegation." This reservation of the British representative must have struck the Somalis very sadly, if they were informed of it. It was gravely out of harmony with the efforts made by the British Military Administration to afford the Somalis opportunities to cultivate some of the fertile arable land on modern lines, which have been noted in previous pages, and the hopes thereby raised. The eagerness with which Somalis had taken to the use of agricultural machinery, whenever they had had the opportunity, was remarked by the Four Power Commission of 1947.

Signor Brusasca (Italian Under-Secretary for the Colonies) objected to the above-mentioned safeguards, and urged instead the Italian draft proposal, which stated vaguely that the Administering Authority should "consider native law and custom and safeguard the interests of the native population," that land and natural resources should not be transferred "from native private persons to non-natives without the consent of the competent authorities." Since hitherto the Italian "competent authorities" had systematically transferred land and natural resources from the native people to the Italian colonists, these clauses were obviously far from adequate. Signor Brusasca, however, thought that "any further restrictions might impede the economic development of the territory"!

All this discussion had the fictitious quality of locking the stable door after the horse is stolen, as the Italian observers, more adequately informed than the members of the Committee concerning the Territory, were fully aware. They, of course, knew that the native people had been evicted from the best of the land long before and that all the natural resources believed to be capable of yielding a profit had passed into Italian hands. Nevertheless, zeal for Italian interests caused Signor Cerulli to follow up the argument of his chief by warning the Committee against what he termed "the social and economic dangers inherent in a total prohibition of land transfers." To avoid restrictions he adduced a number of excuses: the Somalis will not cultivate, the cultivating natives are more primitive and uncivilised, the Italians had to encourage Arab immigration* to get the soil tilled, because of the unwillingness and incapacity of the native people. Moreover, Italy intends to spend ten milliards of lire a year on the territory.

The Italian colonists had probably experienced some anxiety lest provisions to restore land to the native people might be included in the Trusteeship Agreement. Some of the colonists had regretted their neglect to comply with the amazingly easy terms the Italian Government had offered them to transform the leases they had acquired so cheaply into full private ownership. Their relief must have been great when they discovered that the draft Trusteeship Agreement, as finally adopted by the Trusteeship Council for ratification by the United Nations, did not interfere with existing leases, or impose any time limit or other restrictions upon new leases. Article 15 provides:

"*The Administering Authority shall not, without the consent in each case of a majority of the members of the Territorial Council, permit the acquisition by non-indigenous persons, or by companies or associations controlled by such persons, of any rights over land in the territory save on lease for a period to be determined by law.*

"*In cases involving the alienation to non-indigenous persons . . . . of areas of agricultural land in excess of one thousand acres, the Administering Authority shall also ask in advance the advice of the Advisory Council.*

"*The Administering Authority shall include in its annual report to the Trusteeship Council a detailed account of such alienations.*"

Article 15 further stipulated that natural resources might not be acquired by non-indigenous persons " save on lease or concession for a period to be determined by law."

With Italy as Administrator and legislator these stipulations might not impose any great obstacle should the Administrator be desirous of selling an estate to any of his compatriots. The draft Agreement does not oblige him to adopt the advice of the Advisory Council, only to ask it, and even this only applies to agricultural land covering more than 1,000 acres. In the Territorial Council he must obtain the consent of a two-thirds majority, but its members are appointed by him and nothing in the Agreement precludes him from appointing a majority of Italians to that body. Ample facilities will doubtless be provided for Italian nationals to secure for themselves anything further they wish of the land and natural resources, the best of which they have already acquired.

---

* The Arabs, who were old residents of the coast before the Italian advent, own only 15,000 hectares of land divided among 1,016 owners; the Italians own 72,842 hectares divided among 175 owners, as well as 94,407 State and 35,037 hectares of Church lands.

Building land within the municipal area of Mogadishu was specially excluded from the above provisions; it might " be disposed of in accordance with regulations prescribed by law "—Italian law!

Mr. Retta, the Ethiopian observer, being invited to express his opinion, emphasised that very great mistakes had been made in Africa by the sale of communal land to private individuals. He naturally viewed the problem from a standpoint which differed considerably from that of Mr. Cerulli, the Italian official, zealously serving Italian imperial interests.

ITALIANS BORN IN THE TERRITORY CLASSED AS "INDIGENOUS PERSONS"

A sadly erroneous definition of the term " indigenous person " was unfortunately given by the Philippines representative and was subsequently attached to the record, as follows, " indigenous persons are those who are born in the Territory, permanently reside therein, and accept citizenship of the Territory." Not unnaturally, the representative of Italy concurred in this definition; numerous sons and daughters of the Italian Colonists would at once be able to qualify as indigenous persons under this definition. There would be nothing to debar them possessing Italian citizenship in addition to that of the Somaliland Territory. Many Italians abroad possess dual citizenship. The above definition of indigenous persons destroys any safeguards designed to prevent the buying up of African lands by Italian or other foreign colonists to the detriment of the native population.

Yet it must also be emphasised that leases and concessions of natural resources, under the draft Agreement approved by the Trusteeship Council, would be granted by the Italian Administrator to the veriest newcomers on lease, without time limit and without consulting either Advisory or Territorial Council; also that the best of all the territory is known to contain had already been seized by the Italian occupiers. Whether this grievous disinheritance of the native people would be allowed to continue after the termination of Italian Trusteeship is open to doubt. The disposal of the land and natural resources of the territory would be a vital test of Italian intentions. The attitude of the Italian negotiators at Geneva afforded no reason to anticipate that ruthless expropriation would be mitigated except by the paucity of the resources still remaining to be annexed.

EDUCATION

The Education provided for the Somalis would be a crucial test of the Trusteeship; it would quickly reveal whether the Italian Government, the local Administrator and the Colonists were prepared to take serious measures to assist the Somalis to rise from their subject position and to become qualified to administer their territory; and, what was more, whether the Italian Government were prepared to provide substantial means for Somali education. The draft Trusteeship Agreement declared that "national independence," with due respect for freedom and democracy, could only be based on "education in the broadest sense."

The Iraqi delegation had prepared a detailed scheme entailing free education at all levels, and instructing the Administering Authority to select annually an adequate number of the best students, without social or political discrimination, for higher academic and technical studies in Egypt, Europe and America, and to train others for modern agriculture, business and crafts, to recruit university graduates from abroad for the Somaliland Secondary Schools until such teachers could be trained in adequate numbers among the indigenous population. Education was to be free at all levels.

These proposals recalled to the Ethiopian observers the programme being carried out by their own Education Department, but the Italian representative opposed the inclusion of such matters in the Trusteeship Agreement. He endeavoured to avoid any definite commitments. It would be enough, Mr. Cerulli stated, to mention the obligation to provide "a system of Public Education." He warned the Committee against drawing up "detailed legislation." The Committee should "omit any reference to illiteracy,"* because there was difficulty in deciding what languages† should be taught in the schools. Thus far, the Arabic script was the only form of writing which had been taught in the Territory, as the Somali language was not generally written. Mr. Cerulli omitted to recall that the Italian Government had forbidden the use of the script, "Osmania,"‡ which had been invented for the Somali language, and had officially discouraged teaching Somalis to read and write Italian.§ The duration of the elementary school course, the languages to be taught, and all such matters, Mr. Cerulli declared, were too technical for the Committee and should be referred to experts.

In view of exalted Italian fascist and post-fascist claims to have conferred great cultural benefits upon African peoples, it may appear startling that the Italian representative thus freely admitting his Government had hitherto evolved no policy whatsoever concerning either the languages to be taught in the schools, or the duration of the elementary school course, in a territory which had lain for half-a-century under Italian rule. This revelation was not, however, surprising to the grave Ethiopian observers. They knew that under Fascism it had been fashionable to propound as scientific truth in pseudo-learned journals and congresses, as well as in the

---

* United Nations Trusteeship Council Committee for Italian Somaliland. Summary Record T/AC. 18/SR.4. 11th January, 1950. Page 7

† United Nations Trusteeship Council Committee for Italian Somaliland. Summary Record T/AC. 18/SR.13. 16th January, 1950. Pages 7-9.

‡ See page 230 above.

§ See "Directions for the Education of Natives" by General Nasi. Pages 213-14 above.

more popular and blatant, that the African races are incapable of assimilating European culture, and that attempts to impart higher education to them must inevitably prove harmful to themselves and to Society. Nevertheless, Mr. Cerulli's efforts to avoid definite educational commitments must be ascribed to his devotion to Italian interests rather than to solicitude for the Somalis. He received some support in his struggle from Mr. Fletcher-Cooke, who urged the Trusteeship Council would be better able to consider the problem of education successfully after receiving full information about the Territory from the annual reports of the Italian Administering Authority, and expressed the conviction that " the Italian Government would not fail to carry out fundamental policies."

Nevertheless, the final result of the discussion on education was embodied in Article 4 of the draft Trusteeship Agreement. As will be seen by reference to the full text at the end of this chapter, it contained an undertaking by the Administering Authority to provide a system of public education, elementary, secondary and vocational, elementary education at least being free of charge; also to establish institutions for teacher training, and to facilitate higher and professional education and cultural advancement in every way. All this, however, was subject to the qualification " as rapidly as possible," which might cover very considerable delay.

The Administering Authority further undertook to provide that " an adequate number of students from among the indigenous population receive university or professional education outside the Territory, so as to ensure that sufficient qualified personnel will be available when the Territory becomes a sovereign State."

The last provision in particular would appear generous, save for the agreement in the discussion that anyone born in the Territory, of whatever racial origin, may be considered " an indigenous person," provided he or she accepts citizenship of the Territory. Unless the United Nations subsequently decide that the term " indigenous " must be confined to the native people of the Territory, or safeguard the educational rights of the native people by some other means, there would be nothing to prevent the restriction to Italians of the promised facilities for higher education.

Despite Mr. Cerulli's efforts, an undertaking by the Administering Authority " to combat illiteracy by all possible means " was included in the draft Agreement. His protest against what would appear on the face of it to be the least of these undertakings might be likened to straining at a gnat and swallowing a camel, but it is obviously the case that if the population remain illiterate, and elementary education be not provided, there can be no question of sending " qualified students " to universities abroad. The absence, or extreme fewness, of indigenous persons qualified to receive university or professional education might even be urged at the close of the ten years' period as a reason for revising the Agreement, in order to secure a considerable, or even an indefinite prolongation of the Italian occupation. Moreover, one must again recall that the term "indigenous" was defined as covering Europeans or other persons of foreign extraction born in the Territory—a matter of which we shall hear further.

The provision that the Administering Authority should provide instruction regarding "the activities of the United Nations and its organs, the basic objectives of the International Trusteeship System, and the Declaration of Human Rights" was also sound, but as in the case of the other stipulations, there was the basic question whether these highly ethical proposals would be translated into practical application by the Administering Authority.

It may be recalled that when the League of Nations was established, the Covenant of the League was a subject of instruction in the schools of Britain and also of other countries, and was regarded with utmost faith and enthusiasm by the teachers and their pupils. When Italy violated the Covenant by invading Ethiopia, the schools were a most active influence in demanding that the full power of the League should be used to frustrate the aggressor. The failure of the Great Powers of the League to honour their pledges under the Covenant was a source of bitter disappointment in the schools, particularly of Britain. Teachers expressed deep resentment that the principles they had been officially urged to propagate had been disregarded. The teaching of the principles of human equality in Somaliland schools would have important results.

"RIGHTS AND DUTIES OF CITIZENSHIP"

Not without a touch of humour, the Philippines draft had incorporated, under the title "The Rights and Duties of Citizens," a portion of the new Italian Constitution adopted since the fall of Fascism. In these passages were included obligations: to establish a minimum age for paid employment, in order to abolish child labour, with the right of the people to form trade unions and other organisations, and to exercise freedom of speech, press, and public meetings, and freedom of movement, which it was stipulated must not be restricted for political reasons; also the right of all adult men and women to vote and to be elected, with other rights and safeguards generally existing in democratic countries.

The Italians in their own draft had proposed to give to the Administrator the right to apply Italian law, if and when he considered appropriate. The Philippines proposal to take over for application in Somaliland the constitutional rights and duties of citizens embodied in the Italian constitution was, however, strongly opposed by the Italian Observer; he protested there would be "practical difficulties in the way of applying to Somalis measures suitable for Italians."

It should be recalled that democratic rights and institutions had never existed, even for the Italians, in the Italian Colonies.

The question whether a few major elementary democratic rights could be accorded to a people who were ostensibly to have complete self-government after a brief ten years was obstinately debated; no agreement could be obtained; the discussion was adjourned. On its resumption, the Philippines representative struggled to get into the Agreement, pledges against imprisonment for debt, torture and cruel punishment, except in cases prescribed by the military laws of war, free access to the Courts, the right of everyone charged with a penal offence to be presumed innocent until found guilty according to law in public trial, with guarantees for his or her defence.

The Italian observer resisted these safeguards: " it would not be proper to include them," he declared, " either in Muslim or in Italian law "; to do so would be " an insult to both Muslims and Italians." His annoyance may be comprehended by recalling the fact that the elementary principles of justice in a civilised community, which the Philippines delegate was seeking to establish, had been notoriously lacking in Italian administration during the still so recent Fascist period. But was that the only reason Mr. Cerulli objected to the precise obligations being inserted in the Agreement? Mr. Ingles, of the Philippines, stoutly defended his proposals; he had taken them from the Italian Constitution; they would give the inhabitants of the territory " welcome guarantees." The French representative attempted to calm the troubled atmosphere by declaring that he would have had no objection to the Philippines proposals, but he was confident that the present democratic Italian authorities would in fact apply all the provisions the Philippines desired. Mr. Ingles eventually secured the inclusion in the annex to the Agreement of the following words:

" *The Administering Authority, in accordance with the principles laid down in its own Constitution and legislation, shall guarantee to all inhabitants of the Territory human rights and fundamental freedoms, and full equality before the law, without distinction as to race, sex, language, political opinion or religion.*"

PROHIBITION OF SLAVERY, FORCED LABOUR, AND CONTROL OF ARMS TRAFFIC

The Philippines draft contained also a clause, which had occurred in agreements concerning Africa since the Brussels Act, prohibiting slavery and the slave trade, forced labour, child marriage and child barter, and directing control of the traffic in arms, drugs and spirituous liquors. Mr. Cerulli resisted this clause also with an assumption of wounded feelings, arguing that Italy was already bound by international engagements to prohibit such practices. The ugly fact that slavery and forced labour were found flourishing under Italian government in the Somaliland Territory by the British forces who took control at the time of the Italian defeat in 1941 was politely ignored by the Committee. Mr. Fletcher-Cooke tactfully suggested it would be undesirable " to risk offending the native population " by attributing to them practices which were unknown in the territory. A generous coat of whitewash was thus passed over Italy's sombre record.

Mr. Gavin, of the International Labour Office, whose request to attend had received an assent not unmixed with opposition, was doubtless accustomed to dealing with similar touchiness and similar subterfuges. He brushed aside excuses, urging that the proposed clause could involve no affront to the Administering Authority. He introduced an array of formal arguments: the Italian Government had ratified the international convention on forced labour in 1934, and in 1935 had applied it to their East Africa territories by legislation (sic!), which had been continued in force by the British Administration. Moreover, the text proposed by the Philippines was identical with that of a similar clause in the Trusteeship Agreement for Western Samoa, negotiated at a time when New Zealand, the Administering Authority, had already ratified the Forced Labour Convention. In view of these forceful arguments, the Committee accepted the clause. The Somaliland people would be able to appeal to it in the event of slavery and forced labour being reimposed, with what success remained to be seen.

*　*　*　*　*　*

On the morning of January 19th, 1950, when the labours of the Somaliland Committee were nearing completion, one of the two Ethiopian Observers, Ato Tesfaie Teguegn, the Ethiopian Minister in Paris and Brussels, was found dead at his bedside. He had been Director of the Ministry of Foreign Affairs in Addis Ababa when the incident of Wal Wal in 1934 cast its shadow over Ethiopian life, and had served through the anxious months which followed, leading up to the Italian invasion of 1935, the tragic war, and the entry of the forces of Marshal Badoglio into Addis Ababa on May 5th, 1936. Ato Tesfaie had been deported by the invaders to the grim penal island of Ponza, where hideously insanitary conditions, foul food, and water yet more foul, disease and sadistic cruelty combined in the destruction of their unfortunate victims. From this torrid devil's island in the Mediteranean, with a group of his compatriots he was removed to a primitive existence in the snows of the Italian Alps. As a sick man he was returned by his gaolers to Ethiopia in the penultimate stage of the Italian occupation, when the Duke of Aosta was making ineffectual efforts to tranquilise Ethiopia in preparation for Italy's approaching entry into World War II. Tranquility in Ethiopia was an essential prerequisite of successful Italian belligerency in Africa, as a catastrophic series of Italian reverses was subsequently to prove.

When Ethiopia was liberated, Ato Tesfaie, deeply shaken in health by the years of hardship, returned to the diplomatic service of his country. In 1941 he was appointed Minister to Cairo; in 1946 he was transferred to Paris, and later served also as Minister to Brussels. The trend of European policies concerning his country were thus clearly revealed to him. He had attended the Paris Conference on the Peace Treaties in 1946, and all the sessions of the

United Nations at which the future of the former colonies had been debated. From the heavy disappointment at Lake Success in December, 1949, when the Somaliland Trusteeship was given to Italy, and a decision on Eritrea was postponed, he had proceeded to Geneva, as an observer of the Trusteeship negotiations. To witness the progress of the aggressor, stage by stage, to the position from which the invasion of 1935 had been launched, had proved too great a strain for this Ethiopian patriot.

On account of Ato Tasfaie's death, his colleague, Ato Abebbe Retta, was unable to be present when the draft Trusteeship Agreement was approved by the Somaliland Committee. Ethiopia's protest against the return of her old aggressor was submitted in writing.

All the members of the United Nations Trusteeship Council, with representatives of the United Nations and of the Governments of the Powers, attended the funeral of the Ethiopian Minister, whose death in those crucial hours had made him the symbol of the agony of his people under the shadow of Italy's return to Africa. His coffin was draped in the flag of his nation, blazoned with the Lion of Judah, the symbol of his ancient people, and encircled by wreaths presented on behalf of Powers by whose international policies he had greatly suffered. The service was conducted at the Church of Notre Dame de Genève, according to the Roman Catholic rites; Ato Tesfaie had been initiated into the Roman Church during his boyhood when a scholar at the Church of the Alliance Française in Addis Ababa. He lies in the cemetery of the Chatelaine,* one of the numerous martyrs of an era of war and massacre whose mortal remains have been laid in Geneva soil.

ITALIAN AGREEMENT FOR SOMALILAND BEFORE THE UNITED NATIONS TRUSTEESHIP COUNCIL

When the draft agreement drawn up by the Somaliland Committee was laid before the Trusteeship Council,† the representatives

---

* No. 12,072 quartier 8. In Paris, on February 8, a memorial service for Ato Tesfaie Teguegne was held at the little Church of Notre-Dame de l'Assumption where he was wont to attend. The Papal Nuncio, Monseigneur Rocalli, Doyen of the Diplomatic Corps, officiated; the President of the French Republic, the French Prime Minister, the Minister of Foreign Affairs, and the Embassies and Ministries of the other Powers were represented in rendering these last obsequies to their Ethiopian diplomatic colleague.

† The Trusteeship Council was composed as follows: Australia, Mr. John D. L. Hood; Argentine, Ambassador Jeronimo Remorino; Belgium, Mr. Pierre Ryckmans; China, Mr. Shia Shun Liu; Dominican Republic, Ambassador Max Henriques Urena; France, Ambassador Roger Garreau; President of the Trusteeship Council; France, M. Henri Laurentie (Deputy Delegate); Iraq, Dr. Mohamed Fadhel Jamali (Permanent Delegate of Iraq to the United Nations); New Zealand, Mr. George Robert Laking; Philippines, Mr. José D. Ingles; United Kingdom, Sir Alan Burns; United States of America, Ambassador Francis B. Sayre; U.S.S.R., No delegate.

Observers were present from the United Nations Economic and Social Council (U.N.E.S.C.O.), the World Health Organisation (W.H.O.), the International Labour Office (I.L.O.), and from I.T.C.

of Italy and Ethiopia were again invited to take their seats at the Council table. Signor Cerulli now displayed, on Italy's behalf, a more assertive attitude, thrusting forward to take the lead. " I must insist," " our legal opinion," " we cannot accept," " the Italian Administering Authority cannot have its powers limited," were often on his lips.

To a large extent, this assertive attitude met a complaisant Council. Mr. Liu, the Chinese representative, in opening the discussion, praised what he termed " the conciliatory spirit " of the Italian delegation in the Somaliland Committee, which, Mr. Liu declared, had made possible the success of the Committee's deliberations. He recalled that ever since the question of the former Italian Colonies first arose the Chinese Government had advocated placing the Somaliland Territory under Italian Trusteeship during the period prior to independence. One may observe here that the Chinese Government would bitterly have opposed the placing of Formosa, or any part of China which Japan had formerly invaded, under Japanese Trusteeship. The glaringly similar character of Sino-Japanese and Ethiopico-Italian relations was, however, ignored by the then Chinese Government, for reasons best known to their own diplomatists.

The Trusteeship Council made but few alterations in the draft which the Somaliland Committee had prepared.

Nevertheless, the Committee's proposal to give the Trusteeship Council the right to make " special investigations and enquiries " in the Somaliland territory, though hitherto the Italian delegation had agreed to it, was struck out of the draft, on the motion of M. Ryckmans, the Belgian delegate, who continually supported Italian claims. Following this deletion, M. Ryckmans and Signor Cerulli endeavoured also to expunge the phrase obliging Italy to " render assistance " to the General Assembly, in such periodical visits as are made by delegations from the Trusteeship Council to all trust territories, and " *in such other arrangements as these bodies may make in accordance with the terms of the present Agreement.*" M. Ryckmans and Signor Cerulli, in the effort to ward off the possibility of additional investigation into Somaliland affairs, urged the rejection of the *italicised* words above. M. Ryckmans declared their inclusion would be interpreted as meaning that " to-morrow the General Assembly, or the fourth Committee, or the Trusteeship Council, may take a fantastic decision right outside the terms of the trusteeship agreement." This attack on the members and institutions of the United Nations does not seem to have found favour, the motion of M. Ryckmans failing to receive a majority.

INTERVENTION ON SECRETARY-GENERAL'S BEHALF

A sensation akin to consternation was caused by the unexpected intervention of Dr. Hoo, the Assistant Secretary-General of the United Nations Organisation, invested with the authority of the Secretary-General, Mr. Trygvie Lie. Dr. Hoo announced that when the draft Agreement prepared by the Somaliland Committee was reviewed at United Nations headquarters, it was found that provision shown to be necessary by experience of United Nations field Missions abroad had not been made for the Advisory Council in Somaliland and for their staff. The draft, he observed, contained no mention of the fact that the Advisory Council was an organ of the United Nations Organisation though the expenses of the Advisory Council would be borne on the Budget of the Organisation. The Organisation would require to place funds—at the least to open a banking account—in Somaliland, and might find it more economical to erect or purchase property than to rent it. Moreover, the United Nations would have archives in the Territory, and would use " codes, sealed pouches for correspondence, and couriers to take correspondence from Mogadishu to Lake Success." These archives, codes and pouches would not be the property of the members or staff of the Advisory Council; they would belong to the United Nations. The draft Trusteeship Agreement should be amended, Dr. Hoo declared, to provide for all these matters.

Moreover, the present draft failed to assure to the members of the Advisory Council full diplomatic privileges; it accorded to them only the privileges of the United Nations Convention on Privileges and Immunities, which were more restricted than diplomatic privileges. Moreover, the staff which the United Nations would provide for the Advisory Council—that is to say, the Secretariat—were also limited by the present draft to the terms of the Convention, which accord to the Secretariat more restricted privileges than to Members of the Council. Whilst the Convention on Privileges and Immunities was sufficient for conferences lasting a few weeks or months in the capitals of Member States, it was wholly insufficient, the Assistant Secretary-General declared, for field Missions of a diplomatic or political character which have to remain in a far-away territory—in this case for ten years.

The Delegate of Colombia, one of the members of the Somaliland Advisory Council, at once assented to the view of the Secretary-General which Dr. Hoo presented, and asked whether the Secretariat had a text prepared which could be immediately inserted in the draft.

The Italian observer and others were far from being thus compliant. Mr. Cerulli very bitterly opposed the demands of the Secretary-General, which would invest the Advisory Council with an importance most unwelcome to Italian views, and, still more objectionable, would maintain a direct and continuous contact between the Advisory Council and the United Nations, to avoid which the Italian Delegation had made strenuous, and hitherto successful, efforts. Had they not, in the Somaliland Committee, secured the rejection of the proposal to allow the Advisory Council to make direct reports to the United Nations? Had they not succeeded in getting that interloping body restricted to a mere expression of their views at the annual routine discussions by the Trusteeship

Council on the various territories under its control which they would be permitted to attend as observers without a vote when Somaliland came up for routine discussion? Had Italy not been favoured by the rejection of a proposal to give liberty to the Advisory Council to travel freely throughout Somaliland and to visit its institutions, on the ground that the Advisory Council was not a supervising body? Such decisions had been as incense to the sanctity of Italian authority, as meat and drink to Italian ambitions for imperial dignity and power. The demand of the Secretary-General to invest the Advisory Council with diplomatic authority and to tie up their utterances and observations, with Lake Success, by a Secretariat, archives, diplomatic correspondence pouches, and couriers, would lend to the Council what might prove a menacing and immediate importance and power of interference. To treat them as nonentities, to oust them into brief annual, biennial, or perhaps even more infrequent remarks, injected into crowded Trusteeship Council sessions, might prove impossible.

Mr. Cerulli had support from Britain, France and Italy for his protest that the United Nations Assembly had not invited Italy to set up an agency of the United Nations in Somaliland, that there would not be a Secretariat organ of the United Nations at Mogadishu. Members of the Advisory Council would need secretarial assistance, he conceded; they would choose such assistance either from persons of their own nationality in whom they had confidence, or if they so desired—Italy had no objection—from members of the Secretariat at Lake Success. These were personal matters; Italy raised no objection from " the legal standpoint " to any such arrangement, but, he insisted, " there will not be any secretariat organ."

Seeking innocuous and plausible reasons for relentless opposition to intervention by the United Nations in Somaliland, Cerulli urged: " What would be the purpose of increasing the staff of the Advisory Council, of setting up a kind of Ministry with their own officials, who in order to justify their presence would presumably ask information from us, so that we, the Administering Authority, would be obliged to set up a parallel bureaucratic organisation which would greatly increase our expenditure; it would be a wheel turning to no purpose—an excessive machinery."

The Assistant Secretary-General replied, with some severity: " The representative of Italy has interpreted the matter rather differently from the way in which we interpret such cases. He said there were three members of the Advisory Council and that each member would be able freely to choose his secretaries, to pick them where he wished, and if he wished, to pick them from the United Nations Secretariat. That is not the Secretariat's interpretation of the position regarding organs of the United Nations." The Advisory Council, Dr. Hoo continued, was an organ of the United Nations. The staff of the Advisory Council would be appointed by the Secretary-General, as provided by Resolution of the General Assembly; they would not be appointed by the three members of the Advisory Council. The representative of Italy suggested that privileges were being asked for the staff in order to send staff in great numbers; on the contrary the number would be kept to the minimum; proposals were being elaborated for credits for six staff members only. There was no relation between the numbers and privileges of the Secretariat. What was asked in the name of the Secretary-General was that the staff of the Advisory Council should receive the same privileges as members of the Secretariat on other visiting missions; "I only ask that the Italian Government should treat the members of the Secretariat as other Governments treat members of the Secretariat in analogous cases."

Replying to other members of the Trusteeship Council, Dr. Hoo said the representative of France, "with his well-known subtlety and acuity, had seen in the proposals of the Secretary-General the introduction of a new right, but in other Trusteeship agreements similar provisions are inconceivable, because we have not sent permanent missions to reside in other territories." To Sir Alan Burns, who had objected to endowing the Secretariat in Somaliland with greater privileges and immunities than they would enjoy in the United States, the Assistant Secretary-General replied firmly, "The whole United Nations is in the United States," and "Somaliland is under Trusteeship, which is not the case with the United States."

Mr. Cerulli sought persistently to avoid anything definite being written into the Trusteeship Agreement, and repeatedly offered an informal arrangement between the Secretary-General and the Italian Government, provided the draft were left as it stood. He added, "These are the limits of my statement." Dr. Hoo, imperturbable, accepted the proposal, "subject to the agreement of the Secretary-General," but only for the staff, not for the Advisory Council. The members of that body, Colombia, Egypt and the Philippines, under Dr. Hoo's prompting, had become solicitous for their own status. Mr. Ingles, of the Philippines, declared that without the essential diplomatic immunities, their work would be "hampered and subject to unforeseen hatreds." The draft presented by his delegation had specified all the privileges the Assistant Secretary-General had enumerated. They had been told all these privileges were covered by the general terms of the compromise formula in the draft.

Eventually it was settled that full diplomatic privileges be accorded to the Advisory Council. Dr. Hoo extracted from Signor Cerulli a definite assurance that the Italian Government would come to an agreement with the Secretary-General concerning the immunities to be granted to the premises of the United Nations in Somaliland and to their staff.

It was therefore established:

1. That the Advisory Council in Somaliland would be an organ of the United Nations;
2. That the Advisory Council be invested with full diplomatic privileges and immunities;

3. That the United Nations would appoint the staff of the Advisory Council, who would enjoy such privileges and immunities as were accorded to members of the United Nations Secretariat on field missions abroad, by direct agreement between the Secretary-General of the United Nations and the Italian Government;

4. That the immunity of the United Nations premises in Somaliland, which would be established in connection with the Advisory Council, would likewise be the subject of direct agreement between the Secretary-General of the United Nations and the Italian Government.

How much this would mean to Italy, Ethiopia and Somaliland would depend upon the Governments, who are the ultimate arbiters of the United Nations—and the peoples exercising a remote, uncertain control upon those Governments.

PROTECTION OF NATIVE RIGHTS TO LAND AND NATURAL RESOURCES

A suggestion of the Belgian delegate, Mr. Ryckmans, tending to modify the provisions of the draft Agreement which preclude the alienation of the land and natural resources was opposed by Sir Alan Burns, who stated that native lands are protected in British Colonies. Dr. Jamali, of Iraq, made a poignant protest against any weakening of the protection proposed by the draft:

"*This article is the fruit of bitter experience of the alienation of land. The Somalis are poor people; with money it is easy to get all their rights from them. A single rich Belgian or American could buy all Somaliland. The Somalis must be protected; in that protection there is no discrimination. As a Trusteeship Council, we must see that their national patrimony is well cared for. Natural resources do not belong to individuals; they belong to the nation as a whole.*"

Dr. Jamali desired to put on record his hope that the Trusteeship Council would in future ensure to all Trust Territories protection against the alienation of land and natural resources. He attempted to overthrow the definition of the term "indigenous," which had been accepted without discussion in the Somaliland Committee, but which might nullify the clauses safeguarding native right. If people of Western origin were accepted as indigenous, they could dispossess the Somalis and turn the territory into a Western Colony. The Iraqi delegation required full protection for the Somalis.

"*Times are changing,*" said Dr. Jamali, "*the days of colonisation are gone; we must begin to think in terms of human equality. Poor peoples must not be made to suffer because there is a richer country. If we allow them to be exploited, we shall be contributing to revolutions and bloodshed in the future. We shall be contributing* to wars. I appeal to everyone around this table to avert future tragedies by taking protective measures."

FRENCH EXPRESSIONS OF RESERVE

Dr. Jamali's definition of the term "indigenous" drew expressions of reserve from the French delegation, who had already made similar reservations in the Trusteeship Council and in the General Assembly concerning the use of this term. The French Government did not desire the mingling of races to be discouraged, or anyone prevented by racial origin from taking part in the life of a community, all the elements of which he had adopted.

Dr. Jamali replied that he also would desire to see freedom of movement for all mankind, the doors of all countries open without discrimination, racial, religious, political, or of any kind; but Western countries had introduced discriminations for their own reasons, one of which was to protect the standard of living. Rich countries would not accept people of a lower standard of living without restriction; for the same reason protection must be provided for very poor peoples like the Somalis, who would be overwhelmed if richer peoples were admitted to their land without safeguards.

That this had already happened to a major extent in Somaliland, and that the vital need was to rectify existing conditions, as well as to prevent further spoliation, again passed without mention.

The Ethiopian observer, if invited to join in the discussion of this problem, could have thrown a more comprehensive and piercing light upon it, recalling that throughout Africa the indigenous people have lost their natural rights and freedoms. Around the entire coast of Ethiopia, where footholds, purely for commercial trading were originally granted by local chiefs to European nationals, often quite freely or for a token payment such as the ten bags of rice exchanged by Captain Moresby * of the East India Company for the cession of Mussa Island to Great Britain.

The European beneficiaries of this confiding largess on the part of African chiefs had established fortifications, claimed and forcibly imposed prerogatives of government, extended their sway along the coast until checked by the presence of other European claimants, pushed their power inland. The people who inhabited the protectorates or colonies thus established around the entire coast of the Horn of Africa had been placed under subjection to European government. Their compatriots of the interior had been deprived of access to the sea, their industry paying toll in import, export and transit charges to the foreign Powers at the ports. Rigid frontiers had been established between the protectorates and colonies and the free land of the interior. A continuous propaganda, conscious or unconscious—deliberate and purposeful in Italy's case—had issued from the European administrations conveying the constant suggestion that the people of the free interior were wilder and more savage and also hostile to the population under European

---

* See Hertslet. "Map of Africa by Treaty," 1894 Edition. Page 832.

rule, because inimical to the instinctive desire of European administrators to take the richer interior also under their own control.

These fundamental factors, which underlie all the problems of Ethiopia and of the adjacent territories, were ignored by all. The Iraqi delegate strove to wring from the Trusteeship Council a somewhat more adequate protection of native interests by substitution for the disputed term, "indigenous person," the phrase, "any person born in Somaliland of parents born in Somaliland." He protested that the really indigenous persons were "those whose forefathers lived in the Territory, not people who have gone there to make a fortune and to exploit the inhabitants, thereby creating further political and economic problems for the country."

ITALIAN CLAIM TO ENCOURAGE ARAB IMMIGRATION USED TO NEGATE PROTECTION OF NATIVE RIGHTS

Signor Cerulli at once strongly opposed any change in the definition of the term "indigenous person." He had been obliged to tolerate the decision to impose restrictions on future sales of the land and natural resources of the territory; he clung to the vagueness of the term "indigenous" and to the wide definition of the term which had been accepted, as a means of evading such restrictions. He had heard reference to "exploitation of the poor by the rich," he said, but retorted, "It will cost about 10 billion lire annually to administer the Territory. I do not see, therefore, any question of the rich exploiting the poor in this case."

Whether the ten billion lire would be mainly spent in holding down the Somalis and in promoting Italian interests, and what share of the expenditure would benefit the Somalis, was the point which would determine how far the poor people would be exploited by the forthcoming Italian regime.

Posing as the champion of Arab immigration to Somaliland, Signor Cerulli went on to declare that "if examined with a knowledge of the facts," the article intended to prevent the alienation of land and natural resources "would appear ridiculous." "Somaliland is a desert," he exclaimed, "land has no real value there; the Somalis do not like to cultivate it." Yet, to render the Territory independent agriculture must be developed; therefore peasant immigration must be encouraged. For climatic reasons, these peasants must be Arabs. Italian administration had always encouraged, and would continue to encourage, the immigration of Arab cultivators.

How little there was of veracity in this statement by the Italian representative is revealed on examination of the facts. There were at the time about 25,000 Arabs in Somaliland, the majority of whom were engaged in trade and approximately 9,000 in agriculture.* The position, which has been more fully dealt with in Chapter XVI,

---

* See Report of the Four-Power Commission of Investigation, January 6—February 22, 1948, Section 1, page 44.

is clearly revealed by the fact that 1,016 Arabs occupied 15,000 hectares of land, and 175 Italian owners and concessionees occupied 72,842 hectares. It was for the broad and fertile lands held by the Italians that forced labour was requisitioned. The Italians held also a further 99,407 hectares under State ownership, and 35,037 owned by the Roman Catholic Church. The 7,862,510 hectares of so-called "communal lands" left to the native people are irrigated, as already explained, only by a deficient rainfall. There is also the vast area of so-called "waste lands," cultivation of which is considered impossible.

ARAB IMMIGRATION CEASED WITH ITALIAN ADVENT

The Arabs thus own and cultivate a mere fraction of the soil of Somaliland. That they cultivate this fraction is not due to Italian initiative, but the result of Arab settlement dating from pre-Italian times. In a letter from the Arab community to the Four Power Commission* it is stated: that a portion of the Arab community, called "Rer Hamar," had settled on the coast 400 to 500 years before, and named it "Benadir"; that the descendants of these early immigrants bear Arabic names, and are to be found at Mogadishu, Afgoi, Brava, and elsewhere; that a second large Arab immigration occurred during the 19th century, upwards of seventy years ago, during the fifty years' reign of the Sultan of Zanzibar, Bargash of Al Bu Said;† that this latter immigration took place before the transfer of the Benadir ports to Italy, since which event Arab immigration had ceased; that members of the Arab families already settled in Somaliland had continued coming and going between Somaliland and Arabia in the course of their trade, except when prevented by restrictions imposed by the occupying Power.

This statement of the Arab community offers additional evidence of the unreality of the claim that Italy encouraged Arab immigration.

It should be observed that when interviewed by the Four Power Commission, the representatives of the Arab community stated that they would not desire to take Somaliland nationality even if the territory were given a government of its own. They desired to be treated as Asians, to enjoy the same rights as Arabs in Arab lands and to remain an alien community in Somaliland.

As the Arabs reject Somaliland citizenship and are determined to remain a group of foreigners in the Territory, the definition of the term "indigenous person" as a person born in and accepting citizenship of the Territory would not apply to them.

Ignoring all the facts, Signor Cerulli adroitly developed his effort to embarrass and discomfort his Iraqi opponent:

---

* Ibid.

† Sultan Sayyid Bargash-bin-Said, of Zanzibar, who died 26th March, 1888, vide Hertslet, "Map of Africa by Treaty," 1894 Edition, page 110 note.
As we have seen, the rule of the Sultans of Zanzibar was confined to the Benadir ports.

"If the speech of the Iraqi delegate could be read or heard on the radio in Somaliland," he asserted, *" the inhabitants would be astonished; they would say that Arabs were speaking against Arab immigration into the Territory. That was the only interpretation they would put upon it. The question of Arab immigration had long been debated, with its pros and cons. The speech of the Iraqi delegate would certainly be understood in Somaliland as meaning that the Arab representative on the Trusteeship Council had taken up a position against Arab immigration. That might disturb public order in the country; there is a very delicate relationship between the Somalis and the Arab section of the population."*

Thus calling to mind the Somali anti-Arab riots which had recurred in recent years, the expert Italian diplomatist drove his thrust home:

" I have adhered to the compromise, but if others withdraw from it, I shall have to reserve completely the position of the Italian delegation, because I do not want public order in Somaliland exposed to the risk of disturbances which delegations here, with the best of intentions, but perhaps not fully aware of local conditions, may cause in the territory."

In all this, there was the sufficiently obvious suggestion that the Arabs in Somaliland might find themselves harrassed, restricted, perhaps even deported by the Italian Administration in the alleged interests of the Somalis.

Dr. Jamali responded that he wanted " to protect everyone in Somaliland, including the Arabs." He had never imagined the Arabs would be invaders or aggressors anywhere. Wherever the Arabs went they were assimilated with the local people and became indigenous. All he wanted was to protect Somalis from outsiders, even his own people, unless they would actually become indigenous people.

Signor Cerulli responded blandly: *" I agree completely with our colleague from Iraq; we have specially encouraged Arab immigration. Nobody more than I represents the tradition of Italian administration. Nobody can recognise more than I do the quality of the Arabs, but the Somalis do not share this opinion. Only a year ago, there were difficulties with the Arabs in Somaliland."*

Signor Cerulli had played a trump card; Article 14 was put to the vote without further discussion. It was carried by ten votes to none, with one abstention; Mr. Ryckmans, of Belgium, had abstained because urban land had not been exempted from the restrictions concerning the sale of land to foreigners. Signor Cerulli and he continued pressing for this exemption, and eventually succeeded in getting it into the draft Agreement, as will be observed by reference to the text.

COMPLETION OF THE DRAFT TRUSTEESHIP AGREEMENT

On January 27th, 1950, the Trusteeship Council completed their revision of the draft Trusteeship Agreement for the Somaliland Territory. In its general terms the Agreement followed the lines of previous Trusteeship Agreements in respect of other Territories. The special features which arose from the fact that Somaliland was a former colony of an ex-enemy State, included the establishment of the Advisory Council, the specific time limit of ten years for the granting of self-government, and the annex containing a declaration of " Constitutional Principles."

ETHIOPIA PROTESTS TO U.N.O.

Ato Abbebe Retta, the Ethiopian Observer, addressed Ethiopia's protest to the Secretary-General of the United Nations in the following terms:

"*Since on the one hand no delimited frontiers exist, and since none have been agreed to, and since the Ethiopian Government has not received satisfaction from the Trusteeship Council on its request for participation in the work of the Council on the basis of the rights accorded Ethiopia by Article 79 of the Charter, the Ethiopian Government is reluctantly obliged to state that under such circumstances it cannot recognise the validity of any agreement prepared or agreed to by the Trusteeship Council on former Italian Somaliland.*

Appendix 1 to Chapter XXII

ITALO-ETHIOPIAN TREATY TO DEFINE THE FRONTIER BETWEEN THE ITALIAN POSSESSIONS IN SOMALILAND AND THE EMPIRE OF ETHIOPIA, 1908.

His Majesty Victor Emmanuel III, King of Italy in his own name and in the name of his successors, by the intermediary of his representative in Addis Ababa, Cavaliere Giuseppe Colli Di Felizzano, cavalry captain; and His Majesty Menelik II, King of Kings of Ethiopia, in his name and that of his successors.

Wishing to define definitely the frontier between the Italian possessions in Somalia and the Provinces of the Ethiopian Empire have decided to sign the following convention.

Art. 1.—The frontier line between the Italian possessions in Somaliland and the Provinces of the Ethiopian Empire begins at Dolo, at the confluence of the Daua and the Ganale, and runs east following the source of the Maidaba and continues as far as the Webbi Shebeli following the territorial limits between the tribes of the Rahanuin, who will be dependents of Italy, and all the tribes to the north of them, who will be dependent on Ethiopia.

Art. 2.—The frontier point on the Webbi Shebeli shall be at the point of junction between the territory of the tribe of Baddi-Addi, which shall remain dependent on Italy, and the territory of the tribes above the Baddi-Addi, whch shall remain dependent on Ethiopia.

Art. 3.—The tribes on the left of the Juba, those of the Rahanuin and those on the Webbi-Shebeli below the frontier point shall be dependent on Italy. The tribes of Digodia of Afgab Jejedi and all the others north of the frontier shall be dependent on Ethiopia.

Art. 4.—From the Webbi Shebeli the frontier runs towards the north-east following the tracing accepted by the Italian Government in 1897. All the territory belonging to the tribes on the coast side will remain dependent on Italy; all the territory of the Ogaden and the land belonging to the tribes on the Ogaden side will remain dependent on Ethiopia.

Art. 5.—The two governments agree to fix practically and on the spot with little delay the above mentioned frontier line.

Art. 6.—The two governments formally agree not to exercise any interference across the frontier line and not to permit the tribes dependent upon them to pass the frontier for the commission of violence prejudicial to the tribes on the other side; but if disputes arise, or incidents between or because of the border tribes on the frontier, the two governments will solve them by mutual agreement.

Art. 7.—The two governments reciprocally agree not to commit, and not to authorise on the part of their dependents, any action which could be the cause of disputes or incidents, or could disturb the tranquillity of the frontier tribes. The present convention shall be submitted for the approbation of the Parliament of the Realm, and the ratification of His Majesty the King.

Made in duplicate copies and of identical tenure in the two languages, Italian and Amharic, one copy will remain in the hands of the Italian Government, and the other in the hands of the Ethiopian Government, written in the city of Addis Ababa, May 16, 1908.

(Seal of the Emperor Menelik).
Signed by Giuseppe Colli Di Fellizzano.

Appendix 2 to Chapter XXII

TRUSTEESHIP COUNCIL DRAFT AGREEMENT.
DRAFT TRUSTEESHIP AGREEMENT FOR THE TERRITORY OF SOMALILAND UNDER ITALIAN ADMINISTRATION.
APPROVED BY THE TRUSTEESHIP COUNCIL FOR SUBMISSION TO THE UNITED NATIONS.

PREAMBLE.

Somaliland to become an Independent Sovereign State; 10 years under Italian Trusteeship.

WHEREAS, Chapters XII and XIII of the Charter of the United Nations provide for an International Trusteeship System;

WHEREAS, by Article 23 of the Treaty of Peace between the Allied and Associated Powers and Italy, signed in Paris on February 10, 1947, Italy renounced all right and title to the Italian territorial possessions in Africa;

WHEREAS, under paragraph 3 of Annex XI of this Treaty, the General Assembly of the United Nations was requested to make recommendations regarding the future status of the territories referred to in Article 23 thereof;

WHEREAS, under paragraph 3 of Annex XI of this Treaty, the Governments of France, of the Union of Soviet Socialist Republics, of the United Kingdom of Great Britain and Northern Ireland, and of the United States of America agreed to accept the recommendation made by the General Assembly of the United Nations in this matter;

WHEREAS, the General Assembly, after having examined the question at its third and fourth sessions, adopted at its 250th plenary meeting on November 21, 1949, a resolution recommending, with respect to the territory formerly known as Italian Somaliland, that the Territory shall be an independent and sovereign state; that its independence shall become effective at the end of ten years from the date of approval of the Trusteeship Agreement by the General Assembly and that, during this period of ten years, the Territory shall be placed under the International Trusteeship System, with Italy as the Administering Authority, aided and advised by an Advisory Council composed of representatives of Colombia, Egypt and the Philippines;

WHEREAS, the Trusteeship Council, as requested by the General Assembly, has negotiated the draft of a Trusteeship Agreement with Italy and approved it at the eighth meeting of its sixth session on January 27, 1950;

WHEREAS, the Government of Italy has accepted responsibility as the Administering Authority of this Territory;

WHEREAS, the Governments of Colombia, Egypt and the Philippines have accepted the responsibility of designating representatives to aid and advise the Administering Authority in their capacity as members of the Advisory Council;

NOW THEREFORE, the General Assembly of the United Nations approves the following terms of Trusteeship for the Territory formerly known as Italian Somaliland:

ARTICLE 1.
Boundaries.

The territory to which this Agreement applies is the Territory formerly known as Italian Somaliland, hereinafter called the Territory, bounded by the Somaliland Protectorate, Ethiopia, Kenya, the Gulf of Aden and the Indian Ocean. Its boundaries shall be those fixed by international agreement and, in so far as they are not already delimited, shall be delimited in accordance with a procedure approved by the General Assembly.

ARTICLE 2.
Italy to be the Administering Authority aided by an Advisory Council.

Italy shall be entrusted with the administration of the Territory and the Government of Italy designated in this Agreement as the Administering

Authority, shall be represented therein by an Administrator. The Administering Authority shall be responsible to the United Nations for the peace, order and good government of the Territory in accordance with the terms of this Agreement.

The Administering Authority shall be aided and advised by an Advisory Council composed of representatives of Colombia, Egypt and the Philippines.

The headquarters of the Administrator and of the Advisory Council shall be in Mogadishu.

ARTICLE 3.
Independence to be effective after ten years.
Obligations of the Administering Authority.

The Administering Authority undertakes to administer the Territory in accordance with the provision of the United Nations Charter relating to the International Trusteeship System as set out in Chapters XII and XIII thereof, the relevant parts of Resolution 289 (IV) of November 21, 1949, of the General Assembly and this Agreement (which includes an Annex containing a Declaration of Constitutional Principles), with a view to making the independence of the Territory effective at the end of ten years from the date of the approval of this Agreement by the General Assembly.

Political Institutions: Progressive Participation of Inhabitants in Organs of Government.

The Administering Authority shall:

1. Foster the development of free political institutions and promote the development of the inhabitants of the Territory towards independence; and to this end shall give to the inhabitants of the Territory a progressively increasing participation in the various organs of Government.

Economic Advancement.

2. Promote the economic advancement and self-sufficiency of the inhabitants, and to this end shall regulate the use of natural resources; encourage the development of fisheries, agriculture, trade and industries; protect the inhabitants against the loss of their lands and resources; and improve the means of transportation and communication;

Social Advancement.

3. Promote the social advancement of the inhabitants, and to this end shall:

    Protect the rights and fundamental freedoms of all elements of the population without discrimination;

    Protect and improve the health of the inhabitants by the development of adequate health and hospital services for all sections of the population;

    Control the traffic in arms and ammunition, opium and other dangerous drugs, alcohol and other spirituous liquors;

    Prohibit all forms of slavery, slave trade and child marriage;

    Apply existing international conventions concerning prostitution;

    Prohibit all forms of forced or compulsory labour, except for essential public works and services, and then only in time of public emergency with adequate remuneration and adequate protection of the welfare of the workers;

And institute such other regulations as may be necessary to protect the inhabitants against any social abuses.

ARTICLE 4.
Education.

The Administering Authority, recognising the fact that education in its broadest sense is the only sure foundation on which any moral, social, political and economic advancement of the inhabitants of the Territory can be based, and believing that national independence with due respect for freedom and democracy can only be established on this basis, undertakes to establish a sound and effective system of education, with due regard for Islamic culture and religion.

Elementary, Secondary, Vocational, Technical Education, "As Rapidly as Possible."

The Administering Authority therefore undertakes to promote the educational advancement of the inhabitants, and to this end undertakes to establish as rapidly as possible a system of public education which shall include elementary, secondary, vocational (including institutions for the training of teachers) and technical schools, to provide free of charge at least elementary education, and to facilitate higher and professional education and cultural advancement in every possible way.

University Education.

In particular, the Administering Authority shall take all appropriate steps:

(a) to provide that an adequate number of qualified students from among the indigenous population receive university or professional education outside the Territory, so as to ensure that sufficient qualified personnel will be available when the Territory becomes a sovereign independent state;

To Combat Illiteracy.

(b) to combat illiteracy by all possible means; and

(c) to ensure that instruction is given in schools and other educational institutions regarding the activities of the United Nations and its organs, the basic objectives of the International Trusteeship System and the Universal Declaration of Human Rights.

ARTICLE 5.

Collaboration with General Assembly of United Nations and Trusteeship Council.

The Administering Authority shall collaborate fully with the General Assembly of the United Nations and with the Trusteeship Council in the discharge of all their functions as defined in Articles 87 and 88 of the Charter of the United Nations.

Accordingly, the Administering Authority undertakes:

Annual Report to United Nations General Assembly.

1. to make to the General Assembly of the United Nations an annual report on the basis of the questionnaire drawn up by the Trusteeship Council in accordance with Article 88 of the Charter of the United Nations and to include in this report information relating to the measures taken to give effect to the suggestions and recommendations of the General Assembly and of the Trusteeship Council;

Accredited Representative for Trusteeship Council.

2. to designate an accredited representative to be present at the sessions of the Trusteeship Council at which the reports of the Administering Authority and petitions relating to conditions in the Territory are considered;

Visits of Trusteeship Council to Territory.

3. to facilitate periodic visits to the Territory as provided for in Article 87 of the Charter of the United Nations at times and in accordance with arrangements to be agreed upon with the Administering Authority;

4. to render assistance to the General Assembly or the Trusteeship Council in the application of these arrangements and of such other arrangements as these organs of the United Nations may make in accordance with the terms of the present Agreement.

ARTICLE 6.
Forces for Order and Defence; Consultation with Advisory Council before Establishing Installations Requisite.

The Administering Authority may maintain police forces and raise volunteer contingents for the maintenance of peace and good order in the Territory.

The Administering Authority, after consultation with the Advisory Council, may establish installations and take all measures in the Territory, including the progressive development of Somali defence forces, which may be necessary, within the limits laid down in the Charter of the United Nations, for the defence of the Territory and for the maintenance of international peace and security.

ARTICLE 7.
Administering Authority full Powers of Legislation: May apply Italian Law.

The Administering Authority shall have full powers of legislation, administration and jurisdiction in the Territory, subject to the provisions of the Charter of the United Nations, of this Agreement and of the Annex attached hereto, and shall have power to apply to the Territory, temporarily and with such modifications as are considered necessary, such Italian laws as are appropriate to the conditions and needs of the Territory and as are not incompatible with the attainment of its independence.

ARTICLE 8.
Functions of Advisory Council.

The Advisory Council shall be fully informed by the Administering Authority on all matters relating to the political, economic, social and educational advancement of the inhabitants of the Territory, including legislation appertaining thereto, and may make to the Administering Authority such observations and recommendations as it may consider will be conducive to the attainment of the objectives of this Agreement.

The Administering Authority shall seek the advice of the Advisory Council on all measures envisaged for the inauguration, development and subsequent establishment of full self-government for the Territory; in particular it shall consult the Advisory Council regarding plans for:
    (a) the establishment and development of organs of self-government;
    (b) economic and financial development;
    (c) educational advancement;
    (d) labour and social advancement; and
    (e) the transfer of the functions of government to a duly constituted independent Government of the Territory.

The Administering Authority shall seek the advice of the Advisory Council on ordinances which, in accordance with Article 5 of Annex to this Agreement, the Administrator of the Territory may make and promulgate in exceptional circumstances.

ARTICLE 9.
Facilities to be Accorded to Advisory Council.

The Advisory Council shall be accorded such facilities and shall have free access to such sources of information as it may require for the performance of its functions.

ARTICLE 10.
Diplomatic Status of Advisory Council.

In the Territory Members of the Advisory Council shall enjoy full diplomatic privileges and immunities, and their staff shall enjoy the privileges and immunities which they would enjoy if the Convention on the Privileges and Immunities of the United Nations were applicable to the Territory.

ARTICLE 11.
Advisory Council to report to Trusteeship Council.

States Members of the Advisory Council, if they are not members of the Trusteeship Council, shall be entitled to participate without vote in the debates of the Trusteeship Council on any question specifically relating to the Territory.

In the course of such debates, Members of the Advisory Council or the majority of the Members, acting in the name of the Advisory Council, or each of the Members acting separately, may make to the Trusteeship Council such oral statements or may submit such written reports or memoranda as they may deem necessary for the Council's proper consideration of any question specifically relating to the Territory.

ARTICLE 12.
Administering Authority: International Agreements.

The Administering Authority undertakes to maintain the application of the international agreements and conventions **which are at present in force in the Territory,** and to apply therein any conventions and recommendations made by the United Nations, or the specialised agencies referred to in Article 57 of the Charter of the United Nations, the application of which would be in the interests of the population and consistent with the basic objectives of the Trusteeship System, the provisions of Resolution 289 (IV) of November 21, 1949, of the General Assembly, and the terms of the present Agreement.

ARTICLE 13.
Co-operation with Specialised Agencies of United Nations.

The Administering Authority shall take all the necessary steps to enable the Territory to co-operate with the Specialised Agencies referred to in Article 57 of the Charter of the United Nations with other international agencies and regional organisations, and to participate in their activities.

ARTICLE 14.
Land and Natural Resources: Protection of Native Interests.

In order to promote the economic and social advancement of the indigenous population, the Administering Authority shall, in framing laws relating to the holding or alienation of land or other natural resources, take into consideration the laws and customs of the indigenous population and respect their rights and safeguard their interests, both present and future.

Two-thirds Majority of Territorial Council Required for Sale of Land, not for Lease.

The Administering Authority shall not, without the consent in each case of a two-thirds majority of the members of the Territorial Council (provided for in Article 4 of the Annex), permit the acquisition by non-indigenous persons, or by companies or associations controlled by such persons of any rights over land in the Territory save on lease for a period to be determined by law.

In cases involving the alienation to non-indigenous persons or to companies or associations controlled by such persons of areas of agricultural land in excess of one thousand acres, the Administering Authority shall also request in advance the advice of the Advisory Council. The Administering Authority shall include in its annual report to the Trusteeship Council a detailed account of such alienations.

Natural Resources only granted to Non-Indigenous Persons on Lease or Concession.

The Administering Authority shall prohibit the acquisition by non-indigenous persons, or by companies or associations controlled by such persons of any rights over any other natural resources in the Territory, save on lease or grant of concession for a period to be determined by law.

Nothing in this Article shall apply to building land within the municipal area of Mogadishu which may be disposed of in accordance with regulations prescribed by law.

ARTICLE 15.
Equal Treatment for States Members of United Nations.

Subject to the provisions of Article 14, 16 and 17 of this Agreement, the Administering Authority shall take all necessary steps to ensure equal treatment in social, economic, industrial and commercial matters for all States Members of the United Nations and their nationals and for its own nationals and to this end:

    (a) shall grant to all nationals of Members of the United Nations and to its own nationals freedom of transit and navigation, including freedom of transit and navigation by air, and the protection of person and property, subject to the requirements of public order and on condition of compliance with the local law;

    (b) shall ensure the same rights to all nationals of Members of the United Nations as to its own nationals, in respect of entry into and residence in the Territory, acquisition of property, both movable and immovable, and the exercise of professions and trades;

    (c) shall not discriminate on grounds of nationality against nationals of any Member of the United Nations, or its own nationals, in matters relating to the grant of concessions for the development of the natural resources of the Territory, and shall not grant concessions having the character of a general monopoly; and

    (d) shall ensure equal treatment in the administration of justice to the nationals of all Members of the United Nations and to its own nationals.

The rights conferred by this article on nationals of Members of the United Nations or on the Administering Authority's own nationals apply equally to companies and associations controlled by such nationals, and organised in accordance with the law of any Member of the United Nations, or with the law of the Administering Authority.

Article 16.
Public Services and Works, Monopolies, etc.

Measures taken to give effect to Article 15 of this Agreement shall be subject always to the overriding duty of the Administering Authority, in accordance with Article 76 of the Charter of the United Nations, to promote the political, economic, social and educational advancement of the inhabitants of the Territory to carry out the other basic objectives of the International Trusteeship System and the provisions of Resolution 288 (IV) of the General Assembly of November 21, 1949, and to maintain peace, order and good government. In particular, the Administering Authority shall be free:

    (a) to organise essential public services and works on such terms and conditions as it thinks just;

    (b) to create monopolies of a purely fiscal character in order to provide the Territory with the fiscal resources which seem best suited to local requirements, or otherwise to serve the interests of the inhabitants;

    (c) where the interests of the economic advancement of the inhabitants may require it, to establish, or permit to be established, for specific purposes, other monopolies or undertakings having in them an element of monopoly, under conditions of proper public control; provided that, in the selection of agencies to carry out the purposes of this paragraph, other than agencies controlled by the Government of the Territory, or those in which that Government participates, the Administering Authority shall not discriminate on grounds of nationality against Members of the United Nations or their nationals.

ARTICLE 17.
Equality of Treatment for Inhabitants and Companies of Somaliland with that accorded to most favoured Nations.

Nothing in this Agreement shall entitle any Member of the United Nations to claim for itself or for its nationals, companies and associations the benefits of Article 15 of this Agreement in any respect in which it does not give to the inhabitants, companies and associations of the Territory equality of treatment with the nationals, companies and associations of the State which it treats most favourably.

ARTICLE 18.
Property owned by Nationals of U.N.O. States Members.

The Administering Authority shall include in its first annual report to the Trusteeship Council a report on the position in the Territory of property belonging to nationals, associations and companies of Members of United Nations.

ARTICLE 19.
Freedom of Religion and Religious Teaching.

The Administering Authority shall in a spirit of religious tolerance, ensure in the Territory complete freedom of conscience and religion and shall guarantee freedom of religious teaching and the free exercise of all forms of worship.

Missionaries of any faith shall be free to enter, travel and reside in the Territory; to acquire and possess property therein, subject to the conditions laid down in Article 14 of the present Agreement; to erect religious buildings and hospitals therein; and to open schools subject to such regulations as may be prescribed by law for the educational advancement of the inhabitants of the Territory.

The provisions of this Article shall be subject only to such limitations as may be necessary for the maintenance of public order and morality.

ARTICLE 20.
Freedom of Speech, Press, Assembly and Petition.

The Administering Authority shall guarantee to the inhabitants of the Territory complete freedom of speech, of the press, of assembly and of petition, without distinction as to race, sex, language, political opinion or religion, subject only to the requirements of public order.

ARTICLE 21.
Freedom of Trusteeship Council and Administering Authority.

Nothing in this Agreement shall affect the right of the Administering Authority or the Trusteeship Council to propose at any future date, the alteration or amendment of this Agreement in the interests of the Territory or for reasons not inconsistent with the basic objectives of the International Trusteeship System.

The provisions of this Agreement shall not be altered or amended except as provided in Articles 79 and 85 of the United Nations Charter.

ARTICLE 22.
Disputes between U.N.O. States Members and Administering Authority to be submitted to International Court of Justice.

If any dispute whatever should arise between the Administering Authority and a State Member of the United Nations relating to the interpretation or the application of the provisions of this Agreement, such dispute, if it cannot be settled by direct negotiation or other means, shall be submitted to the International Court of Justice, provided for in Chapter XIV of the Charter of the United Nations.

ARTICLE 23.
Agreement to be Approved by U.N.O. General Assembly; Italy to Administer Meanwhile.

The present Agreement, of which the Declaration of Constitutional Principles attached hereto as an Annex is an integral part, shall enter into force as soon as it is approved by the General Assembly of the United Nations and ratified by Italy.

Provisional Administration by Italy.

Nevertheless, after the Trusteeship Council and Italy have agreed upon the terms of trusteeship, and pending approval of this Agreement by the General Assembly, the Administering Authority shall provisionally administer the Territory in accordance with the provisions of the Charter of the United Nations and of this Agreement, and shall assume this provisional administration at a time and pursuant to arrangements for the orderly transfer of administration agreed upon between Italy and the United Kingdom of Great Britain and Northern Ireland.

ARTICLE 24.
The Agreement ceases to be in force ten years after approval by U.N.O. General Assembly.

The present Agreement shall cease to be in force ten years after the date of the approval of the Trusteeship Agreement by the General Assembly at the conclusion of which the Territory shall become an independent sovereign State.

ARTICLE 25.
Eighteen months before Termination of Agreement Italy must submit plan for Transfer to Independent Government.

The Administering Authority shall submit to the Trusteeship Council at least 18 months before the expiration of the present Agreement, a plan for the orderly transfer of all the functions of government to a duly constituted independent Government of the Territory.

ANNEX.
DECLARATION OF CONSTITUTIONAL PRINCIPLES.
Preamble.

In view of the recommendation made by the General Assembly of the United Nations at its Fourth Regular Session with respect to placing the territory formerly known as Italian Somaliland under the International Trusteeship System with Italy as the Administering Authority;

Considering the provisions of the Charter of United Nations which establish an International Trusteeship System, the terms of this Trusteeship Agreement, of which this Declaration is an integral part, and in accordance with the provisions of Resolution 289 (IV) of the General Assembly;

Gradual Development of Institutions for Independent Self-Government.

For the purpose of solemnly guaranteeing the rights of the inhabitants of the Territory and of providing, in accordance with democratic principles, for the gradual development of institutions designed to ensure the establishment of full self-government and independence, and the attainment of the basic objectives of the International Trusteeship System in conformity with the Charter of the United Nations;

It is hereby declared:

ARTICLE 1.
Sovereign Authority to be exercised by Italy on behalf of People of the Territory.

The sovereignty of the Territory is vested in its people and shall be exercised by the Administering Authority on their behalf and in the manner prescribed herein by decision of the United Nations.

ARTICLE 2.
Status of Citizenship for People of the Territory.

The Administering Authority shall take the necessary steps to provide for the population of the Territory a status of citizenship of the Territory and to ensure their diplomatic and consular protection when outside the limits of the Territory and of the Territory of the Administering Authority.

ARTICLE 3.
Executive Powers of Administrator.

The Administrator shall be the chief executive officer of the Territory.

ARTICLE 4.
Consultative Territorial Council Appointed by Administrator.

The Administrator shall appoint a Territorial Council, composed of inhabitants of the Territory and representative of its people.

Defence and Foreign Affairs: No Consultation.

In all matters other than defence and foreign affairs, the Administrator shall consult the Territorial Council.

The legislative authority shall normally be exercised by the Administrator after consultation with the Territorial Council until such time as an elective legislature has been established.

ARTICLE 5.
Exceptional Circumstances.

In exceptional circumstances the Administrator may, after consultation with the Advisory Council, make and promulgate such ordinances as in his opinion the circumstances demand.

These ordinances shall be laid before the Territorial Council as soon as may be practicable and the Administering Authority shall include an account of all such ordinances in its annual report to the Trusteeship Council.

ARTICLE 6.
Administering Authority Answerable to Trusteeship Council.

In matters relating to defence and foreign affairs as in other matters, the Administering Authority shall be accountable to the Trusteeship Council, and shall take into account any recommendations which the Council may see fit to make.

ARTICLE 7.
Judicial System.

The Administering Authority shall establish a judicial system and shall ensure the absolute independence of the judiciary. The Administering Authority shall also ensure that representatives of the indigenous population be progressively entrusted with judicial functions and that the jurisdiction of courts of first instance be progressively widened.

As may be appropriate in each case, the Administering Authority shall apply local legislation, Islamic law, and local customary law.

ARTICLE 8.
Restricted Rights and Freedoms "Consistent with the Development of the Inhabitants."

The Administering Authority, in accordance with the principles laid down in its own Constitution and legislation, shall guarantee to all inhabitants of the Territory human rights and fundamental freedoms and full equality before the law without distinction as to race, sex, language, political opinion or religion.

ARTICLE 9.

The Administering Authority shall guarantee to all the inhabitants of the Territory full civil rights, and also such political rights as are consistent with the progressive political, social, economic and educational development of the inhabitants and with the development of a democratic representative system, due regard being paid to traditional institutions.

In particular, it shall guarantee:
1. the preservation of their personal and successional status with due regard to its evolutionary development;
2. their personal liberty, which may not be restricted except by warrant of judicial authority and only in cases and in accordance with regulations prescribed by law;
3. the inviolability of domicile, to which the competent authority may have access only by due legal process and in a manner prescribed in accordance with local customs and subject to the guarantees for the protection of personal liberty;
4. the freedom and secrecy of communication and correspondence, which may be limited only by means of a warrant of judicial authority stating the reasons and subject to the guarantees prescribed by law;
5. the rights of property, subject to expropriation carried out for a public purpose, after payment of fair compensation, and in accordance with regulations prescribed by law;
6. the free exercise of professions and occupations in accordance with local customs and with regulations prescribed by law;
7. the right to compete for public employment in accordance with regulations prescribed by law; and
8. the right to emigrate and to travel, subject to such regulations as may be prescribed by law for healh and security reasons.

ARTICLE 10.
Human Rights Declaration: A Standard of Achievement.

The Administering Authority accepts as a standard of achievement for the Territory the Universal Declaration of Human Rights adopted by the General Assembly of the United Nations on December 10, 1948.

Appendix 3, Chapter XXII

PROVISIONS OF THE UNITED NATIONS CHARTER CONCERNING TRUSTEESHIP.

CHAPTER XII
INTERNATIONAL TRUSTEESHIP SYSTEM

Article 75

The United Nations shall establish under its authority an international trusteeship system for the administration and supervision of such territories as may be placed thereunder by subsequent individual agreements. These territories are hereinafter referred to as trust territories.

Article 76

The basic objectives of the trusteeship system, in accordance with the Purposes of the United Nations laid down in Article 1 of the present Charter, shall be:—
    a. to further international peace and security;
    b. to promote the political, economic, social, and educational advancement of the inhabitants of the trust territories, and their progressive development towards self-government or independence as may be appropriate to the particular circumstances of each territory

and its peoples and the freely expressed wishes of the peoples concerned, and as may be provided by the terms of each trusteeship agreement;

c. to encourage respect for human rights and for fundamental freedoms for all without distinction as to race, sex, language, or religion, and to encourage recognition of the interdependence of the peoples of the world; and

d. to ensure equal treatment in social, economic, and commercial matters for all Members of the United Nations and their nationals, and also equal treatment for the latter in the administration of justice, without prejudice to the attainment of the foregoing objectives and subject to the provisions of Article 80.

Article 77

1. The trusteeship system shall apply to such territories in the following categories as may be placed thereunder by means of trusteeship agreements:—

a. territories now held under mandate;

b. territories which may be detached from enemy states as a result of the Second World War; and

c. territories voluntarily placed under the system by states responsible for their administration.

2. It will be a matter for subsequent agreement as to which territories in the foregoing categories will be brought under the trusteeship system and upon what terms.

Article 78

The trusteeship system shall not apply to territories which have become Members of the United Nations, relationship among which shall be based on respect for the principle of sovereign equality.

Article 79

The terms of trusteeship for each territory to be placed under the trusteeship system, including any alteration or amendment, shall be agreed upon by the states directly concerned, including the mandatory power in the case of territories held under mandate by a Member of the United Nations, and shall be approved as provided for in Articles 83 and 85.

Article 80

1. Except as may be agreed upon in individual trusteeship agreements, made under Articles 77, 79, and 81, placing each territory under the trusteeship system, and until such agreements have been concluded, nothing in this Chapter shall be construed in or of itself to alter in any manner the rights whatsoever of any states or any peoples or the terms of existing international instruments to which the Members of the United Nations may respectively be parties.

2. Paragraph 1 of this Article shall not be interpreted as giving grounds for delay or postponement of the negotiation and conclusion of agreements for placing mandated and other territories under the trusteeship system as provided for in Article 77.

Article 81

The trusteeship agreement shall in each case include the terms under which the trust territory will be administered and designate the authority which will exercise the administration of the trust territory. Such authority, hereinafter called the administering authority, may be one or more states or the Organisation itself.

Article 82

There may be designated, in any trusteeship agreement, a strategic area or areas which may include part or all of the trust territory to which the agreement applies, without prejudice to any special agreement or agreements made under Article 43.

Article 83

1. All functions of the United Nations relating to strategic areas, including the approval of the terms of the trusteeship agreements and of their alteration or amendment, shall be exercised by the Security Council.

2. The basic objectives set forth in Article 76 shall be applicable to the people of each strategic area.

3. The Security Council shall, subject to the provisions of the trusteeship agreements and without prejudice to security considerations, avail itself of the assistance of the Trusteeship Council to perform those functions of the United Nations under the trusteeship system relating to political, economic, social, and educational matters in the strategic areas.

Article 84

It shall be the duty of the administering authority to ensure that the trust territory shall play its part in the maintenance of international peace and security. To this end the administering authority may make use of volunteer forces, facilities, and assistance from the trust territory in carrying out the obligations towards the Security Council undertaken in this regard by the administering authority, as well as for local defence and the maintenance of law and order within the trust territory.

Article 85

1. The functions of the United Nations with regard to trusteeship agreements for all areas not designated as strategic, including the approval of the terms of the trusteeship agreements and of their alteration or amendment, shall be exercised by the General Assembly.

2. The Trusteeship Council, operating under the authority of the General Assembly, shall assist the General Assembly in carrying out these functions.

CHAPTER XIII

THE TRUSTEESHIP COUNCIL

Composition

Article 86

1. The Trusteeship Council shall consist of the following Members of the United Nations: —

    a. those Members administering trust territories.

    b. such of those Members mentioned by name in Article 23 as are not administering trust territories; and

    c. as many other Members elected for three-year terms by the General Assembly as may be necessary to ensure that the total number of members of the Trusteeship Council is equally divided between those Members of the United Nations which administer trust territories and those which do not.

2. Each member of the Trusteeship Council shall designate one specially qualified person to represent it therein.

Functions and Powers

Article 87

The General Assembly and, under its authority, the Trusteeship Council, in carrying out their functions, may: —

    a. consider reports submitted by the administering authority;

    b. accept petitions and examine them in consultation with the administering authority;

    c. provide for periodic visits to the respective trust territories at times agreed upon with the administering authority; and

    d. take these and other actions in conformity with the terms of the trusteeship agreements.

Article 88

The Trusteeship Council shall formulate a questionnaire on the political, economic, social, and educational advancement of the inhabitants of each trust territory, and the administering authority for each trust territory within the competence of he General Assembly shall make an annual report to the General Assembly upon the basis of such questionnaire.

Voting

Article 89

1. Each member of the Trusteeship Council shall have one vote.
2. Decisions of the Trusteeship Council shall be made by a majority of the members present and voting.

Procedure

Article 90

1. The Trusteeship Council shall adopt its own rules of procedure, including the method of selecting its President.
2. The Trusteeship Council shall meet as required in accordance with its rules, which shall include provision for the convening of meetings on the request of a majority of its members.

Article 91

The Trusteeship Council shall, when appropriate, avail itself of the assistance of the Economic and Social Council and of the specialised agencies in regard to matters with which they are respectively concerned.

Appendix 4, Chapter XXII.

ITALIAN DRAFT AGREEMENT.

DRAFT TRUSTEESHIP AGREEMENT FOR SOMALILAND.

PREPARED BY THE ITALIAN GOVERNMENT FOR SUBMISSION TO THE TRUSTEESHIP COUNCIL.

Preamble.

WHEREAS Article 75 of the Charter of the United Nations, signed at San Francisco on June 26, 1945, provides for the establishment of an International Trusteeship System for the administration and supervision of such territories as may be placed thereunder by individual agreements;

WHEREAS, under Article 77 of the said Charter, the International Trusteeship System may be applied to territories which may be detached from enemy States as a result of the Second World War;

WHEREAS, in application of paragraph 3 of Annex XI of the Treaty of Peace between Italy and the Allied and Associated Powers, signed at Paris on February 10, 1947, the General Assembly of the United Nations has been requested to decide the disposal of the territories referred to in Article 23 of the said Treaty;

WHEREAS under paragraph 3 of Annex XI of the aforementioned Treaty of Peace, the Four Powers agreed to accept the recommendation made by the General Assembly of the United Nations in the matter.

Italian Trusteeship No Time Limit.

WHEREAS the said Assembly, at its fourth regular session, recommended that Italian Somaliland, until it becomes autonomous and independent, be placed under the International Trusteeship System with Italy as the Administering Authority;

WHEREAS the Italian Government has accepted responsibility as the Administering Authority of this Territory;

NOW THEREFORE the General Assembly of the United Nations approves the following terms of Trusteeship for Somaliland:

ARTICLE 1.
January 1935 Boundary, i.e. Walwal under Italian Administration.

The Territory to which this Agreement applies is the Territory known as Somaliland (hereinafter called the Territory), bounded by British Somaliland, Ethiopia, Kenya, the Gulf of Aden and the Indian Ocean.

The boundaries of the Territory are those resulting from the treaties and conventions concluded between the Italian Government and the adjoining States with effect from January 1, 1935.

ARTICLE 2.

Italy shall be entrusted with the administration of the Territory, and the Italian Government (designated in this Agreement as the Administering Authority) shall assume responsibility for such administration with respect to the United Nations.

The administration of the Territory shall be in the hands of an administrator appointed by the Administering Authority and responsible to it.

The Administering Authority shall avail itself of the co-operation of an Advisory Council composed of representatives of Colombia, Egypt and the Philippines.

ARTICLE 3.
Advisory Council.

The Advisory Council, which shall have its headquarters at Mogadishu, shall assist the Administering Authority:

(a) in problems of primary importance respecting the political, economic, social and educational advancement of the inhabitants of the Territory;

(b) in programmes of a general nature reflecting the economic prosperity of the Territory;

(c) in problems relating to the participation of the Territory in the maintenance of international peace and security;

(d) in questions regarding the annual reports of the Administering Authority to the organs of the United Nations;

(e) in any dispute, as referred to in Article 17 of the present Agreement, which may arise;

(f) in all other matters concerning which the Administering Authority may request advice.

The States that are members of the Advisory Council but are not members of the Trusteeship Council shall be invited to participate, without vote, in the debates of the Trusteeship Council on any question relating to the Territory.

ARTICLE 4.
Relations with United Nations.

The Administering Authority undertakes to administer the Territory in such a manner as to achieve the basic objectives of the International Trusteeship System laid down in Article 76 of the United Nations Charter; and further undertakes to collaborate fully with the General Assembly of the United Nations and the Trusteeship Council in the discharge of all their functions as defined in Articles 87 and 88 of the said Charter.

Accordingly the Administering Authority undertakes:

1. To make to the General Assembly of the United Nations an annual report on the basis of the questionnaire drawn up by the Trusteeship Council in accordance with the said Article 88, and this report shall include information relating to the measures taken to give effect to the suggestions and recommendations of the General Assembly and of the Trusteeship Council, and to appoint an accredited representative together, if necessary, with experts to attend the meetings of the General Assembly and of the Trusteeship Council at which such reports will be examined;

2. To appoint an accredited representative, assisted where necessary by experts, to participate, in consultation with the General

Assembly and with the Trusteeship Council, in the examination of petitions presented to these bodies;

3. To facilitate such periodic visits to the Territory as the General Assembly or the Trusteeship Council may decide to arrange and to settle the dates and the details of the organisation and carrying out of these visits;

4. To render assistance to the General Assembly or the Trusteeship Council in the application of these arrangements and of such other arrangements as these bodies may make in accordance with the terms of the present Agreement.

ARTICLE 5.
Power to establish Military, Naval and Air Installations.

The Administering Authority shall be responsible for the peace, order, good government and defence of the Territory, and shall ensure that it shall play its part in the maintenance of international peace and security.

ARTICLE 6.

For the above-mentioned purposes, and in order to fulfil the obligations arising under the Charter of the United Nations, the present Agreement and the Declaration attached hereto, the Administering Authority:

1. Shall have full powers of legislation, administration and jurisdiction in the Territory, subject to the provisions of the United Nations Charter of the present Agreement and of the Declaration attached hereto, and shall have power to apply to the said Territory, temporarily and with such modifications as are considered necessary, such Italian laws as are appropriate to the conditions and needs of the Territory;

2. Shall have power to establish in the Territory whatever military, naval and air installations are necessary for the defence of the Territory, to maintain its own armed forces and to raise volunteer contingents in the Territory and to take, within the limits specified in the United Nations Charter, any measures which in its opinion are likely to ensure respect for the laws and the maintenance of order within the Territory, the participation of the said Territory in the maintenance of international peace and security as well as respect for such undertakings relative to collaboration as the Administering Authority may be required to give to the Security Council.

ARTICLE 7.
Legislative Provisions for Advisory Council to be issued by Administrator after Trusteeship Agreement Approved by U.N.O.

The Administering Authority shall, in conformity with the principles contained in the Declaration attached to the present Agreement, take any measures which in its opinion are likely to assure to the inhabitants of the Territory an ever increasing share in the central and local administration of the said Territory, to initiate and progressively develop their participation in the advisory and legislative bodies of the Territory and to promote in the Territory the early attainment of the objectives set forth in Article 76 b of the United Nations Charter and recommended at the fourth regular session of the General Assembly with respect to the said Territory. In particular, an Advisory Council to advise the Central Administration shall be set up at Mogadishu under legislative provisions to be issued by the Administrator within six months of the approval of the present Agreement.

ARTICLE 8.
International Agreements " at present in force in the Territory to be maintained."

The Administering Authority undertakes to maintain the application to the Territory of the international agreements and conventions which are at present in force in the Territory, and to apply therein any such conventions and recommendations concluded and made by the United Nations and by the specialised agencies referred to in Article 57 of the Charter as are likely to be in the interest of the inhabitants and not inconsistent with the basic obligations of the Trusteeship System and the terms of the present Agreement.

In addition the Administering Authority shall, in the interest of the Territory, take measures deemed likely to cause the Territory to play its part in international co-operation of every kind, in keeping with the spirit of the United Nations Charter, and shall guarantee the participation of the Territory, in the interest of the inhabitants, in the international specialised agencies and in international governmental and non-governmental organisations interested in promoting the education and progress of the said inhabitants.

ARTICLE 9.
Land and Natural Resources.

In order to promote the economic and social advancement of the native populations, the Administering Authority shall, in establishing standards relating to property or the transfer of land and to rights to natural resources, consider native law and customs, and shall respect the rights and safeguard the interests, both present and future, of the said population.

Land or rights to natural resources belonging to native private persons shall not be alienated or transferred in favour of non-natives, save with the previous consent of the competent authorities. Real rights over land or natural resources belonging to native private persons shall not be created in favour of non-natives without the consent of the same authorities.

ARTICLE 10.
Equal Treatment for Members of United Nations.

Subject to the provisions of Article 12 of this Agreement, the Administering Authority shall take all necessary steps to ensure equal treatment in social, economic, industrial and commercial matter for all members of the United Nations and their nationals and to this end:

1. Shall ensure the same rights to all nationals of Members of the United Nations as to its own nationals in respect of entry into and residence in the Territory, freedom of transit and navigation, including freedom of transit and navigation by air, acquisition of property both movable and immovable, the protection of persons and property, and the exercise of professions, trades, industry and commerce consistent with the requirements of public order and in conformity with local laws;

2. Shall not discriminate on grounds of nationality against nationals of any Member of the United Nations in matters relating to the grant of concessions for the development of the natural resources of the Territory, and shall not grant concessions having the character of a general monopoly;

3. Shall ensure equal treatment in the administration of justice to the nationals of the States Members of the United Nations.

The rights conferred by this Article on nationals of States Members of the United Nations apply equally to companies and associations organised in accordance with the law of any such State.

Measures taken to give effect to the equality of treatment referred to in this Article shall be subject to the reserve that such measures do not prejudice the attainment of the basic objectives of the Trusteeship System as prescribed in Article 76 of the United Nations Charter and particularly in paragraph b of that Article, and reciprocity on the part of the States Members of the United Nations in respect of the Territory, its inhabitants and the companies and associations legally organised in the said Territory shall be an implied condition in the taking of such measures.

ARTICLE 11.

Nothing in this Agreement shall entitle any Member of the United Nations to claim for itself or for its nationals or for companies and associations organised in accordance with its laws the benefits referred to in the preceding Article in any respect in which it does not give to the Territory, its inhabitants and companies and associations legally organised in the Territory equality of treatment with the nationals, companies and associations of the State to which the afore-mentioned State Member grants most-favoured treatment by agreement.

ARTICLE 12.
Public Services, etc.

Measures taken to give effect to Article 10 of this Agreement shall be subject always to the overriding duty of the United Nations and of the Administering Authority, in accordance with Article 76 of the Charter, to promote the political, economic, social and educational advancement of the inhabitants of the Territory, to carry out the other basic objectives of the Trusteeship System, and to maintain peace, public order and good government in the Territory.

The Administering Authority shall in particular be free, subject to the provisions of the regulations which shall be applied to the Territory:

    1. To provide for the organisation of public services and the execution of public works on such terms and conditions as it thinks proper;

    2. To create in the Territory, in the interest of the inhabitants, monopolies of a purely fiscal character in order to provide the said Territory with the fiscal resources which seem best suited to local requirements;

    3. To establish or to permit to be established, where the interests of the economic advancement of the inhabitants of the Territory may require it and under conditions of proper control by the competent public authorities, public enterprises or joint undertakings for specific purposes in conformity with Article 76, paragraph d, of the United Nations Charter.

ARTICLE 13.
Religion and Missionaries.

The Administering Authority shall ensure in the Territory complete freedom of conscience and religion and shall guarantee freedom of religious teaching and the free exercise of all forms of worship.

Missionaries who are nationals of any State Member of the United Nations shall be free to enter, travel and reside in the Territory; to acquire and possess property therein, subject to the conditions laid down in Article 9 of the present Agreement; to erect religious buildings and to open schools and hospitals therein.

The provisions of this Article shall be subject only to such limitations as may be necessary for the maintenance of public order and morality and for the educational advancement of the inhabitants of the Territory.

ARTICLE 14.
Education.

The Administering Authority shall consider as its particular objective the development of education in all forms and of all grades for the benefit of the population of the Territory. It shall ensure the operation in the Territory of elementary, secondary and technical schools for the indigenous population. In the interests of the said population it shall in addition make it possible for students to receive advanced and professional education.

ARTICLE 15.
Freedom Subject to Requirements of Public Order.

The Administering Authority shall guarantee to the inhabitants of the Territory complete freedom of speech, of the press, of assembly and of petition, without distinction as to race, sex, language or religion, subject only to the requirements of public order.

ARTICLE 16.

Nothing in this Agreement shall affect the right of the Administering Authority to propose at any future date, the alteration or amendment of this Agreement in the interests of the Territory or for reasons not inconsistent with the basic objectives of the Trusteeship System.

The terms of this Agreement shall not be altered or amended **except** as provided in Articles 79 and 85 of the United Nations Charter.

ARTICLE 17.

Disputes to be submitted to International Court of Justice.

Any dispute whatever between the Administering Authority and a State Member of the United Nations relating to the interpretation or the application of the provisions of this Agreement shall, if it cannot be settled by direct negotiation or other means, be submitted to the International Court of Justice, as provided for in Chapter XIV of the United Nations Charter.

ARTICLE 18.

The present Agreement, an integral part of which is the attached Declaration on the constitutional principles that guarantee the rights of the inhabitants of the Territory and provide for the establishment of institutions intended to prepare the way for the complete self-government of the said Territory, shall enter into force as soon as it is approved by the General Assembly of the United Nations.

The Power entrusted with the administration of the Territory accepts, however, to put these provisions into practice on a provisional basis until such time as this approval is given.

DECLARATION ATTACHED TO THE TRUSTEESHIP AGREEMENT FOR SOMALILAND.

In view of the recommendation made by the General Assembly of the United Nations, at its fourth regular session, with respect to placing the Territory of Italian Somaliland under the International Trusteeship System with Italy as the Administering Authority;

Considering the basic provisions of the United Nations Charter regulating the application of the International Trusteeship System and the terms of the Trusteeship Agreement relating to the Territory of Somaliland, of which this Declaration is an integral part;

For the purpose of solemnly guaranteeing the rights of the inhabitants of the Territory and of ensuring the realisation of the objectives of Trusteeship of the said Territory in conformity with the United Nations Charter and the special resolutions adopted by the General Assembly at the aforementioned regular session;

The Italian Government, as Administering Authority declares that:

1. The Administering Authority shall take the necessary steps to give the indigenous population a status of citizenship in their own Territory.

This will ensure diplomatic and consular protection to the inhabitants of the Territory whenever they are outside the said Territory or the territory of the Administering Authority.

2. The Administering Authority shall guarantee to all inhabitants of the Territory respect for fundamental human rights and full equality before the law without distinction as to race, sex, language or religion.

3. The Administering Authority shall, as regards the administration of justice, provide for the institution of a judiciary system guaranteeing the absolute independence of the judiciary, and ensuring the progressively increasing assignment of judicial functions to the native judiciary and the full application of Islamic law and local customary law.

Limitation of Civil and Political Rights.

4. The Administering Authority shall guarantee to all the inhabitants of the Territory full civil and political rights consistent, as regards the exercise of such rights, with the progressive political, social, economic and educational development of the inhabitants and with the advancement of traditional institutions towards democratic representative systems.

In particular, it shall guarantee to them: (a) the preservation of their personal and successional status and the civil advancement of the same; (b) individual liberty, which may be restricted only in the cases and according to the regulations established by law; (c) the inviolability of domicile, to which the competent authority may have access only by virtue of the law and in the manner prescribed in accordance with local customs; (d) the recognition and the guarantee of property, except in cases of expropriation carried out in the general interest and after payment of just compensation, and subject to other restrictions established by law; (e) the free exercise of professions, trades and economic activities in accordance with existing local customs and in conformity with such regulations as shall be enacted; (f) the right to compete for public employment in conformity with regulations which shall be enacted and which shall determine the particular conditions of eligibility; (g) the right to emigrate and to travel, subject to the restrictions determined by law for health and security reasons.

5. The Administering Authority shall, in order to guide the Territory towards full autonomy, bring about an increasing participation of the inhabitants in public, legislative and administrative offices, through the establishment of central and local representative organs.

In particular, the Administrative Authority shall provide, at its central, regional and municipal organs, for the establishment of appropriate advisory councils appointed by the Administrator, in which at least one half of the members shall be native inhabitants. The functions of the councils shall be defined by law.

XXIII

ITALIAN RETURN TO SOMALILAND

ITALIAN PARLIAMENT FACES TRUSTEESHIP OF SOMALILAND

The question of Italy's return to Somaliland now passed to the Italian Parliament. During the Geneva discussions, the Italian Government were completing their naval, military and airforce preparations for re-occupying the Territory and their negotiations with the British Administration for the transfer of power. The question whether the Trusteeship would cost a hundred thousand million lire, or a mere ten or fifteen thousand million, was being placidly discussed by Ministers and Press. Official complacency was suddenly disturbed by the intervention of a Republican Member of the Italian Parliament, Senator Conti, who laid an interpellation before the President of the Council whereby he requested information concerning the preparations the Government were making to accept the Trusteeship of Somaliland. He protested that if Press reports of these doings were correct, the prerogatives of Parliament under the new post-Fascist Republican Constitution had been violated, as Article 80 of the Constitution provided that no international agreement could be concluded without Parliamentary sanction. Consequently Parliament had the right to decide whether the proposed Trusteeship should be accepted, and, if so, to discuss and determine the conditions of acceptance and the method of Administration. The newspaper " Tempo " reported that " this singular interpellation " was regarded in official circles as " inopportune, in fact more than disturbing." As a result of it, Signor de Gasperi's Government were obliged to seek sanction for the Somaliland Trusteeship and for the expenditure it would involve from both Houses of Parliament.

GENERAL NASI'S APPOINTMENT

Whilst the necessary Bills were pending, it was officially announced that the Administrator of Somaliland under Italian Trusteeship would be General Guglielmo Nasi, who had been Governor of Somaliland and Harar under the Mussolini regime, and for some time Assistant Governor-General of Ethiopia under the brutal Fascist Viceroy, Marshal Rudolfo Graziani, notorious as the perpetrator of the Addis Ababa massacre of February 19,

20 and 21, 1937, in which 30,000 Ethiopians were done to death by every means which vicious sadistic Fascism could devise. Italian official telegrams, left behind in Addis Ababa, prove with irrefutable accuracy the monstrous atrocities systematically executed under Graziani's orders, and the participation of General Nasi in this regime of inhuman crime. A selection of these Italian official telegrams and circulars submitted by the Ethiopian Government to the United Nations War Crimes Commission and published by the Ethiopian Government in 1949, includes some which were signed by General Nasi, and which glaringly expose his utter unsuitability for the task of guiding the Somali people to independent self-government. The appointment to Somaliland of an officer who was a war criminal, and was also reputed to be the most efficient of the Italian Generals who resisted the liberating forces in 1941, was obviously an act of the Italian Government which must heighten Ethiopian anxieties concerning Italy's future behaviour on the border.

General Nasi's instructions concerning education have already been quoted. In a telegram of April 23, 1937, * he advised Marshal Graziani that in order to procure more surrenders of Ethiopian Chiefs, it would be expedient not to execute immediately all who surrendered in response to Italian promises that their lives would be spared, but to allow the Court procedure to take its course. " I assure you," he added, " that it will act with the utmost severity, and will end with capital punishment for the leaders most compromised and dangerous. Wizards and soothsayers will be shot without trial." The so-called " wizards and soothsayers," whose intended destruction was thus cursorily announced, were the bards and minstrels of Ethiopia who sang in the villages at marriages, christenings, funerals and other notable occasions, and accompanied the caravans, praising great men and women, eulogising brave deeds. They played their part in encouraging the resistance to the Italian invaders, predicting the Emperor Haile Sellassie's return, and the ultimate liberation of the Ethiopian people. Graziani, having learnt of their activities, telegraphed as follows† to Lessona, the Italian Minister of the Colonies, the Vice-Governor-General of Ethiopia and other high Fascist officials, on March 19, 1937, declaring his determination to liquidate the bards:

> "*The political department of the police have informed me that among the most dangerous disturbers of public order one must count the ambulant singers, the soothsayers and sorcerers, who perfidiously spread among the primitive, ignorant and superstitious populace the most improbable news of catas-*

---

* *Documents on Italian War Crimes*, submitted to the United Nations War Crimes Commission by the Imperial Ethiopian Government. Vol. I, *Italian Telegrams* and *Circulars*, published by the Ministry of Justice, Addis Ababa, pp. 11, 12.

† Translated from Italian original reproduced in " La Civilisation de l'Italie Fasciste en Ethiopie," published by the Press and Information Department of the Ethiopian Government, Addis Ababa, 1946, page 63.

trophic events; complete destruction of entire populations by the Italians; forthcoming attacks against the capital by imposing rebel forces with foreign aid, the early return of the Emperor at the head of an imposing army, etc. . . . Convinced of the need to uproot completely this evil plant, I have given orders that all strolling singers, clairvoyants and sorcerers of the town and its environs, be arrested and shot. To-day, a total of 76 have been arrested and eliminated. This measure has produced an excellent impression and a feeling of calm among the indigenous population. By a special order, it has been forbidden on pain of death to exercise such professions in future.   *GRAZIANI."*

Mussolini, who was on a visit to Tripoli at the time, was telegraphically informed of this proceeding, and replied on March 20, 1937,* expressing his approval and declaring the extermination must continue:

"*27/ M. Secret. The events in Spain, distorted by the dirty British Press, with the terrible defeats of the Italian volunteers—news of which, filtering through from the Negus via Jibuti, might reach Addis Ababa and raise some remnants of illusion. I approve what has been done concerning the sorcerers and the rebels. It must continue as long as the situation is not definitely and radically tranquilised.*   *MUSSOLINI."*

It was recollected in Britain that the British Somaliland Protectorate was conquered by General Nasi in August, 1940, and that it was Nasi who during the Ethiopian campaigns of 1941 had opposed British forces to the bitter end at Gondar, after being beaten out of the Gojjam mountains by the Emperor's army of liberation under Orde Wingate, a victory by the latter, which in view of the disparity of the opposing forces, could justly be likened to the triumph of David over Goliath.

In view of this sombre history of the Administrator designated for Somaliland, some efforts were made to endow the appointment with a peculiar halo of excellence: Count Sforza described General Nasi as an emeritus who would be able to give most valuable counsel and guidance to the Government on all pertaining to Somaliland. Signor Piacentini, a member of the Italian diplomatic service, even went so far as to allege that the Emperor Haile Sellassie had said to him: " If ever I meet General Nasi I will grasp his hand; I am sorry not to have known him on account of his goodness to the Ethiopian people."

ETHIOPIAN GOVERNMENT DENOUNCES GENERAL NASI AS WAR CRIMINAL

Such absurdities were given their quietus by a statement of the Ethiopian Government protesting against the appointment of

---

* Ibid, page 65.

General Nasi and drawing the attention of the United Nations to General Nasi's record in terms of unmistakable severity, as follows:

" 1. *General Nasi actively participated in the Fascist regime during the Italian invasion and occupation of Ethiopia. He has been listed as a War Criminal by the Allied War Crimes Commission. (List No. 8, May, 1948, of the United Nations War Crimes Commission).*

" 2. *He is one of the Senior Italian Officers who, with General Graziani, waged the 1935-36 Italo-Ethiopian war. Therefore his return to East Africa, where he participated in the initiation, planning and launching from Somaliland of the aggressive war against Ethiopia, is a great menace to the security of Ethiopia. In this connection it must be remembered that General Nasi was at one time Governor of Harar Province, and later became Vice-Governor of Ethiopia. Consequently the Imperial Ethiopian Government view with serious concern his appointment in Somaliland, where under the Fascist regime he was Governor of the Province of Harar and Somaliland combined.*

" 3. *The Imperial Ethiopian Government are in possession of ample documentary evidence, proving beyond any doubt his anti-educational policy. They have, therefore, no doubt that no one is less fitted than General Nasi, in view of his policies, even to maintain the status quo of illiterate people, still less to guide the destiny of the very people who, under the United Nations Mandate, Italy is expected to prepare for independence in ten years.*

" *In view of Ethiopia's intimate knowledge and experience of General Nasi's activities, the Imperial Ethiopian Government trust the United Nations will not let this most undesirable appointment go unnoticed."*

TRUSTEESHIP BILLS: STORMY PASSAGE

Under the shock of the Ethiopian protest, which appeared in the Italian newspapers at that juncture, the Bills to ratify the Somaliland draft Trusteeship Agreement and to vote 6,000,000,000 lire (£3,500,000) for the initial cost of taking over the territory were debated in the Italian Parliament. There was no exultation, no rejoicing; the temper of both Houses was tense and painful.

There appeared to be no glory in a mere ten years trusteeship under League of Nations auspices. There was timorous, even panic-stricken fear of armed opposition by the Somali people which would result in heavy loss of life by the Italians and the necessity of hugely increasing military expenditure. There was already the necessity of assuming a heavy preliminary expenditure, and the unpleasant anticipation of an annual burden of 20,000,000,000 lire per annum, and perhaps a great deal more, without the shadow of a hope of securing any appreciable return in the course of ten years

TENTS FOR SOMALILAND: Italian soldiers at the Arenaccia Barracks, Naples, in training for the Italian Expeditionary Force for Somaliland under Italian Trusteeship, January, 1950.—From the Italian periodical, " Incom."

Stuart tanks and Staghound armoured cars for use in Somaliland were assembled at Caserta, Salerno, S. Maria Capua Vetere and at the Arenaccia Barracks in Naples, while the Italian Trusteeship was debated, January, 1950.

Volunteers enrolling for Somaliland under Trusteeship.
—From the Italian periodical, " Incom."

Awaiting Execution.

from a territory which during half a century had shown a continuous and ever increasing loss.

The Government had their majority, on whom they could call in support of their decision to accept the Trusteeship, willy nilly; but even in the ranks of their regular supporters there was disquiet and reluctance; the parties of the left, particularly the Communists and the Nenni Socialists who hitherto had been loudest in demanding the return of the African Colonies, were now prepared to oppose the Bills for the Trusteeship with utmost bitterness. The cry, " lavishing money in Africa, while Italians are lacking bread!" might easily become a devastating election propaganda.

The Nenni Socialists issued a hostile statement:

"*The directorate recognises in the Government's proposal to accept for 10 years the Trusteeship of Somaliland a sign of the old levity with which the country was in the past pledged to African adventures.*

"*Considers it derisory on the part of the United Nations to entrust to Italy the mandate for Somaliland, which compromises us in the eyes of the African peoples as accomplices of European colonialism, while offering no interest for Italian labour, and this after having closed the door in Libya to the earnestly requested return of 80,000 families of peasants, artisans and traders.*

"*And is unanimous with the Parliamentary groups in rejecting the Government's project, to the end that neither a soldier shall be exposed in Somaliland to the danger of ambushes or guerrilla actions, nor a penny shall be withdrawn from the schemes to solve the problems of life and reconstruction, particularly urgent in the southern and island provinces.*"

It was, as will be noted, a highly equivocal statement, its reference to Libya revealing determination to continue making political capital by fanning Italian Imperialist aspirations towards North Africa. The repudiation of European Colonialism lacked validity on the moral plane, coming as it did from a Party which had hitherto demanded the return to the Italian Government of all the former Italian Colonies in Africa.

From November 2, when Count Sforza moved that the Trusteeship measures be discussed by the Chamber as a matter of urgency, the Somaliland Bills had a stormy passage. Senator Conti, whose intervention had compelled the Government to obtain Parliamentary sanction for these measures, and other Republicans, and all the Socialists, left, right and centre, maintained consistent opposition. Even the Monarchist editor, Senator Tullio Benedetti, was against the Trusteeship. He declared the old colonial mentality out-of-date, " in view of what has happened in India, Indonesia, Egypt and now in Chinese Turkistan." He deplored that France and Britain had not co-operated in the Trusteeship, and declined to vote at all.

Count Sforza appealed for rapid assent to the Bills, on the ground that the troops must sail immediately in order to take over from the British Administration before the season of rain and the monsoon wind. He endeavoured to avoid opposition by declaring that General Nasi had not been appointed as permanent Administrator of Somaliland.

It was not the Government's intention to employ a military man for this position even were his qualifications of the highest, as in General Nasi's case. The Government intended to select as Administrator a civil servant, probably a diplomatist by career. General Nasi had been appointed only to take over power from the British and to remain until after the season of rain and the monsoon.

GENERAL NASI EXECUTED PRISONERS, WOMEN, CHILDREN AND WOUNDED

There was a good deal of perturbation by this time in Government circles concerning General Nasi's appointment. Opposition was not placated by Count Sforza's statement.

Giancarlo Pajetta, a Communist Deputy, roused consternation in the Chamber by reading from the pages of Italian Government publications on Italy's conquest and rule in Ethiopia in the years 1935 onward. These documents, published with exultant pride during the period of easy victories over an unarmed people, and the fierce excitement of acquiring vast territories, were now heard in an atmosphere of anxious and horrified suspense:

" *Destroyed, burned, put in the bag .... the rebel Mijjertines left 60 more dead on the field—It is just the story of a village.*"

In fact, it was a village of the Mijjertine people who inhabit Somilaland, now consigned to Italian Trusteeship.

Pajetta continued reading:

"*In front of us was a mountain of dead, heaped up pell-mell in the quarry, which had become a trap for them .... Bring the petrol can! Bring the torch .... We felt all aflame with ardour!*

"*What satisfaction to raise above the heap of their corpses the victorious flag! To-night we feel savage, bestially savage!*"

" It was Giani, the Fascist poet, who wrote that ! " Pajetta said. " I will not bring out those photographs of Ethiopians with heads cut off and feet burnt, which were carried in the pockets of the Fascist legions. I will not cite a single Ethiopian document, only a document which was written and officially published here in Italy, which extols the Italian Commanders in East Africa, and by means of which General Nasi has made such a career that he has even become your advisor." The volume Pajetta thus described was, "The First Year of the Empire," edited by the Governor-General of Italian East Africa, issued by the Office of the Military General Staff and published by the Topographical Office.* From this document he read a series of horrifying despatches. The first of them was addressed by Marshal Graziani to General Nasi and other Commanders:

"*Telegram* 18474. *The column sent to undertake reprisals has destroyed the whole country; only in this way can we impart a political impression of our prestige and our superiority. This is the reveille which should ring in the end of the rains, to-day, September 24.* GRAZIANI."

Nasi did not wait to have the reveille sounded a second time; he at once despatched a punitive expedition against Ras Desta,† under the command of General Geloso who acted with so much unsparing vigour as to receive Graziani's praise. In the course of the operations, as reported in a telegram read by Pajetta, "one of the columns under General Nasi's command inflicted on the rebels the following losses: 200 killed, 350 prisoners, 200 members of their families and servants captured."

The facts concerning the capture and execution of Ras Desta were next read by Pajetta from the same official document.‡ It should be recalled that this courageous Ethiopian patriot commanded regular troops; that he maintained the defence of his country according to the recognised rules of civilised warfare, and that he never at any stage made submission to the Italians. Nevertheless, when gravely wounded, he was surrounded and captured by the Italian forces, and was executed by the order of General Nasi himself. The event was announced in the following telegram from the Military Command under General Nasi's orders to Italian official circles:

"*The justice of God has indicated clearly the condemnation of the rebel chiefs. To-day Ras Desta was captured and shot by Column Tucci. Give maximum publicity.*"

The author of the official volume, from which Pajetta was reading, doubtless the Governor-General himself, added, "Divine Justice has spoken." "Evidently," observed Pajetta, with sarcasm, "in this case the man sent by Providence§ was General Nasi, who executed the commandment of God by ordering the shooting of a high Ethiopian officer entitled to the respect due to a prisoner of

---

* *Il primo anno dell'Impero*, edito dal Governo Generale dell'A.O.I., Ufficio di Stato Maggiore, a cura dell'Ufficio topografico.

† Ras Desta Dimtu, Governor of Sidamo, was the husband of the Emperor Haile Sellassie's eldest daughter. He was a reformer and a courageous patriot. Captured when gravely wounded, he was carried to the place of execution, and photographed, amid a crowd of exultant captors, before he was killed.

‡ Ibid.

§ The reference of Pajetta was to the designation by Pope Benedict XV of Mussolini as "a man sent by Providence."

war." As this official volume, edited by the Governor-General indicated, General Nasi directed the entire cycle of operations in the zone of Arussi and Bale. From the Column Tucci, which formed part of his troops, came the following despatch:

"*After the encounter of March 16, 1937, we executed about 500 rebels.*"

Pajetta read on:

"*On October 15, 1936, General Nasi, then Governor and Commander of the Italian forces at Harrar, in a report on the military operations in the region of Garamulata, states that the Air Force was able to identify and to bomb a mass of Ethiopian rebels in flight. He comments: ' The lesson we gave them was terrible, because in addition to the human victims, the rebels lost all their houses, which were given to the flames, with all their grain and the greater part of their cattle.'*" (*Pages* 124 *and* 125.)

The reading of a number of telegrams followed:

"*October 21, 1936. Telegram No. 7856. About a dozen rebels executed. Captured arms and 2,700 head of cattle, and burned all Ethiopian dwellings. Signed, General Nasi.* (*Page* 155.)

"*October 25, 1936. Tel. No. 7076. Shot three rebels at Mount Tita and two rebels at Bivio Kunni. Signed General Nasi.*" (*Page* 188.)

(" Shot " in the above quotations and those following always means prisoners shot without trial).

"*October 26, 1936. Tel. No. 8137. Prisoners shot have confirmed a reunion with Simmelis. Signed General Nasi.* (*Page* 263.)

"*November 4, 1936. Tel. No. 8561. Captured and shot five Ethiopian rebels. Signed General Nasi.* (*Page* 254).

"*November 6, 1936. Tel. No. 8723. At Arbà shot native leaders implicated in the rebellion. Signed General Nasi.* (*Page* 263).

"*November 8, 1936. Tel. No. 88727. Enemy losses in action 5th inst. are about 500, amongst whom are 50 wounded women and children and are now in our camp. Signed General Nasi.* (*Page* 276).

"*November 8, 1936. Tel. No. 89078. ' This telegram is signed like the others by General Nasi. It is interesting because it clearly shows the attitude of this war criminal when confronted with those who have submitted to the Italian Government. He indicates the procedure to be followed by Italian officers in cases of submission*':

"*1. Shoot those who come to submit after fighting up to the previous day.*

" 2. Disarm and intern.

" 3. Make use of them.

" Which method to adopt in each case is left to the judgment of the gallant officers commanding the columns." (Page 280).

" Some of them, it was doubtless thought, might serve as spies and provocative agents," interjected Pajetta. He continued his reading:

" February 25, 1937. Tel. No. 2540. Various groups of Ethiopian regular soldiers who had attempted to offer resistance from entrenched positions have been captured and shot. Signed, General Nasi." (Page 379.)

" They were not ' partisans,' not ' rebels,' not ' bandits ': they were regular soldiers," the reader interjected and continued with the official text:

" February 26, 1937. Tel. No. 259. Summarily shot Cagnasmac Tadesse, head of the Ethiopians in this region. Signed, General Nasi." (Page 381.)

" February 27, 1937. Tel. No. 2671. Have shot Barambaras Uec, of the zone Tulu Baltu, and others for connivance with Fitaurari Bahade. Signed, General Nasi." (Page 383.)

WOMEN AND BABIES ALSO SHOT!

Then was read out the wildest, most reckless iniquity:

" March 5, 1937. Tel. No. 2862. Column Cubeddu in clearing up Tamada zone, captured 20 more rebels. They were immediately shot including women and babies. Signed General Nasi." (Page 388.)*

" Not even Kesselring," Pajetta commented, " gave such ferocious orders! You make use of worse criminals than the Nazis!" He read on:

" March 6, 1937. Tel. No. 2880. In western Bale the commander of the column Dallo has ordered the shooting of 29 ex-Ascari. Signed, General Nasi. (Page 390.)

" April 14, 1937. Tel. No. 2914-138. Clearing up battlefield confirms utter defeat of the enemy. Counted on ground 132 dead and many others in adjacent localities, besides numerous wounded, all of whom we have shot together with the prisoners. Signed General Nasi. (Page 436)."

" He is a criminal," Pajetta cried, " a real hyena, who massacres even the wounded!"

---

* The Italian reads as follows: " Data Marzo 5, 1937, tel, n. 2862: " Colonna Cubeddu prosequendo rastrallamento zona Tamada, ha catturato altri 20 ribelli subito passati per le armi anche donne et bambini. Firmato Generale Nasi. (pag 388, vol. cit)."

Count Sforza—the newspaper "Unita" reported—was visibly agitated; he muttered excitedly to De Gasperi, who, pallid and immobile, vouchsafed not a word, but made a pretence of consulting some documents on the desk before him.

These terrible despatches from the generals in the field had been published to popularise the conquest of the Empire, and to preserve them for posterity. Their authenticity could not be denied. "We all read these despatches at the time they were published," declared Pajetta.

Count Sforza retorted that General Nasi's appointment was only temporary; there was no time now to seek a permanent Administrator. "There is the monsoon, we must bow to the exigencies of the climate."

Pajetta answered scornfully:

"It does not interest me that you will appoint another Administrator six months hence. This is the man you chose as your Counsellor and are sending to Somaliland to take power. You said he is a General emeritus able to advise you; that he is exactly what is needed out in Somaliland. You could have chosen an emeritus among the diplomatists; you preferred to choose General Nasi, because he has commanded already in those parts. You said the 'Dubats'* were 'enthusiastic' when they heard the news of his appointment."

COUNT SFORZA

In view of the irrefutable evidence of the despatches, Count Sforza replied with difficulty: General Nasi had been recommended to him by Italians living in Africa as an understanding and competent man. He had never seen, he said, the documents published by the military General Staff which Pajetta had cited, though he had wearily gone through numbers of such documents; he deprecated the reading of them at this time, and attempted to extenuate the atrocities they recorded by protesting, "Pajetta would have been nearer to historic reality if he had said these events happened not during the war, but during the rebellion."

This was obviously incorrect, notably so concerning the execution of Ras Desta, who was a commander of regular forces and defending his country against aggression. Many of the despatches quoted were sent before the Italian conquest of Ethiopia had even been proclaimed in Rome; but for Ethiopia the war never ended till Italian rule was defeated and expelled; the Ethiopian Government and people never surrendered, never admitted defeat, never accepted conquest. A fitting retort was given by Pajetta: "Honourable Sforza, these events occurred when you urged the Ethiopians to rebel against fascism." Count Sforza's discomfort was palpable; again he protested, "In any case, Nasi is only going

---

* "Dubats"—native irregulars who were employed by the Italians to raid into the Ethiopian Ogaden.

out for the transfer of military power, after which a civil Administrator will be appointed." It was evident, nevertheless, that General Nasi had been selected for his military qualities, and that warlike operations were anticipated.

Cavinato, of the Socialist Unitary Party, and Dugoni, of the Socialist Party of Italy, now declared the opposition of their parties to accepting the Administration of Somaliland. Belloni, of the Republican Party, moved a resolution to decline the Trusteeship, and at the same time to send a message of friendship to the Somali people and to the peoples whose governments had confided the Trusteeship to Italy.

DE GASPERI

Signor De Gasperi, the Prime Minister, then rose to throw his influence into the scale for acceptance. He attempted to cast about the Italian return to Africa an atmosphere of ethical and humane sentiment, with a liberal dose of that flattery of Italian national self-esteem and desire for fame and power which has been a favourite stock-in-trade of party politics in the peninsula ever since the creation of United Italy. He raised again the slogan, sounded with so much bombast in Mussolini's time, "Italy's civilising mission to backward peoples." He announced, as though it were a matter of vast importance, the decision of his Cabinet to terminate the Ministry of Italian Africa; this, he declared, would close one cycle of Italian policy in Africa and inaugurate a new one—Trusteeship Administration. The change was, however, purely one of formal designation; even the personnel of the new Ministry remained the same as the old. He urged that Italy could not renounce the Trusteeship of Somaliland after insisting upon it at the United Nations; to do so would be "a great error," and "a negation of faith in a better world."

The frontier problem he dismissed briefly. The British, in accord with Ethiopia, would indicate a provisional frontier which would remain until a permanent frontier had been stabilised by the United Nations. Count Sforza had already stigmatised as absurd the statement that the British were endeavouring to secure a permanent zone between their protectorate of Somaliland and their Colony of Kenya, by means of which British Somaliland would be directly connected with the Indian Ocean, and Britain could direct Ethiopian imports and exports through her own territory, instead of allowing them to pass through Italy's Somaliland territory.

The cost of the Colony, Signor De Gasperi stated, would be 20,000,000,000 lire per annum, according to the experts, but he hoped it could be immediately brought down to 16,000,000,000 or 17,000,000,000 lire, and eventually to 4,000,000,000 or 5,000,000,000 lire per annum. Many Deputies, however, predicted that the cost of "the Somaliland adventure" would far exceed the estimate of the experts.

As the *New York Times* correspondent observed, the Italian Parliament voted reluctantly for the Trusteeship. The Government were able to rely on their majority, but substantial opposition votes in both Chamber and Senate showed the project for a costly ten years' Trusteeship lacked popular appeal.* A few months before, hardly a voice had been raised in opposition to the general clamour for the return to Africa.

A crop of rumours still circulated concerning the position of General Nasi; he was already in Mogadishu; he had merely acted as the " technical adviser " in Italy of the " security force," as the Italian army in Somaliland would be called; his duties were practically at an end, there was " not much likelihood of his being required in Somaliland." He had been officially invited to exculpate himself of the dreadful charges made against him—a matter of difficulty, certainly, since his own official despatches were his accusers; he had refused to exculpate or excuse himself, and was no longer willing to go at all to Somaliland. Though Nasi would not be there, another Fascist General of Mussolini's Roman Empire would be in command, General Arturo Ferrara, who in 1925 had participated in De Vecchi's brutal " fascist reconquest " of Somaliland, and subsequently had served in Ethiopia under Graziani, in 1936-37. The Secretary-General in Somaliland, Signor Pompeo Gorini, had also a long record of employment in Mussolini's fascist empire. The *Eritrea Nuova* observed that Gorini was successively Chief of the Personnel in Italian Somaliland, and an official in the High Commissariat for Jubaland, when that territory was ceded to Italy by Britain; that he was a member of the fascist Government mission to Hungary; that he was successively Director of Civil Affairs in Cyrenaica during Graziani's oppression of that territory, Director of Civil and Economic Affairs in the Ministry of the Colonies, and Secretary-General to the Governor of Harar

---

* CHAMBER OF DEPUTIES:
  Motion to permit immediate discussion of Somaliland Trusteeship Bill:
    Ayes 259
    Noes 168
    Abstentions .. 6

    Majority 91

  Bill to allocate funds for the occupation of the Trusteeship territory:
    Ayes 287
    Noes 153

    Majority 134

SENATE
  Motion to discuss the Somaliland Trusteeship Bill:
    Ayes 164
    Noes 93

    Majority 71

The principle being thus decided, the Senate subsequently passed the Bill by a show of hands.

during the Italian occupation of Ethiopia. Subsequently, he was sent as one of the Italian representatives to London in connection with the Italian liquidation of the Bank of Ethiopia. It will be remembered that the Italian Government took legal action in London to obtain the assets of the Bank of Ethiopia which had been invested abroad, as part of the Italian policy of annexing all Ethiopian property in all parts of the world.

Eventually, Signor Giovanni Fornari was appointed Chief Administrator; he arrived in the territory on April 6th and was greeted by the Members of the Advisory Council who had already taken up residence there.

ITALIAN TROOPS SAIL FOR SOMALILAND

As soon as the funds for the expedition had been voted in the Chamber, the " Auriga " and the " Assiria," the first Italian naval transports for Somaliland sailed from Naples for the Port of Augusta, in Sicily, there " to await the decision of the Senate." The " Assiria " was loaded with tanks, armoured cars, arms and equipment of every sort for the military installations in respect of which Italy, according to the Trusteeship Agreement, should have consulted the Advisory Council. The " Auriga " contained soldiers and carabinieri, officers and men, 900 in all, the first batch of the 5,500 troops *Il Tempo* announced were to be sent to Somaliland, in respect of whom the Advisory Council ought also to have been consulted. The Italian Government was desirous of avoiding popular demonstrations against the expedition, which might so easily have occurred if the Nenni Socialists had attempted to follow up their slogan, "Not a penny, not a man for Somaliland," by mustering crowds to oppose with their bodies the starting of the troop trains, or if the Communists had staged a fight.

These Parties were doubtless too much concerned with Italian internal affairs, too uncertain of their African policy and of the trend of Italian public opinion towards the former colonies, to make the embarkation of the troops an occasion of disturbance. The " Auriga " and the " Assiria " slipped away quietly in the evening, watched only by the Chiefs of Staff and a few junior officers, without cheers or bunting.

The nervousness of the Italian Government concerning the reactions of the Somalis to the Italian arrival was much greater than any anxiety they may have felt in respect of the doings of the Left parties in Italy. A silent departure from Sicily also was considered desirable; the troops who were waiting at Augusta, as though it were zero hour in wartime, were recalled to their ship in the middle of the night, as soon as the telegram that the Bills had been passed by the Senate was received. No spectacular send-off was permitted. The soldiers were bidden to travel " like tourists," all arms being concealed. Each man was furnished with a guidebook for Somalia, an edition of 208 pages for the officers and of 84 pages for the ranks, containing topographical information, a vocabulary, and instructions for conduct—"not to ridicule the proud Somalis," "not to arouse their resentment by amorous advances to their women." "Moreover, for health reasons, one must be careful, venereal diseases (malattie specifiche dell' amore), leprosy and smallpox were prevalent."

A correspondent of the Italian newspaper *L'Europeo* described the examination of the guidebook by the officers on board the "Auriga." None of them, he declared, would obey the instructions concerning the women; they had volunteered for Africa in quest of "women and adventure." "All spoke of the women with enthusiasm; they know the Somalis are most beautiful."

Subsequent contingents set sail with less of secrecy, though without popular jubilations. On March 27, Prime Minister, De Gasperi, accompanied by the Minister of Defence, took the salute at Caserta as the troops of the Somaliland "Security Force," in battle dress with steel helmets, marched past in a silence akin to funereal. Addressing the forces bound for Somaliland, De Gasperi stated this was not an expedition of conquest, or a military enterprise, it was a mission of peace and civilisation; the officials were to administer a territory under United Nations Trusteeship, to prepare it for self-government, the soldiers were to preserve security with order.

Among the Somali people there was a sombre calm. They did not offer resistance to the return of their old rulers as had been threatened at Lake Success. On the contrary, eager foreign Press correspondents reported statements by the Somali Youth League officials that Italy was to be given a fair chance of fulfilling her undertakings. Much effort had been directed to persuade the Somali leaders to adopt a tolerant and hopeful attitude; they had been urged to take their share in rendering possible the independence and self-government, which the United Nations had planned for them, to be effected in the stipulated time.

On arrival in Somaliland the Italian troops were placed under the control of the British G.O.C. East Africa, Lieut.-General Sir Arthur Dowler. They were immediately marched to internment camps, where they would remain until their numbers would be complete, and the time would come for the British Administration to hand over power to them and sail for home.

The advent of the Italian forces was termed, "Operation Caesar," their reception by the British was termed, "Operation Union Jack." All that was left to maintain the *armour propre* of the British Military Administration and its Chief Administrator, Brigadier G. M. Gamble, in resigning to the defeated enemy the territory Britain had liberated, was to conduct the handover with due efficiency, and to preserve the oft-praised discipline, smartness and *esprit de corps* of British forces till the end. Brigadier Gamble, in a conference with British and Italian Press correspondents, referred to "considerable local objection in the past to the return of Somaliland to Italy." He emphasised the necessity of preserving peace and order during the change from one Administration to another, and explained that he had urgently requested the Italians to refrain from flag-flying and demonstrations which might excite the local population.

The British Administration worked actively in the meantime to ease the Italian assumption of power. Italian officers were introduced to their British counterparts in the British Somaliland Protectorate; they were facilitated in touring the territory they were to command, and in offering to the Somali police force a transfer to Italian service with the same pay and conditions, as well as in opening recruitment of additional Somali forces in all parts of the territory. The British decision to discard the native forces employed by the Italians and to man their Somalia Gendarmerie with entirely new recruits had given satisfaction to some Somalis, but had created among the former native soldiers and police an anti-British element. The returning Italian administrators did not complicate their arrival by any hint of displacing Britain's Somali protégés. Let them remain tranquil till Italian power was established.

Already the 5,500 Italians of the new Security Force numbered many more than the white soldiers whom the British had used in the Territory at any time, though the British forces had of late been substantially increased. When these Italian forces had been augmented and the military police force, the carabinieri, had been added, Somalis whom the British had encouraged with notions of self-government could be dealt with. They would be faced by an overwhelming array of force, having regard to the powerful modern military, naval and air equipment with which the Italians were furnished.

A special correspondent of the English weekly, "East Africa and Rhodesia," declared, "The order of the day for Somalis is non-resistance and non-violence." He remarked that the phrase was worth remembering, for otherwise it would be easy to regard with "unwarranted complacency a transfer of sovereignty, which is both unpopular, and to many European and Somali minds unfair," but which appeared to have been effected "without evoking the expected resentment of a people who have unquestionably been led to expect a different future." The correspondent added, "the self-appointed task of the Somali Youth League is to fight for Somali independence and it must be credited with sufficient powers of discernment to select the battlegrounds which give it the best chance of success."

The future relations of the Italians and the native people remained under the shadow of a great suspense. On March 7, as reported in the "Giornale d'Italia," of Milan, two prominent Somalis were stabbed in the streets of Mogadishu by adherents of Italy, Mussor Bogor, the hereditary and chosen prince of the Mijjerteins, and Haji Dirie Herze, the only Somali representative in the Chamber of Commerce, who during the visit of the Four Power Commission of Investigation, had spoken up strongly against Italian rule.

The Italo-Ethiopian Boundary

As the Ethiopian Government had foretold, the question of the boundary already appeared as a potential source of conflict. In the Italian press, claims to thrust the frontier further into Ethiopia were already being urged. Both the oil wells which the Sinclair Company of U.S.A. was boring at Gomburru Hills, in the Ogaden, and the wells at Wal Wal, were mentioned as Italian interests. The " Governo " of Rome, declared that a disputed zone had always existed in the Ethiopian Ogaden, adjacent to the Italian Colony, that only the presence of Italy had maintained " a certain elasticity of transhumance," that " the Ethiopian fitauraris " would prevent the tribes under Italian trusteeship from migrating north in the dry season to obtain water at the wells of the Ogaden, and that unless the zone of wells were brought under Italian trusteeship, the tribes under Italy must " either see their cattle perish or become Ethiopian subjects." It was because Italy desired to establish " a true and proper frontier," in order that the tribes of the Italian colony might not be " abandoned to famine," that the Wal Wal incident had resulted, " Governo " declared. This new version of the Wal Wal incident was, of course, entirely false. The wells of the Ogaden are essential to the Ethiopian subjects permanently resident there; Ethiopia did not oppose the seasonal migration of the tribes according to their immemorial custom, when the Europeans settled on the coasts in the latter part of the nineteenth century, and thereby established frontiers where none had formerly existed. The Anglo-Ethiopian Treaty of 1897 made provision for these migrations between Ethiopia and the British Somaliland Protectorate. On the other hand, the boundary of the Italian colony, which was drawn on the map and agreed by the Emperor Menelik II and the Italian negotiators in 1908, seems to have been planned with due attention to the watering and grazing habits of the local tribes, in order to avoid the necessity of seasonal migrations by them across the border. In practice such migrations do not occur it appears. An Englishman of great experience in the area writes on this point:

" The only migrations of the tribes with their cattle which occur are within the known borders of Somalia and are inter-tribal, not inter-territorial. Proof of this is to be found in the fact that the question of migrations between former Italian Somaliland and Ethiopia never arose during the nine years of British occupation there."

The same official comments: *No recognised border Commission having yet carried out a survey no accepted border yet exists. The Italians claim a line which the Ethiopians refute. The local inhabitants are the scapegoats. How can the inhabitants keep to boundaries which are not yet marked? Even the United Nations do not know where one territory ends and the other begins!*

" The small adjustments made by the British Administration on the ground, at Ferfer and at Godderefort, before handing over to

the Italians, can make no difference to the necessity, or otherwise, of tribal migrations for cattle grazing.

"*The most regrettable aspect of the whole frontier question is the responsibility put upon uneducated tribesmen, who have never seen a map, and have no boundary stones or lines to guide them in keeping within what is supposed to be their own territorial limit. If inadvertently they cross the border they are fined, imprisoned, fired on, or have their cattle confiscated. Such a situation is a disgraceful kind of thing to exist in this century.*"

This honest expression of opinion by an Englishman who has seen, at first hand, the suffering daily caused by the frontiers the foreigner has established is worthy of honest consideration. The right and satisfactory solution is not to transfer more territory from indigenous to foreign Government.

BRITISH ADMINISTRATION DEMARCATES PROVISIONAL BOUNDARY

The British Government had given an undertaking to the Trusteeship Council to establish a provisional frontier by March 1, to be observed pending a decision by the United Nations. Unjustified Italian claims being already indicated, it was evident that negotiations if opened with Italy would be protracted much beyond the date assigned for completion. The Menelik frontier of 1908, which Italy had demanded at that period, was known and marked on the map; the British adopted the obvious course of fixing the provisional frontier on that line. The United Kingdom Government, therefore, instructed the British Administration on the spot to establish an equitable frontier, access to water for the tribes on either side of the line being a guiding consideration.

Count Sforza's Protest Against British Provisional Boundary

After the hand-over of power by the British Administration to the Italian, Count Sforza issued a protest against the provisional boundary the British Administration had established. He complained that the frontier had been pushed back 30 miles "in relation to what was for years the frontier of Somaliland." Thereby he claimed territory illegally occupied "for years" by the forces of Mussolini's Italy. He added:

"*As the frontier was fixed without consulting them, the Italian Government reserve their position concerning the legal aspect and such practical difficulties as may occur.*"

A Military Regime

The new Italian regime in Somaliland immediately shaped itself as a military occupation. Mr. Ralph Chapman, Somaliland correspondent of the "New York Herald Tribune," wrote from Mogadishu:

"Heavily armed troops are everywhere, artillery practice is held within a few miles of Mogadishu, fighter planes roar overhead."

"Signor Fornari, the Chief Administrator, emphasised the military rule in two recent speeches. On one occasion he said: 'It is our duty to see that the law is respected and that those who violate it are punished.' Another time he said: 'Every deviation, every infraction of the law will, of course, be relentlessly punished.' This is scarcely the atmosphere conducive to instilling democratic ideas in the minds of the uneducated natives."

Somali Youth League members, declared Mr. Chapman, "are constantly circulating stories of Italian atrocities. They list alleged machine gunning of women and children, murders in outlying districts, lootings and mass arrests."

These Somali allegations received striking confirmation from a broadcast on the B.B.C. Overseas Service, in which it was reported that Italian forces had opened fire upon crowds at Baidoa, Magherita and Kismayu, about April 15, a fortnight after the completion of the British hand-over. Somewhat earlier, when the Italians were already recruiting the native battalions for their security force, Italian troops fired on a peaceful Somali demonstration at Galkayu. The incident arose through the objection of Somali elders to the recruitment of their youths for Italian military purposes. This incident was reported in an Aden newspaper, "Fatat ul Jezirah." News of it was also received by the present writer direct from Somaliland.

Mohamud Mohamed Faccia, a prominent leader of the Somali Youth League, who had fled from the Trusteeship Territory to Ethiopia, wrote to this writer from Addis Ababa:

"*I am a refugee from my country, having been driven to seek refuge in this motherland of ours. I am not alone; I have arrived with friends who are also refugees. We have left our country and our families on account of the Italians.*

"*Since my arrival here I have received letters from Mogadishu, informing me that very many Somalis have been arrested by the Italian Administration, on the pretext that they are spies.*

"*News from Somaliland is scarce, but some of the diabolical work Italy has already started trickles through the Italian iron curtain. I am in receipt of a letter from Mogadishu, which reads:* 'The Italians are putting certain Somalis in prison, charging them as spies for Ethiopia! They are trying to suppress the Somali Youth League, the well-known anti-Italian force. If this is just the beginning it can be guessed the end will be terrible.'"*

Italian Intrigues Across the Frontier

†In a further letter Mohamud Mohamed Faccia alleged that the Italians were active in espionage against Ethiopia, and were attempting to cause disruption in the neighbouring Ethiopian Ogaden. He wrote:—

"*There is strong Italian propaganda in the Ogaden. The Italian Administration has sent there many ex-Yusbashis‡ and Sheikhs for propaganda against the Ethiopian Government. The*

---

* Published in "New Times and Ethiopia News," May 13, 1950 (No. 730).

† "New Times and Ethiopia News," July 1, 1950 (No. 737).

‡ Native petty officer in the Italian Colonial forces.

Sheikhs tell the Ogaden people: *The Ethiopians in Addis Ababa are Christians."*

Mohamud Mohamed Faccia further stated that Italy was " reversing the unifying process undertaken by the British Administration among the Somalis. Britain encouraged the people to think in terms of one word, Somali, whereas the Italians now do everything to replant the tribal divisions in the minds of the people. Every Somali is obliged to give, not only his name, but his tribe, and sub-tribe. This is what Mussolini did.

" We have seen 'Battaglione Arabo-Somalo.'* and we are expecting to see ' Camerati Camice Nere : † this is the voice of Mussolini ! "

Political Persecution

Information from various sources in Somaliland began to indicate the operation, by the Italian Administration, of definite policies, which reproduced those of the Fascist Administration in conquered Ethiopia.

The first of them was the destruction of all Somali leadership which might be opposed to the Italian regime: the dismissal or imprisonment on trumped-up charges of members of the Somali Youth League who had held high rank in the Somali Police Force, ‡ inspectors, sergeants and others, whose trials were held in secret, the Italian Courts being closed to the public; imprisonment of the Somali intelligentsia, and all Somalis hostile to the Italians.

§ In pursuance of this policy, Aden Abdi Mohamed Abshir and Farah Segulle, all of whom were Somali police inspectors when the British handed over to the Italians, were imprisoned. Farah Segulle was arrested in the street in Mogadishu, on June 24, and charged with " insulting the Italian police," and " inciting an unknown Somali." He was employed at the time of his arrest as interpreter to the British Consul ! The Branch Secretary of the Somali Youth League at Baidoa and all his committee were imprisoned. The Somali Youth League branches in the Upper Juba area were closed. All Mijjertine Somalis were forcibly removed from the Baidoa area; the Baidoa Division was made a Rahawein reserve. A renewal of Somali Arab conflicts was reported. The Arabs, as traders, were largely at the mercy of the Italian Administration, who, by the system of licences they had established, had the power totally to destroy the trade of any or all the Arabs unless they conformed to Italian policy. It was alleged that the Italians were scheming to oust the Somali Youth League by inducing the Arabs to form a Muslim League in Somaliland

---

* Arab-Somali Battalion.

† Black Shirt comrades.

‡ The Somalia Gendarmerie had been disbanded at the time of the Mogadishu riot of 1947 and replaced by the Somali Police Force.

§ Vide " New Times and Ethiopia News," August 19, 1950 (No. 744).

under Italo-Arab control which would displace the existing Youth League representation on the Central Muslim League in Nairobi, and, more important for the Somaliland territory, would monopolise native representation on the Territorial Council formed under the Trusteeship Agreement, from which it was hoped to exclude the Youth League.

Confirmation of the above reports from European and Somali sources in Mogadishu was subsequently received in a further communication from Mohamud Mohamed Faccia. Announcing the incarceration in the Mogadishu Central Prison of the Committee of the Somali Youth League Branch in Dolo and of the secretary, Mohamed Yusef, he bitterly remarked: " Mogadishu prison is the foremost training institution of the Italian master trainer to whom the United Nations have confided the Somali people." He added that, so far from assisting the Somalis to gain administrative experience, the Italians selected their local assistants not from among the Somalis but from among the Arabs.

Concerning fighting at Baidoa, which others had reported, he explained that the rival protagonists were the Somali Youth League and the pro-Italian Hizbia Dikil Mirifle. The latter had made use of hand-grenades stamped "Esercito Italiano, 1950," an obvious indication that these missiles had issued from the arsenals of the Administration, and the gravest feature of the affray.

Another Mogadishu correspondent wrote: —

" *The worthlessness of the Trusteeship Agreement is apparent from its fruit.**

" *In the first forty-seven days of the Italian Trusteeship more than 300 members of the Somali Youth League from all parts of Somaliland had been thrown into prison.*"

Fascist " Old Colonials "

He declared that the officers and officials of the new regime had all served under Mussolini and instanced Secretary-General Gorini, formerly in the Fascist Government of Harar, Dr. Gualtiero Bernadelli, Political Secretary, formerly Regional Commissioner in Somalia, Dr. Gabbarri, Regional Commissioner, formerly in the Fascist Government of Harar in Ethiopia during the Italian occupation.

There had been fighting, he added, at Baidoa between the Somali Youth League and Somalis under Italian influence, and armed raids and assaults had been made upon groups and individuals of the Somali Youth League, without any attempt to punish this violence, or to give protection against it on the part of the Italian authorities.

It appeared that the Italians, as in Fascist times, were organising among Somalis whom they had suborned to be their tools, a

---

* Vide " New Times and Ethiopia News," August 26, 1950 (No. 745).

movement similar to the Fascist Party in Italy, with its armed squads of "Black Shirt" thugs and assassins, who carried out murderous attacks on the political opponents of Mussolini and his gang.

The Aden newspaper, "Ellenehada," asserted that the Italian Administrator, on taking control of Somaliland, announced to the people of Kismayu:—

"*During the daily hoisting and lowering of the Italian flag all pedestrians in the various streets shall halt, all who are seated shall stand, in honour of the Italian flag.*

"*It is incumbent on every Somali and every African resident in Somaliland, whether civilian or soldier, to halt and salute, in the appropriate manner, any Italian seen passing by.*

"*Anyone violating this decree is liable to six months imprisonment, or a fine of 1,000 shillings.*"

"*The Ellenehada*" added: "*This proclamation having been officially announced, the Somali people appealed to the United Nations Advisory Council, reminding them that the Somalis had begged the United Nations not to allow Italy to return to her former colony to indulge in her fascist activities. They also openly told the Italians the Somalis do not want them. As a result seven Somalis were killed by the Italians.*"

This tragic situation, following as it did on the fallen hope of salvation from an Italian return by British aid, caused thoughtful Somalis to turn towards union with Ethiopia as the sole solution offering a prospect of ultimate happiness and progress.

A Somali correspondent wrote: "I believe that a good part of our young people will pass into Ethiopia and will find there hospitality and work under our Emperor Haile Sellassie. I know that Somalis who have reached Ethiopia are fully satisfied and very grateful for the reception they have had from the Ethiopian Government and people."

Exclusive Economic Policy

The other governing policy of the new Italian Trusteeship Administration, which reproduced that of the old Fascist regime, was that of an exclusive economic connection with Italy. This was contrary to Article 10 of the draft Trusteeship Agreement, which stipulated that the same rights must be assured in the Territory for all nationals of members of the United Nations as for Italians.

"It is obvious," wrote Mr. Ralph Chapman in "Montreal Daily Star," "that Italy hopes to gain such an economic hold on Somaliland in ten years that it will make little difference whether or not Somaliland then becomes politically independent in name."

The same correspondent reported in the "New York Herald Tribune," the bitter complaint of a business man that Somaliland would be "virtually an Italian colony in a couple of years," and the allegation by many non-Italians that Italy was establishing an economic strangle hold upon the territory.

There was indeed no doubt that the Italian Administration was working steadily to ensure that whatever else might eventually happen to the territory it should be economically tied to Italy.

Already, as we have seen, the Italians had possessed themselves of the best of the land and all natural resources of the country worth having, which they had thus far discovered, Mr. Chapman reported, on the authority of the Italian Chief Administrator, that numerous permits to prospect for minerals were now being issued.

The commerce of the territory was being confined to trade with Italy. Import licences, except to Italy, were issued only "without currency"; in other words no cash remittances were permitted from Somaliland except to Italy. In the case of exports to non-Italian areas, remittance of proceeds back to Somaliland must be guaranteed before a licence is issued. Signor Brusasca, in the Italian Chamber of Deputies, on February 4th, 1950, declared that leases up to 99 years could be granted, though the Trusteeship was only for ten years.

Mr. Chapman emphasised the disadvantage to all concerned of being compelled to trade exclusively with Italy. He instanced the case of a member of the secretariat of the United Nations Advisory Council who desired to import a British Singer sewing machine for his wife, but was informed that he must purchase it from Italy. Italian consumer goods, Mr. Chapman argued, were "far more expensive than similar items from the sterling area, and many goods were not available at all in Italy." Extra shipping charges, taxes and so forth resulted from the obligation to purchase all imports, whatever their origin, through Italy. All this, as well as an increase in the charge for trading licences and numerous other matters, had caused a serious rise in the cost of living. Trade was reported to be stagnating.

Though the Trusteeship Agreement stipulated that nationals of members of the United Nations must have the right to move freely in the Territory, passengers on British aircraft in transit to other locations descending at Mogadishu were forbidden to enter the town, and were detained in a small waiting room at the aerodrome. No one was permitted to contact or speak to passengers. Permits were requisite for entry to the airport (as well as to the docks) and were issued on payment of a Somal (equal to one shilling), but applicants were screened by the Italian police, who usually refused admission.

Numerous petitions complaining of the Italian Administration were addressed to the United Nations Advisory Council, and the pathetic hope was expressed that the forthcoming United Nations Assembly would refuse to sanction the continuance of the Italian Trusteeship.

The Somalis had been prevailed upon to give Italian Trusteeship a trial, and to avoid all disorders which would be regarded as evidence that Somaliland was not ripe for independence. They had refrained from concerted action, only to find themselves attacked piecemeal. Dismissed all from responsible employment, not one could feel secure from imprisonment or violence.

A glimpse of race relations is afforded by the letter of a Somali schoolboy, whose friend, a youth of fifteen years, wrote from the trust territory. He related that some Italian children and their dogs were chasing a Somali child, while their parents and the Italian police were laughing at the sport. The child was severely bitten, and crying in pain and terror. The Somali youth tried to help him by throwing a stick at the dogs and shouting to the children to desist. He was thereupon arrested, and brought before a judge, who said : " If you repeat such conduct you will be punished. Today you will merely have 20 lashes on your back."

The following report has been received by the writer from the leaders of the Somali Youth League in Mogadishu:—

REPORT FROM SOMALILAND

TRUSTEESHIP AGREEMENT ONLY A SCRAP OF PAPER

Italy has been offered a very good opportunity to show her change of heart by the United Nations in allowing her to resume the administration of her former Colony Somalia as a Trustee Power. The conditions in the Trusteeship Agreement, on which Italy was to administer Somalia, are beautifully worded, but since Italy resumed the administration over Somalia experience has shown that to the Italians the Trusteeship Agreement is just a document without value or meaning, and remains only on paper. This reminds one of Mussolini's famous speech, when declaring war against the allies, and thus violating all the peace pacts and mutual agreements with Great Britain, France, and their allies : "Le carte sono state fatte da uomini come noi, e noi le strappiamo," i.e. papers are made by men like us, and we shall tear them up.

ITALIANIZATION OF SOMALILAND ADMINISTRATION

During the British Administration.—The Somaliland Police Force consisted of only 58 British Officers and 2,000 Somali ranks. In the interior, almost all police stations and posts were run by Somali Inspectors or Sergeants. Some of these stations covered districts inhabited by a population of 50,000 to 100,000, with an area of about 100 to 200 square miles. The British Police Officers were merely acting as a sort of a guidance for the Somali Inspectors and Sergeants; they acted as Divisional or District Superintendents, and occupied the higher administrative and technical positions in the running of the Police Force.

Somali Police Dismissed, Imprisoned or Fled

To-day, Somalia is policed by the so called Carabinieri, and the 58 British Officers in the Somaliland Police Force have been replaced by over two Battalions of Carabinieri. During the first week of April, 1950, all Somali Inspectors and Sergeants, who were in charge of police stations and posts, were replaced by Carabinieri Officers and N.C.O's. All Somali leading and intelligent Police Officers were arrested and imprisoned, kept in jail for months without being informed of the charge against them, convicted and sentenced to terms of imprisonment (with hard labour) ranging from one to five years. Others were dismissed from the service, and some, who were arrested in April, are still detained in jail without trial. The following are some of the victims:

> Chief Inspector Farah Segulle, Inspector Aden Abdi, Inspector Mohamed Abshir, Sub-Inspector Ahmed Shire, Sub-Inspector Abshir Abdurahman, Sub-Inspector Abdullahi Ahmed, Sub-Inspector Mohamed Mire, Sgt. Ahmed Iasa, Sgt. Mohamed Ahmed Anagel, Sgt. Sheik Ussen Ali, Sgt. Jama Yassin, Sgt. Farah Ali, Sgt. Hassan Mohamed, Sgt. Ahmed Aden, Sgt. Mohamed Hersi, Sgt. Mohamed Ali, Sgt. Issa Mohamed, Sgt. Mohamed Ismail, Sgt. Jama Mohamed, Sgt. Mohamed Aden, Sgt. Farah Dirshe, Sgt. Abdi Mohamed, Sgt. Abdullahi Elmi, Sgt. Issa Wehelie, and Sgt. Issa Hersi.

These were the well-known leading officers who were arrested in the capital and other administrative centres, but large numbers of other ranks have suffered likewise in the interior. Hundreds have been dismissed, after a period of detention, for reasons best known to the Italian authorities. A large number of other Inspectors, Sergeants, and other ranks gave up their career for fear of being sent to jail and emigrated to Ethiopia and other adjacent territories. These include:

> Chief Inspector Daud Timayare, Inspector Khaliph Shire, Inspector Jama Aden, Sub-Inspector Issa Farah, Sub-Inspector Ali Farah, Sub-Inspector Abdurahman Omar, Inspector Abdurahman Mumin and many other Sgts. and N.C.O's.

All these officers were either accused of having been "anti-Italian" during their service with the British Administration, or of being "pro-British."

During the British Administration, all investigation and detection work was left entirely in the hands of the Somali police officers. This was due to the fact that, being Somalis, they understood the language, the mentality and the various ways and methods of dealing with the local people—as is natural after all.

TRUSTEESHIP OBLIGATION TO TRAIN SOMALIS VIOLATED

To-day, the remainder of the Somali police officers are removed from all responsible positions and are made to work under Italian Carabinieri N.C.O's and Constables. The highest Somali Officer in the Police Force is subordinate to a Carabiniere Constable. This is quite contrary to the Trusteeship Agreement, which binds Italy—even in the Provisional Administration (see Art. 23 para. 2 of T.A.)—to prepare the ground for the complete independence of the Territory within the short period of ten years, and in the meantime, to give more responsible positions to the Somalis in the administration of their country. As a matter of fact, instead of doing so, the Italians have removed all Somali officials who were holding responsible positions during the British Administration, and replacing them by Italians.

SOMALI CIVIL SERVANTS ALSO DISMISSED

This has not only been done in the police force, but also in the Civil Administration. Nearly all Somali officials, Sub-Accountants, District and Chief Clerks, Cashiers, Post-Masters, Typists, Filing-Registering-Despatching Clerks, W/T and Telephone Operators, etc., have been replaced by Italians. Quite a large number of the Somalis who occupied such positions were arrested and imprisoned, or discharged from service early in April of this year. Many others went into exile to Ethiopia and other adjacent countries to avoid being arrested and imprisoned by the worthy descendants of Nero. Those who are still retained in the service of the Administration are hanging around the offices, chewing the time and buying " caffe latte " (coffee with milk—famous Italian drink) during office hours. They are purposely treated so that they may get " fed up," and give up their posts. In other words this is a part of the long-term scheme, which is the policy of the Italian Administration here, to find jobs for Italians, so as to solve the critical problem of unemployment in Italy. Some of the victims known to the writer in person are:

> Legal Officer Advocate, C. L. Salole; Sub-Accountant, Ibrahim Hassan; Cashier, Abdi Hussein; District Clerks, Ahmed Aden, Ahmed Dahir, Ali Hussein, Ahmed Mohamed; Cashiers, Abdulkadir Issa, Mohamed Nur; Clerks, Ahmed Aden Gabah, Jama Khalaph Koshin; Post Masters, Abdi Haji Hussein, Ahmed Shire Egal, Ahmed Atto Mohamud, Mohamed Hersi; Interpreters, Adan Salan and Nur Ahmed—to name the more outstanding ones.

BRITISH POLICY OF SOMALIZATION REVISED BY ITALY

It will be recalled that a policy of gradual Somalization of the Administration was pursued since 1946 by the British Administration, and that one of the Provincial Commissioners' conferences, presided over by the Chief Administrator, adopted a resolution creating Somali administrative officials. What a pity for those British Officers, who sacrificed nine years of their lives in Somalia, to see such an end of the brilliant work carried out by them, with great patience and sacrifice, during the nine years of their Administration in Somalia! Perhaps these officers will now console themselves in the knowledge that their work has been destroyed by the so-called Bevin-Sforza Plan?

What does the so-called "New Italy" intend by importing thousands of Italian civilian clerks and carabinieri constables into Somalia? Surely clerical and constabulary work can be done by the Somalis. Or does Italy intend that these Italian clerks and constables shall lead Somalia to independence? I do not argue that Italy must not have white troops in Somalia. The so-called Italian Security Corps—which is composed of about eight thousand men is one thing; the Italian carabinieri as police is another. A policeman must know the local language and mentalities, and the way to deal with the public he serves. The carabinieri may be useful in Italy, but they are quite useless here in Somalia as a police force.

POWERS OF THE CARABINIERI

Events have proved beyond doubt that the carabinieri here are like the Gestapo and the S.S. in Germany. Proof of this:

You will find every carabiniere—at all times and even in his off-duty hours when walking out in town—armed with a fully loaded Bretta sub-machine gun, and automatic pistol and handcuffs. One finds hundreds of carabinieri, in various groups at every corner in Mogadishu, stopping Somalis in the streets by challenging them with their machine guns, ordering them to put up their hands and searching them. Carabinieri walk into Somali houses without notice, and carry out searches without a warrant, terrorising women and children, offering no explanation as to what they are searching for. Very often these searches are carried out during the absence of the owners, using force to make an entry, breaking open all doors and boxes. On completion of the searches, nothing is done to repair the damage. Doors and boxes are left wide open. Thieves take great advantage of this to steal property in the house. Hundreds of Somalis whose houses were searched in their absence and whose property was thus damaged or stolen, and who complained of the matter to the carabinieri have been sent to jail on framed-up charges, such as "simulating evidence of an offence," under Art. 367 of Mussolini's penal code.

The carabinieri, as a force, are soldiers rather than police, and as such, are taught to kill. They are in fact, "Military Police." The crimes and mischief committed by the Italian carabinieri in Somalia resemble those of the Nazi armies in occupied Europe during the second world war. They are invested with full judicial powers; apart from being executives. The lowest carabiniere holds as much power as a judicial officer. He does not require arrest, search or remand warrants. He has judicial power to issue expulsion orders to Somalis within and outside the Territory, powers of which the carabinieri take the greatest advantage at the expense of the poor Somalis. In addition to these powers, the carabinieri are also in charge of the prison, which completes the chain of the power: to arrest, search, imprison and carry out the execution of the sentence.

TERRIBLE PRISON CONDITIONS: PRISONERS TIED TOGETHER AND PILED UP LIKE SACKS

Thousands of Somalis have been dragged to prison, where they are left for months without being informed of the charges against them. When they request to know with what they are charged, the poor Somalis are told by the carabinieri that, according to the Italian Law the authorities are not obliged to inform them of the charge.

All remand prisoners are made to work from the first day of their arrest. Any person who protests against being made to work before trial is inhumanly beaten, placed in the well-known " celle di morte "—i.e., death cells—where it is difficult even to breathe owing to lack of ventilation, and where the prisoner is deprived of food and water for days.

The food supplied to prisoners is totally unfit for human consumption. It consists of unsifted coffee-like and millet flour ground with the husks. No fruit, vegetables, meat, milk or tea are supplied. It so happened one day that on an inspection tour the Director of the Central Prison noticed the remains of a prisoner's ration lying on the floor of the cell; he cried out angrily, " Who has deposited this human excrement here?" At the same time he pointed to the bits of the cooked millet lying on the floor. One of the prisoners explained that the droppings were from the ration supplied to the prisoners by the Administration.

Adult and juvenile prisoners share the same cells, receive the same punishments in the Courts, and are subjected to the same labour. During the British Administration juvenile offenders were sent to an approved school in the town of Merca. (Proc. of 1943 refers.)

PRISON POPULATION UNDER BRITAIN AND ITALY COMPARED

During the nine years of British Administration, the highest number of prisoners in the Mogadishu prisons was seven hundred persons; nearly half of these prisoners were from the Ogaden, due to the disturbances existing then in that province. At the time of the handing over there were about 427 prisoners in Mogadishu prison. During May, 1950, there were over three thousand prisoners in Mogadishu. This also occurred in out-stations, but although the writer is not in a position to give the exact number of prisoners in all up-country stations, it has been possible to ascertain the figures for the undermentioned four.

In the Isha Baidoa District, the average number of prisoners during the British Administration was 40. In May this year there were 511; in Kismayu Districts 25, as against 475; in Merca District 35, as against 306; in Villabruzzi 15, as against 89. At least four-fifths of these were political prisoners, and consisted of Somali Youth League members, including branch committee members, S.Y.L. sympathisers, amongst them chiefs, sheikhs, notables and influential men, police officers and other administrative staff. Many of these S.Y.L. leaders and other influential men were flown by air from various up-country stations and brought to Mogadishu Central Prison, tied together in bunches, with ropes attached to their waists from one to another and their hands tied behind them. Political prisoners and criminals are tied together; no distinction is made whatsoever. Thus S.Y.L. leaders, chiefs, sheikhs, influential men, police inspectors, sergeants, and other administrative officials share cells with thieves, murderers and other habitual delinquents. Ten to twenty prisoners are placed in small cells which were intended to accommodate three; in consequence, prisoners lie one on top of the other likes piles of sacks or sardines.

BACK TO 1941

The prisons have now gone back to those wretched conditions which were found by the British in February, 1941. Prison cells have become filthy; no whitewash or disinfections have been employed since Italy resumed the Administration over Somalia. No sanitation exists in the prisons and no professional medical officer has yet visited them. There is an Italian dresser at the Mogadishu Central Prison, but he never goes round to visit the prisoners. Sick prisoners are never attended to at once. The Carabinieri Guards take only one case out of ten to the Italian dresser, and all the medicine the sick prisoner gets is only purgative, no matter what sickness he may be suffering from.

FASCIST LAW STILL OPERATES

The laws on which Somalia is at present administered are those of the Fascist regime of Mussolini. In 1941, when British troops occupied Somalia, the fascist penal code was amended and all measures contrary to democratic principles of law were cancelled and substituted by British proclamations.

On resuming the administration of the Territory, the first thing the Italians did was to reinstate all fascist law cancelled by the British Administration. This was done by means of an official Bulletin.

How can Mussolini's Penal Code and U.N.O.'s Charter go together? Mussolini's laws were made with the sole purpose of colonialising—in its worst form—whereas the Charter of the United Nations is based on democratic constitutional principles. These cannot go together!

As far as the Somalis are concerned, the law under which they are tyrannised is that of the fascists, camouflaged by a beautifully worded Trusteeship Agreement which only exists on paper.

Proof of this: The Italians have enforced the whole of the old fascist laws, thus disregarding completely the provisions in Art. 7 of the Trusteeship Agreement, which reads as follows:—

"The Administering Authority shall have full powers of legislation, administration and jurisdiction in the Territory, **subject to the provisions of the Charter of the United Nations, of this Agreement, and of the Annex attached hereto, and shall have power to apply to the Territory, temporally—and with such modifications as are considered necessary, such Italian laws as are appropriate to the conditions and needs of the Territory, and as are not incompatible with the attainment of its independence.**"

THE JUDICIARY

Art. 7 of the Annex to the Trusteeship Agreement, which is itself an integral part of the Trusteeship Agreement, reads: "The Administering Authority shall establish a judicial system and shall ensure the **absolute independence of the judiciary.**" Yet the courts are—as in the totalitarian States—mere instruments in the hands of the hated carabinieri, whose incredible and barbarous activities have been described above.

In Somalia, there exist two courts: an Assize Court in the capital and District Courts in the interior. The Assize Court is run by a single judge, whose decision is supposed to be final.

POWERS OF RESIDENT, EXECUTIVE AND JUDICIAL

The District Courts are run by "Residenti" (District Commissioners), who hold the power of a Chief Executive, as well as that of a Chief Judiciary. These so-called "Residenti" have no legal qualifications; they try the poor unfortunate Somalis according to the dictates of their own fascist mentality.

Under Italian Law here, every person is presumed guilty from the moment he is arrested by the carabinieri until he proves otherwise, whereas according to the democratic conception of justice, and in the words of Art. 11 of the Universal Declaration of Fundamental Human Rights, accepted by Italy as a standard of achievement for the Territory (vide Art. 10 of the Annex to T.A.): "Every person who is accused of an offence is presumed innocent until proof of his guilt is legally established before a Court of Justice, in which he is assured of all necessary guarantees for his defence."

Every arrested person is sent to jail by the carabinieri, on their own warrant, after keeping him under their custody for an unlimited period, whereas in the British Administration the police were only allowed to detain people for a period not exceeding twenty-four hours, at the end of which time the arrested person was either to be released or taken before the magistrate, who holds the power either to issue a remand warrant, if he deems fit, or to release the prisoner on bail. It is worthy of note that the word "Bail" has no place in the judiciary of Somalia. There has been no single case of any person being let out on bail, despite many requests.

HOW COURT CASES ARE CONDUCTED

After sending the accused to jail, the carabinieri later submit their findings, including a full history of the person in question, with special attention to his past and present political activities and views, and in addition to this, their recommendations as to what punishment the person should receive. So it naturally happens that the Court, if he is brought to the Court at all, opens when the judge has already formed an opinion on the case, having read through the findings, reports and recommendations of the carabinieri. He is therefore prejudiced against the defendant in the first place. Because of this influence and the consequent prejudice, the judge, before listening to the defence, addresses to the defendant questions which are absolutely irrelevant to the charge. The following are a few examples of questions which are now very common in the Courts of Somalia: "What political party do you belong to?" "What is your tribe?" "Were you in Mogadishu on the 11th January, 1948?" "Have you been working for the British Administration and, if so, in what capacity and for how long?" If the defendant protests that these questions have no bearing on the charge, the judge severely reprimands him and orders him to answer the questions put to him without further argument.

It is to be noted that under the British Administration the judge never knew anything about the case until it was brought before him for trial, so that he was in a position to start the case with an open mind, and without having any preconceived ideas. He therefore tried the case on the evidence produced before him from both sides—namely, the prosecution and the defence.

Another interesting point in the Italian Court procedure is that there is no public prosecutor in the whole of Somalia, except and only in the Assize Court in Mogadishu. In all District Courts the District Commissioners are invested with the functions of public prosecutors, in addition to that of judges.

Normally prisoners are not brought before a Court for trial. The judge studies the case submitted by the carabinieri, from which he makes his judgment. This always means conviction, for the judge is only acquainted with one side of the story. Thereupon he fills an official form which is called "Decreto Penale"—i.e. penal decree—concerning the case. These forms are later taken, in great bundles, from the Court to the prison by a Carabiniere, who parades the prisoners and distributes the forms to them, calling out their names and at the same time announcing the sentence inscribed on the form. Sentences may vary from 14 days to three years imprisonment with hard labour, a fine up to a thousand shillings, or both.

Cases of the few prisoners who are fortunate enough to be tried before a Court of Law are heard "in camera," to prevent the public discovering the irregularities of Italian Court procedure.

The denial of the right of entry to the Courts is another violation of Art. 10 of the Universal Declaration of Human Rights on the part of the Italian Administration.

The so-called "Decreto Penale" has proved an effective means of achieving the aim of the Italians to suppress their political opponents. Hundreds of Somali Youth League members and their supporters, including branch secretaries and committee members, chiefs, sheikhs, elders and other influential men and administrative officials, in every town and village all over the territory, have been arrested and sentenced to from six months to three years hard labour, by means of the "Decreto Penale." Under this "Decreto Penale" the accused is not allowed to be represented by an advocate.

XXIV

SOMALILAND AND THE FUTURE.

What future awaits the people of the former Italian Somaliland Colony, who have suffered fifty years of oppression, hardship, and frustration?

One would plead for them the right to achieve those natural aspirations for freedom, education and progress, which large numbers of them have conceived despite the limitations of a hard, nomadic existence in waterless scrublands, despite enslavement to forced labour in the fertile, river-irrigated regions seized by the foreigner, in abject political and economic subjection to alien invaders for half a century. Freedom for them, as for all peoples, must mean release from the position of an inferior race dominated by a foreign Power.

The United Nations had become the arbiter of their future, but the rivalries of other Powers, which had prevented a decision by the Council of Foreign Ministers and by the Paris Conference, cast their deepening shadow over the fortunes of the Somalis at Lake Success; Italy's imperial ambitions still pursued them.

In the decision to place them under Italian trusteeship, albeit with a promise that their territory would become a free and independent self-governing State in ten years' time, Italy's demand for colonial prestige predominated. The political aspect of the Italian Government's demand for trusteeship, and of the Somaliland problem, as viewed by other nations, completely obscured the practical and permanently fundamental questions: whether the territory could be rendered self-supporting, what the cost of its administration would be, how that cost would, or could be met. There was no discussion of the form of the Trusteeship administration. As we have seen, the vague sketch presented by the Indian Delegation was accepted without discussion or vote, as a mere guiding suggestion, not intended to convey any compulsive authority, or to bind the Italian Administrator in the slightest degree. No pledge was given, or asked, concerning the basis on which the Somali people would be progressively associated with and incorporated into the administration of their land under the trusteeship, or how they would be educated and trained for assuming the responsibility of government after ten years. No decision was made, or stipulation suggested, that the Trusteeship agreement must contain compulsory provisions for at least a minimum of elementary, secondary and higher education to equip the population at large for intelligent and successful self-government, and also to educate a corps of administrators.

Such matters, it is true, were regarded as being within the province of the Trusteeship Council, to which was referred the drafting of the Trusteeship Agreement in consultation with the Italian Administering Authority. The Trusteeship Council had been wholly concerned up to that time with long-term (apparently permanent) trusteeship; it was half composed by the Powers administering such trusteeship. It proved indisposed to lay upon Italy, the short-term administrator, a compulsory programme and timetable. No special instructions, in view of Italy's past aggression and misgovernment and of the short period of the trusteeship, were given by the General Assembly to the Trusteeship Council.

In support of the claim to the reunion of Eritrea to the Ethiopian State, and its re-incorporation into the Ethiopian administrative system, the Ethiopian Government had early presented a memorandum containing an administrative programme and budget for the provincial administration, with special elaboration of their proposals for elementary and secondary schools in the reincorporated territory, for hospitals and public health services, reconstruction and development of the ports of Massawa and Assab and other improvements and amenities for which funds were in reserve.

The Italian Government had not considered any such programme necessary to recommend their claim to Trusteeship of Somaliland; nor had either the General Assembly or the Political Committee called for such information and plans. The Italian Delegation offered no evidence that during the projected Trusteeship, they either would, or could, render the territory self-supporting in ten years' time, or any guarantee to carry out works of education and development, or to devote any sum to such purposes.

In order to form a wise judgment for the future of the territory, careful consideration of economic possibilities is obviously essential. The Report compiled by the Four Power Commission of 1948 afforded some data for such consideration, but neither the matter therein contained, nor any other source of information upon which an estimate might have been based, was submitted to any sort of systematic examination, despite the dismal record of half a century in which first Italy, then Britain had found the administration of the territory impossible without a subsidy by the occupying Power.

Little argument is needed to demonstate that no government, be it native or foreign, can without adequate sources of revenue provide an efficient administration suited to a progressive modern State, with the numerous personnel required for the many departments of State—foreign affairs, defence, justice, agriculture, industry and trade, transport, communications, light, power and, above all, educational and other social institutions for the welfare of the people. The fact that the people have been hitherto starved of education and of administrative and economic opportunities renders the task of the administration and the need of revenue all the greater, for the Government is obliged to do for the entire people what many are able to do for themselves in a prosperous community where numerous persons possess ample incomes. Without adequate revenue there cannot be either an efficient administration, or the education required to develop from the population the administrators and technicians who are needed to maintain the life of the community.

Nor can a State without adequate revenue employ administrators and technicians in sufficient numbers from abroad—a short-term necessity until the population has been trained—though there is no full and genuine independence for a people so long as they lack the capacity to man their own essential services. Some foreigners all States employ for special requirements, but to rely entirely on foreign personnel for all services calling for proficiency in the arts and sciences means a large and continued dependence on other nations, which in the long run is highly unsatisfactory.

To achieve such cultural progress in the people of the ex-colony as would fit them to become a self-governing community, liberal facilities for education would be needed, as well as the raising of their material conditions of life. The enterprise of preparing the people for self-government necessitates a considerable expenditure, which neither the Italian, nor the British Government had undertaken in this field. The territory has hitherto failed to produce sufficient revenue to maintain the administration of the colony even with purely nominal social services, which cannot on the most modest and favourable view be considered at all adequate.

If Italy were now to undertake a lavish expenditure, entailing extremely heavy sacrifices, she would probably fail to make the territory any more self-supporting than it was in Mussolini's time. One may aptly recall here the facts already cited concerning the natural resources of the territory, and in particular the statement of the Four Power Commission—which is not denied in any quarter, and is based on ample official evidence—that approximately one-half the total area is waste land; and of the remainder, 80 per cent. is pasture, the major part of the arable land being irrigated only by deficient rainfall.

The Commission further stated there is no timber industry in the territory, because such timber as exists "could be processed only with difficulty," and it is estimated that the yield of commercial timber, whilst difficult of access, would at best be no more than "400 to 700 cubic feet per acre. Under Italian administration all timber was imported from Italy." The mineral resources of the territory appear to be insignificant. The Italians made many prospecting expeditions to discover wealth in this direction, but no mineral deposits of substantial value were discovered. As the Commission of Investigation stated, "the economic structure of

Italian Somaliland has been characterised up to the present time by the impossibility of the territory meeting its elementary requirements."

One must recall the already quoted statement on the economic possibilities of the Italian Somaliland colony by Maurizio Rava, who prepared the incident at Wal Wal, and was given the responsibility of effecting preliminary measures for the conquest of Ethiopia. Governor Rava declared that only when joined to Ethiopia could Italian Somaliland be rendered economically worth holding. Even when the Somaliland colony, Ethiopia and Eritrea had all been combined as an Italian Empire, without the hindrance of the present frontiers and the expenditure thereby entailed, the whole great area was a huge loss to Italy, because of the determined hostility of the people.

The Somaliland Colony proved a heavy disappointment to a succession of Italian Governments who dissipated there an unending stream of revenue which was urgently needed in Italy.

The Benadir Ports under the almost nominal rule of the Sultans of Zanzibar were not lacking in prosperity in the simple fashion of olden times. They were self-supporting of necessity, for no Power existed to subsidise them. They had a favourable balance of trade. They made no claim to own or control the hinterland. Their position was that of free commercial centres trading with the people of the locality. Nevertheless from the time Italy took over the ports a subsidy became unavoidable, and both the subsidy and the adverse balance of trade were continually augmented.

The deficit economy of the territory was due in the main, one might almost say entirely, to the requirements of the Italian officials and colonists who demanded a higher standard of life and comfort than the territory could produce, and whose attempts to make it more productive were in every case unsuccessful. By one or more expedients, export bounties and tariffs, import restrictions, monopolies in the Italian market, direct subsidies from the Italian State, slave labour at starvation rates with penal sanctions imposed by Government officials, the Italian enterprises in the colony, and the Italian administration there, were all artificially supported; otherwise they would all have been bankrupt and could not have been maintained.

It should be noted that under the Sultan of Zanzibar, the coastal area was not, as now, isolated from the rest of Somaliland and the richer lands beyond. It was not barred off by frontiers, with customs, transit dues, currency restrictions. Moreover the aspirations of the people were then simpler; there was no urge for an education such as is to-day required; the functions of government were smaller; departments of Public Health, piped water supplies, and so forth were not contemplated.

We have reviewed the impecuniosity of the co-called democratic period of Italian rule and the relative lavishness of Fascist expenditure; both were alike insolvent, save for the Italian State subsidy, but the subsidy and the gap between revenue and expenditure were enormously greater in the Fascist period.

We may observe that in the neighbouring British Protectorate, though prudence in financial matters is a marked characteristic, there would also be insolvency save for the subsidy of the United Kingdom Government; so modest is the administration that in 1949 there was still only 1 per cent. of literacy in the population, only 2 per cent. of the children were at school. The staff of the Government elementary schools were all Somalis, few had had any professional training, there were no Secondary schools and only 7 scholarships for study abroad instituted only in 1947 under the Colonial Development and Welfare Scheme. There were no agricultural schools.*

Ethiopia under Italian administration was extremely insolvent. Yet prior to the Italian usurpation she was an independent self-supporting State, without a National Debt, and was making steady progress. She had a railway as well as the telegraph, telephone and radio communications. At the time of the Italian invasion, she had some 4,000 boys and girls attending modern schools in the capital, a number of modern provincial schools, and some 40 students studying abroad.

After the reckless insolvency of the Italian interregnum, liberated Ethiopia became self-supporting within three years, despite the grievous destruction of life and treasure caused by war, enemy occupation, and war again—a travail of seven years, and the difficulties occasioned by the World War.

Not only is Ethiopia again fully self-supporting, the progress she was making before the Italian invasion has been resumed and accelerated; by 1948 50,000 boys and girls were at modern schools in Ethiopia†, about 400 studying abroad at Ethiopian Government expense; all former State activities were resumed and extended; Ethiopian Civil airlines, several new industries and new agricultural enterprises were established, a considerable number of schools and administrative offices, dwelling houses, roads and bridges were built; water and electric light were newly supplied to several towns. All this is not without meaning.

The Emperor Haile Sellassie is undoubtedly an administrator of great genius, animated by a rare devotion to his people, and with a remarkable gift for assiduous toil. Moreover, he is surrounded by a corps of able and devoted Ministers, and the people are stirred by a surge of patriotism and strong desire for national progress. Certainly the work of administration is greatly facilitated by the unity among the people, their trust in their Govern-

---

* Non-self governing territories, summaries and analyses of information transmitted to the Secretary-General of the United Nations during 1949; Lake Success, 1950. Part II, pp. 230-239.

† It is interesting to note that in 1949 17 per cent. of the elementary school population of Ethiopia were Moslems, as were 20 per cent. of the Ethiopian candidates for London Matriculation, and 22 per cent. of the Ethiopian students sent abroad for higher education at State expense—Vide "New Times and Ethiopia News," July 22, 1950. No. 740.

ment, and ardent affection for their Sovereign. It is a broad fact that the insolvency of the European colonies on the Ethiopian seaboard and their failure to afford education and progress to the indigenous people contrast markedly with the advances made by Ethiopia. Her ability to effect national development without foreign subsidies is a challenge to European colonial administration on the Horn of Africa which calls for a new approach by them towards government in that area. Granted that these seaboard colonies are less productive than the Ethiopian interior, one would submit that European government on the Horn of Africa has failed to make adequate use of the human resources of the locality. It has relied upon European administrators who have not been furnished with the capital, the experience or the instructions which would have enabled them to initiate the full development of the natural possibilities of the territory, and to bring the people of the area into the business of development as close and willing co-operators, to train them to occupy not the subordinate, but the leading rôle. It is in relation to the human element that the Ethiopian Government has the unmistakable advantage over European Government which, having ample resources in capital and technicians, has not applied these to the territories in question. Imported European personnel has been costly, insufficient in numbers and lacking in the diverse qualifications required for the administration of law and justice, for the social services, medicine, surgery, education of the various grades. Even such obvious necessities as transport, water supplies, agriculture, prospecting for natural resources have been neglected. The European administrator holding aloof from the native population, having social contact only with the handful of other white residents, had no real knowledge of the people. He never indentified himself with the natives; indeed, he would have repudiated with indignation any suggestion that he had done so. Advice against intercourse with the native on equal terms, or any show of familiarity is found in the memoirs of Colonial administrators. A post in the Colonies was too often regarded as a mere station where one changed on the road to a pension.

In the British Protectorate the soldier has been paramount; the maintenance of order and the holding of the territory for its ports on the way to the East have been the outstanding aim of a static government, leaving the tribes to go their immemorial way unchanged, but imposing relatively high taxation, as Jardine observed.*

In the Italian colonies the aim has been to exploit the territory as a field for Italian enterprise and a source of raw materials for Italian industries—the indigenous people being ruthlessly subordinated to Italian ends. The effort to develop the colonies in order to promote Italy's own prosperity failed totally. Her vast East African Empire proved useless to Italy when the World War

---

* Vide page 30 above.

came; she was defeated by forces numerically smaller and with more slender equipment than her own. At the outset of the war when Britain had scarcely a handful of troops to defend the British Somaliland Protectorate the Somali soldiers there fought valiantly against the Italians; they knew enough of Italian rule in the rest of Somaliland to hate and fear it, but after the British defeat they abandoned resistance; there was no long, steadfast struggle such as the Ethiopian defence of their ancient liberties and national government.

In the Italian colony, there was not merely a refusal by the Somalis to support their Italian masters in opposing the British invasion. There was a general desertion by the Somalis from the side of Italy, an active support of the British invaders who were hailed as liberators. Somali troops attacked the Italian officers, as revealed by the letters of Italian officers which have been quoted in an earlier chapter. No proof could be greater of the total failure of Italian administration to benefit and to win the respect of the Somaliland population.

To make a lavish expenditure in Somaliland, despite her own gravely impoverished condition, with the honourable intention to withdraw at the close of ten years, leaving the territory intact with its resources available for the benefit of its native population, would involve an unprecedented degree of disinterested sacrifice for an alien people, which nothing in Italy's colonial history suggests she is prepared to make.

This was another aspect which failed to receive consideration from the United Nations, though a number of them, notably Mexico, had taken action to prevent the exploitation of their own natural resources by foreign interests. The Mexican Government had gone even to the verge of war to recover Mexican oil from foreign control. Even if the people of the Somaliland ex-colony had now been liberated politically from Italian rule, they would still have been involved in many difficulties resulting from the seizure of the best of their resources by the Italians during the sixty years of alien occupation.

When the draft Trusteeship Agreement came to be discussed by the Somaliland Committee at Geneva a provision against alienating native land was suggested; it was opposed, as we have seen, by the Italian negotiators on the ground that too rigorous an application of this principle might militate against the rapid development of the territory, a cynical reservation in view of the known facts. The provisions actually in the draft were exceedingly weak and could place little handicap on the transfer to the Italians of what is left of the Somaliland resources.

The protests of the Ethiopians and Somalis against the presence of Dr. Cerulli at Lake Success did not deter the De Gasperi Government from employing this Fascist administrator also at Geneva. Well able to baffle less fully informed delegations, he fought meticulously every suggestion which might limit or hamper Italian freedom of action.

As soon as the Somaliland trusteeship had been secured for Italy large scale military equipment—tanks, armoured cars, artillery, wireless installations—became the primary consideration of the Italian Government. The elimination of Somalis from such administrative functions as they had exercised under the British Administration was systematically pursued. To have held some minor clerical or police office under the British was to incur Italian official disfavour. To have been " pro-British " during the British occupation of the territory was now a punishable offence.

Eighteen months before the termination of the Trusteeship Agreement, when in conformity with its terms, the Italian Administration must present the final plan for the independent self-government of the territory, all the economic and political problems which the Fourth Assembly of the United Nations failed to contemplate, will present themselves anew. The territory will still suffer a deficit economy. The Somalis will still lack education and administrative experience.

There is little doubt that the Italian Government will attempt one of the two following alternatives :—

1. To prolong the Trusteeship, as the Italian Press suggested as soon as the Fourth Assembly adopted the Ten Years' Trusteeship solution. (Count Sforza himself hinted that if the period of Italian administration were short, the needed capital investments would not be obtainable).

2. To establish a bogus self-government, entirely controlled by the Italian Colonists, in which the Somali people would remain subordinate as before, and with the economy already inextricably linked to that of Italy.

Economic dependence exclusively upon Italy, as we have seen, is the policy already operated by the Italian Administration, though such a policy is totally contrary to the Trusteeship Agreement, and to the Charter of the United Nations. As an appendage of Italy, the territory will have the old chronic deficit, which will have to be met by the Italian exchequer, as formerly.

It is obvious already that the administration of Italy as Trustee will differ little from that of Italy as Imperial Ruler. If Italian Trusteeship is to follow the pattern of Italian government in the pre-fascist period the subsidy from the Italian exchequer will be meagre. Life in the colony will be harder for the Italian colonists than in fascist times; they will endeavour to ease their own position by further exploitation of the Somali people; forced labour—which the Italians of the colony declared to the Four Power Commission was beneficial to the Somalis—will be reintroduced and rigorously enforced; wages will be the lowest possible, hours of toil the longest, conditions of labour harsh in every respect.

If the neo-fascists were to gain control in Italy, expenditure on the territory would tend to be more lavish, its products highly protected by tariffs and bounties, as in fascist times. The military forces, both Italian and native, would be increased. Some measure of artificial prosperity might be created for the Italian colonists.

Inevitably the aim of the neo-fascist administration would be aggressive, espionage in Ethiopia, border raids represented as having been initiated on the Ethiopian side, attempts to subborn Ethiopian local chiefs, intrigues and false charges against Ethiopia—all the pernicious tactics of Mussolini's dictatorship would be revived in full measure, culminating in a major invasion.

Though these tendencies under a frankly neo-fascist or imperialist regime would attain their most aggressive form, they are already strongly manifest under the ostensibly democratic and temperate rule of the Administration headed by Signor De Gasperi and Count Sforza. As we have seen already, an exclusive autarchy has been established in the economic field; already Count Sforza has demanded a frontier enclosing Ethiopian territory which Italy invaded in Mussolini's time; already inspired articles in the Italian Press lay claim to include in the Italian Colony, wells which Italian maps prior to the Wal Wal incident of 1934 indicate as clearly belonging to Ethiopian territory; the vilifying of Ethiopia in the Italian Press, and the manufacture and publication of entirely fictitious incidents has become a systematic campaign.

The Menace to Ethiopia

The peril to Ethiopia of a return of Italian Administration on her southern frontier must not be ignored. The danger of invasion might even be greater from the south than from Eritrea, the lowland country being more penetrable than the mountain terrain of the north, and the possibility of obtaining entry unobserved and unresisted being infinitely greater in the sparsely populated nomadic areas of the south than in the arable lands which lie on the Ethiopian side of the Eritrean border.

If such an invasion were attempted, what course would be taken by the Four Great Powers, and by the United Nations as a whole ? Should we see repeated the flight from the Charter, as from the Covenant of 1935 and 1936, the recognition of a conquest as in 1937, the appeasement which culminated in the world war of 1939-45 ?

Apart from the peril to Ethiopia, there can be no doubt of the utterly tragic consequences to the native population of the former Somaliland colony which are already evident under Italian Trusteeship.

The Italian people as a whole can certainly reap no benefit; the economy of the Italian State, which is still suffering severely from the war into which it was dragged by the fascist experiment, must now stagger more heavily by reason of the colonial burden. Some realisation of this fact was manifested by the large minority opposition to the acceptance of the Somaliland Trusteeships Bill in the Italian Senate and Chamber of Deputies. The mention of such sums as 1.000 million lire for the colonies aroused protests on behalf of Calabria and other starving Italian districts.

Somali Yearning for Unity

The yearning of progressive Somalis in the Italian ex-colony for union with the rest of Somaliland is essentially sound and reasonable, as well as being socially and historically justified. At the time of the Italian defeat many forward thinking Somalis foresaw that union of the Somalilands could only be successfully realised within Ethiopia, the Somalilands being part of a great entity comprising the whole of the Horn of Africa. They saw that to divide the Somalilands from the grain-producing Ethiopian highlands would be economically a most serious act of unwisdom, to which the people of Ethiopian Somaliland would never willingly assent; they had not ceased to protest against being administratively divided from Ethiopia during the seven years of British military occupation.

When the scheme for a "greater Somaliland," including the British, French and ex-Italian territories, plus the Ethiopian Ogaden, to be established apart from the Ethiopian realm, was advocated by the British Military Administration, it gained weight from the pledge that by this means British support against the return of Italy would be assured. Moreover, the dominant group in the Somali Youth League, which had been helped into existence by the British Administration, was influenced by the fact that many of its members were employed by the Administration.

Since the withdrawal of British support for Greater Somaliland and the decision of the British Government to vote for the return of the Italians, the desire for reunion with Ethiopia has been rapidly regaining ground, as the solution which offers the only possible hope of liberation for the Somali people.

Events have already out-run all speculations; the new Italian regime has already been shaped as a grim tyranny. The former Fascists, the "Old Colonials," have returned. The imprisonment and persecution of the Somali leaders is in full operation. Refugees from the terror are fleeing to Ethiopia for refuge. The exclusive autarchy is in being.

EUROPE AND THE HORN OF AFRICA; BROAD CONSIDERATIONS

One would urge a broader and more objective consideration of the future of the territories which line the Ethiopian seaboard, and which were only divided from their hinterland by European intervention.

One would suggest that the policy of segmenting into separate States the great area comprised by the Horn of Africa is from every aspect retrograde. It is diametrically opposed to the effort towards unity, co-operation and harmony implicit in the conception of the United Nations. The unity towards which the nations of Europe are painfully and tentatively striving is obstructed by the conflicting ambitions of various highly national States which have repeatedly waged war on each other, and which have developed competing national economies difficult now to assimilate. On the Horn of Africa no comparable difficulties exist. The economy of the territories surrounding Ethiopia is not based on a separate territorial existence; these colonies depend on Ethiopia and form with Ethiopia an economic entity. France, were her seaboard in the hands of alien and competing Governments able to impose tariffs and currency regulations upon her commerce, would suffer grievously. The United States of America would scarcely have risen to its present importance in world economy if the Union of the States had not been achieved.

The suggestion of separatist independence for the former colonies on the Ethiopian seaboard may appear genuinely attractive to the organisers of the societies which have adopted that slogan, but such independence would be purely the recognition of a separation imposed by foreign conquest. The independence of the former colonies could not transform them into other than small, economically poor territories, unable to provide an adequate administration, to defend themselves against aggression, to develop a happy and prosperous society, to cast off the trammels they suffered at the hands of governments from distant lands overseas.

The sentiment of hostility and estrangement towards the people of free Ethiopia in the great land mass of which the seaboard colonies are geographically a part was intrinsically opposed to the interests of the people in the seaboard colonies as well as in the interior. It was in the main artificially imbibed from the foreign rulers of the colonial territories. In the case of the Italian rulers we know that the indigenous inhabitants were deliberately indoctrinated, province against province, religion against religion, and were repeatedly employed to attack their brothers in Ethiopia in order to extend the territory of the colonial power which was their own oppressor. In so far as such estrangement was a spontaneous growth or still exists, it is but the legacy of a primitive existence in which tribe attacked and looted tribe in the absence of any conception of nationhood. Historically the lack of a developed sense of African solidarity was one of the principal factors which enabled foreign invaders to subject and partition the African continent and to destroy its ancient freedom. This process is graphically described in the " History of Nigeria," by Sir Alan Burns.

The distastrous policy of Somalis advocating a United Somalia under British trusteeship is dead. It led to its own annihilation as, relying on the advice and succumbing to the influence of the British Military Administration, it appealed for the trusteeship of a British Government which had abandoned Somaliland to the Italians; it appealed for a United Nations trusteeship to an international organisation which had no desire of assuming the burden of governing Somaliland ; it turned its back on its compatriots in Ethiopia who were busy in building up a free and progressive country. Even if the disastrous policy had not gone aground on these rocks it was doomed, as there is no hope for the Horn of Africa if it is to remain a handful of fragmented territories with its economy shackled by artificial frontiers cutting ports from hinterland, and hinterland from ports; nor is there any hope of real political independence and security as long as the Ethiopian people —including the populations of Eritrea and Somaliland—do not stand united in the face of possible invasion from Italy and other aggressive powers. "Unity is strength" is always a forceful motto; it becomes decisive when it is realised that the self-preservation of the Horn of Africa depends on the ability of the government of Addis Ababa to import through its own ports the means of self-defence, and on the availability for the population of the whole area of a single government, capable by strength and by the ability of playing off possible enemies against each other, to maintain the national freedom of the area. Africa fell essentially because the boot was on the other foot, that is to say, because a handful of European Powers, often acting in unison, as by the arrangements of the Berlin Congress, were able to play one African village against its neighbour, one tribe against its cousins.

It is because they are grasping these realities and because events—their betrayal by Britain, the return of Italy and the refuge afforded by Ethiopia to the Somali escaping from the persecution of an ill-conceived trusteeship—are drumming these realities into the minds of even those very Somalis who were once led into the wilderness by the British Administration, that the situation is clarifying. The logic of events is bringing about the reunion of the Ethiopian people. To-day Somaliland is becoming clearly divided into two groups: the hirelings of Italy and the patriotic resistance to Italian rule. Day by day, month by month the ranks of the hirelings will be reduced in numbers and become ever more discredited among their compatriots, for constantly, with each new indignity imposed on the Somalis by the occuping Power, the overflowing bitterness with which the oppression is regarded by the Somalis will be augmented; as the Italians more and more become aware of the popular hatred, more and more will the oppressors have to rely on local Arab and other non-Somali elements to serve their purposes. Meanwhile as the Somalia Conferenza and other pro-Italians dwindle in numbers, the Somalis of the Youth League are being thrust into contact with their neighbours of free Ethiopia, and as the refugees from Somaliland flow into Ethiopia a new sense of union with Ethiopia is being reborn among the leaders of Somaliland.

Even the leaders of the Somali Youth League, living in Britain, who placed their faith in the policy of finding a way of escape from Italian oppression through British, or latterly through Four Power Trusteeship, and had been deeply committed to that policy, resolved to place before the Fifth Assembly of the United Nations a demand for Ethiopian Trusteeship as their first preference, and failing that, a joint trusteeship of Ethiopia and Britain.

Since their return the Italians have made it crystal clear that in colonial affairs, at least, the "New Italy" is merely a replica of the old.

Now that the attempt to secure an acceptable solution by the expedient of trusteeship has failed, Somalis, many of them the most far-sighted and influential, who had first believed that union to Ethiopia would be the best policy for their people to adopt, are returning strongly to that view. Somalis who have fled from Italian persecution to Ethiopia have there communed with their co-religionists who are Ethiopian subjects; from them they have learnt to appreciate the status of citizenship which Ethiopians enjoy and the economic advantages which are theirs in a country governed not by a European Power but by people of their own race.

Somalis who have journeyed to Harar, Dire Dawa, Addis Ababa have discovered among the inhabitants there prosperous merchants, Members of Parliament, government employees, judges in the courts, children in the schools, who are natives of Ethiopian Somaliland where their forebears lived of old before the creation of the colonial frontiers. From the patriots of Ethiopia, who courageously defended their national independence in lone isolation from 1935 to 1941, the Somali refugees are gaining a wider view of freedom, a new stimulus and a new hope. To them Ethiopia has become indeed "this Motherland."

In Ethiopia there is no colour bar, no question of doubt or mystery as to whether the dark coloured people, as such, can achieve the highest that human understanding can attain. The Ethiopian is in possession; he is not confined to a reservation nor relegated as a subordinate to a minor clerical or interpreter's position; the land is his and all its products. It is his prerogative, as it is of the European in his own land, to learn from his own errors, to achieve from his own efforts.

But the Italian Trusteeship is a grim fact. To the happy prospect of progress, wrought out of the reunion of a people, there is a darker alternative, a danger which cannot be ignored, a danger which as these lines are penned has become a tragic reality, striking down the advance guard of the Somali leaders as they follow their avocations or in their homes. In a previous chapter reference has been made to some of the cruel incidents of the present oppression in Somaliland.

The past rôle imposed by their Italian masters on the Somali quislings was to demand Italian trusteeship. Their present role is to play the part of the Fascist squadristi in Italy, to make war on Somalis who are opponents of Italian rule; for this warfare they are armed from the arsenals of the Italian State by the "old colonials" of the Administration, in accordance with the maxim, "who is not with us is against us."

Given the limited possibilities of the colony, the Fascist traditions in which the present Italian colonial officials have been steeped, the evil forces deliberately engendered in Somaliland upon which no staying hand from Rome has been imposed, the danger of war across the frontier of which the Ethiopians gave warning to the Fourth Assembly of the United Nations, remains an ever-present peril.

www.ingramcontent.com/pod-product-compliance
Lightning Source LLC
Chambersburg PA
CBHW021912180426
43198CB00034B/130